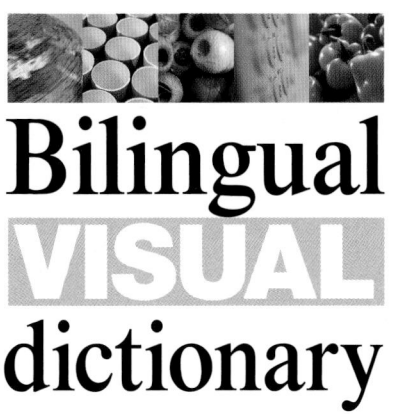

Bilingual VISUAL dictionary

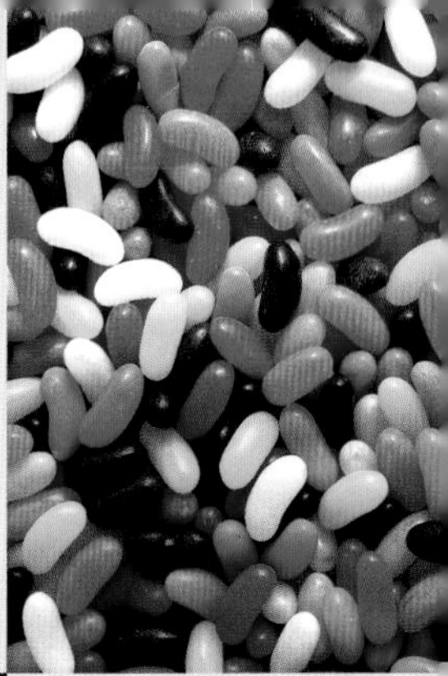

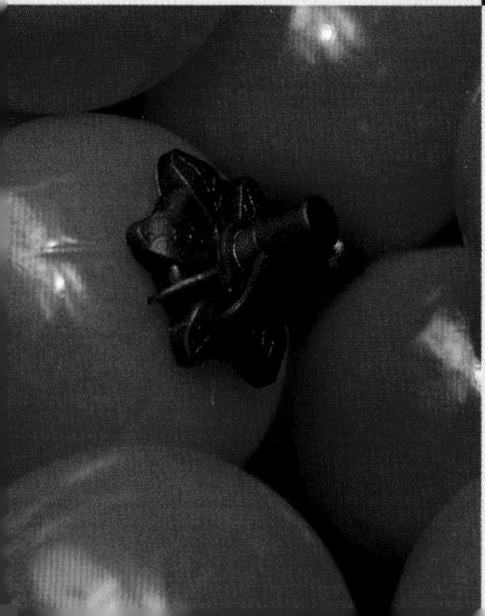

TOP-FLITE
XL
Titleist

Bilingual VISUAL dictionary

Penguin Random House

DK LONDON
Managing Editor Christine Stroyan
Managing Art Editor Anna Hall
Jacket Design Development Manager Sophia MTT
Jacket Editor Emma Dawson
Producer, Pre-Production Andy Hillard
Senior Producer Jude Crozier
Art Director Karen Self
Associate Publishing Director Liz Wheeler
Publishing Director Jonathan Metcalf

DK INDIA
Editor Arpita Dasgupta
Assistant Editor Ishita Jha
Assistant Art Editor Garima Agarwal
DTP Designers Vishal Bhatia, Rakesh Kumar, Anita Yadav
Jacket Designer Tanya Mehrotra
Jackets Editorial Coordinator Priyanka Sharma
Managing Jackets Editor Saloni Singh
Senior Managing Editor Rohan Sinha
Preproduction Manager Balwant Singh
Production Manager Pankaj Sharma

Hindi Translation by Yatra Books
Hindi Typing by Manipal Digital Systems Pvt. Ltd

First American Edition, 2008
This edition published in the United States in 2019 by DK Publishing, 1450 Broadway, 8th Floor, New York, NY 10018

19 20 21 22 23 10 9 8 7 6 5 4 3 2 1
001–312718–Apr/2019

Published in Great Britain by Dorling Kindersley Limited.

A catalog record for this book is available from the Library of Congress.
ISBN: 978-1-4654-8115-3

Printed in China

A WORLD OF IDEAS:
SEE ALL THERE IS TO KNOW

www.dk.com

contents
viṣaya sūchī
विषय सूची

42
health
svāsthya
स्वास्थ्य

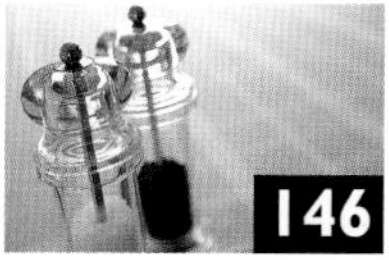

146
eating out
bāhar khānā
बाहर खाना

252
leisure
manorañjan
मनोरंजन

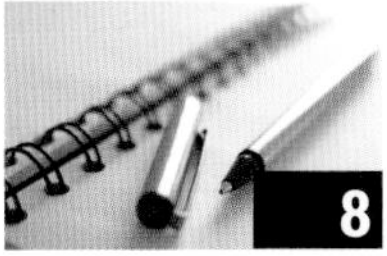
8
about the dictionary
śabdkoś ke bāre meṃ
शब्दकोश के बारे में

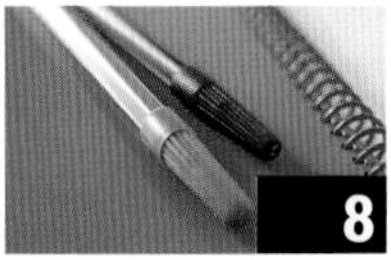
8
pronunciation tips
ucchāraṇ sujhāv
उच्चारण सुझाव

10
people
log
लोग

28
appearance
veśbhūṣā
वेशभूषा

56
home
ghar
घर

92
services
sevāyeṃ
सेवाएं

102
shopping
ḳharīdārī
ख़रीदारी

116
food
khādya padārth
खाद्य पदार्थ

160
study
adhyayan
अध्ययन

170
work
kārya
कार्य

192
transportation
parivahan
परिवहन

218
sports
khelkūd
खेलकूद

278
environment
paryāvaraṇ
पर्यावरण

302
reference
sandarbh
संदर्भ

324
indexes
tālikāyeṃ
तालिकाएं

360
acknowledgments
ābhār
आभार

people • लोग

body | शरीर 12
face | चेहरा 14
hand | हाथ 15
foot | पैर 15
muscles | मांशपेशियाँ 16
skeleton | अस्थिपंजर 17
internal organs आंतरिक अंग 18
reproductive organs जननांग 20
family | परिवार 22
relationships | संबंध 24
emotions | भावनाएं 25
life events जीवन की खास घटनाएं 26

appearance • वेशभूषा

children's clothing बाल परिधान 30
men's clothing पुरुष परिधान 32
women's clothing महिला परिधान 34
accessories सहायक वस्तुएं 36
hair | बाल 38
beauty | सौंदर्य 40

health • स्वास्थ्य

illness | बीमारी 44
doctor | चिकित्सक 45
injury | चोट 46
first aid | प्राथमिक चिकित्सा 47
hospital | अस्पताल 48
dentist | दंत चिकित्सक 50
optometrist | दृष्टि परीक्षक 51
pregnancy | गर्भावस्था 52
childbirth | शिशु जन्म 53
alternative therapy वैकल्पिक चिकित्सा 54

home • घर

house | मकान 58
internal systems घरेलू उपकरण 60
living room | बैठक 62
dining room | भोजन कक्ष 64
kitchen | रसोई 66
kitchenware | रसोई उपकरण 68
bedroom | शयन कक्ष 70
bathroom | स्नानघर 72
nursery | शिशुगृह 74
utility room घरेलू कार्य कक्ष 76
workshop | कार्यशाला 78
toolbox | औज़ार पेटी 80
decorating | गृह सज्जा 82
garden | बग़ीचा 84
garden plants बगीचे के पौधे 86
garden tools बग़ीचे के उपकरण 88
gardening | बाग़बानी 90

services • सेवाएं

emergency services आपातकालीन सेवाएं 94
bank | बैंक 96
communications | संचार 98
hotel | होटल 100

shopping • ख़रीदारी

shopping center ख़रीदारी केंद्र 104
department store डिपार्टमेंटल स्टोर 105
supermarket सुपर बाज़ार 106
drugstore | दवाई विक्रेता 108
florist | फूल विक्रेता 110
newsstand समाचार पत्र विक्रेता 112
candy store | कन्फेक्शनर 113
other stores | अन्य दुकानें 114

food • खाद्य पदार्थ

meat | मांस 118
fish | मछली 120
vegetables | सब्ज़ियां 122
fruit | फल 126
grains and legumes अनाज एवं दालें 130
herbs and spices औषधि एवं मसाले 132
bottled foods बोतलबंद खाद्य पदार्थ 134
dairy products | डेयरी उत्पाद 136
breads and flours ब्रेड एवं आटा 138
cakes and desserts केक और मिष्ठान्न 140
delicatessen पके भोजन की दुकान 142
drinks | पेय 144

eating out • बाहर खाना

café | कैफ़े 148
bar | बार 150

restaurant । रेस्तरां 152
fast food । फ़ास्ट फ़ूड 154
breakfast । सुबह का नाश्ता 156
dinner । डिनर 158

study • अध्ययन

school । विद्यालय 162
math । गणित 164
science । विज्ञान 166
college । महाविद्यालय 168

work • कार्य

office । कार्यालय 172
computer । कंप्यूटर 176
media । मीडिया 178
law । क़ानून 180
farm । खेत 182
construction । निर्माण कार्य 186
occupations । व्यवसाय 188

transportation • परिवहन

roads । सड़कें 194
bus । बस 196
car । कार 198
motorcycle । मोटरबाइक 204
bicycle । साइकिल 206
train । रेलगाड़ी 208
aircraft । वायुयान 210
airport । हवाई अड्डा 212
ship । जहाज़ 214
port । बंदरगाह 216

sports • खेलकूद

football अमेरिकन फुटबॉल 220
rugby । रग्बी 221
soccer । सॉकर 222
hockey । हॉकी 224
cricket । क्रिकेट 225
basketball । बास्केट बॉल 226
baseball । बेसबॉल 228
tennis । टेनिस 230
golf । गोल्फ़ 232
track and field । एथलेटिक्स 234
combat sports मल्ल क्रीड़ा 236
swimming । तैराकी 238
sailing । पाल नौकायन 240
horseback riding । घुड़सवारी 242
fishing । मछली पकड़ना 244
skiing । स्कीइंग 246
other sports अन्य खेलकूद 248
fitness । स्वस्थता 250

leisure • मनोरंजन

theater । थिएटर 254
orchestra । वाद्यवृंद 256
concert । कॉन्सर्ट 258
sightseeing । सैर-सपाटा 260
outdoor activities बाहरी गतिविधियां 262
beach । तट 264
camping । शिविर लगाना 266
home entertainment घरेलू मनोरंजन 268
photography फ़ोटोग्राफ़ी 270
games । खेल 272
arts and crafts कला और शिल्प 274

environment • पर्यावरण

space । अंतरिक्ष 280
Earth । पृथ्वी 282
landscape । भूदृष्य 284
weather । मौसम 286
rocks । पाषाण 288
minerals । खनिज 289
animals । पशु 290
plants । वनस्पति 296
city । शहर 298
architecture । वास्तुशिल्प 300

reference • संदर्भ

time । समय 304
calendar । कैलेंडर 306
numbers । अंक 308
weights and measures भार और मापक 310
world map । विश्व मानचित्र 312
particles and antonyms उपसर्ग, प्रत्यय और विलोम शब्द 320
useful phrases उपयोगी वाक्यांश 322

about the dictionary

The use of pictures is proven to aid understanding and the retention of information. Working on this principle, this highly illustrated English–Hindi bilingual dictionary presents a large range of useful current vocabulary in the two languages.

The dictionary is divided thematically and covers most aspects of everyday life in detail, from the restaurant to the gym, the home to the workplace, outer space to the animal kingdom. You will also find additional words and phrases for conversational use and for extending your vocabulary.

This is an essential reference tool for anyone interested in languages—practical, stimulating, and easy to use.

A few things to note

The Hindi terms in the dictionary use the Devnagari script, and are accompanied by their romanized versions, showing you how to pronounce each word. The entries in the dictionary are always presented in the same order—English, the romanization, and then Hindi. Where no suitable Hindi words exist, or are not commonly used, we have retained the English words, but the romanization has been adapted to show how native Hindi speakers would pronounce them.

Verbs are indicated by a (v) after the English, for example: **attend (v)**

There are two indexes at the back of the book—English and Hindi—that you can use to look up a word and find out on which page it appears. In the Hindi index, the masculine and feminine nouns are indicated by "m" and "f," and the transitive and intransitive verbs are indicated by "tr" and "itr."

pronunciation tips

This book romanizes Hindi by dropping the "a" normally used to represent the Hindi vowel "अ" that is attached to all Hindi consonants. Traditionally, "लोग" (people) would be transcribed as "loga," but we have used "log" to help you pronounce it more accurately. The exception to this is the Hindi consonant "य," represented by the roman "ya," where we have retained the "a" to keep the pronunciation accurate. For example, स्वास्थ्य is romanized as "svāsthya."

The *nukta* is the dot below the consonants "क़," "ख़," "ग़," "ज़," and "फ़," used to denote Urdu pronunciation. Consonants with *nuktas* are romanized using a dot under the roman consonant. They are pronounced with greater stress.

The dot under "ṃ" is a half consonant, and is used to denote the sound "ang" as in "kangaroo."

Guide to romanization

अ	आ	इ	ई	उ	ऊ	ऋ	
a	ā	i	ī	u	ū	ṛ	
ए	ऐ	ओ	औ	अं	:		
e	ai	o	au	ṃ	ḥ		
क	क़	ख	ख़	ग	ग़	घ	ङ
k	ḳ	kh	ḳh	g	g̣	gh	ṅ
च	छ	ज	ज़	झ	ञ		
ch	chh	j	z	jh	ñ		
ट	ठ	ड	ड़	ढ	ढ़	ण	
ṭ	ṭh	ḍ	ṛ	ḍh	ṛh	ṇ	
त	थ	द	ध	न			
t	th	d	dh	n			
प	फ	फ़	ब	भ	म		
p	ph	f	b	bh	m		
य	र	ल	व				
ya	r	l	v				
श	ष	स	ह				
ś	ṣ	s	h				
क्ष	त्र	ज्ञ					
kṣ	tr	jña					

free audio app

The audio app contains all the words and phrases in the book, spoken by native speakers in both Hindi and English, making it easier to learn important vocabulary and improve your pronunciation.

how to use the audio app

- Search for "Bilingual Visual Dictionary" and download the free app on your smartphone or tablet from your chosen app store.
- Open the app and scan the barcode (or enter the ISBN) to unlock your Visual Dictionary in the Library.
- Download the audio files for your book.
- Enter a page number, then scroll up and down through the list to find a word or phrase.
- Tap a word to hear it.
- Swipe left or right to view the previous or next page.
- Add words to your Favorites.

शब्दकोश के बारे में

तस्वीरों के ज़रिये किसी जानकारी को समझना और उसे ग्रहण करना हमेशा सहायक सिद्ध होता है। यह चित्रात्मक द्विभाषी शब्दकोश इसी सिद्धांत के आधार पर तैयार किया गया है, जिसमें अंग्रेजी और हिन्दी भाषाओं के कई उपयोगी शब्द दिए गए हैं।

यह शब्दकोश विषयों के आधार पर विभाजित है और इसमें रोज़मर्रा के जीवन से जुड़े अनेक पक्ष समेटे गए हैं, जिनमें रेस्तरां से जिम, घर से दफ़्तर और अंतरिक्ष से लेकर प्राणी जगत तक के क्षेत्र शामिल हैं। शाब्दिक क्षमता और बातचीत के कौशल को निखारने के लिए इसमें अतिरिक्त शब्द और वाक्यांश भी दिए गए हैं।

यह संदर्भ पुस्तक व्यावहारिक, उत्साहवर्धक और प्रयोग में आसान है। भाषाओं में दिलचस्पी रखने वाले व्यक्तियों के लिए यह एक अत्यावश्यक उपकरण सिद्ध होगी।

ध्यान देने योग्य बातें

इस शब्दकोश में हिन्दी मूल देवनागरी लिपि में लिखी गई हैं। शब्दों के उच्चारण को स्पष्ट करने के लिए उनका रोमन लिप्यंतरण दिया गया है। इस शब्दकोश में शब्दों को इस क्रम में प्रस्तुत किया गया है – अंग्रेज़ी, हिन्दी रूप का रोमन में लिप्यंतरण और फिर देवनागरी में हिन्दी रूप। ऐसी स्थितियों में जहां अंग्रेज़ी शब्दों के समुचित हिन्दी पर्याय नहीं हैं या उनका आम चलन में प्रयोग नहीं होता है, वहां हमने मूल अंग्रेज़ी के शब्दों को ही रखा है। उनके रोमन लिप्यंतरण को उनके हिन्दी उच्चारण के अनुसार लिखा गया है।

क्रियाओं को अंग्रेज़ी शब्द के बाद (v) के द्वारा निर्दिष्ट किया गया है, जैसे: **attend (v)**

इस शब्दकोश के अंत में अंग्रेज़ी और हिन्दी तालिकाएं दी गई हैं जिनमें किसी भी शब्द को देखकर आप उसकी पृष्ठ संख्या जान सकते हैं। हिन्दी तालिका में संज्ञा के स्त्रीलिंग और पुलिंग रूप को "f" और "m" के द्वारा बताया गया है। सकर्मक और अकर्मक क्रियाओं को "tr" और "itr" से चिह्नित किया गया है।

कोश का प्रयोग कैसे करें

आप भले ही व्यापार के लिए, शौक़ के लिए या विदेश में छुट्टी मनाने जाने के लिए कोई नई भाषा सीख रहे हों या पहले से सीखी हुई किसी भाषा का अपना शब्द ज्ञान बढ़ाना चाहते हों, आपके लिए यह शब्दकोश काफ़ी सहायक होगा और आप कई तरह से इसका प्रयोग कर सकते हैं।

कोई नई भाषा सीखते समय उस भाषा में प्रयोग होने वाले समानार्थी शब्दों (वे शब्द जिनका एक जैसा अर्थ होता है) और भिन्नार्थी शब्दों (वे शब्द जो एक जैसे दिखते हैं, परंतु उनके अर्थ अलग होते हैं) पर ध्यान ज़रूर दें। आप यह भी देख सकते हैं कि भाषाएं किस तरह एक–दूसरे को प्रभावित करती हैं। उदाहरण के लिए, अंग्रेज़ी भाषा में भोजन संबंधित अनेक शब्द यूरोपीय भाषाओं से लिए गए हैं और दूसरी तरफ़ इस भाषा ने संस्कृति व तकनीक के क्षेत्र में बहुत से शब्द उन्हें प्रदान किए हैं।

सीखने के लिए व्यावहारिक अभ्यास

- आप अपने घर, दफ़्तर या कॉलेज में घूमते हुए, उन पन्नों को देखने का प्रयास करें, जो इन क्षेत्रों से संबंधित हैं। फिर इस पुस्तक को बंद करके अपने आसपास नज़र दौड़ाएं और यह देखें कि आपको कितनी चीज़ों के नाम याद हैं।
- किसी एक विशेष पन्ने पर दिए गए शब्दों का प्रयोग करके छोटी कहानी, पत्र या संवाद लिखने का प्रयास करें। इससे आपको शब्द और वर्तनी याद रखने में मदद मिलेगी। अगर आप कोई बड़ा आलेख लिखना चाहते हैं, तो दो–तीन शब्दों को मिलाकर छोटे–छोटे वाक्य बनाकर शुरुआत करें।
- यदि चित्रों की सहायता से आपको अधिक याद रहता है तो इस कोश में दिए गए चित्रों को अलग काग़ज़ पर बनाएं और बिना देखे उनसे संबंधित शब्दों को लिखें।

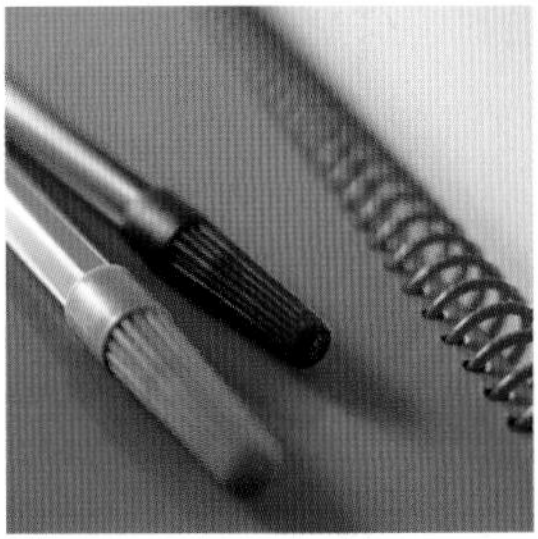

निःशुल्क श्रव्य ऐप

इस ऐप में इस पुस्तक के सारे हिन्दी/अंग्रेज़ी शब्द और वाक्यांश शामिल हैं, जो उन भारतीयों द्वारा रिकॉर्ड किए गए हैं, जिनकी मातृ भाषा हिन्दी है। इस ऐप के प्रयोग से महत्वपूर्ण शब्दों की जानकारी पाना और उनके सही उच्चारण सीखना आसान हो जाएगा।

श्रव्य ऐप का प्रयोग कैसे करें

- "Bilingual Visual Dictionary"– इस वाक्य को अपने स्मार्टफ़ोन या टैबलेट के ऐप स्टोर में ढूंढें और डाउनलोड करें।
- ऐप को खोलें और बारकोड को स्कैन करें या आई. एस. बी. एन. खुद टाइप करें। ऐसा करने से शब्दावली खुल जाएगी।
- पुस्तक संबंधित श्रव्य फ़ाइलें डाउनलोड कर लें।
- पृष्ठ संख्या टाइप करें, जिसके परिमाणस्वरूप उस पन्ने की शब्द सूची प्रत्यक्ष होगी। इस सूचीपत्र में आप शब्द या वाक्यांश ढूंढ़ सकते हैं।
- किसी शब्द या वाक्यांश का उच्चारण सुनने के लिए, उसे चुनें (टैप करें)।
- अगला या पिछला पन्ना देखने के लिए दायें या बायें जाएं।
- विशेष शब्दों को पसंदीदा अनुभाग में अलग से जमा किया जा सकता है।

people
log
लोग

body • śarīr • शरीर

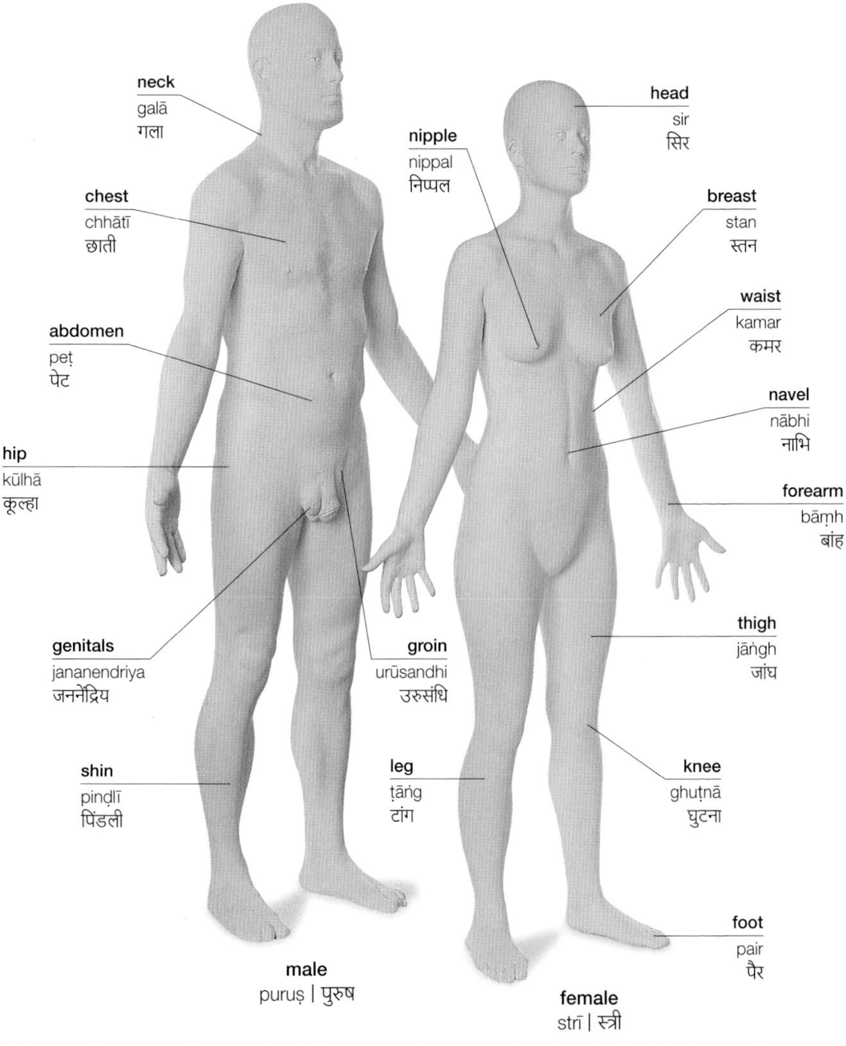
neck
galā
गला
chest
chhātī
छाती
abdomen
peṭ
पेट
hip
kūlhā
कूल्हा
genitals
jananendriya
जननेंद्रिय
shin
pinḍlī
पिंडली
nipple
nippal
निप्पल
head
sir
सिर
breast
stan
स्तन
waist
kamar
कमर
navel
nābhi
नाभि
forearm
bāṃh
बांह
thigh
jāṅgh
जांघ
groin
urūsandhi
उरुसंधि
leg
ṭāṅg
टांग
knee
ghuṭnā
घुटना
foot
pair
पैर
male
puruṣ | पुरुष
female
strī | स्त्री

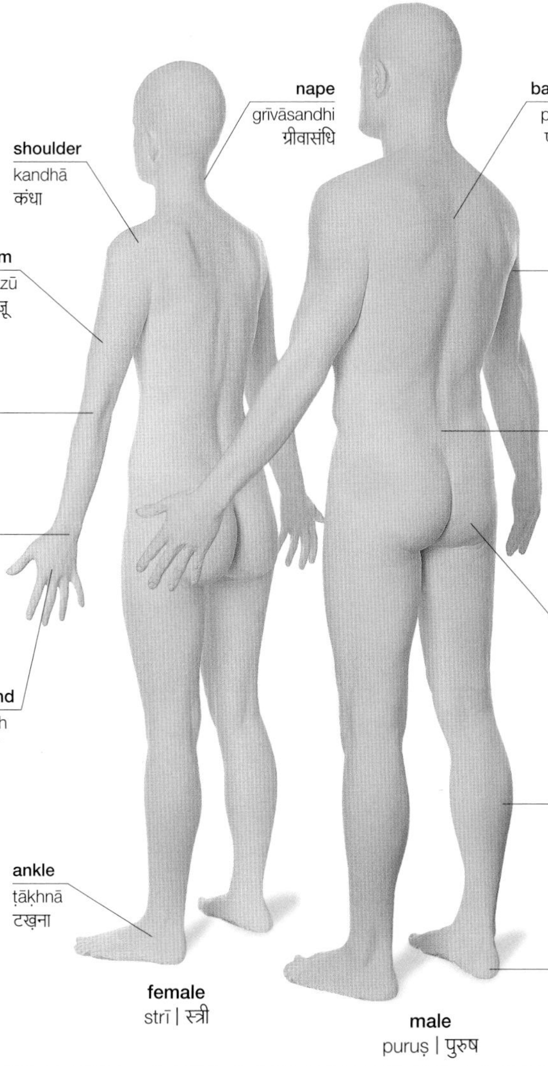
nape
grīvāsandhi
ग्रीवासंधि
back
pīṭh
पीठ
shoulder
kandhā
कंधा
arm
bāzū
बाज़ू
armpit
bagal
बग़ल
elbow
kohnī
कोहनी
small of back
kaṭiparak kṣetr
कटिपरक क्षेत्र
wrist
kalāī
कलाई
buttock
nitamb
नितंब
hand
hāth
हाथ
calf
piṇḍlī
पिंडली
ankle
ṭāk̲hnā
टख़ना
heel
eṛī
एड़ी
female
strī | स्त्री
male
puruṣ | पुरुष

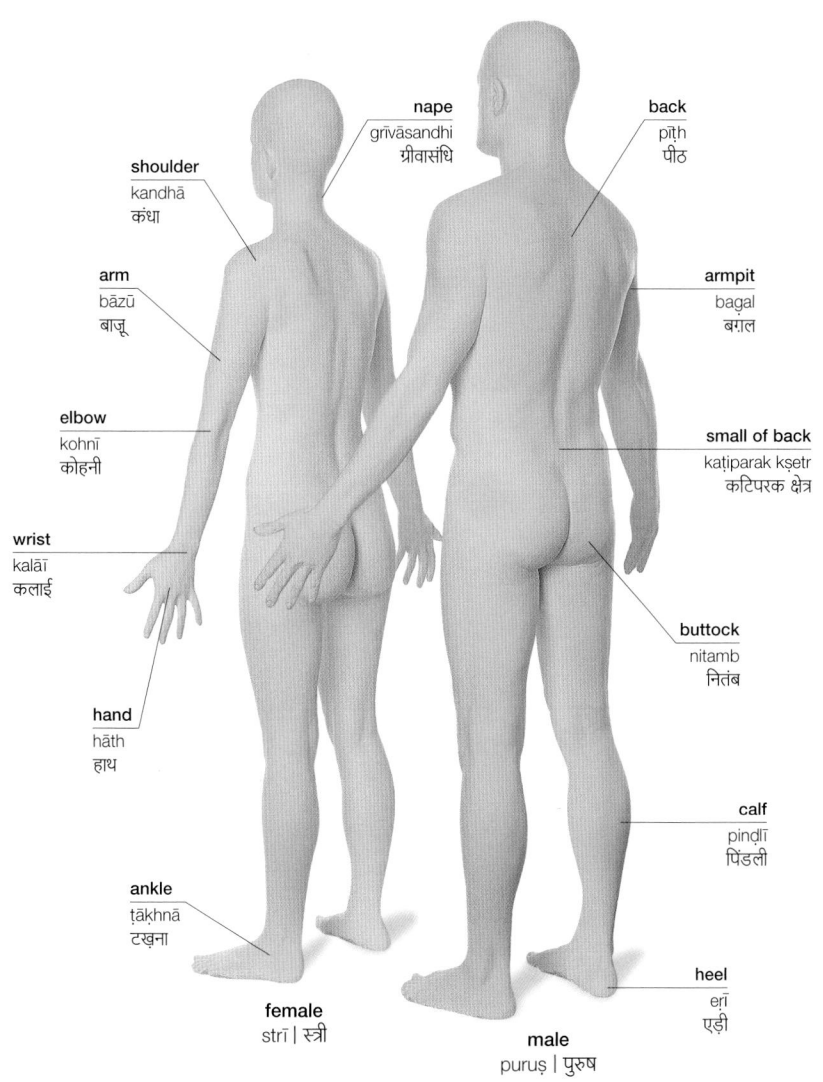

face • chehrā • चेहरा

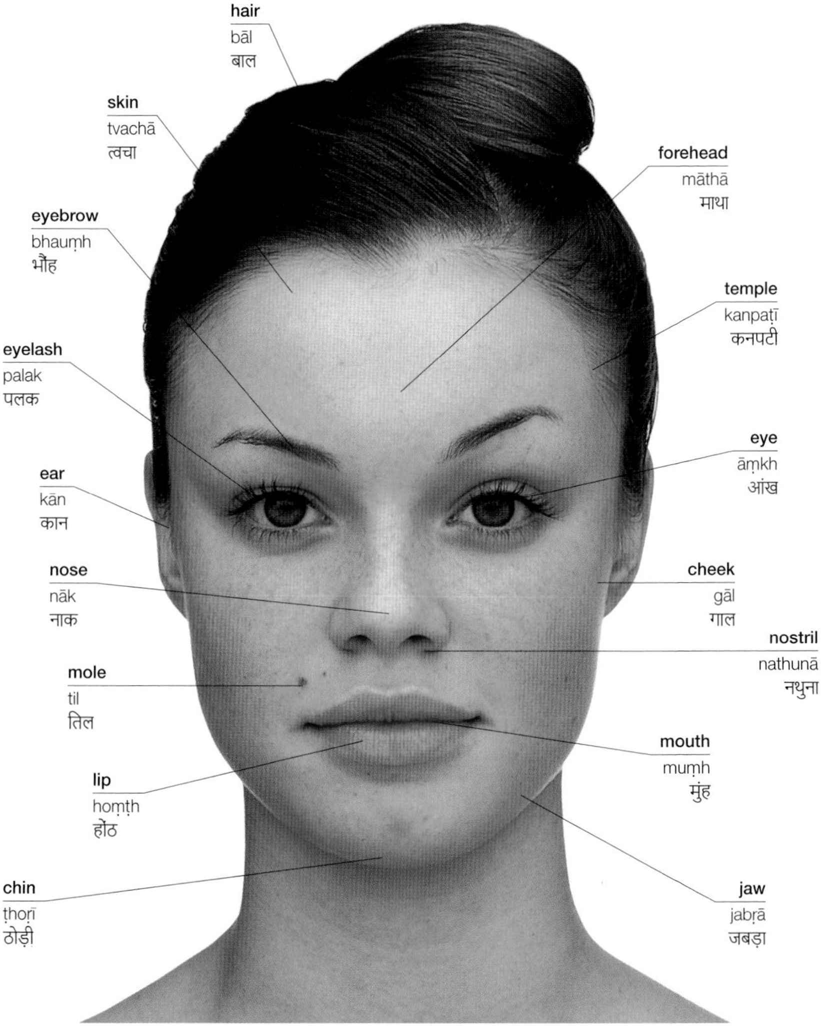
hair
bāl
बाल
skin
tvachā
त्वचा
forehead
māthā
माथा
eyebrow
bhauṃh
भौंह
temple
kanpaṭī
कनपटी
eyelash
palak
पलक
eye
āṃkh
आंख
ear
kān
कान
nose
nāk
नाक
cheek
gāl
गाल
nostril
nathunā
नथुना
mole
til
तिल
mouth
muṃh
मुंह
lip
hoṃṭh
होंठ
chin
ṭhoṛī
ठोड़ी
jaw
jabṛā
जबड़ा

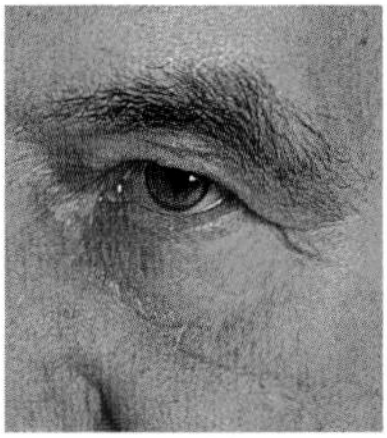

wrinkle
jhurriyāṃ | झुर्रियां

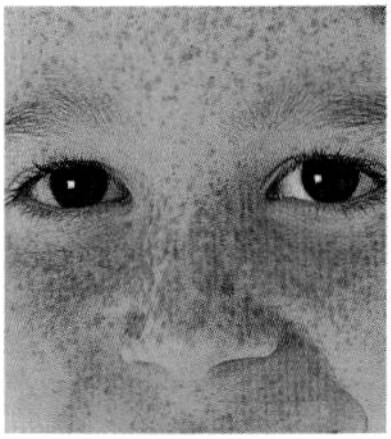

freckle
jhāīṃ | झाईं

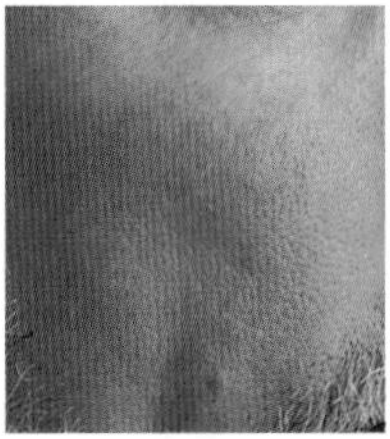

pore
rom chhidr | रोमछिद्र

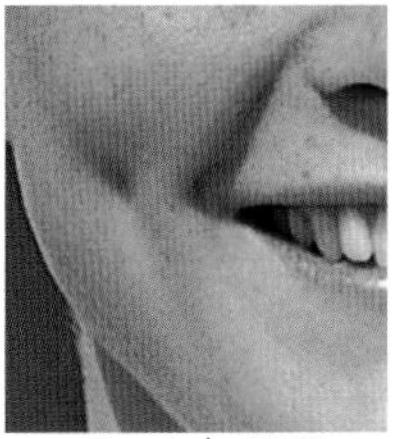

dimple | gāl kā gaḍḍhā | गाल का गड्ढा

hand • hāth • हाथ

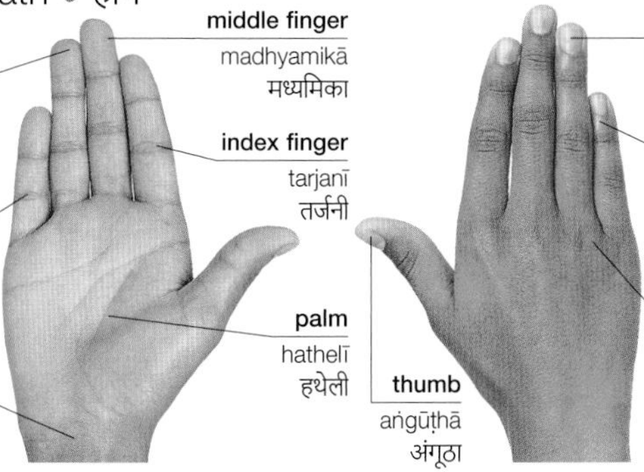

fist
muṭṭhī | मुट्ठी

foot • pair • पैर

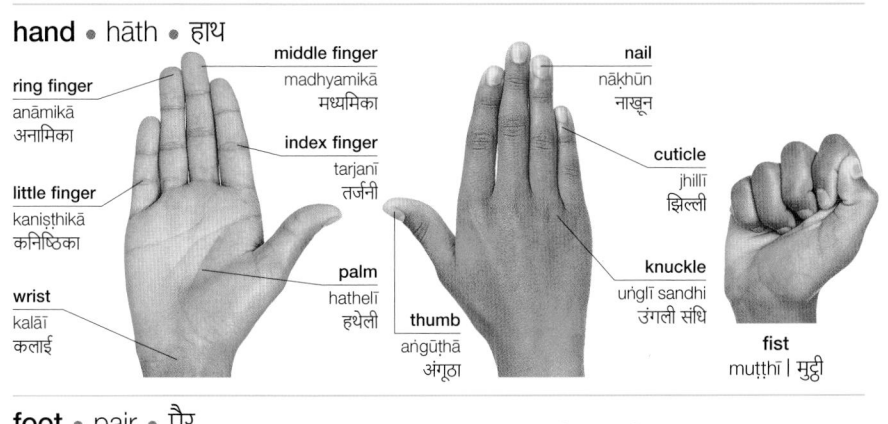

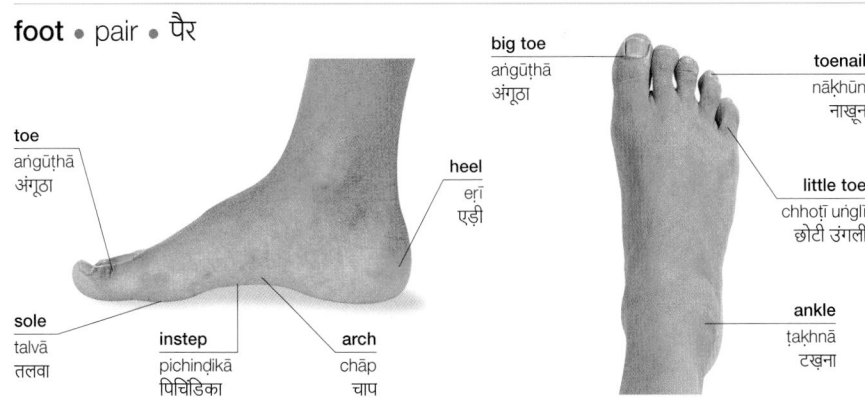

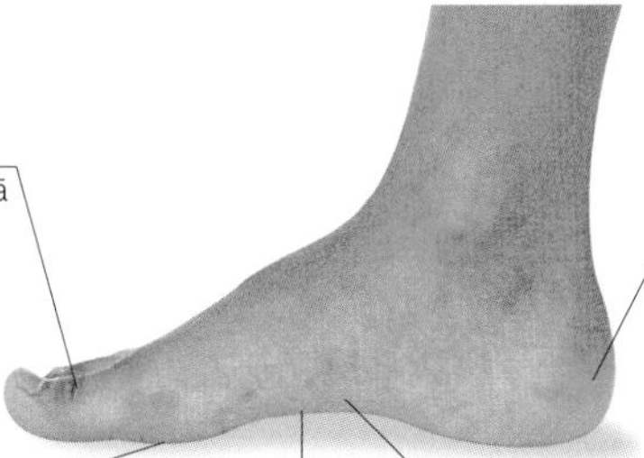

muscles • māṃspeśiyāṃ • मांसपेशियां

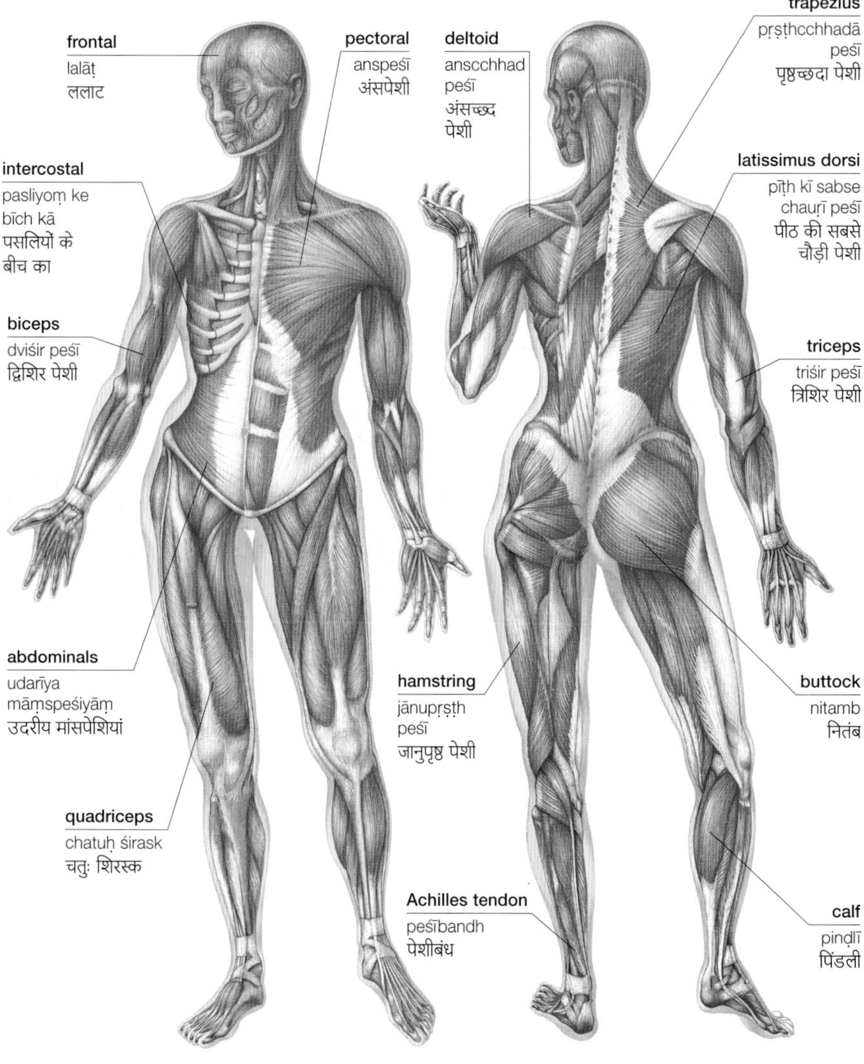
frontal
lalāṭ
ललाट
pectoral
anspeśī
अंसपेशी
deltoid
anscchhad
peśī
अंसच्छद
पेशी
trapezius
pṛṣṭhcchhadā
peśī
पृष्ठच्छदा पेशी
intercostal
pasliyoṃ ke
bīch kā
पसलियों के
बीच का
latissimus dorsi
pīṭh kī sabse
chauṛī peśī
पीठ की सबसे
चौड़ी पेशी
biceps
dviśir peśī
द्विशिर पेशी
triceps
triśir peśī
त्रिशिर पेशी
abdominals
udarīya
māṃspeśiyāṃ
उदरीय मांसपेशियां
hamstring
jānupṛṣṭh
peśī
जानुपृष्ठ पेशी
buttock
nitamb
नितंब
quadriceps
chatuḥ śirask
चतुः शिरस्क
Achilles tendon
peśībandh
पेशीबंध
calf
piṇḍlī
पिंडली

skeleton • asthipanjar • अस्थिपंजर

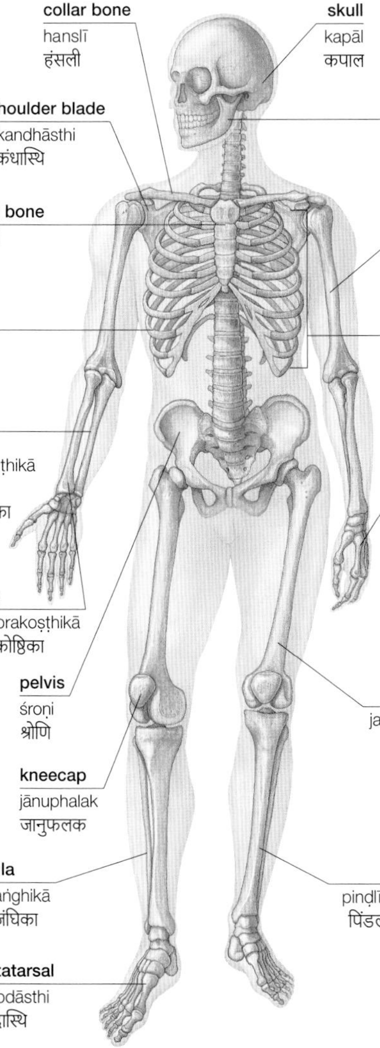
collar bone
hanslī
हंसली
skull
kapāl
कपाल
shoulder blade
skandhāsthi
स्कंधास्थि
jaw
jabṛā
जबड़ा
breast bone
urosthi
उरोस्थि
humerus
pagaṇḍikā
पगंडिका
rib
paslī
पसली
rib cage
paslī panjar
पसली पंजर
ulna
antaḥ
prakoṣṭhikā
अंतः
प्रकोष्ठिका
metacarpal
panje kī asthi
पंजे की अस्थि
radius
bahiḥ prakoṣṭhikā
बहिः प्रकोष्ठिका
pelvis
śroṇi
श्रोणि
femur
jaṅghāsthi
जंघास्थि
kneecap
jānuphalak
जानुफलक
fibula
upjaṅghikā
उपजंघिका
tibia
pinḍlī kī haḍḍī
पिंडली की हड्डी
metatarsal
prapdāsthi
प्रपदास्थि

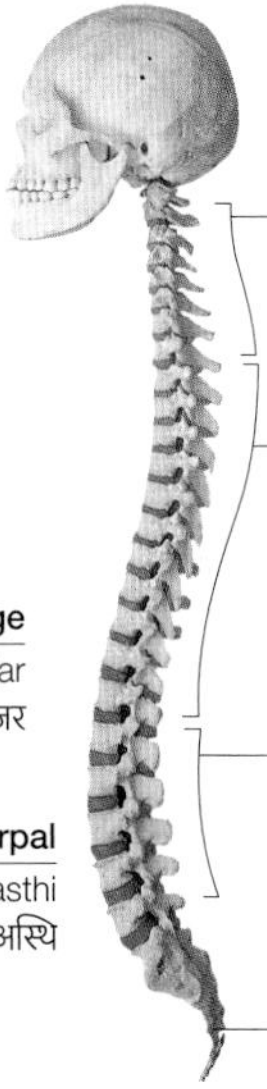
cervical vertebrae
grīvā kaśerukāeṃ
ग्रीवा कशेरुकाएं
thoracic vertebrae
vakṣīya kaśerukāeṃ
वक्षीय कशेरुकाएं
lumbar vertebrae
kaṭiparak kaśerukāeṃ
कटिपरक कशेरुकाएं
tailbone
puchhāsthi
पुच्छास्थि

spine
merudanḍ | मेरुदंड

joint • joṛ • जोड़

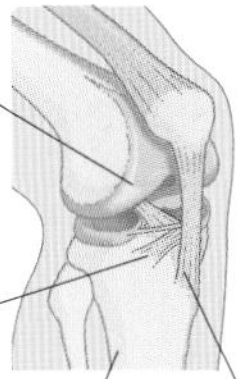
cartilage
upāsthi
उपास्थि
ligament
snāyu jāl
स्नायु जाल
bone
asthi
अस्थि
tendon
kanḍrā
कंडरा

internal organs • āntarik aṅg • आंतरिक अंग

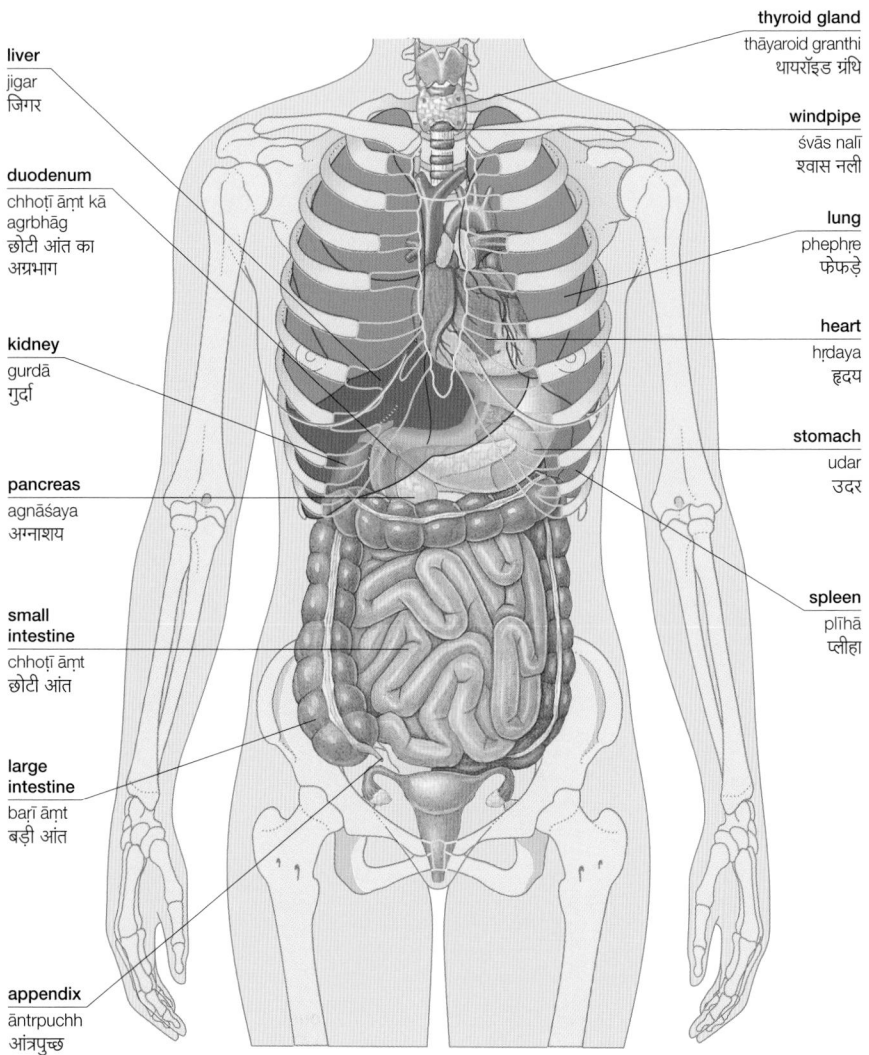

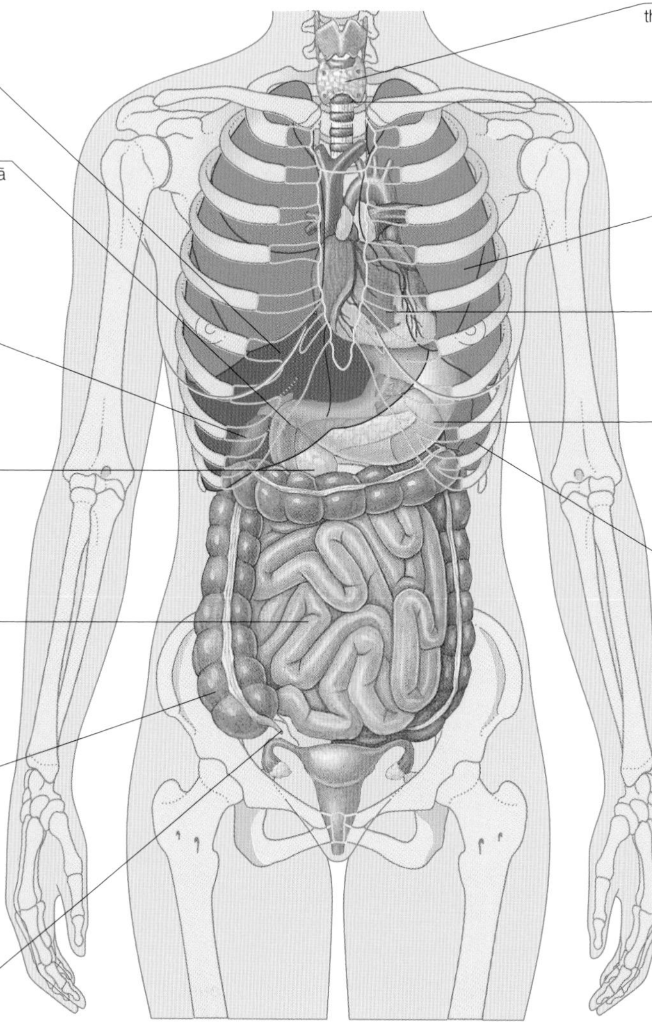
liver
jigar
जिगर
duodenum
chhoṭī āṃt kā agrbhāg
छोटी आंत का अग्रभाग
kidney
gurdā
गुर्दा
pancreas
agnāśaya
अग्नाशय
small intestine
chhoṭī āṃt
छोटी आंत
large intestine
baṛī āṃt
बड़ी आंत
appendix
āntrpuchh
आंत्रपुच्छ
thyroid gland
thāyaroid granthi
थायरॉइड ग्रंथि
windpipe
śvās nalī
श्वास नली
lung
phephṛe
फेफड़े
heart
hṛdaya
हृदय
stomach
udar
उदर
spleen
plīhā
प्लीहा

head • sir • सिर

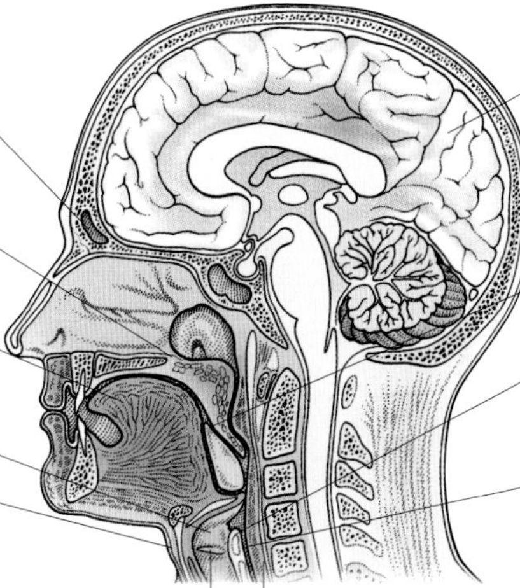

body systems • śarīr tantr • शरीर तंत्र

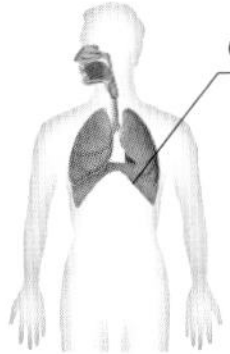

respiratory
śvasan | श्वसन

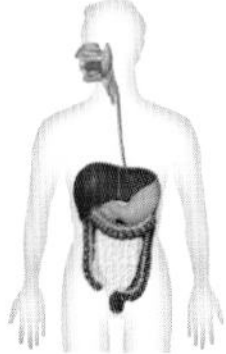

digestive
pāchak | पाचक

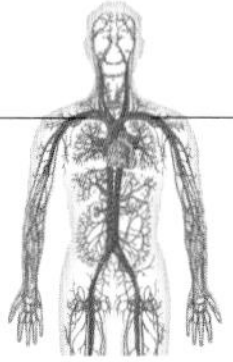

cardiovascular
hṛdaya evam raktvāhinī
हृदय एवं रक्तवाहिनी

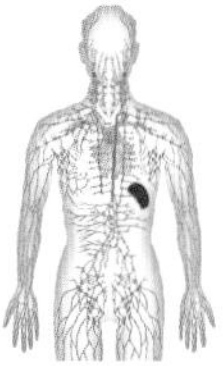

lymphatic
lasikā
लसिका

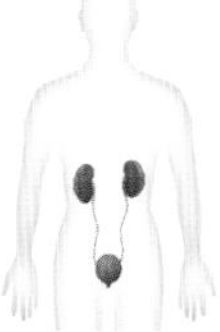

urinary
mūtr | मूत्र

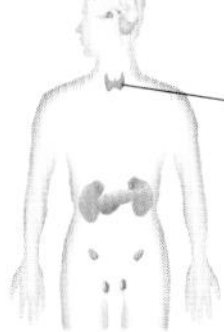

endocrine
antaḥ srāvī | अंतः स्रावी

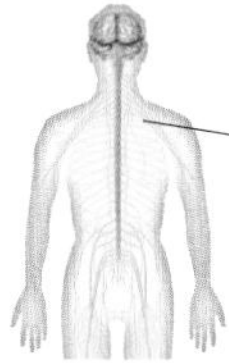

nervous
snāyu | स्नायु

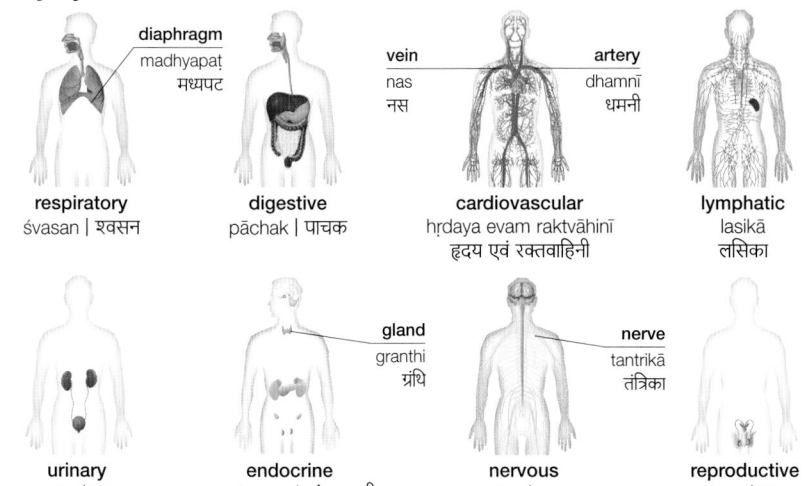

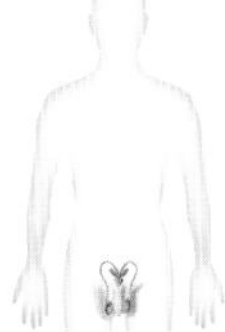

reproductive
prajnan | प्रजनन

reproductive organs • jananāṅg • जननांग

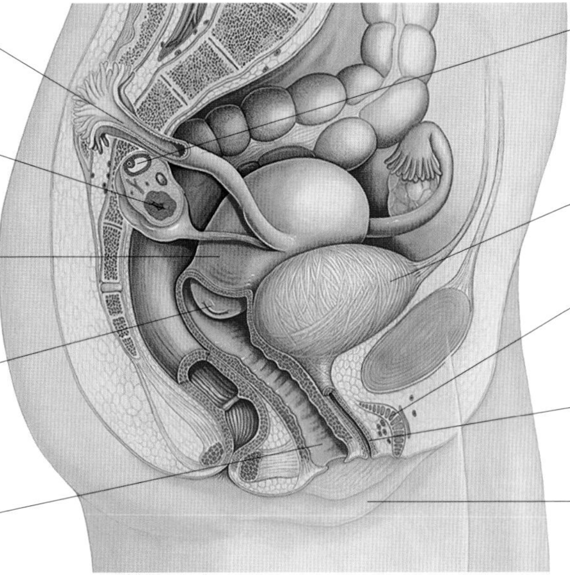

female | strī | स्त्री

reproduction • prajnan • प्रजनन

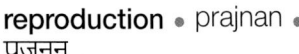

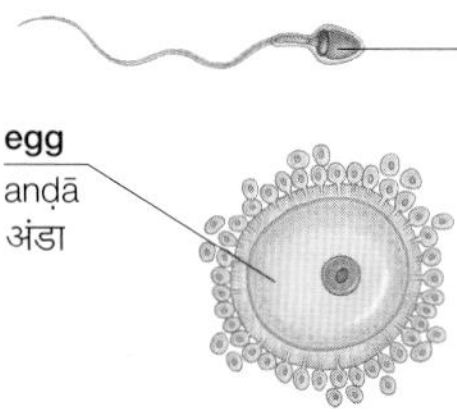

fertilization | niṣechan | निषेचन

vocabulary • śabdāvalī • शब्दावली

hormone
hārmon
हारमोन

impotent
napunsak
नपुंसक

infertile
anurvar
अनुर्वर

ovulation
bīj janan
बीजजनन

menstruation
māhvārī
माहवारी

intercourse
sambhog
संभोग

conceive
garbhdhāraṇ karnā
गर्भधारण करना

fertile
urvar
उर्वर

sexually transmitted disease
yaun rog
यौन रोग

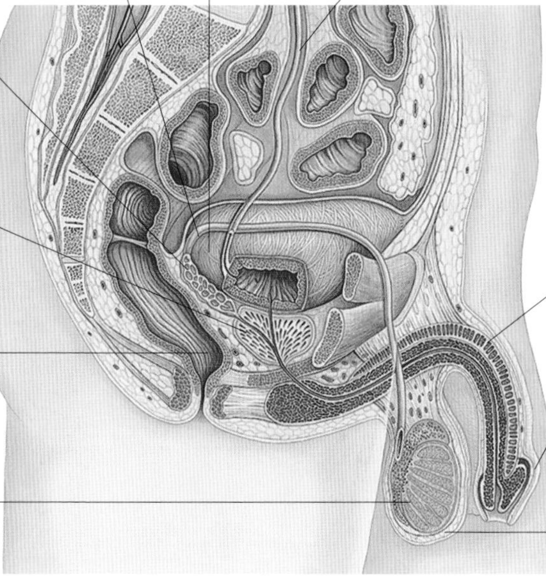

male | puruṣ | पुरुष

contraception • garbhnirodh • गर्भनिरोध

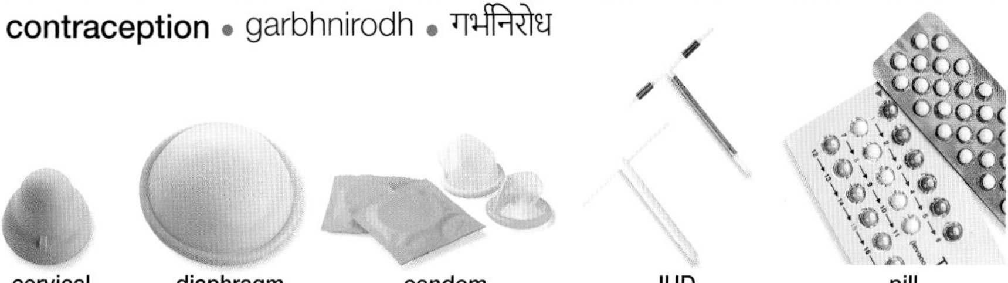

cervical cap
kaip
कैप

diaphragm
ḍāyafrām
डायफ्राम

condom
kanḍom
कंडोम

IUD
kopar-ṭī
कॉपर-टी

pill
garbh nirodhak goliyāṃ
गर्भ निरोधक गोलियां

family • parivār • परिवार

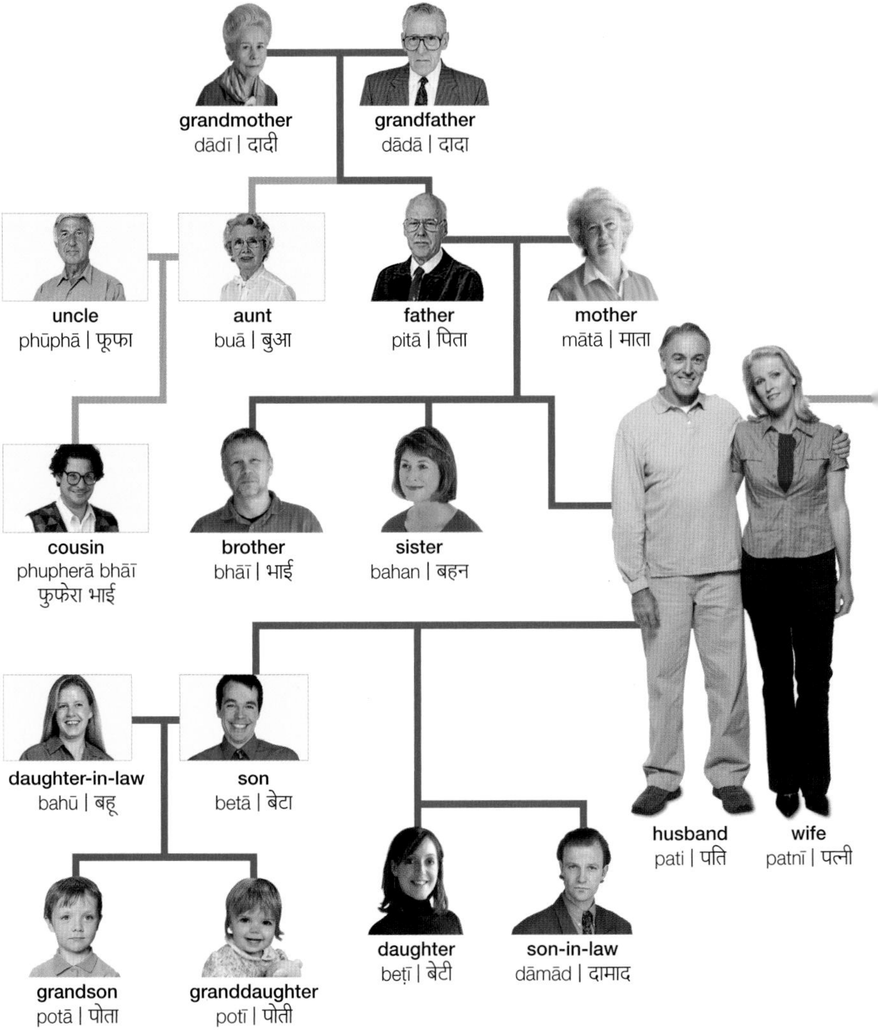
grandmother
dādī | दादी
grandfather
dādā | दादा
uncle
phūphā | फूफा
aunt
buā | बुआ
father
pitā | पिता
mother
mātā | माता
cousin
phupherā bhāī
फुफेरा भाई
brother
bhāī | भाई
sister
bahan | बहन
daughter-in-law
bahū | बहू
son
betā | बेटा
husband
pati | पति
wife
patnī | पत्नी
grandson
potā | पोता
granddaughter
potī | पोती
daughter
beṭī | बेटी
son-in-law
dāmād | दामाद

vocabulary • śabdāvalī • शब्दावली

relatives riśtedār रिश्तेदार	**parents** mātā-pitā माता-पिता	**grandparents** dādā-dādī/nānā-nānī दादा-दादी/नाना-नानी	**stepfather** sautele pitā सौतेले पिता	**stepson** sautelā beṭā सौतेला बेटा	**generation** pīṛhī पीढ़ी
partner sāthī साथी	**children** bacche बच्चे	**grandchildren** nātī-nātin/potā-potī नाती-नातिन/पोता-पोती	**stepmother** sautelī mātā सौतेली माता	**stepdaughter** sautelī beṭī सौतेली बेटी	**twins** juṛvāṃ जुड़वां

mother-in-law
sās | सास

father-in-law
sasur | ससुर

brother-in-law
sāṛhū | साढ़ू

sister-in-law
sālī | साली

niece
bhānjī | भानजी

nephew
bhānjā | भानजा

titles • sambodhan • संबोधन

Mrs.
śrīmatī | श्रीमती

Mr.
śrī | श्री

Miss/Ms.
kumārī | कुमारी

stages • avasthāeṃ • अवस्थाएं

baby
śiśu | शिशु

child
bacchā | बच्चा

boy
laṛkā | लड़का

girl
laṛkī | लड़की

teenager
kiśorī | किशोरी

adult
vayask | वयस्क

man
ādmī | आदमी

woman
aurat | औरत

relationships • sambandh • संबंध

manager
prabandhak
प्रबंधक

assistant
sahāyak
सहायक

business partner
kārōbārī
sājhedār
कारोबारी
साझेदार

employer
mālik
मालिक

employee
karmchārī
कर्मचारी

colleague
sahyogī
सहयोगी

office
kāryālaya | कार्यालय

neighbor
paṛosī | पड़ोसी

friend
dost | दोस्त

acquaintance
parichit | परिचित

pen pal
patr mitr | पत्र मित्र

boyfriend
puruṣ mitr
पुरुष मित्र

girlfriend
mahilā mitr
महिला मित्र

couple | yugal | युगल

fiancé
maṅgetar
मंगेतर

fiancée
maṅgetar
मंगेतर

engaged couple | bhāvī var-vadhū | भावी वर-वधू

emotions • bhāvnāeṃ • भावनाएं

happy
ḳhuś | खुश

sad
dukhī | दुखी

excited
utsāhit | उत्साहित

bored
ūb | ऊब

surprised
āścharyachakit
आश्चर्यचकित

scared
bhayabhīt | भयभीत

angry
gussā | गुस्सा

confused
bhramit | भ्रमित

worried
chintit | चिंतित

nervous
ghabrāyā | घबराया

proud
garvit | गर्वित

confident
ātmaviśvāsī | आत्मविश्वासी

embarrassed
lajjit | लज्जित

shy
śarmānā | शर्माना

vocabulary • śabdāvalī • शब्दावली

sigh (v) āh bharnā आह भरना	**shout (v)** chillānā चिल्लाना	**laugh (v)** haṃsnā हंसना	**cry (v)** ronā रोना
shocked sadmā lagnā सदमा लगना	**yawn (v)** ubāsī lenā उबासी लेना	**upset** pareśān परेशान	

life events • jīvan kī ḳhās ghaṭnāeṃ • जीवन की ख़ास घटनाएं

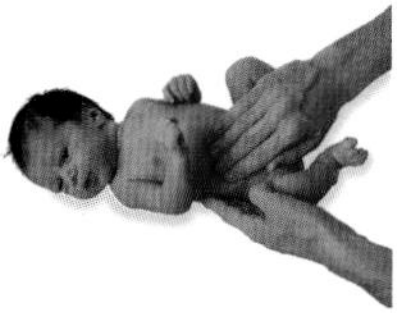

be born (v)
paidā honā | पैदा होना

start school (v) | skūl ārambh karnā | स्कूल आरम्भ करना

make friends (v) | dost banānā | दोस्त बनाना

graduate (v) | snātak honā | स्नातक होना

get a job (v)
naukrī pānā | नौकरी पाना

fall in love (v)
prem honā | प्रेम होना

get married (v)
śādī karnā | शादी करना

have a baby (v)
santān honā | संतान होना

wedding | vivāh | विवाह

divorce
talāḳ | तलाक़

funeral
antyeṣṭi | अंत्येष्टि

vocabulary • śabdāvalī • शब्दावली

christening
nāmkaraṇ
नामकरण

bar mitzvah
yahūdī upnayan
यहूदी उपनयन

anniversary
sālgirah
सालगिरह

emigrate (v)
utpravās karnā
उत्प्रवास करना

retire (v)
sevānivṛtt honā
सेवानिवृत्त होना

die (v)
marnā
मरना

make a will (v)
vasīyat banānā
वसीयत बनाना

birth certificate
janm pramāṇpatr
जन्म प्रमाणपत्र

wedding reception
vivāh bhoj
विवाह भोज

honeymoon
hanīmūn
हनीमून

celebrations • utsav • उत्सव

birthday party
janmdin kī partī
जन्मदिन की पार्टी

card
kārḍ
कार्ड

present
tohfā
तोहफ़ा

birthday
janmdin | जन्मदिन

Christmas
krismas | क्रिसमस

New Year
nav varṣ | नव वर्ष

carnival
kārnival | कार्निवल

procession
śobhāyātrā
शोभायात्रा

ribbon
riban
रिबन

Thanksgiving
thaiṅks giviṅg | थैंक्स गिविंग

Easter
īsṭar | ईस्टर

Halloween
hailovīn | हैलोवीन

festivals • tyohār • त्योहार

Passover | yahūdī parv
यहूदी पर्व

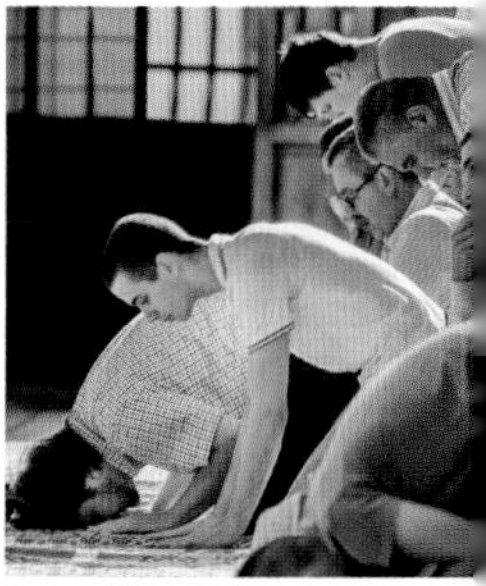

Ramadan
ramzān | रमज़ान

Diwali
dīvālī | दीवाली

appearance
veśbhūṣā
वेशभूषा

children's clothing • bāl paridhān • बाल परिधान

baby • śiśu • शिशु

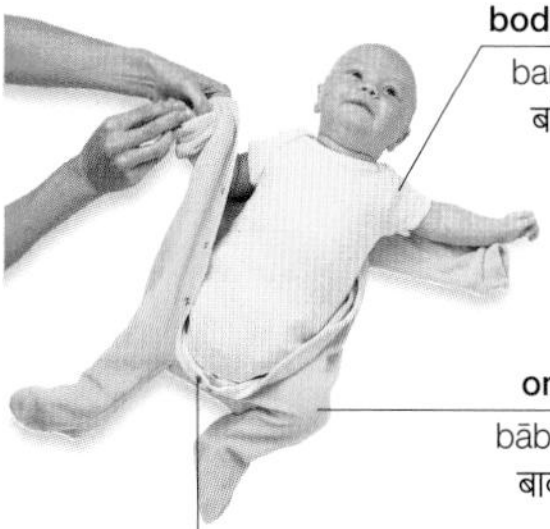

bodysuit
baniyān
बनियान

onesie
bābā sūṭ
बाबा सूट

snap
ṭich baṭan kā sūṭ
टिच बटन का सूट

sleeper | slīp sūṭ
स्लीप सूट

snowsuit
garm sūṭ | गर्म सूट

romper
rompar sūṭ | रोम्पर सूट

bib
bib | बिब

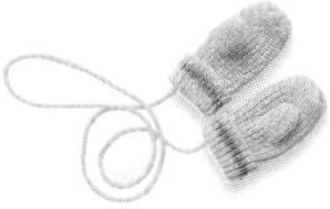

mittens
dastāne
दस्ताने

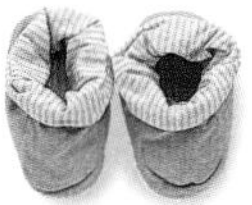

booties
bebī jūte
बेबी जूते

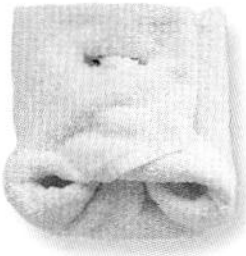

cloth diaper
ṭairī naipī
टैरी नैपी

disposable diaper
dispozebal naipī
डिस्पोज़ेबल नैपी

plastic pants
plāsṭik kī laṅgoṭī
प्लास्टिक की लंगोटी

toddler • chhoṭā bacchā • छोटा बच्चा

sun hat
ṭopī | टोपी

apron
epran | एप्रन

shorts
nikar
निकर

overalls
ḍāṅgarī
डांगरी

T-shirt
ṭī śarṭ
टी शर्ट

skirt
skarṭ
स्कर्ट

child • bacchā • बच्चा

dress
ḍres
ड्रेस

sandals
saiṇḍil
सैंडिल

summer
garmī | गर्मी

hood
ṭopī
टोपी

raincoat
barsātī | बरसाती

jeans
jīns
जीन्स

backpack
piṭṭhū baig
पिट्ठू बैग

fall | śarad ṛtu
शरद ऋतु

toggle
lambā
baṭan
लंबा बटन

duffel coat
garm koṭ
गर्म कोट

scarf
skārf
स्कार्फ़

parka
barsātī koṭ
बरसाती कोट

rain boots
veliṅgṭan
būṭ
वेलिंगटन बूट

winter
sardī
सर्दी

bathrobe
ḍresiṅg gāun
ड्रेसिंग गाउन

nightgown
nāiṭī
नाइटी

slippers
chappal
चप्पल

nightwear
rātri pośāk | रात्रि पोशाक

logo
logo
लोगो

atheltic shoes
ṭrenars
ट्रेनर्स

soccer uniform
fuṭbol sṭrip
फ़ुटबॉल स्ट्रिप

jogging suit
ṭraik sūṭ
ट्रैक सूट

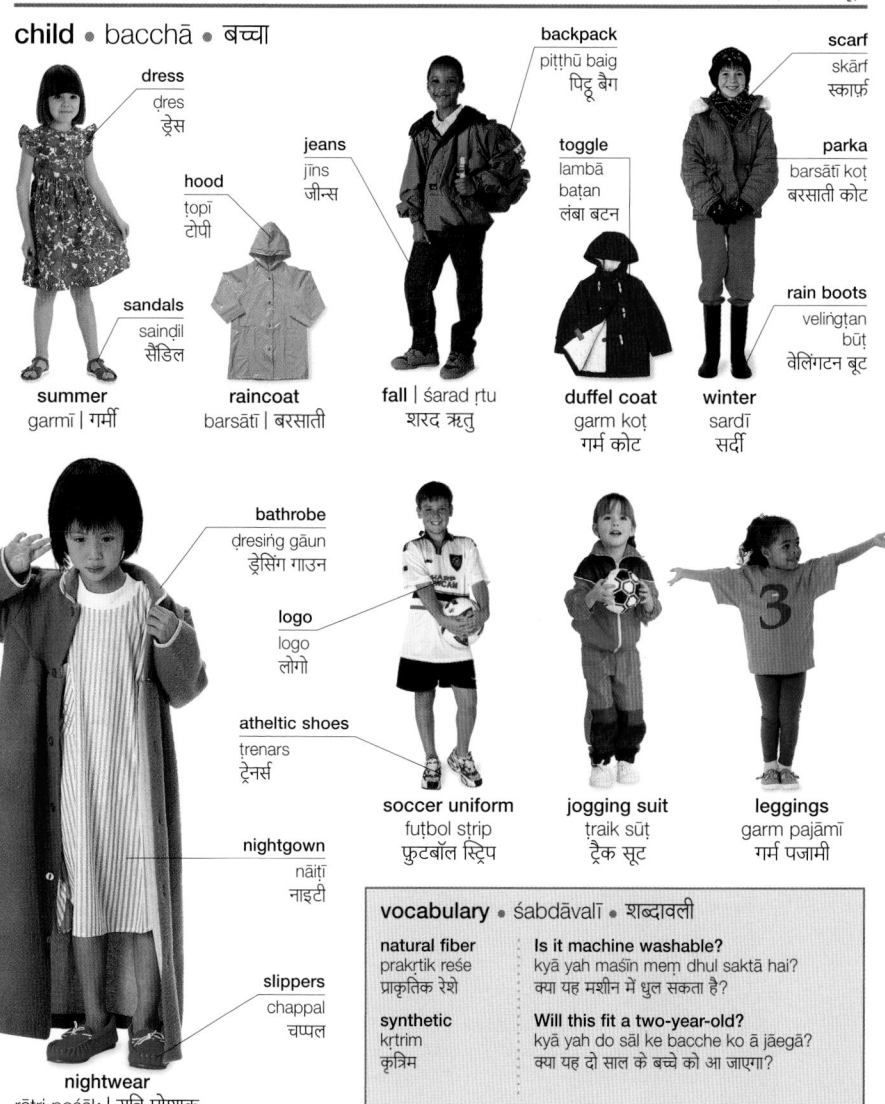

leggings
garm pajāmī
गर्म पजामी

vocabulary • śabdāvalī • शब्दावली

natural fiber
prakṛtik reśe
प्राकृतिक रेशे

synthetic
kṛtrim
कृत्रिम

Is it machine washable?
kyā yah maśīn meṃ dhul saktā hai?
क्या यह मशीन में धुल सकता है?

Will this fit a two-year-old?
kyā yah do sāl ke bacche ko ā jāegā?
क्या यह दो साल के बच्चे को आ जाएगा?

men's clothing • puruṣ paridhān • पुरुष परिधान

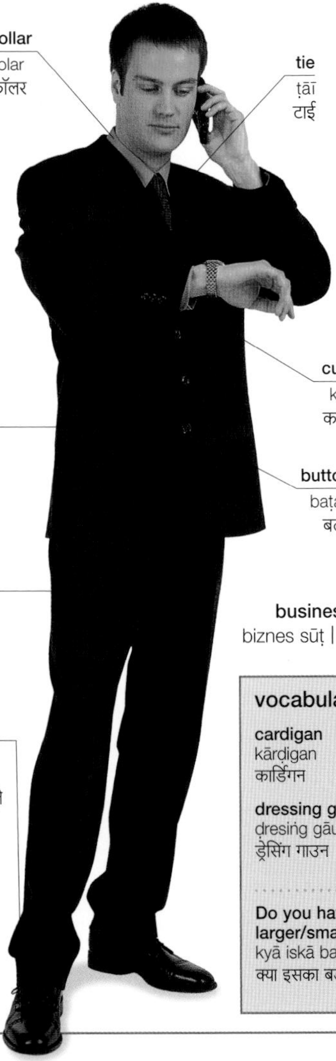

business suit
biznes sūṭ | बिज़नेस सूट

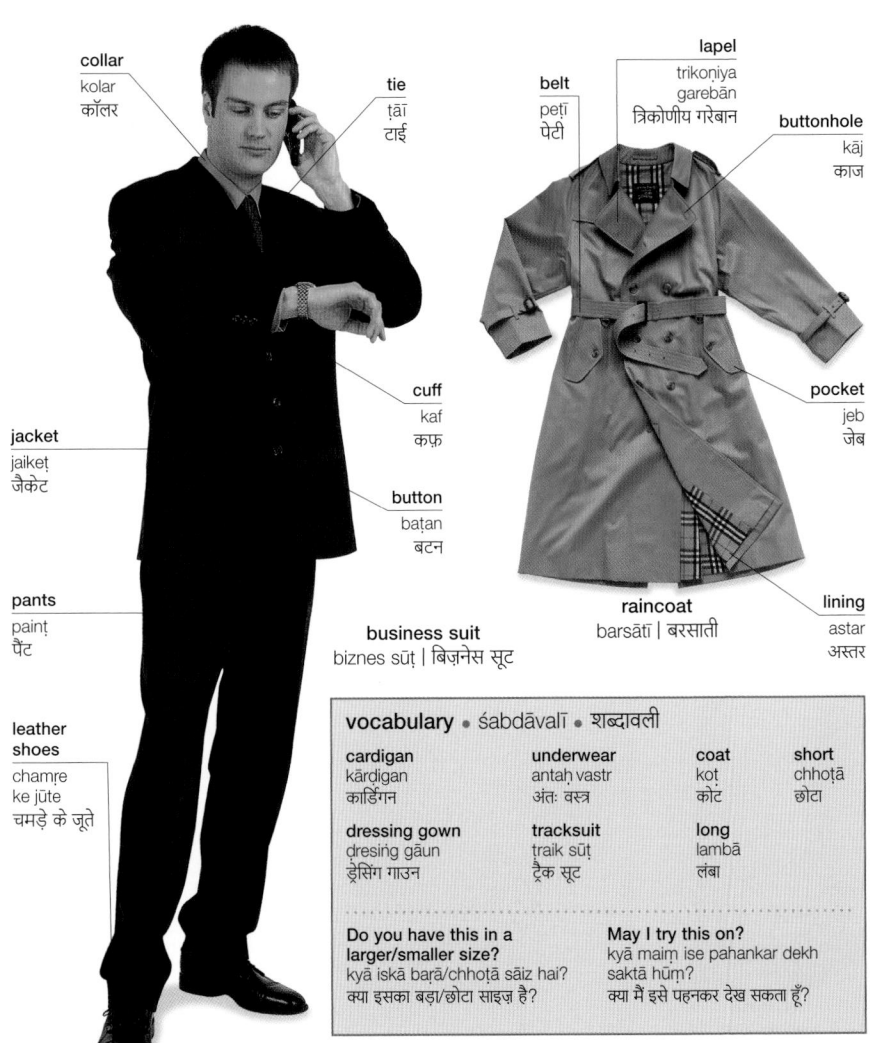

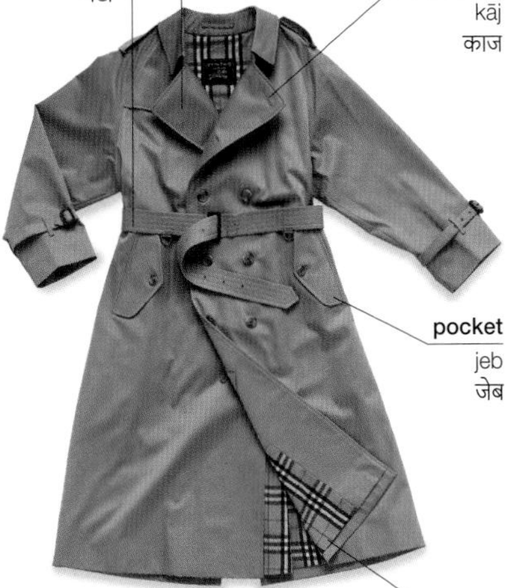

raincoat
barsātī | बरसाती

vocabulary • śabdāvalī • शब्दावली

cardigan
kārḍigan
कार्डिगन

dressing gown
dresiṅg gāun
ड्रेसिंग गाउन

underwear
antaḥ vastr
अंतः वस्त्र

tracksuit
ṭraik sūṭ
ट्रैक सूट

coat
koṭ
कोट

long
lambā
लंबा

short
chhoṭā
छोटा

Do you have this in a larger/smaller size?
kyā iskā baṛā/chhoṭā sāiz hai?
क्या इसका बड़ा/छोटा साइज़ है?

May I try this on?
kyā maiṃ ise pahankar dekh saktā hūṃ?
क्या मैं इसे पहनकर देख सकता हूँ?

blazer
blezar | ब्लेज़र

sport coat | sporṭs jaikeṭ | स्पोर्ट्स जैकेट

vest
vāskaṭ | वास्कट

casual wear
rozmarrā ke vastr
रोज़मर्रा के वस्त्र

parka
barsātī koṭ | बरसाती कोट

sweatshirt
sveṭ śarṭ | स्वेट शर्ट

shirt
ķamīz | क़मीज़

sweater
sveṭar | स्वेटर

pajamas
pajāmā sūṭ | पजामा सूट

undershirt
baniyān | बनियान

shorts
nikar | निकर

briefs
chaḍḍī | चड्डी

boxer shorts | boksar shorts | बॉक्सर शॉर्ट्स

socks
moze | मोज़े

women's clothing • mahilā paridhān • महिला परिधान

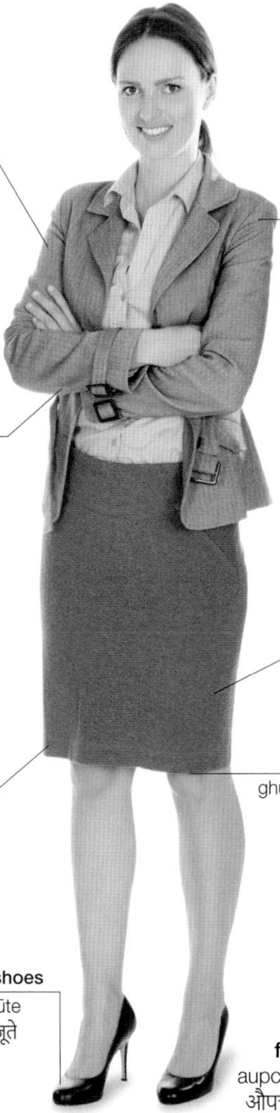

formal
aupchārik vastr
औपचारिक वस्त्र

evening dress
gāun
गाउन

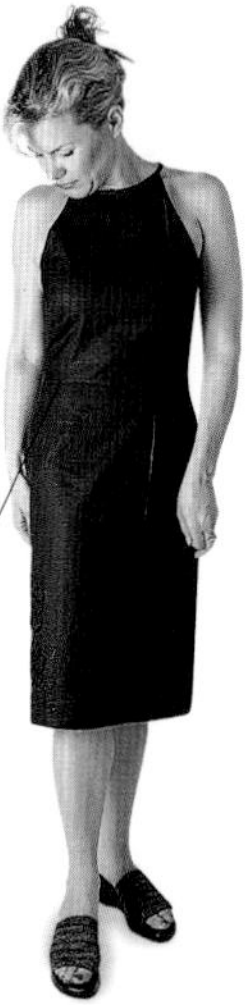

dress
paridhān | परिधान

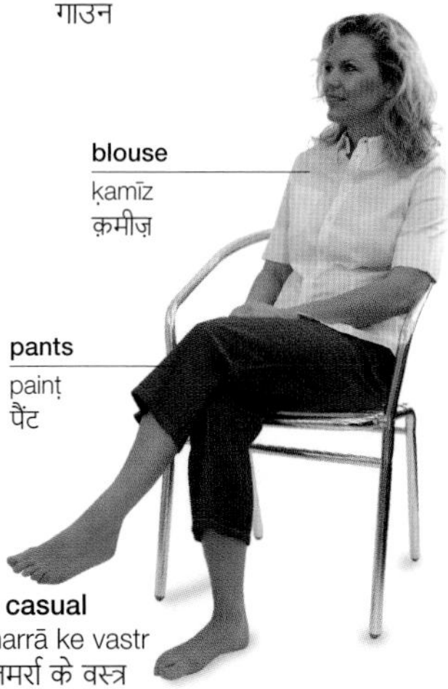

casual
rozmarrā ke vastr
रोज़मर्रा के वस्त्र

lingerie • adhovastr • अधोवस्त्र

robe
ḍresiṅg gāun
ड्रेसिंग गाउन

slip
slip | स्लिप

camisole
śamīz | शमीज़

bustier
aṅgiyā
अंगिया

stockings
lambe moze
लंबे मोज़े

panty hose
taṅg pajāmī
तंग पजामी

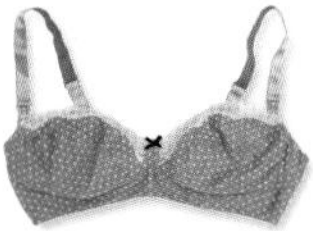

bra
brā | ब्रा

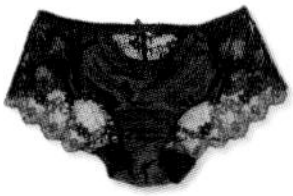

panties
nikar | निकर

nightgown
nāiṭī | नाइटी

wedding • vivāh • विवाह

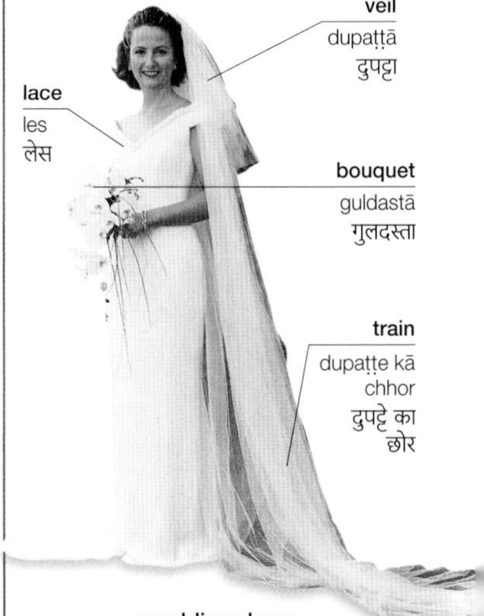

wedding dress
vivāh kī pośāk | विवाह की पोशाक

vocabulary • śabdāvalī • शब्दावली

corset
cholī
चोली

garter
geṭis
गेटिस

shoulder pad
śolḍar paiḍ
शोल्डर पैड

waistband
kamarband
कमरबंद

tailored
sile vastr
सिले वस्त्र

halter neck
ḍorī vālā galā
डोरी वाला गला

underwire
anḍarvāyarḍ
अंडरवायर्ड

sports bra
sporṭs brā
स्पोर्ट्स ब्रा

accessories • sahāyak vastueṃ • सहायक वस्तुएं

cap
ṭopī | टोपी

hat
ṭop | टोप

scarf
gulūband | गुलूबंद

buckle
baksuā
बकसुआ

belt
peṭī | पेटी

handkerchief
rumāl | रुमाल

bow tie
bo-ṭāī | बो-टाई

tiepin
ṭāī pin | टाई-पिन

gloves
dastāne | दस्ताने

handle
hatthā
हत्था
tip
nok
नोक

umbrella
chhātā | छाता

jewelry • zevar • ज़ेवर

pendant
lokeṭ | लॉकेट

brooch
jaṛāū pin | जड़ाऊ पिन

cuff links
kaflink | कफ़लिंक

link
kaṛī
कड़ी

bracelet
bresleṭ | ब्रेसलेट

clasp
baksuā
बकसुआ
stone
ḳīmtī patthar
क़ीमती पत्थर

chain
chen | चेन

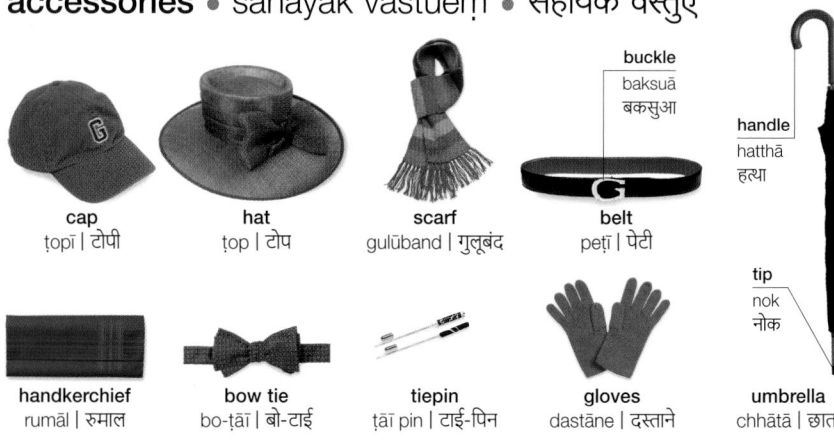

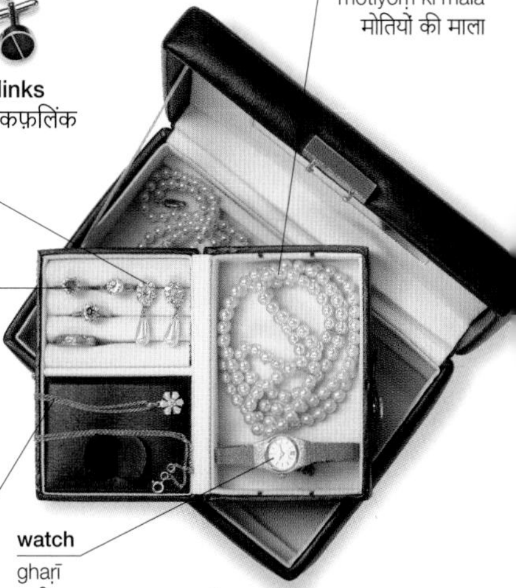
strand of pearls
motiyoṃ kī mālā
मोतियों की माला
earrings
bunde
बुंदे
ring
aṅgūṭhī
अंगूठी
necklace
hār
हार
watch
ghaṛī
घड़ी

jewelry box
zevar peṭī | ज़ेवर पेटी

bags • baig • बैग

wallet
volet̩ | वॉलेट

change purse
baṭuā | बटुआ

shoulder bag
śolḍar baig | शोल्डर बैग

duffel bag
bistar band | बिस्तर बंद

briefcase
brīfkes | ब्रीफ़केस

handbag
hainḍ baig | हैंड बैग

backpack
piṭṭhū baig | पिट्ठू बैग

shoes • jūte-chappal • जूते-चप्पल

lace-up
fīte vāle jūte | फ़ीते वाले जूते

boot
būṭ
बूट

hiking boot
būṭ
बूट

sneaker
ṭrenar
ट्रेनर

flip-flop
chappal
चप्पल

dress shoe
chamṛe ke jūte
चमड़े के जूते

high-heeled shoe
ūṃchī eṛī ke jūte
ऊंची एड़ी के जूते

wedge
chauṛī eṛī ke chappal
चौड़ी एड़ी के चप्पल

sandal
sainḍil
सैंडिल

slip-on
jūtiyāṃ
जूतियां

pump
pamp śūz
पंप शूज़

hair • bāl • बाल

comb
kaṇghā
कंघा

comb (v)
kaṇghī karnā | कंघी करना

brush
braś
ब्रश

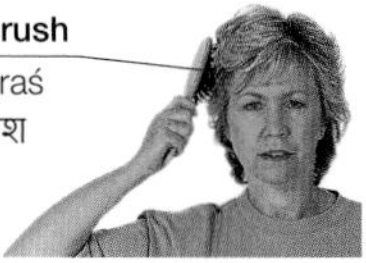

brush (v)
braś karnā | ब्रश करना

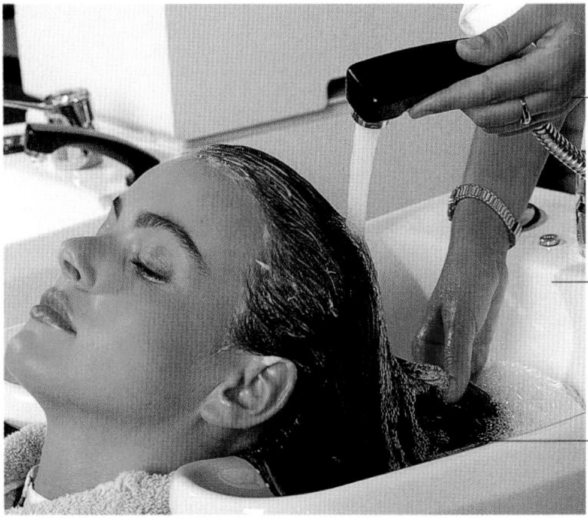

hairdresser
heyar ḍraisar
हेयर ड्रेसर

sink
besin
बेसिन

client
grāhak
ग्राहक

wash (v)
bāl dhonā | बाल धोना

rinse (v)
bāl dhonā | बाल धोना

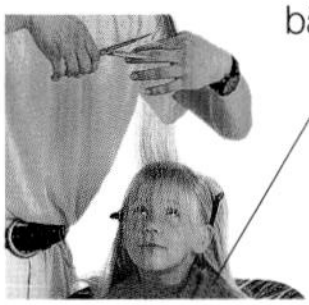

robe
vastr
वस्त्र

cut (v)
bāl kāṭnā | बाल काटना

blow-dry (v)
bāl sukhānā | बाल सुखाना

set (v) | bāl seṭ karnā | बाल सेट करना

accessories • saundarya prasādhan • सौंदर्य प्रसाधन

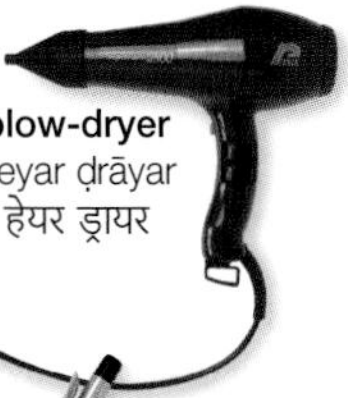

blow-dryer
heyar ḍrāyar
हेयर ड्रायर

shampoo
śaimpū | शैम्पू

conditioner
kanḍiśnar | कंडिशनर

gel
jail | जैल

hairspray
heyar spre | हेयर-स्प्रे

curling iron
karliṅg chimṭā
कर्लिंग चिमटा

scissors
ḳaiṃchī
क़ैंची

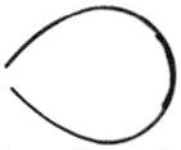

headband
heyar bainḍ
हेयर बैंड

hair straightener
bāl sidhā karne kā upkaraṇ
बाल सीधा करने का उपकरण

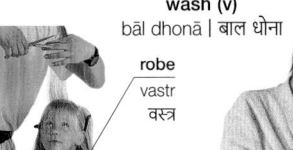

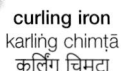

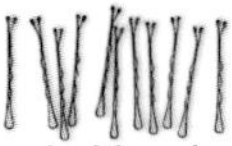

bobby pins
heyar pin
हेयर पिन

styles • keś sajjā • केश सज्जा

ponytail
ponī ṭel | पोनी टेल

braid
choṭī | चोटी

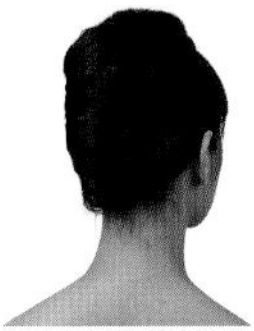

French twist
french jūṛā | फ़्रेंच जूड़ा

bun
jūṛā | जूड़ा

pigtails
do choṭī | दो चोटी

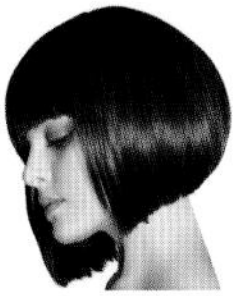

bob
bob | बॉब

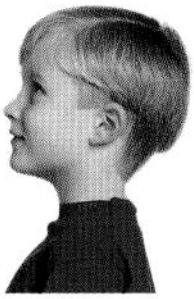

crop
krop | क्रॉप

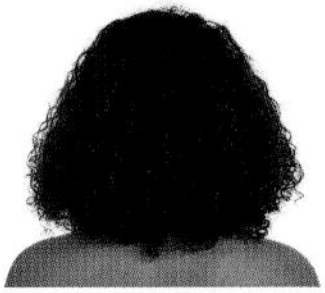

curly
ghuṅghrāle | घुंघराले

perm
parm | पर्म

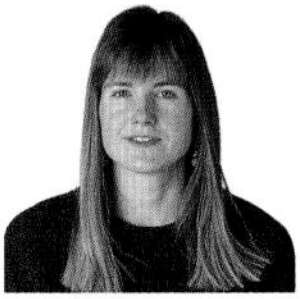

straight
sīdhe bāl | सीधे बाल

roots
jaṛeṃ
जड़ें

highlights
haīlāiṭ | हाईलाइट

bald
ganjā | गंजा

wig
vig | विग

colors • raṅg • रंग

blonde
sunahrā
सुनहरा

brunette
kālā-bhūrā
काला-भूरा

auburn
sunahrā bhūrā
सुनहरा-भूरा

red
lāl bhūrā
लाल भूरा

black
kālā | काला

gray
sleṭī | स्लेटी

white
safed | सफ़ेद

dyed | raṅge
hue | रंगे हुए

vocabulary • śabdāvalī • शब्दावली

trim (v)
chhāṃṭnā
छांटना

straighten (v)
sīdhā karnā
सीधा करना

barber
nāī
नाई

dandruff
rūsī
रूसी

split ends
domuṃhe bāl
दोमुंहे बाल

greasy
tailīya
तैलीय

dry
rūkhe
रूखे

normal
sāmānya
सामान्य

scalp
śirovalk
शिरोवल्क

hairband
bāloṃ kā fītā
बालों का फ़ीता

beard
dāṛī
दाड़ी

mustache
mūchhe
मूंछें

beauty • saundarya • सौंदर्य

makeup • sāj-śṛṅgār • साज-श्रृंगार

eyebrow pencil
āī bro pensil | आई ब्रो पेंसिल

eyebrow brush
āī bro braś | आई ब्रो ब्रश

tweezers
chimṭī | चिमटी

lip gloss
lip gloss
लिप ग्लॉस

lip brush
lip braś
लिप ब्रश

lip liner
lip lāinar | लिब लाइनर

brush
braś | ब्रश

concealer
kansīlar | कंसीलर

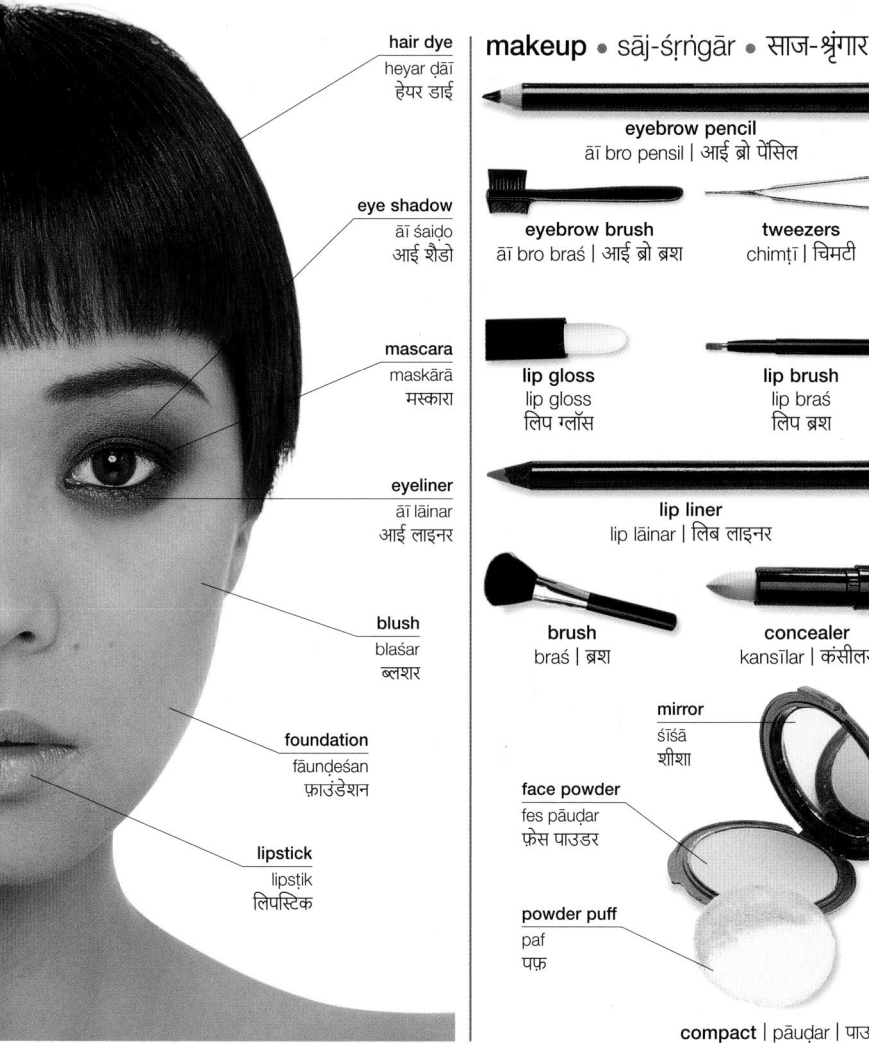

compact | pāuḍar | पाउडर

beauty treatments • sundarya upchār • सौंदर्य उपचार

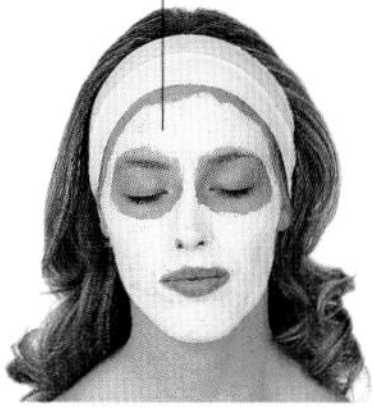

face mask
fes paik
फ़ेस पैक

facial
feśiyal | फ़ेशियल

sunbed
san beḍ | सन बेड

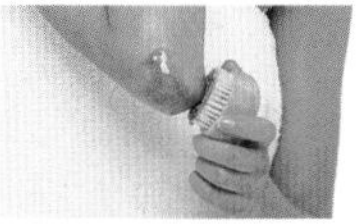

exfoliate (v)
mṛt tvachā utārnā
मृत त्वचा उतारना

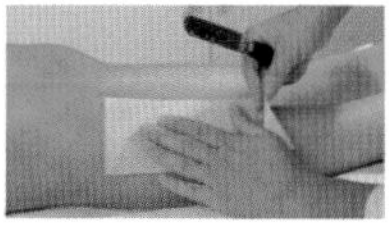

wax
vaiks | वैक्स

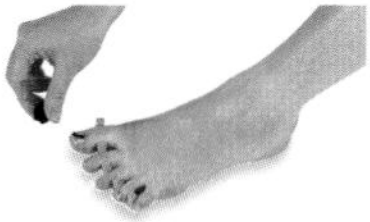

pedicure
pairoṃ kī safāī
पैरों की सफ़ाई

manicure • hāthoṃ kī safāī • हाथों की सफ़ाई

nail file
nel fāilar
नेल फ़ाइलर

nail polish remover
nel poliś rimūvar
नेल पॉलिश रिमूवर

nail polish
nel poliś
नेल पॉलिश

nail scissors
nakh kaiṃchī
नख क़ैंची

nail clippers
nel kaṭar
नेल कटर

toiletries • saundarya prasādhan • सौंदर्य प्रसाधन

cleanser
klīnzar
क्लीज़र

toner
ṭonar
टोनर

moisturizer
moiścharāizar
मॉइश्चराइज़र

self-tanning lotion
ṭain karne kī krīm
टैन करने की क्रीम

perfume
itr
इत्र

eau de toilette
parfyūm spre
परफ़्यूम स्प्रे

vocabulary • śabdāvalī • शब्दावली

complexion
raṅg rūp
रंग-रूप

fair
gorī
गोरी

dry
rūkhī
रूखी

anti-wrinkle
jhurrī-nivārak
झुर्री-निवारक

oily
tailīya
तैलीय

sensitive
saṃvedanśīl
संवेदनशील

shade
raṅg
रंग

hypoallergenic
elarjī rodhak
एलर्जी रोधक

dark
kālī
काली

tattoo
gudnā
गुदना

cotton balls
rūī ke phāhe
रूई के फाहे

tan
bhūre raṅg kā honā
भूरे रंग का होना

health

svāsthya

स्वास्थ्य

illness • bīmārī • बीमारी

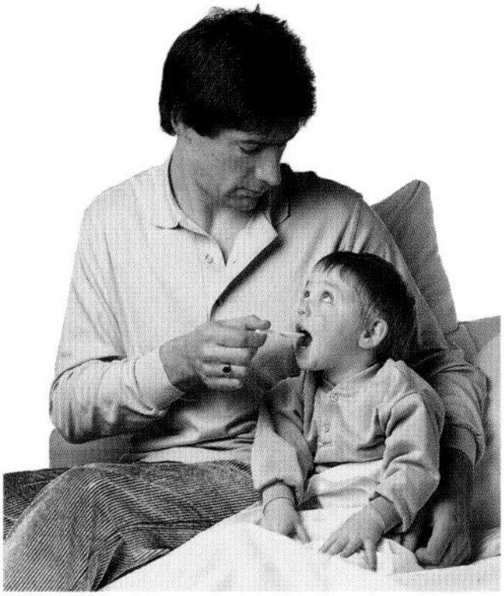

fever
buḳhār | बुख़ार

headache
sirdard
सिरदर्द

nosebleed
naksīr
नकसीर

cough
khāṃsī
खांसी

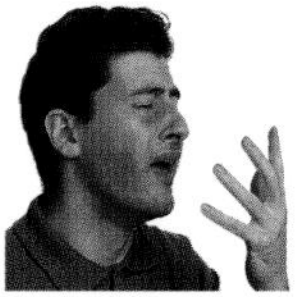

sneeze
chhīṃk | छींक

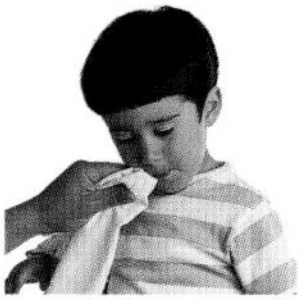

cold
zukām | ज़ुकाम

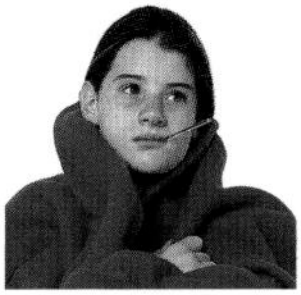

flu
flū | फ़्लू

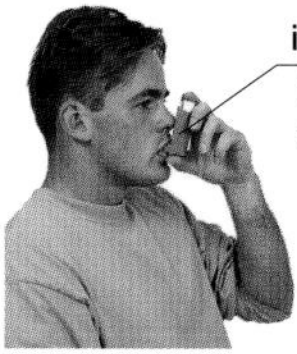

inhaler
inhelar
इनहेलर

asthma
damā | दमा

cramps
maroṛ | मरोड़

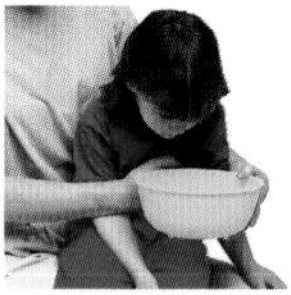

nausea
mitlī | मितली

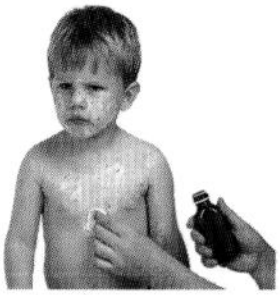

chicken pox
chhoṭī chechak | छोटी चेचक

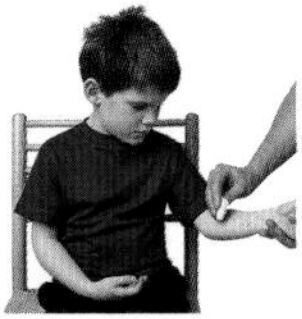

rash
funsī | फ़ुंसी

vocabulary • śabdāvalī • शब्दावली

stroke pakṣāghāt पक्षाघात	**diabetes** madhumeh मधुमेह	**eczema** khāj खाज	**chill** sardī सर्दी	**vomit (v)** ulṭī karnā उल्टी करना	**diarrhea** dast दस्त
blood pressure raktchāp रक्तचाप	**allergy** elarjī एलर्जी	**infection** saṅkramaṇ संक्रमण	**stomachache** peṭ dard पेट दर्द	**epilepsy** mirgī मिरगी	**measles** khasrā खसरा
heart attack dil kā daurā दिल का दौरा	**hayfever** parāgaj jvar परागज ज्वर	**virus** viṣāṇu विषाणु	**faint (v)** behoś honā बेहोश होना	**migraine** ādhāsīsī आधासीसी	**mumps** kanpeṛā कनपेड़ा

doctor • chikitsak • चिकित्सक

consultation • parāmarś • परामर्श

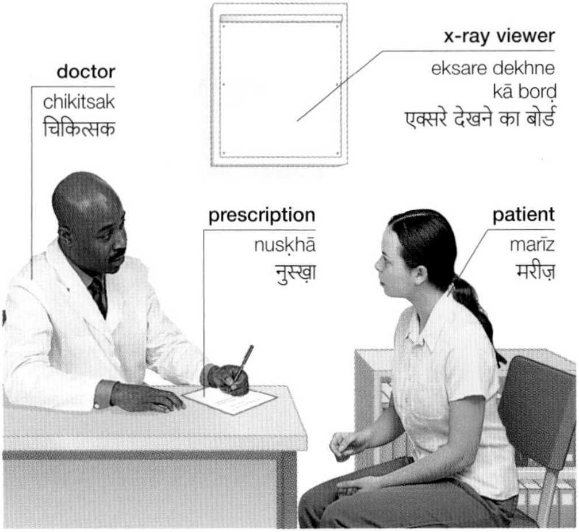

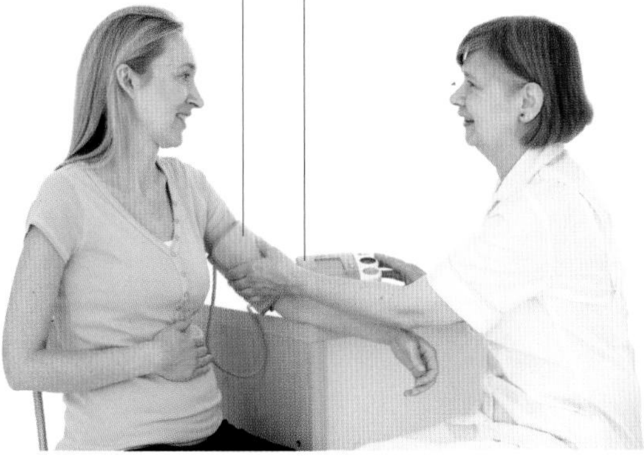

vocabulary • śabdāvalī • शब्दावली

appointment
milne kā samaya
मिलने का समय

doctor's office
śalya chikitsā
शल्य चिकित्सा

waiting room
pratīkṣā kakṣ
प्रतीक्षा कक्ष

vaccination
ṭīkā
टीका

thermometer
tharmāmīṭar
थर्मामीटर

medical examination
śārīrik jāṃch
शारीरिक जांच

I need to see a doctor.
mujhe ḍokṭar ko dikhānā hai
मुझे डॉक्टर को दिखाना है।

It hurts here.
yahāṃ dard ho rahā hai
यहां दर्द हो रहा है।

injury • choṭ • चोट

sprain | moch | मोच

sling
sliṅg paṭṭī
स्लिंग पट्टी

fracture | haḍḍī ṭūṭnā
हड्डी टूटना

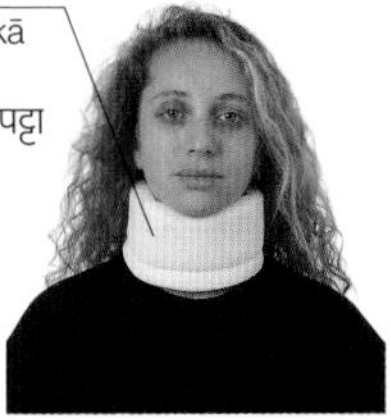

neck brace
gardan kā paṭṭā
गर्दन का पट्टा

whiplash | gale kī moch
गले की मोच

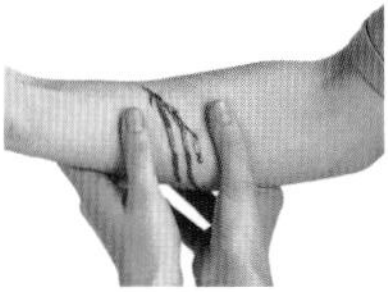

cut
kaṭnā | कटना

graze
ragaṛ | रगड़

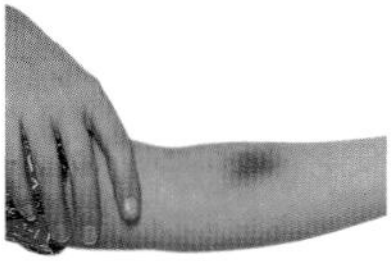

bruise
kharoṃch | खरोंच

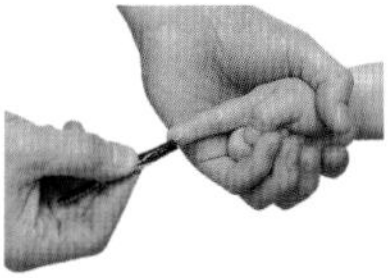

splinter
khapcchī | खपच्ची

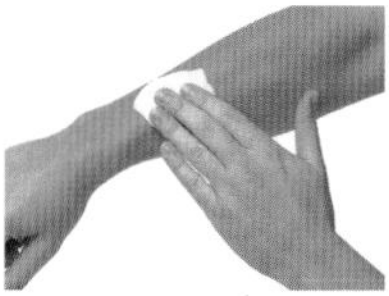

sunburn
dhūp se jalnā
धूप से जलना

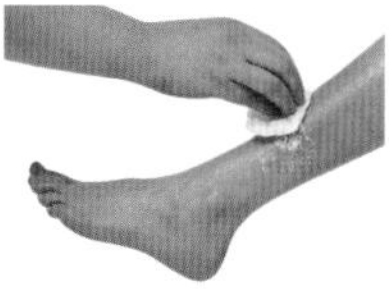

burn
jalnā
जलना

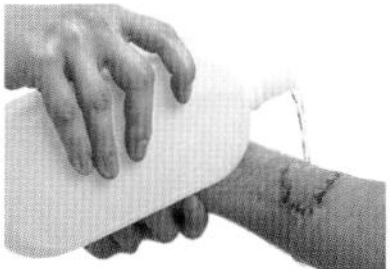

bite
kāṭā huā
काटा हुआ

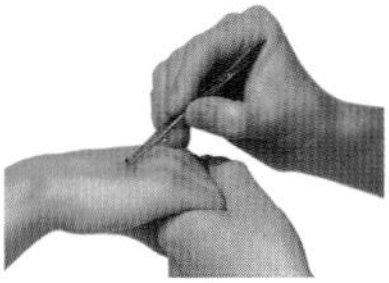

sting
ḍaṅk
डंक

vocabulary • śabdāvalī • शब्दावली

accident durghaṭnā दुर्घटना	**hemorrhage** raktsrāv रक्तस्राव	**poisoning** viṣpān विषपान	**Will he/she be all right?** kyā vah ṭhīk ho jāegā/jāegī? क्या वह ठीक हो जाएगा/जाएगी?
emergency āpātkāl आपातकाल	**blister** chhālā छाला	**electric shock** bijlī kā jhaṭkā बिजली का झटका	**Where does it hurt?** kahāṃ dard ho rahā hai? कहां दर्द हो रहा है?
wound ghāv घाव	**concussion** āghāt आघात	**head injury** sir kī choṭ सिर की चोट	**Please call an ambulance.** kṛpyā embulens bulāie कृपया एम्बुलेंस बुलाइए।

first aid • prāthmik chikitsā • प्राथमिक चिकित्सा

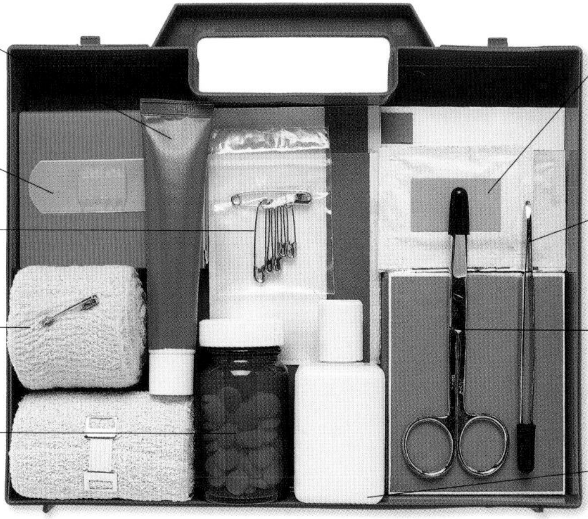

first-aid kit | prāthmik chikitsā peṭī | प्राथमिक चिकित्सा पेटी

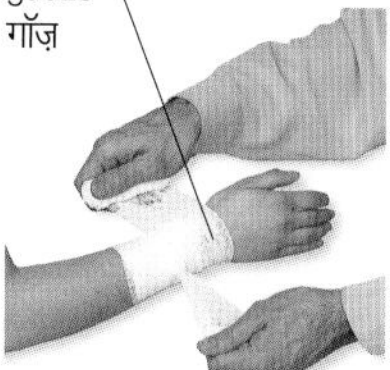

dressing
marham paṭṭī | मरहम पट्टी

splint | khapachī | खपची

adhesive tape
chipakne vālā ṭep
चिपकने वाला टेप

resuscitation | hoś meṃ lānā/kritrim śvasan
होश में लाना/कृत्रिम श्वसन

vocabulary • śabdāvalī • शब्दावली

shock sadmā सदमा	**pulse** nāṛī नाड़ी	**choke (v)** dam ghuṭnā दम घुटना
unconscious behoś बेहोश	**breathing** sāṃs सांस	**sterile** saṅkramaṇ rahit संक्रमण रहित

Can you help?
kyā āp madad kar sakte haiṃ?
क्या आप मदद कर सकते हैं?

Do you know first aid?
kyā āp prāthmik chikitsā jānte haiṃ?
क्या आप प्राथमिक चिकित्सा जानते हैं?

hospital • aspatāl • अस्पताल

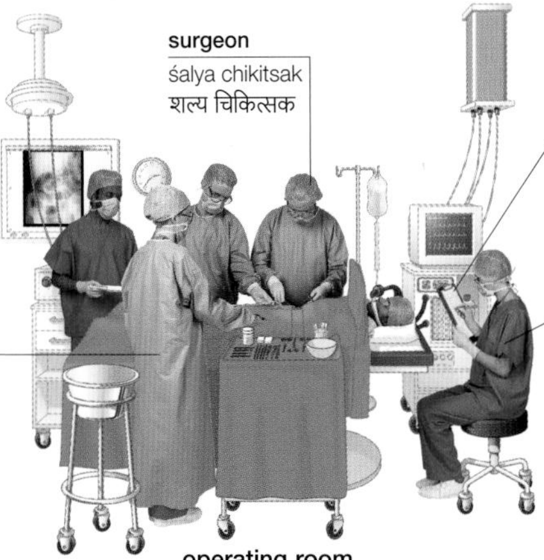

surgeon
śalya chikitsak
शल्य चिकित्सक

chart
chārṭ
चार्ट

nurse
nars
नर्स

anesthetist
niśchetan chikitsak
निश्चेतन चिकित्सक

operating room
śalya kakṣ | शल्य कक्ष

blood test
ḳhūn kī jāṃch
ख़ून की जांच

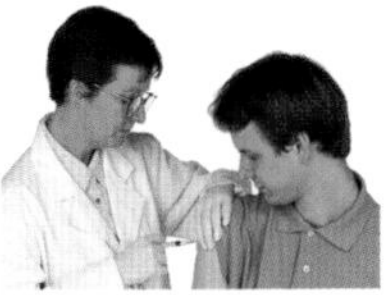

injection
sūī lagānā | सुई लगाना

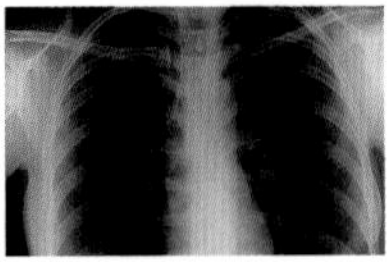

X-ray
eks-re | एक्स-रे

gurney
trolī
ट्रॉली

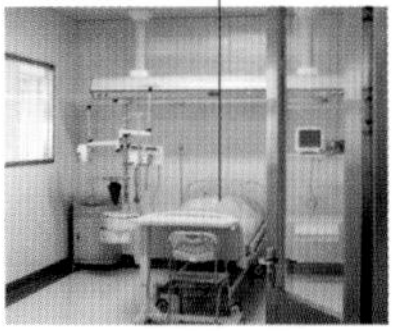

emergency room
āpātkālīn kakṣ
आपातकालीन कक्ष

call button
kol baṭan
कॉल बटन

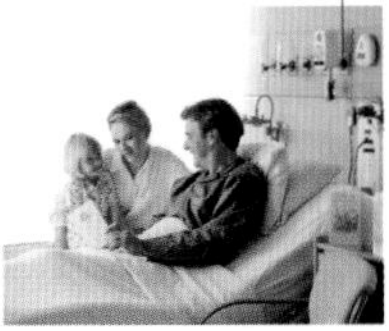

ward
kakṣ | कक्ष

wheelchair
vhīlcheyar | व्हीलचेयर

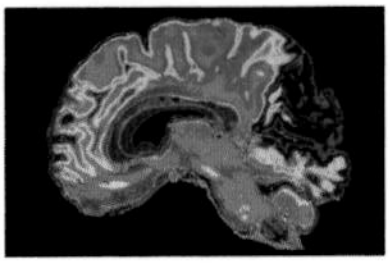

scan
skain | स्कैन

vocabulary • śabdāvalī • शब्दावली

operation śalya chikitsā शल्य चिकित्सा	**discharged** chhuṭṭī denā छुट्टी देना	**visiting hours** milne kā samaya मिलने का समय	**children's ward** bacchoṃ kā vorḍ बच्चों का वॉर्ड	**intensive care unit** gahan chikitsā kakṣ गहन चिकित्सा कक्ष
admitted bhartī भर्ती	**clinic** chikitsālaya चिकित्सालय	**maternity ward** prasūti kakṣ प्रसूति कक्ष	**private room** nijī kamrā निजी कमरा	**outpatient** bāhya rogī बाह्य रोगी

departments • vibhāg • विभाग

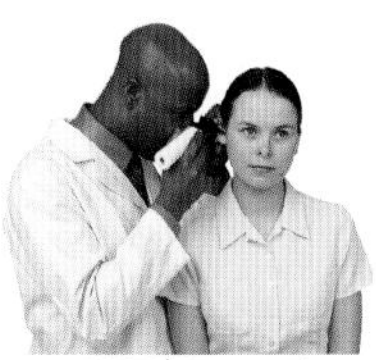

ENT | kān, nāk, evam galā chikitsā
कान, नाक एवं गला चिकित्सा

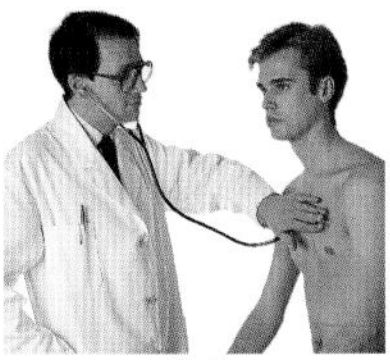

cardiology
hṛdaya chikitsā
हृदय चिकित्सा

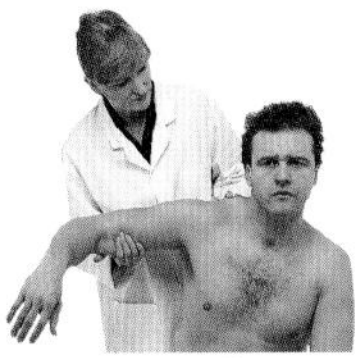

orthopedics
asthi chikitsā
अस्थि चिकित्सा

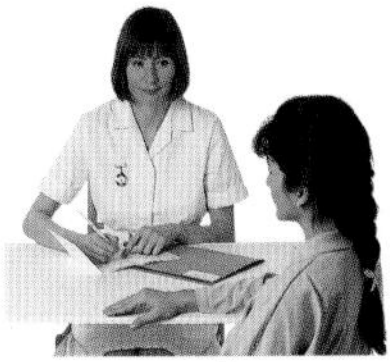

gynecology
strī rog chikitsā
स्त्री-रोग चिकित्सा

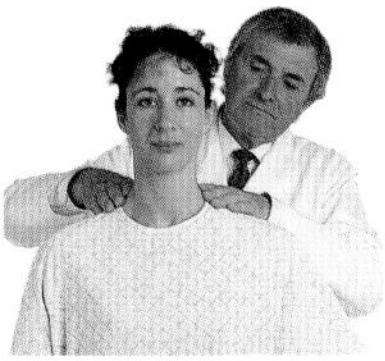

physiotherapy
vyāyām chikitsā
व्यायाम चिकित्सा

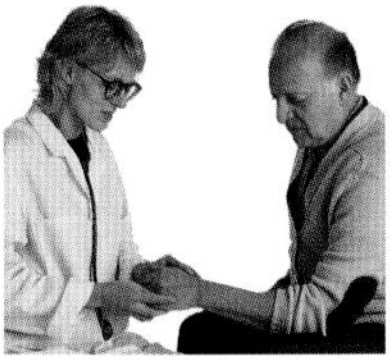

dermatology
tvachā chikitsā
त्वचा चिकित्सा

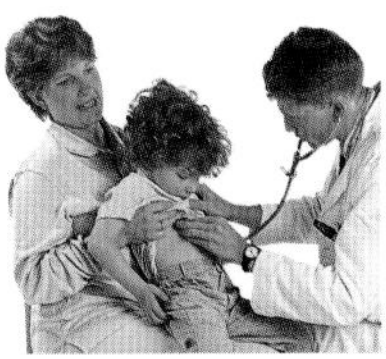

pediatrics
bāl chikitsā
बाल चिकित्सा

radiology
vikiraṇ chikitsā
विकिरण चिकित्सा

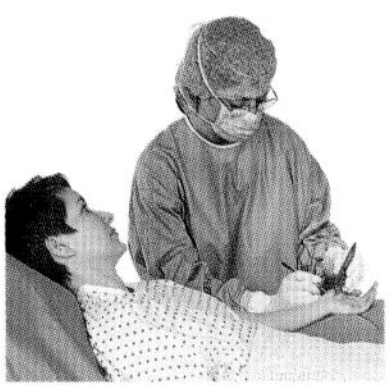

surgery
śalya chikitsā
शल्य चिकित्सा

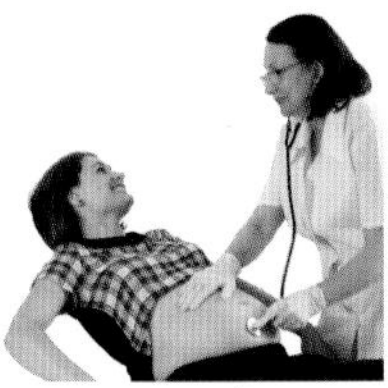

maternity
prasūti
प्रसूति

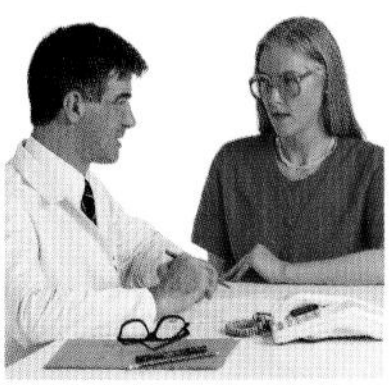

psychiatry
manochikitsā
मनोचिकित्सा

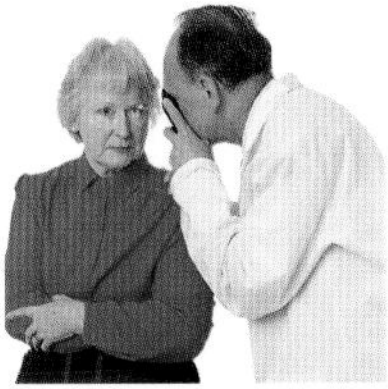

ophthalmology
netr chikitsā
नेत्र चिकित्सा

vocabulary • śabdāvalī • शब्दावली

neurology
snāyu vijñān
स्नायु विज्ञान

oncology
kainsar vijñān
कैंसर विज्ञान

urology
mūtr vijñān
मूत्र विज्ञान

plastic surgery
plāsṭik sarjarī
प्लास्टिक सर्जरी

endocrinology
antaḥ srāvikī
अंतः स्राविकी

referral
sifāriś
सिफ़ारिश

pathology
rog nidān
रोग निदान

test
jāṃch
जांच

result
pariṇām
परिणाम

specialist
parāmarśdātā
परामर्शदाता

dentist • dant chikitsak • दंत चिकित्सक

tooth • dāṃt • दांत

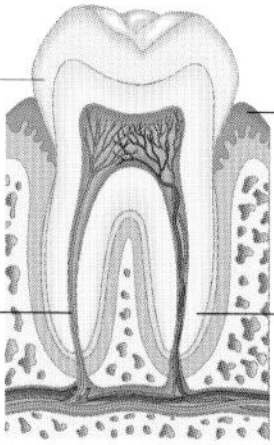

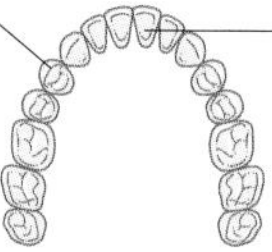

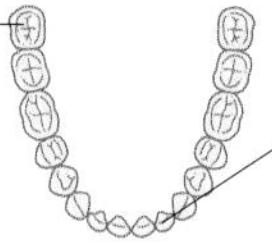

check-up • jāṃch • जांच

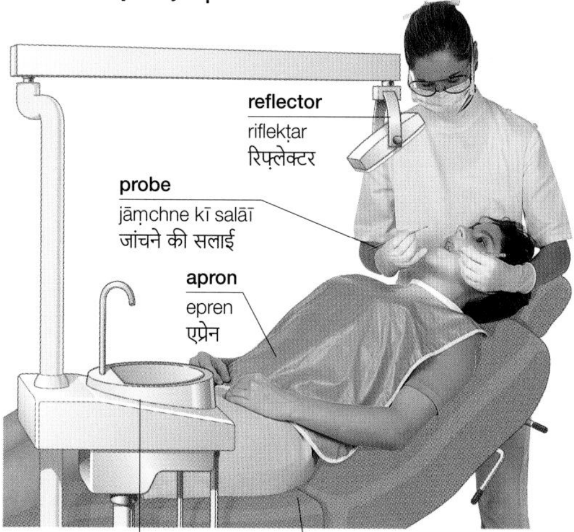

vocabulary • śabdāvalī • शब्दावली

toothache
dāṃt kā dard
दांत का दर्द

plaque
plāk
प्लाक

decay
saṛan
सड़न

filling
bharāvan
भरावन

drill
chhed karnā
छेद करना

dental floss
denṭal flos
डेंटल फ़्लॉस

extraction
dāṃt ukhāṛnā
दांत उखाड़ना

crown
upri dant
उपरि दंत

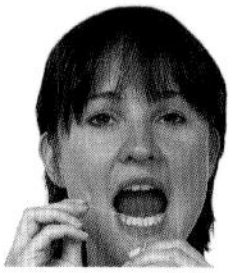

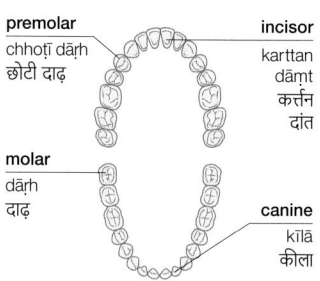

floss (v)
dhāge se safāī karnā
धागे से सफ़ाई करना

brush (v)
braś karnā
ब्रश करना

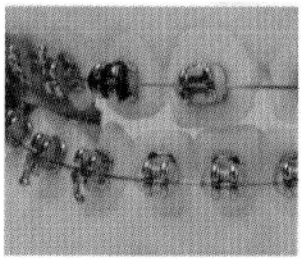

braces
tār kasnā
तार कसना

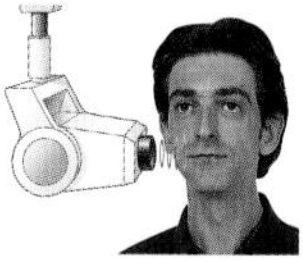

dental x-ray
dāṃtoṃ kā eksare
दांतों का एक्सरे

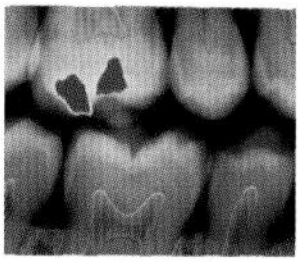

x-ray film
eksare film
एक्सरे फ़िल्म

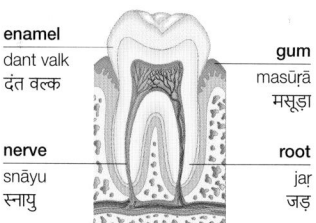

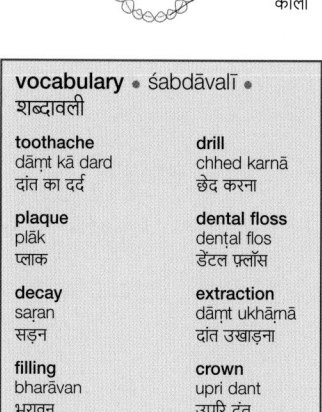

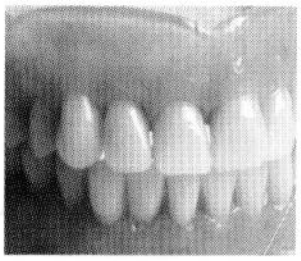

dentures
naklī battīsī
नक़ली बत्तीसी

optometrist • dṛṣṭi parīkṣak • दृष्टि परीक्षक

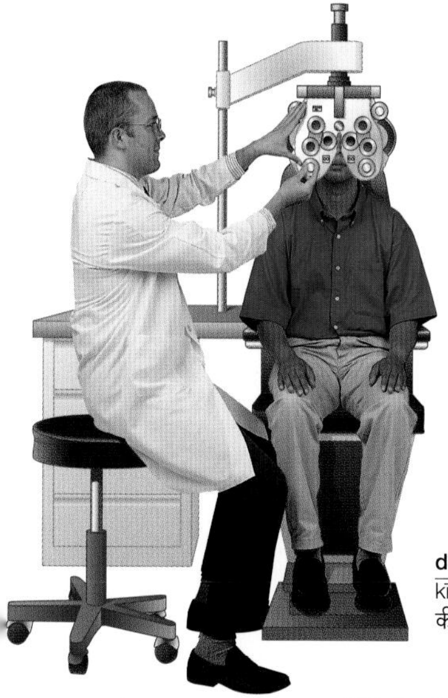

eye test | āṃkhoṃ kī jāṃch | आँखों की जांच

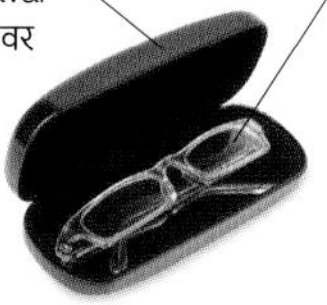

case
kavar
कवर

lens
lens
लेंस

glasses
chaśmā | चश्मा

frame
frem
फ़्रेम

sunglasses
dhūp kā chaśmā | धूप का चश्मा

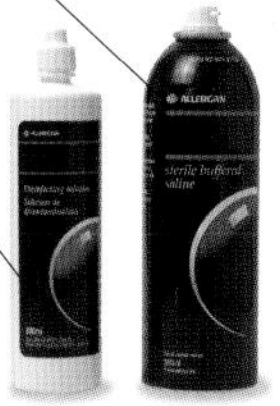

cleaning fluid
lens sāf karne
kā dṛavya
लेंस साफ़ करने का द्रव्य

disinfectant solution
kīṭaṇunāśak rasdravya
कीटाणुनाशक रसद्रव्य

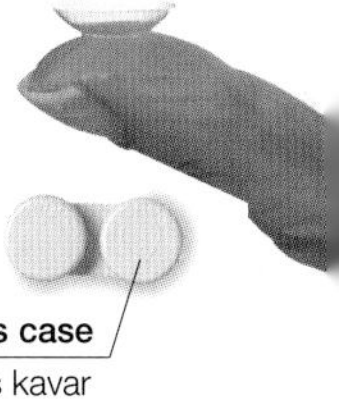

lens case
lens kavar
लेंस कवर

contact lenses | konṭekṭ lens | कॉन्टेक्ट लेंस

eye • āṃkh • आंख

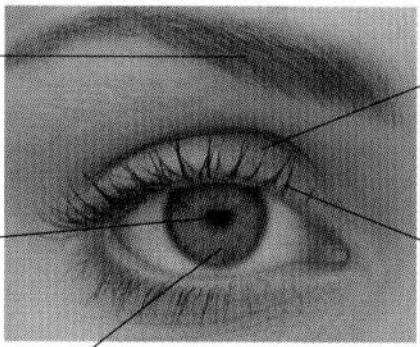

eyebrow
bhauṃh
भौंह

eyelid
palak
पलक

pupil
putlī
पुतली

eyelash
baraunī
बरौनी

iris
uptārā
उपतारा

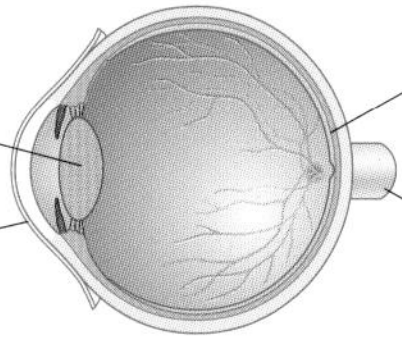

retina
dṛṣṭi paṭal
दृष्टि पटल

lens
lens
लेंस

cornea
korniyā
कोर्निया

optic nerve
dṛṣṭi tantrikā
दृष्टि तंत्रिका

vocabulary • śabdāvalī • शब्दावली

vision
dṛṣṭi
दृष्टि

farsighted
dīrgh dṛṣṭi
दीर्घ दृष्टि

nearsighted
alp dṛṣṭi
अल्प दृष्टि

bifocal
bāyafokal
बायफ़ोकल

astigmatism
dṛṣṭi vaiṣamya
दृष्टि वैषम्य

tear
āṃsū
आंसू

cataract
motiyābind
मोतियाबिंद

diopter
śīśā parakhne
kī ikāī
शीशा परखने की
इकाई

pregnancy • garbhāvasthā • गर्भावस्था

pregnancy test
garbhāvasthā jāṃch
गर्भावस्था जांच

scan
skain
स्कैन

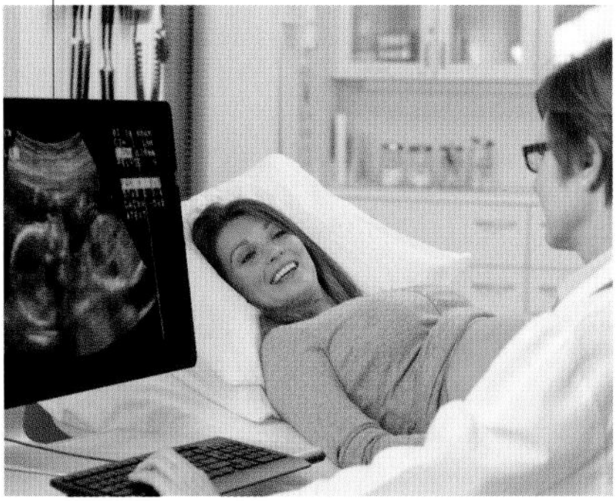

ultrasound
alṭrāsāunḍ | अल्ट्रासाउंड

umbilical cord
nābhi-rajju
नाभि-रज्जु

placenta
garbhnāl
गर्भनाल

cervix
garbhaśaya dvār
गर्भाशय द्वार

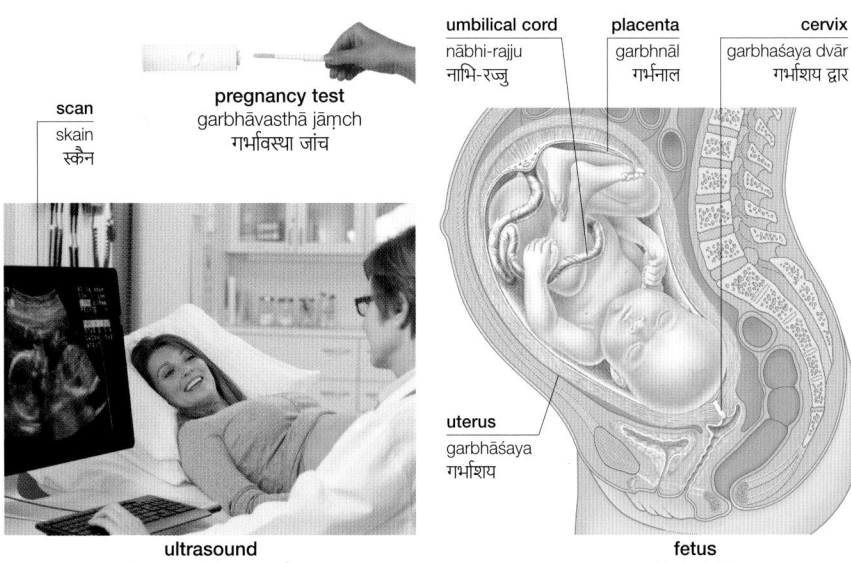

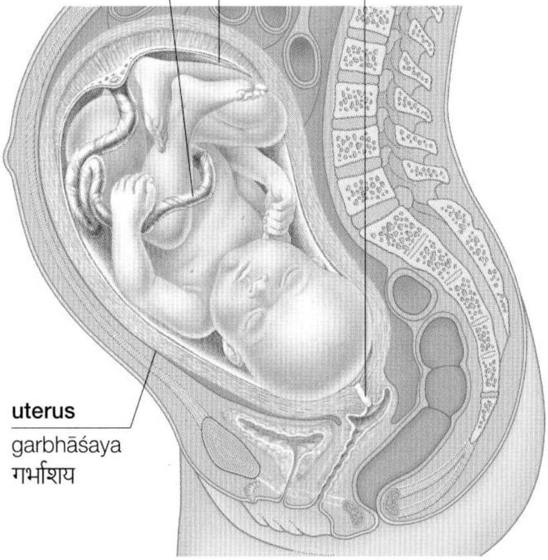

uterus
garbhāśaya
गर्भाशय

fetus
bhrūṇ | भ्रूण

vocabulary • śabdāvalī • शब्दावली

ovulation bījjanan बीजजनन	**prenatal** janm pūrv जन्म पूर्व	**contraction** saṅkuchan संकुचन	**dilation** phailāv फैलाव	**delivery** prasav प्रसव	**breech birth** ulṭā bhrūṇ उल्टा भ्रूण
conception garbhādhān गर्भाधान	**womb** bacchedānī बच्चेदानी	**break water (v)** pānī jānā पानी जाना	**epidural** epiḍyūral एपिड्यूरल	**birth** janm जन्म	**premature** samaya pūrv समय पूर्व
pregnant garbhvatī गर्भवती	**trimester** trimās त्रिमास	**amniotic fluid** ulv drav उल्व द्रव	**episiotomy** bhagacchhedan भगच्छेदन	**miscarriage** garbhpāt गर्भपात	**gynecologist** strī rog viśeṣajñ स्त्री-रोग विशेषज्ञ
expecting garbhvatī गर्भवती	**embryo** aviksit bhrūṇ अविकसित भ्रूण	**amniocentesis** sīrinj se ulv drav nikālnā सीरिंज से उल्व-द्रव निकालना	**cesarean section** operation prasav ऑपरेशन प्रसव	**stitches** ṭāṃke टांके	**obstetrician** prasav viśeṣajñ प्रसव विशेषज्ञ

childbirth • śiśu janm • शिशु जन्म

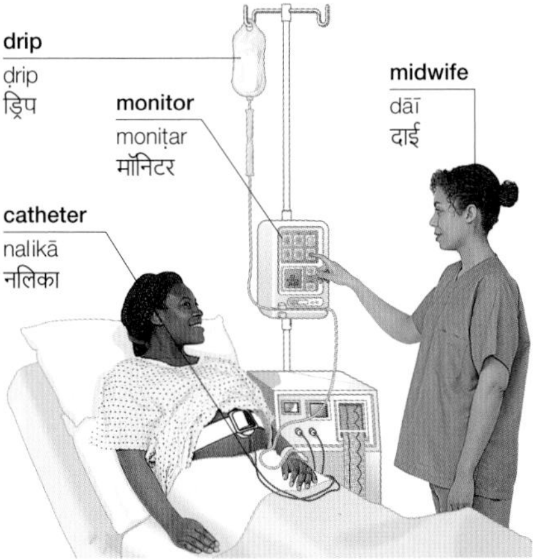

induce labor (v)
kṛtrim prasav karānā | कृत्रिम प्रसव कराना

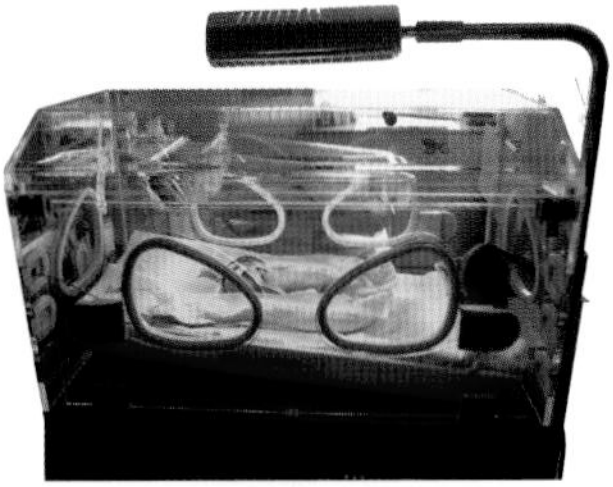

incubator | ūṣmak | ऊष्मक

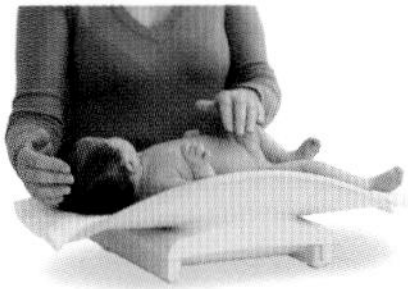

birth weight
janm bhār | जन्म भार

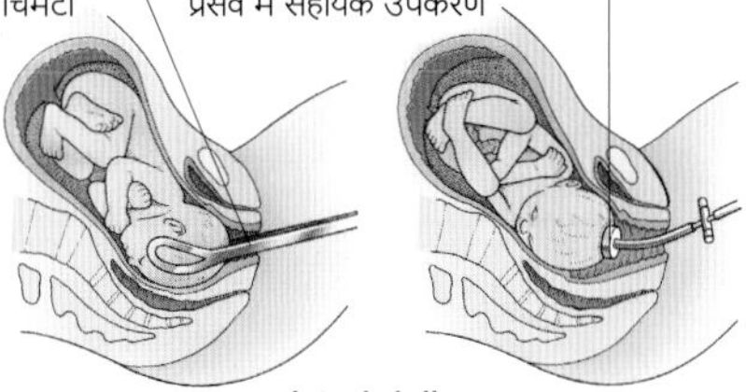

assisted delivery
upkaraṇ dvārā prasav | उपकरण द्वारा प्रसव

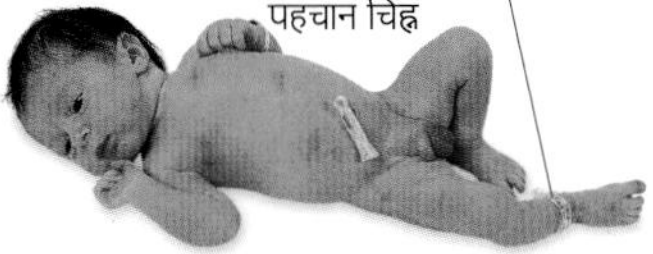

newborn baby
navjāt śiśu | नवजात शिशु

nursing • stanpān • स्तनपान

breast pump
stan pamp
स्तन पंप

nursing bra
narsiṅg brā
नर्सिंग ब्रा

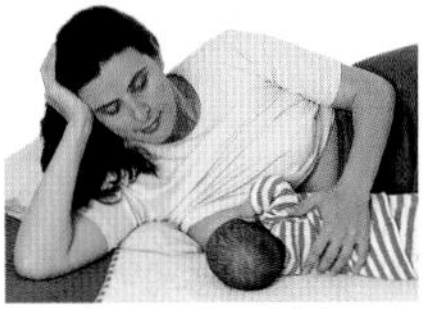

breastfeed (v)
stanpān karānā
स्तनपान कराना

nursing pads
paid
पैड

alternative therapy • vaikalpik chikitsā • वैकल्पिक चिकित्सा

yoga
yog | योग

massage
māliś | मालिश

shiatsu
śiyātsu | शियात्सु

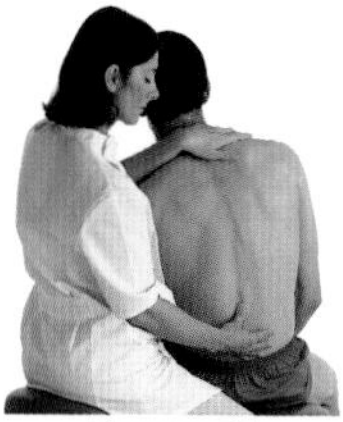

chiropractic
merudaṇḍ upchār
मेरुदंड उपचार

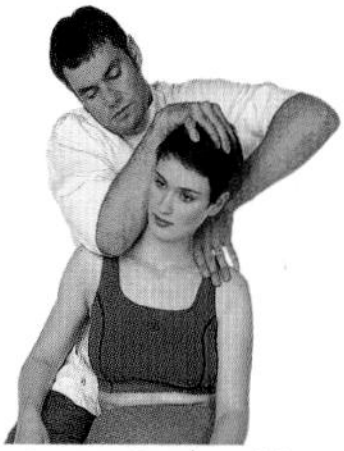

osteopathy | asthi chikitsā | अस्थि चिकित्सा

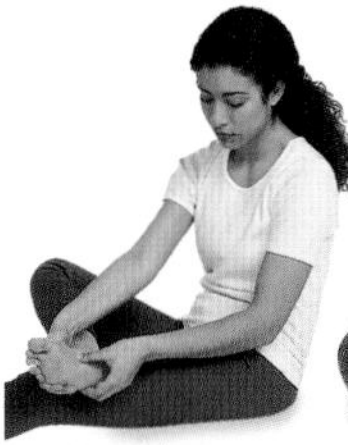

reflexology | rifleksolojī
रिफ़्लेक्सोलॉजी

meditation
dhyān | ध्यान

counselor
parāmarśdātā
परामर्शदाता

group therapy
samūh chikitsā | समूह चिकित्सा

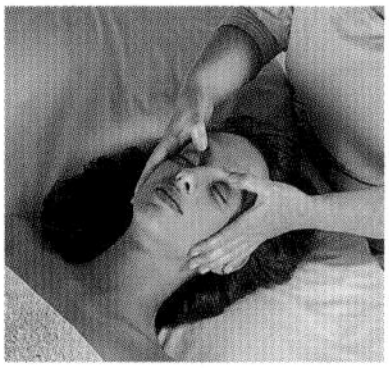

reiki
rekī | रेकी

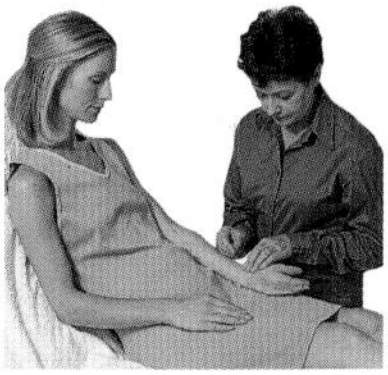

acupuncture
ekyūpaṅkchar
एक्यूपंक्चर

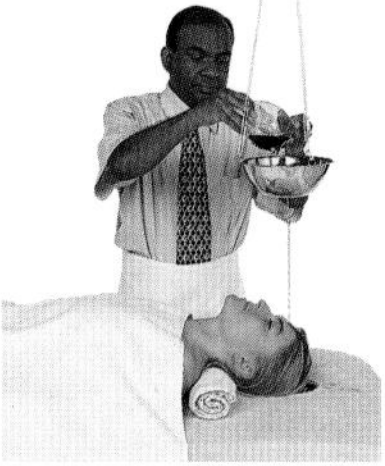

ayurveda
āyurved | आयुर्वेद

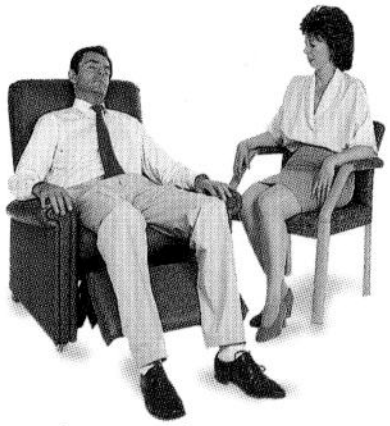

hypnotherapy
sammohan chikitsā
सम्मोहन चिकित्सा

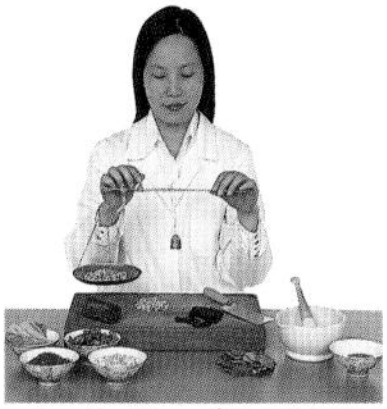

herbalism | jaṛī-būṭī sevan | जड़ी-बूटी सेवन

essential oils
sugandhit tel
सुगंधित तेल

aromatherapy
sugandh chikitsā
सुगंध चिकित्सा

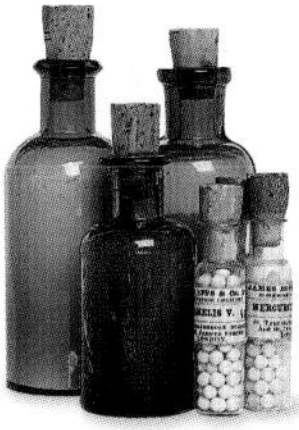

homeopathy
homyopaithī
होम्योपैथी

acupressure
ekyūpraiśar
एक्यूप्रैशर

therapist
chikitsak
चिकित्सक

psychotherapy
manochikitsā | मनोचिकित्सा

vocabulary • śabdāvalī • शब्दावली

supplement
pūrak
पूरक

hydrotherapy
jal chikitsā
जल चिकित्सा

feng shui
feṅg śuī
फ़ेंग शुई

herb
jaṛī-būṭī
जड़ी-बूटी

relaxation
tanāv mukti
तनाव मुक्ति

stress
tanāv
तनाव

naturopathy
prākṛtik chikitsā
प्राकृतिक चिकित्सा

crystal healing
krisṭal chikitsā
क्रिस्टल चिकित्सा

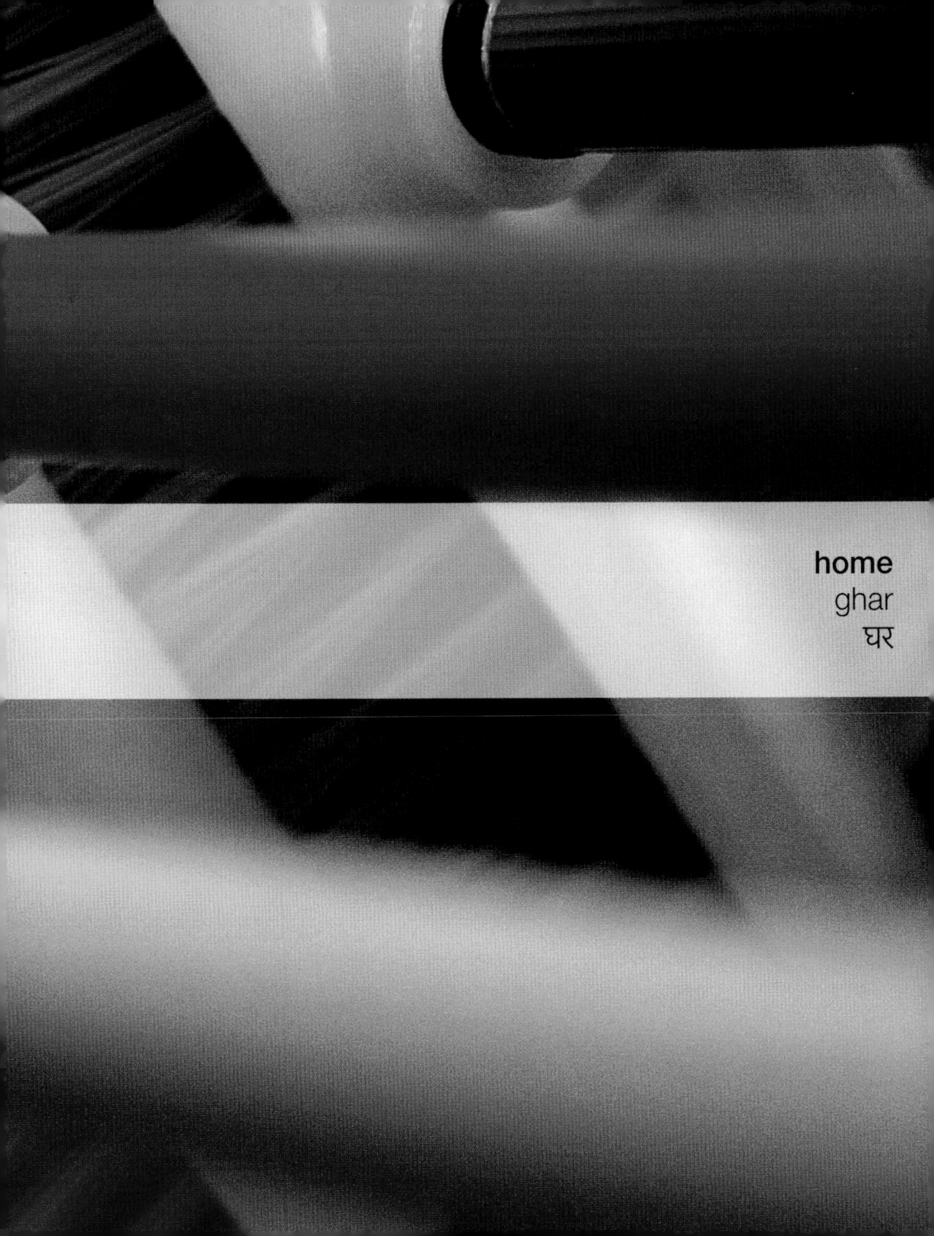

home
ghar
घर

house • makān • मकान

gutter
gaṭar
गटर

roof
chhat
छत

chimney
chimnī
चिमनी

dormer window
ḍormar khiṛkī
डोर्मर खिड़की

wall
dīvār
दीवार

eaves
chhajjā
छज्जा

shingle
ṭāil
टाइल

shutter
kapāṭ
कपाट

porch
dvārmanḍap
द्वारमंडप

window
khiṛkī
खिड़की

addition
atirikt bhāg
अतिरिक्त भाग

path
rāstā
रास्ता

front door
mukhyadvār
मुख्यद्वार

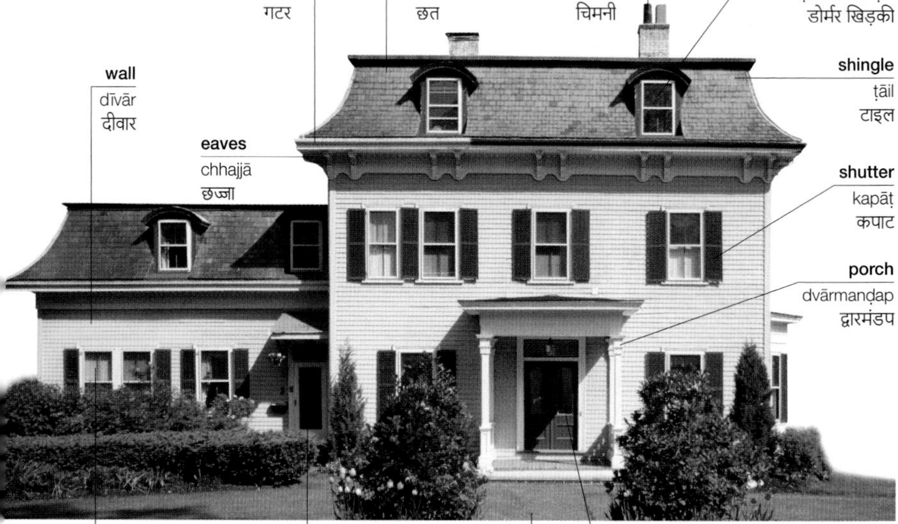

vocabulary • śabdāvalī • शब्दावली

single-family ekal ghar एकल घर	**tenant** kirāedār किराएदार	**row house** chhat vālā छत वाला	**garage** gairej गैरेज	**burglar alarm** chor ghanṭī चोर घंटी	**rent (v)** kirāe par lenā किराए पर लेना
townhouse śahrī makān शहरी मकान	**bungalow** banglā बंगला	**landlord** makān mālik मकान मालिक	**attic** aṭārī अटारी	**courtyard** āṅgan आंगन	**rent** kirāyā किराया
duplex saṭā huā ghar सटा हुआ घर	**basement** tahkhānā तहख़ाना	**porch light** dvārmanḍap battī द्वारमंडप बत्ती	**room** kamrā कमरा	**floor** manzil मंज़िल	**mailbox** laiṭar box लैटर बॉक्स

entrance • praveś dvār • प्रवेश द्वार

foyer
galiyārā | गलियारा

doorbell
darvāze kī ghaṇṭī
दरवाज़े की घंटी

doormat
pāyadān
पायदान

door knocker
kuṇḍā
कुंडा

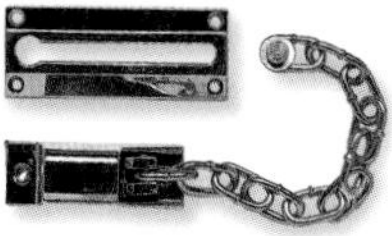

door chain | darvāze kī kaṛī | दरवाजे की कड़ी

lock
tālā | ताला

bolt
chaṭkhanī | चटख़नी

apartment • flaiṭ • फ़्लैट

apartment building
apārṭmenṭ | अपार्टमेंट

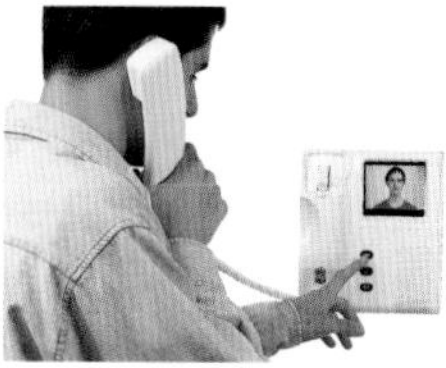

intercom
antaḥ sanchār | अंतः संचार

elevator
lifṭ | लिफ्ट

internal systems • gharelū upkaraṇ • घरेलू उपकरण

blade
paṅkh | पंख

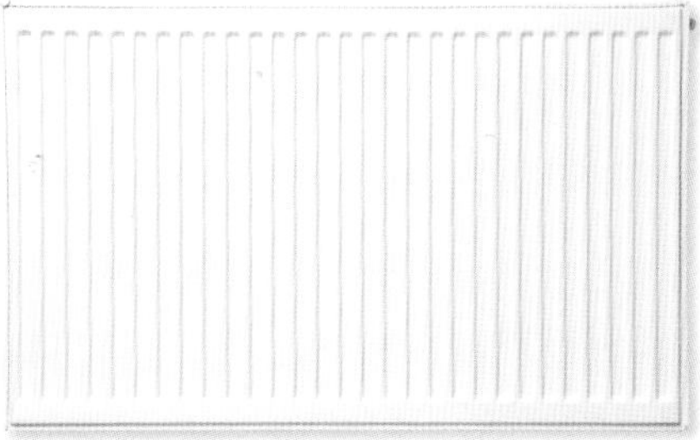

fan | paṅkhā | पंखा

convector heater
bloar | ब्लोअर

radiator | reḍieṭar | रेडिएटर

space heater | hīṭar | हीटर

electricity • bijlī • बिजली

ground
arthiṅg
अर्थिंग

pin
pin
पिन

neutral
nyūṭral | न्यूट्रल

live
lāiv
लाइव

energy-saving bulb
bijli bachāne vālā balb
बिजली बचाने वाला बल्ब

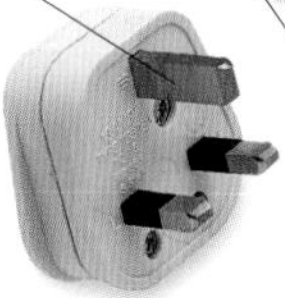

plug
plag | प्लग

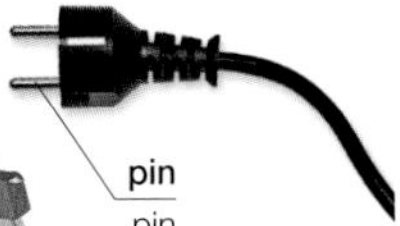

wires
tār | तार

vocabulary • śabdāvalī • शब्दावली

voltage	fuse	outlet	household current	direct current
volṭej	fyūz	sokeṭ	men saplāī	ḍāyarekṭ karanṭ
वोल्टेज	फ़्यूज़	सॉकेट	मेन सप्लाई	डायरेक्ट करंट
amp	fuse box	switch	transformer	alternating current
empīyar	fyūz box	svich	transformer	olṭarneṭiṅg karanṭ
एम्पियर	फ़्यूज़ बॉक्स	स्विच	ट्रांसफ़ॉर्मर	ऑल्टरनेटिंग करंट
power	generator	power outage	electric meter	
ūrjā	jenreṭar	bijlī kaṭautī	bijlī kā mīṭar	
ऊर्जा	जेनरेटर	बिजली कटौती	बिजली का मीटर	

plumbing • nalsāzī • नलसाज़ी

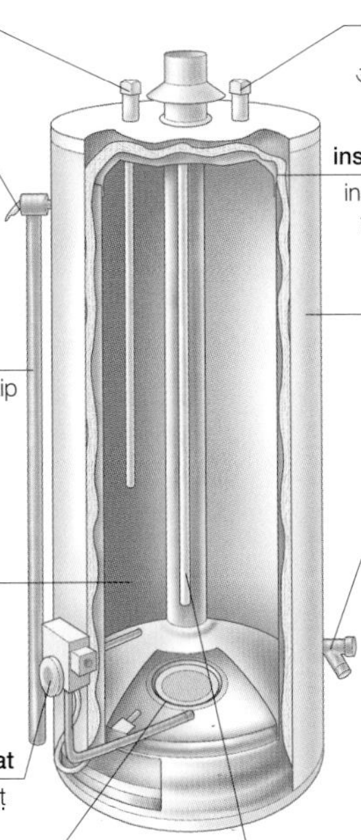

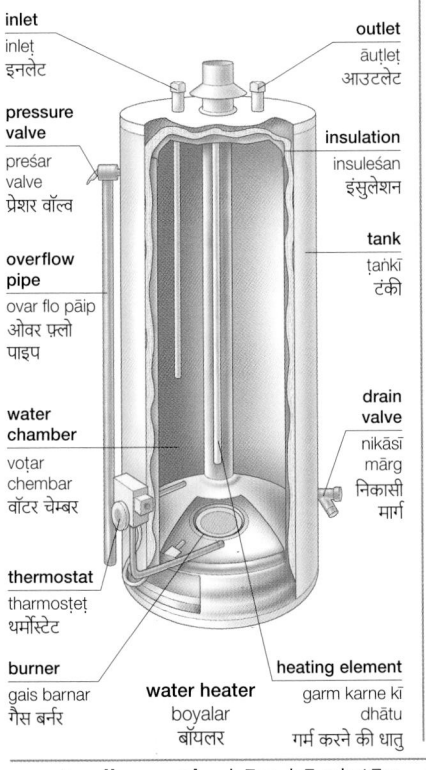

water heater
boyalar
बॉयलर

sink • siṅk • सिंक

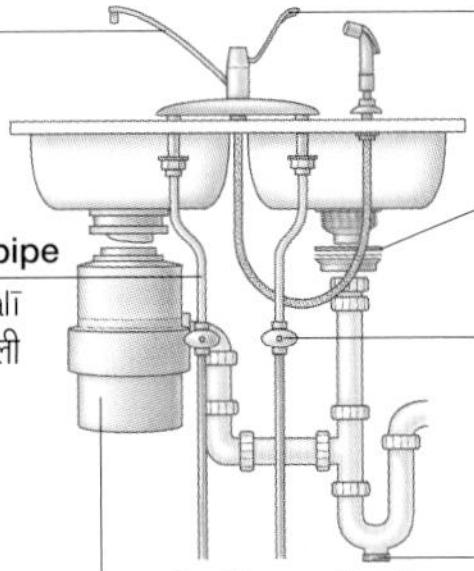

toilet • śauchālaya • शौचालय

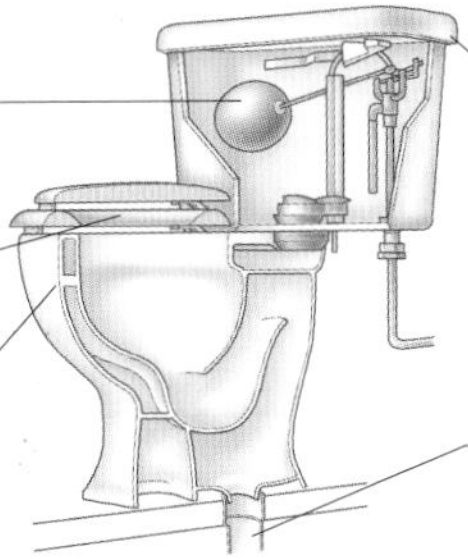

waste disposal • kūṛe kā nipṭān • कूड़े का निपटान

recycling bin
punarchakraṇ pātr
पुनर्चक्रण पात्र

trash can
kūṛedān
कूड़ेदान

sorting unit
chhaṃṭāī yūniṭ
छंटाई यूनिट

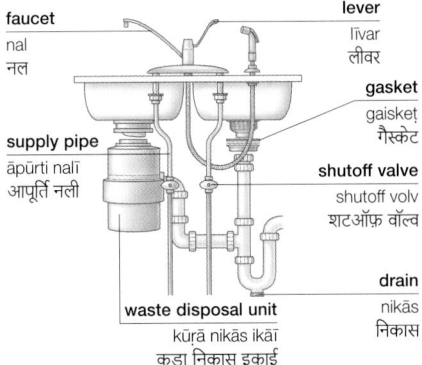

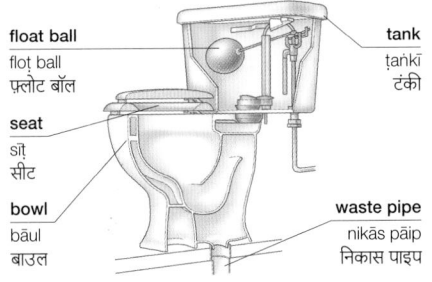

organic waste
jaivik kūṛā
जैविक कूड़ा

living room • baiṭhak • बैठक

curtain
pardā | पर्दा

sheer curtain
jālīdār pardā
जालीदार पर्दा

Venetian blind
veneśiyan blāinḍ
वेनेशियन ब्लाइंड

roller shade | rolar blāinḍ | रोलर ब्लाइंड

study | paṛhne kā kamrā | पढ़ने का कमरा

dining room • bhojan kakṣ • भोजन कक्ष

vocabulary • śabdāvalī • शब्दावली

serve (v)
parosnā
परोसना

eat (v)
khānā
खाना

set the table (v)
mez lagānā
मेज़ लगाना

hungry
bhūkhā
भूखा

tablecloth
mezpoś
मेज़पोश

breakfast
nāśtā
नाश्ता

dinner
rāt kā bhojan
रात का भोजन

hostess
mahilā mezbān
महिला मेज़बान

lunch
dopahar kā bhojan
दोपहर का भोजन

full
bharā huā
भरा हुआ

portion
hissā
हिस्सा

meal
bhojan
भोजन

host
mezbān
मेज़बान

guest
mehmān
मेहमान

place mat
ṭebal maiṭ
टेबल मैट

Can I have some more, please?
kyā mujhe aur mil saktā hai?
क्या मुझे और मिल सकता है?

I've had enough, thank you.
aur nahīṃ chāhie, dhanyavād
और नही चाहिए, धन्यवाद।

That was delicious.
khānā svādiṣṭ thā
खाना स्वादिष्ट था।

crockery and cutlery • bartan aur chhurī-kāṃṭe • बर्तन और छुरी-कांटे

teaspoon
chhoṭā chammach
छोटा चम्मच

mug
mag
मग

coffee cup
kofī kā pyālā
कॉफ़ी का प्याला

teacup
chāya kā pyālā
चाय का प्याला

plate
pleṭ
प्लेट

bowl
kaṭorā
कटोरा

wine glass
vāin gilās
वाइन गिलास

tumbler
gilās
गिलास

French press
kofī kī ketlī
कॉफ़ी की केतली

teapot
ketlī
केतली

pitcher
jag
जग

eggcup
aṇḍe kā kap
अंडे का कप

glassware
kāṃch ke gilās
कांच के गिलास

napkin ring
naipkin riṅg
नैपकिन रिंग

side plate
chhoṭī pleṭ
छोटी प्लेट

dinner plate
baṛī pleṭ
बड़ी प्लेट

soup bowl
sūp kī pleṭ
सूप की प्लेट

soup spoon
sūp kā chammach
सूप का चम्मच

napkin
naipkin
नैपकिन

fork
kāṃṭā
कांटा

place setting
bartan lagāne kā tarīkā
बर्तन लगाने का तरीक़ा

spoon
chammach
चम्मच

knife
chhurī
छुरी

kitchen • rasoī • रसोई

shelves
ḳhāne
ख़ाने

backsplash
splaiśbaik
स्प्लैशबैक

faucet
nal
नल

sink
siṅk
सिंक

drawer
darāz
दराज़

ventilation hood
chimnī
चिमनी

ceramic stovetop
sṭov
स्टोव

countertop
khānā banāne kī jagah
खाना बनाने की जगह

oven
ovan
ओवन

cabinet
almārī
अलमारी

appliances • upkaraṇ • उपकरण

microwave oven
māikrovev ovan | माइक्रोवेव ओवन

electric kettle
ketlī
केतली

toaster
ṭosṭar
टोस्टर

mixing bowl
miksiṅg bāul
मिक्सिंग बाउल

blade
bleḍ
ब्लेड

food processor
fūḍ prosesar
फ़ूड प्रोसेसर

lid
ḍhakkan
ढक्कन

blender
blenḍar
ब्लेंडर

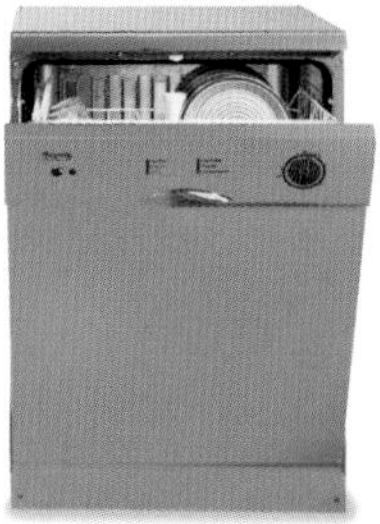

dishwasher
bartan dhone kī maśīn
बर्तन धोने की मशीन

ice maker
baraf jamāne kī jagah
बर्फ़ जमाने की जगह

refrigerator
refrījaretar
रेफ़्रीजरेटर

shelf
khānā
ख़ाना

freezer
frīzar
फ्रीज़र

crisper
krispar
क्रिस्पर

side-by-side refrigerator
frij | फ्रिज

vocabulary • śabdāvalī • शब्दावली

burner
barnar
बर्नर

stovetop
stov
स्टोव

garbage can
kūredān
कूड़ेदान

draining board
drening bord
ड्रेनिंग बोर्ड

freeze (v)
jamānā
जमाना

defrost (v)
pighlānā
पिघलाना

sauté (v)
halkā bhūnnā
हल्का भूनना

steam (v)
bhāp se pakānā
भाप से पकाना

cooking • khānā pakānā • खाना पकाना

peel (v)
chhīlnā | छीलना

slice (v)
kāṭnā | काटना

grate (v)
ghisnā | घिसना

pour (v)
uṛelnā | उड़ेलना

mix (v)
milānā | मिलाना

whisk (v)
pheṃṭnā | फेंटना

boil (v)
ubālnā | उबालना

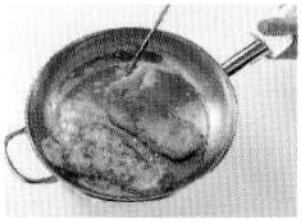

fry (v)
talnā | तलना

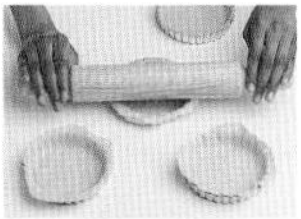

roll (v)
belnā | बेलना

stir (v)
chalānā | चलाना

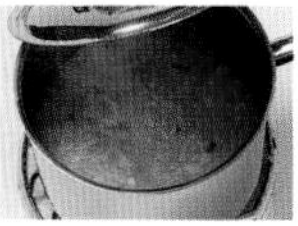

simmer (v)
khadaknā
खदकना

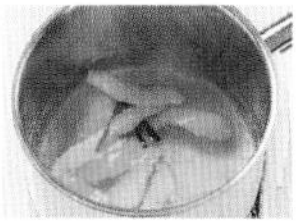

poach (v)
pānī meṃ pakānā
पानी में पकाना

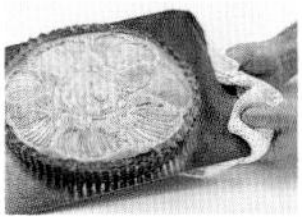

bake (v)
bek karnā
बेक करना

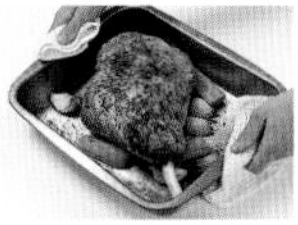

roast (v)
bhūnnā
भूनना

broil (v) | tandūr meṃ bhūnnā
तंदूर में भूनना

kitchenware • rasoī upkaraṇ • रसोई उपकरण

cutting board
sabzī kāṭne kā takhtā | सब्ज़ी काटने का तख़्ता

bread knife
breḍ kāṭne kī chhurī
ब्रेड काटने की छुरी

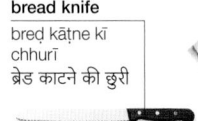

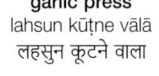

kitchen knife
chākū
चाकू

cleaver
chāpaṛ
चापड़

knife sharpener
chākū tez karne vālā
चाकू तेज करने वाला

meat tenderizer
māṃs kūṭne kā auzār | मांस कूटने का औज़ार

skewer
sīkh | सीख

peeler | chhīlne vālā chākū
छीलने वाला चाकू

apple corer | bīj nikālne kī salāī
बीज निकालने की सलाई

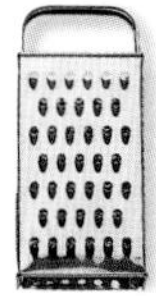

grater
kaddūkas
कद्दूकस

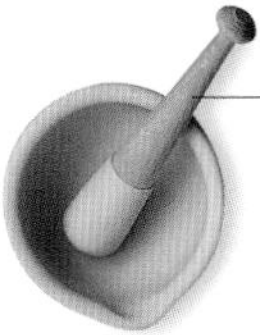

pestle
mūsal
मूसल

mortar
kharal | खरल

masher
meśar | मेशर

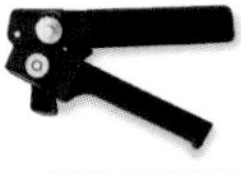

can opener
kain opnar
कैन ओपनर

bottle opener
botal opnar
बोतल ओपनर

garlic press
lahsun kūṭne vālā
लहसुन कूटने वाला

serving spoon
parosne kā chammach
परोसने का चम्मच

slotted spatula
palṭā | पलटा

colander
chhalnā | छलना

spatula
spaichulā | स्पैचुला

wooden spoon
lakṛī kā chammach
लकड़ी का चम्मच

slotted spoon
kalchhī | कलछी

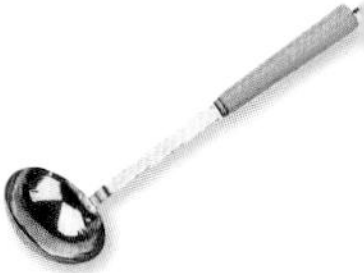

ladle
chamchā | चमचा

carving fork | ghumāvdār kāṃṭā | घुमावदार कांटा

ice-cream scoop
skūp | स्कूप

whisk
pheṃṭnī | फेंटनी

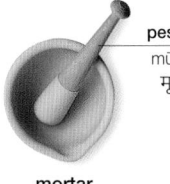

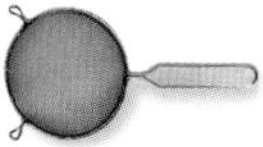

sieve
chhannī | छन्नी

frying pan
frāiṅg pain
फ़्राइंग पैन

saucepan
ḍegchī
डेगची

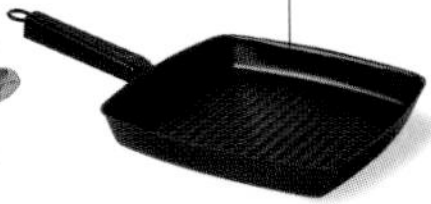

grill pan
gril pain
ग्रिल पैन

wok
kaṛāhī
कड़ाही

earthenware dish
miṭṭī kā bartan
मिट्टी का बर्तन

mixing bowl
miksiṅg bāul
मिक्सिंग बाउल

soufflé dish
sūfle bartan
सूफ़ले बर्तन

gratin dish
grāṭin ḍiś
ग्राटिन डिश

ramekin
remikīn
रेमिकीन

casserole dish
kaisrol
कैसरोल

baking cakes • kek banānā • केक बनाना

scale | tarāzū
तराज़ू

measuring cup
māpak jag
मापक जग

cake pan | kek banāne kā sāṃchā
केक बनाने का सांचा

pie pan | pāī banāne kā sāṃchā
पाई बनाने का सांचा

quiche pan | flain banāne kā sāṃchā
फ़्लैन बनाने का सांचा

pastry brush
pesṭrī braś | पेस्ट्री ब्रश

rolling pin
belan | बेलन

piping bag | pāipiṅg baig | पाइपगि बैग

muffin pan
mafin ṭre
मफ़िन ट्रे

cookie sheet
bekiṅg ṭre
बेकिंग ट्रे

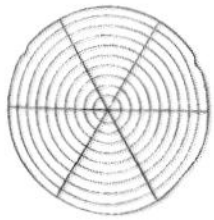

cooling rack
kūliṅg raik
कूलिंग रैक

oven mitt
ovan ke dastāne
ओवन के दस्ताने

apron
epren
एप्रेन

bedroom • śayan kakṣ • शयन कक्ष

wardrobe
almārī
अलमारी

bedside lamp
sāiḍ laimp
साइड लैम्प

headboard
palaṅg kā sirhānā
पलंग का सिरहाना

nightstand
sāiḍ ṭebal
साइड टेबल

chest of drawers
darāzoṃ kī almārī
दराज़ों की अलमारी

drawer
darāz
दराज़

bed
palaṅg
पलंग

mattress
gaddā
गद्दा

bedspread
palaṅgpoś
पलंगपोश

pillow
takiyā
तकिया

hot-water bottle | garm panī kī thailī
गर्म पानी की थैली

clock radio
reḍiyo ghaṛī
रेडियो घड़ी

alarm clock
alārm ghaṛī
अलार्म घड़ी

box of tissues
ṭiśyū boks
टिश्यू बॉक्स

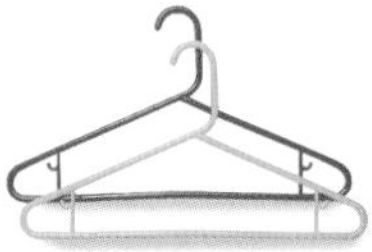

coat hanger
koṭ kā haiṅgar
कोट का हैंगर

bed linen • chādar va takiyā gilāf ādi • चादर व तकिया गिलाफ़ आदि

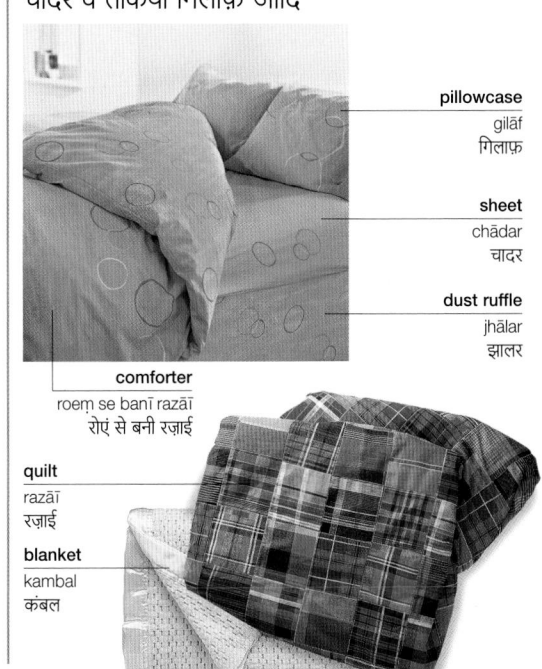

vocabulary • śabdāvalī • शब्दावली

twin bed siṅgal palaṅg सिंगल पलंग	**footboard** pāyadān पायदान	**insomnia** anidrā अनिद्रा	**wake up (v)** jāgnā जागना	**make the bed (v)** bistar lagānā बिस्तर लगाना
full bed ḍabal palaṅg डबल पलंग	**bedspring** gadde kā spriṅg गद्दे का स्प्रिंग	**go to bed (v)** sone jānā सोने जाना	**get up (v)** uṭhnā उठना	**snore (v)** ḳharrāṭe lenā खर्राटे लेना
electric blanket vidyut kambal विद्युत कंबल	**carpet** ḳālīn कालीन	**go to sleep (v)** sonā सोना	**set the alarm (v)** alārm lagānā अलार्म लगाना	**closet** antarnirmit almārī अंतर्निर्मित अलमारी

bathroom • snānghar • स्नानघर

bathtub
bāth ṭab | बाथ टब

bidet
biḍe | बिडे

vocabulary • śabdāvalī • शब्दावली

medicine cabinet
davāī kī almārī
दवाई की अलमारी

bath mat
snānghar kī chaṭāī
स्नान की चटाई

toilet paper
ṭoyaleṭ rol
टॉयलेट रोल

shower curtain
śovar kā pardā
शॉवर का पर्दा

take a shower (v)
phuhāre meṃ nahānā
फुहारे में नहाना

take a bath (v)
nahānā
नहाना

dental hygiene • dāṃtoṃ kī safāī • दांतों की सफाई

toothbrush
ṭūthbraś | टूथब्रश

toothpaste
ṭūthpesṭ | टूथपेस्ट

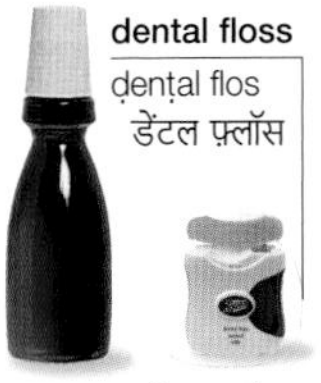

mouthwash
māuthvoś | माउथवॉश

sponge
spanj | स्पंज

pumice stone
jhāmak | झामक

back brush | pīṭh kā braś | पीठ का ब्रश

deodorant
ḍiyoḍrenṭ | डियोडरेंट

soap dish
sābundānī
साबुनदानी

soap
sābun
साबुन

face cream
krīm
क्रीम

shower gel
śāvar jail
शॉवर जैल

bubble bath
babbal bāth
बब्बल बाथ

bathrobe | ḍresiṅg gāun | ड्रेसिंग गाउन

hand towel
chhoṭā tauliyā
छोटा तौलिया

bath towel
tauliyā
तौलिया

towels
taulie | तौलिए

body lotion
boḍī lośan | बॉडी लोशन

talcum powder
ṭelkam pāuḍar
टेल्कम पाउडर

shaving • hajāmat • हजामत

electric razor
ilekṭrik rezar
इलेक्ट्रिक रेज़र

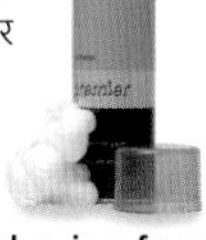

shaving foam
śeviṅg fom
शेविंग फ़ोम

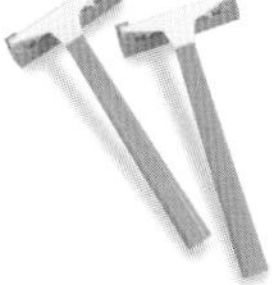

disposable razor
ḍispozebal rezar
डिस्पोज़ेबल रेजर

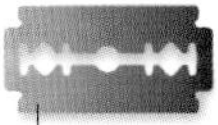

razor blade
rezar bleḍ
रेज़र ब्लेड

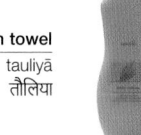

aftershave
āfṭar śev
आफ़्टर शेव

nursery • śiśugṛh • शिशुगृह

baby care • śiśu dekhbhāl • शिशु देखभाल

sponge
spanj
स्पंज

baby bath
śiśu snān | शिशु स्नान

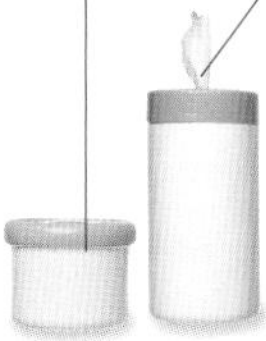

diaper rash cream
naipī raiś krīm
नैपी रैश क्रीम

wet wipe
nam ṭiśyu
नम टिश्यु

potty
poṭī | पॉटी

changing mat | kapṛe badalne kī gaddī | कपड़े बदलने की गद्दी

sleeping • sonā • सोना

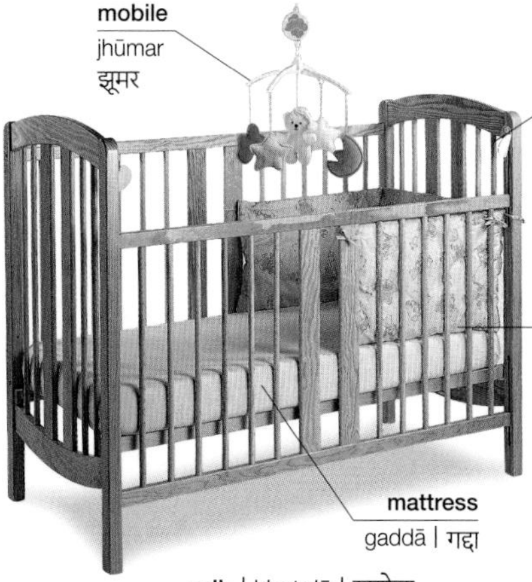

mobile
jhūmar
झूमर

bars
sīṃkhche
सीख़चे

bumper
bampar
बम्पर

mattress
gaddā | गद्दा

crib | khaṭolā | खटोला

sheet
chādar
चादर

blanket
kambal
कंबल

fleece
ūnī chādar
ऊनी चादर

bedding
bichhaunā | बिछौना

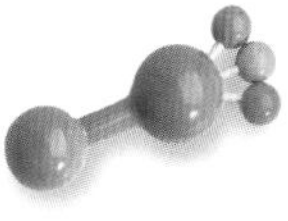

rattle
jhunjhunā | झुनझुना

bassinet | mozes bāsket
मोज़स बास्केट

playing • khelnā • खेलना

doll
guṛiyā
गुड़िया

stuffed toy
mulāyam khilaune
मुलायम खिलौने

dollhouse
guṛiyā ghar
गुड़िया घर

playhouse
khel ghar | खेल घर

teddy bear
teḍī biyar
टेडी बियर

toy
khilaunā
खिलौना

toy basket | khilaune kī ṭokrī | खिलौने की टोकरी

ball
gend
गेंद

playpen
khel bāṛā | खेल बाड़ा

safety • surakṣā • सुरक्षा

child lock
bacchoṃ kā tālā
बच्चों का ताला

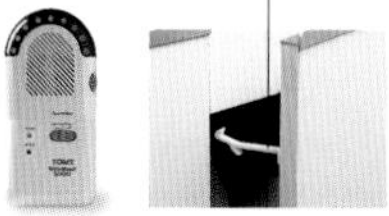

baby monitor
bebī moniṭar
बेबी मॉनिटर

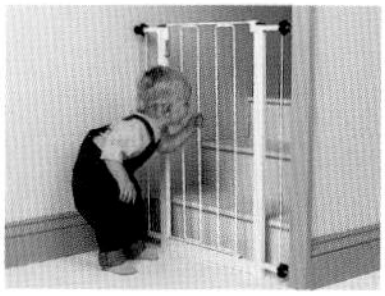

stair gate
sīṛhiyoṃ kā geṭ
सीढ़ियों के गेट

eating • khānā • खाना

high chair
ūṃchī kursī | ऊँची कुर्सी

nipple
nippal
निप्पल

drinking cup
pīne kā kap
पीने का कप

bottle
botal | बोतल

going out • bāhar jānā • बाहर जाना

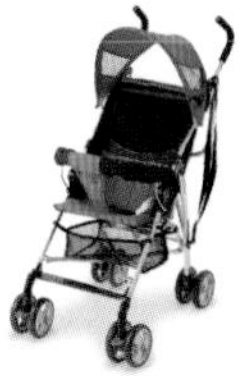

stroller | hāth gāṛī | हाथ गाड़ी

hood
chhatrī
छतरी

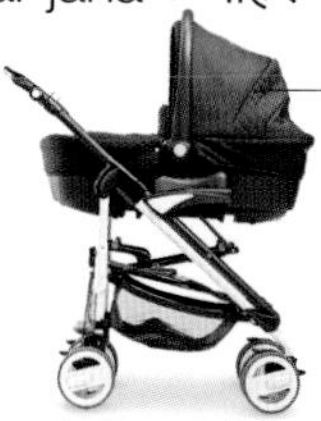

baby carriage
bagghī | बग्घी

carrier
pālnā | पालना

diaper
laṅgoṭī
लंगोटी

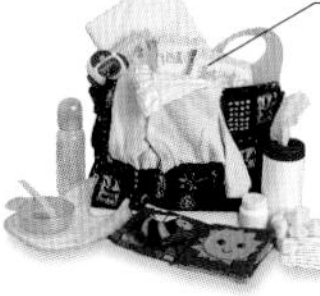

diaper bag | bacchoṃ kā thailā | बच्चों का थैला

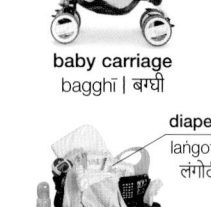

baby sling | śiśu paṭṭā
शिशु पट्टा

utility room • gharelū kārya kakṣ • घरेलू कार्य कक्ष

laundry • londrī • लॉन्ड्री

dirty laundry
gande kapṛe
गंदे कपड़े

laundry basket
gande kapṛoṃ kī ṭokrī | गंदे कपड़ों की टोकरी

washing machine
kapṛe dhone kī maśīn | कपड़े धोने की मशीन

washer-dryer
vośar ḍrāyar
वॉशर-ड्रायर

tumble dryer
ḍrāyar
ड्रायर

clean clothes
dhule kapṛe
धुले कपड़े

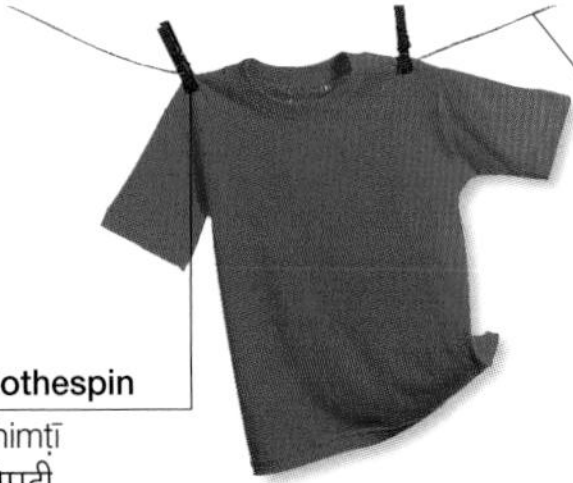

clothesline
alganī
अलगनी

clothespin
chimṭī
चिमटी

dry (v)
sukhānā | सुखाना

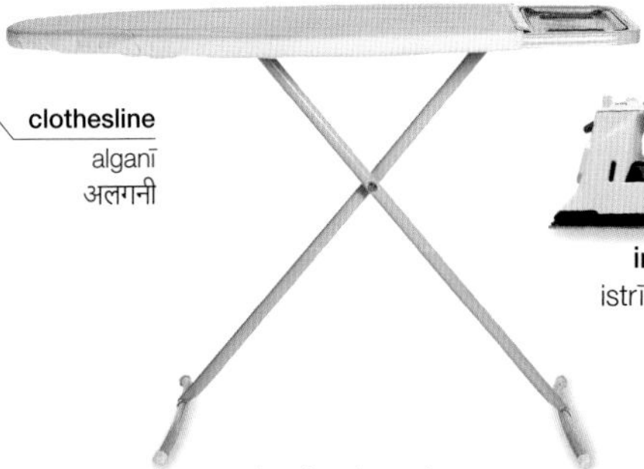

ironing board
istrī kā taḳhtā | इस्त्री का तख़्ता

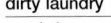

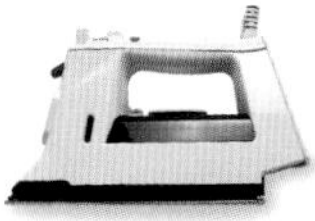

iron
istrī | इस्त्री

vocabulary • śabdāvalī • शब्दावली

rinse (v)
khaṅgālnā
खंगालना

load (v)
kapṛe maśīn meṃ ḍālnā
कपड़े मशीन में डालना

spin (v)
kapṛe nichoṛnā
कपड़े निचोड़ना

spin dryer
kapṛe nichoṛne vālā
कपड़े निचोड़ने वाला

iron (v)
istrī karnā
इस्त्री करना

fabric softener
kapṛe ka kanḍiśnar
कपड़े का कंडिशनर

How do I operate the washing machine?
vośiṅg maśīn kaise chalāūṃ?
वॉशिंग मशीन कैसे चलाऊँ?

cleaning equipment • safāī upkaraṇ • सफ़ाई उपकरण

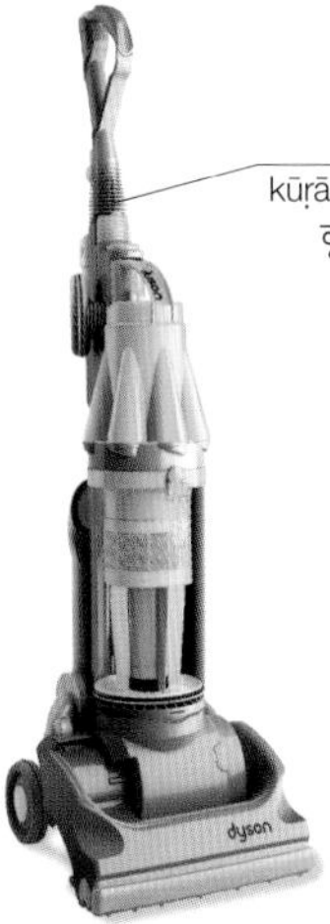

suction hose
kūṛā khīṃchne kī nalī
कूड़ा खीचने की नली

vacuum cleaner | vekyūm klīnar | वेक्यूम क्लीनर

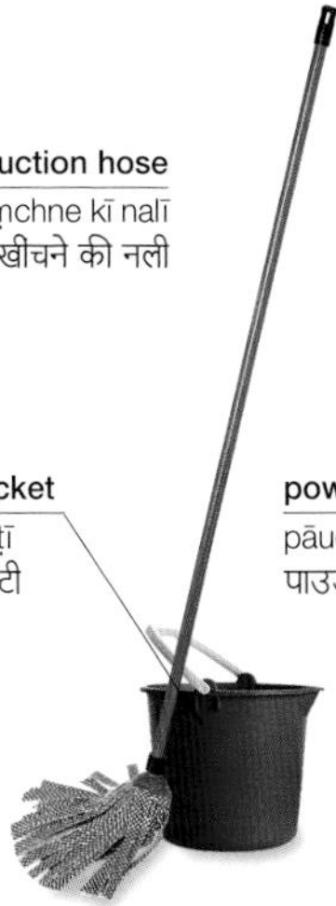

bucket
bālṭī
बाल्टी

mop
pochhā | पोछा

brush
braś
ब्रश

dustpan | kūṛe kā panjā | कूड़े का पंजा

bleach
blīch | ब्लीच

powder
pāuḍar
पाउडर

liquid
dravya
द्रव्य

detergent
ḍiṭarjenṭ | डिटर्जेंट

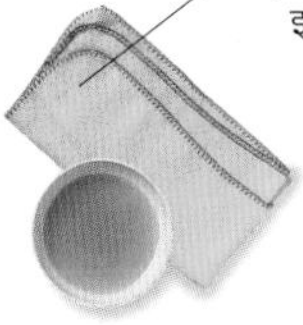

dust cloth
jhāṛan
झाड़न

polish
poliś | पॉलिश

activities • gatividhiyāṃ • गतिविधियां

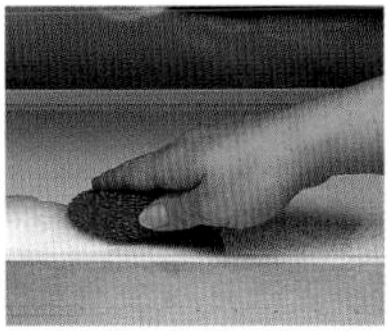

clean (v)
safāī karnā | सफ़ाई करना

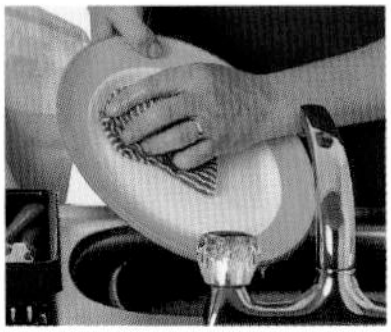

wash (v)
dhonā | धोना

wipe (v)
poṃchhnā | पोंछना

scrub (v)
ghisnā | घिसना

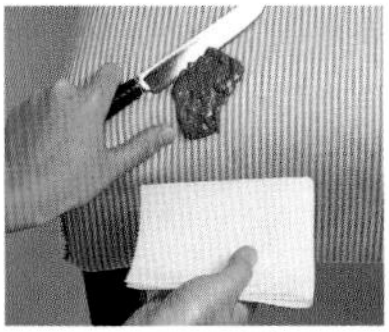

scrape (v)
khurachnā | खुरचना

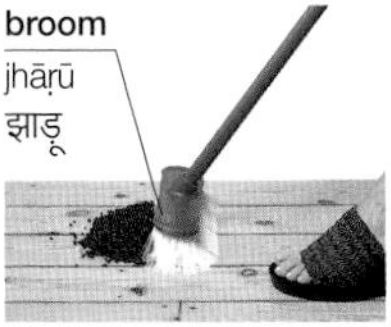

sweep (v)
jhāṛū lagānā | झाड़ू लगाना

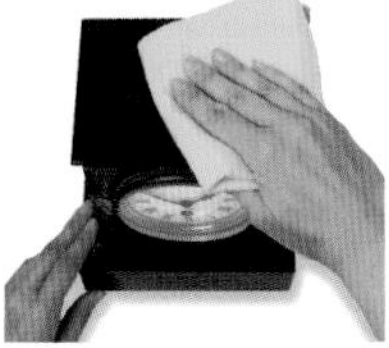

dust (v)
dhūl jhāṛnā | धूल झाड़ना

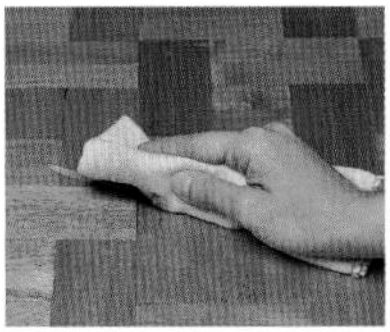

polish (v)
chamkānā | चमकाना

workshop • kāryaśālā • कार्यशाला

chuck
chakkā
चक्का

drill bit
chhed karne kī suī
छेद करने की सुई

jigsaw
chhoṭā ārā
छोटा आरा

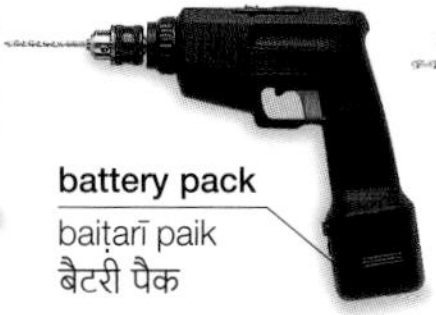

battery pack
baiṭarī paik
बैटरी पैक

cordless drill
kordles ḍril
कॉर्डलेस ड्रिल

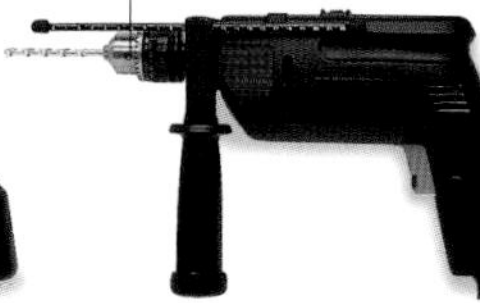

electric drill
vidyut ḍril/vedhnī
विद्युत ड्रिल/वेधनी

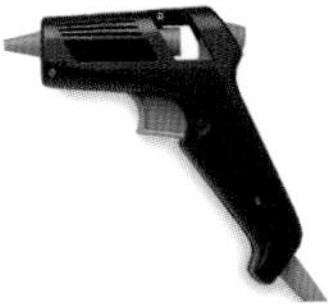

glue gun
gond gan | गोंद गन

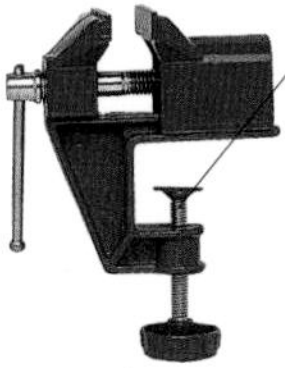

clamp
śikanjā/paṭṭī
शिकंजा/पट्टी

vise
śikanjā | शिकंजा

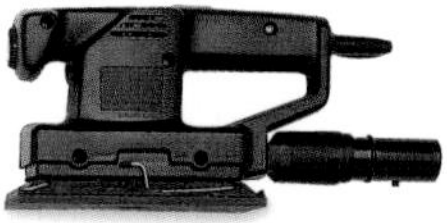

sander
saiṇḍar | सैंडर

blade
bleḍ
ब्लेड

circular saw
gol ārī | गोल आरी

workbench
kām karne kī mez
काम करने की मेज़

wood glue
lakṛī kā gond
लकड़ी का गोंद

router
rūṭar
रूटर

wood shavings
lakṛī kī chhīlan
लकड़ी की छीलन

tool rack
auzār raik
औज़ार रैक

bit brace
biṭ bres
बिट ब्रेस

extension cord
atirikt tār
अतिरिक्त तार

techniques • vidhiyāṃ • विधियां

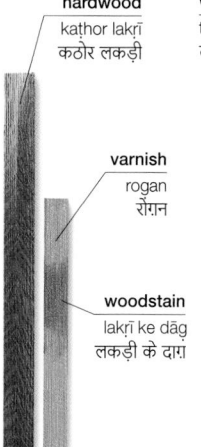

cut (v)
kāṭnā | काटना

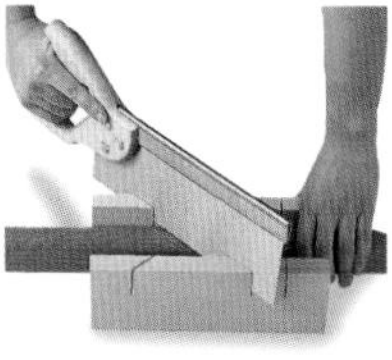

saw (v)
chīrnā | चीरना

drill (v)
chhed karnā | छेद करना

hammer (v)
ṭhoknā | ठोकना

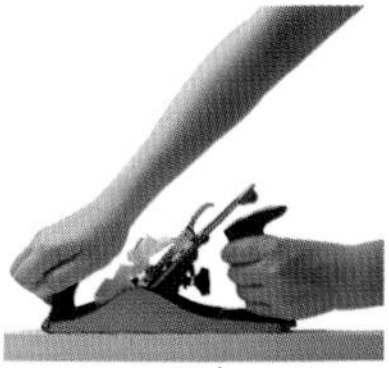

plane (v) | randā karnā | रंदा करना

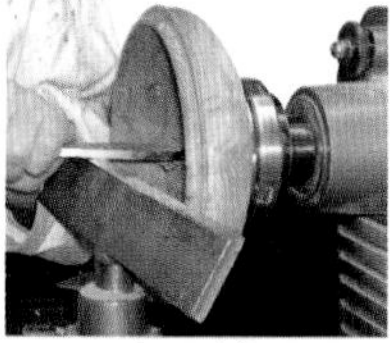

turn (v)
kharādnā | खरादना

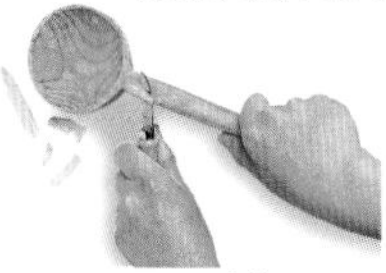

carve (v)
nakḳāśī karnā | नक़्क़ाशी करना

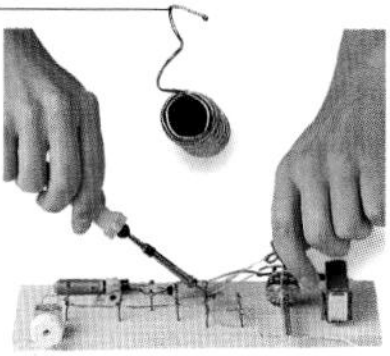

solder (v) | ṭāṃkā lagānā | टांका लगाना

materials • sāmān • सामान

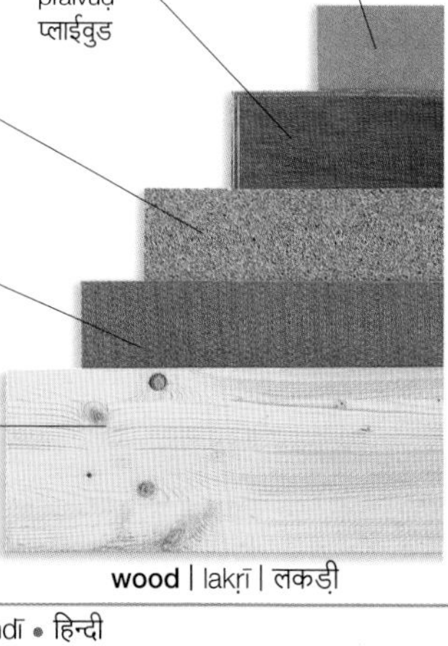

wood | lakṛī | लकड़ी

cable
kebal | केबल

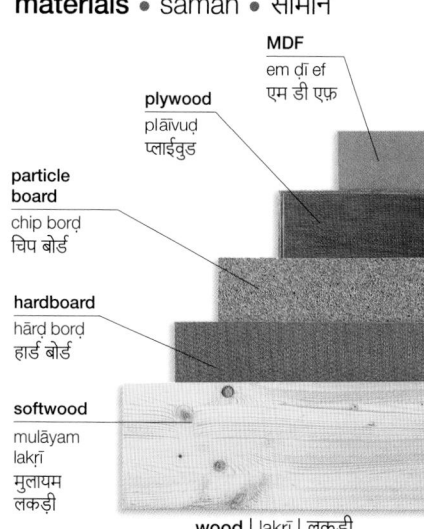

metal | dhātu | धातु

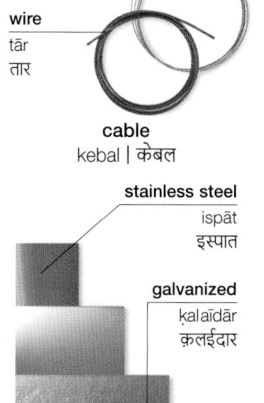

toolbox • auzār peṭī • औज़ार पेटी

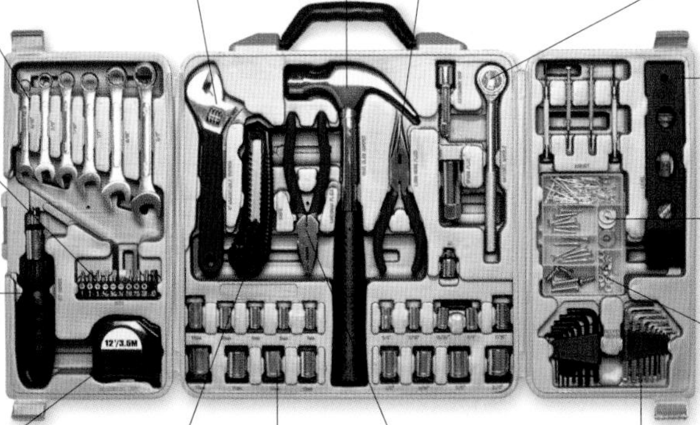

drill bits • ḍriliṅg maśīn ke vajr • ड्रिलिंग मशीन के वज्र

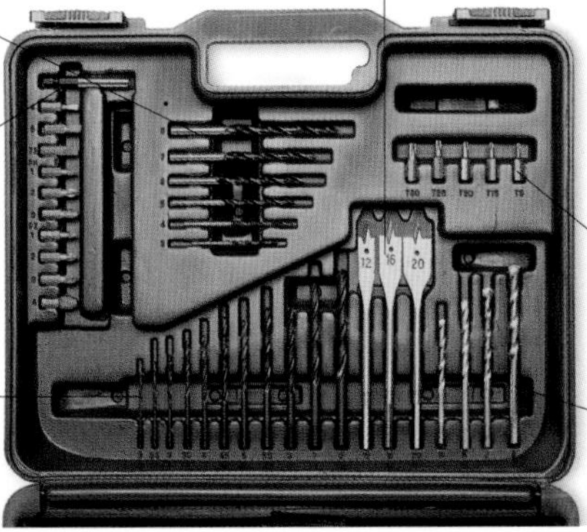

phillips screwdriver
filips pechkas
फ़िलिप्स पेचकस

nail
kīl | कील

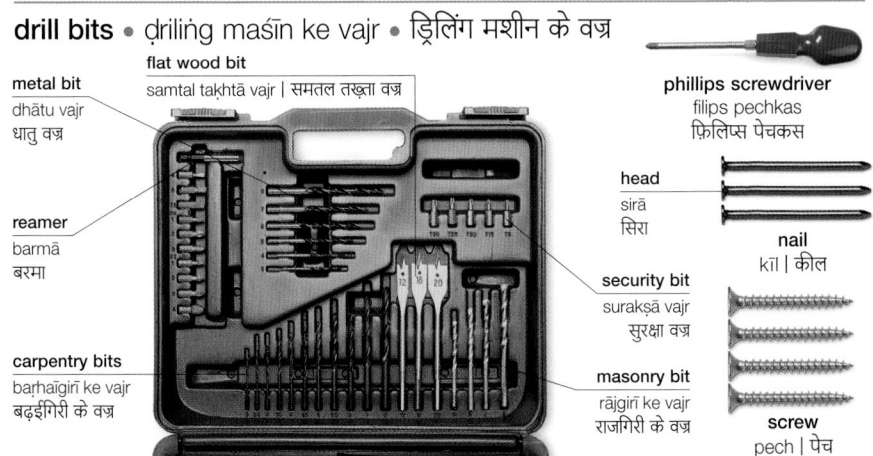

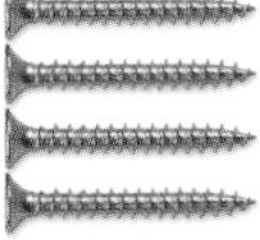

screw
pech | पेच

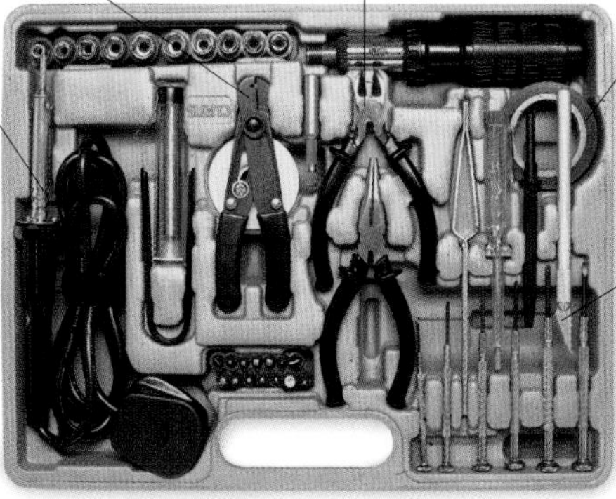

wire strippers
tār chhīlne kā plās
तार छीलने का प्लास

wire cutters
tār kāṭne kā yantr
तार काटने का यंत्र

soldering iron
ṭāṃke kā upkaraṇ
टांके का उपकरण

electrical tape
bijlī kā ṭep
बिजली का टेप

craft knife
chhurī
छुरी

solder
ṭāṃkā lagāne kā tār
टांका लगाने का तार

fretsaw
patlī ārī
पतली आरी

tenon saw | chul ārā | चुल आरा

safety goggles
surakṣā chaśmā
सुरक्षा चश्मा

plane
randā | रंदा

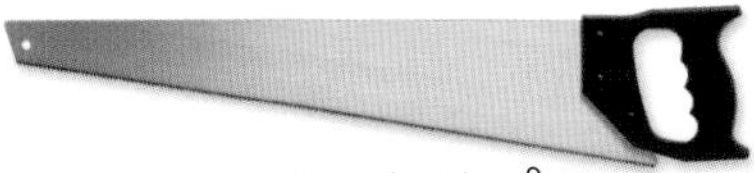

handsaw | ārī | आरी

miter block
mīṭar blok
मीटर ब्लॉक

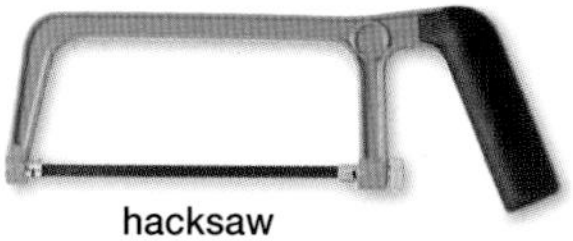

hacksaw
dāṃtedār ārī | दांतेदार आरी

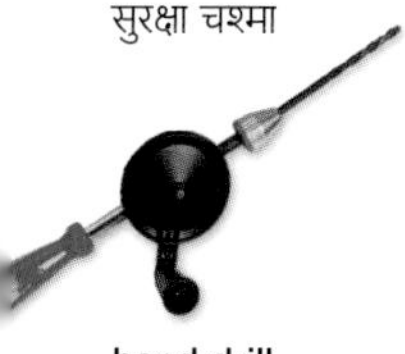

hand drill
haiṇḍ ḍril
हैंड ड्रिल

steel wool
tār
तार

sandpaper
regmāl
रेगमाल

wrench
rinch
रिंच

chisel
chhenī | छेनी

whetstone
sān | सान

pipe cutter | pāip kaṭar | पाइप कटर

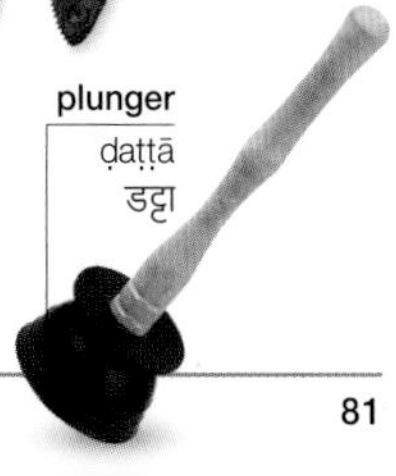

plunger
ḍaṭṭā
डट्टा

file
retī | रेती

decorating • gṛh sajjā • गृह सज्जा

scissors
kaiṃchī | क़ैंची

utility knife
chhurī | छुरी

plumb line
sāhul ḍorī | साहुल डोरी

scraper
khurachnī | खुरचनी

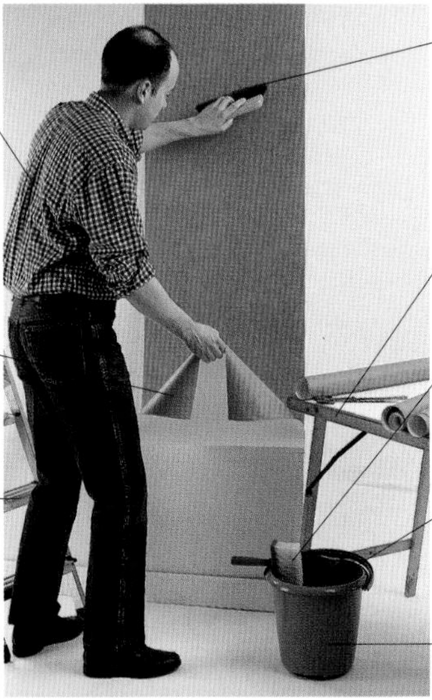

wallpaper (v) | volpepar lagānā | वॉलपेपर लगाना

strip (v) | khurachnā | खुरचना

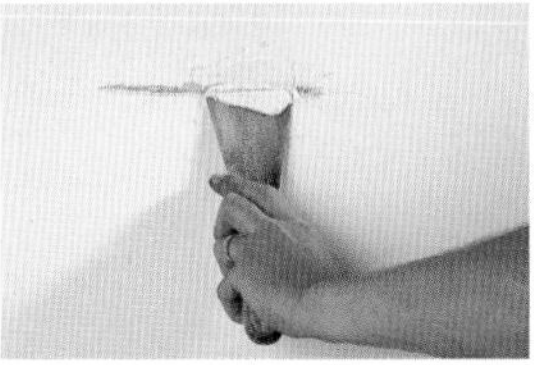

fill (v) | bharnā | भरना

sand (v)
ghisāī karnā | घिसाई करना

plaster (v)
palastar karnā | पलस्तर करना

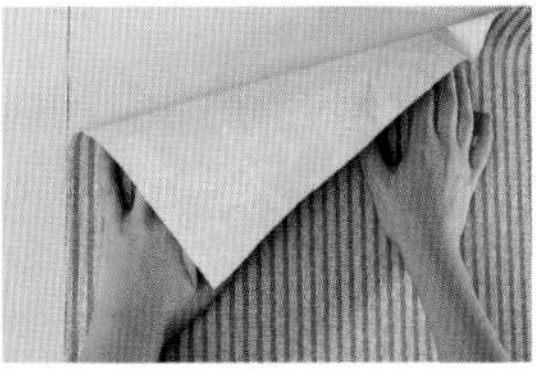

hang (v)
laṭkānā | लटकाना

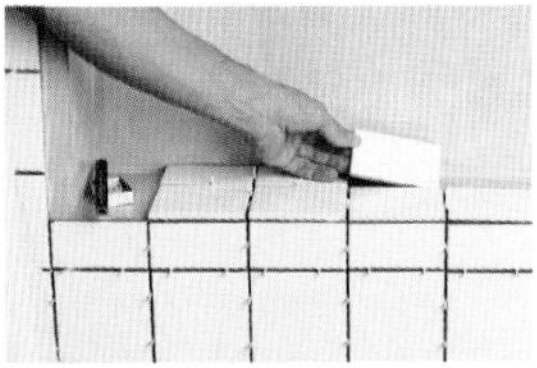

tile (v)
ṭāil lagānā | टाइल लगाना

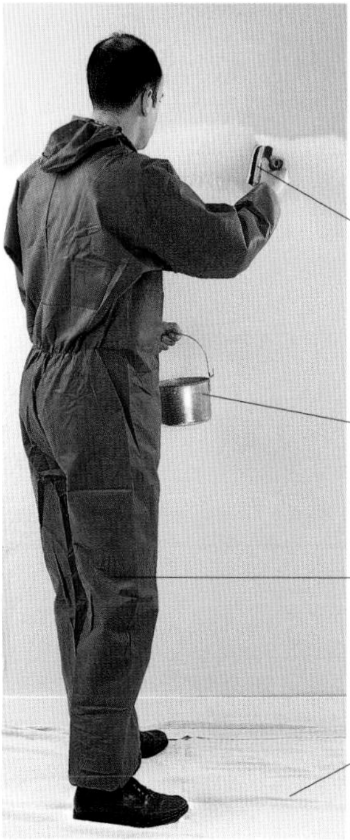

roller
rolar
रोलर

paint tray
penṭ ṭre | पेंट ट्रे

paint
penṭ | पेंट

brush
braś
ब्रश

paint can
penṭ kā ḍibbā
पेंट का डिब्बा

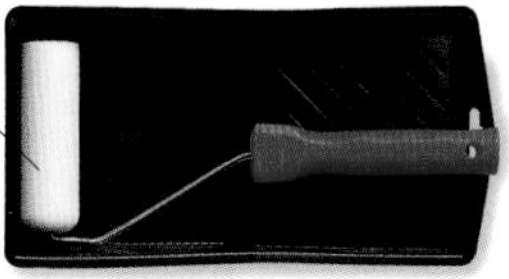

sponge
spanj
स्पंज

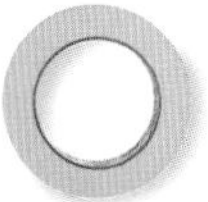

masking tape
apārdarśī ṭep
अपारदर्शी टेप

sandpaper
regmāl
रेगमाल

coveralls
ūprī vastr
ऊपरी वस्त्र

turpentine
tārpīn
तारपीन

drop cloth
gandī darī
गंदी दरी

paint (v)
raṅgnā | रंगना

filler
filar | फ़िलर

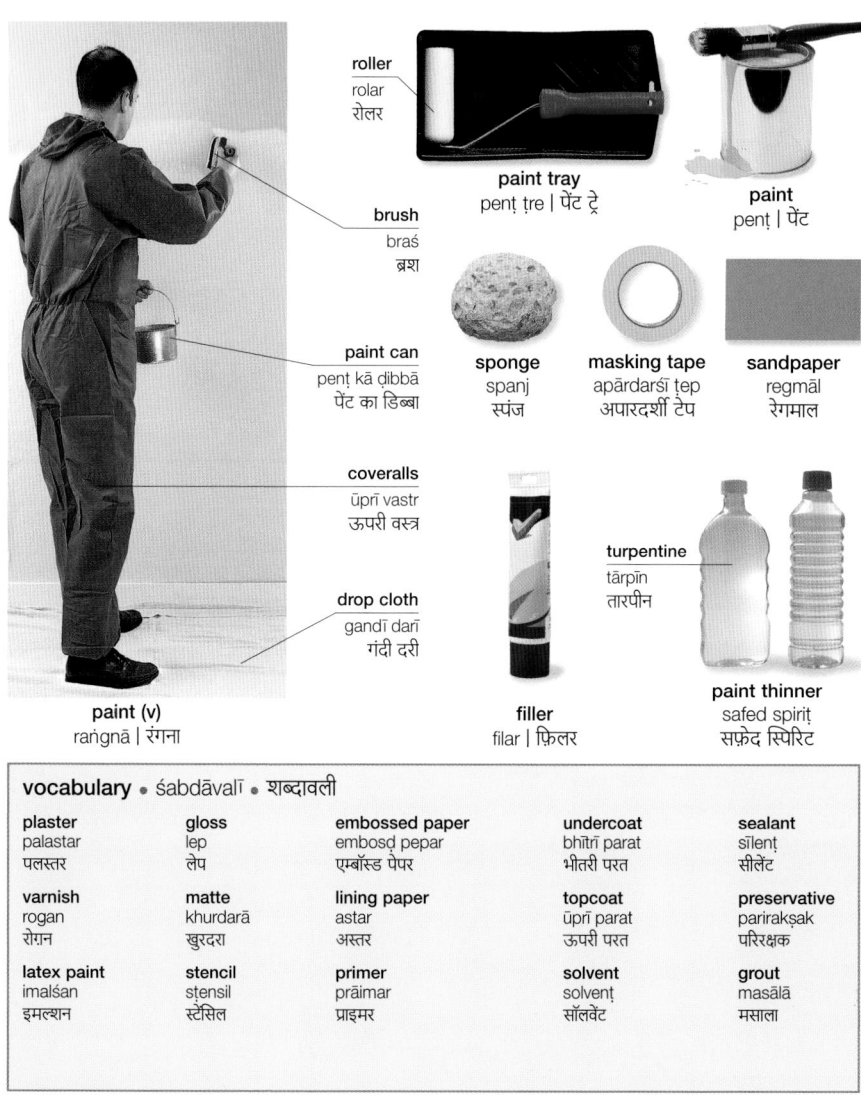

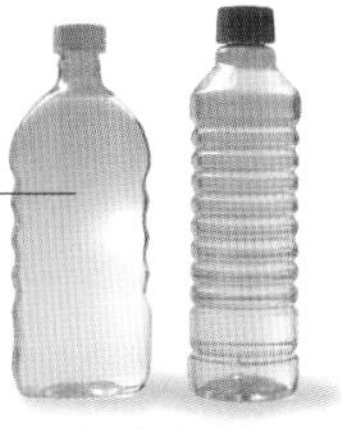

paint thinner
safed spiriṭ
सफ़ेद स्पिरिट

---

vocabulary • śabdāvalī • शब्दावली

plaster palastar पलस्तर	**gloss** lep लेप	**embossed paper** embosḍ pepar एम्बॉस्ड पेपर	**undercoat** bhītrī parat भीतरी परत	**sealant** sīlenṭ सीलेंट
varnish rogan रोग़न	**matte** khurdarā खुरदरा	**lining paper** astar अस्तर	**topcoat** ūprī parat ऊपरी परत	**preservative** parirakṣak परिरक्षक
latex paint imalśan इमल्शन	**stencil** sṭensil स्टेंसिल	**primer** prāimar प्राइमर	**solvent** solvenṭ सॉल्वेंट	**grout** masālā मसाला

garden • bagīchā • बग़ीचा

garden styles • bagīche kī śailiyāṃ • बग़ीचे की शैलियां

patio garden | upvan/bagīchī | उपवन/बग़ीची

roof garden
chhat bagīchī
छत बग़ींची

rock garden
pathrīlā bāg | पथरीला बाग़

formal garden | bagīchā | बग़ीचा

courtyard | āṅgan | आंगन

cottage garden
kuṭīr udyān
कुटीर उद्यान

herb garden
auṣadhi udyān
औषधि उद्यान

water garden
jal udyān
जल उद्यान

garden features • bagīche kī rūp sajjā • बग़ीचे की रूप सज्जा

hanging basket
jhūltī ṭokrī | झूलती टोकरी

trellis
bāṛā/jālī | बाड़ा/जाली

arbor
latāmaṇḍap
लतामंडप

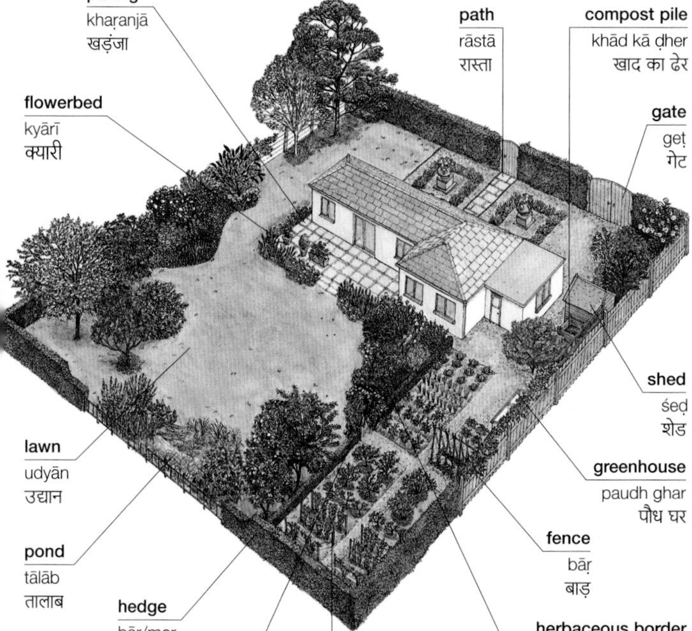

deck
chabūtrā | चबूतरा

fountain | favvārā | फ़व्वारा

soil • miṭṭī • मिट्टी

topsoil
ūprī miṭṭī | ऊपरी मिट्टी

sand
ret | रेत

chalk
khaṛiyā | खड़िया

silt
gād | गाद

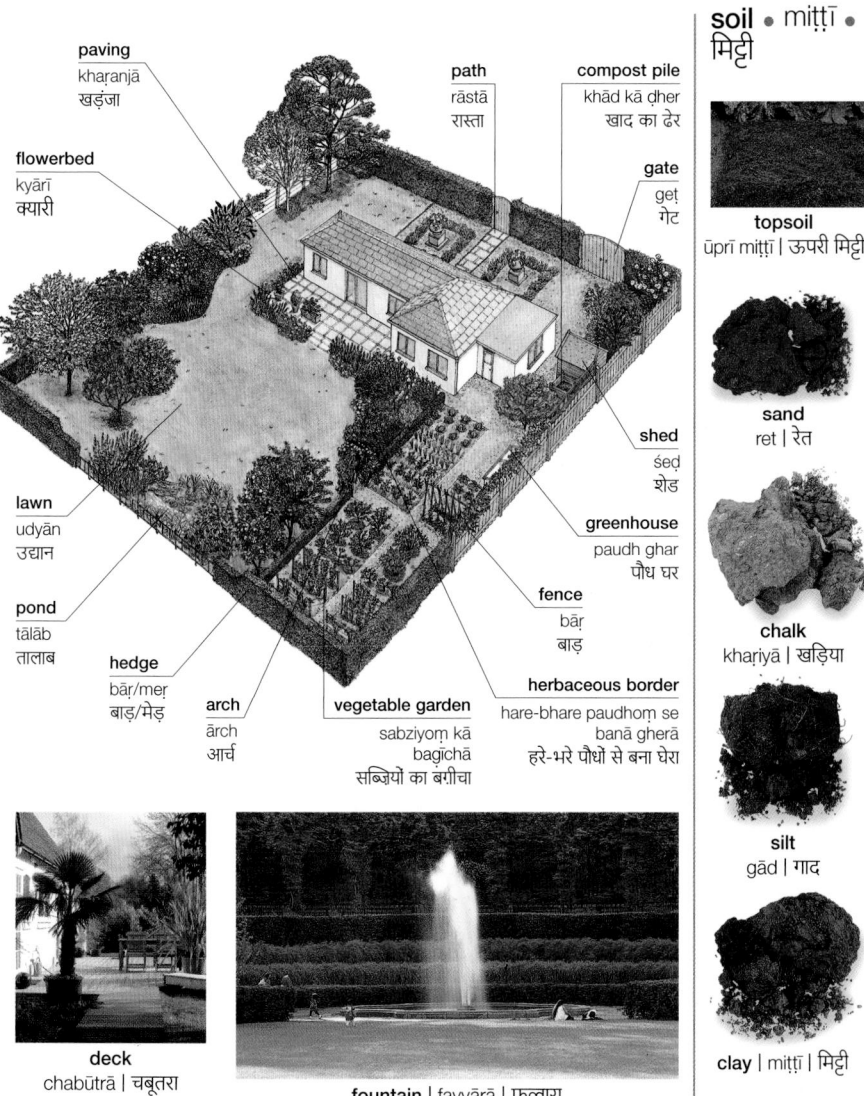

clay | miṭṭī | मिट्टी

garden plants • bagīche ke paudhe • बगीचे के पौधे

types of plants • paudhoṃ ke prakār • पौधों के प्रकार

annual | vārṣikī paudh
वार्षिकी पौध

biennial | dvivārṣik paudh | द्विवार्षिक पौध

perennial
bārahmāsī | बारहमासी

bulb
balb | बल्ब

fern
parṇāṅg | पर्णाङ्ग

cattail
jalbeṃt | जलबेंत

bamboo
bāṃs | बांस

weeds
ghās-pāt | घास-पात

herb
jaṛī-būṭī | जड़ी-बूटी

water plant
jalīya paudh | जलीय पौध

tree
peṛ | पेड़

palm
tāṛ | ताड़

conifer
śaṅku vṛkṣ | शंकु वृक्ष

evergreen
sadābahār | सदाबहार

deciduous
parṇpātī | पर्णपाती

topiary
kaṭāī-chhaṃṭāī
कटाई-छंटाई

alpine
parvatīya paudhe
पर्वतीय पौधे

succulent
ārdr paudh
आर्द्र पौध

cactus
kaikṭas
कैक्टस

potted plant
gamle ke paudhe
गमले के पौधे

shade plant
chhāyādār paudhe
छायादार पौधे

climber
latā
लता

flowering shrub
phūloṃ kī jhāṛī
फूलों की झाड़ी

ground cover
grāunḍ kavar
ग्राउंड कवर

creeper
bel
बेल

ornamental
sajāvaṭī
सजावटी

grass
ghās
घास

garden tools • bagīche ke upkaraṇ • बगीचे के उपकरण

shovel
phāvṛā
फावड़ा

fork
kāṃṭā auzār
कांटा औज़ार

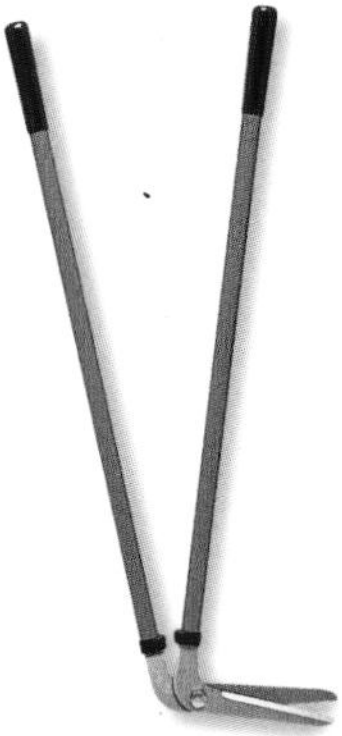
long-handled shears
lambe hatthe kī kaiṃchī
लंबे हत्थे की क़ैंची

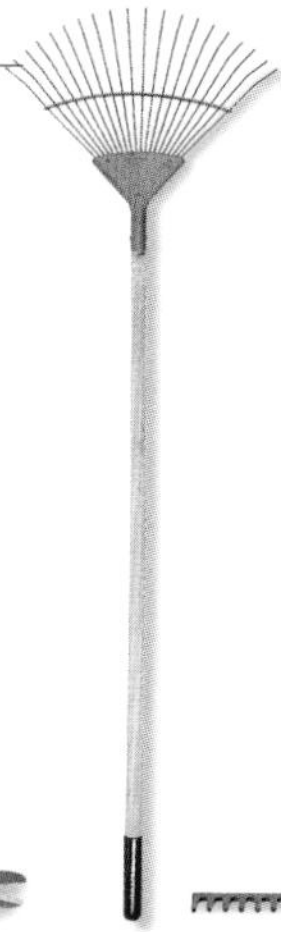
lawn rake
jhāṛū
झाड़ू

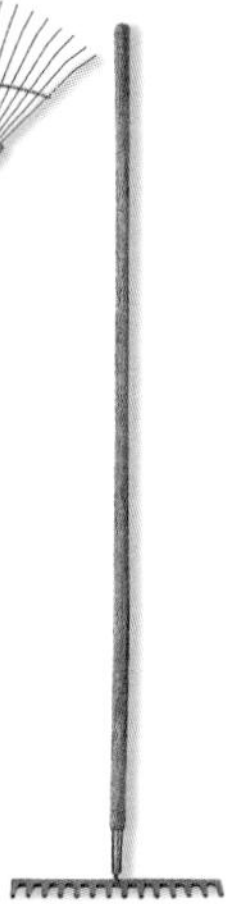
rake
pāṃchā
पांचा

hoe
khurpā | खुरपा

compost
khād | खाद

seeds
bīj | बीज

bone meal
asthi chūrṇ
अस्थि चूर्ण

gravel
bajrī | बजरी

gardening basket | ṭre/ṭokrī | ट्रे/टोकरी

grass bag
ghās kā thailā
घास का थैला

motor
moṭar
मोटर

shield
pleṭ
प्लेट

trimmer | katarne kā auzār
कतरने का औज़ार

lawnmower
ghās kāṭne kī maśīn
घास काटने की मशीन

handle
hatthā
हत्था

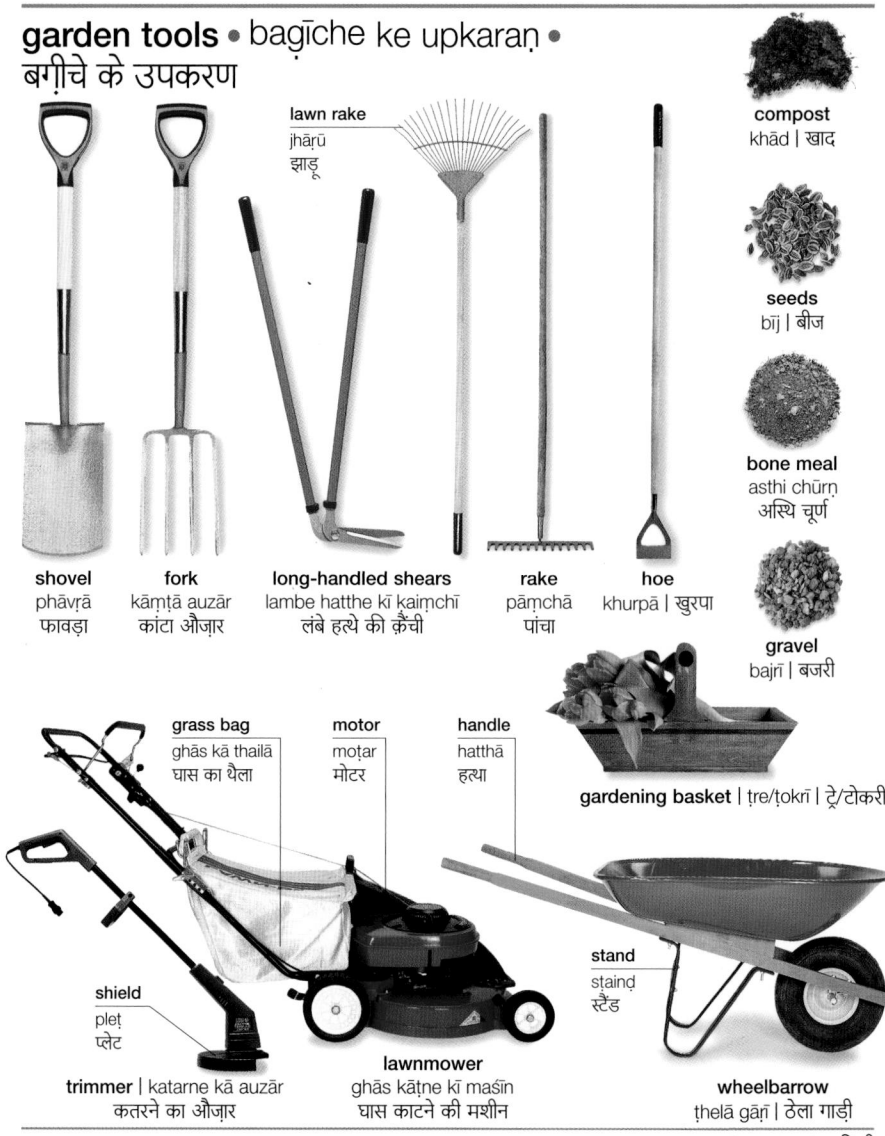

stand
staiṇḍ
स्टैंड

wheelbarrow
ṭhelā gāṛī | ठेला गाड़ी

hand fork
kurednī | कुरेदनी

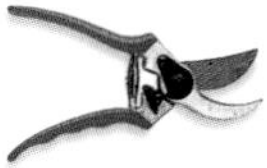

pruners
kaṭar | कटर

gardening gloves
bāgbānī ke dastāne
बाग़बानी के दस्ताने

trowel
khurpī | खुरपी

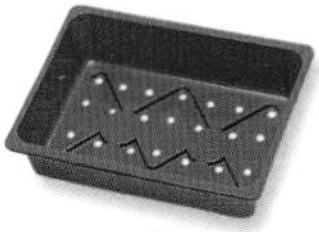

seed tray
bīj ṭre | बीज ट्रे

twine
ḍorī
डोरी

labels
lebal
लेबल

twist ties
chimṭiyāṃ
चिमटियां

ring ties
chhalle
छल्ले

canes
beṃt | बेंत

blade
phal
फल

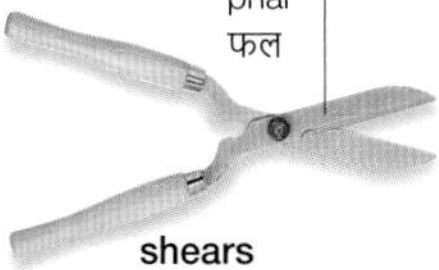

shears
baṛī kaiṃchī
बड़ी कैंची

hand saw
ārī | आरी

pesticide
kīṭnāśak
कीटनाशक

sieve
chhalnī
छलनी

plant pot
gamlā
गमला

rubber boots | rabaṛ ke jūte | रबड़ के जूते

watering • sīṃchnā • सींचना

watering can
phuhārā
फुहारा

spray
hazārā
हज़ारा

spray bottle
pichkārī | पिचकारी

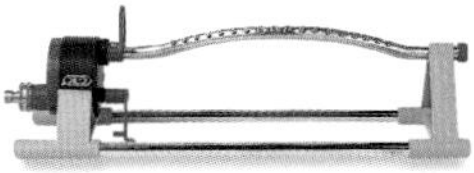

sprinkler
hazārā
हज़ारा

nozzle
ṭoṃṭī
टोंटी

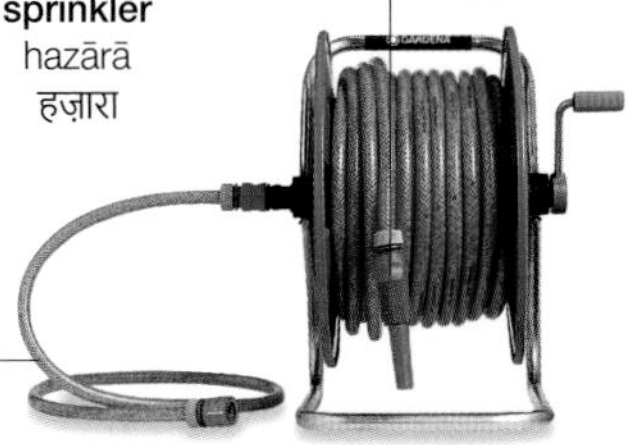

hose
rabaṛ nalī
रबड़ नली

hose reel | huchkā | हुचका

gardening • bāġbānī • बाग़बानी

mow (v) | ghās kāṭnā | घास काटना

sod (v)
ghās bichhānā
घास बिछाना

spike (v)
khūṃṭā ṭhoknā
खूंटा ठोकना

rake (v)
buhārnā
बुहारना

trim (v)
chhāṃṭnā
छांटना

dig (v)
khodnā | खोदना

sow (v)
bonā | बोना

top-dress (v)
khād ḍālnā | खाद डालना

water (v)
sīṃchnā | सींचना

train (v) | ākār denā
आकार देना

deadhead (v) | sūkhe patte nikālnā | सूखे पत्ते निकालना

spray (v)
chhiṛaknā | छिड़कना

graft (v) | ḳalam bāṃdhnā | क़लम बांधना

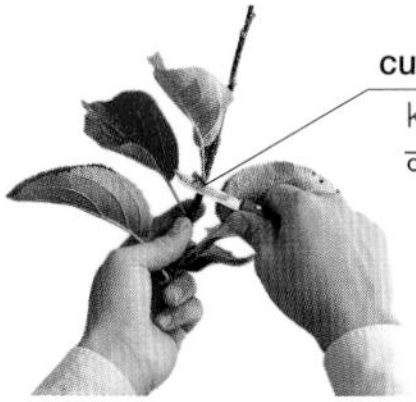

propagate (v)
baṛhānā | बढ़ाना

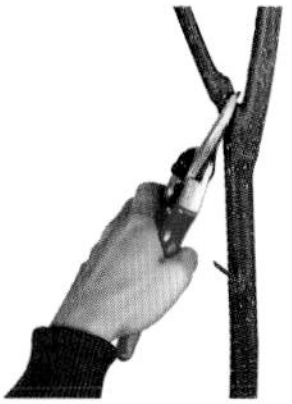

prune (v)
chhāṃṭnā | छांटना

stake (v) | khūṃṭī se bāṃdhnā | खूंटी से बांधना

transplant (v)
pratiropit karnā
प्रतिरोपित करना

weed (v)
nirāī
निराई

mulch (v)
ghās-pāt se ḍhaknā
घास-पात से ढकना

harvest (v)
fasal kāṭnā
फ़सल काटना

vocabulary • śabdāvalī • शब्दावली

cultivate (v)
khetī karnā
खेती करना

fertilize (v)
urvar banānā
उर्वर बनाना

sift (v)
chhānnā
छानना

organic
jaiv
जैव

seedling
bījaropaṇ
बीजारोपण

pot (v)
gamle meṃ ḍālnā
गमले में डालना

subsoil
avmṛdā
अवमृदा

tend (v)
dekhbhāl karnā
देखभाल करना

pick (v)
chunnā/toṛnā
चुनना/तोड़ना

aerate (v)
havā lagānā
हवा लगाना

drainage
morī
मोरी

fertilizer
urvarak
उर्वरक

weedkiller
kharpatvār nāśak
खरपतवार नाशक

JKL
5
TUV
8
0

services
sevāeṃ
सेवाएं

emergency services • āpātkālīn sevāeṃ • आपातकालीन सेवाएं

ambulance • embulens • एंबुलेंस

ambulance
embulens | एंबुलेंस

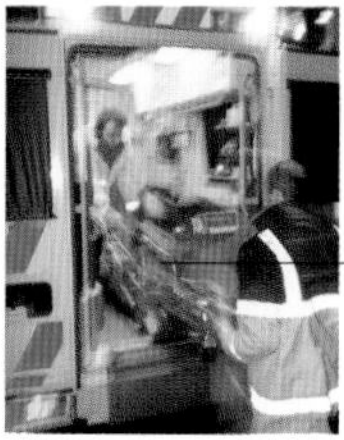

paramedic
parāchikitsak | पराचकित्सक

police • pulis • पुलिस

police officer
pulis adhikārī | पुलिस अधिकारी

handcuffs
hathkaṛī
हथकड़ी

police car
pulis kār | पुलिस कार

police station
pulis chaukī
पुलिस चौकी

vocabulary • śabdāvalī • शब्दावली

captain darogā दरोगा	**suspect** saṃdigdh संदिग्ध	**complaint** śikāyat शिकायत	**arrest** giraftār गिरफ़्तार
crime jurm जुर्म	**assault** hamlā हमला	**investigation** jāṃch जांच	**cell** havālāt हवालात
detective jāsūs जासूस	**fingerprint** uṃgliyoṃ kī chhāp उंगलियों की छाप	**burglary** chorī चोरी	**charge** ārop आरोप

fire department • damkal dastā • दमकल दस्ता

fire | āg | आग

fire fighters
agniśāmak karmī
अग्निशामक कर्मी

fire station
damkal kendr
दमकल केंद्र

fire escape
āpātkālīn rakṣā mārg
आपातकालीन रक्षा मार्ग

fire engine
damkal | दमकल

smoke alarm
smok alārm
स्मोक अलार्म

fire alarm
fāyar alārm
फ़ायर अलार्म

ax
kulhāṛī
कुल्हाड़ी

fire extinguisher
agniśāmak upkaraṇ
अग्निशामक उपकरण

hydrant
pānī kā nal
पानी का नल

I need the police/fire department/ambulance. I mujhe pulis/damkal dasta/embulens bulānī hai I मुझे पुलिस/दमकल दस्ता/एंबुलेंस बुलानी है।

There's a fire at...
...meṃ āg lagī hai
... में आग लगी है।

There's been an accident.
ek durghaṭnā huī hai
एक दुर्घटना हुई है।

Call the police!
pulis ko bulāo!
पुलिस को बुलाओ!

bank • baiṅk • बैंक

customer
grāhak
ग्राहक

window
khiṛkī
खिड़की

teller
ḳhazānchī
ख़ज़ांची

brochures
parchī
पर्ची

counter
kāunṭar
काउंटर

deposit slips
jamā parchī
जमा पर्ची

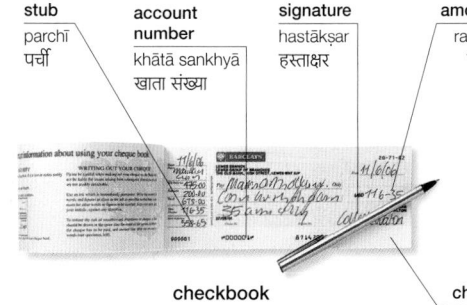

branch manager
baink prabandhak
बैंक प्रबंधक

debit card
ḍebiṭ kārḍ
डेबिट कार्ड

credit card
kreḍiṭ kārḍ
क्रेडिट कार्ड

stub
parchī
पर्ची

account number
khātā sankhyā
खाता संख्या

signature
hastākṣar
हस्ताक्षर

amount
raḳam
रक़म

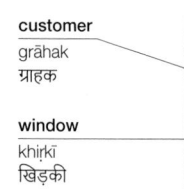

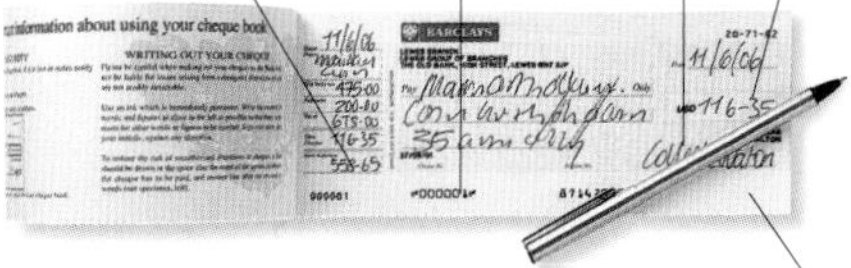

checkbook
chek buk
चेक बुक

check
chek
चेक

vocabulary • śabdāvalī • शब्दावली

savings bachat बचत	**mortgage** bandhak बंधक	**payment** bhugtān भुगतान	**deposit (v)** jamā karnā जमा करना	**checking account** chālū khātā चालू खाता
tax kar कर	**overdraft** ovar ḍrāfṭ ओवर ड्राफ़्ट	**automatic payment** pratyakṣ bhugtān प्रत्यक्ष भुगतान	**bank charge** baink prabhār बैंक प्रभार	**savings account** bachat khātā बचत खाता
loan ṛiṇ ऋण	**interest rate** byāj dar ब्याज दर	**withdrawal slip** āharaṇ parchī आहरण पर्ची	**bank transfer** baink antraṇ बैंक अंतरण	**PIN** pin पिन

money
dhan | धन

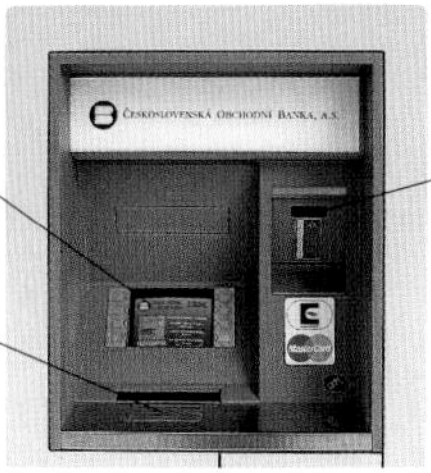

ATM
eṭīem | एटीएम

foreign currency • videśī mudrā • विदेशी मुद्रा

currency exchange
videśī mudrā vinimaya kendr
विदेशी मुद्रा विनिमय केंद्र

traveler's check
yātrī chek | यात्री चेक

exchange rate
vinimaya dar
विनिमय दर

finance • vitt • वित्त

financial advisor
vittīya salāhkār
वित्तीय सलाहकार

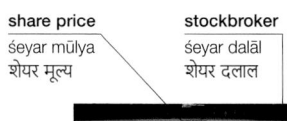

stock exchange
śeyar bāzār | शेयर बाज़ार

vocabulary • śabdāvalī • शब्दावली

cash (v)
nakad nikālnā
नक़द निकालना

denomination
mūlyavarg
मूल्यवर्ग

commission
dalālī
दलाली

investment
niveś
निवेश

stocks
sṭok
स्टॉक

shares
śeyar
शेयर

dividends
lābhānś
लाभांश

accountant
lekhākār
लेखाकार

portfolio
niveś sūchī
निवेश सूची

equity
śeyar pūnjī
शेयर पूंजी

Can I change this please?
kyā ise badlā jā saktā hai?
क्या इसे बदला जा सकता है?

What's today's exchange rate?
vartmān vinimaya dar kyā hai?
वर्तमान विनिमय दर क्या है?

communications • sanchār • संचार

postal worker
ḍāk karmī
डाक कर्मी

window
khiṛkī
खिड़की

scale
vazan-māpī
वज़न-मापी

counter
kāunṭar
काउंटर

post office
ḍākghar | डाकघर

mail carrier
ḍākiyā | डाकिया

postmark
mohar
मोहर

stamp
ḍāk ṭikaṭ
डाक टिकट

address
patā
पता

zip code
ḍāk koḍ
डाक कोड

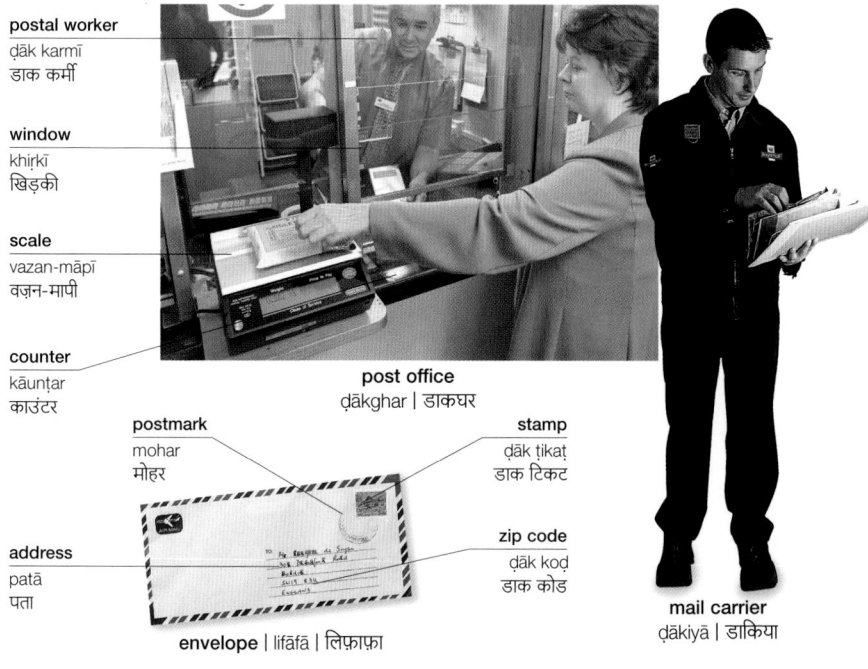

envelope | lifāfā | लिफ़ाफ़ा

vocabulary • śabdāvalī • शब्दावली

letter patr पत्र	**return address** vāpsī kā patā वापसी का पता	**delivery** vitraṇ वितरण	**fragile** nāzuk vastu नाज़ुक वस्तु	**do not bend (v)** kripyā moṛeṃ nahīṃ कृपया मोड़ें नहीं
by airmail havāī ḍāk dvārā हवाई डाक द्वारा	**signature** hastākṣar हस्ताक्षर	**money order** posṭal order पोस्टल ऑर्डर	**mailbag** ḍāk thailā डाक थैला	**this way up** ise ūpar rakheṃ इसे ऊपर रखें।
registered mail rajisṭarḍ ḍāk रजिस्टर्ड डाक	**pickup** saṅgrah संग्रह	**postage** ḍāk vyaya डाक व्यय	**telegram** tār तार	**fax** faiks फ़ैक्स

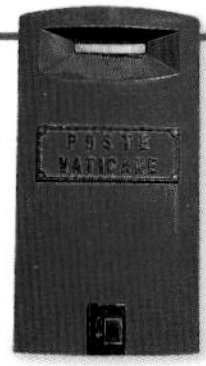

mailbox
ḍākpeṭī | डाकपेटी

letter slot
patrpeṭī | पत्रपेटी

package
pārsal | पार्सल

courier
kūriyar | कूरियर

telephone • dūrbhāṣ • दूरभाष

handset
haiṇḍ seṭ
हैंडसेट

base station
fon sṭaiṇḍ
फ़ोन स्टैंड

answering machine
ānsariṅg maśīn
आंसरिंग मशीन

cordless phone
kordles fon
कॉर्डलेस फ़ोन

video phone
vīḍiyo fon | वीडियो फ़ोन

phone booth
ṭelīfon boks
टेलीफ़ोन बॉक्स

smartphone
smārṭfon
स्मार्टफ़ोन

keypad
kī paiḍ
की-पैड

cell phone
mobāil fon
मोबाइल फ़ोन

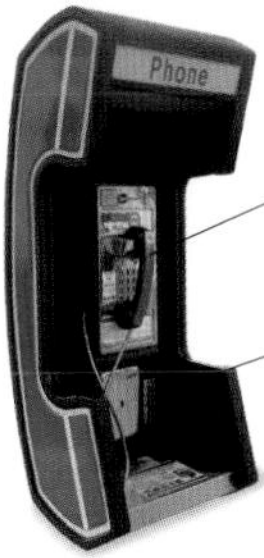

receiver
risīvar
रिसीवर

coin return
sikkā vāpsī
सिक्का वापसी

payphone
pī sī o fon
पी सी ओ फ़ोन

vocabulary • śabdāvalī • शब्दावली

dial (v)
nambar milānā
नंबर मिलाना

collect call
revars chārj kol
रिवर्स चार्ज कॉल

directory assistance
ḍāyarek ṭarī pūchhtāchh
डायरेक्टरी पूछताछ

app
aip
ऐप

answer (v)
uttar denā
उत्तर देना

text (SMS)
es em es
एस एम एस

voice message
dhvani sandeś
ध्वनि संदेश

passcode
pāskoḍ
पासकोड

operator
prachālak
प्रचालक

busy
vyast
व्यस्त

disconnected
sampark ṭūṭnā
संपर्क टूटना

Can you give me the number for...?
kyā āp mujhe … kā nambar de sakte haiṃ?
क्या आप मुझे... का नंबर दे सकते हैं?

What is the area code for...?
… ke lie ḍāyaling koḍ kyā hai?
... के लिए डायलिंग कोड क्या है?

Text me!
mujhe es em es bhejeṃ!
मुझे एस एम एस भेजें!

hotel • hoṭal • होटल

lobby • lobī • लॉबी

guest
mehmān
मेहमान

room key
kamre kī chābī
कमरे की चाबी

messages
sandeś
संदेश

pigeonhole
koṣṭh
कोष्ठ

receptionist
svāgat adhikārī
स्वागत अधिकारी

register
rajisṭar
रजिस्टर

counter
kāunṭar
काउंटर

reception | svāgat | स्वागत

luggage
sāmān
सामान

cart
ṭrolī
ट्रॉली

porter | darbān | दरबान

elevator | lifṭ | लिफ़्ट

room number
kamrā nambar
कमरा नंबर

rooms • kamre • कमरे

single room
siṅgal kamrā
सिंगल कमरा

double room
ḍabal kamrā
डबल कमरा

twin room
ṭvin kamrā
ट्विन कमरा

private bathroom
nijī snānghar
निजी स्नानघर

services • sevāeṃ • सेवाएं

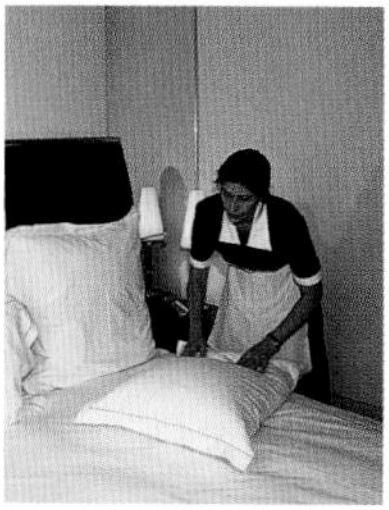

maid service
parichārikā sevā
परिचारिका सेवा

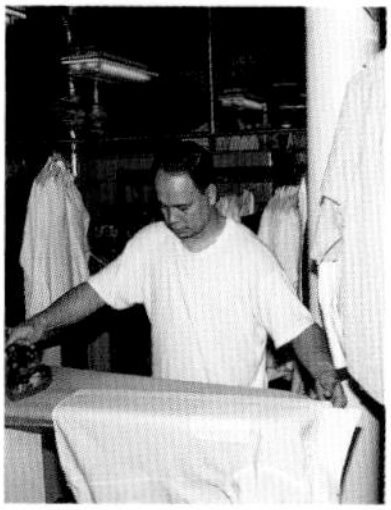

laundry service
londṛī sevā
लॉन्ड्री सेवा

room service | rūm sarvis | रूम सर्विस

mini bar
minī bār | मिनी बार

restaurant
restrāṃ
रेस्तरां

gym
vyāyāmśālā
व्यायामशाला

swimming pool
taranṭāl
तरणताल

vocabulary • śabdāvalī • शब्दावली

bed and breakfast
rahnā aur nāśtā
रहना और नाश्ता

all meals included
ful borḍ
फुल बोर्ड

some meals included
hāf borḍ
हाफ़ बोर्ड

Do you have any vacancies?
kyā āpke yahāṃ kamrā ḳhālī hai?
क्या आपके यहां कमरा खाली है?

I have a reservation.
maiṃne kamrā ārakṣit karāyā huā hai
मैंने कमरा आरक्षित कराया हुआ है।

I'd like a single room.
mujhe ek siṅgal kamrā chāhie
मुझे एक सिंगल कमरा चाहिए।

I'd like a room for three nights.
mujhe tīn rātoṃ ke lie ek kamrā chāhie
मुझे तीन रातों के लिए एक कमरा चाहिए।

What is the charge per night?
ek rāt kā kirāyā kitnā hai?
एक रात का किराया कितना है?

When do I have to check out?
mujhe kab kamrā ḳhālī karnā hai?
मुझे कब कमरा ख़ाली करना है?

shopping
kẖarīdārī
ख़रीदारी

shopping center • ḳharīdārī kendr • ख़रीदारी केंद्र

atrium
prāṅgaṇ
प्रांगण

sign
nām
नाम

elevator
lifṭ
लिफ़्ट

third floor
dūsrī manzil
दूसरी मंज़िल

second floor
pahlī manzil
पहली मंज़िल

escalator
svachālit sīṛhiyāṃ
स्वचालित सीढ़ियां

ground floor
bhūtal
भूतल

customer
grāhak
ग्राहक

vocabulary • śabdāvalī • शब्दावली

luggage department
sāmān vibhāg
सामान विभाग

shoe department
jūtā chappal vibhāg
जूता चप्पल विभाग

children's department
bāl vibhāg
बाल विभाग

store directory
sṭor nirdeśikā
स्टोर निर्देशिका

salesclerk
bikrī sahāyak
बिक्री सहायक

customer services
grāhak sevāeṃ
ग्राहक सेवाएं

fitting rooms
chenjiṅg rūm
चेंजिंग रूम

restroom
prasādhan
प्रसाधन

baby changing room
bāl suvidhā kendr
बाल-सुविधा केंद्र

How much is this?
iskī kyā ḳīmat hai?
इसकी क्या क़ीमत है?

May I exchange this?
kyā ise badlā jā
saktā hai?
क्या इसे बदला जा सकता है?

department store • ḍepārṭmenṭal sṭor • डिपार्टमेंटल स्टोर

menswear
puruṣ paridhān
पुरुष परिधान

womenswear
mahilā paridhān
महिला परिधान

lingerie
adhovastr
अधोवस्त्र

perfumes
itr ityādi
इत्र इत्यादि

cosmetics
saundarya
सौंदर्य

linens
chādar takiyā ādi
चादर तकिया आदि

home furnishings
gṛh sāj-sajjā
गृह साज-सज्जा

notions
bisāt
बिसात

kitchenware
bartan
बर्तन

china
chīnī miṭṭī ke bartan
चीनी मिट्टी के बर्तन

electriconics
bijlī kā sāmān
बिजली का सामान

lighting
lāiṭiṅg
लाइटिंग

sportswear
sporṭs | स्पोर्ट्स

toys
khilaune | खिलौने

stationery | lekhan sāmagrī | लेखन सामग्री

groceries
fūḍ hol | फ़ूड हॉल

supermarket • supar bāzār • सुपर बाज़ार

grocery cart | ṭrolī | ट्रॉली

basket | ṭokrī | टोकरी

780863 185779

bar code
bār koḍ | बार कोड

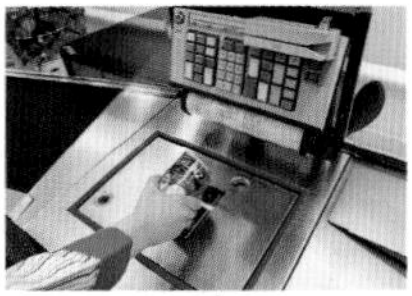

scanner | skainar
स्कैनर

bakery
bekrī
बेकरी

dairy
dugdh utpād
दुग्ध उत्पाद

cereals
anāj
अनाज

canned food
ḍibbāband khādya padārth
डिब्बाबंद खाद्य पदार्थ

candy
mīṭhe khādya
मीठे खाद्य

vegetables
sāg-sabzī
साग-सब्ज़ी

fruit
phal
फल

meat and poultry
māṃsāhārī khādya padārth
मांसाहारी खाद्य पदार्थ

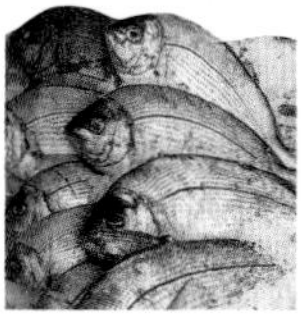

fish
machhlī
मछली

deli
delī
डेली

frozen food
frozan āhār
फ़्रोज़न आहार

prepared food
suvidhājanak bhojan
सुविधाजनक भोजन

drinks
peya padārth
पेय पदार्थ

household products
gharelū vastueṃ
घरेलू वस्तुएं

toiletries
saundarya prasādhan
सौंदर्य प्रसाधन

baby products
śiśu utpād
शिशु उत्पाद

electrical goods
bijlī kī vastueṃ
बिजली की वस्तुएं

pet food
paśu āhār
पशु आहार

magazines | patrikāeṃ | पत्रिकाएं

drugstore • davāī vikretā • दवाई विक्रेता

dental care
dant surakṣā
दंत सुरक्षा

feminine hygiene
strī svacchhatā sāmān
स्त्री-स्वच्छता सामान

deodorants
ḍiyoḍarenṭ
डियोडरेंट

vitamins
viṭāmin
विटामिन

pharmacy
davāḳhānā
दवाख़ाना

pharmacist
auṣadh vitrak
औषध वितरक

cough medicine
khāṃsī kī davāī
खांसी की दवाई

herbal remedies
jaṛī-būṭī auṣadh
जड़ी-बूटी औषध

skin care
tvachā surakṣā
त्वचा सुरक्षा

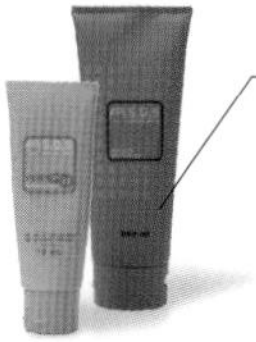

aftersun lotion
āfṭarsan
आफ़्टरसन

sunscreen
sanskrīn | सनस्क्रीन

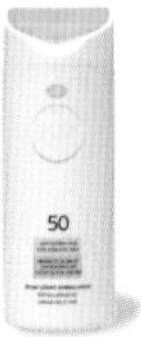

sunblock
san blok
सन ब्लॉक

insect repellent
macchhar avrodhak
मच्छर अवरोधक

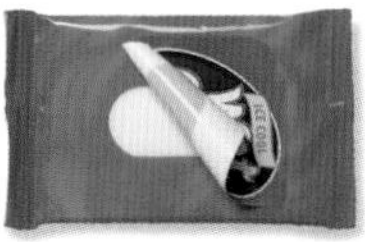

wet wipe
namīyukt ṭiśyū
नमीयुक्त टिश्यू

tissue
ṭiśyū | टिश्यू

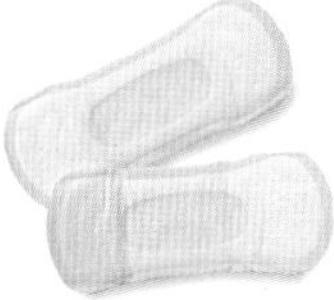

sanitary napkin | sainiṭ arī paid | सैनिटरी पैड

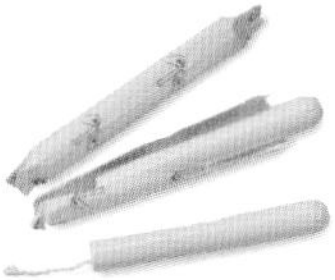

tampon
ṭempon | टेम्पोन

panty liner | painṭī lāinar | पैंटी लाइनर

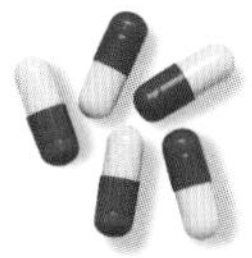

capsule
kaipsūl | कैप्सूल

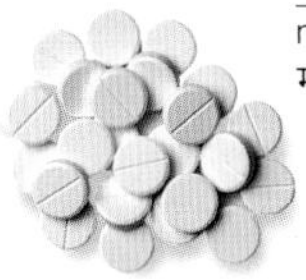

pill
goliyāṃ | गोलियां

measuring spoon
māpak chammach
मापक चम्मच

syrup
sirap | सिरप

instructions
nirdeś
निर्देश

inhaler | śvās yantr
श्वास यंत्र

cream
krīm | क्रीम

ointment
marham | मरहम

gel
jail | जैल

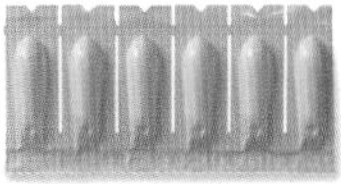

suppository
guhyavarti | गुह्यवर्ति

dropper
ḍropar
ड्रॉपर

drops
ḍrops | ड्रॉप्स

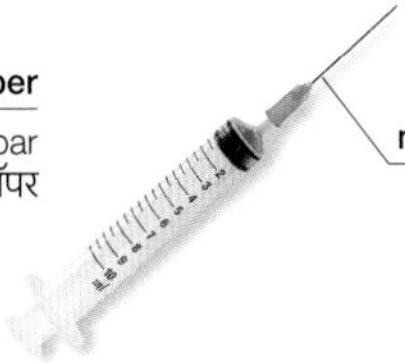

needle
sūī
सूई

syringe
sirinj | सिरिंज

spray
spre | स्प्रे

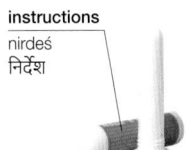

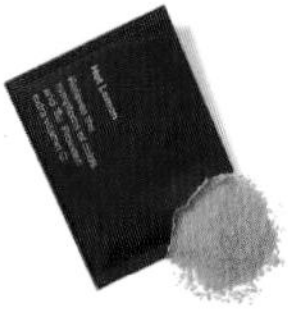

powder
pāuḍar | पाउडर

vocabulary • śabdāvalī • शब्दावली

iron
āyaran
आयरन

calcium
kailśiyam
कैल्शियम

magnesium
maignīśiyam
मैग्नीशियम

multivitamins
bahu viṭāmin
बहु विटामिन

insulin
insulin
इंसुलिन

side-effects
viprīt prabhāv
विपरीत प्रभाव

expiration date
samāpti tithi
समाप्ति तिथि

travel-sickness pills
mitlī kī davā
मितली की दवा

disposable
ḍispozebal
डिस्पोज़ेबल

soluble
ghulanśīl
घुलनशील

dosage
ḳhurāk
ख़ुराक

medication
upchār
उपचार

medicine
davāī
दवाई

laxative
ḳabzḳuśā
क़ब्ज़कुशा

diarrhea
dast
दस्त

throat lozenge
ḳharāś kī davā
ख़राश की दवा

painkiller
dardnāśak
दर्दनाशक

sedative
praśāmak
प्रशामक

sleeping pill
nīṃd kī golīyāṃ
नींद की गोलियां

anti-inflammatory
sūjan rodhī
सूजन रोधी

florist • phūl vikretā • फूल विक्रेता

stocks
sṭoks | स्टॉक्स

gerbera
jarberā | जरबेरा

foliage
phūl-patte | फूल-पत्ते

rose
gulāb | गुलाब

freesia
frīziyā | फ़्रीज़िया

orchid
orkiḍ | ऑरकिड

peony
piyoni | पियोनि

daffodil
ḍaifoḍil
डैफ़ोडिल

tulip | ṭyūlip | ट्यूलिप

arrangements • sajāvaṭ • सजावट

bouquet
guldastā | गुलदस्ता

dried flowers | sūkhe phūl | सूखे फूल

potpourri
sūkhe phūl | सूखे फूल

wreath
puṣp chakr | पुष्प चक्र

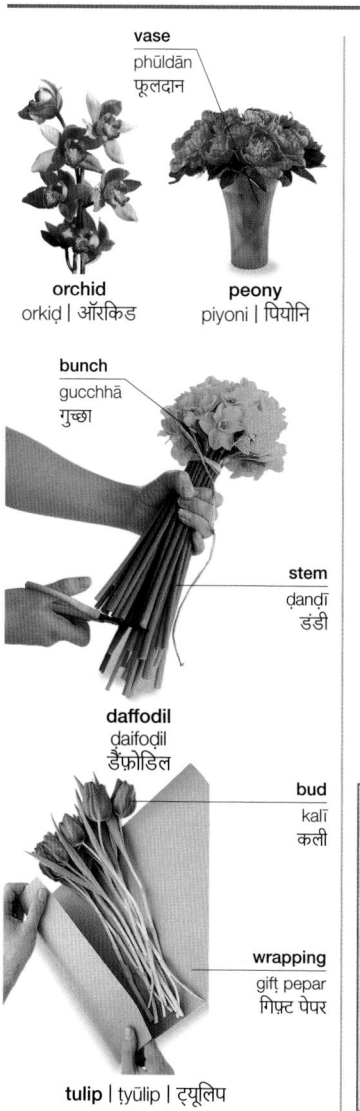

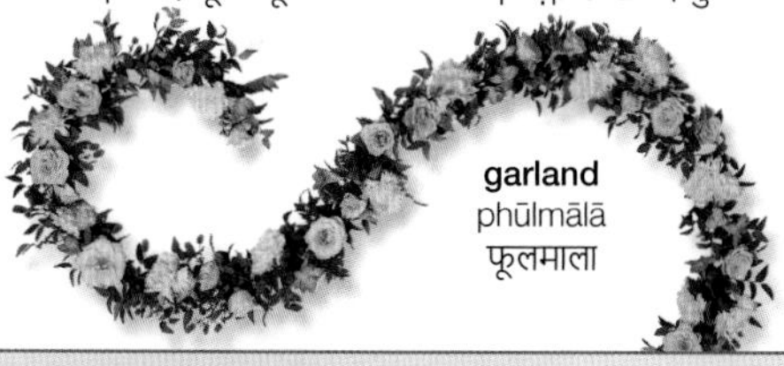

vocabulary • śabdāvalī • शब्दावली

Can I have them wrapped?
āp inheṃ kāgaz meṃ lapeṭ deṇge?
आप इन्हें काग़ज़ में लपेट देंगे?

Can I attach a message?
kyā ek sandeś lag saktā hai?
क्या एक संदेश लग सकता है?

Can I have a bunch of... please?
kyā mujhe ... kā gucchhā mil saktā hai?
क्या मुझे... का गुच्छा मिल सकता है?

Can you send them to...?
kyā āp unheṃ ... ko bhej sakte haiṃ?
क्या आप उन्हें... को भेज सकते हैं?

newsstand • samāchār patr vikretā • समाचार पत्र विक्रेता

cigarettes
sigreṭ
सिगरेट

pack of cigarettes
sigreṭ kī ḍibbī
सिगरेट की डिब्बी

stamps
ḍāk ṭikaṭ
डाक टिकट

postcard
posṭ kārḍ | पोस्ट कार्ड

comic book
chitrkathā | चित्रकथा

magazine
patrikā | पत्रिका

newspaper
samāchār patr | समाचार पत्र

smoking • dhūmrpān • धूम्रपान

tobacco
tambāḳū | तंबाकू

lighter
lāiṭar | लाइटर

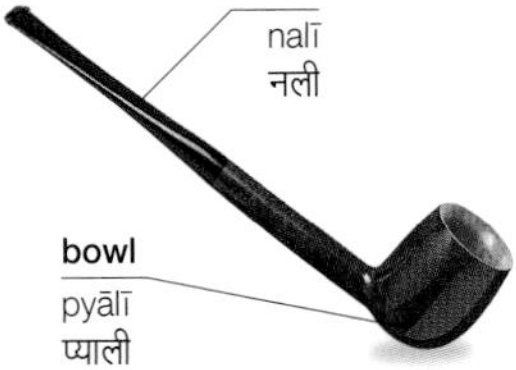

stem
nalī
नली

bowl
pyālī
प्याली

pipe
pāip | पाइप

cigar
sigār | सिगार

candy store • kanfekśnar • कन्फेक्शनर

box of chocolates
choklet̤ box
चॉकलेट बॉक्स

snack bar
snaiks bār
स्नैक्स बार

potato chips
krisps
क्रिस्प्स

candy store | t̤ofī kī dukān | टॉफ़ी की दुकान

vocabulary • śabdāvalī • शब्दावली

milk chocolate
dūdh kī choklet̤
दूध की चॉकलेट

dark chocolate
sādī choklet̤
सादी चॉकलेट

white chocolate
safed choklet̤
सफ़ेद चॉकलेट

pick and mix
milī-julī goliyāṃ
मिली-जुली गोलियां

caramel
kairāmal
कैरामल

truffle
t̤rafal
ट्रफ़ल

cookie
biskut̤
बिस्कुट

confectionery • kanfekśnarī • कन्फेक्शनरी

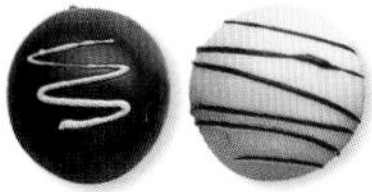

chocolate
choklet̤ | चॉकलेट

chocolate bar
choklet̤ kī pat̤t̤ī
चॉकलेट की पट्टी

hard candy
kaind̤ī | कैंडी

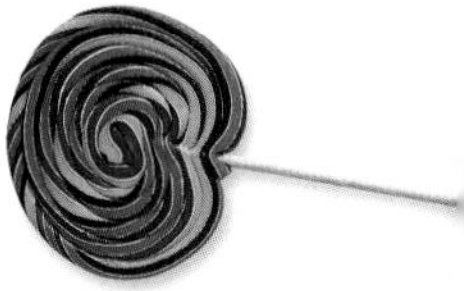

lollipop
lolīpop | लॉलीपॉप

toffee | t̤ofī | टॉफ़ी

nougat | girī kī choklet̤
गिरी की चॉकलेट

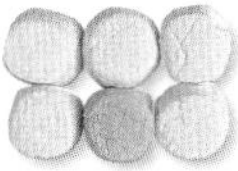

marshmallow
mārśmailo
मार्शमैलो

mint
mint̤ tofī | मिंट टॉफ़ी

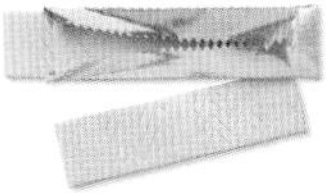

chewing gum
chyūiṅg gam | च्यूइंग गम

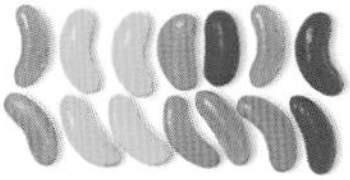

jellybean
jailībīn | जैलीबीन

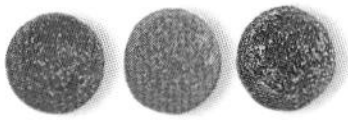

gumdrop
frūt̤ gam | फ़्रूट गम

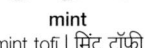

licorice
mulet̤hī kaind̤ī
मुलेठी कैंडी

other stores • anya dukāneṃ • अन्य दुकानें

bakery
bekrī
बेकरी

pastry shop
kek kī dukān
केक की दुकान

butcher shop
ḳasāī kī dukān
क़साई की दुकान

fish counter
machhlī kī dukān
मछली की दुकान

produce stand | phal evam sabziyoṃ kī dukān
फल एवं सब्ज़ियों की दुकान

grocery store
pansārī kī dukān
पंसारी की दुकान

shoe store
jūte kī dukān
जूते की दुकान

hardware store
hārḍveyar shop
हार्डवेयर शॉप

antique store | prāchīn vastuoṃ kī dukān
प्राचीन वस्तुओं की दुकान

gift shop
upahāroṃ kī dukān
उपहारों की दुकान

travel agency
ṭreval ejensī
ट्रेवल एजेंसी

jewelry store
sunār kī dukān
सुनार की दुकान

bookstore
kitāboṃ kī dukān
किताबों की दुकान

record store
rikorḍ kī dukān
रिकॉर्ड की दुकान

liquor store
śarāb kī dukān
शराब की दुकान

pet store
pāltū jānvaroṃ kī dukān
पालतू जानवरों की दुकान

furniture store
farnīchar kī dukān
फ़र्नीचर की दुकान

boutique
buṭīk
बुटीक

vocabulary • śabdāvalī • शब्दावली

real estate office
propartī ḍīlar
प्रॉपर्टी डीलर

garden center
bagbānī kī dukān
बाग़बानी की दुकान

dry cleaner
ḍraī klīnar
ड्राई क्लीनर

laundromat
londrī
लॉन्ड्री

camera store
kaimre kī dukān
कैमरे की दुकान

art supply store
ārt śop
आर्ट शॉप

secondhand store
saikand haind śop
सैकंड हैंड शॉप

health food store
svāsthya āhār kī dukān
स्वास्थ्य आहार की दुकान

tailor shop | darzī kī dukān | दर्ज़ी की दुकान

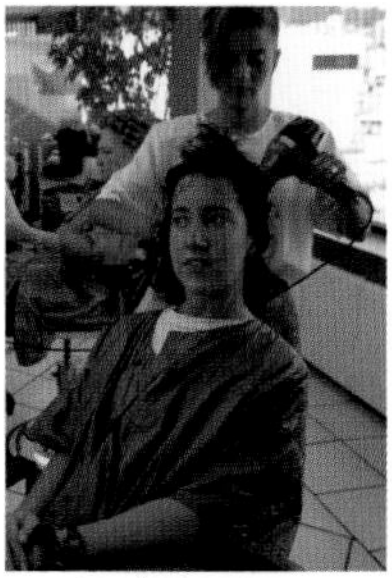

salon | nāī kī dukān
नाई की दुकान

market | bāzār | बाज़ार

food
khādya padārth
खाद्य पदार्थ

meat • māṃs • मांस

butcher
ḳasāī
क़साई

knife sharpener
chākū/chhurī tez
karne kā upkaraṇ
चाकू/छुरी तेज़
करने के उपकरण

meat hook
mīṭ huk
मीट हुक

scale
tarāzū
तराज़ू

lamb
maṭan | मटन

bacon
bekan | बेकन

sausages
sosejes | सॉसेजेस

liver
kalejī | कलेजी

vocabulary • śabdāvalī • शब्दावली

pork sūar kā māṃs सूअर का मांस	**venison** mrg māṃs मृग मांस	**variety meat** chhīchhṛe छीछड़े	**free range** jaṅglī जंगली	**red meat** lāl māṃs लाल मांस
beef go māṃs गो मांस	**rabbit** ḳhargoś ख़रगोश	**cured** sanrakṣit संरक्षित	**organic** jaivik जैविक	**lean meat** binā charbī kā māṃs बिना चर्बी का मांस
veal bachhṛe kā māṃs बछड़े का मांस	**tongue** jībh जीभ	**smoked** dhūmrit धूम्रित	**white meat** safed māṃs सफ़ेद मांस	**cooked meat** pakā huā māṃs पका हुआ मांस

cuts • māṃs ke ṭukṛe • मांस के टुकड़े

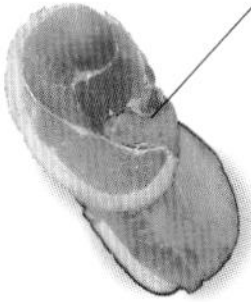

slice
ḳatlā | क़तला

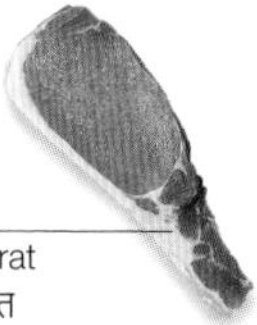

bacon strip
jaṅghā kā māṃs
जंघा का मांस

ground meat
ḳīmā | क़ीमा

fillet
machhlī kā ṭukṛā
मछली का टुकड़ा

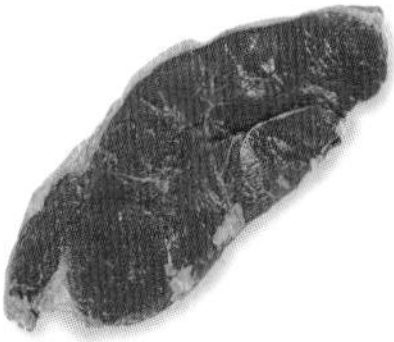

rump steak | kamar kā māṃs | कमर का मांस

sirloin steak | puṭṭhe kā māṃs | पुट्ठे का मांस

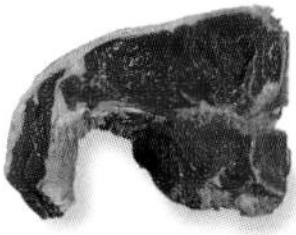

rib
paslī | पसली

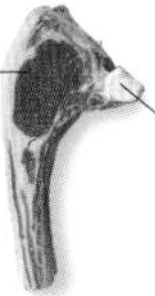

chop
chop | चॉप

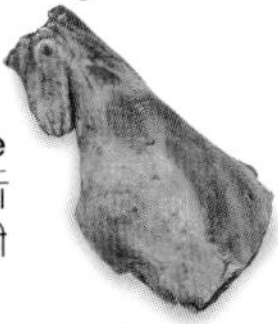

joint
joṛ | जोड़

heart
dil | दिल

poultry • pakṣī-māṃs • पक्षी-मांस

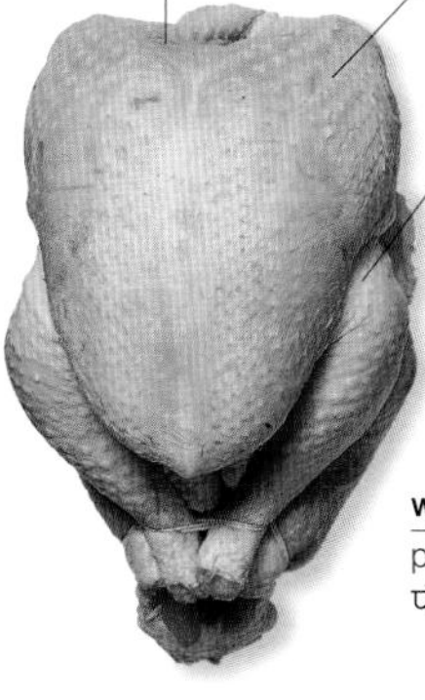

turkey | ṭarkī | टर्की

pheasant
tītar | तीतर

quail | baṭer | बटेर

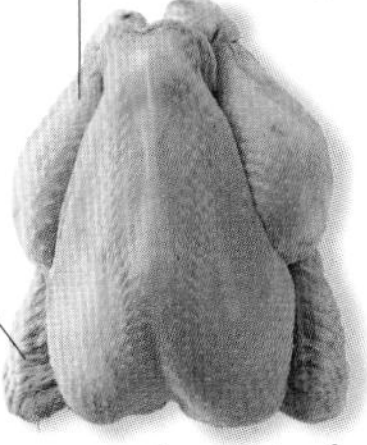

chicken | murg̣ | मुर्ग़

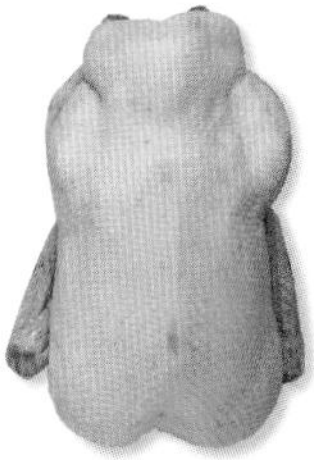

duck | bataḳh | बतख़

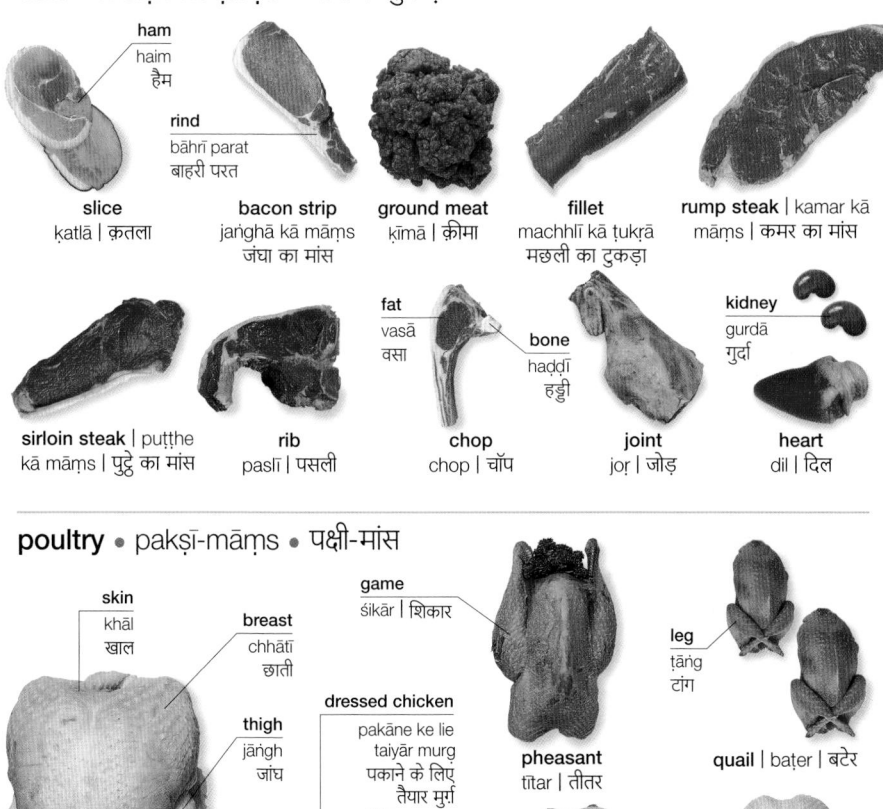

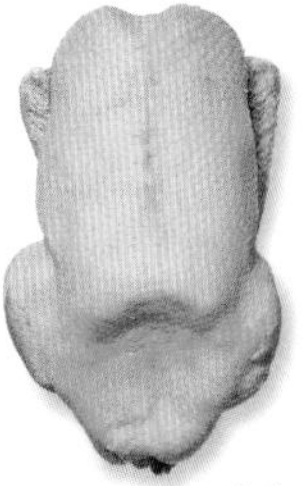

goose | hans | हंस

fish • machhlī • मछली

fish counter
machhlī kī dukān | मछली की दुकान

monkfish
maṅk fiś | मंक फ़िश

mackerel | maikaral machhlī | मैकरल मछली

trout | ṭrāuṭ machhlī
ट्राउट मछली

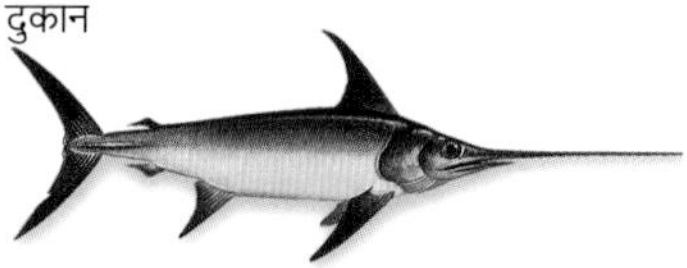

swordfish
khaṅg mīn
खंग मीन

Dover sole
sol machhlī
सोल मछली

lemon sole
laiman sol
लैमन सोल

haddock
haiḍok | हैडॉक

sardine
sārḍin | सार्डिन

skate | śaṅkuchi machhlī | शंकुचि मछली

whiting | viṭīṅg | विटींग

sea bass | sī bās | सी बास

salmon | sāman machhlī | सामन मछली

cod | coḍ machhlī
कॉड मछली

sea bream
sī brīm | सी ब्रीम

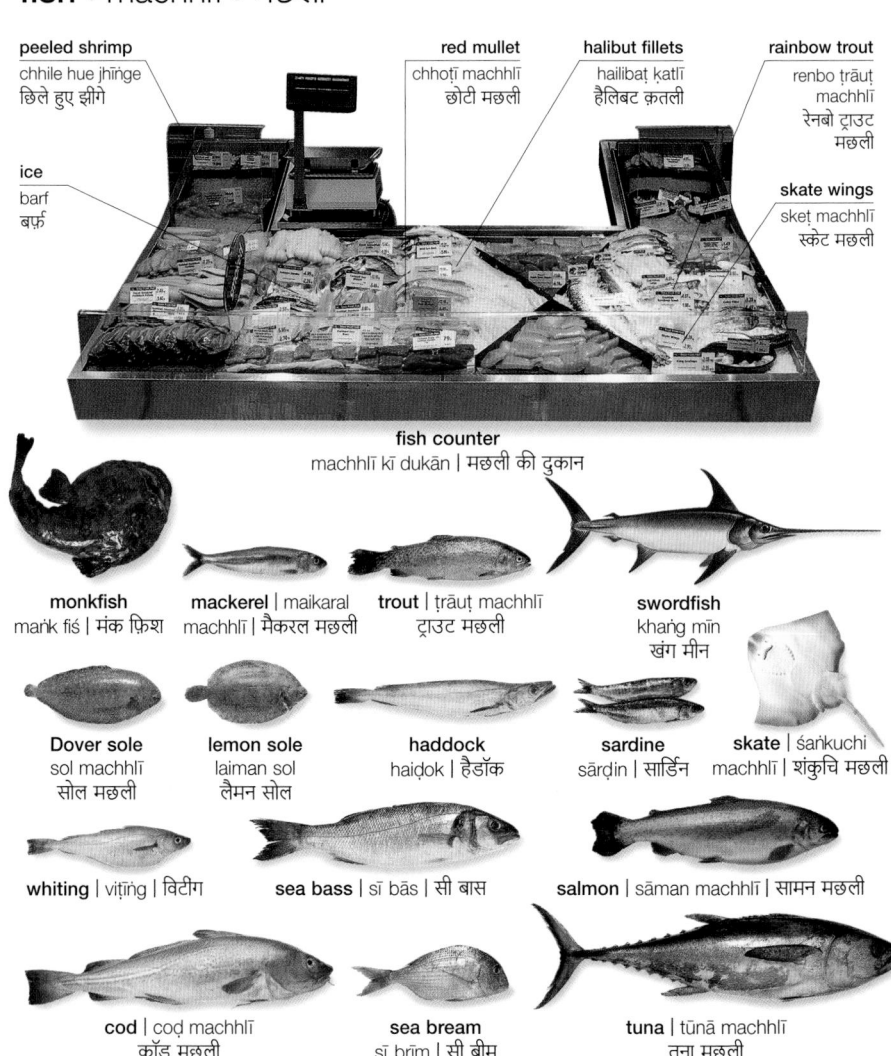

tuna | tūnā machhlī
तूना मछली

seafood • samudrī bhojan • समुद्री भोजन

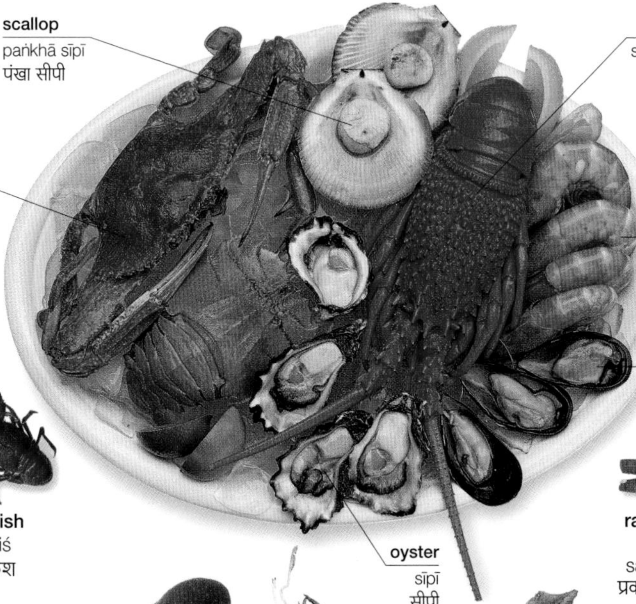

crayfish
krefiś
क्रेफ़िश

razorshell clam
ek prakār kā samudrī jīv | एक प्रकार का समुद्री जीव

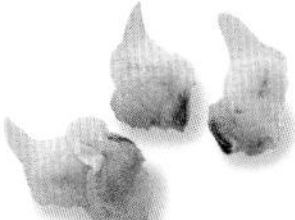
cockle | cockle sīpī | कॉकल सीपी

octopus
aṣṭbhuj | अष्टभुज

cuttlefish
kaṭal fiś | कटल फ़िश

squid
skviḍ | स्क्विड

clam
baṛī sīpī | बड़ी सीपी

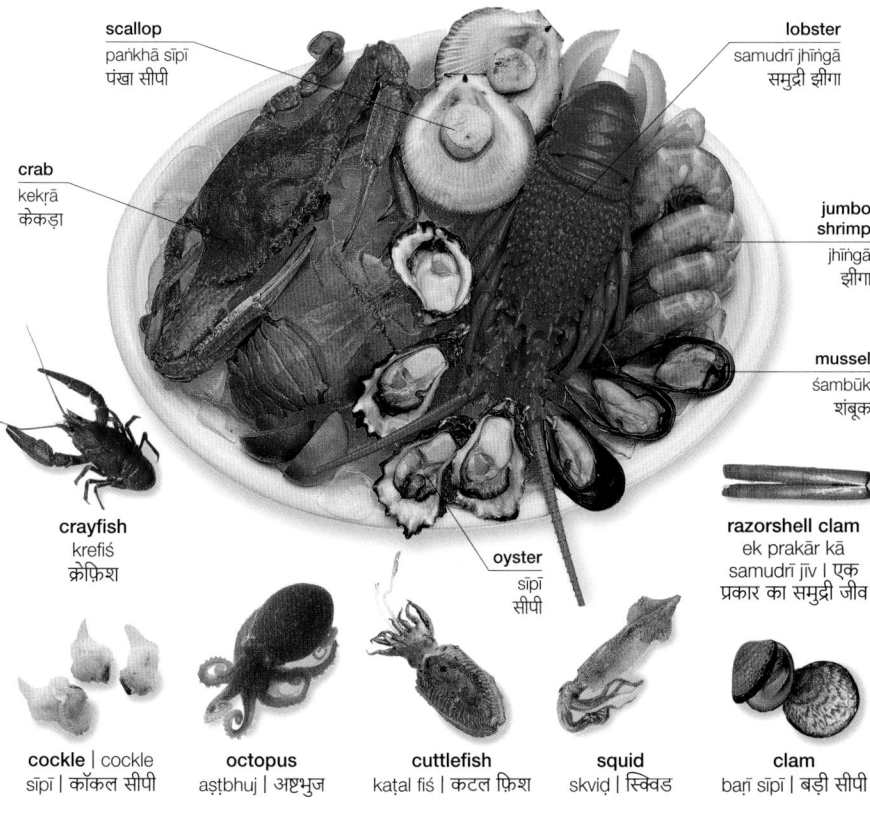

vocabulary • śabdāvalī • शब्दावली

fresh	tāzā	ताज़ा
frozen	saṃśītit	संशीतित
cleaned	svacchh	स्वच्छ
filleted	ḳatle kiyā huā	क़तले किया हुआ
smoked	dhūmrit	धूम्रित
skinned	khāl rahit	खाल रहित
tail	pūṃchh	पूंछ
bone	kāṃṭe	कांटे
fillet	ḳatlā	क़तला
scale	mīn śalk	मीन शल्क
salted	lavaṇit	लवणित
loin	śroṇik māṃs	श्रोणिक मांस

Will you clean it for me?
kyā āp ise sāf kar deṅge?
क्या आप इसे साफ़ कर देंगे?

vegetables 1 • sabziyāṃ • सब्ज़ियां 1

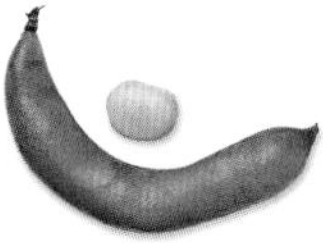

fava bean
bāklā
बाकला

seed
bīj
बीज

runner bean
guār kī phalī
गुआर की फली

green bean
frānsbīn
फ्रांसबीन

pea
maṭar
मटर

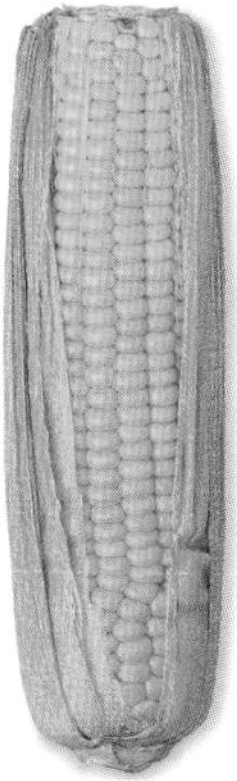

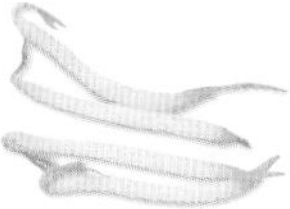

bean sprout
aṅkurit phalī
अंकुरित फली

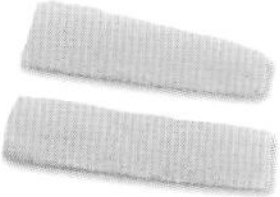

bamboo
bāṃs
बांस

pod
phalī
फली

okra
bhinḍī
भिंडी

corn
mīṭhī makaī
मीठी मकई

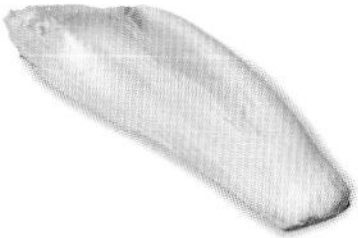

chicory
chikorī
चिकोरी

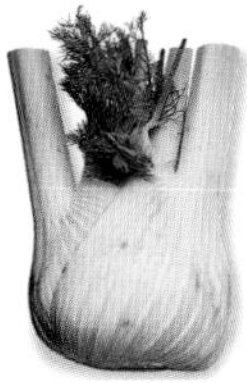

fennel
soā
सोआ

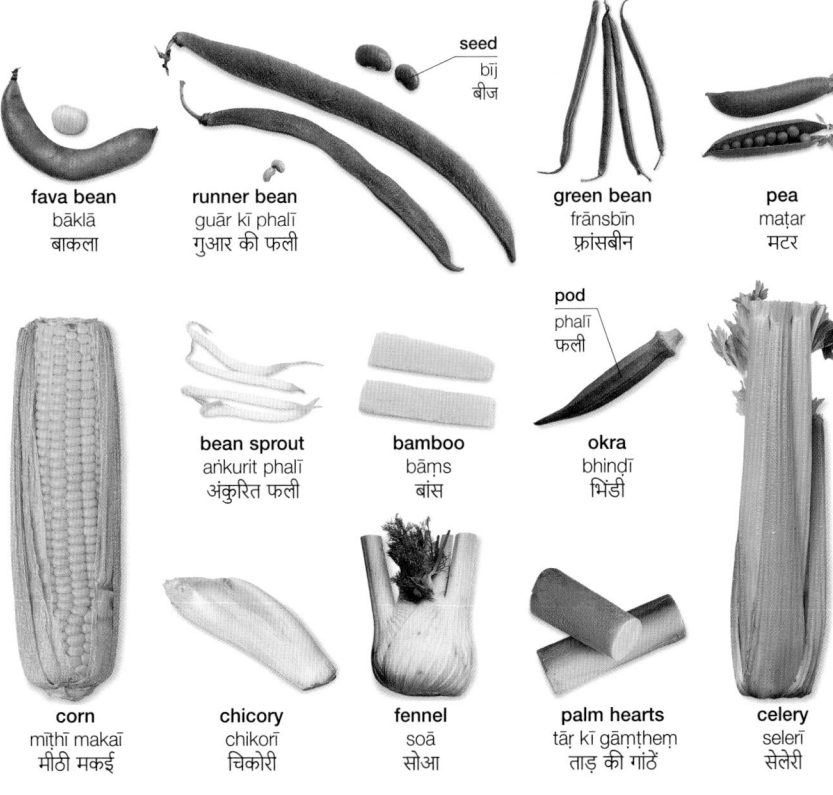

palm hearts
tāṛ kī gāṃṭheṃ
ताड़ की गांठें

celery
selerī
सेलेरी

vocabulary • śabdāvalī • शब्दावली

leaf
pattī
पत्ती

floret
chhoṭā phūl
छोटा फूल

tip
nok
नोक

organic
jaivik
जैविक

stalk
ḍanṭhal
डंठल

kernel
girī
गिरी

heart
bhītrī gāṃṭh
भीतरी गांठ

plastic bag
plāsṭik baig
प्लास्टिक बैग

Do you sell organic vegetables?
āp jaivik sabziyāṃ bechte haiṃ?
आप जैविक सब्ज़ियां बेचते हैं?

Are these grown locally?
kyā ye āspās ugāī jātī haiṃ?
क्या ये आसपास उगाई जाती हैं?

arugula
roket salād
रॉकेट सलाद

watercress
voṭarcres
वॉटरक्रेस

radicchio
lāl pattāgobhī
लाल पत्तागोभी

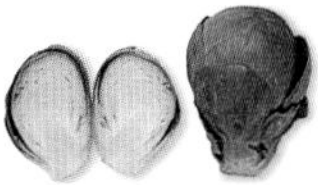

Brussel sprout
gāṃṭh gobhī
गांठ गोभी

Swiss chard
svis chārḍ | स्विस चार्ड

kale
kel pattī | केल पत्ती

sorrel
sorel pattī | सॉरेल पत्ती

endive | enḍāiv
pattī | एनडाइव पत्ती

dandelion
ḍenḍiliyan
डेंडिलियन

spinach
pālak
पालक

kohlrabi
śalgam
शलग़म

bok choy
pāk-choī
पाक-चोई

lettuce
salād pattā | सलाद पत्ता

broccoli
broklī | ब्रोकली

cabbage
bandgobhī | बंदगोभी

spring greens
harā salād pattā
हरा सलाद पत्ता

vegetables 2 • sabziyāṃ • सब्ज़ियां 2

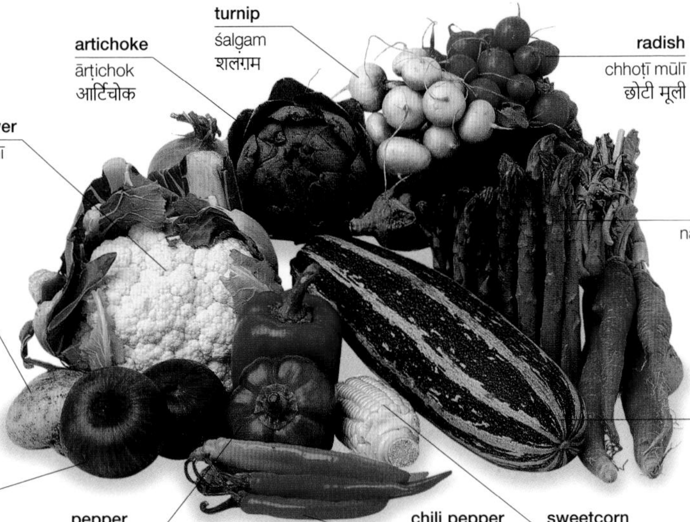

vocabulary • śabdāvalī • शब्दावली

cherry tomato
bebī ṭamāṭar
बेबी टमाटर

carrot
gājar
गाजर

breadfruit
breḍfrūṭ
ब्रेडफ़्रूट

new potato
nayā ālū
नया आलू

celeriac
ek prakār kā kand
एक प्रकार का कंद

taro root
kachālū
कचालू

cassava
kasāvā
कसावा

water chestnut
siṅghāṛā
सिंघाड़ा

frozen
frozan
फ़्रोज़न

raw
kacchā
कच्चा

hot (spicy)
tīkhā
तीखा

sweet
mīṭhā
मीठा

bitter
kaṛvā
कड़वा

firm
saḳht
सख़्त

flesh
gūdā
गूदा

root
jaṛ
जड़

May I have one kilo of potatoes, please?
kyā mujhe ek kilo ālū deṇge?
क्या मुझे एक किलो आलू देंगे?

What's the price per kilo?
ek kilo kitne kā hai?
एक किलो कितने का है?

What are those called?
inheṃ kyā kahte haiṃ?
इन्हें क्या कहते हैं?

sweet potato
śakarkandī
शकरकंदी

yam
jimīkand
जिमीकंद

beet
chukandar
चुकंदर

rutabaga
svīḍan kā śalgam
स्वीडन का शलग़म

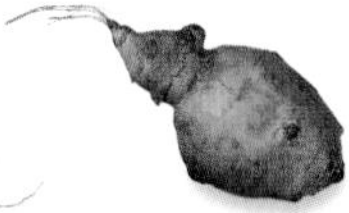

Jerusalem artichoke
yerūśalam ārṭichok
येरुशलम आर्टिचोक

horseradish
nāgarmothā
नागरमोथा

parsnip
pīlī gājar
पीली गाजर

ginger
adrak
अदरक

eggplant
baiṅgan
बैंगन

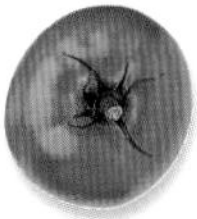

tomato
ṭamāṭar
टमाटर

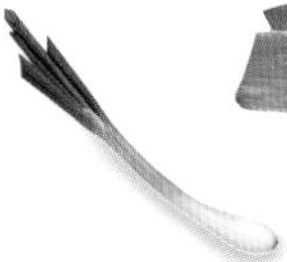

scallion
harā pyāz
हरा प्याज़

leek
līk
लीक

shallot
pyāz
प्याज़

clove
kalī
कली

garlic
lahsun
लहसुन

truffle
gucchhī
गुच्छी

mushroom
maśrūm
मशरूम

cucumber
khīrā
खीरा

zucchini
toraī
तोरई

butternut squash
peṭhā
पेठा

acorn squash
banjuphal
बंजुफल

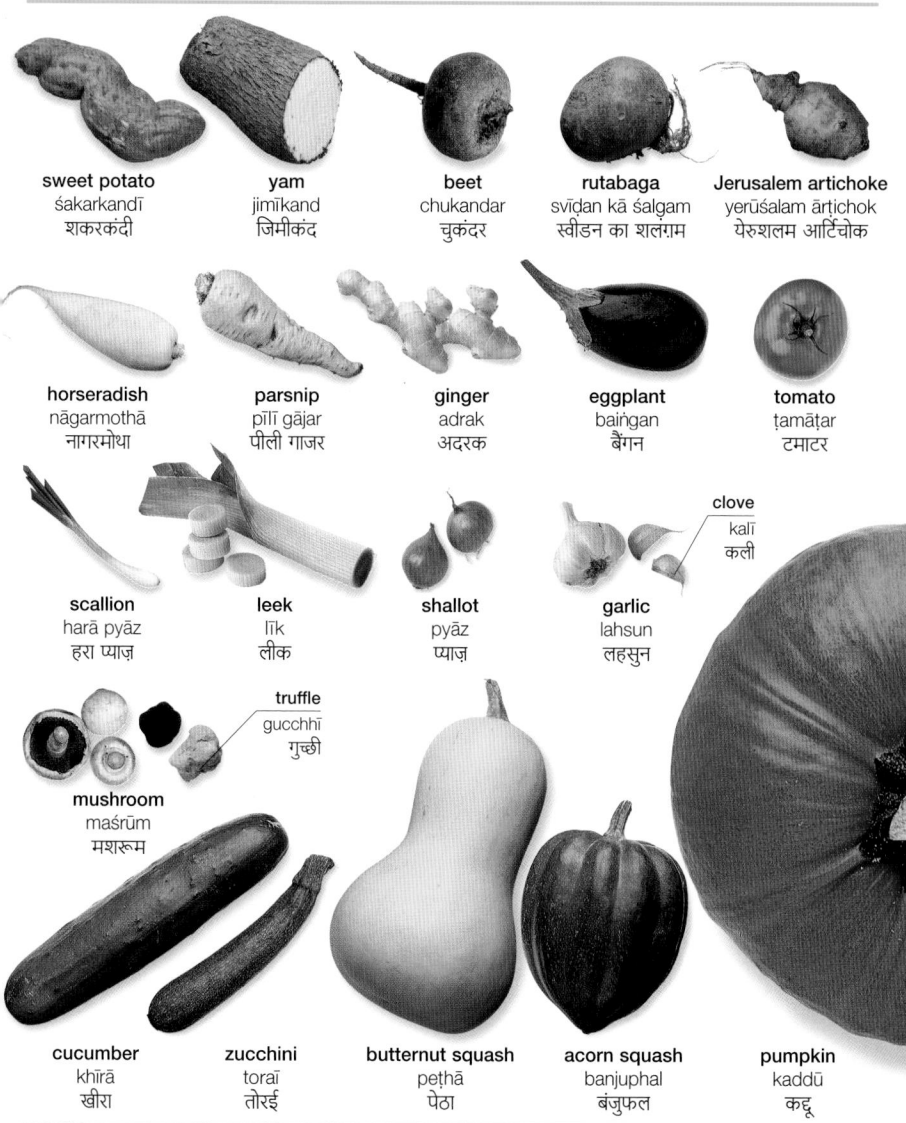

pumpkin
kaddū
कद्दू

fruit 1 • phal • फल 1

citrus fruit • khaṭṭe phal • खट्टे फल

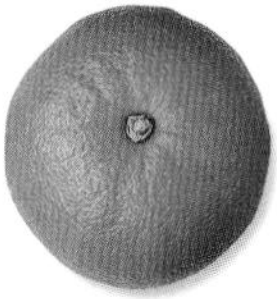

orange
santrā | संतरा

clementine
mālṭā | माल्टा

ugli fruit
aglī frūṭ | अगली फ्रूट

pith
bhītrī chhilkā
भीतरी छिलका

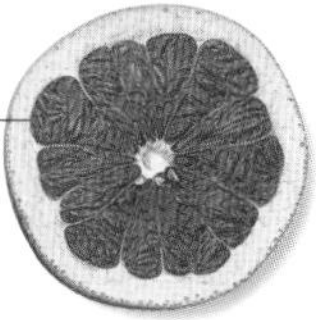

grapefruit
chakotrā | चकोतरा

tangerine
nāraṅgī | नारंगी

segment
phāṃk
फांक

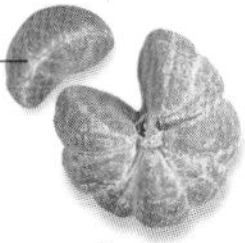

satsuma
jāpānī santrā
जापानी संतरा

zest
chhilkā
छिलका

lime
nībū | नीबू

lemon
khaṭṭā | खट्टा

kumquat
kummkāṭ | कुम्मकाट

stone fruit • guṭhlīdār phal • गुठलीदार फल

peach
āṛū | आड़ू

nectarine
śaftālū | शफ़तालू

apricot
ḳhubānī
ख़ुबानी

plum
ālū buḳhārā
आलू बुख़ारा

cherry
cherī
चेरी

pear
nāśpātī
नाशपाती

apple
seb | सेब

basket of fruit
phaloṃ kī ṭokrī | फलों की टोकरी

berries and melons • ber aur sardā • बेर और सर्दा

strawberry
sṭroberī | स्ट्रॉबेरी

raspberry
rasbharī | रसभरी

melon
kharbūz
खरबूज़

grapes
aṃgūr | अंगूर

blackberry
blaikberī | ब्लैकबेरी

red currant
reḍ karanṭ | रेड करंट

black currant
blaik karanṭ
ब्लैक करंट

cranberry
krainberī
क्रैनबेरी

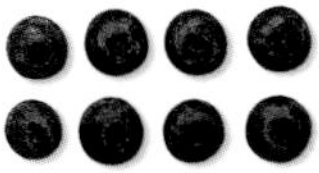

blueberry
jāmun | जामुन

white currant
vhāiṭ karanṭ
व्हाइट करंट

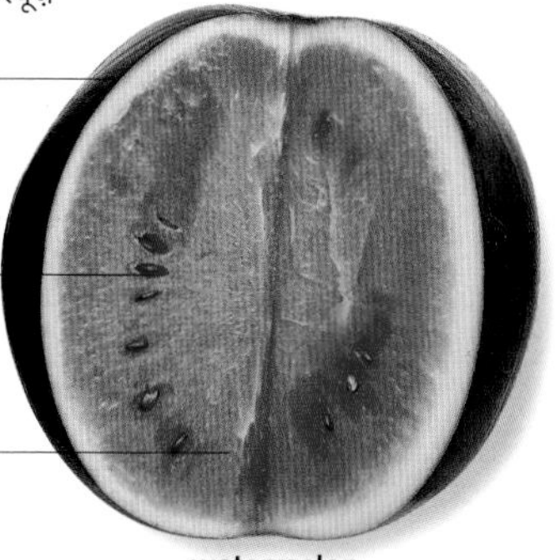

watermelon
tarbūz
तरबूज़

loganberry
loganberī
लोगनबेरी

gooseberry
jharberī
झरबेरी

vocabulary • śabdāvalī • शब्दावली

rhubarb revāchīnī रेवाचीनी	**sour** khaṭṭā खट्टा	**crisp** kurkurā कुरकुरा	**juice** jūs जूस	**Are they ripe?** kyā ye pake hue haiṃ? क्या ये पके हुए हैं?
fiber reśedār रेशेदार	**fresh** tāzā ताज़ा	**rotten** saṛā huā सड़ा हुआ	**core** bīj बीज	**Can I try one?** kyā maiṃ ek chakh lūṃ? क्या मैं एक चख लूं?
sweet mīṭhā मीठा	**juicy** rasīlā रसीला	**pulp** gūdā गूदा	**seedless** bīj rahit बीज रहित	**How long will they keep?** ye kab tak ṭhīk raheṇge? ये कब तक ठीक रहेंगे?

fruit 2 • phal • फल 2

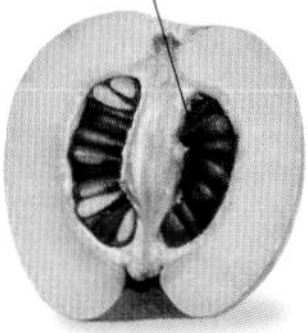

quince
kīns | कीन्स

passion fruit
paiśan frūṭ
पैशन फ्रूट

banana
kelā | केला

guava
amrūd | अमरूद

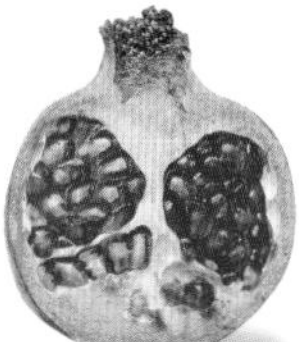

pomegranate
anār | अनार

persimmon
tendū phal
तेंदू फल

feijoa
fehoā | फ़ेहोआ

prickly pear
nākh | नाख

starfruit
kamrakh
कमरख

mangosteen
maṅguṣṭh
मंगुष्ठ

nuts and dried fruit • meve aur girī • मेवे और गिरी

pine nut
chilgozā | चिलगोज़ा

pistachio
pistā | पिस्ता

cashew
kājū | काजू

peanut
mūṅgphalī | मूंगफली

hazelnut
pahāṛī bādām
पहाड़ी बादाम

brazilnut
brāzīlnaṭ | ब्राज़ीलनट

pecan
pīkan | पीकन

almond
bādām | बादाम

walnut
akhroṭ | अख़रोट

chestnut
chesṭnaṭ | चेस्टनट

macadamia
maikāḍemiyā
मैकाडेमिया

fig
anjīr | अंजीर

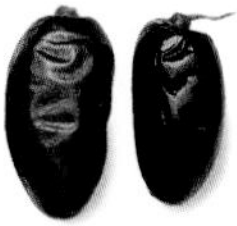

date
khajūr | खजूर

prune
sūkhā alūchā
सूखा अलूचा

sultana
bījrahit kiśmiś
बीजरहित किशमिश

raisin
kiśmiś
किशमिश

currant
munakkā
मुनक़्क़ा

shell
khol
ख़ोल

flesh
girī
गिरी

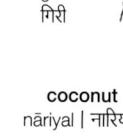

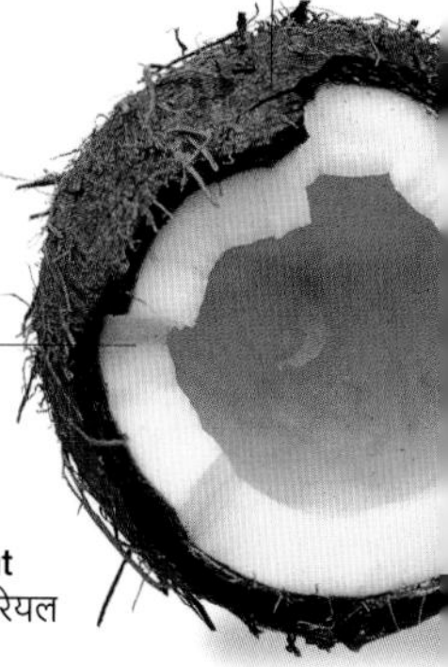

coconut
nāriyal | नारियल

vocabulary • śabdāvalī • शब्दावली

green
harā
हरा

hard
sakht
सख़्त

kernel
girī
गिरी

salted
lavaṇit
लवणित

roasted
bhunā
भुना

tropical fruit
uṣṇdeśīya phal
उष्णदेशीय फल

shelled
chhilkā rahit
छिलका रहित

ripe
pakā
पका

soft
narm
नर्म

desiccated
sukhāyā huā
सुखाया हुआ

raw
kacchā
कच्चा

seasonal
mausmī
मौसमी

candied fruit
page phal
पगे फल

whole
sābut
साबुत

grains and legumes • anāj evam dālem̩ • अनाज एवं दालें

grains • anāj • अनाज

wheat
gehūm̩ | गेहूं

oats
jaī | जई

barley
jau | जौ

millet
jvār | ज्वार

corn
makkā | मक्का

quinoa
kinoyā | किनोया

vocabulary • śabdāvalī • शब्दावली

seed bīj बीज	**fragranced** k̲husbūdār खुशबूदार	**long-grain** baṛā dānā बड़ा दाना
husk bhūsī भूसी	**cereal** khādyānn खाद्यान्न	**short-grain** chhoṭā dānā छोटा दाना
kernel girī गिरी	**whole-grain** sābut साबुत	**fresh** tāzā ताज़ा
dry sukhā सूखा	**soak (v)** bhigonā भिगोना	**quick cooking** jaldī pakne vālā जल्दी पकने वाला

rice • chāval • चावल

white rice | safed chāval | सफ़ेद चावल

brown rice | brāun rāis | ब्राउन राइस

wild rice | jaṅglī chāval | जंगली चावल

arborio rice | puḍiṅg rāis | पुडिंग राइस

processed grains • saṅsādhit anāj • संसाधित अनाज

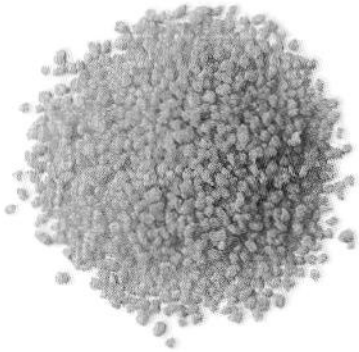

couscous
khaskhas | खसखस

cracked wheat
daliyā | दलिया

semolina
sūjī | सूजी

bran
chokar | चोकर

legumes • dāleṃ • दालें

butter beans
sem
सेम

haricot beans
safed rājmā
सफ़ेद राजमा

red kidney beans
rājmā
राजमा

adzuki beans
aḍukī bīn
अडुकी बीन

fava beans
bāklā
बाकला

soybeans
soyābīn
सोयाबीन

black-eyed peas
lobiyā
लोबिया

pinto beans
chitrā rājmā
चितरा राजमा

mung beans
sābut mūṅg
साबुत मूंग

flageolet beans
sūkhī frānsbīn
सूखी फ़्रांसबीन

brown lentils
kālī masūr
काली मसूर

red lentils
lāl masūr
लाल मसूर

green peas
maṭar
मटर

chickpeas
kābulī chane
काबुली चने

split peas
maṭrā
मटरा

seeds • bīj • बीज

pumpkin seed
kaddū ke bīj
कद्दू के बीज

mustard seed
rāī | राई

caraway
safed zīrā
सफ़ेद ज़ीरा

sesame seed
til | तिल

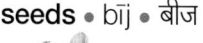

sunflower seed
sūrajmukhī ke bīj
सूरजमुखी के बीज

herbs and spices • auṣadhi evam masāle • औषधि एवं मसाले

spices • masāle • मसाले

vanilla | vainilā (paudhā) | वैनिला (पौधा)

nutmeg
jāyaphal
जायफल

mace
jāvitrī | जावित्री

turmeric
haldī | हल्दी

cumin
zīrā | ज़ीरा

bouquet garni
masālom̥ kī poṭlī
मसालों की पोटली

allspice
lavaṅg badar
लवंग बदर

peppercorn | kālī mirch | काली मिर्च

fenugreek
methī | मेथी

chili powder
mirch | मिर्च

saffron
kesar | केसर

cardamom
ilāyachī | इलायची

curry powder
śorbe kā masālā
शोरबे का मसाला

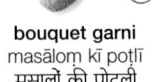

paprika
pisī mirch
पिसी मिर्च

garlic
lahsun | लहसुन

sticks
chhāl
छाल

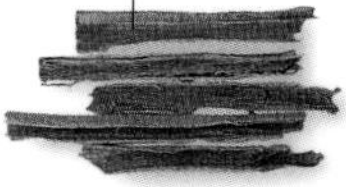

cinnamon
dālchīnī | दालचीनी

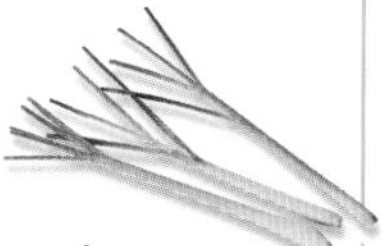

lemon grass
leman grās
लेमन ग्रास

cloves
lauṅg
लौंग

star anise
sṭār enīs
स्टार एनीस

ginger
adrak
अदरक

herbs • auṣadhi • औषधि

fennel | soā | सोआ

fennel seeds
moṭī sauṃf
मोटी सौंफ़

bay leaf
tezpattā | तेज़पत्ता

parsley
pārsli | पारस्लि

chives
jambū | जंबू

mint
pudīnā | पुदीना

thyme
ajvāyan | अजवायन

sage | kapūr kā
pattā | कपूर का पत्ता

tarragon
ṭairāgan | टैरागन

marjoram
marūā | मरूआ

basil
tulsī | तुलसी

oregano
origāno | ऑरिगानो

cilantro
dhaniyā | धनिया

dill
śatpuṣpikā
शतपुष्पिका

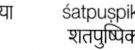

rosemary
rozmerī | रोज़मेरी

bottled foods • botalband khādya padārth • बोतलबंद खाद्य पदार्थ

oils | tel | तेल

sweet spreads • jaim, śahad ityādi • जैम, शहद इत्यादि

sauces and condiments • chaṭnī sos ityādi • चटनी, सॉस इत्यादि

mayonnaise
myonīz | म्योनीज़

cider vinegar
seb sirkā
सेब सिरका

balsamic vinegar
bolsam sirkā
बॉल्सम सिरका

malt vinegar
mālṭ kā sirkā
माल्ट का सिरका

wine vinegar
vāin sirkā
वाइन सिरका

vinegar | sirkā | सिरका

bottle
botal
बोतल

ketchup
ṭamāṭar sos
टमाटर सॉस

english mustard
iṅgliś masṭarḍ
इंगलिश मस्टर्ड

french mustard
french masṭarḍ
फ्रेंच मस्टर्ड

chutney
chaṭnī
चटनी

sauce
sos
सॉस

whole-grain mustard
sābut sarsoṃ
साबुत सरसों

peanut butter
pīnaṭ baṭar
पीनट बटर

chocolate spread
chokleṭ spraiḍ
चॉकलेट स्प्रैड

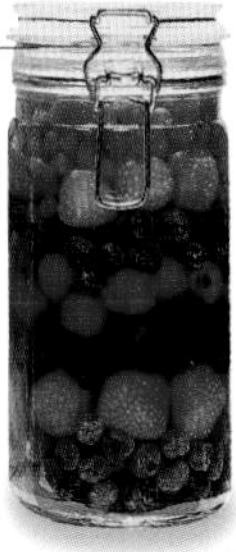

canning jar
sīlband jār
सीलबंद जार

preserved fruit
sanrakṣit phal
संरक्षित फल

vocabulary • śabdāvalī • शब्दावली

corn oil
makaī kā tel
मकई का तेल

peanut oil
mūṅgphalī kā tel
मूंगफली का तेल

vegetable oil
vanaspati tel
वनस्पति तेल

canola oil
tilhan kā tel
तिलहन का तेल

cold-pressed oil
kold-praisd tel
कोल्ड-प्रैस्ड तेल

dairy products • ḍeyarī utpād • डेयरी उत्पाद

cheese • chīz • चीज़

rind
paprī
पपड़ी

semi-hard cheese
ardh saḳht chīz
अर्ध सख़्त चीज़

semi-soft cheese
ardh mulāyam chīz
अर्ध मुलायम चीज़

blue cheese
blū chīz
ब्लू चीज़

soft cheese
mulāyam chīz
मुलायम चीज़

grated cheese
kaddūkas kiyā chīz
कद्दूकस किया चीज़

hard cheese
ṭhos chīz | ठोस चीज़

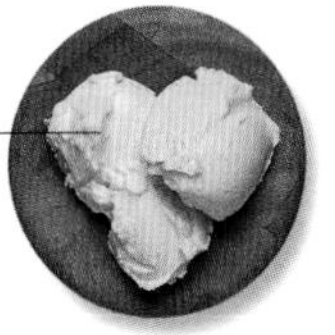

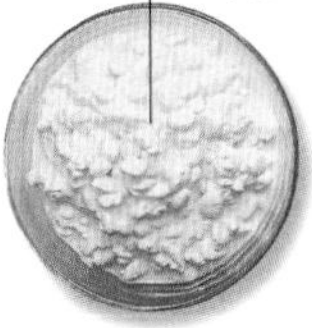

cottage cheese
panīr
पनीर

cream cheese
krīm chīz
क्रीम चीज़

fresh cheese | tāzā chīz | ताज़ा चीज़

milk • dūdh • दूध

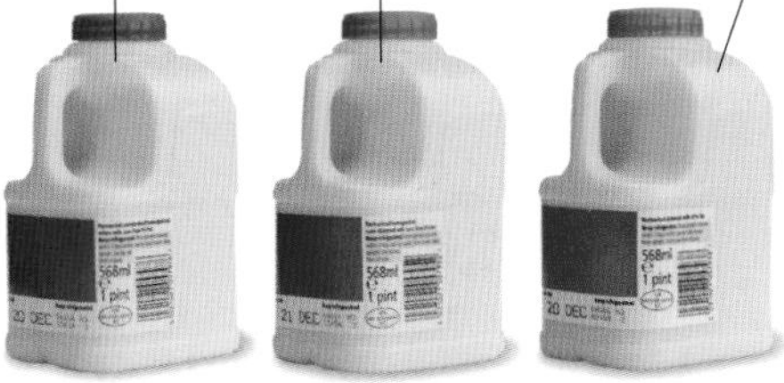

whole milk
ful krīm dūdh
फुल क्रीम दूध

reduced-fat milk
ardh-malāīrahit dūdh
अर्ध-मलाईरहित दूध

skim milk
krīm rahit dūdh
क्रीम रहित दूध

cow's milk | gāya kā dūdh | गाय का दूध

milk carton
dūdh kā ḍibbā
दूध का डिब्बा

goat's milk
bakrī kā dūdh
बकरी की दूध

condensed milk
kanḍensḍ milk
कंडेंस्ड मिल्क

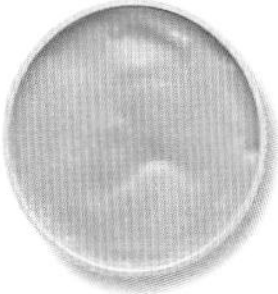

butter
makkhan | मक्खन

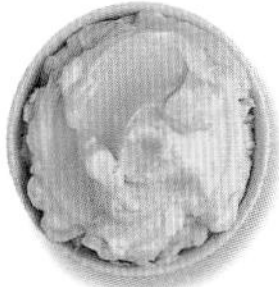

margarine
kṛtrim makkhan
कृत्रिम मक्खन

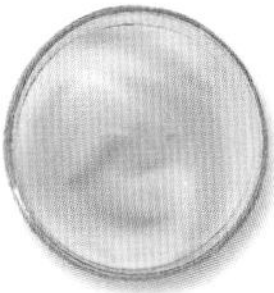

cream
krīm | क्रीम

half-and-half
patlī krīm | पतली क्रीम

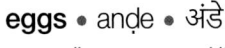

heavy cream
gaṛhī krīm
गाढ़ी क्रीम

whipped cream
phemṭī huī krīm
फेंटी हुई क्रीम

sour cream
khaṭṭī krīm
खट्टी क्रीम

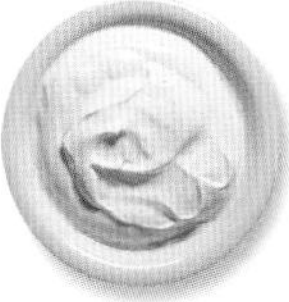

yogurt
dahī
दही

ice cream
āiskrīm
आइसक्रीम

eggs • aṇḍe • अंडे

yolk
zardī
ज़र्दी

egg white
safed bhāg
सफ़ेद भाग

shell
chhilkā
छिलका

eggcup
aṇḍe kā kap
अंडे का कप

soft-boiled egg | ublā aṇḍā | उबला अंडा

hen's egg
murgī kā aṇḍā
मुर्गी का अंडा

duck egg
batakh kā aṇḍā
बतख़ का अंडा

goose egg
hans kā aṇḍā
हंस का अंडा

quail egg
baṭer kā aṇḍā
बटेर का अंडा

vocabulary • śabdāvalī • शब्दावली

pasteurized
pāscharīkṛt
पास्चरीकृत

unpasteurized
apāscharīkṛt
अपास्चरीकृत

milk shake
milkśek
मिल्कशेक

frozen yogurt
ṭhanḍā dahī
ठंडा दही

salted
namkīn
नमकीन

unsalted
namak rahit
नमक रहित

sheep's milk
bheṛ kā dūdh
भेड़ का दूध

buttermilk
chhāchh
छाछ

lactose
dugdh śarkarā
दुग्ध शर्करा

fat-free
vasā rahit
वसा रहित

homogenised
samāṅgīkṛt dūdh
समांगीकृत दूध

powdered milk
pāuḍar dūdh
पाउडर दूध

breads and flours • breḍ evam āṭā • ब्रेड एवं आटा

bakery | bekrī | बेकरी

making bread • breḍ banānā • ब्रेड बनाना

white flour
maidā | मैदा

brown flour
gehūṃ kā āṭā | गेहूं का आटा

whole-wheat flour
āṭā | आटा

yeast
khamīr | खमीर

sift (v)
chhānnā | छानना

mix (v)
milānā | मिलाना

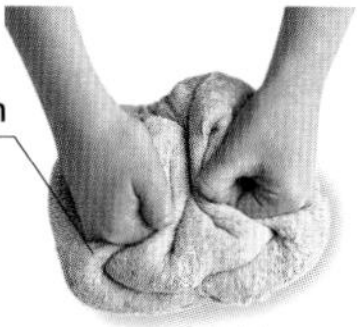

knead (v)
gūṃdhnā | गूंधना

bake (v)
bek karnā | बेक करना

white bread
maidā breḍ | मैदा ब्रेड

brown bread
brāun breḍ | ब्राउन ब्रेड

whole-wheat bread
āṭe kī breḍ | आटे की ब्रेड

multigrain bread
miśrit anāj breḍ
मिश्रित अनाज ब्रेड

corn bread
makaī breḍ | मकई ब्रेड

soda bread
soḍā breḍ | सोडा ब्रेड

sourdough bread
khamīrī breḍ
खमीरी ब्रेड

flat bread
chapṭī breḍ | चपटी ब्रेड

bagel
begal ban | बेगल बन

bun
safed ban | सफ़ेद बन

roll
rol | रोल

fruit bread
frūṭ breḍ | फ्रूट ब्रेड

seeded bread
bījyukt breḍ | बीजयुक्त ब्रेड

naan bread
nān | नान

pita bread
piṭā breḍ | पीटा ब्रेड

crispbread
kurkurī breḍ | कुरकुरी ब्रेड

vocabulary • śabdāvalī • शब्दावली

bread flour moṭā āṭā मोटा आटा	**rise (v)** phūlnā फूलना	**prove (v)** ūpar uṭhnā ऊपर उठना	**breadcrumbs** breḍ kā chūrā ब्रेड का चूरा	**slicer** slāisar स्लाइसर
self-rising flour mahīn āṭā महीन आटा	**all-purpose flour** āṭā आटा	**glaze (v)** chamak ānā चमक आना	**flute** flūṭ फ़्लूट	**baker** bekar बेकर

cakes and desserts • kek aur miṣṭhānn • केक और मिष्ठान्न

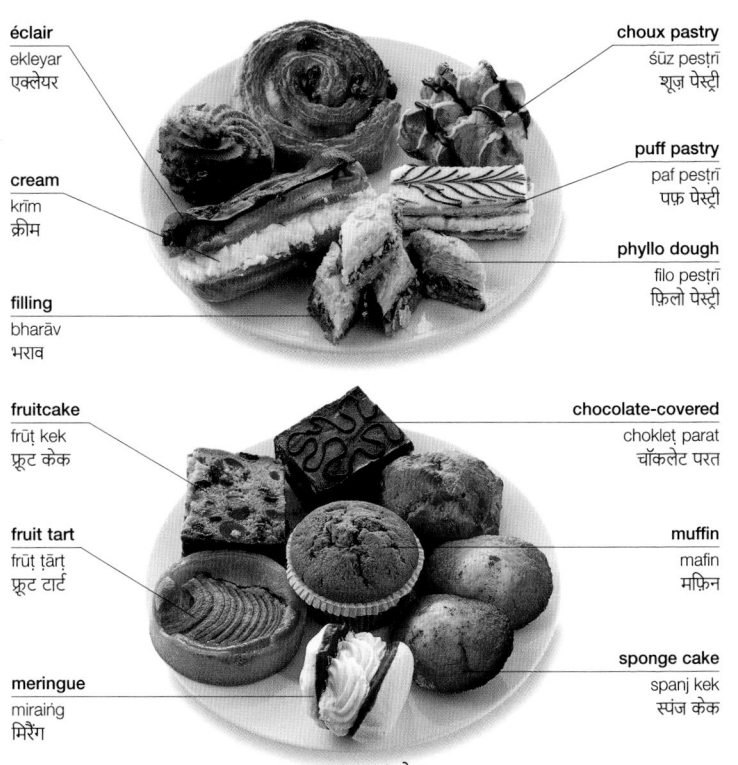

cakes | kek | केक

vocabulary • śabdāvalī • शब्दावली

rice pudding khīr खीर	**bun** ban बन	**pastry** pesṭrī पेस्ट्री	**crème pâtissèrie** krīm pesṭrī क्रीम पेस्ट्री
celebration samāroh समारोह	**custard** kastarḍ कस्टर्ड	**slice** ṭukṛā टुकड़ा	**chocolate cake** chokleṭ kek चॉकलेट केक

May I have a slice please?
kyā ek ṭukṛā le lūṃ?
क्या एक टुकड़ा ले लूँ?

chocolate chip
choklet̩ chip biskut̩
चॉकलेट चिप बिस्कुट

Florentine
florent̩āin
फ़्लोरेन्टाइन

cookies | biskut̩ | बिस्कुट

ladyfinger
spanj fiṅgar
स्पंज फ़िंगर

trifle
t̩rāifal
ट्राइफ़ल

mousse
mūs pud̩iṅg | मूस पुडिंग

sherbet
sorbet̩ | सॉर्बेट

cream pie
krīm pāī | क्रीम पाई

crème caramel | krīm kairāmal | क्रीम कैरामल

celebration cakes • samāroh kek • समारोह केक

top tier
ūprī chakr
ऊपरी चक्र

decoration
sajāvat̩
सजावट

ribbon
riban
रिबन

bottom tier
nichlā chakr
निचला चक्र

frosting
āisiṅg
आइसिंग

marzipan
bādām parat
बादाम परत

wedding cake | śādī kā kek | शादी का केक

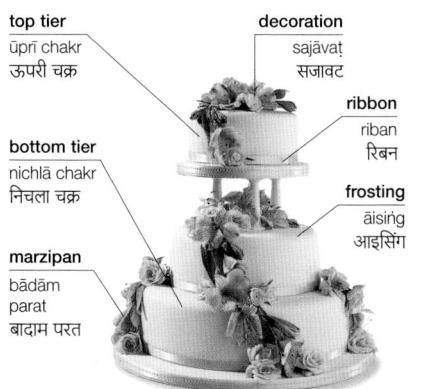

birthday candles
mombattī
मोमबत्ती

blow out (v)
phūṃk se bujhānā
फूंक से बुझाना

birthday cake | janmdin kā kek | जन्मदिन का केक

delicatessen • pake bhojan ki dukān • पके भोजन की दुकान

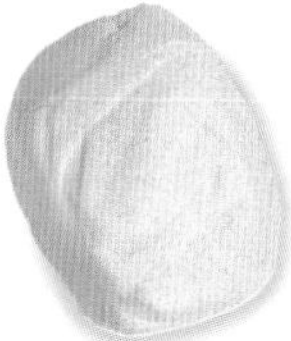

mozzarella
mozerelā | मोज़ेरेला

Brie
brī chīz | ब्री चीज़

goat cheese | bakrī ke dūdh kā chīz | बकरी के दूध का चीज़

cheddar
cheḍar chīz | चेडर चीज़

Parmesan | ek prakār kā iṭeliyan chīz | एक प्रकार का इटेलियन चीज़

Camembert | ek prakār kā french chīz | एक प्रकार का फ़्रेंच चीज़

Edam | eḍām chīz | एडाम चीज़

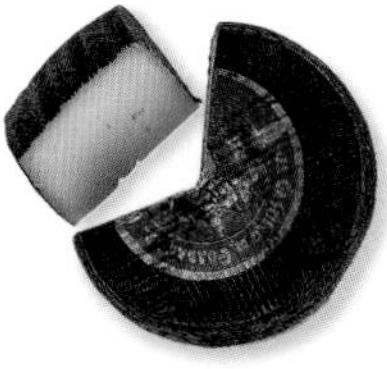

Manchego | manchego chīz | मनचेगो चीज़

potpie
pāī
पाई

cooked meat
pakā huā māṃs
पका हुआ मांस

ham
haim
हैम

black olive
kālā zaitūn
काला ज़ैतून

chili pepper
mirch
मिर्च

sauce
chaṭnī
चटनी

bread roll
breḍ rol
ब्रेड रोल

green olive
harā zaitūn
हरा ज़ैतून

sandwich counter
saiṇḍvich kāunṭar | सैंडविच काउंटर

smoked fish
dhūmit machhlī
धूमित मछली

capers
kaipars
कैपर्स

prosciutto | iṭeliyan haim | इटेलियन हैम

chorizo
speniś sosej
स्पेनिश सॉसेज

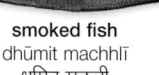

stuffed olive | bharvāṃ zaitūn | भरवां ज़ैतून

vocabulary • śabdāvalī • शब्दावली

in oil tel meṃ pakā तेल में पका	**marinated** masāle meṃ lipṭā मसाले में लिपटा	**in brine** namkīn pānī meṃ rakhā नमकीन पानी में रखा
smoked dhūmrit धूम्रित	**salted** namkīn नमकीन	**cured** sanrakṣit संरक्षित

Take a number, please.
kṛpyā nambar le leṃ
कृपया नंबर ले लें।

Can I try some of that please?
ise chakh sakte haiṃ?
इसे चख सकते हैं?

May I have six slices of that, please?
kyā mujhe iske chhah pīs denge?
क्या मुझे इसके छह पीस देंगे?

drinks • peya • पेय

water • pānī • पानी

bottled water
botalband pānī
बोतलबंद पानी

sparkling
bulbuledār
बुलबुलेदार

still
sthir
स्थिर

mineral water
minral voṭar | मिनरल वॉटर

tap water | nal kā pānī | नल का पानी

tonic water
ṭonik voṭar
टॉनिक वॉटर

soda water
soḍā voṭar
सोडा वॉटर

hot drinks • garm peya • गर्म पेय

teabag
ṭī baig
टी बैग

loose-leaf tea
khulī chāya pattī
खुली चाय पत्ती

tea | chāya | चाय

beans
kofī ke bīj
कॉफ़ी के बीज

ground coffee
pisī kofī
पिसी कॉफ़ी

coffee | kofī | कॉफ़ी

hot chocolate
hoṭ chokleṭ
हॉट चॉकलेट

malted drink
mālṭ vālā peya
माल्ट वाला पेय

soft drinks • śītal peya • शीतल पेय

tomato juice
ṭamāṭar kā jūs
टमाटर का जूस

straw
sṭro
स्ट्रॉ

grape juice
aṃgūr kā jūs
अंगूर का जूस

lemonade
śikanjī
शिकंजी

orangeade
santare kā jūs
संतरे का जूस

cola
kolā
कोला

alcoholic drinks • madya peya • मद्य पेय

gin
jin | जिन

can
kain
कैन

beer
bīyar | बीयर

hard cider | seb kī vāin | सेब की वाइन

bitter
charparā | चरपरा

stout
sṭāuṭ | स्टाउट

vodka
vodkā | वोदका

whiskey
vhiskī | व्हिस्की

rum
ram | रम

brandy
brānḍī | ब्रांडी

port
porṭ | पोर्ट

dry
sādī
सादी

sherry
śerī | शेरी

campari
kampārī | कमपारी

rosé
gulābī
गुलाबी

white
safed
सफ़ेद

red
lāl
लाल

liqueur
likar | लिकर

tequila
ṭakīlā | टकीला

champagne
śaimpen | शैम्पेन

wine
vāin | वाइन

eating out
bāhar khānā
बाहर खाना

café • kaife • कैफ़े

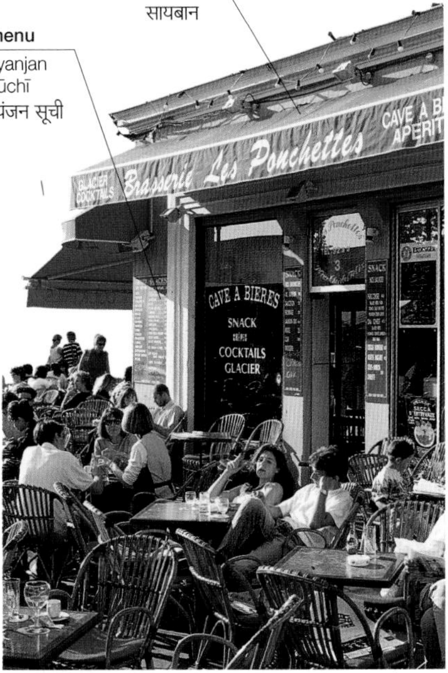

sidewalk café | roḍ sāiḍ kaife | रोड साइड कैफ़े

patio café | khulā kaife | खुला कैफ़े

snack bar | snaik bār | स्नैक बार

coffee • kofī • कॉफ़ी

filter coffee
filṭar kofī | फ़िल्टर कॉफ़ी

espresso
espraiso | एस्प्रैसो

cappuccino
kepyūchīno | केप्यूचीनो

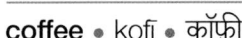

iced coffee
āisḍ kofī | आइस्ड कॉफ़ी

tea • chāya • चाय

herbal tea
auṣadhīya chāya
औषधीय चाय

chamomile tea | babūnā kī chāya
बबूना की चाय

green tea | harī chāya
हरी चाय

tea with milk
dūdh vālī chāya
दूध वाली चाय

black tea
kālī chāya
काली चाय

tea with lemon
nībū vālī chāya
नीबू वाली चाय

mint tea
pudīne vālī chāya
पुदीने वाली चाय

iced tea
ṭhanḍī chāya
ठंडी चाय

juices and milkshakes • jūs evam milkśek • जूस एवं मिल्कशेक

chocolate milkshake
chokleṭ milkśek
चॉकलेट मिल्कशेक

strawberry milkshake
sṭroberī milkśek
स्ट्रॉबेरी मिल्कशेक

orange juice
santare kā jūs
संतरे का जूस

apple juice
seb kā jūs
सेब का जूस

pineapple juice
anannās kā jūs
अनन्नास का जूस

tomato juice
ṭamāṭar kā jūs
टमाटर का जूस

coffee milkshake
kofī milkśek
कॉफ़ी मिल्कशेक

food • khādya padārth • खाद्य पदार्थ

whole-wheat bread
brāun breḍ
ब्राउन ब्रेड

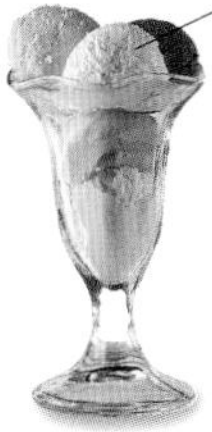

scoop
skūp
स्कूप

toasted sandwich | ṭosṭeḍ saindvich | टोस्टेड सैंडविच

salad
salād | सलाद

ice cream
āiskrīm | आइसक्रीम

pastry
pesṭrī | पेस्ट्री

bar • bār • बार

glasses
gilās
गिलास

dispenser
opṭik
ऑप्टिक

cash register
tijorī
तिजोरी

bartender
bārṭenḍar
बारटेंडर

beer tap
bīyar ṭaip
बीयर टैप

coffee machine
kofī maśīn
कॉफ़ी मशीन

ice bucket
āis baketṭ
आइस बकेट

bar stool
bār kursī
बार कुर्सी

ashtray
aiśṭre
ऐशट्रे

coaster
kosṭar
कोस्टर

bar counter
bār kāunṭar
बार काउंटर

bottle opener
botal opnar
बोतल ओपनर

lever
līvar
लीवर

corkscrew | korkskrū | कॉर्कस्क्रू

tongs
chimṭā
चिमटा

stirrer
peya hilāne kī ḍanḍī
पेय हिलाने की डंडी

measure
māpak
मापक

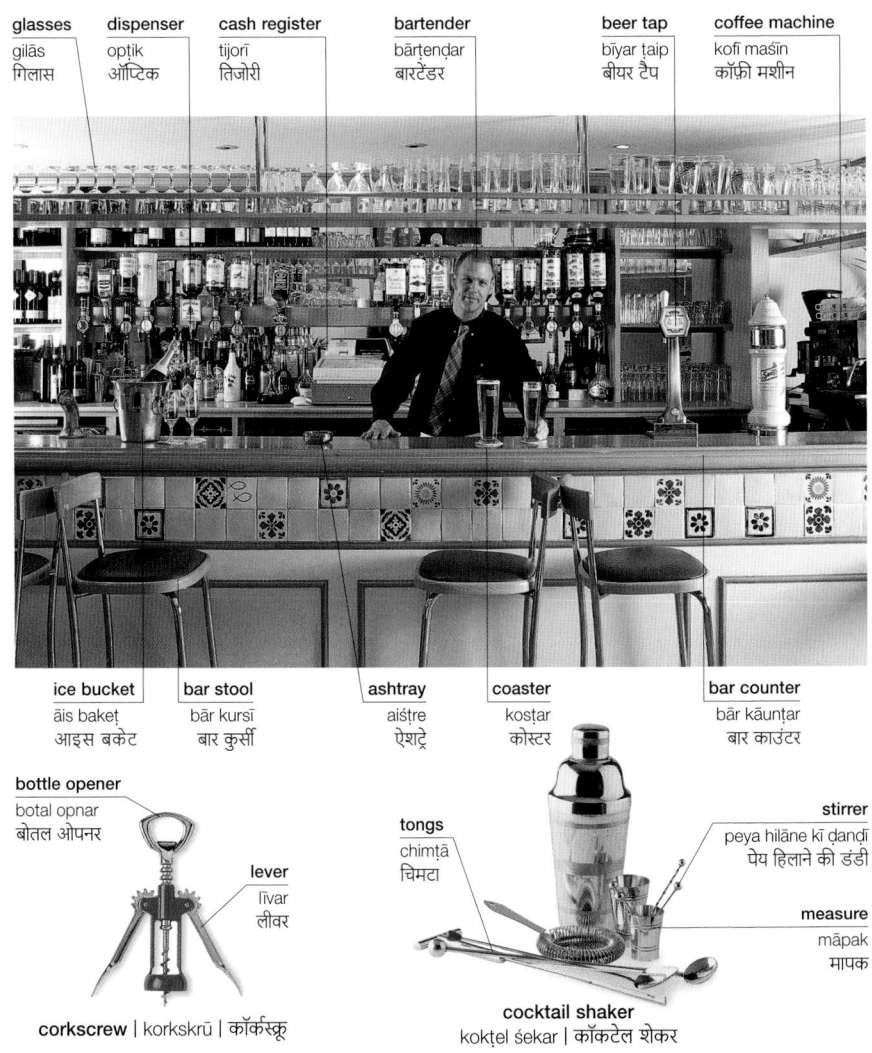

cocktail shaker
kokṭel śekar | कॉकटेल शेकर

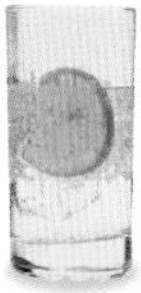

gin and tonic
jin aur ṭonik
जिन और टॉनिक

pitcher
jag
जग

scotch and water
skoch aur pānī
स्कॉच और पानी

ice cube
barf
बर्फ़

rum and cola
ram aur kok
रम और कोक

screwdriver
vodkā aur santrā
वोदका और संतरा

martini
mārṭinī | मार्टिनी

cocktail
kokṭel | कॉकटेल

wine
vāin | वाइन

beer
bīyar | बीयर

shot
ek śoṭ | एक शॉट

single
siṅgal
सिंगल

double
ḍabal
डबल

measure
māp | माप

without ice | barf rahit
बर्फ़ रहित

ice and lemon
barf va nīmbū
बर्फ़ व नींबू

with ice | barf ke sāth | बर्फ़ के साथ

bar snacks • bār snaiks • बार स्नैक्स

potato chips | kurkurā namkīn | कुरकुरा नमकीन

cashews
kājū
काजू

peanuts
mūngfalī
मूंगफ़ली

almonds
bādām
बादाम

nuts | meve | मेवे

olives | zaitūn | ज़ैतून

restaurant • restrāṃ • रेस्तरां

table setting
mez sajjā
मेज़ सज्जा

sous chef
sahāyak rasoiyā
सहायक रसोइया

chef
rasoiyā
रसोइया

kitchen
rasoī | रसोई

glass
gilās
गिलास

tray
ṭre
ट्रे

server
bairā | बैरा

vocabulary • śabdāvalī • शब्दावली

receipt rasīd रसीद	**specials** viśeṣ विशेष	**price** mūlya मूल्य	**customer** grāhak ग्राहक	**à la carte** menū ke anusār मेनू के अनुसार	**service charge included** sevā sammilit सेवा सम्मिलित
wine list vāin sūchī वाइन सूची	**dessert cart** pesṭrī ṭrolī पेस्ट्री ट्रॉली	**check** bil बिल	**salt** namak नमक	**lunch menu** dopahar kā menū दोपहर का मेनू	**service charge not included** sevā sammilit nahīṃ सेवा सम्मिलित नही
tip bakhśīś बख़्शीश	**pepper** kālī mirch काली मिर्च	**bar** bār बार	**buffet** bufe बुफ़े	**dinner menu** sandhyākālīn menū संध्याकालीन मेनू	

menu
vyanjan sūchī
व्यंजन सूची

child's meal
bāl āhār | बाल-आहार

order (v)
orḍar denā | ऑर्डर देना

pay (v)
dām chukānā | दाम चुकाना

courses • bhojan ke daur • भोजन के दौर

apéritif
ārambh peya
आरंभ पेय

appetizer
sṭārṭar | स्टार्टर

soup
sūp | सूप

entrée
men kors | मेन कोर्स

side order
sāiḍ orḍar | साइड ऑर्डर

dessert | misṭhānn | मिष्ठान्न

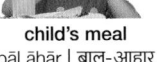

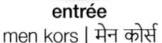

coffee | kofī | कॉफ़ी

A table for two, please.
kṛpyā do logoṃ ke lie ṭebal batāeṃ
कृपया दो लोगों के लिए टेबल बताएं।

Can I see the menu/wine list, please?
kyā menu/vāin lisṭ dikhāeṇge?
क्या मेनू/वाइन लिस्ट दिखाएंगे?

Is there a fixed-price menu?
kyā yah ek dām menū hai?
क्या यह एक दाम मेनू है?

Do you have any vegetarian dishes?
kyā yahāṃ śākāhārī khānā haï?
क्या यहां शाकाहारी खाना है?

Could I have the check/a receipt, please?
kyā mujhe bil/rasīd mil saktī hai?
क्या मुझे बिल/रसीद मिल सकती है?

Can we pay separately?
kyā ham alag-alag bil de sakte haiṃ?
क्या हम अलग-अलग बिल दे सकते हैं?

Where is the restroom, please?
śauchālaya kahāṃ haiṃ?
शौचालय कहाँ हैं?

fast food • fāsṭ fūḍ • फ़ास्ट फ़ूड

burger meal | bargar mīl | बर्गर मील

home delivery
hom ḍilīvarī | होम डिलीवरी

street vendor
sṭrīṭ sṭol | स्ट्रीट स्टॉल

vocabulary • śabdāvalī • शब्दावली

pizzeria
pizzā pārlar
पिज़्ज़ा पार्लर

burger bar
bargar bār
बर्गर बार

menu
vyanjan sūchī
व्यंजन सूची

eat-in
restrāṃ meṃ khānā
रेस्तरां में खाना

to go
paik karvāke le jānā
पैक करवाके ले जाना

reheat (v)
dubārā garm karnā
दुबारा गर्म करना

ketchup
ṭamāṭar sos
टमाटर सॉस

Can I have that to go please?
kyā āp ise paik kar sakte haiṃ?
क्या आप इसे पैक कर सकते हैं?

Do you deliver?
kyā āp ḍilīvar karte haiṃ?
क्या आप डिलीवर करते हैं?

hamburger
haim bargar
हैम बर्गर

chicken burger
chikan bargar
चिकन बर्गर

veggie burger
vej bargar
वेज बर्गर

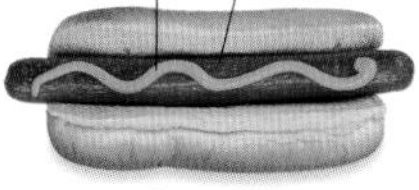

hot dog
hoṭ ḍog | हॉट डॉग

sandwich
saiṇḍvich
सैंडविच

club sandwich
klab saiṇḍvich
क्लब सैंडविच

open-faced sandwich
khulā saiṇḍvich
खुला सैंडविच

wrap
rol | रोल

kebab
kabāb | कबाब

chicken nuggets | chikan nageṭs | चिकन नगेट्स

crepes
maide kā chīlā
मैदे का चीला

fish and chips
talī machhlī aur chips
तली मछली और चिप्स

ribs
chāṃp
चांप

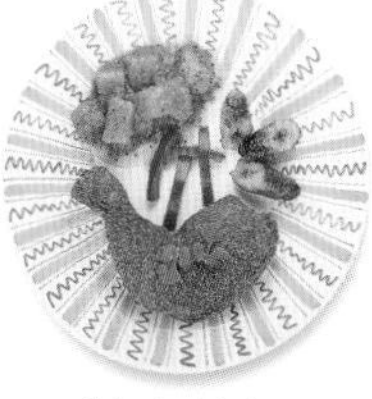

fried chicken
frāiḍ chikan
फ़्राइड चिकन

pizza
pizzā
पिज़्ज़ा

breakfast • subah kā nāśtā • सुबह का नाश्ता

milk
dūdh
दूध

cereal
sīriyal
सीरियल

jam
jaim
जैम

dried fruit
meve
मेवे

ham
haim
हैम

cheese
chīz
चीज़

crispbread
kurkurī breḍ
कुरकुरी ब्रेड

breakfast buffet
brekfāsṭ bufe | ब्रेकफ़ास्ट बुफ़े

marmalade
mārmleḍ
मार्मलेड

pâté
mīṭ kā pesṭ
मीट का पेस्ट

butter
makkhan
मक्खन

fruit juice
phaloṃ kā ras
फलों का रस

coffee
kofī
कॉफ़ी

breakfast table
nāśte kī mez | नाश्ते की मेज़

hot chocolate
hot chokleṭ
हॉट चॉकलेट

croissant
krosāṃ ban
क्रोंसां बन

tea
chāya
चाय

drinks
peya padārth | पेय पदार्थ

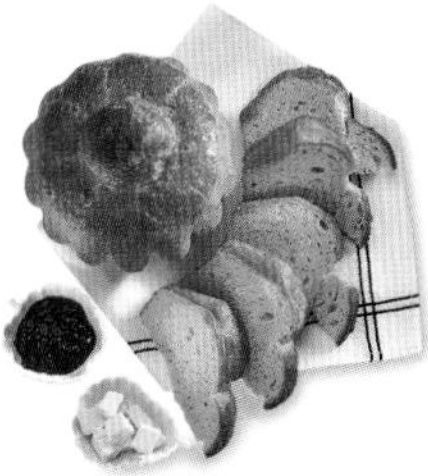

brioche
mīṭhe ban | मीठे बन

bread
breḍ | ब्रेड

tomato
ṭamāṭar
टमाटर

black pudding
blaik puḍiṅg
ब्लैक पुडिंग

toast
ṭosṭ
टोस्ट

sausage
sosej
सॉसेज

fried egg
frāiḍ anḍā
फ़्राइड अंडा

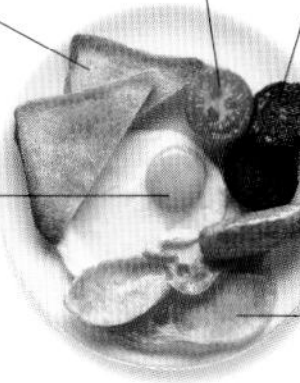

bacon
bekan
बेकन

English breakfast
aṅgrezī nāśtā | अंग्रेज़ी नाश्ता

kippers
kipars | किपर्स

French toast
french ṭosṭ
फ़्रेंच टोस्ट

yolk
zardī
ज़र्दी

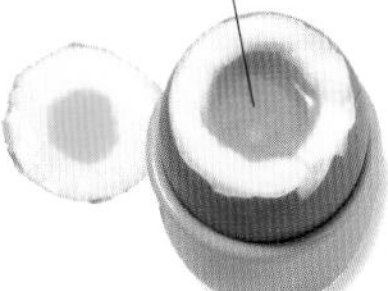

soft-boiled egg
ublā anḍā
उबला अंडा

scrambled eggs
anḍe kī bhurjī | अंडे की भुर्जी

whipped cream
krīm
क्रीम

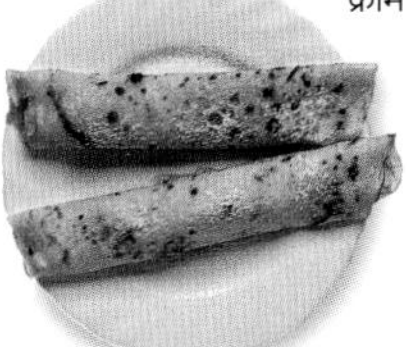

crepes
painkek | पैनकेक

waffles
vofals | वॉफ़ल्स

oatmeal
daliyā | दलिया

fruit yogurt
frūṭ dahī
फ़्रूट दही

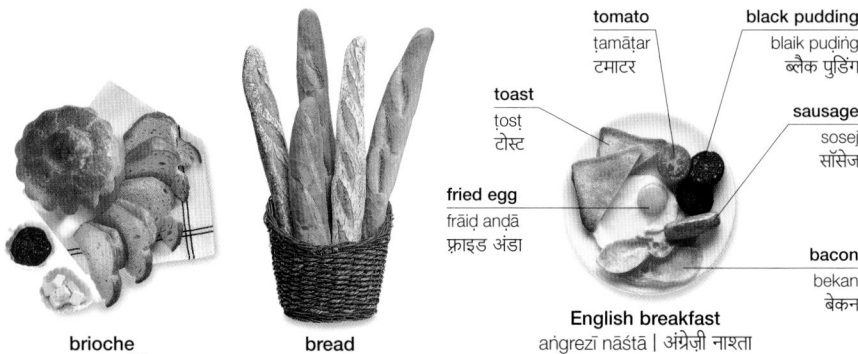

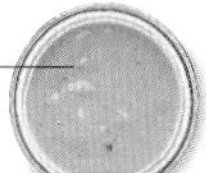

fresh fruit
tāze phal | ताज़े फल

dinner • ḍinar • डिनर

soup
sūp | सूप

broth
śorbā | शोरबा

stew
dampuḳht | दमपुख़्त

curry
rasedār | रसेदार

roast
bhunā | भुना

potpie
pāī | पाई

soufflé
sūfle | सूफ़ले

kebab
kabāb | कबाब

meatballs
kofte | कोफ़्ते

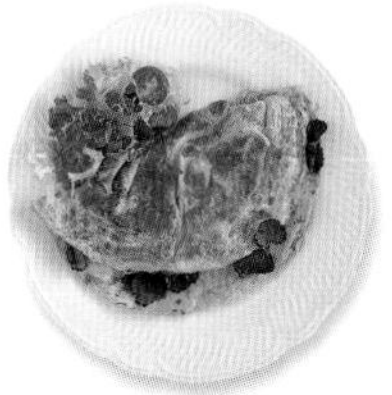

omelet
omleṭ | ऑमलेट

stir-fry | kam tel meṃ bhunā | कम तेल में भुना

pasta
pāstā | पास्ता

rice
chāval | चावल

tossed salad | miśrit salād | मिश्रित सलाद

green salad
harā salād | हरा सलाद

dressing
ḍresiṅg | ड्रेसिंग

techniques • vidhiyāṃ • विधियां

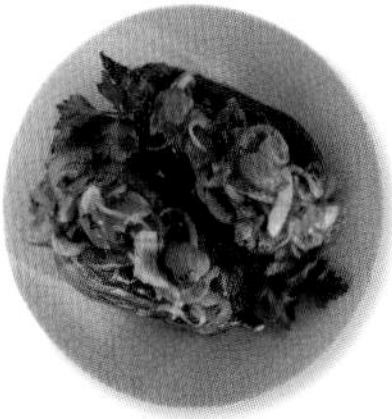

stuffed
bharvāṃ | भरवां

in sauce | sos meṃ
सॉस में

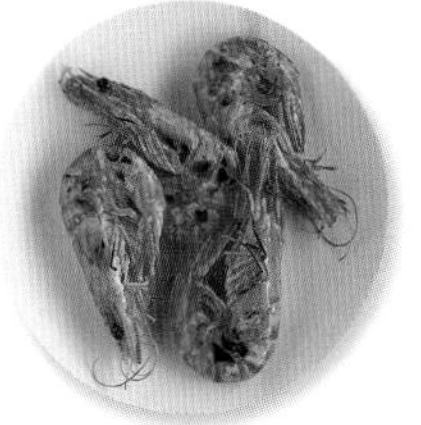

grilled
bhunā huā | भुना हुआ

marinated | masāle meṃ
lipṭā | मसाले में लिपटा

poached
pochḍ | पोच्ड

mashed
maslā huā | मसला हुआ

baked | bek kiyā
huā | बेक किया हुआ

pan fried | kam tel meṃ
pakā | कम तेल में पका

fried
talā huā | तला हुआ

pickled
achārit | अचारित

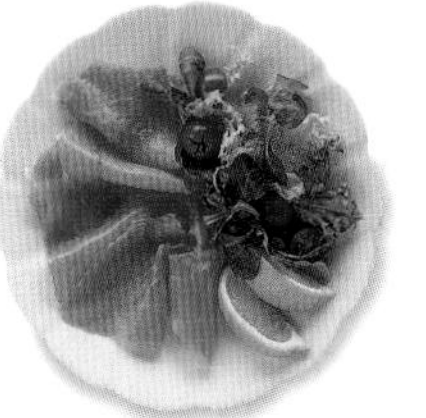

smoked
dhūmrit | धूम्रित

deep-fried
talā huā | तला हुआ

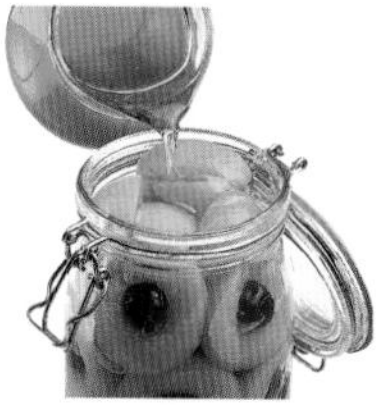

in syrup | sirap meṃ
banā | सिरप में बना

dressed | ḍresiṅg kiyā
huā | ड्रेसिंग किया हुआ

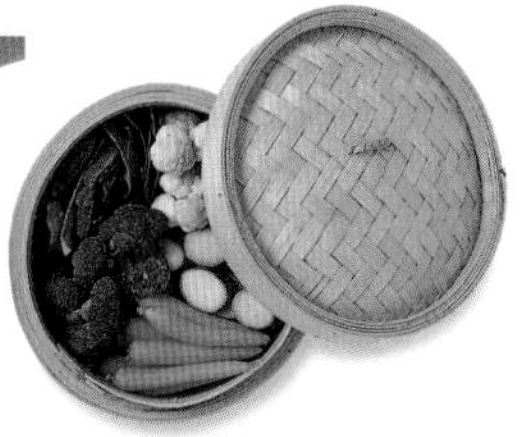

steamed | bhāp meṃ
pakā | भाप में पका

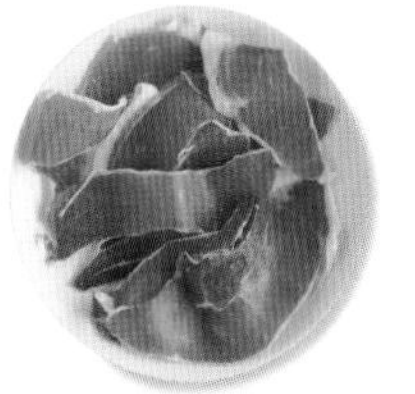

cured
sanrakṣit | संरक्षित

study
adhyayan
अध्ययन

school • vidyālaya • विद्यालय

whiteboard
vāiṭborḍ
वाईटबोर्ड

student
chhātr
छात्र

teacher
adhyāpikā
अध्यापिका

desk
bench
बेंच

classroom | kakṣā | कक्षा

schoolbag
skūl bastā
स्कूल बस्ता

schoolgirl
skūl chhātrā
स्कूल छात्रा

schoolboy
skūl chhātra | स्कूल छात्र

vocabulary • śabdāvalī • शब्दावली

history itihās इतिहास	**science** vijñān विज्ञान	**physics** bhautikī भौतिकी
languages bhāṣāeṃ भाषाएं	**art** kalā कला	**chemistry** rasāyan śāstr रसायन शास्त्र
literature sāhitya साहित्य	**music** saṅgīt संगीत	**biology** jīv vijñān जीव विज्ञान
geography bhūgol भूगोल	**math** gaṇit गणित	**physical education** vyāyām śikṣā व्यायाम शिक्षा

activities • gatividhiyāṃ • गतिविधियां

read (v) | paṛhnā | पढ़ना

write (v) | likhnā | लिखना

spell (v) | uchchāraṇ karnā | उच्चारण करना

draw (v)
chitr banānā | चित्र बनाना

digital projector
ḍijiṭal projekṭar
डिजिटल प्रोजेक्टर

nib
nib
निब

pen
pen | पेन

colored pencil
raṅgīn pensil
रंगीन पेंसिल

pencil
pensil | पेंसिल

pencil sharpener
pensil śārpnar
पेंसिल शार्पनर

eraser
rabaṛ | रबड़

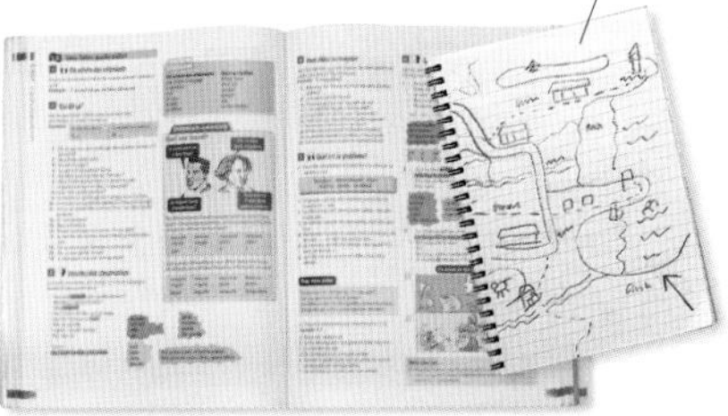

notebook
kopī | कॉपी

textbook | pāṭhya pustak | पाठ्य पुस्तक

pencil case
pensil kes | पेंसिल केस

ruler
paimānā | पैमाना

question (v) | praśn pūchhnā | प्रश्न पूछना

answer (v)
uttar denā | उत्तर देना

discuss (v) | vichār-vimarś karnā | विचार-विमर्श करना

learn (v)
sīkhnā | सीखना

vocabulary • śabdāvalī • शब्दावली

principal
mukhyādhyāpak/
mukhyādhyāpikā
मुख्याध्यापक /
मुख्याध्यापिका

lesson
adhyāya
अध्याय

question
praśn
प्रश्न

take notes (v)
noṭs lenā
नोट्स लेना

answer
uttar
उत्तर

homework
gṛhkārya
गृहकार्य

test
parīkṣā
परीक्षा

essay
nibandh
निबंध

grade
śreṇī
श्रेणी

year
varṣ
वर्ष

dictionary
śabdkoṣ
शब्दकोष

encyclopaedia
viśvakoś
विश्वकोश

math • gaṇit • गणित

shapes • ākṛtiyāṃ • आकृतियां

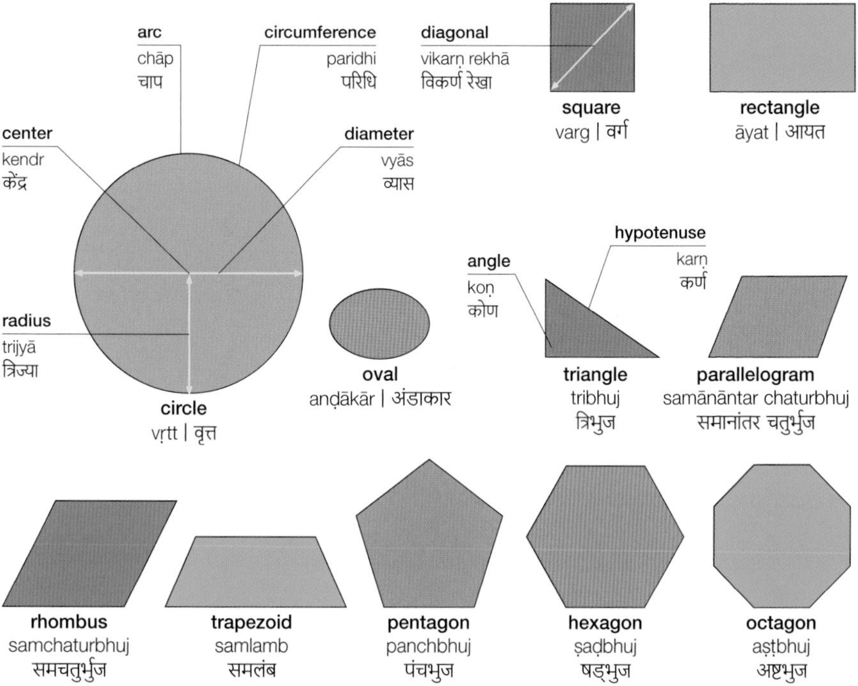

solids • ghanākṛtiyāṃ • घनाकृतियां

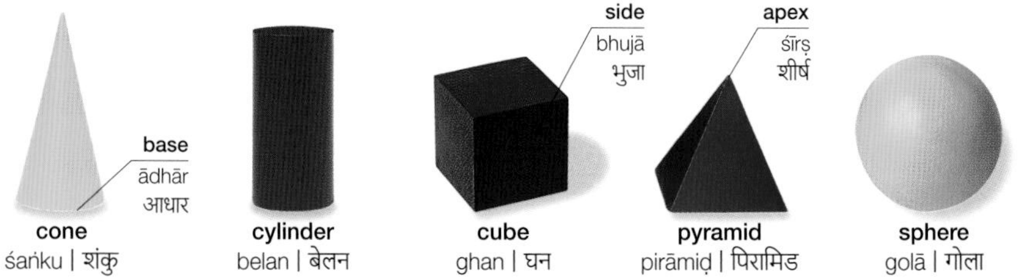

lines • rekhāeṃ • रेखाएं

straight
sīdhī | सीधी

parallel
samānāntar | समानांतर

perpendicular
lamb | लंब

curved
vakr | वक्र

measurements • māpak • मापक

volume
parimāṇ | परिमाण

numerator
aṅś
अंश

denominator
har
हर

fraction
bhinn | भिन्न

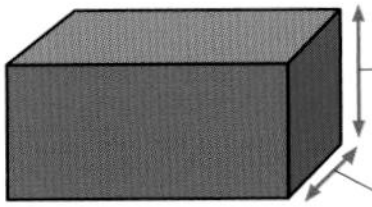

height
ūṃchāī
ऊंचाई

depth
gahrāī
गहराई

dimensions
āyām | आयाम

width
chauṛāī
चौड़ाई

length
lambāī
लंबाई

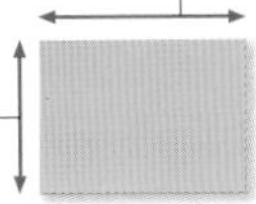

area
kṣetraphal | क्षेत्रफल

equipment • upkaraṇ • उपकरण

triangle
samkoṇak
समकोणक

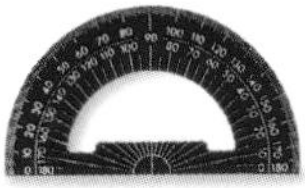

protractor
koṇmāpak/ḍī
कोणमापक/डी

ruler
paimānā
पैमाना

compass
parkār
परकार

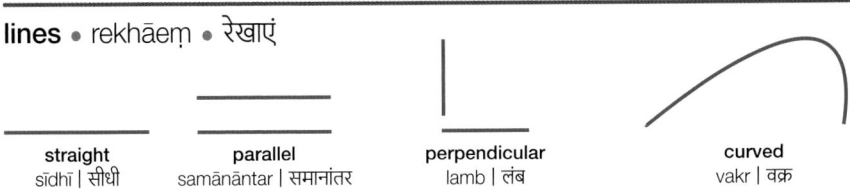

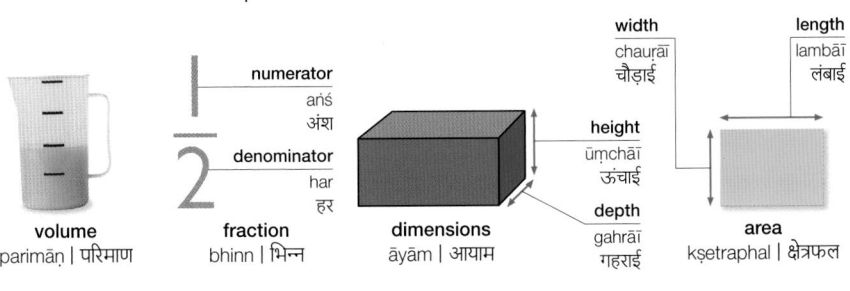

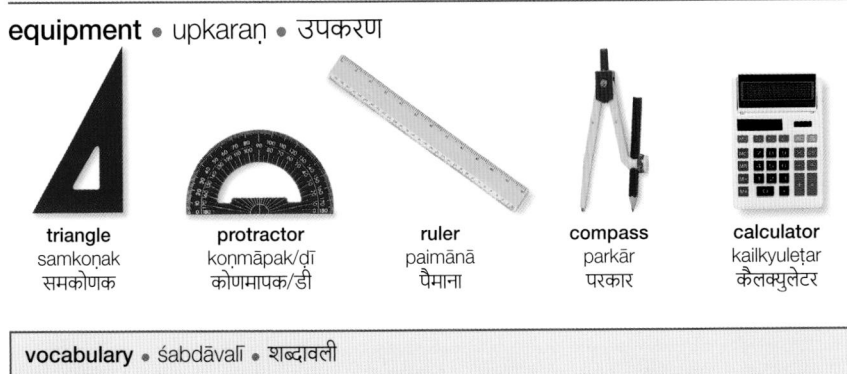

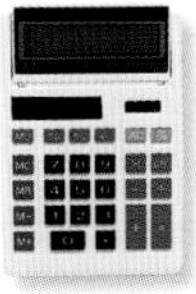

calculator
kailkyuleṭar
कैलक्युलेटर

vocabulary • śabdāvalī • शब्दावली

geometry
rekhāgaṇit
रेखागणित

arithmetic
aṅkgaṇit
अंकगणित

plus
jamā
जमा

minus
ghaṭā
घटा

times
gunā
गुना

divided by
bhājak
भाजक

equals
barābar
बराबर

count (v)
ginnā
गिनना

add (v)
joṛnā
जोड़ना

subtract (v)
ghaṭānā
घटाना

multiply (v)
guṇā karnā
गुणा करना

divide (v)
bhāg denā
भाग देना

equation
samīkaraṇ
समीकरण

percentage
pratiśat
प्रतिशत

science • vijñān • विज्ञान

laboratory
prayogśālā | प्रयोगशाला

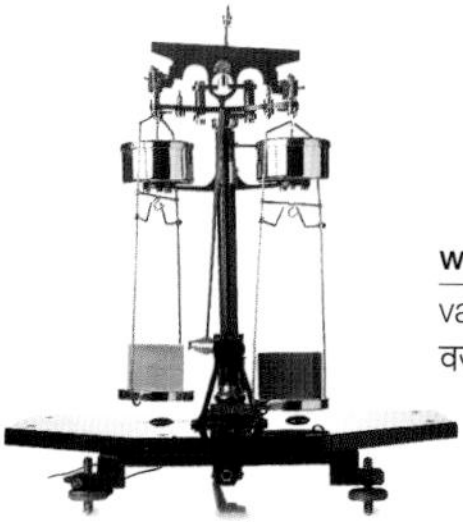

scale
tarāzū | तराज़ू

spring balance
spriṅg tulā | स्प्रिंग तुला

tripod
tipāī | तिपाई

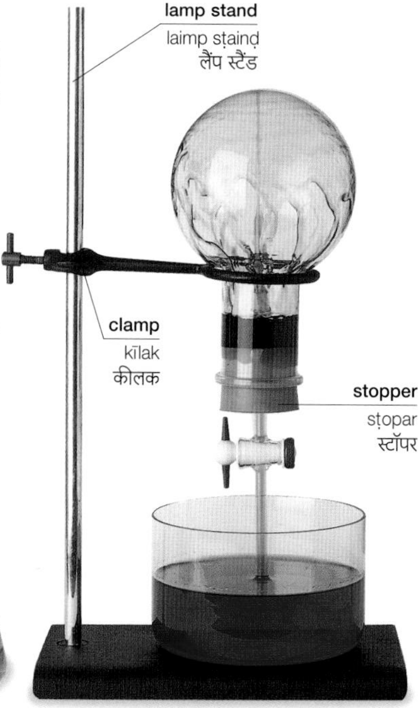

experiment | prayog | प्रयोग

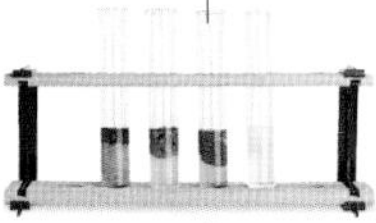

rack
raik | रैक

timer
ṭāimar | टाइमर

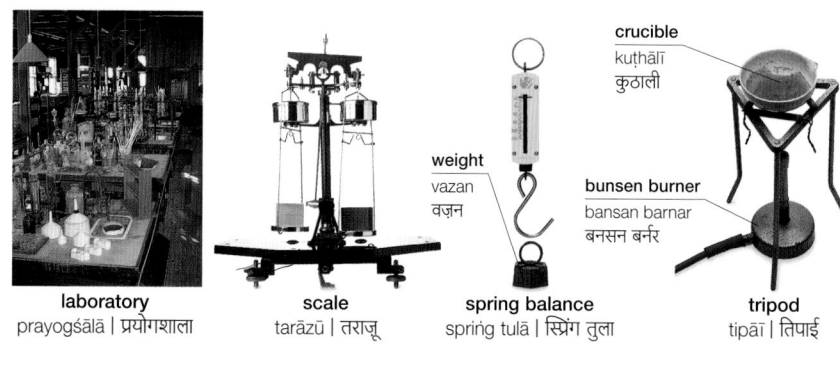

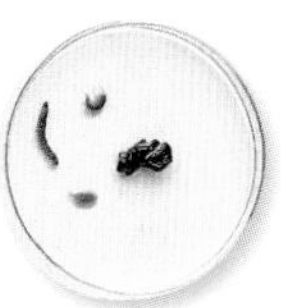

petri dish
peṭrī ḍiś | पेट्री डिश

thermometer
tharmāmīṭar | थर्मामीटर

syringe
sirinj | सिरिंज

tweezers
chhoṭī chimṭī | छोटी चिमटी

scalpel
chāḳū | चाक़ू

dropper
ḍropar | ड्रॉपर

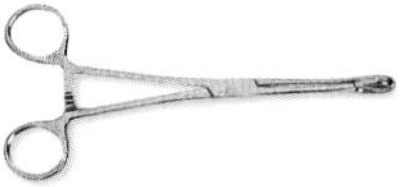

forceps
forsep | फ़ॉरसेप

tongs
baṛī chimṭī | बड़ी चिमटी

spatula
spaichulā | स्पैचुला

pestle
mūsal
मूसल

mortar
kharal | खरल

filter paper
filṭar pepar | फ़िल्टर पेपर

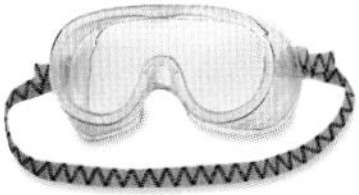

safety goggles | surakṣā chaśmā | सुरक्षा चश्मा

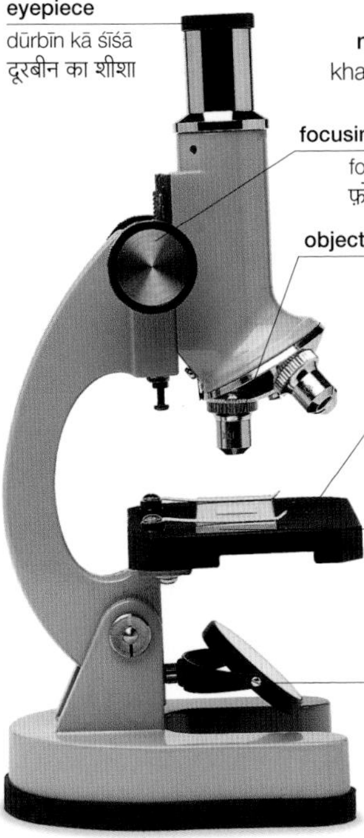

eyepiece
dūrbīn kā śīśā
दूरबीन का शीशा

focusing knob
fokas nob
फ़ोकस नॉब

objective lens
lens
लेंस

stage
tal
तल

slide
slāiḍ
स्लाइड

mirror
śīśā
शीशा

microscope
sūkṣmdarśī | सूक्ष्मदर्शी

pipette
nalikā | नलिका

glass stirring rod
kāṃch kī chhaṛ
कांच की छड़

beaker
bīkar | बीकर

magnet
chumbak
चुंबक

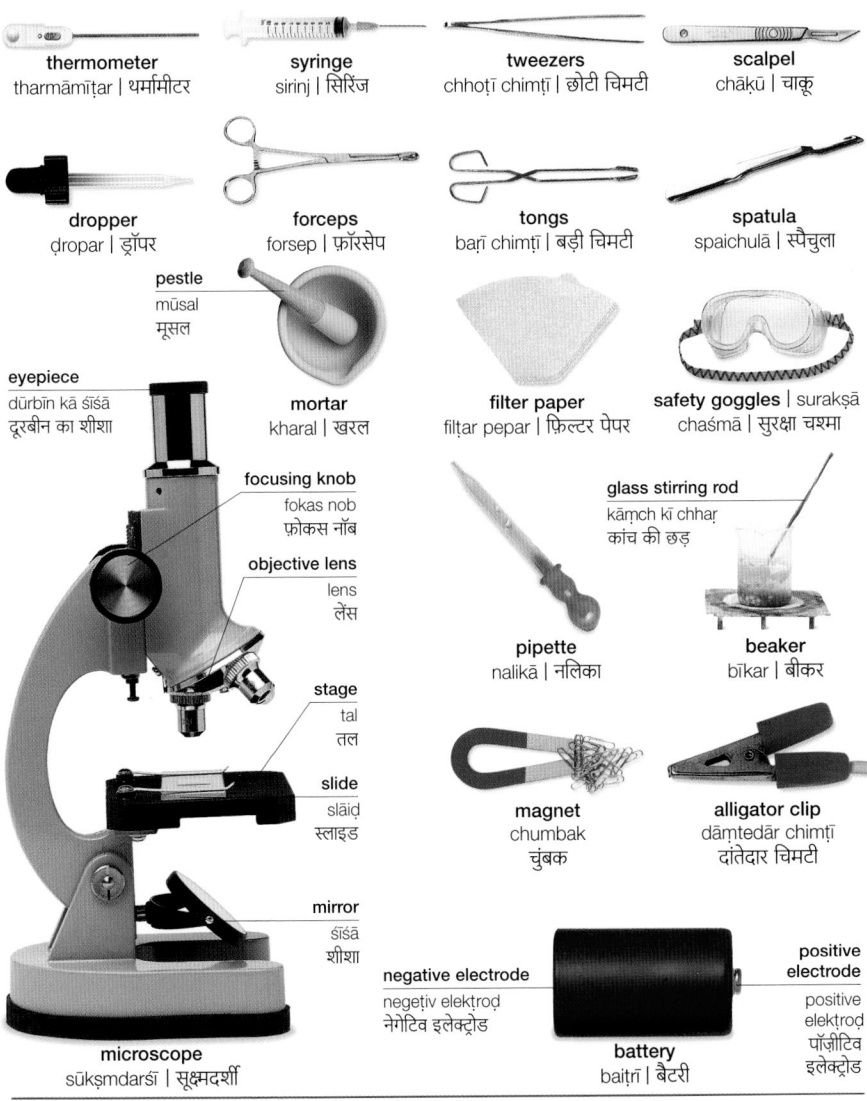

alligator clip
dāṃtedār chimṭī
दांतेदार चिमटी

negative electrode
negeṭiv elekṭroḍ
नेगेटिव इलेक्ट्रोड

positive electrode
positive elekṭroḍ
पॉज़ीटिव इलेक्ट्रोड

battery
baiṭrī | बैटरी

college • mahāvidyālaya • महाविद्यालय

campus | parisar | परिसर

library | pustakālaya | पुस्तकालय

vocabulary • śabdāvalī • शब्दावली

library card
pustakālaya kārḍ
पुस्तकालय कार्ड

reading room
adhyayan kakṣ
अध्ययन कक्ष

reading list
adhyayan sūchī
अध्ययन सूची

due date
deya tithi
देय तिथि

help desk
pūchhtāchh
पूछताछ

borrow (v)
udhār lenā
उधार लेना

reserve (v)
surakṣit karnā
सुरक्षित करना

renew (v)
navīkṛt karvānā
नवीकृत करवाना

loan
udhār
उधार

book
pustak
पुस्तक

title
śīrṣak
शीर्षक

aisle
galiyārā
गलियारा

undergraduate
pūrvsnātak
पूर्वस्नातक

professor
prādhyāpak
प्राध्यापक

lecture hall
lekchar thiyeṭar | लेक्चर थियेटर

graduate
snātak
स्नातक

gown
choṅgā | चोंगा

graduation ceremony
snātak samāroh | स्नातक समारोह

schools • vidyālaya • विद्यालय

model
moḍal
मॉडल

art school | kalā
mahāvidyālaya | कला महाविद्यालय

music school
saṅgīt vidyālaya | संगीत विद्यालय

dance school
nṛtya akādmī | नृत्य अकादमी

vocabulary • śabdāvalī • शब्दावली

scholarship chhātrvṛtti छात्रवृत्ति	**research** anusandhān अनुसंधान	**dissertation** śodh nibandh शोध निबंध	**medicine** āyurvijñān आयुर्विज्ञान	**philosophy** darśan śāstr दर्शन शास्त्र
diploma diplomā डिप्लोमा	**master's** viśārad विशारद	**department** vibhāg विभाग	**zoology** prāṇī vijñān प्राणी विज्ञान	**literature** sāhitya साहित्य
degree upādhi उपाधि	**doctorate** ḍokṭreṭ डॉक्ट्रेट	**law** kānūn क़ानून	**physics** bhautikī भौतिकी	**art history** kalā kā itihās कला का इतिहास
postgraduate snātakottar स्नातकोत्तर	**thesis** śodh prabandh शोध प्रबंध	**engineering** abhiyāntrikī अभियांत्रिकी	**political science** rājnīti राजनीति	**economics** arthśāstr अर्थशास्त्र

work
kārya
कार्य

office 1 • kāryālaya • कार्यालय 1

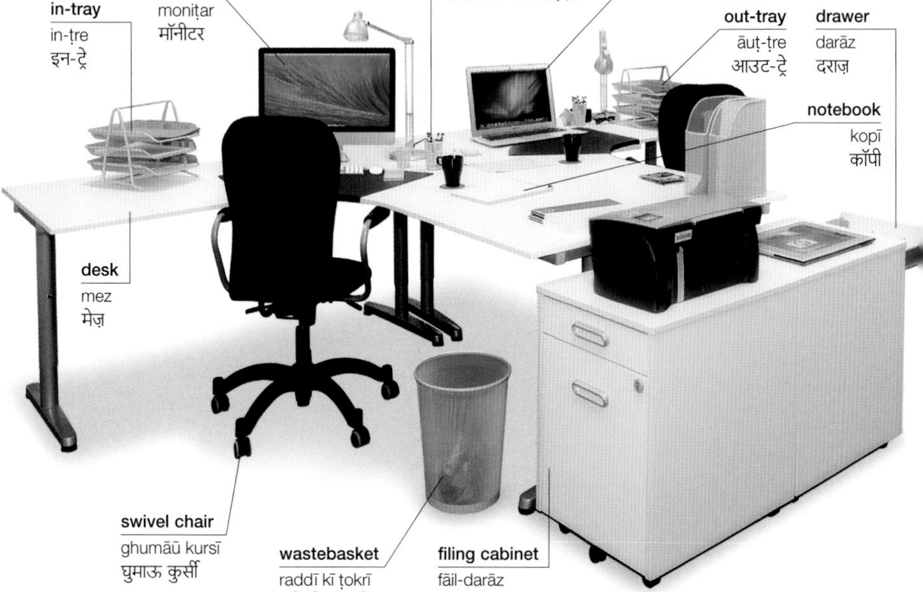

office equipment • kāryālayī upkaraṇ • कार्यालयी उपकरण

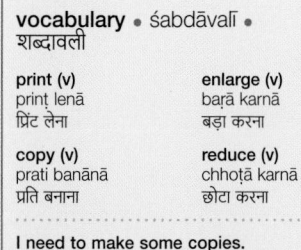

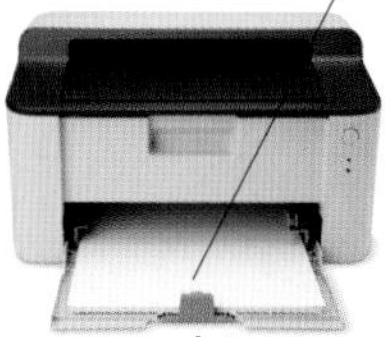

vocabulary • śabdāvalī • शब्दावली

print (v)
print lenā
प्रिंट लेना

copy (v)
prati banānā
प्रति बनाना

enlarge (v)
baṛā karnā
बड़ा करना

reduce (v)
chhoṭā karnā
छोटा करना

I need to make some copies.
mujhe kuchh pratiyāṃ banānī haiṃ
मुझे कुछ प्रतियां बनानी हैं।

office supplies • kāryālayī vastueṃ • कार्यालयी वस्तुएं

compliments slip
preṣak parchī
प्रेषक पर्ची

letterhead
laiṭar haiḍ
लैटर हैड

envelope
lifāfā | लिफ़ाफ़ा

box file
boks fāil
बॉक्स फ़ाइल

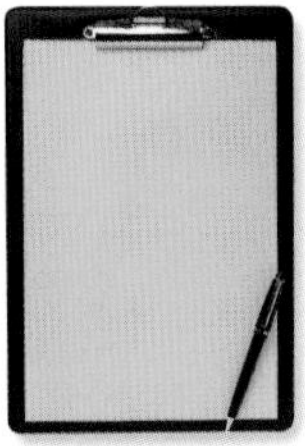

clipboard
klip borḍ
क्लिप बोर्ड

notepad
noṭ paiḍ
नोट पैड

tab
ṭaib
टैब

hanging file
haiṅgiṅg fāil
हैंगिंग फाइल

divider
vibhājak
विभाजक

expanding file
konsarṭīnā fāil
कॉनसर्टीना फ़ाइल

binder
līvar ārch fāil
लीवर आर्च फ़ाइल

personal organizer
nijī orgenāizar
निजी ऑर्गेनाइज़र

staples
sṭepals
स्टेपल्स

stapler
sṭeplar
स्टेप्लर

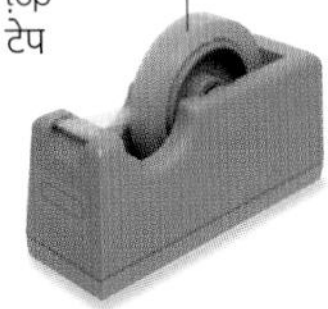

tape
ṭep
टेप

tape dispenser
ṭep ḍispensar
टेप डिस्पेंसर

hole punch
hol panch
होल पंच

ink pad
syāhī paiḍ
स्याही पैड

rubber stamp
rabaṛ kī mohar
रबड़ की मोहर

rubber band
rabaṛ bainḍ
रबड़ बैंड

bulldog clip
baṛī klip
बड़ी क्लिप

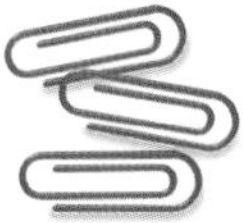

paper clip
pepar klip
पेपर क्लिप

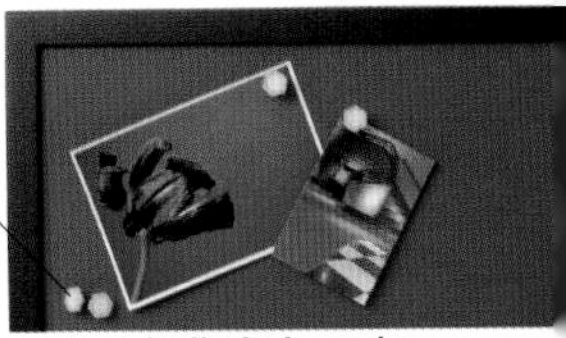

thumbtack
ḍroiṅg pin
ड्रॉइंग पिन

bulletin board
sūchanā paṭṭ | सूचना पट्ट

office 2 • kāryālaya • कार्यालय 2

meeting | sabhā/mīṭiṅg | सभा/मीटिंग

vocabulary • śabdāvalī • शब्दावली

meeting room
sabhā kakṣ
सभा कक्ष

agenda
kāryasūchī
कार्यसूची

attend (v)
upasthit rahnā
उपस्थित रहना

chair (v)
adhyakṣtā karnā
अध्यक्षता करना

What time is the meeting?
mīṭiṅg kis samaya hai?
मीटिंग किस समय है?

What are your office hours?
āpake kāryālay kā samay kyā hai?
आपके कार्यालय का समय क्या है?

presentation | prastutikaraṇ | प्रस्तुतिकरण

business • vyavsāya • व्यवसाय

businessman
vyavsāyī
व्यवसायी

businesswoman
mahilā vyavsāyī
महिला व्यवसायी

business lunch | biznes lanch | बिज़नेस लंच

business trip | biznes ṭrip | बिज़नेस ट्रिप

appointment
milne kā samaya
मिलने का समय

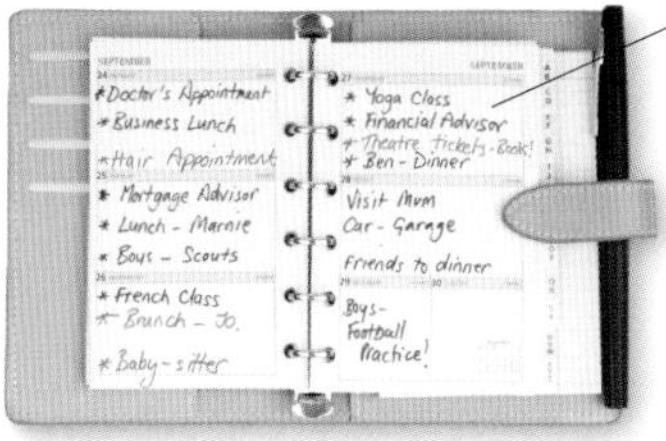

day planner | ḍāyarī | डायरी

CEO
prabandh nideśak
प्रबंध निदेशक

client
grāhak
ग्राहक

business deal
vyāvsāyik saudā | व्यावसायिक सौदा

vocabulary • śabdāvalī • शब्दावली

company
kampanī
कंपनी

head office
pradhān kāryālaya
प्रधान कार्यालय

regional office
śākhā
शाखा

staff
karmchārī varg
कर्मचारी वर्ग

salary
vetan
वेतन

payroll
vetansūchī
वेतनसूची

accounting department
lekhā vibhāg
लेखा विभाग

marketing department
vipṇan vibhāg
विपणन विभाग

sales department
bikrī vibhāg
बिक्री विभाग

legal department
ḳānūnī vibhāg
क़ानूनी विभाग

customer service department
grāhak sevā vibhāg
ग्राहक सेवा विभाग

human resources department
kārmik vibhāg
कार्मिक विभाग

computer • kampyūṭar • कंप्यूटर

printer
prinṭar
प्रिंटर

screen
skrīn
स्क्रीन

scanner
skainar
स्कैनर

laptop
laipṭop | लैपटॉप

key
kī | की

keyboard
kunjīpaṭal
कुंजीपटल

mouse
māus | माउस

speaker
spīkar | स्पीकर

hardware | hārḍveyar | हार्डवेयर

memory stick
memorī sṭik | मेमोरी स्टिक

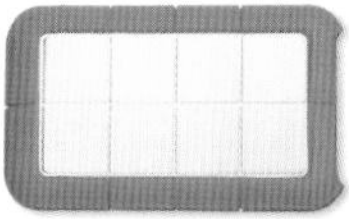

external hard drive
bāharī hārḍ ḍrāiv
बाहरी हार्ड ड्राइव

vocabulary • śabdāvalī • शब्दावली

memory
memorī
मेमोरी

RAM
raim
रैम

bytes
bāiṭs
बाइट्स

system
sisṭam
सिस्टम

software
sofṭveyar
सॉफ़्टवेयर

application
eplīkeśan
एप्लीकेशन

program
progrām
प्रोग्राम

network
neṭvark
नेटवर्क

server
sarvar
सर्वर

port
porṭ
पोर्ट

processor
prosesar
प्रोसेसर

power cord
vidyut tār
विद्युत तार

tablet
taibleṭ | टैबलेट

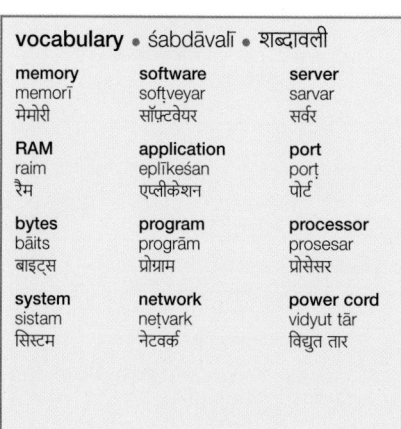

smartphone
smārṭfon | स्मार्टफ़ोन

desktop • desktọp • डेस्कटॉप

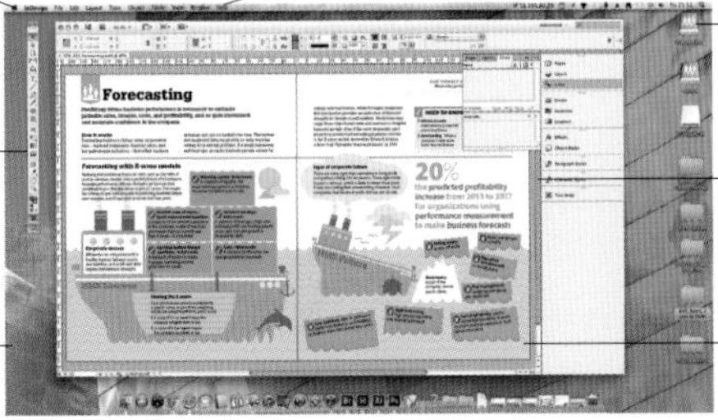

menubar
menū bār
मेनू बार

font
fonṭ
फ़ॉन्ट

toolbar
ṭūlbār
टूलबार

icon
āikan
आइकन

scrollbar
skrolbār
स्क्रोलबार

wallpaper
volpepar
वॉलपेपर

window
vinḍo
विंडो

file
fāil | फाइल

folder
folḍar | फोल्डर

trash | ṭraiś | ट्रैश

internet • inṭarneṭ • इंटरनेट

browser
brāuzar
ब्राउज़र

website
vebsāiṭ
वेबसाइट

browse (v)
brāuz | ब्राउज़

email • ī-mel • ई-मेल

email address
ī-mel patā
ई-मेल पता

inbox
inboks
इनबॉक्स

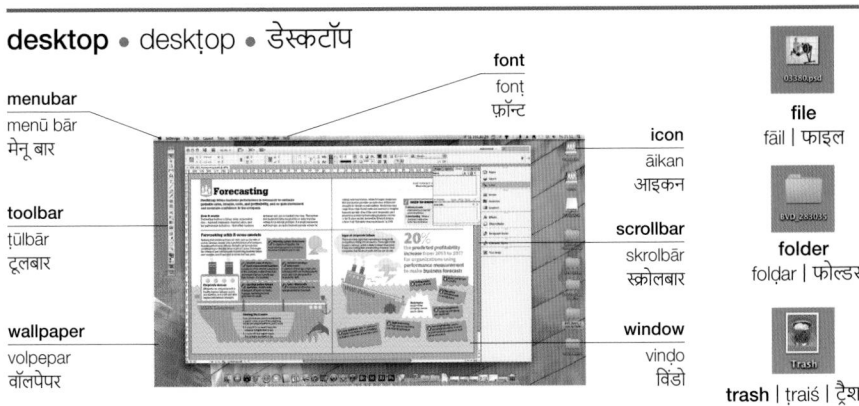

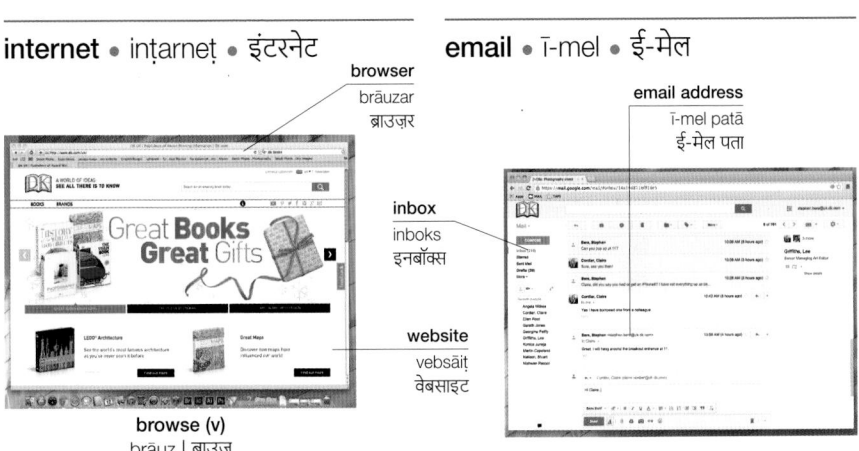

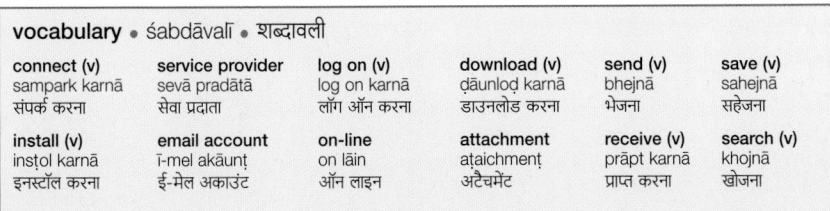

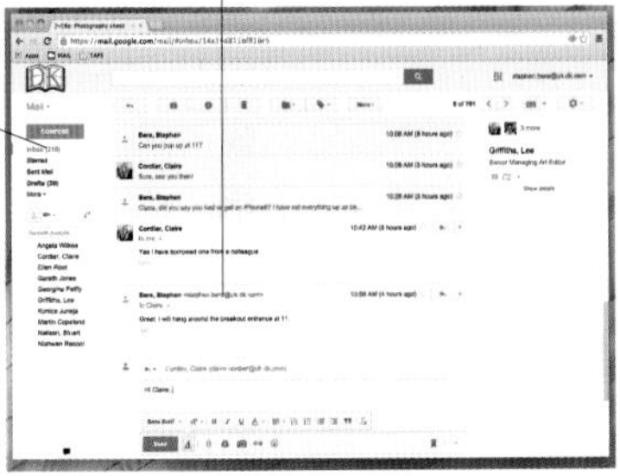

vocabulary • śabdāvalī • शब्दावली

connect (v)
sampark karnā
संपर्क करना

service provider
sevā pradātā
सेवा प्रदाता

log on (v)
log on karnā
लॉग ऑन करना

download (v)
ḍāunloḍ karnā
डाउनलोड करना

send (v)
bhejnā
भेजना

save (v)
sahejnā
सहेजना

install (v)
insṭol karnā
इनस्टॉल करना

email account
ī-mel akāunṭ
ई-मेल अकाउंट

on-line
on lāin
ऑन लाइन

attachment
aṭaichmenṭ
अटैचमेंट

receive (v)
prāpt karnā
प्राप्त करना

search (v)
khojnā
खोजना

media • mīḍiyā • मीडिया

television studio • ṭelīvizan stūḍiyo • टेलीविज़न स्टूडियो

vocabulary • śabdāvalī • शब्दावली

channel chainal चैनल	**news** samāchār समाचार	**press** pres प्रेस	**soap opera** nāṭak नाटक	**cartoon** kārṭūn कार्टून	**live** sīdhā prasāraṇ सीधा प्रसारण
programming progrāmiṅg प्रोग्रामिंग	**documentary** vṛttchitr वृत्तचित्र	**television series** ṭelīvizan śṛiṅkhlā टेलीविज़न शृंखला	**game show** gem śo गेम शो	**prerecorded** pūrv rikorḍeḍ पूर्व रिकॉर्डेड	**broadcast (v)** prasārit karnā प्रसारित करना

interviewer
sākṣātkārkartā
साक्षात्कारकर्ता

reporter
patrakār | पत्रकार

teleprompter
ṭelī prompṭar
टेली प्रॉम्प्टर

anchor | samāchār
vāchak | समाचार वाचक

actors
abhinetā | अभिनेता

sound boom
sāunḍ būm | साउंड बूम

clapper board | klaipar
borḍ | क्लैपर बोर्ड

movie set
film seṭ | फ़िल्म सेट

radio • reḍiyo • रेडियो

sound technician
sāunḍ takniīśiyan
साउंड तकनीशियन

mixing desk
miksing ḍesk
मिक्सिंग डेस्क

microphone
māikrofon
माइक्रोफोन

recording studio | rikorḍing sṭūḍiyo | रिकॉर्डिंग स्टूडियो

vocabulary • śabdāvalī • शब्दावली

radio station reḍiyo sṭeśan रेडियो स्टेशन	**frequency** āvṛtti आवृत्ति
broadcast prasāraṇ प्रसारण	**volume** dhvani star ध्वनि स्तर
wavelength vevlainth वेवलैंथ	**DJ** ḍīje डीजे
long wave long vev लॉन्ग वेव	**short wave** śort vev शॉर्ट वेव
tune (v) chainal seṭ karnā चैनल सेट करना	**medium wave** mīḍiyam vev मीडियम वेव
analog enālog एनालॉग	**digital** ḍijiṭal डिजिटल

law • ḳānūn • क़ानून

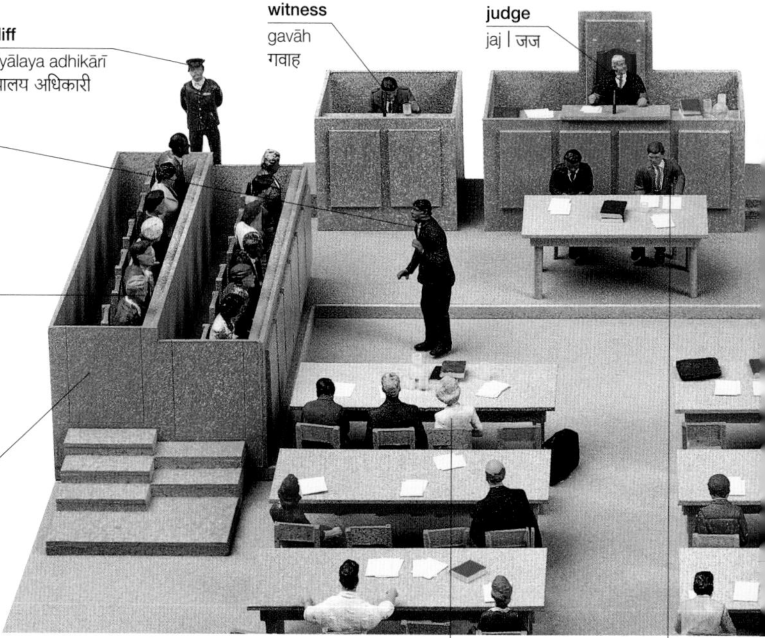

vocabulary • śabdāvalī • शब्दावली

lawyer's office
vakīl kā kāryālaya
वकील का कार्यालय

legal advice
ḳānūnī salāh
क़ानूनी सलाह

client
muvakkil
मुवक्किल

summons
saman
समन

statement
bayān
बयान

warrant
vāranṭ
वारंट

writ
riṭ
रिट

court date
nyāyālaya kī tārīḳh
न्यायालय की तारीख़

plea
pairavī
पैरवी

court case
muḳaddmā
मुक़द्दमा

charge
abhiyog
अभियोग

accused
abhiyukt
अभियुक्त

defendant
prativādī
प्रतिवादी

stenographer
āśulipik
आशुलिपिक

defense
bachāv pakṣ
बचाव पक्ष

suspect
sandigdh
संदिग्ध

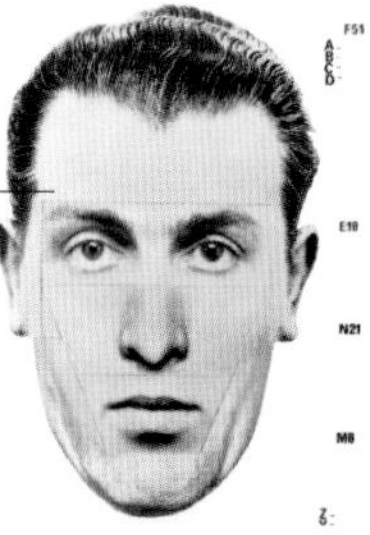

composite sketch
anumānit tasvīr
अनुमानित तस्वीर

criminal
aprādhī
अपराधी

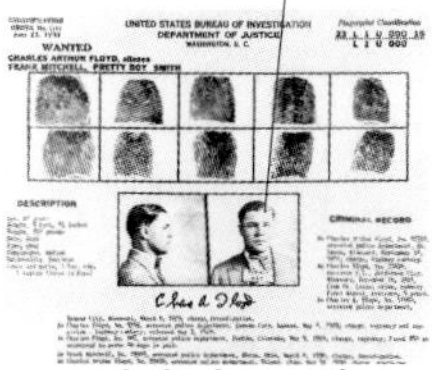

criminal record
āprādhik rikorḍ
आपराधिक रिकॉर्ड

prison guard | jel kā pahredār | जेल का पहरेदार

cell | jel kī koṭhrī | जेल की कोठरी

prison
jel | जेल

vocabulary • śabdāvalī • शब्दावली

evidence
sabūt
सबूत

verdict
faislā
फ़ैसला

innocent
beḳasūr
बेक़सूर

guilty
doṣī
दोषी

acquitted
abhimukt
अभिमुक्त

sentence
daṇḍādeś
दंडादेश

bail
zamānat
ज़मानत

appeal
apīl
अपील

parole
pairol
पैरोल

I want to see a lawyer.
mujhe ek vakīl chāhie
मुझे एक वकील चाहिए।

Where is the courthouse?
nyāyālaya kahāṃ hai?
न्यायालय कहां है?

Can I post bail?
kyā mujhe zamānat bharne milegī?
क्या मुझे ज़मानत भरने मिलेगी?

farm 1 • khet • खेत 1

farmer
kisān
किसान

tractor
ṭrekṭar | ट्रेक्टर

combine
kaṭāī maśīn | कटाई मशीन

types of farms • khetoṃ ke prakār • खेतों के प्रकार

crop farm
khetī yogya bhūmi
खेती योग्य भूमि

dairy farm
deyarī fārm
डेयरी फ़ार्म

sheep farm
bheṛoṃ kā bāṛā
भेड़ों का बाड़ा

poultry farm | murgī pālan kendr | मुर्गी पालन केंद्र

pig farm
sūar pālan kendr
सूअर पालन केंद्र

fish farm
machhlī pālan kṣetr
मछली पालन क्षेत्र

fruit farm
phaloṃ kā bāg
फलों का बाग

vineyard
aṃgūr kā bāg
अंगूर का बाग़

actions • khetoṃ ke kāmkāj • खेतों के कामकाज

plow (v)
jotnā | जोतना

sow (v)
bonā | बोना

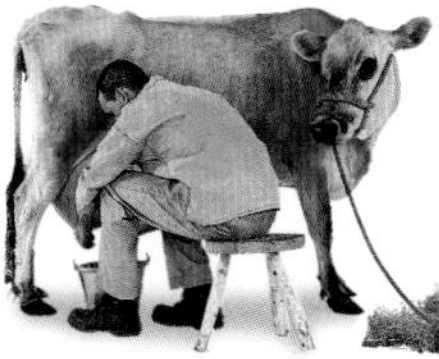

milk (v)
dūdh duhnā | दूध दुहना

feed (v)
charnā | चरना

water (v)
sīṃchnā | सींचना

harvest (v)
fasal kāṭnā | फ़सल काटना

vocabulary • śabdāvalī • शब्दावली

herbicide vanaspatināśak वनस्पतिनाशक	**herd** jhuṇḍ झुंड	**trough** nāṃd नांद
pesticide kīṭnāśak कीटनाशक	**silo** khattī खत्ती	**plant (v)** ropnā रोपना

farm 2 • khet • खेत 2

crops • fasal • फ़सल

wheat
gehūṃ | गेहूं

corn
makaī | मकई

barley
jau | जौ

rapeseed | safed sarsoṃ | सफ़ेद सरसों

sunflower
sūrajmukhī | सूरजमुखी

bale
gaṭṭhā | गट्ठा

hay
sūkhī ghās | सूखी घास

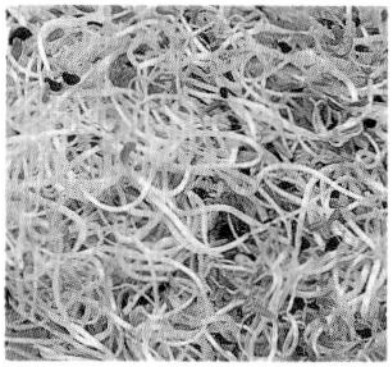

alfalfa
alfālfā | अल्फ़ाल्फ़ा

tobacco
tambākū | तंबाकू

rice
dhān | धान

tea
chāya | चाय

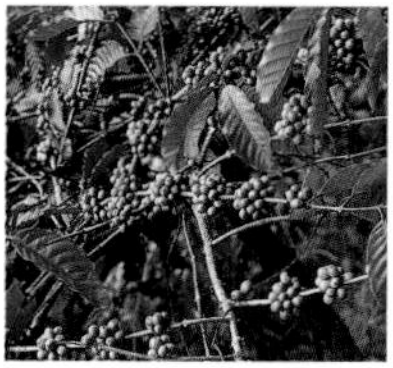

coffee
kofī | कॉफ़ी

scarecrow
bijūkā
बिजूका

flax
alsī
अलसी

sugarcane
gannā
गन्ना

cotton
kapās
कपास

livestock • paśudhan • पशुधन

pig
sūar | सूअर

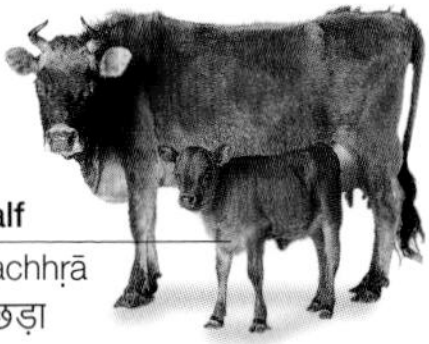

cow
gāya | गाय

bull
bail | बैल

sheep
bheṛ | भेड़

lamb
meṛhā | मेढ़ा

goat
bakrī | बकरी

horse
ghoṛā | घोड़ा

donkey
gadhā | गधा

chicken
murgī | मुर्गी

rooster
murgā | मुर्गा

turkey
ṭarkī | टर्की

duck
batakh | बतख़

stable
astabal | अस्तबल

pen
bāṛā | बाड़ा

chicken coop
daṛbā | दड़बा

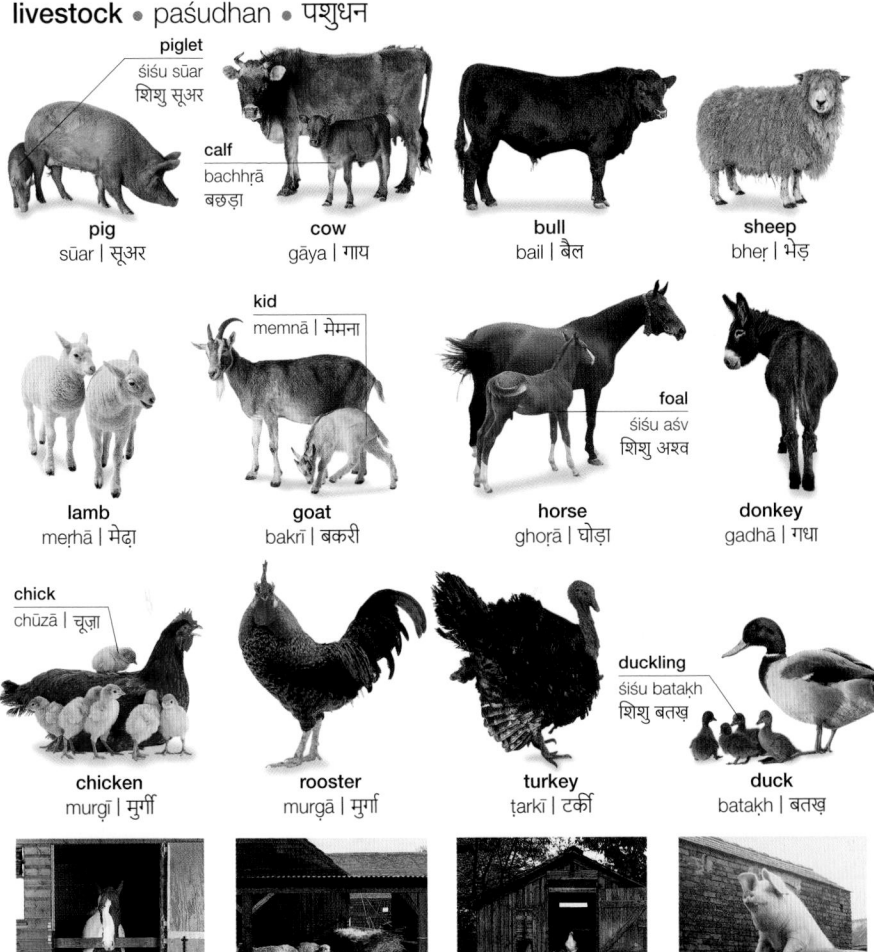

pigsty
sūarbāṛā | सूअरबाड़ा

construction • nirmāṇ kārya • निर्माण कार्य

scaffolding
pāṛ | पाड़

pallet
taḳhte
तख़्ते

ladder
sīṛhī
सीढ़ी

window
khiṛkī
खिड़की

rafter
kaṛī/śahtīr
कड़ी/शहतीर

forklift
kren
क्रेन

construction site
nirmāṇ sthal
निर्माण स्थल

lintel
chaukhaṭ
चौखट

wall
dīvār
दीवार

girder
garḍar
गर्डर

hard hat
ṭop
टोप

build (v)
nirmāṇ karnā | निर्माण करना

toolbelt
auzār peṭī
औज़ार पेटी

beam
śahtīr
शहतीर

construction worker
rājgīr | राजगीर

cement
sīmenṭ
सीमेंट

cement mixer | sīmenṭ miksar | सीमेंट मिक्सर

materials • sāmān • सामान

brick
īṃṭ | ईंट

lumber
imāratī lakṛī | इमारती लकड़ी

roof tile
paṭiyā | पटिया

cinder block
kankrīṭ blok | कंक्रीट ब्लॉक

tools • auzār • औज़ार

mortar
gārā | गारा

trowel
kannī | कन्नी

level
talmāpī | तलमापी

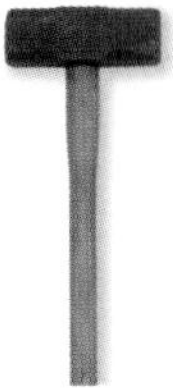

sledgehammer
hathauṛā | हथौड़ा

handle
hatthā
हत्था

pickax
kudāl | कुदाल

shovel
belchā | बेलचा

machinery • maśīnarī • मशीनरी

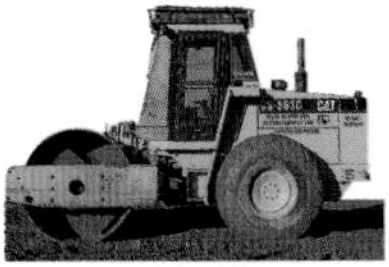

road roller
roḍ rolar | रोड रोलर

dump truck
ḍampar | डम्पर

support
ādhār stambh
आधार स्तंभ

hook
huk
हुक

crane | kren | क्रेन

roadwork • saṛak nirmāṇ kārya • सड़क निर्माण कार्य

asphalt
tārkol
तारकोल

cone
kon
कोन

jackhammer
nyūmaiṭik ḍril
न्यूमैटिक ड्रिल

excavator
yāntrik khudāī
यांत्रिक खुदाई

occupations 1 • vyavasāya • व्यवसाय 1

carpenter
baṛhaī | बढ़ई

electrician | bijlī mistrī
बिजली मिस्त्री

plumber
nalsāz | नलसाज़

construction worker
rājgīr | राजगीर

gardener
mālī | माली

vacuum cleaner
vekyūm klīnar
वेक्यूम क्लीनर

cleaner
safaī karmī | सफ़ाई कर्मी

mechanic
mistrī | मिस्त्री

butcher
ḳasāī | क़साई

hairdresser | keś prasādhak | केश प्रसाधक

fish seller
machhlī vikretā
मछली विक्रेता

produce seller
sabzī vikretā
सब्ज़ी विक्रेता

florist
phūl vikretā
फूल विक्रेता

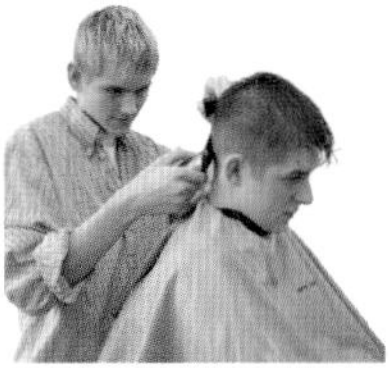

barber
nāī | नाई

jeweler
sunār | सुनार

salesperson | dukān sahāyak | दुकान सहायक

realtor | bhūsam-patti dalāl | भूसंपत्ति दलाल

optometrist | dṛṣṭi parīkṣak | दृष्टि परीक्षक

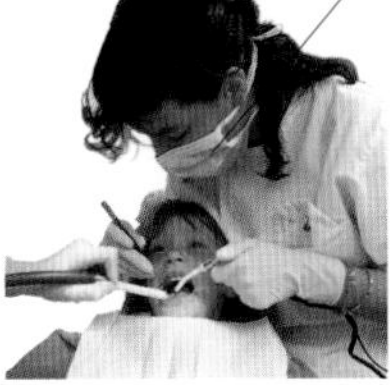

dentist | dant chikitsak | दतं चिकित्सक

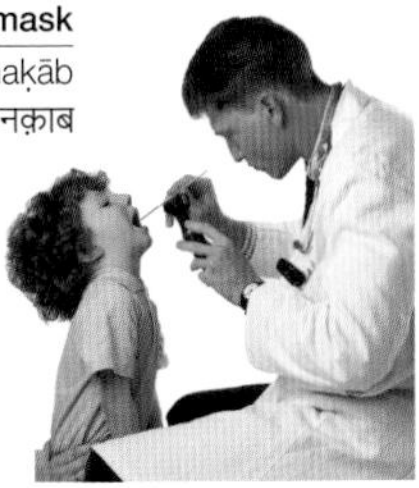

doctor
chikitsak | चिकित्सक

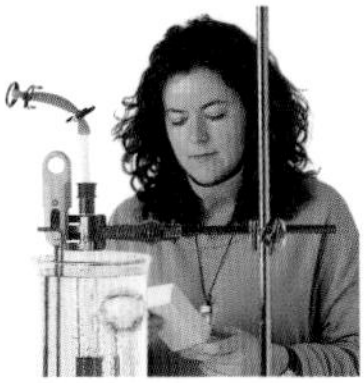

pharmacist
auṣadhkārak | औषधकारक

nurse
nars | नर्स

veterinarian | paśu chikitsak | पशु चिकित्सक

farmer
kisān | किसान

fisherman
machhuārā | मछुआरा

soldier
sainik | सैनिक

police officer | pulis karmī | पुलिस कर्मी

security guard
surakṣā karmī | सुरक्षा कर्मी

sailor
nāvik | नाविक

firefighter
fāyarmain | फ़ायरमैन

occupations 2 • vyavasāya • व्यवसाय 2

lawyer
vakīl | वकील

accountant
lekhākār | लेखाकार

architect
vāstukār | वास्तुकार

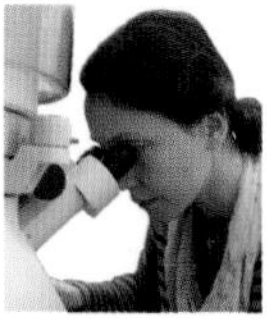

scientist
vaijñānik | वैज्ञानिक

teacher
adhyāpak | अध्यापक

librarian
pustakālaya adhyakṣ
पुस्तकालय अध्यक्ष

receptionist
svāgatkartā | स्वागतकर्ता

mail carrier
ḍākiyā | डाकिया

bus driver
bas chālak | बस चालक

truck driver
ṭrak chālak | ट्रक चालक

taxi driver | ṭaiksī chālak | टैक्सी चालक

pilot | vimān chālak | विमान चालक

flight attendant | vimān parichārikā | विमान परिचारिका

travel agent | ṭraival ejenṭ | ट्रैवल एजेंट

chef
rasoiyā | रसोइया

musician
saṅgītkār | संगीतकार

tutu
baile skarṭ
बैले स्कर्ट

dancer
nartakī | नर्तकी

actress
abhinetrī | अभिनेत्री

singer
gāyikā | गायिका

waitress
parichārikā | परिचारिका

bartender
bārṭenḍar | बारटेंडर

sportsman
khilāṛī | खिलाड़ी

sculptor
mūrtikār | मूर्तिकार

painter
chitrakār | चित्रकार

photographer
chhāyākār | छायाकार

anchor | samāchār
vāchak | समाचार वाचक

notes
noṭs
नोट्स

journalist
patrakār | पत्रकार

editor
sampādak | संपादक

designer
ḍizāinar | डिज़ाइनर

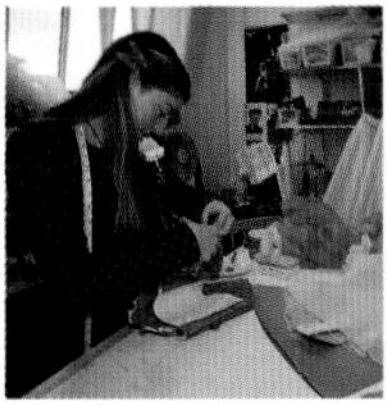

seamstress
darzin | दर्ज़िन

tailor
darzī | दर्ज़ी

transportation

parivahan

परिवहन

roads • saṛkeṃ • सड़कें

freeway
hāīve
हाईवे

toll booth
ṭol būth
टोल बूथ

road markings
mārg chihn
मार्ग चिह्न

on-ramp
sāiḍ kī saṛak
साइड की सड़क

one-way street
ek diśā mārg
एक दिशा मार्ग

divider
vibhājak
विभाजक

interchange
jaṅkśan
जंक्शन

traffic light
yātāyāt battī
यातायात बत्ती

right lane
bhītrī len
भीतरी लेन

middle lane
madhya len
मध्य लेन

left lane
bāhrī len
बाहरी लेन

off-ramp
nikās ḍhalān
निकास ढलान

traffic
yātāyāt
यातायात

overpass
flāī ovar
फ़्लाई ओवर

shoulder
saṛak kā kinārā
सड़क का किनारा

truck
ṭrak
ट्रक

median strip
kendrīya ārakṣaṇ
केंद्रीय आरक्षण

underpass
bhūmigat mārg
भूमिगत मार्ग

crosswalk
paidal pārpath
पैदल पारपथ

emergency phone
āpātkālīn dūrbhāṣ
आपातकालीन दूरभाष

disabled parking
viklāṅg
pārkiṅg sthal
विकलांग
पार्किंग स्थल

traffic jam
yātāyāt jām | यातायात जाम

satnav
jī pī es | जीपीएस

parking meter
pārkiṅg mīṭar
पार्किंग मीटर

traffic policeman
yātāyāt puliskarmī
यातायात पुलिसकर्मी

vocabulary • śabdāvalī • शब्दावली

roundabout
gol chakkar
गोल चक्कर

tow away (v)
ṭo karnā
टो करना

detour
parivartit mārg
परिवर्तित मार्ग

guardrail
ṭakkar avrodh
टक्कर अवरोध

park (v)
pārk karnā
पार्क करना

pass (v)
āge nikālnā
आगे निकालना

drive (v)
gāṛī chalānā
गाड़ी चलाना

reverse (v)
pīchhe karnā
पीछे करना

roadwork
saṛak nirmāṇ kārya
सड़क निर्माण कार्य

divided highway
dvaya vāhan mārg
द्वय वाहन मार्ग

Is this the road to...?
kyā... jāne kā yahī mārg hai?
क्या... जाने का यही मार्ग है?

Where can I park?
maiṃ kahāṃ pārk karūṃ?
मैं कहां पार्क करूँ?

road signs • yātāyāt saṅket • यातायात संकेत

do not enter
praveś niṣedh
प्रवेश निषेध

speed limit
gati sīmā
गति सीमा

hazard
khatrā
खतरा

no stopping
ruknā manā hai
रुकना मना है

no right turn
dāeṃ muṛnā niṣedh
दाएं मुड़ना निषेध

bus • bas • बस

driver's seat
chālak sīṭ
चालक सीट

handrail
haiṇḍrel
हैंडरेल

automatic door
svachālit darvāzā
स्वचालित दरवाज़ा

front wheel
āge kā pahiyā
आगे का पहिया

luggage hold
sāmān kakṣ
सामान कक्ष

door | darvāzā | दरवाज़ा

long-distance bus | bas | बस

types of buses • basoṃ ke prakār • बसों के प्रकार

route number
rūṭ nambar
रुट नंबर

driver
chālak
चालक

double-decker bus
ḍabal-ḍekar bas
डबल-डेकर बस

tram
ṭrām | ट्राम

streetcar
trolī bas | ट्रॉली बस

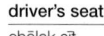

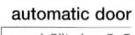

school bus | skūl bas | स्कूल बस

rear wheel
pichhlā pahiyā
पिछला पहिया

window
khiṛkī
खिड़की

stop button
sṭop baṭan
स्टॉप बटन

bus ticket
bas ṭikaṭ | बस टिकट

bell
ghanṭī | घंटी

bus station
bas aḍḍā | बस अड्डा

bus stop
bas sṭop
बस स्टॉप

vocabulary • śabdāvalī • शब्दावली

schedule
samaya sūchī
समय सूची

fare
kirāyā
किराया

wheelchair access
vhīlcheyar suvidhā
व्हीलचेयर सुविधा

bus shelter
bas khaṛī karne kī jagah
बस खड़ी करने की जगह

Do you stop at...?
kyā āp ... par rokeṅge?
क्या आप ... पर रोकेंगे?

Which bus goes to...?
... ke lie kaun sī bas jātī hai?
... के लिए कौन सी बस जाती है?

minibus
minī bas | मिनी बस

tour bus | paryaṭak bas | पर्यटक बस

shuttle bus | śaṭal bas | शटल बस

car 1 • kār • कार 1

exterior • bāhrī svarūp • बाहरी स्वरूप

roofrack
kairiyar | कैरियर

tailgate | ḍikkī kā darvāzā
डिक्की का दरवाज़ा

seat belt
sīṭ belṭ | सीट बेल्ट

car seat
śiśu sīṭ | शिशु सीट

types • prakār • प्रकार

electric car
bijlī se chalne vālī kār
बिजली से चलने वाली कार

hatchback
haichbaik | हैचबैक

sedan
salūn | सलून

station wagon
vaigan | वैगन

convertible
kanvarṭibal
कन्वर्टिबल

sports car
sporṭs kār
स्पोर्ट्स कार

minivan
pīpul kairiyar
पीपुल कैरियर

four-wheel drive
for-vhīl ḍrāiv
फ़ोर-व्हील ड्राइव

vintage
vinṭej kār | विंटेज कार

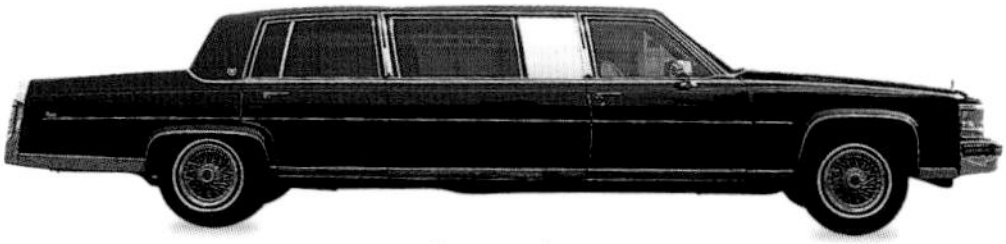

limousine
limozīn | लिमोज़ीन

gas station • peṭrol sṭeśan • पेट्रोल स्टेशन

gas pump
peṭrol pamp
पेट्रोल पंप

price
mūlya
मूल्य

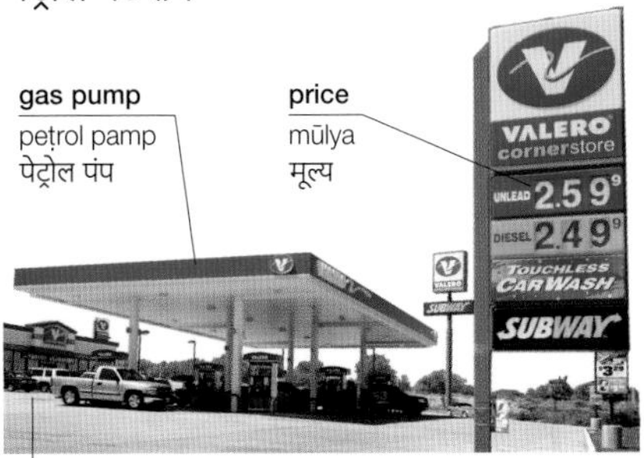

forecourt
dālān
दालान

vocabulary • śabdāvalī • शब्दावली

oil tel तेल	**leaded** sīsā yukt सीसा युक्त	**car wash** kār dhulāī कार धुलाई
gasoline peṭrol पेट्रोल	**diesel** ḍīzal डीज़ल	**antifreeze** enṭī frīz एंटी फ्रीज़
unleaded sīsā rahit सीसा रहित	**garage** gairej गैरेज	**windshield washer fluid** skrīnvoś स्क्रीनवॉश

Fill it up, please.
kṛpyā pūrī ṭaṅkī bhar deṃ
कृपया पूरी टंकी भर दें।

car 2 • kār • कार 2

interior • inṭīriyar • इंटीरियर

backseat
pichhlī sīṭ | पिछली सीट

headrest
sirhānā | सिरहाना

door lock
darvāze kā lok
दरवाज़े का लॉक

armrest
ārmresṭ
आर्मरेस्ट

handle
haindil
हैंडिल

vocabulary • śabdāvalī • शब्दावली

two-door	**four-door**	**automatic**	**brake**	**accelerator**
do-darvāzā	chār-darvāzā	svachālit	brek	aiksīlreṭar
दो-दरवाज़ा	चार-दरवाज़ा	स्वचालित	ब्रेक	ऐक्सीलरेटर
hatchback	**manual**	**ignition**	**clutch**	**air-conditioning**
tīn-darvāzā	mānav-chālit	ignīśan	klach	vātānukūlan
तीन-दरवाज़ा	मानव-चालित	इग्नीशन	क्लच	वातानुकूलन

Can you tell me the way to...?
kyā āp mujhe... jāne kā rāstā batāeṅge?
क्या आप मुझे... जाने का रास्ता बताएंगे?

Where is the parking lot?
kār pārkiṅg kahāṃ hai?
कार पार्किंग कहां है?

Can I park here?
kyā maiṃ yahāṃ gāṛī khaṛī kar
saktā hūṃ?
क्या मैं यहां गाड़ी खड़ी कर सकता हूँ?

controls • niyantraṇ • नियंत्रण

left-hand drive | bāīṃ or kī ḍrāiv | बाईं ओर की ड्राइव

right-hand drive | dāīṃ or kī ḍrāiv | दाईं ओर की ड्राइव

car 3 • kār • कार 3

mechanics • yāntrikī • यांत्रिकी

washer fluid reservoir
skrīn voś ḍibbā
स्क्रीन वॉश डिब्बा

dipstick
ḍipasṭik
डिपस्टिक

air filter
vāyu chhalnī
वायु छलनी

brake fluid reservoir
brek dravya ḍibbā
ब्रेक द्रव्य डिब्बा

battery
baiṭrī
बैटरी

bodywork
boḍīvark
बॉडीवर्क

coolant reservoir
kūlenṭ ḍibbā
कूलेंट डिब्बा

cylinder head
silenḍar
सिलेंडर

pipe
pāip
पाईप

sunroof
kār kī chhat
कार की छत

radiator
reḍieṭar
रेडिएटर

fan
paṅkhā
पंखा

engine
injan
इंजन

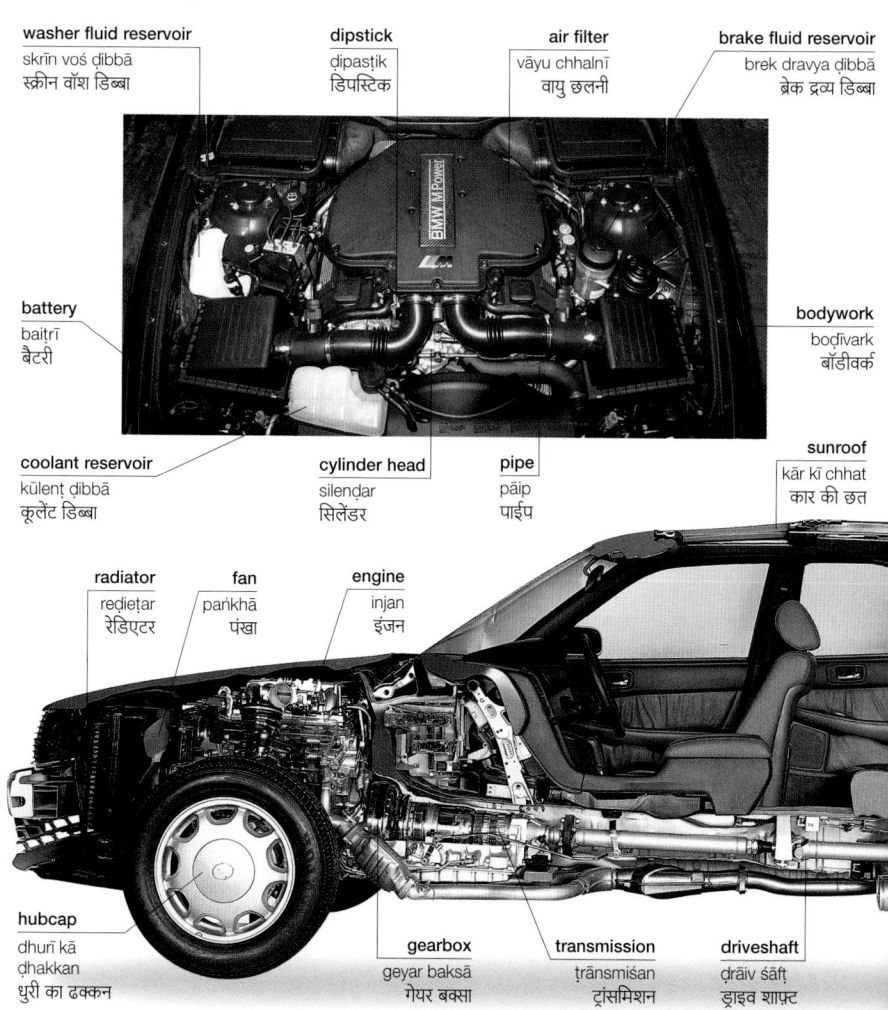

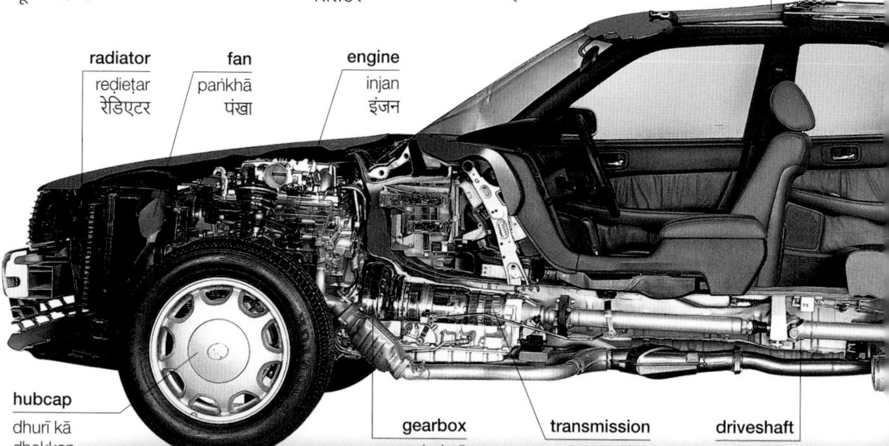

hubcap
dhurī kā ḍhakkan
धुरी का ढक्कन

gearbox
geyar baksā
गेयर बक्सा

transmission
ṭrānsmiśan
ट्रांसमिशन

driveshaft
ḍrāiv śāfṭ
ड्राइव शाफ़्ट

flat tire • paṅkchar • पंक्चर

change a tire (v)
ṭāyar badalnā | टायर बदलना

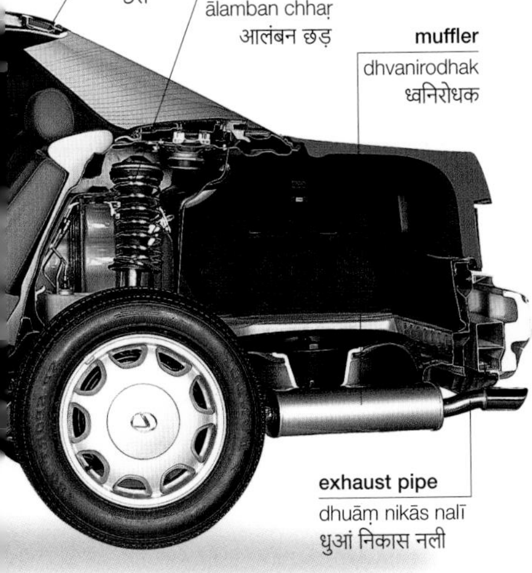

vocabulary • śabdāvalī • शब्दावली

car accident
kār durghaṭnā
कार दुर्घटना

breakdown
brek ḍāun
ब्रेक डाउन

insurance
bīmā
बीमा

tow truck
ṭo ṭrak
टो ट्रक

mechanic
maikenik
मैकेनिक

tire pressure
ṭāyar preśar
टायर प्रेशर

fuse box
fyūz boks
फ़्यूज़ बॉक्स

spark plug
spārk plag
स्पार्क प्लग

fan belt
fain belṭ
फ़ैन बेल्ट

turbocharger
ṭarbo chārjar
टर्बो चार्जर

distributor
vitrak
वितरक

chassis
chesis
चेसिस

parking brake
haiṇḍ brek
हैंड ब्रेक

alternator
pratyāvartak
प्रत्यावर्तक

cam belt
kem belṭ
केम बेल्ट

timing
ṭāimiṅg
टाइमिंग

gas tank
peṭrol ṭaṅkī
पेट्रोल टंकी

My car won't start.
merī kār sṭārṭ nahīṃ ho rahī
मेरी कार स्टार्ट नहीं हो रही।

My car has broken down.
merī gāṛī kharāb ho gaī hai
मेरी गाड़ी खराब हो गई है।

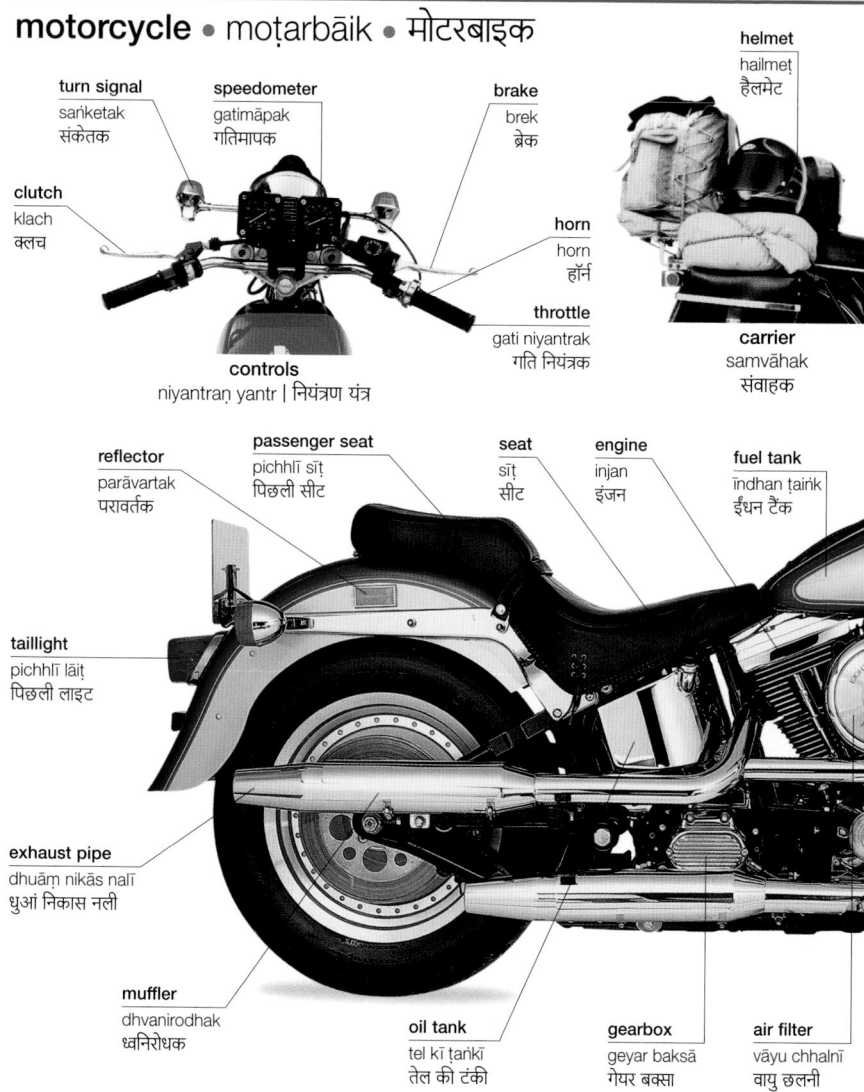

motorcycle • moṭarbāik • मोटरबाइक

controls
niyantraṇ yantr | नियंत्रण यंत्र

carrier
samvāhak
संवाहक

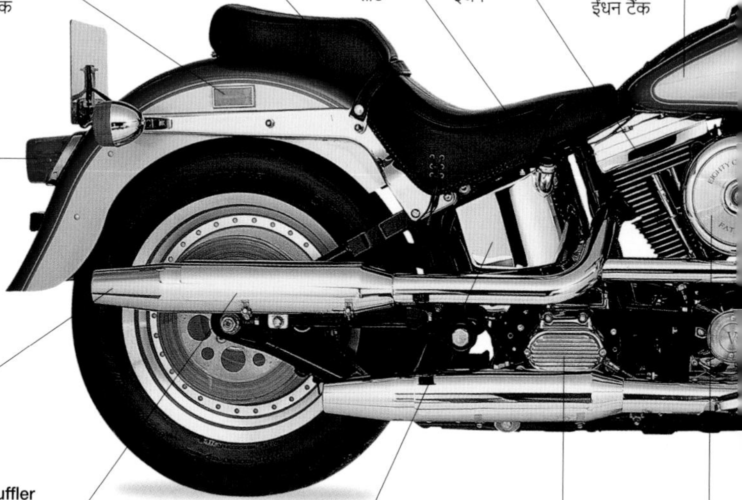

clothing | vastr | वस्त्र

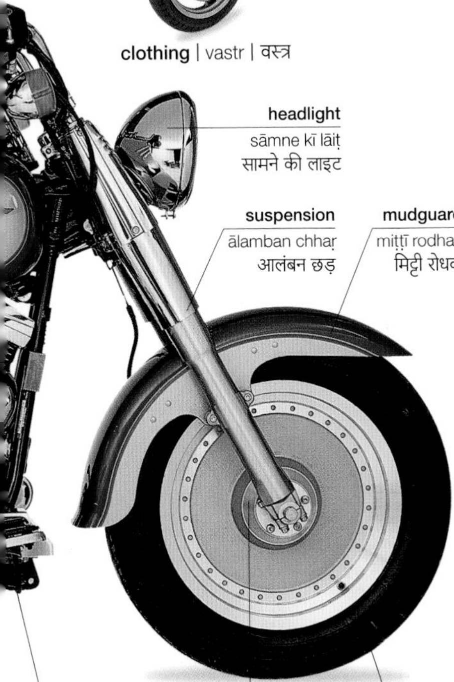

types • prakār • प्रकार

racing bike | resiṅg bāik | रेसिंग बाइक

tourer | moṭar sāikil | मोटर साइकिल

dirt bike | ḍarṭ bāik | डर्ट बाइक

scooter | skūṭar | स्कूटर

bicycle • sāikil • साइकिल

tandem | do sīṭoṃ vālī sāikil
दो सीटों वाली साइकिल

racing bike
resiṅg bāik
रेसिंग बाइक

mountain bike
māunṭen bāik
माउंटेन बाइक

touring bike
ṭūriṅg bāik | टूरिंग बाइक

road bike
roḍ bāik | रोड बाइक

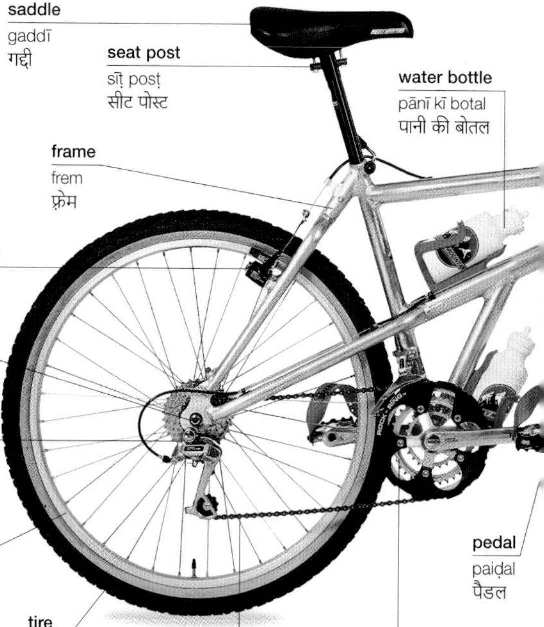

bike lane | sāikil len | साइकिल लेन

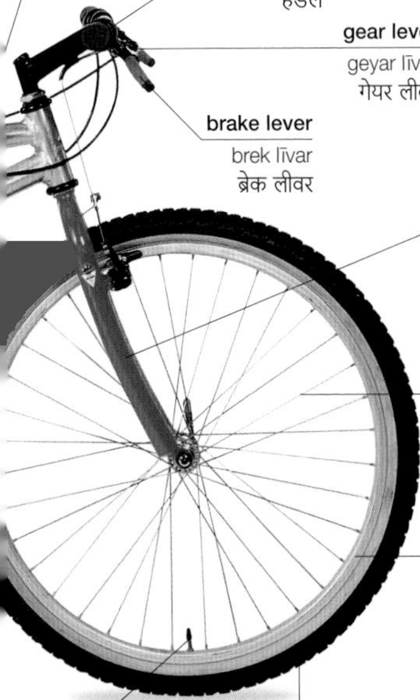

crossbar
krosbār
क्रॉसबार

handlebar
haiṇḍal
हैंडल

gear lever
geyar līvar
गेयर लीवर

brake lever
brek līvar
ब्रेक लीवर

fork
chimṭā
चिमटा

spoke
tīlī
तीली

wheel
pahiyā
पहिया

valve
vālv
वाल्व

tread
ṭāyar par ḍizāin
टायर पर डिज़ाइन

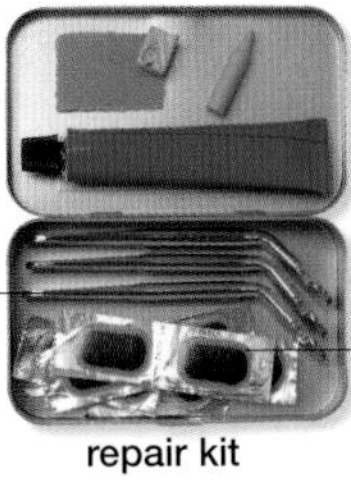

tire lever
ṭāyar līvar
टायर लीवर

patch
ṭyūb chippī
ट्यूब चिप्पी

repair kit
marammat kā sāmān | मरम्मत का सामान

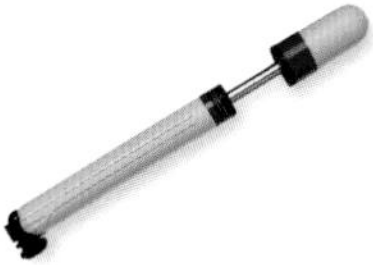

pump
pamp
पंप

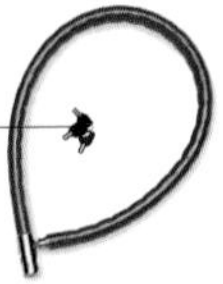

key
chābī
चाबी

lock
tālā
ताला

inner tube
bhītrī ṭyūb
भीतरी ट्यूब

child seat
śiśu sīṭ
शिशु सीट

vocabulary • śabdāvalī • शब्दावली

headlight laimp लैंप	**kickstand** kiksṭaiṇḍ किकस्टैंड	**brake block** brek blok ब्रेक ब्लॉक	**basket** ṭokrī टोकरी	**toe clip** ṭo klip टो क्लिप	**brake (v)** roknā रोकना
rear light pichhe kī lāiṭ पीछे की लाइट	**bike rack** bāik raik बाइक रैक	**cable** tār तार	**dynamo** ḍāyanamo डायनमो	**toe strap** ṭo sṭrep टो स्ट्रेप	**cycle (v)** sāikil chalānā साइकिल चलाना
reflector parāvartak परावर्तक	**training wheels** sṭeblāizars स्टेबलाइज़र्स	**sprocket** chakradant चक्रदंत	**flat tire** paṅkchar पंक्चर	**pedal (v)** paiḍal mārnā पैडल मारना	**change gears (v)** geyar badalnā गेयर बदलना

train • relgāṛī • रेलगाड़ी

train station | relve sṭeśan | रेलवे स्टेशन

types of train • relgāṛī ke prakār • रेलगाड़ी के प्रकार

steam train | bhāp chālit relgāṛī
भाप चालित रेलगाड़ी

diesel train | ḍīzal relgāṛī | डीज़ल रेलगाड़ी

electric train
vidyut relgāṛī | विद्युत रेलगाड़ी

high-speed train
tez gati relgāṛī | तेज़ गति रेलगाड़ी

monorail | ekpaṭrī relgāṛī
एकपटरी रेलगाड़ी

subway | bhūmigat relgāṛī
भूमिगत रेलगाड़ी

tram
ṭrām | ट्राम

freight train
mālgāṛī | मालगाड़ी

luggage rack
sāmān kī jagah
सामान की जगह

window
khiṛkī
खिड़की

door
darvāzā
दरवाज़ा

track
paṭrī
पटरी

seat
sīṭ
सीट

compartment | ḍibbā | डिब्बा

ticket gates
ṭikaṭ bairiyar | टिकट बैरियर

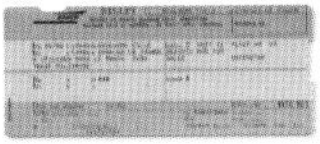

ticket
ṭikaṭ | टिकट

dining car | bhojanyān | भोजनयान

public address system
jan sūchnā praṇālī
जन सूचना प्रणाली

schedule
samaya sārṇī
समय-सारणी

concourse | relve parisar | रेलवे परसिर

sleeping compartment
śayan yān | शयन यान

vocabulary • śabdāvalī • शब्दावली

railroad network
rel neṭvark
रेल नेटवर्क

express train
antar nagarīya relgāṛī
अंतर नगरीय रेलगाड़ी

rush hour
vyast samaya
व्यस्त समय

subway map
bhūmigat nakśā
भूमिगत नक़्शा

delay
vilamb
विलंब

fare
kirāyā
किराया

ticket office
ṭikaṭ ghar
टिकट घर

ticket inspector
ṭikaṭ nirīkṣak
टिकट निरीक्षक

transfer (v)
badalnā
बदलना

live rail
chālū paṭrī
चालू पटरी

signal
signal
सिग्नल

emergency lever
āpātkālīn līvar
आपातकालीन लीवर

aircraft • vāyuyān • वायुयान

airliner • yātrī vimān • यात्री विमान

cockpit
chālak kakṣ
चालक कक्ष
exit
nikās dvār
निकास द्वार
engine
injan
इंजन
fuselage
fyūzilej
फ़्यूज़िलेज
wing
paṅkh
पंख
tail
sirā
सिरा
rudder
raḍar | रडर
nose
agra bhāg
अग्र भाग
nosewheel
nāsā pahiyā
नासा पहिया
landing gear
lainḍiṅg giyar
लैंडिंग गियर
aileron
pichhlī patvār
पिछली पतवार
fin
paṅkh
पंख
tailplane
pichhlā samtal paṅkh
पिछला समतल पंख

cabin • kebin • केबिन

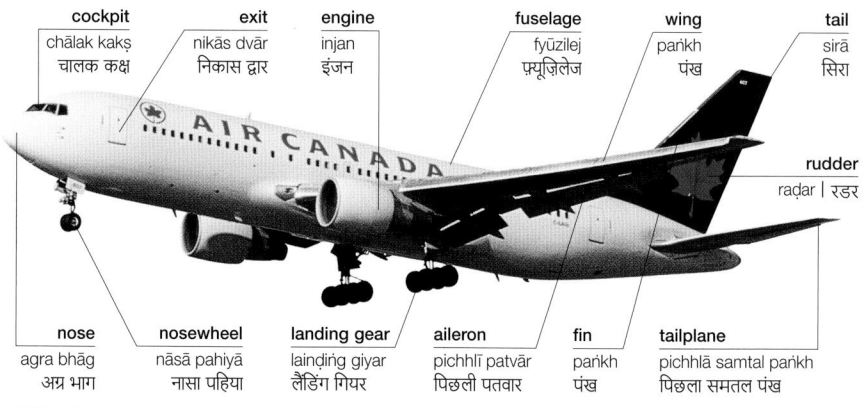

emergency exit
āpātkālīn nikās
आपातकालीन निकास
flight attendant
vimān parichārikā
विमान परिचारिका
overhead bin
ūprī lokar
ऊपरी लॉकर
window
khiṛkī
खिड़की
air vent
vāyu chhidr
वायु छिद्र
reading light
paṛhne kī battī
पढ़ने की बत्ती
row
ḳatār
क़तार
seat
sīṭ
सीट
tray-table
ṭre-ṭebal
ट्रे-टेबल
armrest
hatthā
हत्था
aisle
galiyārā
गलियारा
seat back
sīṭ kī pīṭh
सीट की पीठ

hot-air balloon
garm havā kā gubbārā
गर्म हवा का गुब्बारा

ultralight
māikrolāiṭ
माइक्रोलाइट

glider
glāiḍar
ग्लाइडर

biplane
bāiplen
बाइप्लेन

propeller
chālak yantr
चालक यंत्र

light aircraft
halkā vayuyān
हल्का वायुयान

seaplane
naukā vimān
नौका विमान

private jet
nijī vimān | निजी विमान

fighter plane
laṛākū vimān | लड़ाकू विमान

missile
misāil | मिसाइल

rotor blade
roṭar bleḍ
रोटर ब्लेड

helicopter
hailīkopṭar | हैलीकॉप्टर

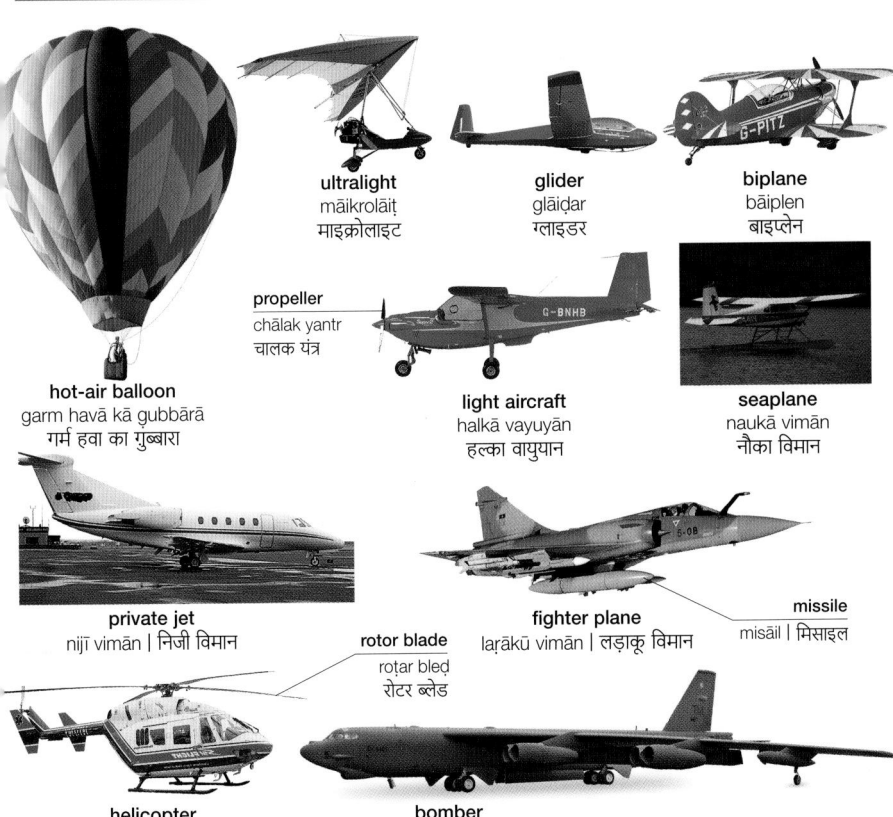

bomber
bamvarṣak | बमवर्षक

vocabulary • śabdāvalī • शब्दावली

pilot
vimān chālak
विमान चालक

copilot
sah-vimān chālak
सह-विमान चालक

take off (v)
uṛān bharnā
उड़ान भरना

fly (v)
uṛnā
उड़ना

land (v)
utarnā
उतरना

altitude
ūṃchāī
ऊंचाई

economy class
sāmānya śreṇī
सामान्य श्रेणी

business class
vyāvasāyik śreṇī
व्यावसायिक श्रेणी

carry-on luggage
hāth kā sāmān
हाथ का सामान

seat belt
sīṭ belṭ
सीट बेल्ट

airport • havāī aḍḍā • हवाई अड्डा

apron
epran
एप्रन

baggage trailer
sāmān gāṛī
सामान गाड़ी

terminal
ṭarminal
टर्मिनल

service vehicle
sevā vāhan
सेवा वाहन

jetway
mārg
मार्ग

airliner | vāyuyān | वायुयान

vocabulary • śabdāvalī • शब्दावली

runway
havāī paṭṭī
हवाई पट्टी

international flight
antarrāṣṭrīya uṛān
अंतरराष्ट्रीय उड़ान

domestic flight
gharelū uṛān
घरेलू उड़ान

connection
sanyojan
संयोजन

flight number
uṛān nambar
उड़ान नंबर

immigration
āpravās
आप्रवास

customs
sīmā śulk
सीमा शुल्क

excess baggage
atirikt sāmān
अतिरिक्त सामान

baggage carousel
sāmān kī chal paṭṭī
सामान की चल पट्टी

security
surakṣā
सुरक्षा

x-ray machine
eks-re maśīn
एक्स-रे मशीन

travel brochure
paryaṭan sūchnā pustikā
पर्यटन सूचना पुस्तिका

vacation
chhuṭṭiyāṃ
छुट्टियां

check in (v)
chek in
चेक इन

control tower
niyantraṇ ṭovar
नियंत्रण टॉवर

book a flight (v)
uṛān buk karnā
उड़ान बुक करना

carry-on luggage
hāth kā sāmān
हाथ का सामान

luggage
sāmān
सामान

cart
ṭrolī
ट्रॉली

check-in desk
chek-in ḍesk
चेक-इन डेस्क

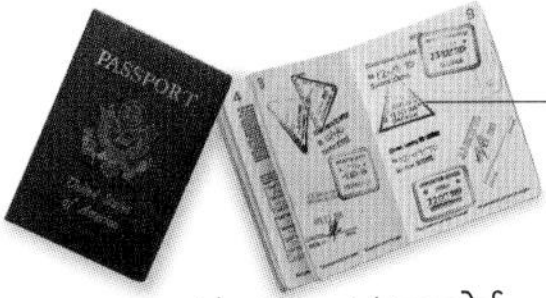

visa
vīzā
वीज़ा

passport | pāsporṭ | पासपोर्ट

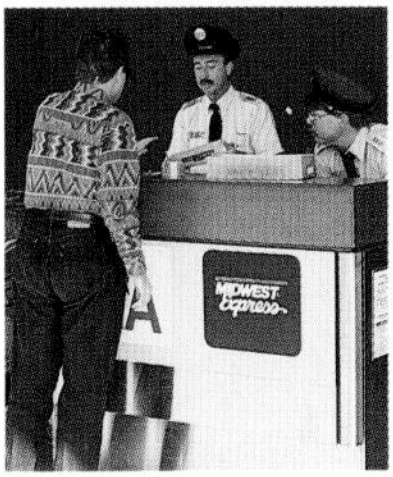

passport control
pāsporṭ kanṭrol
पासपोर्ट कंट्रोल

boarding pass
borḍiṅg pās
बोर्डिंग पास

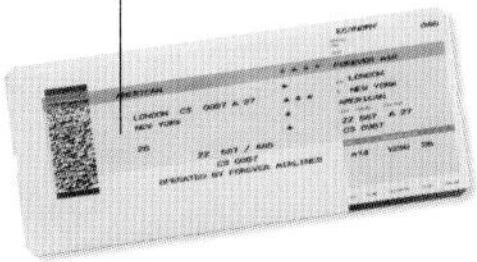

ticket
ṭikaṭ
टिकट

gate number
dvār saṃkhyā
द्वार संख्या

departure lounge
prasthān kakṣ | प्रस्थान कक्ष

destination
gantavya sthān
गंतव्य स्थान

departures
prasthān
प्रस्थान

arrivals
āgman
आगमन

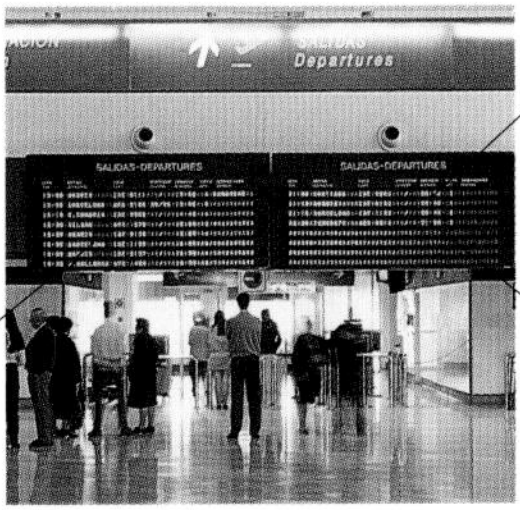

information screen
sūchnā skrīn | सूचना स्क्रीन

duty-free shop
śulk mukt dukān
शुल्क मुक्त दुकान

baggage claim
sāmān vāpsī
सामान वापसी

taxi stand
ṭaiksī ḳatār
टैक्सी-क़तार

car rental
kirāe kī kār
किराए की कार

ship • jahāz • जहाज़

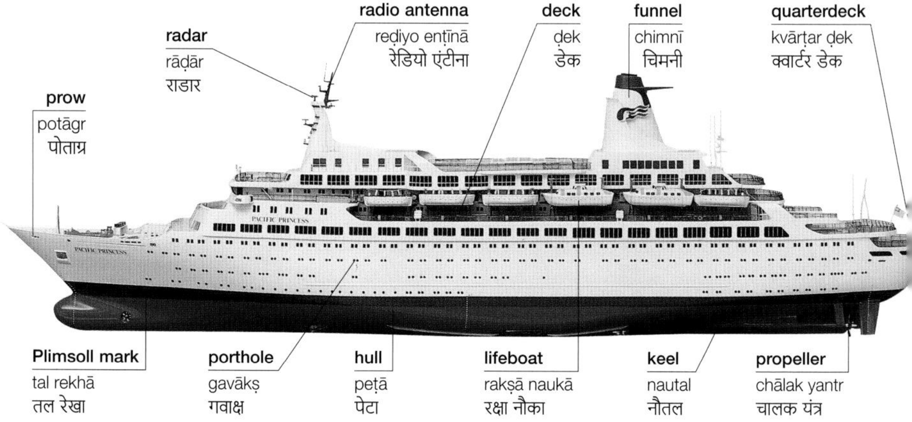

ocean liner | samudrī jahāz | समुद्री जहाज़

bridge
potādhikārī kakṣ
पोताधिकारी कक्ष

engine room
injan kakṣ
इंजन कक्ष

cabin
kaibin | कैबिन

galley
pot | पोत

vocabulary • śabdāvalī • शब्दावली

dock
dok
डॉक

port
bandargāh
बंदरगाह

gangway
mārgikā
मार्गिका

anchor
laṅgar
लंगर

bollard
rakṣā stambh
रक्षा-स्तंभ

windlass
charkhī
चरखी

captain
kaptān
कप्तान

speedboat
moṭar naukā
मोटर नौका

rowboat
chappū vālī nāv
चप्पू वाली नाव

canoe
ḍoṅgī
डोंगी

other ships • anya jahāz • अन्य जहाज़

ferry | yātrī vāhak jahāz | यात्री वाहक जहाज़

inflatable dinghy | havā bharī ḍoṅgī | हवा भरी डोंगी

hydrofoil | jal patrak
जल पत्रक

yacht
krīṛā naukā | क्रीड़ा नौका

catamaran
donāvā | दोनावा

tugboat
karṣ naukā | कर्ष नौका

hovercraft
hovar krāfṭ | होवर क्राफ़्ट

container ship
māl pot | माल पोत

sailboat
pāl naukā | पाल नौका

freighter | mālvāhak
मालवाहक

oil tanker
tel pot | तेल पोत

aircraft carrier | vāyuyān vāhak | वायुयान वाहक

battleship
jaṅgī jahāz | जंगी जहाज़

submarine
panḍubbī | पनडुब्बी

port • bandargāh • बंदरगाह

warehouse
mālgodām
मालगोदाम

crane
kren
क्रेन

forklift
kren
क्रेन

access road
praveś mārg
प्रवेश मार्ग

customs house
sīmā śulk chaukī
सीमा शुल्क चौकी

dock
godī
गोदी

container
māl ḍibbā
माल डिब्बा

quay
jahāz ghāṭ
जहाज़ घाट

cargo
kārgo
कार्गो

container port | māl vāhak bandargāh
माल वाहक बंदरगाह

ferry terminal
yātrī jahāz ṭarminal
यात्री जहाज़ टर्मिनल

ferry
yātrī jahāz
यात्री जहाज़

ticket office
ṭikaṭ ghar
टिकट घर

passenger
yātrī
यात्री

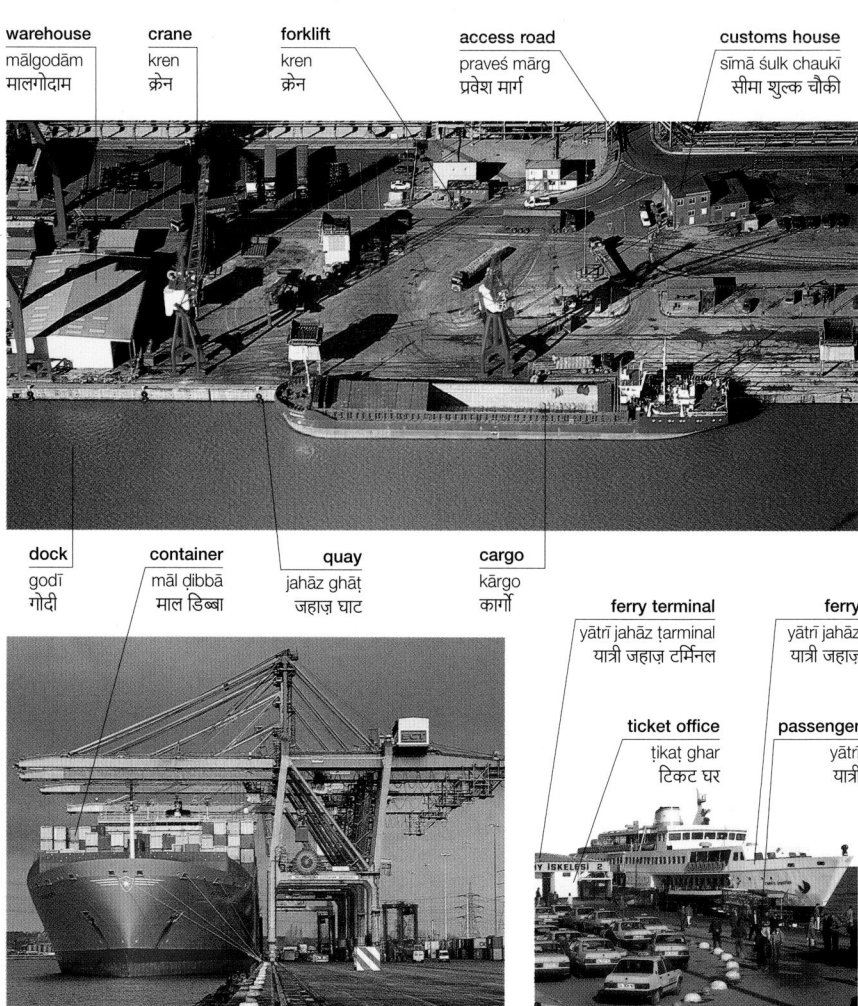

passenger port
yātrī bandargāh | यात्री बंदरगाह

fishing port | matsya bandargāh | मत्स्य बंदरगाह

marina | taṭvartī ḳasbā | तटवर्ती क़स्बा

harbor | bandargāh | बंदरगाह

pier | potghāṭ | पोतघाट

jetty | jeṭī | जेटी

shipyard | pot nirmāṇ ghāṭ
पोत निर्माण घाट

lighthouse | prakāś stambh | प्रकाश स्तंभ

buoy
boyā | बोया

vocabulary • śabdāvalī • शब्दावली

coast guard
taṭrakṣak
तटरक्षक

harbor master
bandargāh pramukh
बंदरगाह प्रमुख

drop anchor (v)
laṅgar ḍālnā
लंगर डालना

dry dock
sūkhā bandargāh
सूखा बंदरगाह

moor (v)
nāv bāndhnā
नाव बांधना

dock (v)
bandargāh meṃ lānā
बंदरगाह में लाना

board (v)
chaṛhnā
चढ़ना

disembark (v)
jahāz se utarnā
जहाज़ से उतरना

set sail (v)
yātrā ārambh karnā
यात्रा आरंभ करना

ULTRA
3
DUNLOP
DDH III
4
DUNLOP
MOLITOR
TOUR
EDITION
1
ProStaff
4
SPRINGS
GOLF CLUB
TOP-FLITE
HOT XL
4
ProStaff
4
RAM TOUR
1
MAXFLI
TOP-FLITE
STRATA
3
DISTANCE

sports
khelkūd
खेलकूद

football • fuṭbol • फ़ुटबॉल

goalpost
gol posṭ
गोल पोस्ट

sideline
sāiḍ lāin
साइड लाइन

referee
refrī
रेफ़री

goal line
gol lāin
गोल लाइन

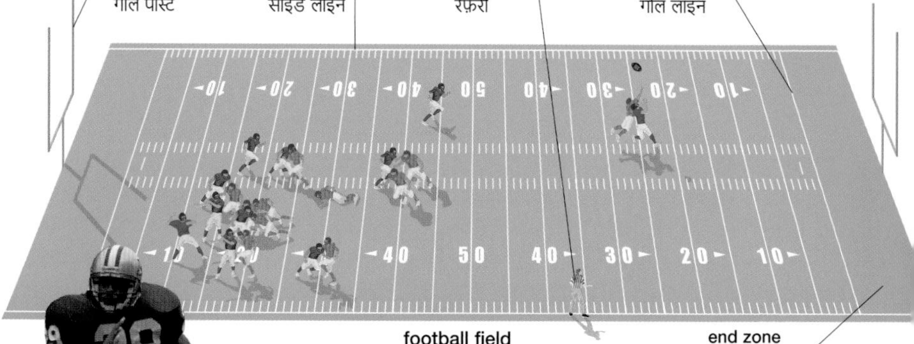

football field
fuṭbol kā maidān | फ़ुटबॉल का मैदान

end zone
samāpti kṣetr
समाप्ति क्षेत्र

football
fuṭbol | फ़ुटबॉल

cleat
jūtā
जूता

football player
fuṭbol khilāṛī
फ़ुटबॉल खिलाड़ी

pads
paid | पैड

helmet
hailmeṭ | हैलमेट

tackle (v)
pratirodh karnā | प्रतिरोध करना

pass (v)
pās denā | पास देना

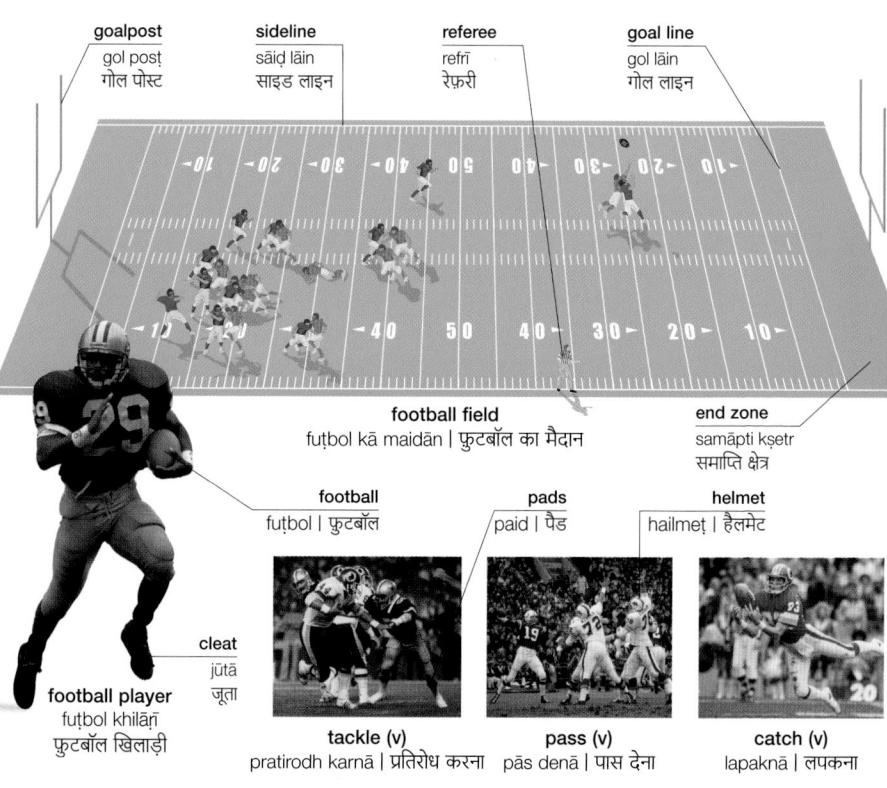

catch (v)
lapaknā | लपकना

vocabulary • śabdāvalī • शब्दावली

time out
samaya samāpt
समय समाप्त

team
ṭīm
टीम

defense
bachāv
बचाव

cheerleader
protsāhak ṭīm netā
प्रोत्साहक टीम नेता

What is the score?
kyā skor huā hai?
क्या स्कोर हुआ है?

fumble
binā soche kik mārnā
बिना सोचे किक मारना

attack
hamlā
हमला

score
skor
स्कोर

touchdown
gend se zamīn chhūnā
गेंद से ज़मीन छूना

Who is winning?
kaun jīt rahā hai?
कौन जीत रहा है?

rugby • ragbī • रग्बी

rugby field | ragbī kā maidān | रग्बी का मैदान

throw (v)
bol pheṃknā
बॉल फेंकना

ball
bol
बॉल

kick (v)
kik mārnā
किक मारना

rugby uniform
ragbī sṭrip
रग्बी स्ट्रिप

pass (v)
bol ek-dūsre ko denā
बॉल एक-दूसरे को देना

tackle (v)
pratirodh karnā
प्रतिरोध करना

try
ṭrāi
ट्राइ

player
khilāṛī
खिलाड़ी

ruck | khilāṛiyoṃ kā dal | खिलाड़ियों का दल

scrum | bol ko ghernā | बॉल को घेरना

soccer • sokar • सॉकर

soccer player
fuṭbolar
फ़ुटबॉलर

soccer ball
fuṭbol
फ़ुटबॉल

soccer uniform
fuṭbol sṭrip
फ़ुटबॉल स्ट्रिप

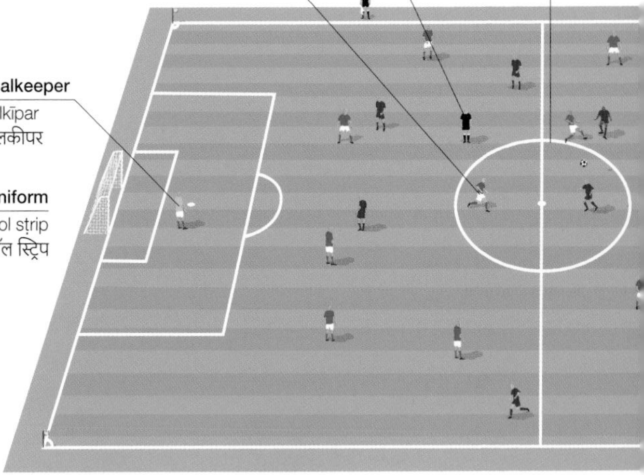

forward
agrim paṅkti kā khilāṛī
अग्रिम पंक्ति का खिलाड़ी

referee
refrī
रेफ़री

center circle
kendrīya gherā
केंद्रीय घेरा

goalkeeper
golkīpar
गोलकीपर

soccer field
fuṭbol maidān | फ़ुटबॉल मैदान

goalpost
gol posṭ
गोल पोस्ट

net
jāl
जाल

crossbar
krosbār
क्रॉसबार

goal | gol | गोल

dribble (v) | gend dhakelnā
गेंद धकेलना

head (v)
sir se mārnā | सिर से मारना

wall
pratirakṣak
paṅkti
प्रतिरक्षक पंक्ति

free kick | frī kik | फ़्री किक

penalty area
penalṭī kṣetr
पेनल्टी क्षेत्र

goal line
gol sīmā
गोल सीमा

goal area
gol kṣetr
गोल क्षेत्र

goal
gol
गोल

defender
pratirakṣak
प्रतिरक्षक

linesman
lāins main
लाइन्स मैन

corner flag
kornar jhaṇḍā
कॉर्नर-झंडा

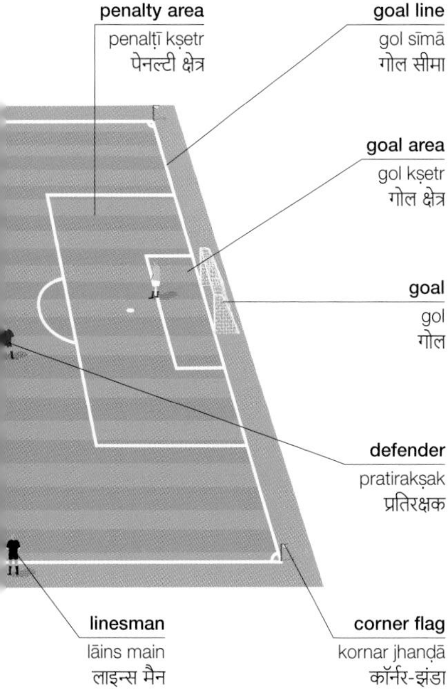

throw-in
bol pheṃknā | बॉल फेंकना

kick (v) | kik mārnā
किक मारना

cleat
jūtā
जूता

pass (v) | pās denā
पास देना

shoot (v) | zor se
mārnā | ज़ोर से मारना

save (v) | gol roknā
गोल रोकना

tackle (v) | pratirodh karnā
प्रतिरोध करना

vocabulary • śabdāvalī • शब्दावली

stadium	**foul**	**yellow card**	**league**	**extra time**
sṭeḍiyam	niyam ullaṅghan	pīlā kārḍ	līg	atirikt samaya
स्टेडियम	नियम उल्लंघन	पीला कार्ड	लीग	अतिरिक्त समय
score a goal (v)	**corner**	**offside**	**tie**	**substitute**
gol dāgnā	kornar	of sāiḍ	anirṇit maich	vaikalpik khilāṛī
गोल दाग़ना	कॉर्नर	ऑफ़ साइड	अनिर्णित मैच	वैकल्पिक खिलाड़ी
penalty	**red card**	**send off**	**halftime**	**substitution**
penalṭī	lāl kārḍ	seṇḍ of	ādhā vakt	vikalp bulānā
पैनल्टी	लाल कार्ड	सेंड ऑफ़	आधा वक़्त	विकल्प बुलाना

hockey • hokī • हॉकी

ice hockey • āis hokī • आइस हॉकी

ice hockey rink
āis hokī kā maidān
आइस हॉकी का मैदान

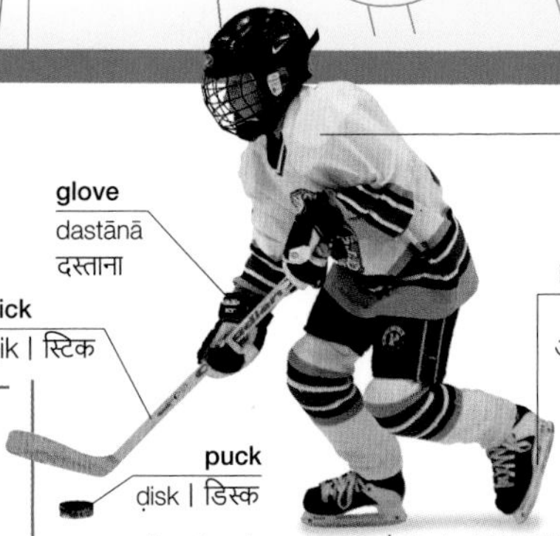

ice hockey player | āis hokī khilāṛī
आइस हॉकी खिलाड़ी

field hockey • fīlḍ hokī • फ़ील्ड हॉकी

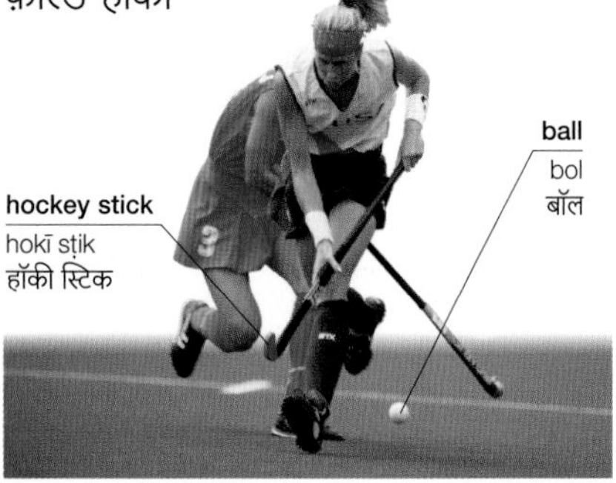

skate (v) | skeṭiṅg karnā | स्केटिंग करना

hit (v)
bol mārnā | बॉल मारना

cricket • kriket̤ • क्रिकेट

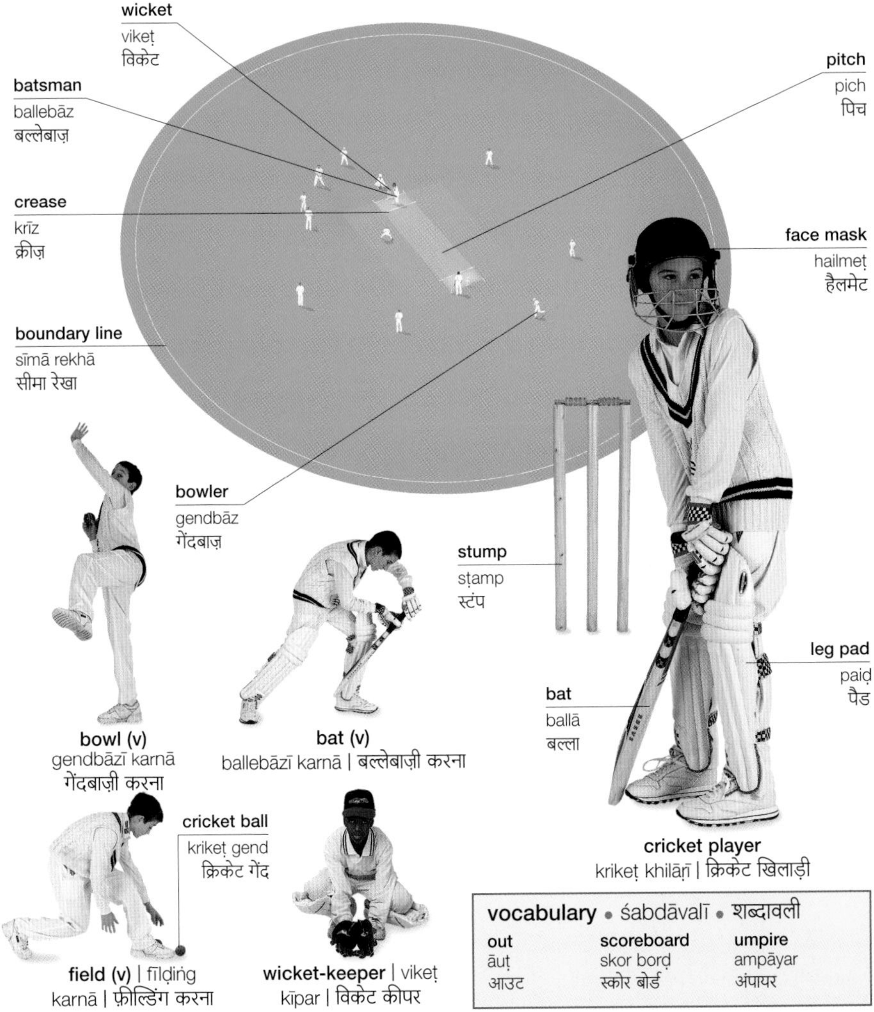

vocabulary • śabdāvalī • शब्दावली

out āut̤ आउट	**scoreboard** skor bord̤ स्कोर बोर्ड	**umpire** ampāyar अंपायर

basketball • bāskeṭ bol • बास्केट बॉल

court | maidān | मैदान

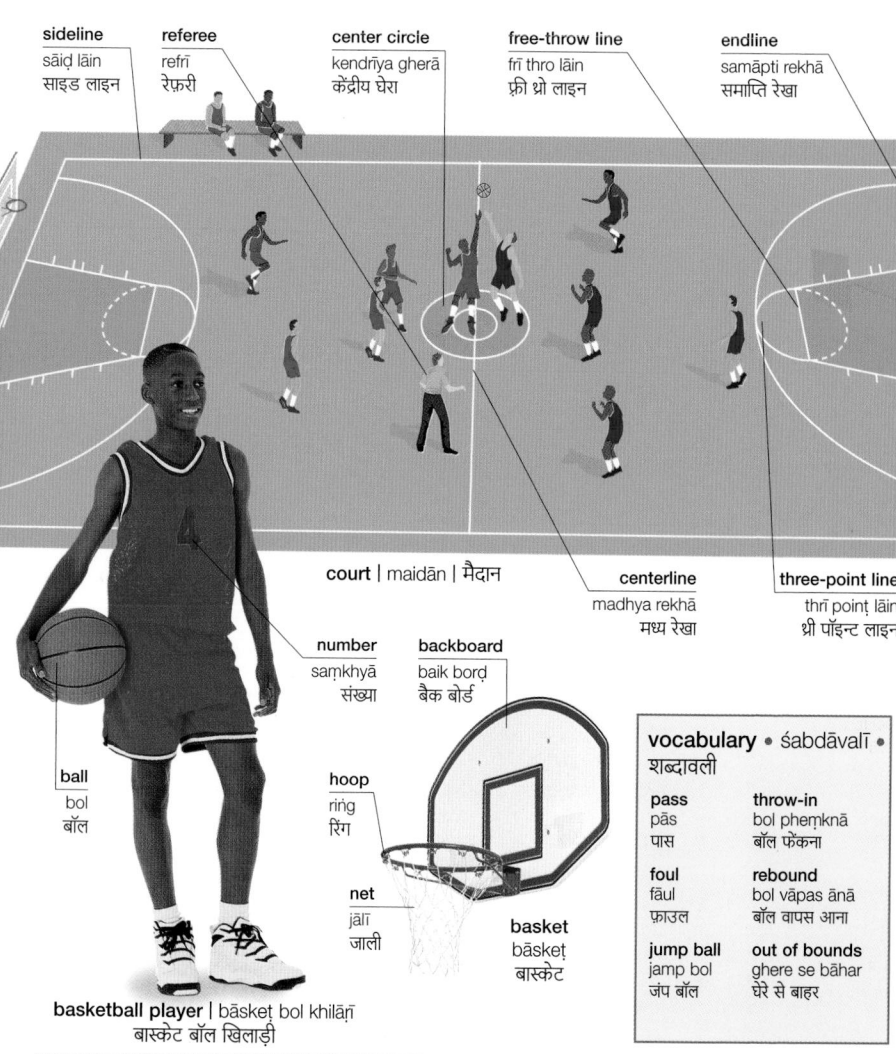

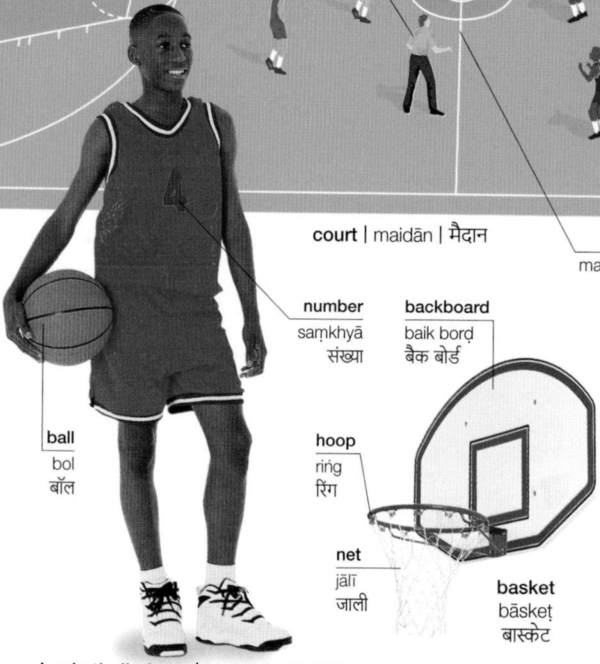

basketball player | bāskeṭ bol khilāṛī
बास्केट बॉल खिलाड़ी

vocabulary • śabdāvalī • शब्दावली

pass pās पास	**throw-in** bol pheṃknā बॉल फेंकना
foul fāul फ़ाउल	**rebound** bol vāpas ānā बॉल वापस आना
jump ball jamp bol जंप बॉल	**out of bounds** ghere se bāhar घेरे से बाहर

actions • gativid hiyāṃ • गतिविधियां

throw (v)
bol pheṃknā
बॉल फेंकना

catch (v)
bol pakaṛnā
बॉल पकड़ना

shoot (v)
gol mārnā
गोल मारना

jump (v)
kūdnā
कूदना

mark (v) | bol niśāne par mārnā | बॉल निशाने पर मारना

block (v) | bol roknā | बॉल रोकना

dribble (v) | ṭappā mārnā | टप्पा मारना

dunk (v) | bol bāskeṭ meṃ ḍālnā | बॉल बास्केट में डालना

volleyball • volībol • वॉलीबॉल

block (v)
bol roknā
बॉल रोकना

net
jāl
जाल

dig (v)
bol lapakne ko taiyār rahnā
बॉल लपकने को तैयार रहना

referee
refrī
रेफ़री

knee support
nī saporṭ
नी सपोर्ट

court | maidān | मैदान

baseball • besbol • बेसबॉल

field • maidān • मैदान

left field
left fīlḍ
लेफ्ट फ़ील्ड

infield
in fīlḍ
इन फ़ील्ड

center field
senṭar fīlḍ
सेंटर फ़ील्ड

bat
ballā
बल्ला

helmet
hailmeṭ
हैलमेट

baseman
besmain
बेसमैन

pitcher's mound
pichar kā sthān
पिचर का स्थान

home plate
vāpas apne sthān par pahumchnā
वापस अपने स्थान पर पहुंचना

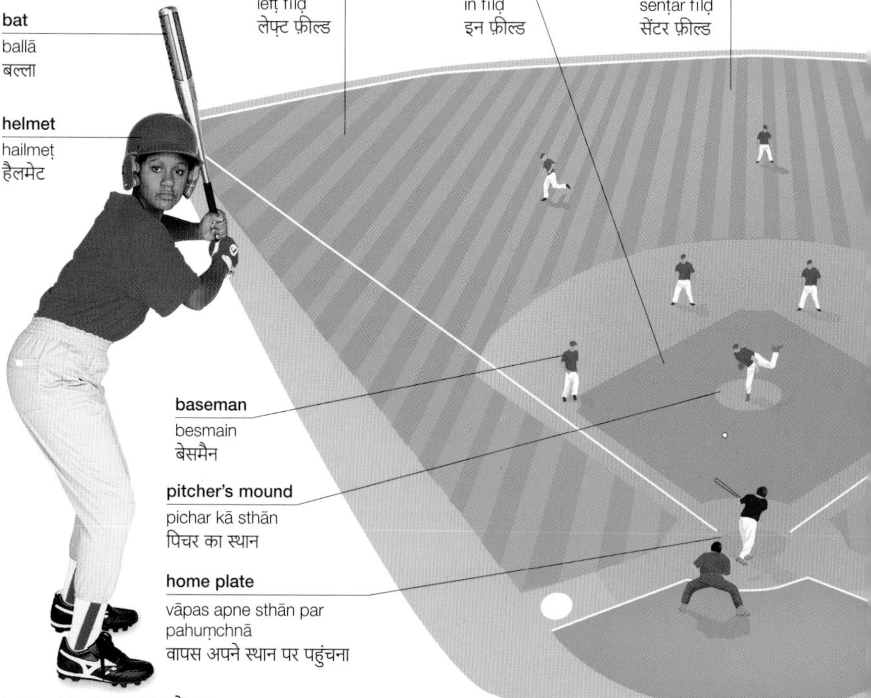

batter | ballebāz़ | बल्लेबाज़

vocabulary • śabdāvalī • शब्दावली		
inning	**safe**	**foul ball**
pārī	surakṣit	fāul gend
पारी	सुरक्षित	फ़ाउल गेंद
run	**out**	**strike**
ran	āuṭ	sṭrāik
रन	आउट	स्ट्राइक

ball
gend
गेंद

glove | dastānā
दस्ताना

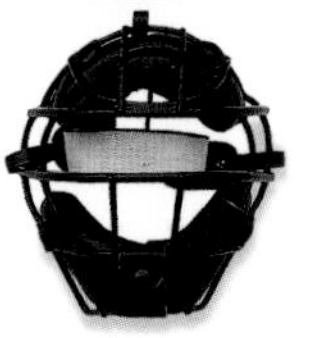

mask | mukhauṭā
मुखौटा

outfield
āuṭ fīlḍ
आउट फ़ील्ड

right field
rāiṭ fīlḍ
राइट फ़ील्ड

foul line
fāul lāin
फ़ाउल लाइन

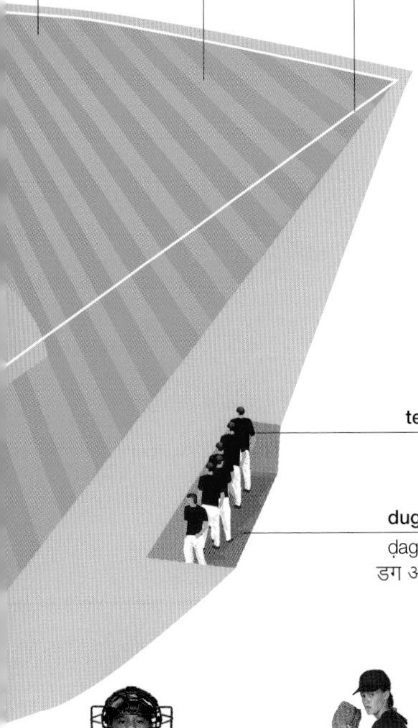

team
ṭīm
टीम

dugout
ḍag āuṭ
डग आउट

catcher
kaichar | कैचर

pitcher
pichar | पिचर

actions • kriyāeṃ • क्रियाएं

throw (v) | bol pheṃknā
बॉल फेंकना

catch (v) | gend
pakaṛnā | गेंद पकड़ना

run (v)
dauṛnā | दौड़ना

field (v) | fīlḍiṅg karnā
फ़ील्डिंग करना

slide (v)
phisalnā
फिसलना

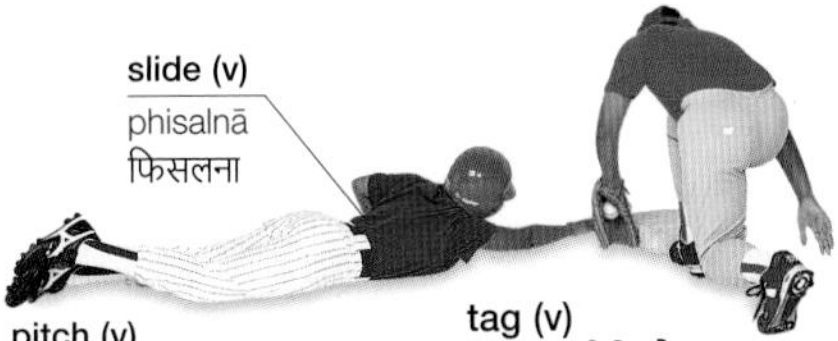

tag (v)
pīchhe dauṛnā | पीछे दौड़ना

pitch (v)
gend
pheṃknā
गेंद
फेंकना

bat (v)
balle se khelnā
बल्ले से खेलना

umpire
ampāyar
अंपायर

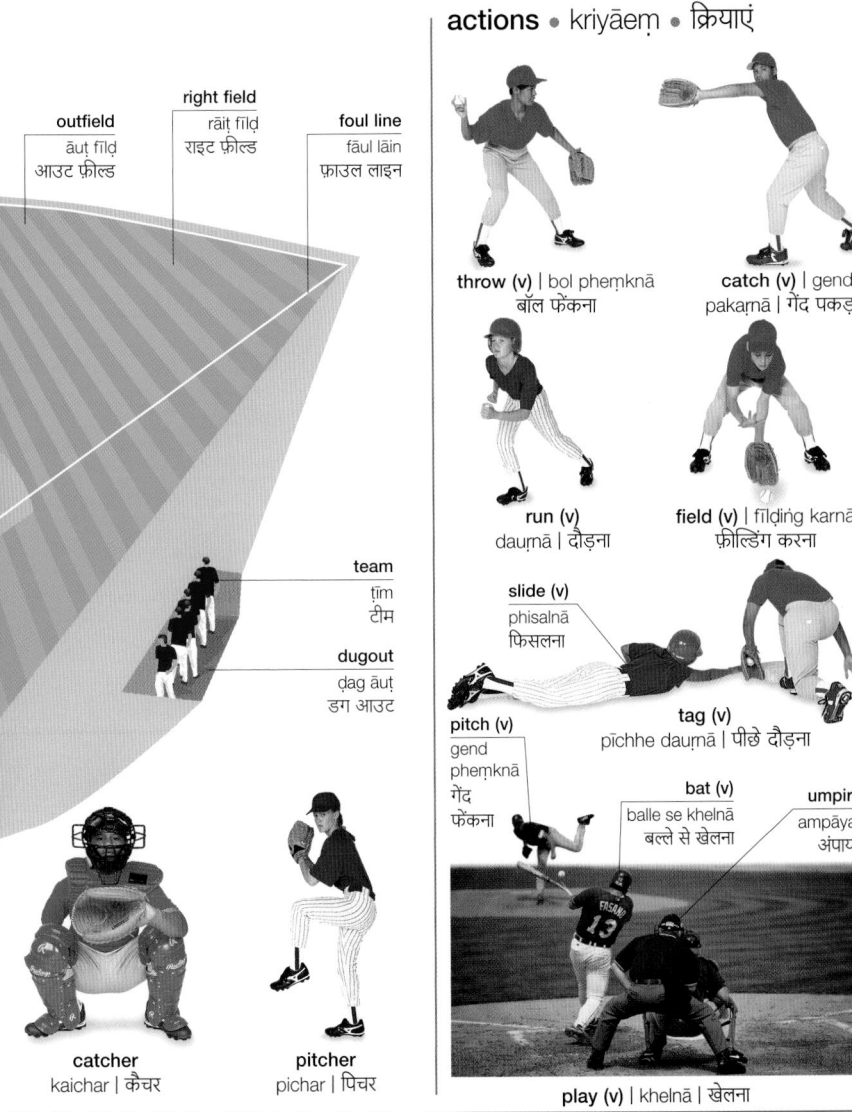

play (v) | khelnā | खेलना

tennis • ṭenis • टेनिस

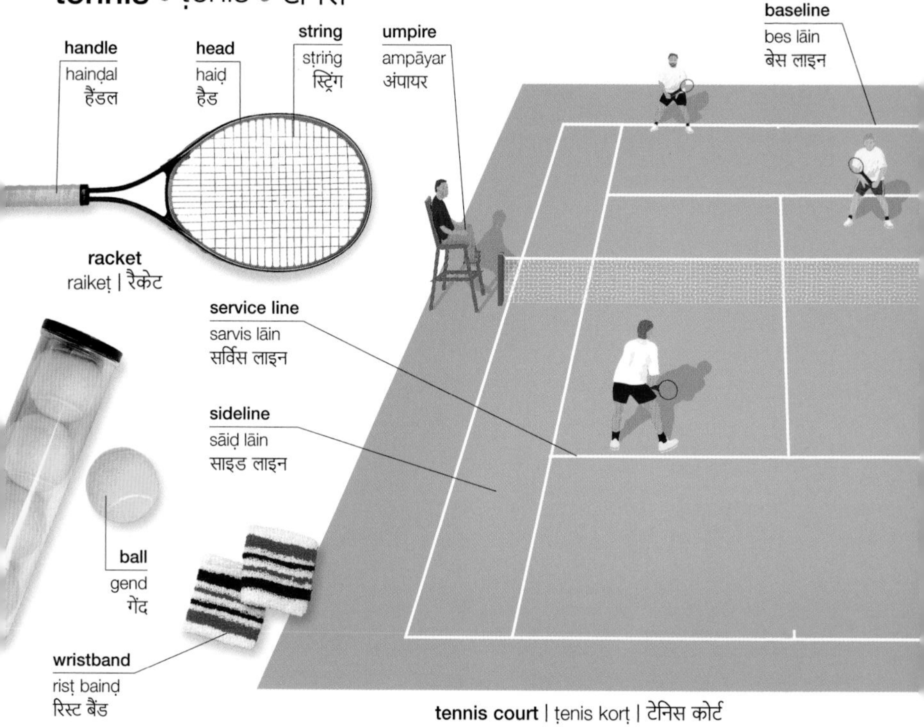

tennis court | ṭenis korṭ | टेनिस कोर्ट

vocabulary • śabdāvalī • शब्दावली

singles ekal एकल	**set** saiṭ सैट	**deuce** barābarī बराबरी	**fault** galat śoṭ ग़लत शॉट	**slice** galat prahār ग़लत प्रहार	**let!** khilāṛī ko roknā खिलाड़ी को रोकना
doubles yugal युगल	**match** maich मैच	**love** śūnya शून्य	**dropshot** ḍropśoṭ ड्रॉप शॉट	**rally** kaṛā pariśram कड़ा परिश्रम	**championship** chaimpiyanśip चैम्पियनशिप
game khel खेल	**spin** spin स्पिन	**tiebreaker** nirṇāyak aṃk निर्णायक अंक	**advantage** anukūl sthiti अनुकूल स्थिति	**linesman** lāins main लाइन्स मैन	**ace** pahlī sarvis se banā aṃk पहली सर्विस से बना अंक

net
neṭ
नेट

smash
zor se mārnā
ज़ोर से मारना

ballboy
bol bvoya
बॉल ब्वॉय

serve (v)
sarvis karnā
सर्विस करना

tennis shoes
ṭenis jūte
टेनिस जूते

player
khilāṛī | खिलाड़ी

strokes • sṭroks • स्ट्रोक्स

serve
sarv | सर्व

volley
volī | वॉली

return
riṭarn | रिटर्न

lob | lob
लोब

forehand
forhainḍ | फ़ोरहैंड

backhand
baikhainḍ | बैकहैंड

racket games • raikeṭ ke khel • रैकेट के खेल

shuttlecock
chiṛiyā
चिड़िया

paddle
baiṭ
बैट

badminton
baiḍminṭan | बैडमिंटन

table tennis
ṭebal ṭenis | टेबल टेनिस

squash
skvaiś | स्क्वैश

racquetball
raikeṭ bol | रैकेट बॉल

golf • golf • गोल्फ़

green
grīn
ग्रीन

bunker
baṅkar
बंकर

flag
jhaṇḍā
झंडा

teeing ground
ṭīiṅg grāunḍ
टीइंग ग्राउंड

hole
hol
होल

swing (v)
śoṭ mārnā
शॉट मारना

fairway
sāf rāstā
साफ़ रास्ता

rou
ūba
khā
ऊब
ख

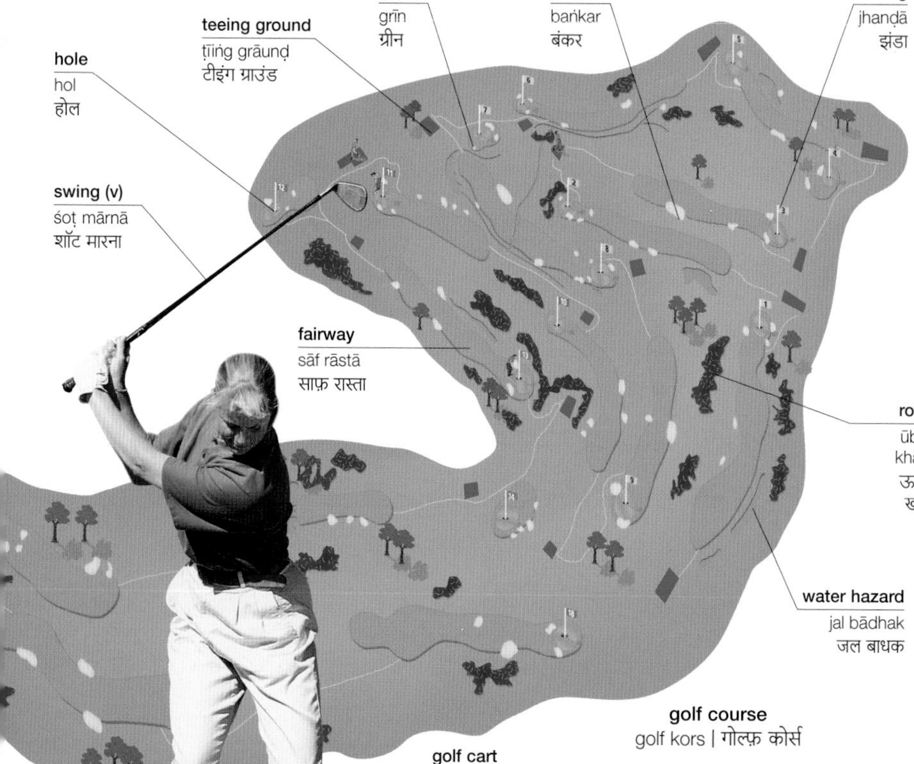

water hazard
jal bādhak
जल बाधक

golf course
golf kors | गोल्फ़ कोर्स

golf cart
baggī
बग्गी

stance
śoṭ mārne kā tarīkā
शॉट मारने का तरीक़ा

golfer | golf khilāṛī | गोल्फ़ खिलाड़ी

clubhouse | klab hāus | क्लब हाउस

equipment • upkaraṇ • उपकरण

golf ball
golf bol
गोल्फ़ बॉल

tee | ṭī | टी

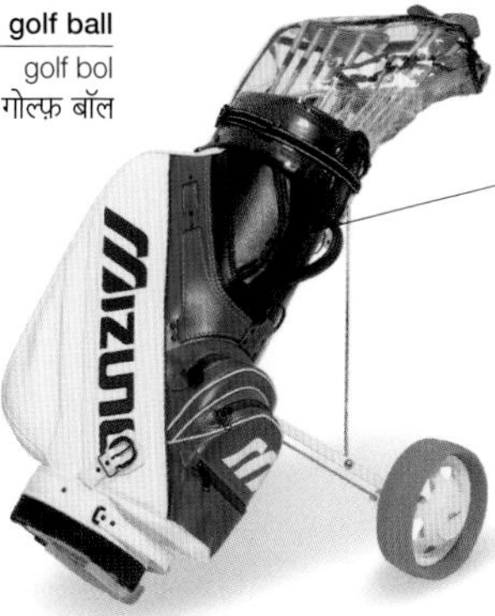

golf bag
golf baig
गोल्फ़ बैग

spikes
kīloṃ vāle jūte
कीलों वाले जूते

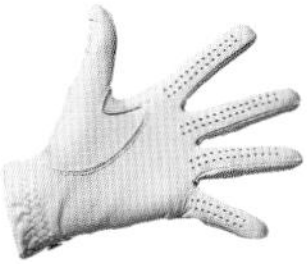

glove
dastānā | दस्ताना

bag cart
golf trolī | गोल्फ़ ट्रॉली

golf shoe
golf ke jūte | गोल्फ़ के जूते

actions • gatividhiyāṃ • गतिविधियां

tee-off (v) | khel ārambh karnā
खेल आरंभ करना

drive (v)
ḍrāiv mārnā
ड्राइव मारना

putt (v) | gend par prahār karnā
गेंद पर प्रहार करना

chip (v)
chip śoṭ lenā
चिप शॉट लेना

golf clubs • golf klab • गोल्फ़ क्लब

wood
vuḍ | वुड

putter
paṭar | पटर

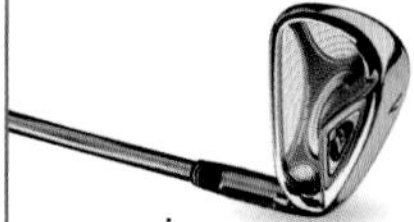

iron
āyaran | आयरन

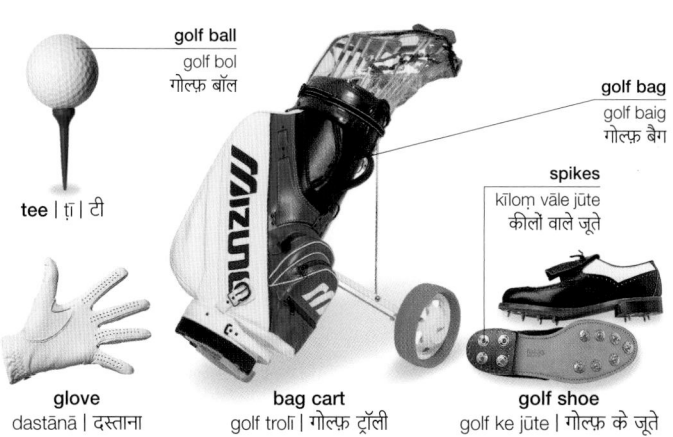

wedge
vej | वेज

vocabulary • śabdāvalī • शब्दावली

par
ausat khel
औसत खेल

under par
nimn khel
निम्न खेल

over par
utkṛṣṭ khel
उत्कृष्ट खेल

hole in one
hol in van
होल इन वन

handicap
haindīkaip
हैंडीकैप

tournament
khel pratiyogitā
खेल प्रतियोगिता

caddy
golf sahāyak
गोल्फ़ सहायक

spectators
darśak
दर्शक

backswing
baiksviṅg
बैकस्विंग

practice swing
praikṭis śoṭ
प्रैक्टिस शॉट

stroke
sṭrok
स्ट्रोक

line of play
khel rekhā
खेल रेखा

track and field • ethleṭiks • एथलेटिक्स

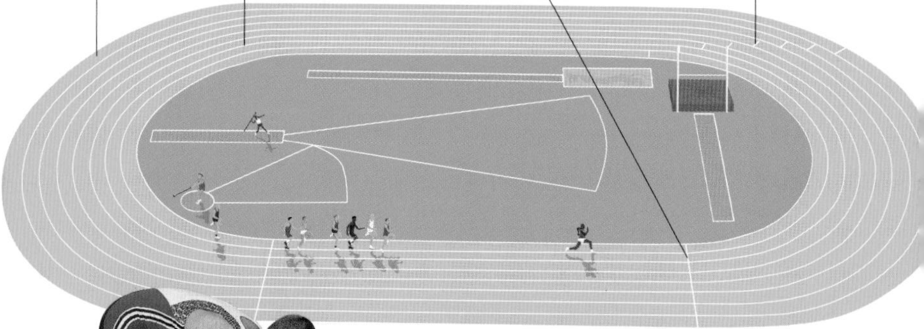

sprinter
tez dhāvak
तेज़ धावक

discus
chakkā pheṃk
चक्का फेंक

shotput
golā pheṃk
गोला फेंक

javelin
bhālā pheṃk
भाला फेंक

vocabulary • śabdāvalī • शब्दावली

race dauṛ दौड़	**record** rikorḍ रिकॉर्ड	**photo finish** barābarī kī dauṛ बराबरी की दौड़	**personal best** apnā viśeṣ pradarśan अपना विशेष प्रदर्शन
time samaya समय	**pole vault** bāṃs kūd बांस-कूद	**marathon** mairāthan मैराथन	**break a record (v)** rikorḍ toṛnā रिकॉर्ड तोड़ना

stopwatch
virām ghaṛī | विराम घड़ी

relay race
rile dauṛ | रिले दौड़

high jump
ūṃchī kūd | ऊंची कूद

long jump
lambī kūd | लंबी कूद

hurdles | bādhā dauṛ | बाधा दौड़

gymnastics • jimnāsṭik • जिमनास्टिक

vault
chhalāṅg mārnā
छलांग मारना

somersault
kalābāzī | कलाबाज़ी

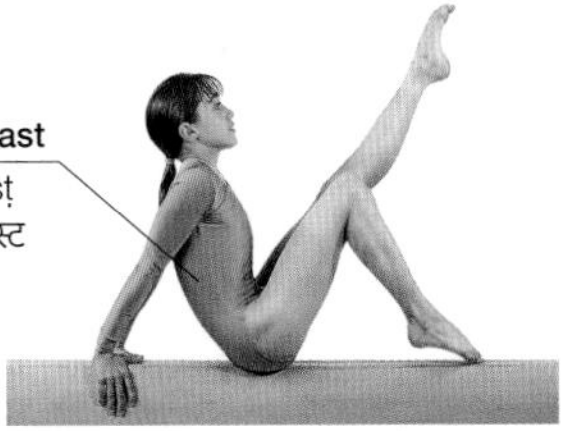

beam | bīm | बीम

floor exercises
zamīnī vyāyām
ज़मीनी व्यायाम

cartwheel
kalābāzī
कलाबाज़ी

rhythmic gymnastics
saṅgītmaya jimnāsṭik
संगीतमय जिमनास्टिक

vocabulary • śabdāvalī • शब्दावली

horizontal bar
āṛī chhaṛ
आड़ी छड़

parallel bars
samānāntar chhaṛeṃ
समानांतर छड़ें

pommel horse
pomel hors
पॉमेल हॉर्स

asymmetric bars
asamān chhaṛeṃ
असमान छड़ें

rings
riṅg
रिंग

podium
poḍiyam
पोडियम

medals
padak
पदक

gold
svarṇ
स्वर्ण

silver
rajat
रजत

bronze
kāṃsya
कांस्य

combat sports • mall krīṛā • मल्ल क्रीड़ा

tae kwon do | tāikvāṅḍo | ताइक्कांडो

karate | karāṭe | कराटे

judo | jūḍo | जूडो

aikido
ekāiḍo | एकाइडो

kendo
kenḍo | केनडो

kung fu
kūṅg fū | कूंग-फ़ू

kickboxing
kik boksiṅg | किक बॉक्सिंग

wrestling
kuśtī | कुश्ती

boxing
mukkebāzī | मुक्केबाज़ी

actions • daṃvpeṃch • दांवपेंच

fall
girnā | गिरना

hold
pakaṛnā | पकड़ना

throw
girānā | गिराना

pin | paṭkanī denā | पटकनी देना

kick
kik | किक

punch
mukkā | मुक्का

strike
mukkā mārnā | मुक्का मारना

chop | nīche vār karnā | नीचे वार करना

jump
kūdnā | कूदना

block
prahār roknā | प्रहार रोकना

vocabulary • śabdāvalī • शब्दावली

boxing ring
boksiṅg riṅg
बॉक्सिंग रिंग

boxing gloves
boksiṅg dastāne
बॉक्सिंग दस्ताने

mouth guard
māuth gārḍ
माउथ गार्ड

round
charaṇ
चरण

bout
śakti parīkṣā
शक्ति परीक्षा

sparring
paiṃtrebāzī
पैंतरेबाज़ी

fist
muṭṭhī
मुट्ठी

knockout
paṭkanī
पटकनी

punching bag
panch baig
पंच बैग

black belt
blaik belṭ
ब्लैक बेल्ट

self-defense
ātmrakṣā
आत्मरक्षा

martial arts
mārśal ārṭs
मार्शल आर्ट्स

capoeira
kepoirā
केपोइरा

sumo wrestling
sūmo kuśtī
सूमो कुश्ती

Tai-Chi
tāī chī
ताई ची

swimming • tairākī • तैराकी

equipment • upkaraṇ • उपकरण

water wings
bāzū paṭṭī | बाज़ू पट्टी

nose clip
noz klip
नोज़ क्लिप

goggles
chaśmā | चश्मा

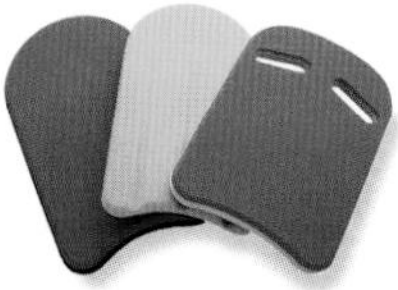

kickboard
floṭ | फ़्लोट

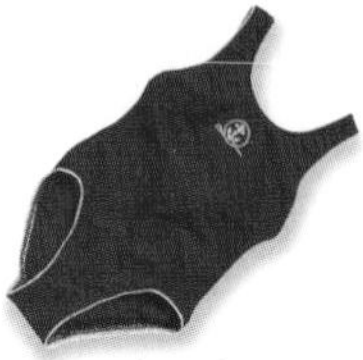

swimsuit
svimsūṭ | स्विमसूट

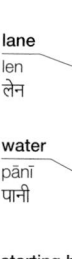

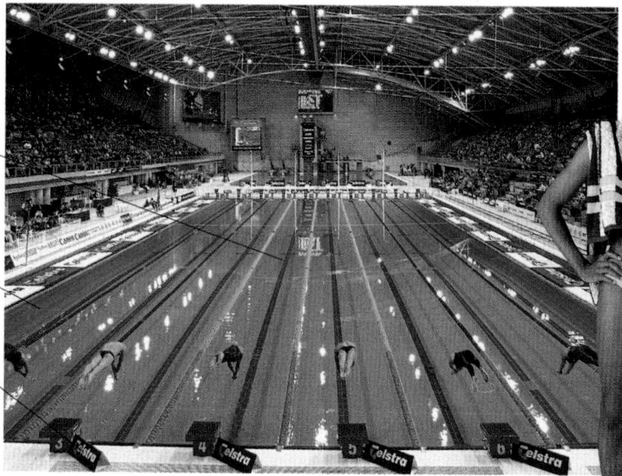

swimming pool | taraṇtāl | तरणताल

swimmer | tairāk | तैराक

dive (v) | ḍāiv mārnā | डाइव मारना

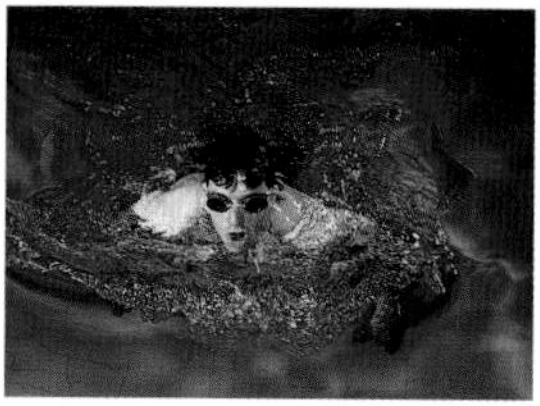

swim (v) | tairnā | तैरना

turn | palaṭnā | पलटना

styles • śailiyāṃ • शैलियां

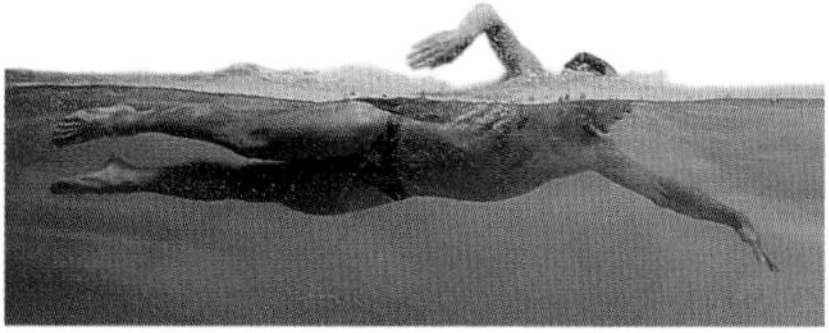

front crawl | franṭ crol | फ़्रंट क्रॉल

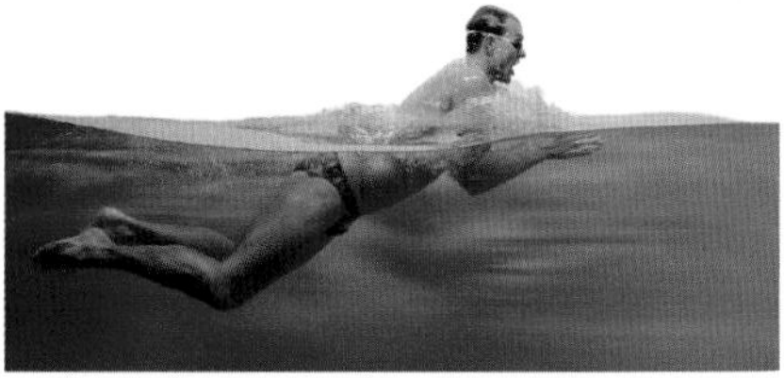

breaststroke | bresṭsṭrok | ब्रेस्टस्ट्रोक

backstroke | baiksṭrok | बैकस्ट्रोक

butterfly | baṭarflāī | बटरफ्लाई

scuba diving • skūbā ḍāiviṅg • स्कूबा डाइविंग

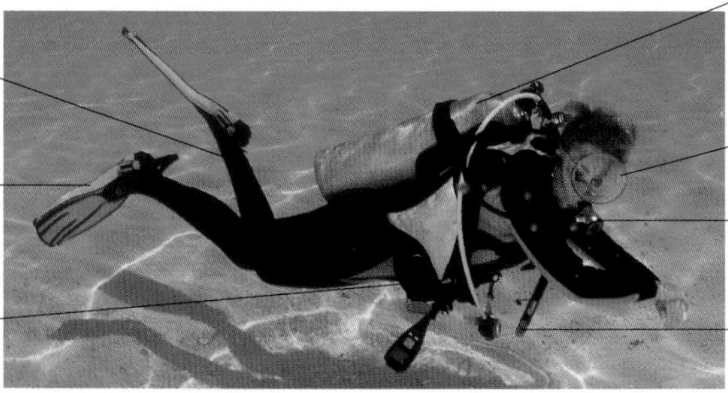

vocabulary • śabdāvalī • शब्दावली

dive ḍāiv डाइव	**racing dive** resiṅg ḍāiv रेसिंग डाइव	**lockers** lokar लॉकर	**water polo** voṭar polo वॉटर पोलो	**shallow end** uthlā chhor उथला छोर	**cramp** nas caṛhnā नस चढ़ना
high dive ūṃchī ḍāiv ऊंची डाइव	**tread water (v)** pānī meṃ pair mārnā पानी में पैर मारना	**lifeguard** jīvan rakṣak जीवन रक्षक	**deep end** gahrā chhor गहरा छोर	**synchronized swimming** siṅkronāizḍ tairākī सिंक्रोनाइज़्ड तैराकी	**drown (v)** ḍūbnā डूबना

sailing • pāl naukāyan • पाल नौकायन

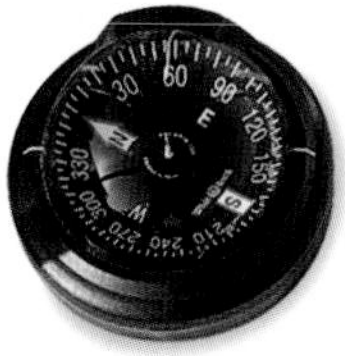

compass
kampās | कंपास

anchor
laṅgar | लंगर

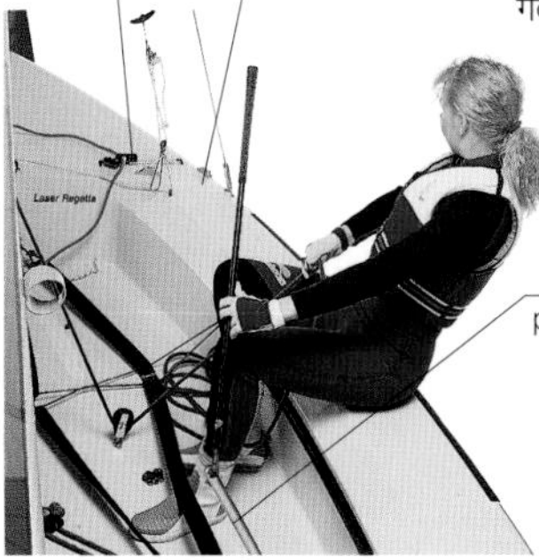

navigate (v) | mārg nirdeśan karnā | मार्ग निर्देशन करना

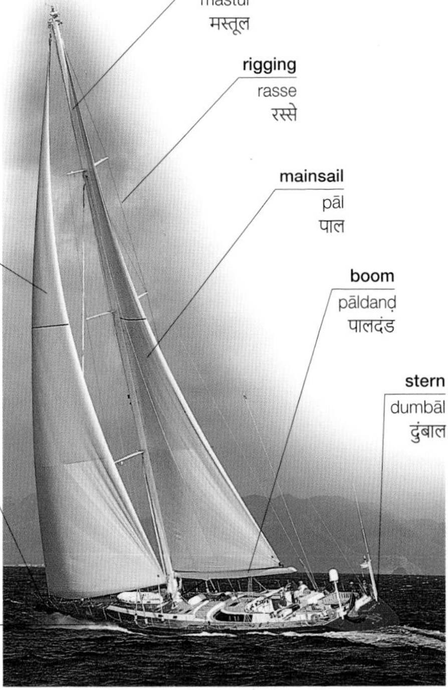

yacht | krīṛā naukā | क्रीड़ा-नौका

safety • surakṣā • सुरक्षा

flare
tīvr prakaś saṅketak
तीव्र प्रकाश संकेतक

life buoy
jīvan rakṣā ṭyūb
जीवन रक्षा ट्यूब

life jacket
rakṣā jaikeṭ
रक्षा जैकेट

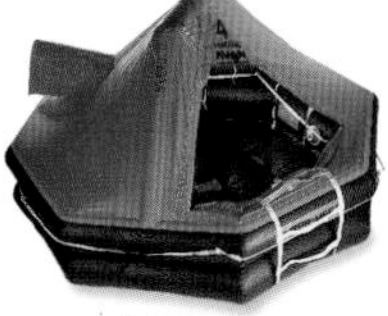

life raft
jīvan rakṣā naukā
जीवन रक्षा नौका

watersports • jalkrīṛā • जलक्रीड़ा

rower
nāvik
नाविक

oar
chappū
चप्पू

row (v) | nāv khenā | नाव खेना

kayak
pansuiyā
पनसुइया

paddle
chhoṭā chappū
छोटा चप्पू

kayaking | naukā vihār | नौका विहार

sail
pāl
पाल

windsurfer
vinḍ sarfar
विंड सर्फ़र

board
borḍ
बोर्ड

footstrap
fuṭ strep
फुट स्ट्रेप

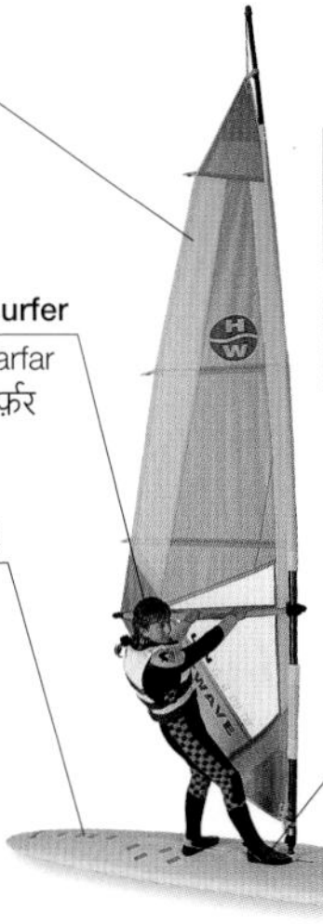

windsurfing | vinḍ sarfiṅg | विंड सर्फ़िंग

surfboard
sarf borḍ
सर्फ़ बोर्ड

surfing
sarfiṅg | सर्फ़िंग

ski
skī | स्की

waterskiing | voṭar skīiṅg | वॉटर स्कीइंग

speedboating | spīḍ boṭiṅg | स्पीड बोटिंग

rafting
naukāyan | नौकायन

jet skiing
jeṭ skīiṅg | जेट स्कीइंग

vocabulary • śabdāvalī • शब्दावली

waterskier voṭar skīar वॉटर स्कीअर	**crew** karmīdal कर्मीदल	**wind** havā हवा	**surf** samudrī lahreṃ समुद्री लहरें	**sheet** naukā pāl नौका पाल	**centerboard** senṭar borḍ सेंटर बोर्ड
surfer sarfar सर्फ़र	**tack (v)** diśā badalnā दिशा बदलना	**wave** lahar लहर	**rapids** tīvr nadī तीव्र नदी	**rudder** patvār पतवार	**capsize (v)** nāv ulaṭnā नाव उलटना

horseback riding • ghuṛsavārī • घुड़सवारी

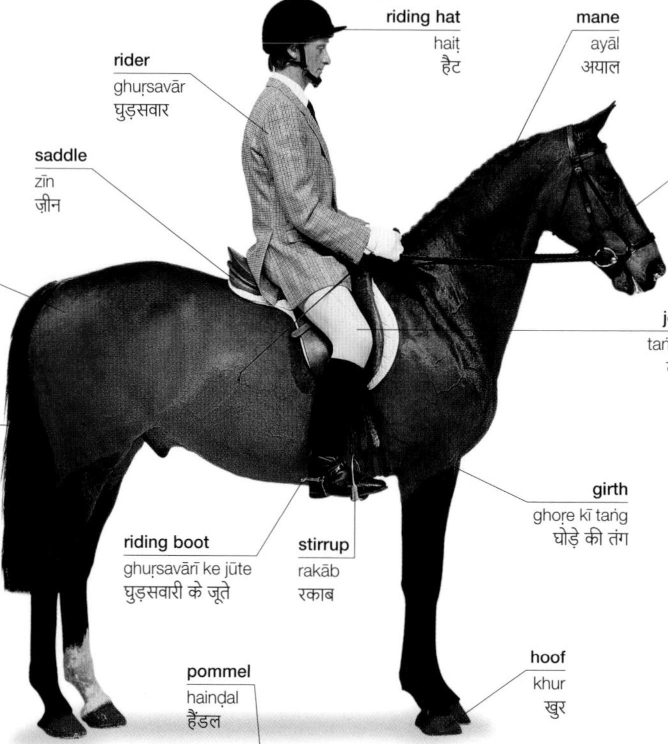

horseshoe
ghuṛnāl | घुड़नाल

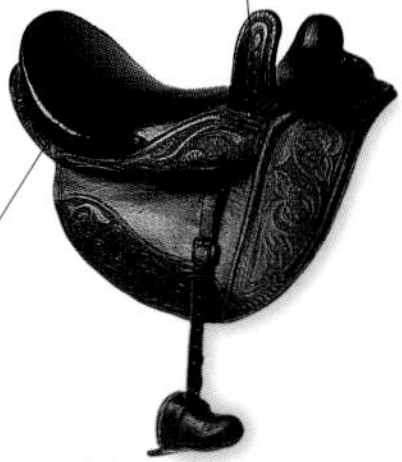

sidesaddle
sāiḍ zīn | साइड ज़ीन

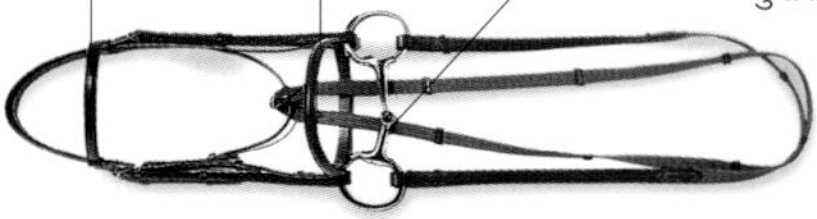

bridle | lagām | लगाम

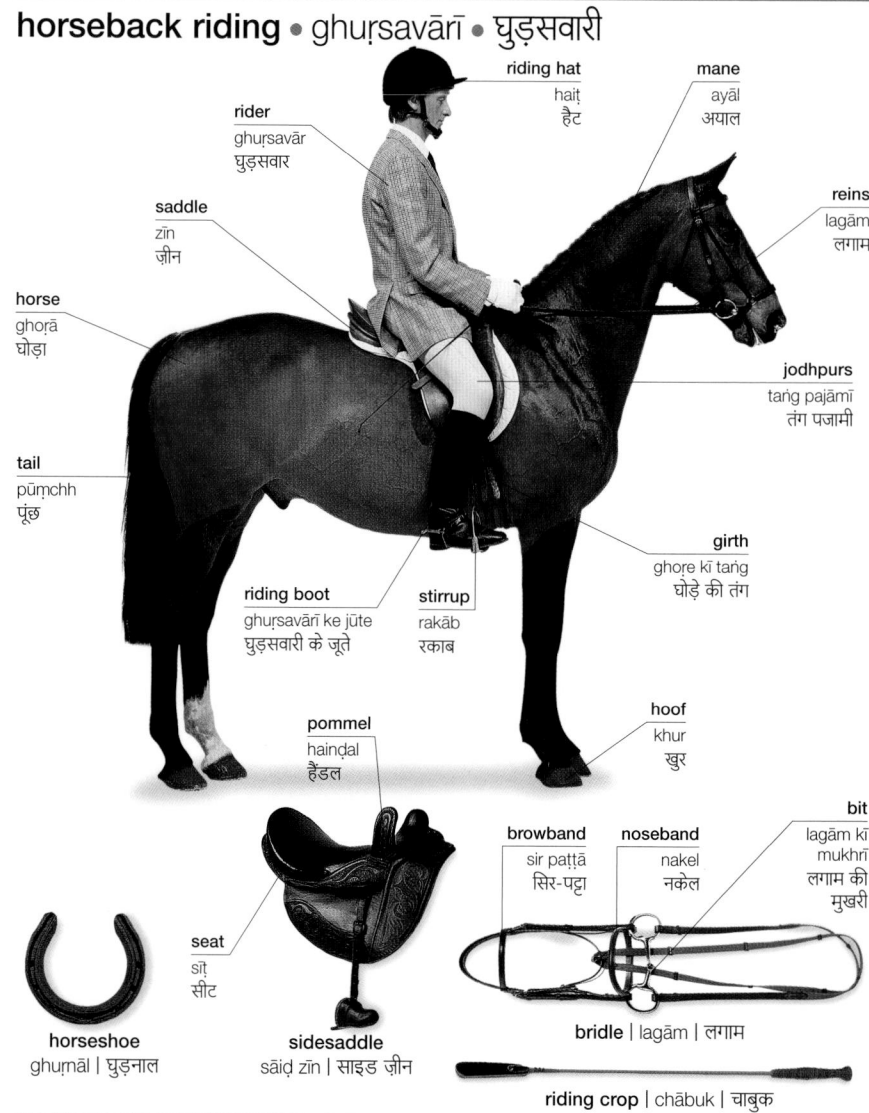

riding crop | chābuk | चाबुक

events • pratispardhā • प्रतिस्पर्धा

racehorse
dauṛ kā ghoṛā | दौड़ का घोड़ा

horse race
ghuṛdauṛ | घुड़दौड़

fence
bāṛ | बाड़

steeplechase
bādhā dauṛ | बाधा दौड़

harness race | ghoṛā gāṛī dauṛ | घोड़ा गाड़ी दौड़

rodeo
ghuṛsavārī khel | घुड़सवारी खेल

showjumping
śo jampiṅg | शो जंपिंग

carriage race
baggī dauṛ | बग्गी दौड़

trail riding
ṭraikiṅg | ट्रैकिंग

dressage
ghoṛā sadhānā | घोड़ा सधाना

polo
polo | पोलो

vocabulary • śabdāvalī • शब्दावली

walk chāl चाल	**canter** ghoṛe kī mand chāl घोड़े की मंद चाल	**jump** kūd कूद	**halter** rassī रस्सी	**paddock** ghoṛoṃ kā bāṛā घोड़ों का बाड़ा	**flat race** sīdhī dauṛ सीधी दौड़
trot dulkī दुलकी	**gallop** sarpaṭ chāl सरपट चाल	**groom** sāīs साईस	**stable** astabal अस्तबल	**arena** khel kā maidān खेल का मैदान	**racecourse** dauṛ kā maidān दौड़ का मैदान

fishing • machhlī pakaṛnā • मछली पकड़ना

sinker | bhār | भार

fishhook | machhlī huk | मछली हुक

bait | machhlī chārā
मछली चारा

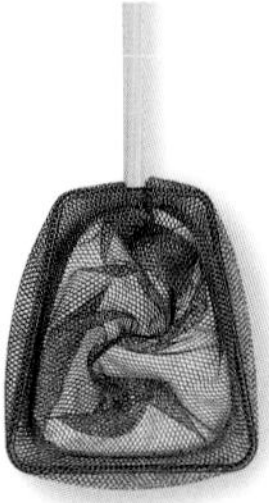

landing net | machhlī pakaṛne kā jāl | मछली पकड़ने का जाल

float
floṭ | फ़्लोट

fly | kṛtrim makkhī
कृत्रिम मक्खी

lure
chārā | चारा

tackle box
upkaraṇ baksā
उपकरण बक्सा

keep net | machhlī rakhne kā jāl | मछली रखने का जाल

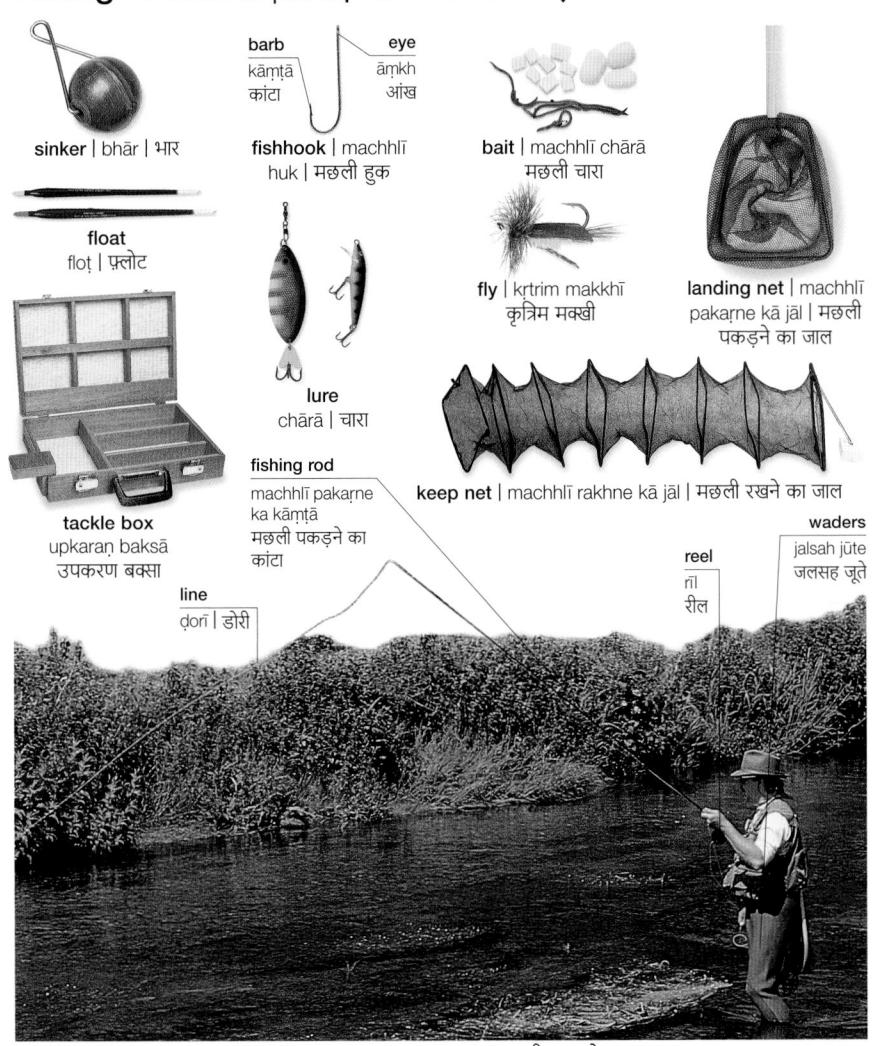

angler | machhlī pakaṛne vālā | मछली पकड़ने वाला

types of fishing • machhlī pakaṛne ke prakār • मछली पकड़ने के प्रकार

freshwater fishing | nadī meṃ machhlī pakaṛnā | नदी में मछली पकड़ना

fly fishing | makkhī se machhlī pakaṛnā | मक्खी से मछली पकड़ना

sport fishing
śaukiyā machhlī pakaṛnā
शौक़िया मछली पकड़ना

deep sea fishing
gahre samudr meṃ machhlī pakaṛnā
गहरे समुद्र में मछली पकड़ना

surfcasting | samudr kināre machhlī pakaṛnā
समुद्र किनारे मछली पकड़ना

activities • gatividhiyāṃ • गतिविधियां

cast (v)
jāl ḍālnā
जाल डालना

catch (v)
pakaṛnā
पकड़ना

reel in (v)
ḍorī khīṃchnā
डोरी खीचना

net (v)
jāl se pakaṛnā
जाल से पकड़ना

release (v)
pānī meṃ chhoṛnā
पानी में छोड़ना

vocabulary • śabdāvalī • शब्दावली

bait (v)
chārā lagānā
चारा लगाना

bite (v)
chārā khānā
चारा खाना

tackle
upkaraṇ
उपकरण

spool
charkhī
चरखी

rain gear
jalrodhak
जलरोधक

pole
bāṃs
बांस

fishing license
fiśiṅg parmiṭ
फ़िशिंग परमिट

marine fishing
samudr meṃ machhlī pakaṛnā
समुद्र में मछली पकड़ना

creel
machhlī kī ṭokrī
मछली की टोकरी

spearfishing
bhāle se machhlī pakaṛnā
भाले से मछली पकड़ना

skiing • skīiṅg • स्कीइंग

ski slope
skī slop
स्की स्लोप
chairlift
cheyarlifṭ
चेयरलिफ़्ट
cable car
kebal kār
केबल कार
ski run
skī mārg
स्की मार्ग
glove
dastānā
दस्ताना
ski pole
skī pol
स्की पोल
safety barrier
surakṣā bairiyar
सुरक्षा बैरियर
ski
skī
स्की
edge
kinārā
किनारा
tip
nok
नोक
ski jacket
skī jaikeṭ
स्की जैकेट
ski boot
skī būṭ
स्की बूट
skier
skīyar | स्कीयर

events • pratispardhāeṃ • प्रतिस्पर्धाएं

downhill skiing | ḍāun hil skīiṅg | डाउन हिल स्कीइंग

slalom | barfānī dauṛ | बर्फ़ानी दौड़

ski jump
skī kūd | स्की कूद

cross-country skiing
kros-kanṭrī skīiṅg
क्रॉस-कंट्री स्कीइंग

winter sports • śaradiya krīṛāeṃ • शरदीय क्रीड़ाएं

ice climbing
āis klāimbiṅg
आइस क्लाइम्बिंग

ice-skating
āis sketiṅg
आइस स्केटिंग

figure skating
figar sketiṅg
फ़िगर स्केटिंग

snowboarding
sno borḍiṅg | स्नो बोर्डिंग

bobsled
slej gāṛī | स्लेज गाड़ी

luge
him vāhan | हिम वाहन

snowmobile
sno mobāil | स्नो मोबाइल

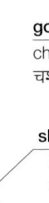

sledding | slej par phisalnā | स्लेज पर फिसलना

vocabulary • śabdāvalī • शब्दावली

alpine skiing
ucch parvatīya skīiṅg
उच्च पर्वतीय स्कीइंग

giant slalom
baṛī barfānī dauṛ
बड़ी बर्फ़ानी दौड़

off-piste
ṭhos barf par skīiṅg
ठोस बर्फ़ पर स्कीइंग

curling
karliṅg khel
कर्लिंग खेल

dogsledding
ḍog slejiṅg
डॉग स्लेजिंग

speed skating
spīḍ sketiṅg
स्पीड स्केटिंग

biathlon
skīiṅg pratiyogitā
स्कीइंग प्रतियोगिता

avalanche
him skhalan
हिम स्खलन

other sports • anya khelkūd • अन्य खेलकूद

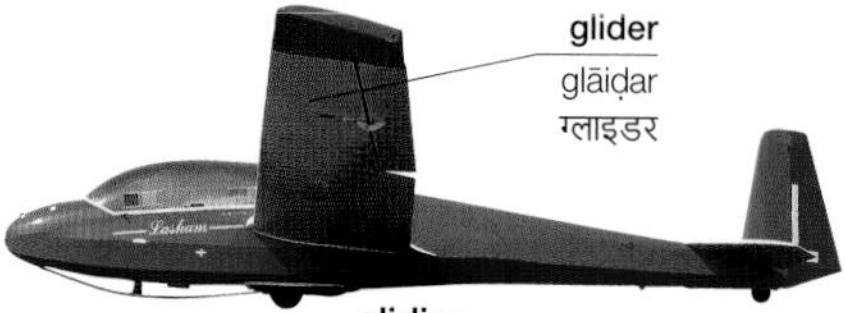

glider
glāiḍar
ग्लाइडर

gliding
glāiḍiṅg
ग्लाइडिंग

hang-glider
haiṅg glāiḍar
हैंग-ग्लाइडर

hang-gliding
haiṅg glāiḍiṅg
हैंग-ग्लाइडिंग

rope
rassī
रस्सी

rock climbing
parvatārohaṇ | पर्वतारोहण

parachute
pairāśūṭ
पैराशूट

parachuting
pairāśūṭ se utarnā | पैराशूट से उतरना

paragliding
pairāglāiḍiṅg | पैराग्लाइडिंग

skydiving
skāiḍāiving | स्काइडाइविंग

rappelling
parvat avrohaṇ | पर्वत अवरोहण

bungee jumping
banjī kūd | बंजी कूद

rally driving
railī ḍrāiviṅg
रैली ड्राइविंग

race-car driver
resiṅg ḍrāivar
रेसिंग ड्राइवर

auto racing
moṭar res
मोटर रेस

motocross
moṭar kros
मोटर क्रॉस

motorcycle racing
moṭarbāik res
मोटरबाइक रेस

skateboard
sket borḍ
स्केट बोर्ड

skateboarding
sket borḍiṅg
स्केट बोर्डिंग

inline skating
inalāin sketiṅg
इनलाइन स्केटिंग

stick
sṭik
स्टिक

lacrosse
kros balle kā khel
क्रॉस बल्ले का खेल

mask
nak̤āb
नक़ाब

foil
talvār
तलवार

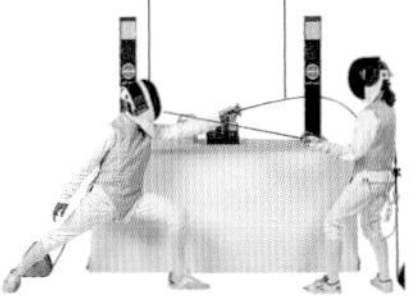

fencing
talvārbāzī
तलवारबाज़ी

pin
pin | पिन

bowling ball
boliṅg bol
बोलिंग बॉल

bowling
boliṅg | बोलिंग

bow
dhanuṣ | धनुष

arrow
tīr
तीर

quiver
tarkaś
तरकश

archery
dhanurvidyā
धनुर्विद्या

target
niśānā | निशाना

target shooting
niśānebāzī
निशानेबाज़ी

pool
pūl biliyarḍ | पूल बिलियर्ड

snooker
snūkar | स्नूकर

fitness • svasthtā • स्वस्थता

exercise bike
vyāyām sāikil
व्यायाम साइकिल

gym machine
jim maśīn
जिम मशीन

bench
bench
बेंच

free weights
vazan
वज़न

bar
chhaṛ
छड़

gym
jim
जिम

rowing machine
roiṅg maśīn
रोइंग मशीन

treadmill
ṭredmil
ट्रेडमिल

elliptical trainer
kros ṭrenar
क्रॉस ट्रेनर

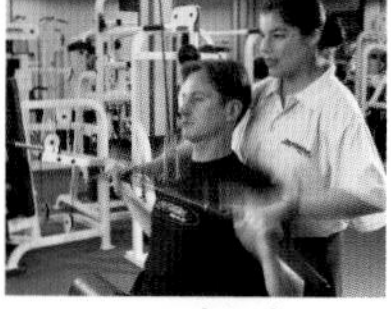

personal trainer
nijī praśikṣak
निजी प्रशिक्षक

stair machine
sṭep maśīn
स्टेप मशीन

swimming pool
taraṇtāl
तरणताल

sauna
vāṣp snān
वाष्प स्नान

exercises • vyāyām • व्यायाम

stretch | sṭrech | स्ट्रेच

lunge
āge jhuknā | आगे झुकना

tights
taṅg pajāmī
तंग पजामी

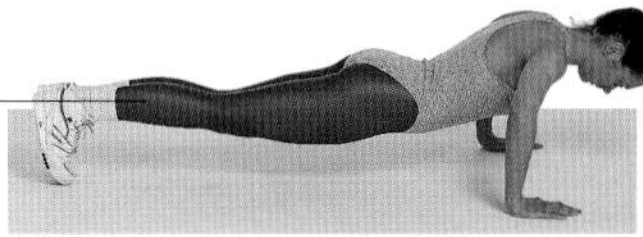

push-up
pres ap | प्रेस अप

squat
skvāṭ
स्क्वॉट

sit-up
siṭ-ap
सिट-अप

dumb bell
ḍamb bel
डंब बेल

bicep curl
ḍole
डोले

leg press
leg pres
लेग प्रेस

chest press
chesṭ pres
चेस्ट प्रेस

sneakers
ṭrenars
ट्रेनर्स

weight bar
vazan chhaṛ
वज़न छड़

weight training
bhārottolan
भारोत्तोलन

jogging
jogiṅg
जॉगिंग

Pilates
pilāṭez
पिलाटेज़

vocabulary • śabdāvalī • शब्दावली

train (v)
abhyās karnā
अभ्यास करना

warm up (v)
māṃspeśiyāṃ garmānā
मांसपेशियां गरमाना

circuit training
sarkiṭ ṭreniṅg
सर्किट ट्रेनिंग

flex (v)
jhukānā
झुकाना

extend (v)
baṛhānā
बढ़ाना

pull up (v)
pul-ap karnā
पुल-अप करना

boxercise
boksiṅg vyāyām
बॉक्सिंग व्यायाम

jumping rope
rassī kūd
रस्सी कूद

jog in place (v)
ek jagah jog karnā
एक जगह जॉग करना

leisure
manoranjan
मनोरंजन

theater • thieṭar • थिएटर

curtain
pardā
पर्दा

wings
pārśv
पार्श्व

set
seṭ
सेट

audience
darśak
दर्शक

orchestra
orkesṭrā
ऑर्केस्ट्रा

stage | manch | मंच

seat
sīṭ
सीट

balcony seats
ūprī dīrghā
ऊपरी दीर्घा

row
ḳatār
क़तार

box
boks
बॉक्स

mezzanine
dīrghā
दीर्घा

balcony
bālkanī
बालकनी

aisle
vīthikā
वीथिका

orchestra seats
sṭol
स्टॉल

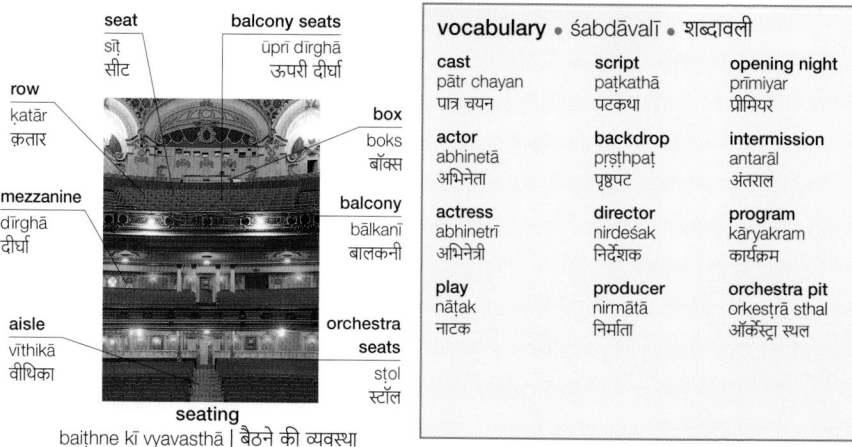

seating
baiṭhne kī vyavasthā | बैठने की व्यवस्था

vocabulary • śabdāvalī • शब्दावली

cast	**script**	**opening night**
pātr chayan	paṭkathā	prīmiyar
पात्र चयन	पटकथा	प्रीमियर
actor	**backdrop**	**intermission**
abhinetā	pṛṣṭhpaṭ	antarāl
अभिनेता	पृष्ठपट	अंतराल
actress	**director**	**program**
abhinetrī	nirdeśak	kāryakram
अभिनेत्री	निर्देशक	कार्यक्रम
play	**producer**	**orchestra pit**
nāṭak	nirmātā	orkesṭrā sthal
नाटक	निर्माता	ऑर्केस्ट्रा स्थल

concert
konsarṭ | कॉन्सर्ट

musical
myūzikal | म्यूज़िकल

costume
veśbhūṣā
वेशभूषा

ballet
baile | बैले

vocabulary • śabdāvalī • शब्दावली

usher
praveśak
प्रवेशक

classical music
śāstrīya saṅgīt
शास्त्रीय संगीत

musical score
svarlipi
स्वरलिपि

soundtrack
dhvani paṭṭī
ध्वनि पट्टी

applaud (v)
tālī bajānā
ताली बजाना

encore
punaḥ prastuti
पुन: प्रस्तुति

What time does it start?
yah kis samaya śurū hogā?
यह किस समय शुरू होगा?

I'd like two tickets for tonight's performance.
mujhe āj rāt ke kāryakram kī do ṭikṭeṃ chāhie
मुझे आज रात के कार्यक्रम की दो टिकटें चाहिए।

opera
operā | ऑपेरा

movies • sinemā • सिनेमा

popcorn
popkorn
पॉपकॉर्न

box office
boks ofis
बॉक्स ऑफ़िस

lobby
lobī
लॉबी

poster
posṭar
पोस्टर

movie theater
sinemā hol | सिनेमा हॉल

screen
pardā | पर्दा

vocabulary • śabdāvalī • शब्दावली

comedy
komeḍī
कॉमेडी

thriller
thrilar
थ्रिलर

horror movie
ḍarāvanī film
डरावनी फ़िल्म

western
paśchimī
पश्चिमी

romance
romāns
रोमांस

science fiction movie
vijñān kathā film
विज्ञान कथा फ़िल्म

adventure movie
romānch kathā
रोमांच कथा

animated movie
ainimeṭeḍ film
ऐनिमेटेड फ़िल्म

orchestra • vādyavṛṅd • वाद्यवृंद

strings • tantrī vādya • तंत्री वाद्य

piano | piyāno | पियानो

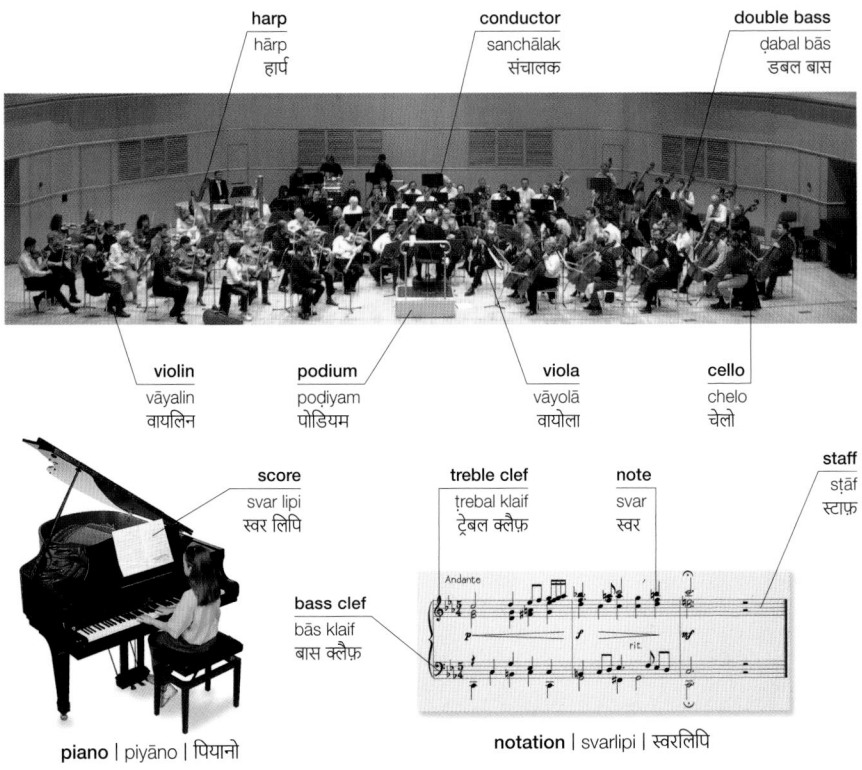

notation | svarlipi | स्वरलिपि

vocabulary • śabdāvalī • शब्दावली

overture pūrvraṅg पूर्वरंग	**sonata** sonāṭā सोनाटा	**rest** virām विराम	**sharp** ucch svar उच्च स्वर	**natural** piyāno kā śvet pardā पियानो का श्वेत पर्दा	**scale** saptak सप्तक
symphony svar saṅgati स्वर संगति	**instruments** vādya yantr वाद्य यंत्र	**pitch** svarmān स्वरमान	**flat** komal sur कोमल सुर	**bar** tālkhanḍ तालखंड	**baton** chhaṛī छड़ी

woodwind • kāṣṭh vādya yantr • काष्ठ वाद्य यंत्र

piccolo
pikolo | पिकॉलो

flute
bāṃsurī | बांसुरी

oboe
obo | ओबो

English horn
aṅgrezī bīn | अंग्रेज़ी बीन

clarinet
klairineṭ
क्लैरिनेट

bass clarinet
mandr klairineṭ
मंद्र क्लैरिनेट

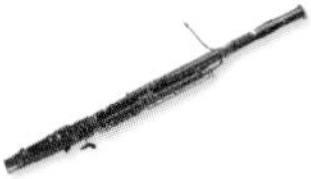
bassoon
basūn
बसून

double bassoon
ḍabal basūn
डबल बसून

saxophone
saiksofon
सैक्सोफ़ोन

percussion • tāl vādya • ताल वाद्य

kettledrum
nagāṛā | नगाड़ा

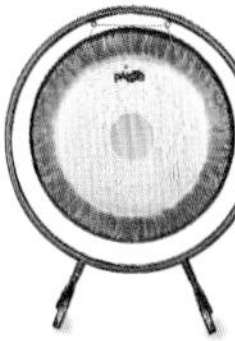
gong
ghanṭā | घंटा

vibraphone
vāibrāfon | वाइब्राफ़ोन

foot pedal
fuṭ paiḍal
फुट पैडल

bongos
baumgo
बौंगो

snare drum
chhoṭā ḍram
छोटा ड्रम

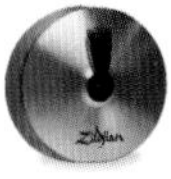
cymbals
manjīrā | मंजीरा

tambourine
ḍaphlī | डफली

triangle
ṭrāieṅgal
ट्राइएंगल

maracas
marākas
माराकस

brass • pītal ke vādya • पीतल के वाद्य

trumpet
ṭrampeṭ | ट्रम्पेट

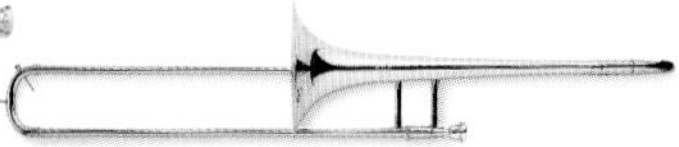
trombone
ṭrombon | ट्रॉमबोन

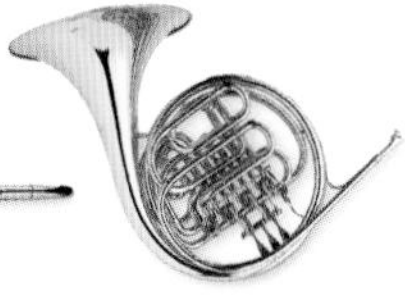
French horn
french horn | फ़्रेंच हॉर्न

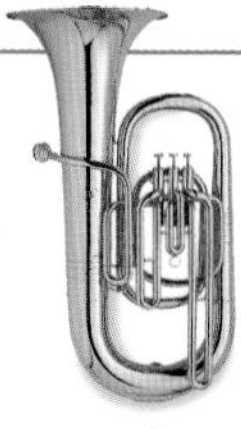
tuba
ṭyūbā | ट्यूबा

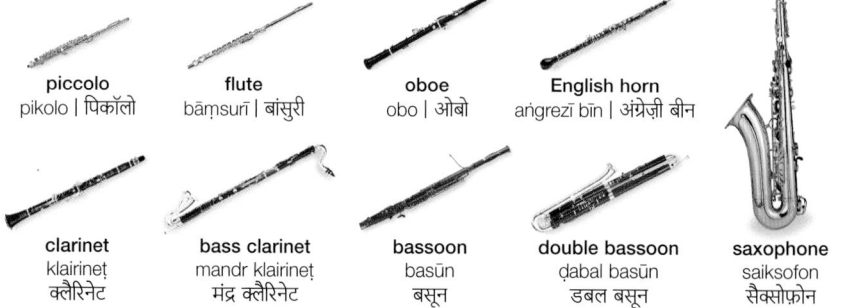

concert • konsarṭ • कॉन्सर्ट

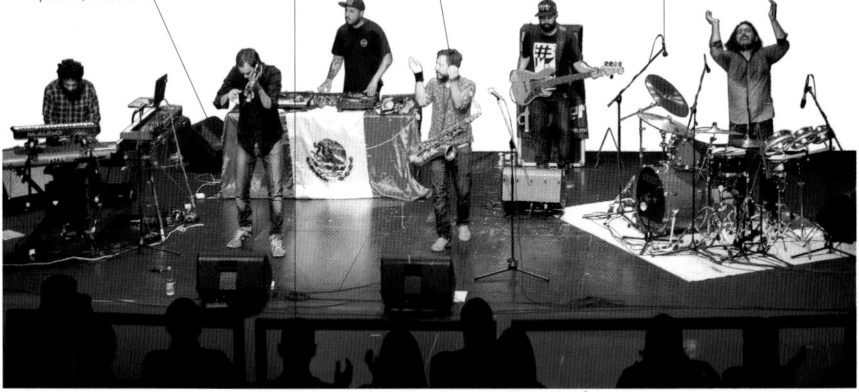

rock concert | rok konsarṭ | रॉक कॉन्सर्ट

instruments • vādya yantr • वाद्य यंत्र

bass guitar | bās giṭār | बास गिटार

keyboard
kī borḍ | की बोर्ड

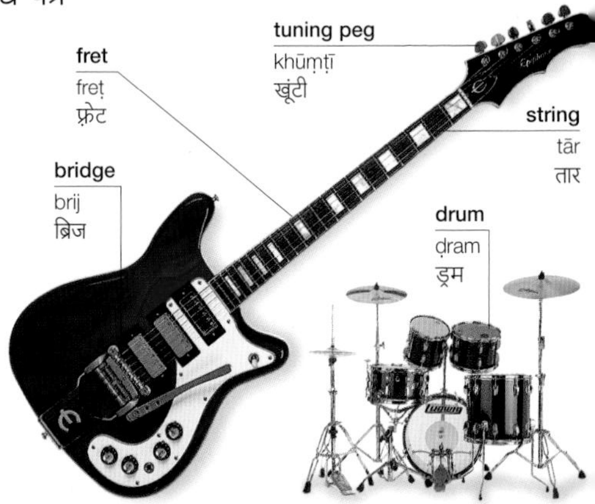

electric guitar
ilekṭrik giṭār | इलेक्ट्रिक गिटार

drum kit
ḍram kiṭ | ड्रम किट

musical styles • saṅgīt śailiyāṃ • संगीत शैलियां

jazz | jaiz | जैज़

blues | blūz | ब्लूज़

punk | paṅk | पंक

folk music
lok saṅgīt | लोक संगीत

pop | pop | पॉप

dance | nṛitya | नृत्य

rap
raip | रैप

heavy metal
rok | रॉक

classical music
śāstrīya saṅgīt | शास्त्रीय संगीत

vocabulary • śabdāvalī • शब्दावली

song	**lyrics**	**melody**	**beat**	**reggae**	**country**	**spotlight**
gānā	gīt	madhur saṅgīt	thāp	raige	kanṭrī myūzik	spoṭ lāiṭ
गाना	गीत	मधुर संगीत	थाप	रैगे	कंट्री म्यूज़िक	स्पॉट लाइट

sightseeing • sair-sapāṭā • सैर-सपाटा

tourist
paryaṭak
पर्यटक

tourist attraction
paryaṭan sthal | पर्यटन स्थल

itinerary
mārg nirdeśikā
मार्ग निर्देशिका

open-top
khulī chhat
खुली छत

tour bus | paryaṭan bas | पर्यटन बस

tour guide
paryaṭan gāiḍ
पर्यटन-गाइड

guided tour
mārgdarśit paryaṭan
मार्गदर्शित पर्यटन

figurine
laghu pratimā
लघु-प्रतिमा

souvenirs
smṛti chihn
स्मृति चिह्न

vocabulary • śabdāvalī • शब्दावली

open
khulā
खुला

entrance fee
praveś śulk
प्रवेश शुल्क

film
film
फ़िल्म

guide book
nirdeśikā
निर्देशिका

closed
band
बंद

batteries
baitriyāṃ
बैटरियां

camcorder
haiṇḍīkaim
हैंडीकैम

camera
kaimrā
कैमरा

directions
nirdeśan
निर्देशन

left
bāyāṃ
बायां

right
dāyāṃ
दायां

straight ahead
sīdh meṃ
सीध में

Where is…?
... kahāṃ hai?
...कहां है?

I'm lost.
maiṃ kho gayā hūṃ
मैं खो गया हूं।

Can you tell me the way to…?
kyā āp mujhe... jāne kā rāstā batā sakte haiṃ?
क्या आप मुझे... जाने का रास्ता बता सकते हैं?

attractions • ramaṇīya sthal • रमणीय स्थल

painting
penṭiṅg
पेंटिंग

exhibit
pradarśit vastu
प्रदर्शित वस्तु

art gallery
kalā dīrghā | कला दीर्घा

monument
smārak | स्मारक

exhibition
pradarśanī | प्रदर्शनी

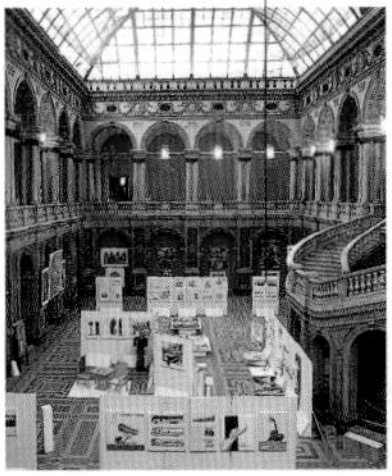

museum
saṅgrahālaya | संग्रहालय

famous ruin
prasiddh khanḍahar
प्रसिद्ध खंडहर

historic building
aitihāsik imārat
ऐतिहासिक इमारत

casino
juāghar | जुआघर

gardens
bāg̣ | बाग़

national park
rāṣṭrīya udyān | राष्ट्रीय उद्यान

information • jānkarī • जानकारी

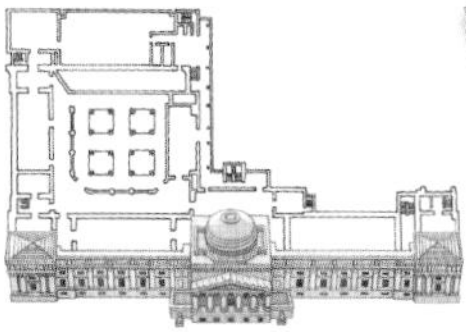

floor plan
bhavan nakśā | भवन नक़्शा

map
nakśā | नक़्शा

times
samaya
समय

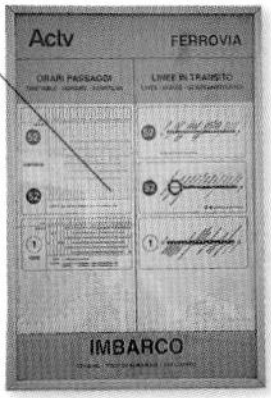

schedule
samaya sāriṇī
समय-सारिणी

tourist information
paryaṭak sūchnā kendr
पर्यटक सूचना केंद्र

outdoor activities • bāhrī gatividhiyāṃ • बाहरी गतिविधियां

footpath
paidal rāstā
पैदल रास्ता

sundial
dhūp gharī
धूप घड़ी

café
kaife
कैफ़े

park | udyān | उद्यान

grass
ghās
घास

bench
bench
बेंच

formal gardens
bagīchā
बग़ीचा

roller coaster
rolar kosṭar
रोलर कोस्टर

fairground
melā sthal | मेला स्थल

theme park
thīm pārk | थीम पार्क

safari park
safārī pārk | सफ़ारी पार्क

zoo
chiṛiyāghar | चिड़ियाघर

activities • gatividhiyāṃ • गतिविधियां

cycling | sāikil chalānā
साइकिल चलाना

jogging
joging | जॉगिंग

skateboarding | skeṭ
borḍiṅg | स्केट बोर्डिंग

rollerblading | rolar
bleḍiṅg | रोलर ब्लेडिंग

bird-watching | pakṣī
nihārnā | पक्षी निहारना

horseback riding
ghuṛsavārī | घुड़सवारी

hiking
padyātrā | पदयात्रा

picnic
piknik | पिकनिक

playground • khel kā maidān • खेल का मैदान

sandbox
ret kā akhāṛā
रेत का अखाड़ा

wading pool
kṛtrim tālāb
कृत्रिम तालाब

swing
jhūlā | झूला

seesaw | sīso | सीसॉ

slide | phisal paṭṭī | फिसल पट्टी

climbing frame
sīṛhīnumā jhūlā | सीढ़ीनुमा झूला

beach • taṭ • तट

sunbathe (v) | sūrya snān karnā | सूर्य स्नान करना

lifeguard
jīvan rakṣak
जीवन रक्षक

lifeguard tower
jīvan rakṣak ṭāvar
जीवन रक्षक टावर

windbreak | havā rodhak | हवा रोधक

boardwalk | vihār sthal
विहार स्थल

deck chair | ḍaik kursī | डैक कुर्सी

sunglasses | dhūp kā chaśmā | धूप का चश्मा

sun hat
haiṭ | हैट

suntan lotion | sanṭain lośan | सनटैन लोशन

sunblock | san blok
सन ब्लॉक

beach ball
bīch bol | बीच बॉल

inflatable ring | rabaṛ kī ṭyūb | रबड़ की ट्यूब

beach towel
bīch tauliyā | बीच तौलिया

swimsuit
tairākī sūṭ
तैराकी सूट

shovel
khurpī
खुरपी

pail
ṭokrī
टोकरी

sandcastle
ret kā mahal
रेत का महल

shell
sīp
सीप

camping • śivir lagānā • शिविर लगाना

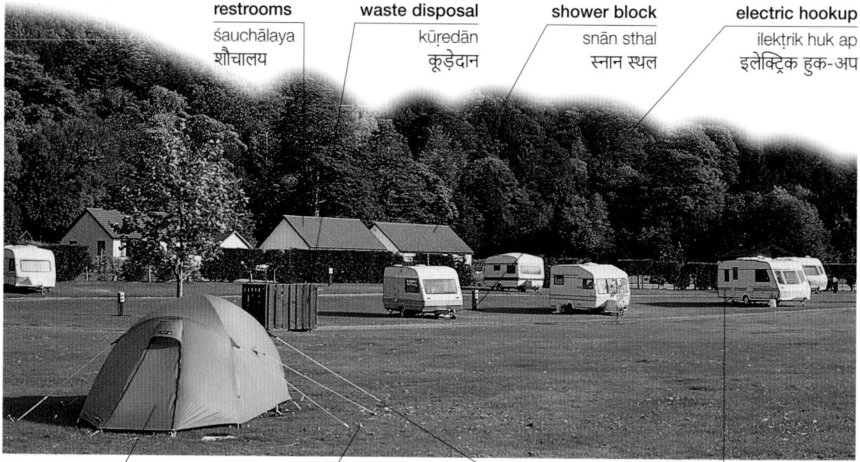

campground
śivir sthal | शिविर स्थल

vocabulary • śabdāvalī • शब्दावली

camp (v)
śivir lagānā
शिविर लगाना

site manager's office
sāiṭ prabandhak kāryālaya
साइट प्रबंधक कार्यालय

sites available
sthān uplabdh
स्थान उपलब्ध

full
pūrā
पूरा

site
sthān
स्थान

pitch a tent (v)
tambū gāṛnā
तंबू गाड़ना

tent pole
tambū kā khambhā
तंबू का खंभा

camp bed
safrī palaṅg
सफ़री पलंग

picnic bench
piknik bench
पिकनिक बेंच

hammock
jhūlā
झूला

camper van
śivir vāhan
शिविर वाहन

trailer
ṭrelar
ट्रेलर

charcoal
kacchā koyalā
कच्चा कोयला

firelighter
āg jalāne kā upkaraṇ
आग जलाने का उपकरण

light a fire (v)
āg jalānā
आग जलाना

campfire
alāv
अलाव

frame
frem
फ़्रेम

ground sheet
darī
दरी

backpack
piṭṭhū
पिट्ठू

vacuum flask
vaikyūm flāsk
वैक्यूम फ़्लास्क

water bottle
pānī kī botal
पानी की बोतल

tent
śivir | शिविर

insect repellent
macchhar avrodhak
मच्छर अवरोधक

flashlight
ṭorch | टॉर्च

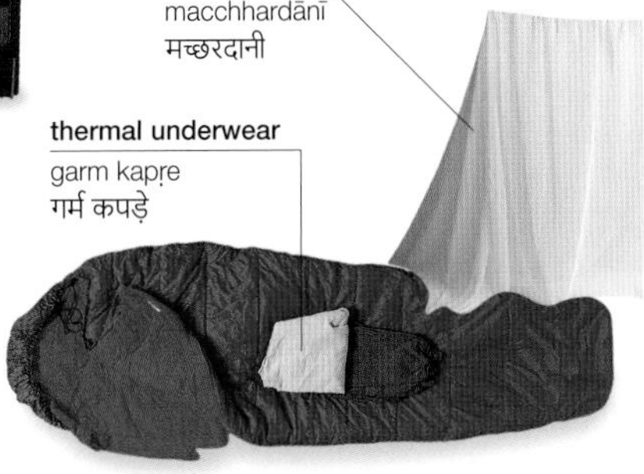

mosquito net
macchhardānī
मच्छरदानी

thermal underwear
garm kapṛe
गर्म कपड़े

sleeping bag
slīpiṅg baig | स्लीपिंग बैग

hiking boots
jūte | जूते

rain gear
voṭarprūf | वॉटरप्रूफ़

camping stove
safrī sṭov | सफ़री स्टोव

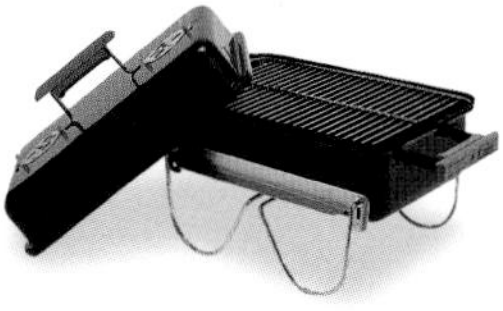

barbecue grill
gril | ग्रिल

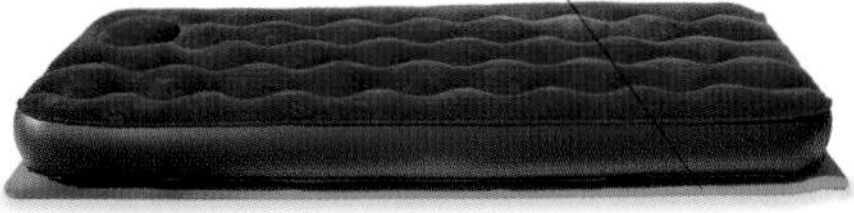

sleeping mat
gaddā
गद्दा

air mattress | havā bharā gaddā | हवा भरा गद्दा

home entertainment • gharelū manoranjan • घरेलू मनोरंजन

digital radio
ḍijiṭal reḍiyo | डिजिटल रेडियो

DVD
ḍīvīḍī
डीवीडी

DVD player
ḍīvīḍī pleyar | डीवीडी प्लेयर

record player
rikorḍ pleyar
रिकॉर्ड प्लेयर

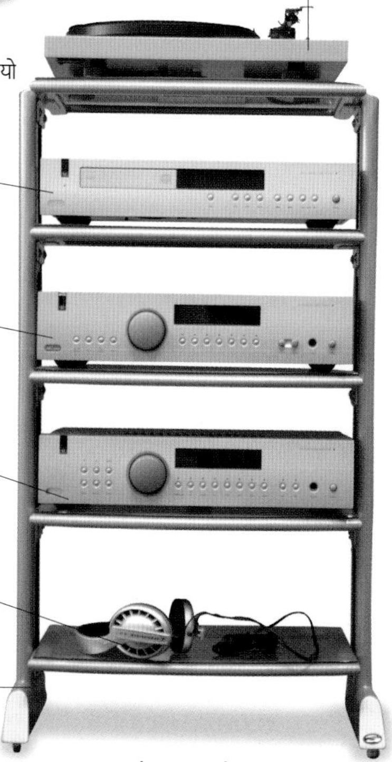

CD player
sīḍī pleyar
सीडी प्लेयर

radio
reḍiyo
रेडियो

amplifier
emplīfāyar
ऐम्प्लीफ़ायर

headphones
haiḍfon
हैडफ़ोन

stand
sṭainḍ
स्टैंड

stereo system
hāī fāī sisṭam | हाई-फ़ाई सिस्टम

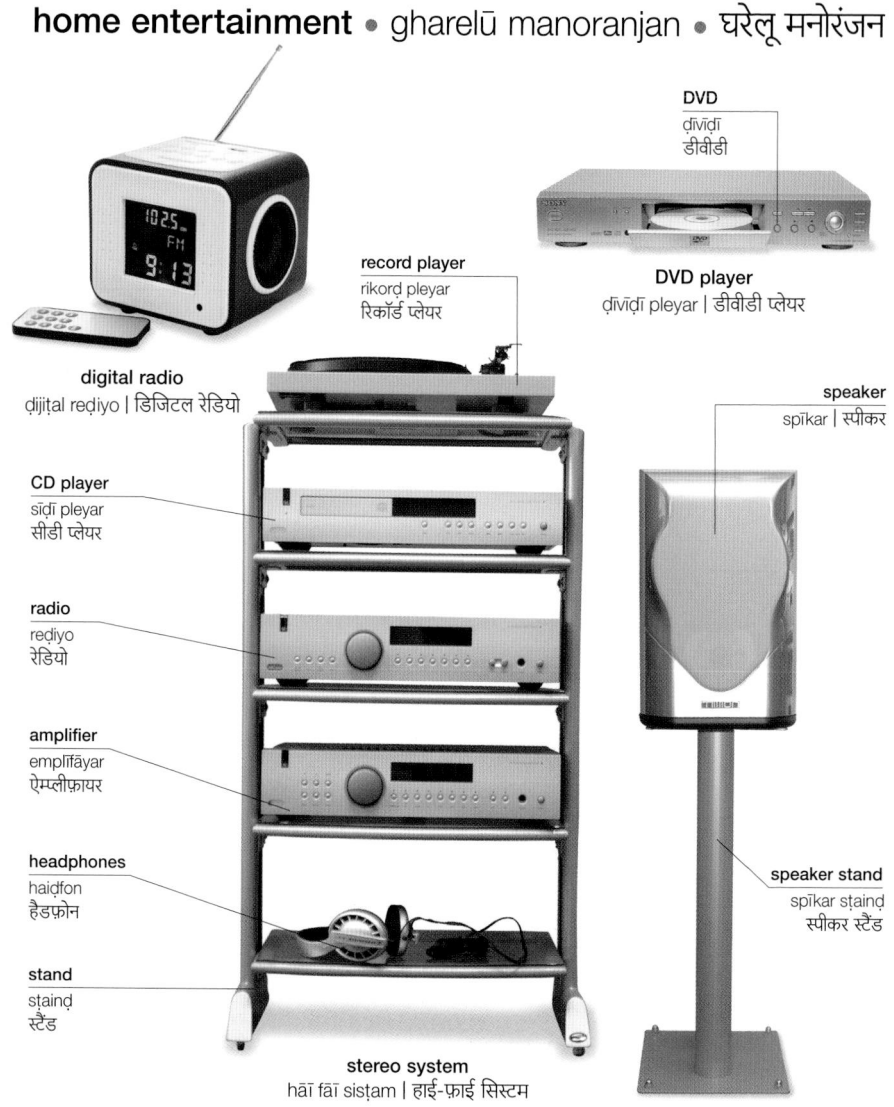

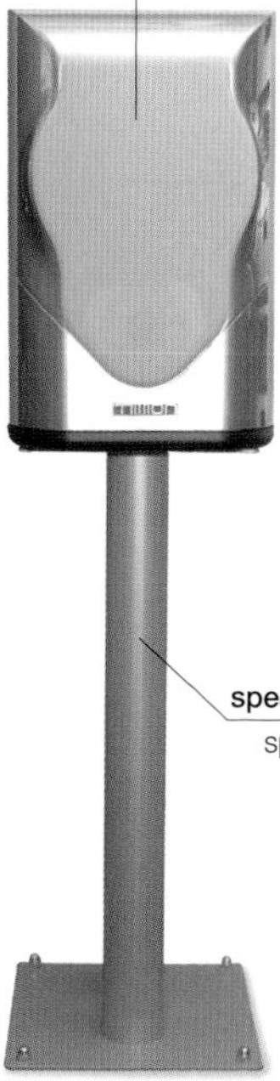

speaker
spīkar | स्पीकर

speaker stand
spīkar sṭainḍ
स्पीकर स्टैंड

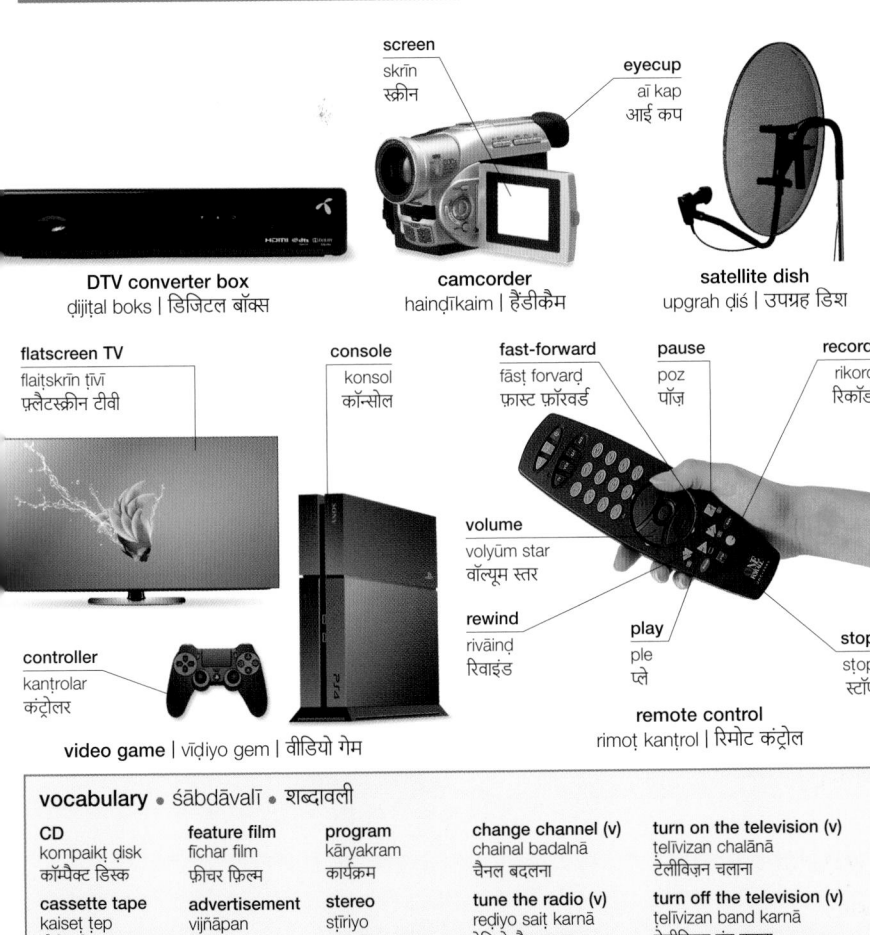

DTV converter box
ḍijiṭal boks | डिजिटल बॉक्स

camcorder
hainḍīkaim | हैंडीकैम

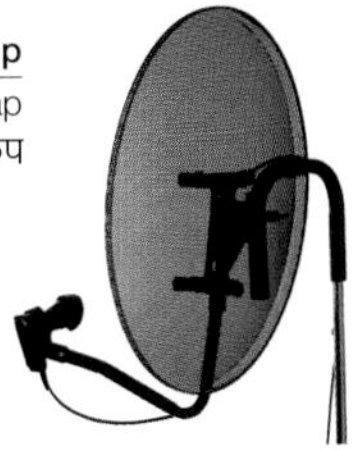

satellite dish
upgrah ḍiś | उपग्रह डिश

video game | vīḍiyo gem | वीडियो गेम

remote control
rimoṭ kanṭrol | रिमोट कंट्रोल

vocabulary • śābdāvalī • शब्दावली

CD
kompaikṭ ḍisk
कॉम्पैक्ट डिस्क

cassette tape
kaiseṭ ṭep
कैसेट टेप

cassette player
kaiseṭ pleyar
कैसेट प्लेयर

streaming
sṭrīmiṅg
स्ट्रीमिंग

feature film
fīchar film
फ़ीचर फ़िल्म

advertisement
vijñāpan
विज्ञापन

digital
ḍijiṭal
डिजिटल

Wi-Fi
wāī fāī
वाई फ़ाई

program
kāryakram
कार्यक्रम

stereo
sṭīriyo
स्टीरियो

cable television
kebal ṭelīvizan
केबल टेलीविज़न

high definition
haī ḍefiniśan
हाइ डेफ़िनिशन

change channel (v)
chainal badalnā
चैनल बदलना

tune the radio (v)
reḍiyo saiṭ karnā
रेडियो सैट करना

watch television (v)
ṭīvī dekhnā
टीवी देखना

turn on the television (v)
ṭelīvizan chalānā
टेलीविज़न चलाना

turn off the television (v)
ṭelīvizan band karnā
टेलीविज़न बंद करना

pay-per-view channel
prati chainal bhugtān
प्रति चैनल भुगतान

photography • foṭogrāfī • फ़ोटोग्राफ़ी

shutter release
śaṭar rilīz
शटर रिलीज़

aperture dial
aparchar niyantrak
अपर्चर नियंत्रक

lens
lens
लेंस

SLR camera | es el ār kaimrā | एस एल आर कैमरा

filter
filṭar | फ़िल्टर

lens cap
lens kaip | लेंस कैप

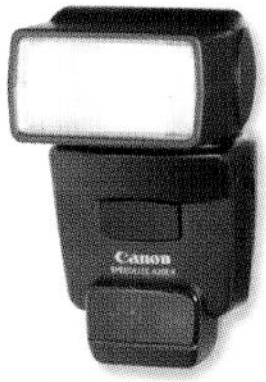

flash gun
flaiś gan | फ़्लैश गन

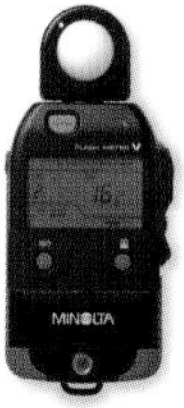

light meter
lāiṭmīṭar | लाइटमीटर

zoom lens
zūm lens | ज़ूम लेंस

tripod
tipāyā sṭaiṇḍ | तिपाया स्टैंड

types of camera • kaimre ke prakār • कैमरे के प्रकार

Polaroid camera
polaroeḍ kaimrā
पोलरॉएड कैमरा

flash
flaiś
फ़्लैश

digital camera
ḍijiṭal kaimrā
डिजिटल कैमरा

camera phone
kaimrāfon
कैमराफ़ोन

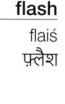

disposable camera
ḍispozebal kaimrā
डिस्पोज़ेबल कैमरा

photograph (v) • foṭo khīṃchnā • फ़ोटो खींचना

film roll
film rīl
फ़िल्म रील

film
film | फ़िल्म

focus (v) | kendrit karnā | केंद्रित करना

develop (v)
film dhonā | फ़िल्म धोना

negative
negeṭiv | नेगेटिव

landscape
prākṛtik dṛśya
प्राकृतिक दृश्य

portrait
vyakti chitr
व्यक्ति चित्र

photograph | tasvīr | तस्वीर

photo album
foṭo elbam | फ़ोटो एल्बम

picture frame | foṭo frem | फ़ोटो फ़्रेम

problems • samasyāeṃ • समस्याएं

underexposed
kam udbhāsit
कम उद्भासित

overexposed
atyadhik udbhāsit
अत्यधिक उद्भासित

out of focus | fokas se bāhar | फ़ोकस से बाहर

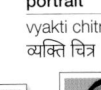

red eye
reḍ āī | रेड आई

vocabulary • śabdāvalī • शब्दावली

viewfinder
dṛśyadarśī
दृश्यदर्शी

camera case
kaimrā kes
कैमरा केस

exposure
udbhāsan
उद्भासन

darkroom
ḍārk rūm
डार्क रूम

print
foṭo prati
फ़ोटो प्रति

matte
khurdarā
खुरदरा

gloss
chiknā
चिकना

enlargement
foṭo baṛī karānā
फ़ोटो बड़ी कराना

I'd like this film processed.
maiṃ yah rīl dhulvānā chāhtā hūṃ
मैं यह रील धुलवाना चाहता हूं।

games • khel • खेल

chess
śatranj | शतरंज

checkers | droṭs | ड्रॉट्स

Scrabble | skraibal | स्क्रैबल

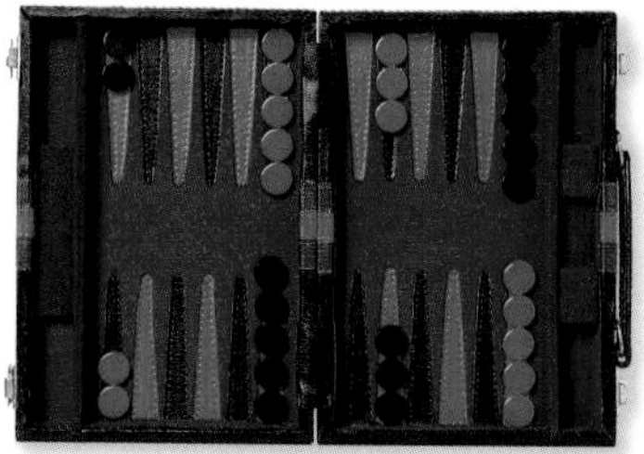

backgammon
baik gaiman | बैक गैमन

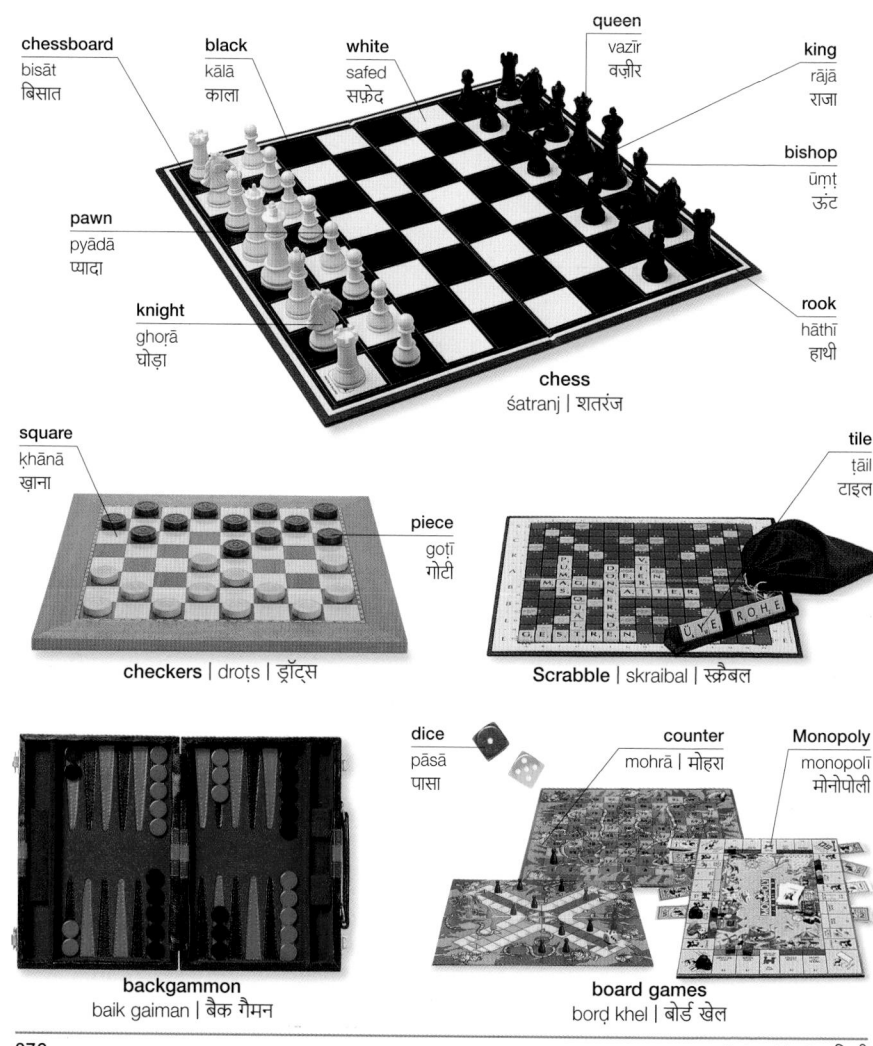

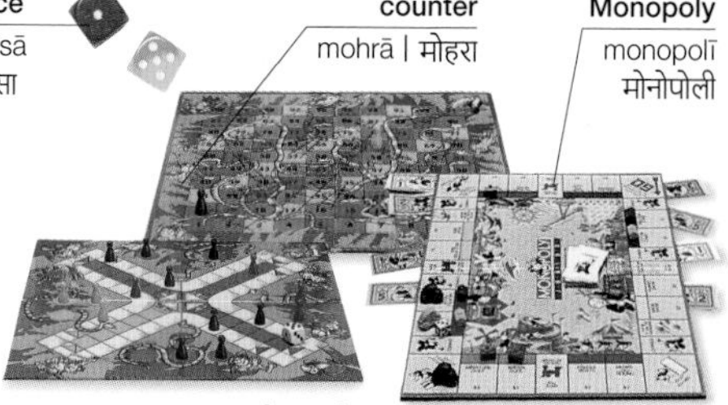

board games
borḍ khel | बोर्ड खेल

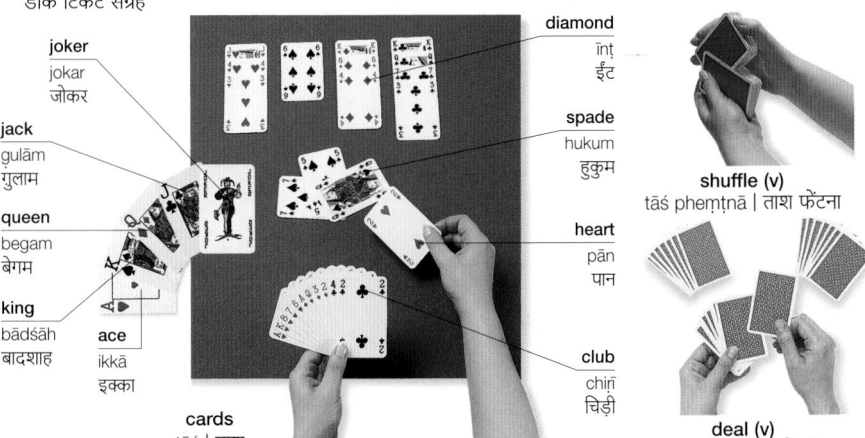

stamp collecting
ḍāk ṭikaṭ saṅgrah
डाक टिकट संग्रह

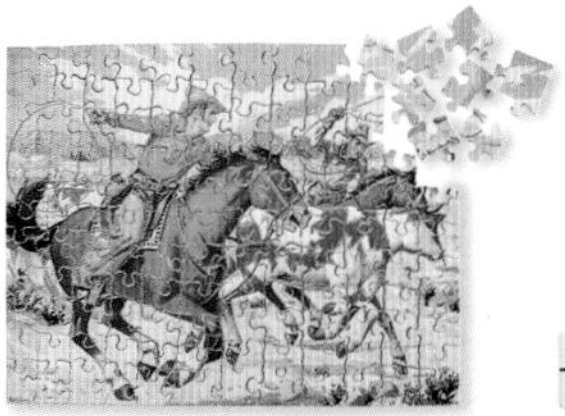

jigsaw puzzle | chitrakhanḍ pahelī | चित्रखंड पहेली

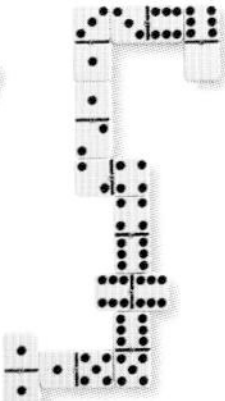

dominoes
ḍominos | डोमिनोस

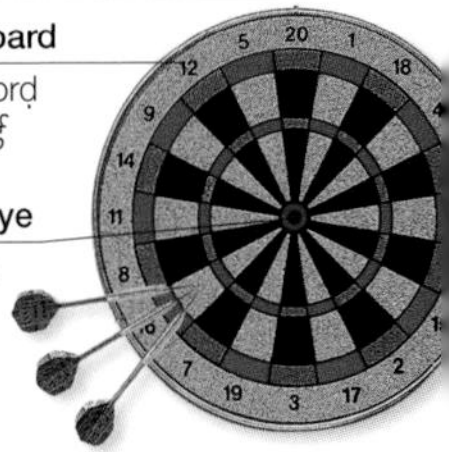

dartboard
ḍārṭ borḍ
डार्टबोर्ड

bullseye
lakṣya
लक्ष्य

darts
ḍārṭs | डार्ट्स

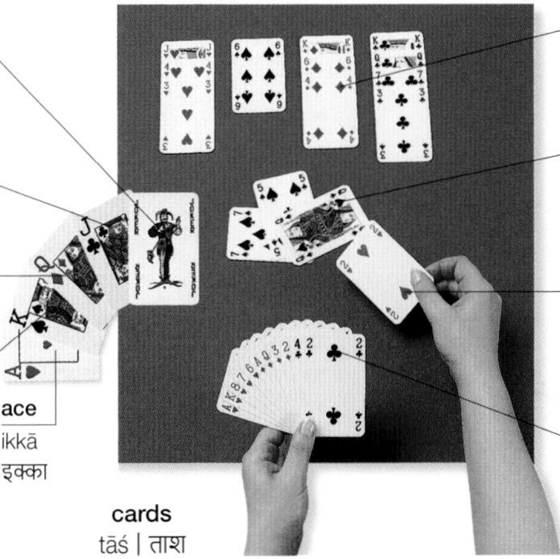

joker
jokar
जोकर

jack
gulām
गुलाम

queen
begam
बेगम

king
bādśāh
बादशाह

ace
ikkā
इक्का

diamond
īnṭ
ईंट

spade
hukum
हुकुम

heart
pān
पान

club
chiṛī
चिड़ी

cards
tāś | ताश

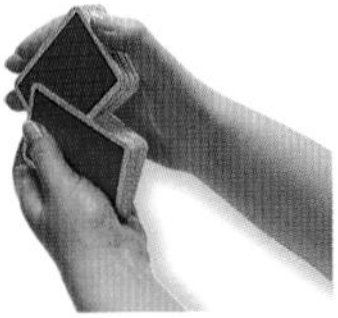

shuffle (v)
tāś phemṭnā | ताश फेंटना

deal (v)
patte bāmṭnā | पत्ते बांटना

vocabulary • śabdāvalī • शब्दावली

move chāl चाल	**win (v)** jītnā जीतना	**loser** parājit पराजित	**point** nambar नंबर	**bridge** brij ब्रिज	**Roll the dice.** pāsā phemko पासा फेंको
play (v) khelnā खेलना	**winner** vijetā विजेता	**game** khel खेल	**score** arjit amk अर्जित अंक	**deck of cards** tāś kī gaḍḍī ताश की गड्डी	**Whose turn is it?** kiskī bārī hai? किसकी बारी है?
player khilāṛī खिलाड़ी	**lose (v)** hārnā हारना	**bet** śart शर्त	**poker** pokar पोकर	**suit** tāś raṅg ताश रंग	**It's your move.** ab tumhārī chāl hai अब तुम्हारी चाल है।

arts and crafts 1 • kalā aur śilp • कला और शिल्प 1

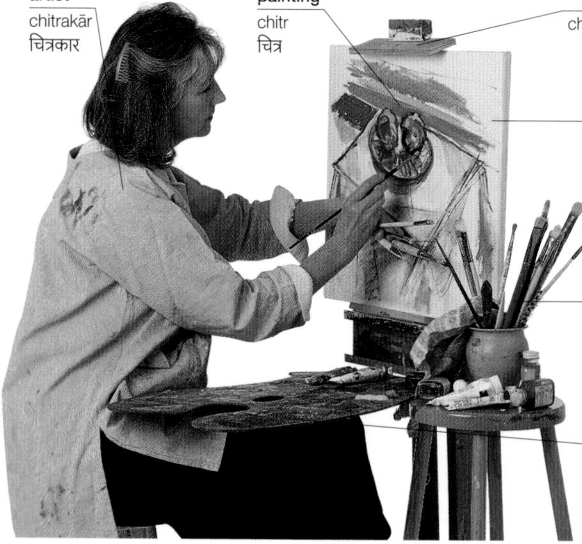

painting | chitrakārī | चित्रकारी

colors • raṅg • रंग

red lāl | लाल	**blue** nīlā | नीला	**yellow** pīlā | पीला	**green** harā | हरा
orange nāraṅgī | नारंगी	**purple** baiṅganī | बैंगनी	**white** safed | सफ़ेद	**black** kālā | काला
gray slēṭī | स्लेटी	**pink** gulābī | गुलाबी	**brown** bhūrā | भूरा	**indigo** nīl | नील

paints • raṅg • रंग

oil paint
tail raṅg | तैल रंग

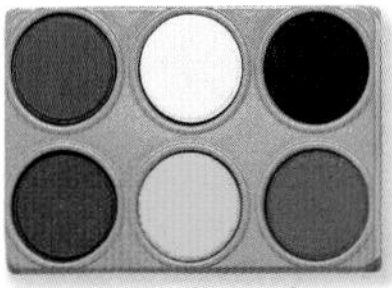

watercolor paint
pānī ke raṅg | पानी के रंग

pastels
raṅgīn khaṛiyā | रंगीन खड़िय

acrylic paint
ekrelik raṅg | एक्रेलिक रंग

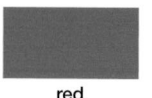

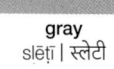

poster paint
pōsṭar raṅg | पोस्टर रंग

other crafts • anya kalāeṃ • अन्य कलाएं

sketch pad
rekhāṅkan paṭal
रेखांकन पटल

sketch
ḳhākā
ख़ाका

pencil
pensil
पेंसिल

charcoal
koyalā battī
कोयला बत्ती

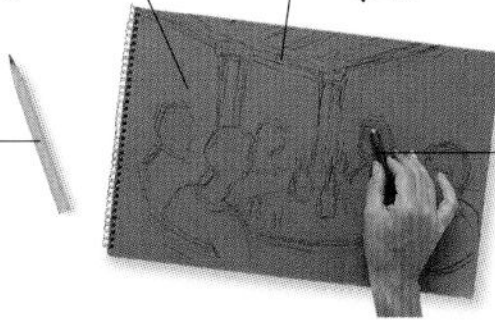

drawing | rekhāṅkan | रेखांकन

ink
syāhī
स्याही

printing
chhapāī | छपाई

engraving
utkīrṇan | उत्कीर्णन

stone
patthar
पत्थर

mallet
muṅgrā
मुंगरा

sculpting
mūrti śilp | मूर्ति शिल्प

chisel
chhainī
छैनी

wood
lakṛī
लकड़ी

woodworking
kāṣṭh-kalā | काष्ठ-कला

modeling tool
hastkalā upkaraṇ
हस्तकला उपकरण

potter's wheel
chāk
चाक

clay
chiknī miṭṭī
चिकनी
मिट्टी

pottery
kumhār karm | कुम्हार कर्म

glue
gond
गोंद

cardboard
gattā
गत्ता

collage | kolāj | कोलाज

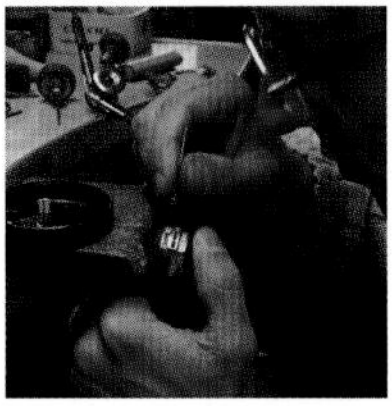

jewelry-making | ābhūṣaṇ-nirmāṇ | आभूषण निर्माण

papier-mâché | pepar māśe | पेपर माशे

origami
origemī | ऑरिगेमी

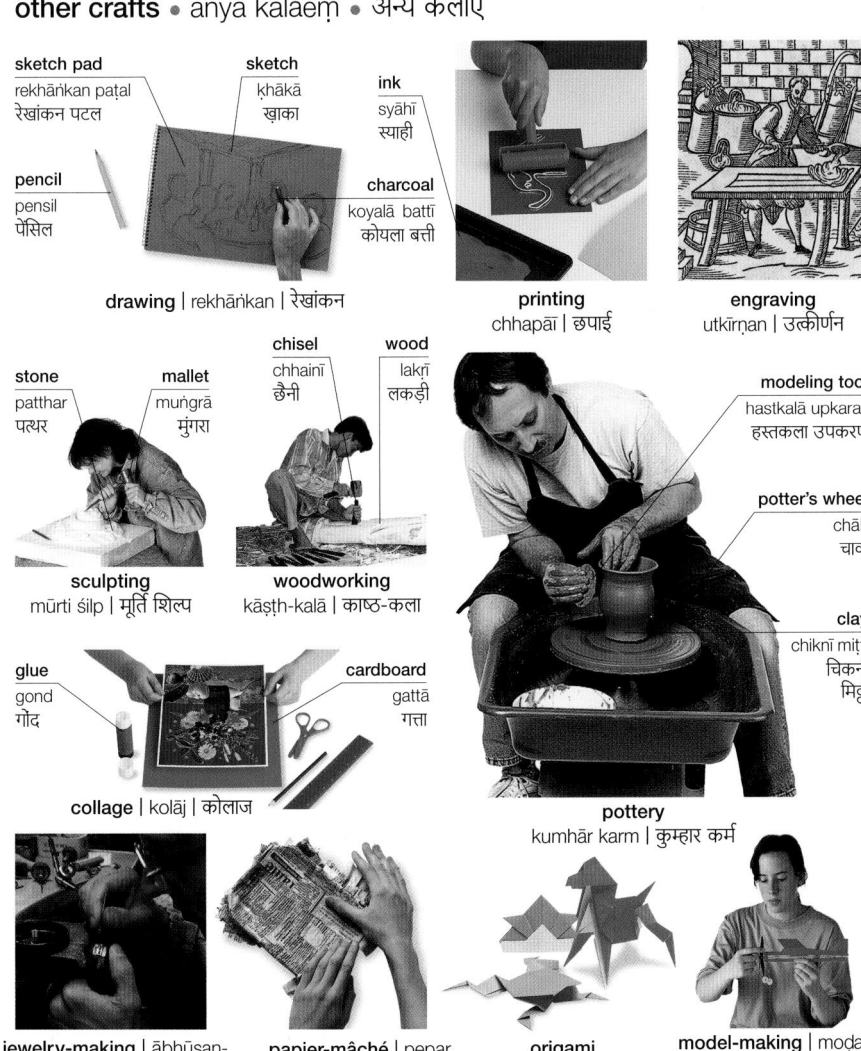

model-making | moḍal banānā | मॉडल बनाना

arts and crafts 2 • kalā aur śilp • कला और शिल्प 2

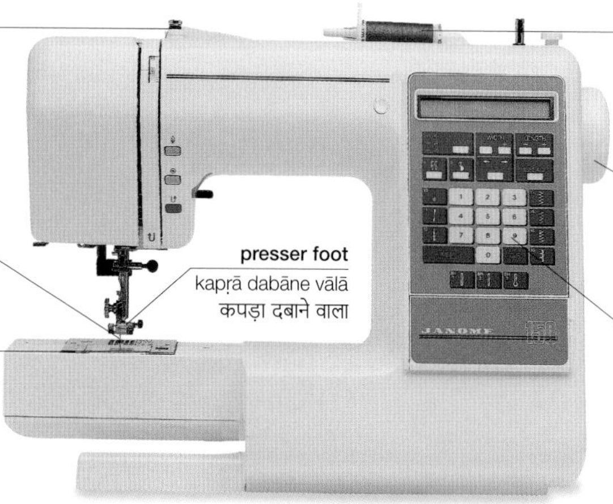

thread guide
dhāgā
धागा

spool of thread
dhāge kī rīl
धागे की रील

needle
sūī
सूई

balance wheel
pahiyā
पहिया

presser foot
kapṛā dabāne vālā
कपड़ा दबाने वाला

needle plate
sūī ke nīche kī pattī
सूई के नीचे की पत्ती

stitch selector
silāī chayan baṭan
सिलाई चयन बटन

sewing machine
silāī maśīn | सिलाई मशीन

scissors
ḳaiṃchī
क़ैंची

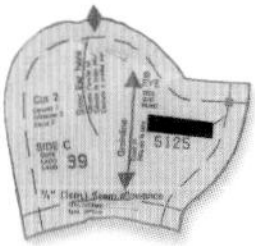

pattern
ḳhākā
ख़ाका

pincushion
pinkuśan
पिनकुशन

pin
pin
पिन

sewing basket
silāī kī ṭokrī | सिलाई की टोकरी

tape measure
inch ṭep
इंच टेप

material
kapṛā | कपड़ा

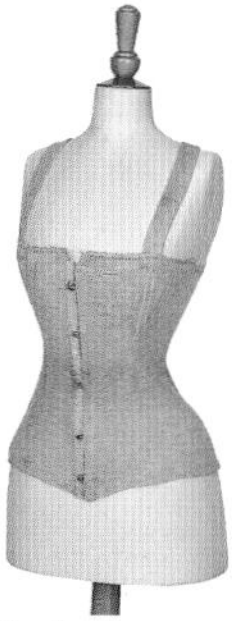

bobbin
phirkī
फिरकी

thread
dhāgā
धागा

eye
āī | आई

hook
huk
हुक

thimble
aṃguśtānā
अंगुश्ताना

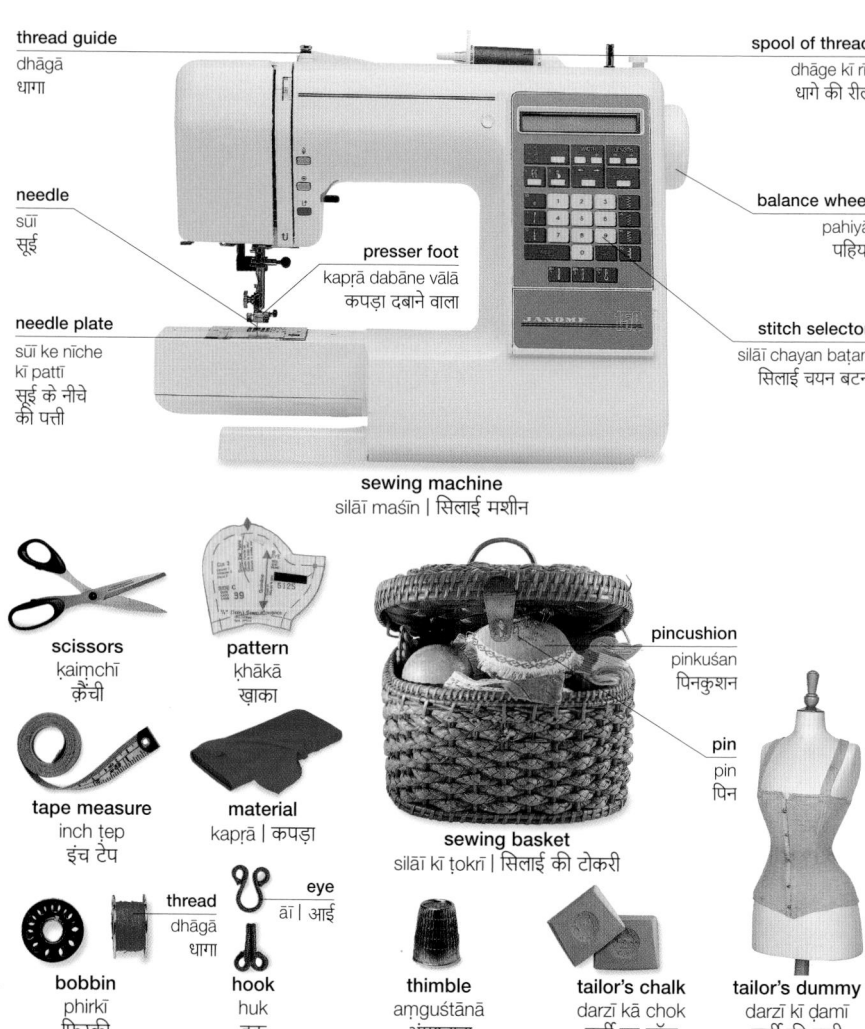

tailor's chalk
darzī kā chok
दर्ज़ी का चॉक

tailor's dummy
darzī kī ḍamī
दर्ज़ी की डमी

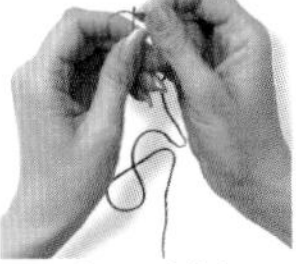

thread (v)
dhāgā ḍālnā
धागा डालना

stitch
bakhiyā
बखिया

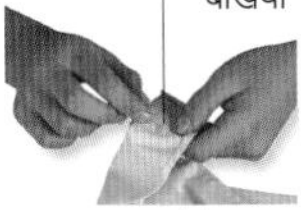

sew (v)
silnā
सिलना

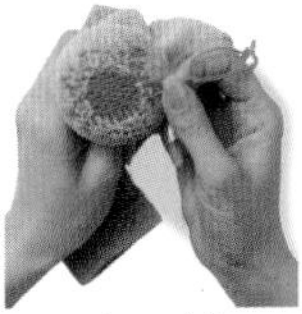

darn (v)
rafū karnā
रफ़ू करना

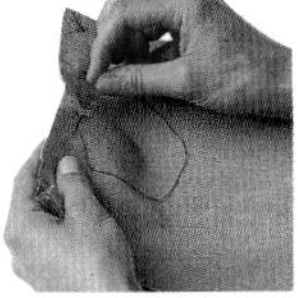

tack (v)
ṭāṃknā
टांकना

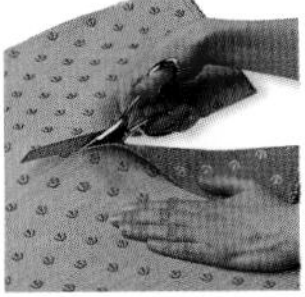

cut (v)
kāṭnā
काटना

needlepoint
sūī kī nok
सूई की नोक

embroidery
kaṛhāī
कढ़ाई

crochet hook
krośiyā huk
क्रोशिया हुक

crochet
krośiyā
क्रोशिया

macramé
jhālar
झालर

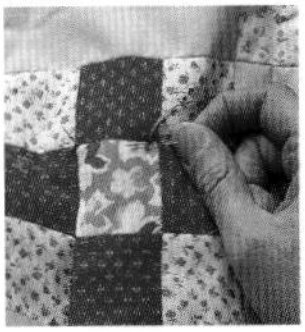

patchwork
paiband
पैबंद

quilting
parat lagānā
परत लगाना

lace bobbin
les bobin
लेस बॉबिन

lace-making
les banānā
लेस बनाना

loom
karghā
करघा

weaving
bunnā
बुनना

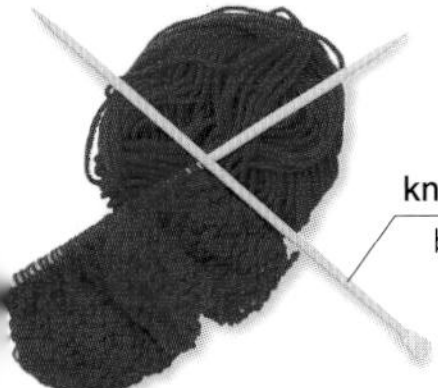

knitting needle
bunne kī salāī
बुनने की सलाई

knitting
bunāī | बुनाई

yarn
ūn
ऊन

skein
lacchhī | लच्छी

vocabulary • śabdāvalī • शब्दावली

unpick (v)
udheṛnā
उधेड़ना

fabric
kapṛā
कपड़ा

cotton
sūtī kapṛā
सूती कपड़ा

linen
linen
लिनेन

polyester
polīesṭar
पॉलीएस्टर

nylon
nāyalon
नायलोन

silk
reśam
रेशम

designer
ḍizāinar
डिज़ाइनर

fashion
faiśan
फ़ैशन

zipper
zip
ज़िप

environment

paryāvaraṇ

पर्यावरण

space • antarikṣ • अंतरिक्ष

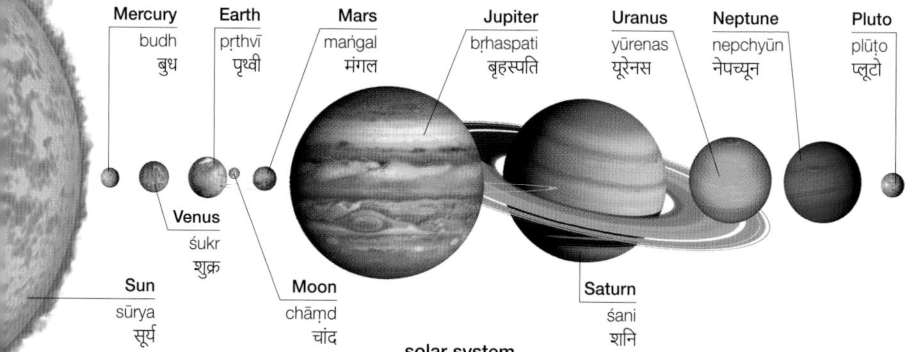

solar system
saur maṇḍal | सौर मंडल

galaxy
tārāsamūh | तारासमूह

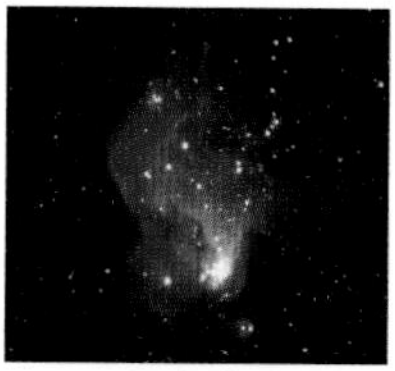

nebula
nihārikā | निहारिका

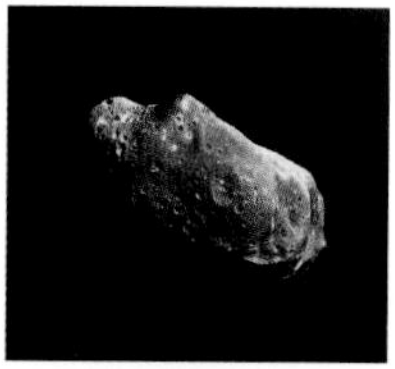

asteroid
grahikā | ग्रहिका

comet
dhūmketu | धूमकेतु

vocabulary • śabdāvalī • शब्दावली

universe brahmāṇḍ ब्रह्मांड	**black hole** blaik hol ब्लैक होल	**full moon** pūrā chāṃd पूरा चांद
orbit kakṣā कक्षा	**planet** grah ग्रह	**new moon** pratipadā kā chāṃd प्रतिपदा का चांद
gravity gurutv गुरुत्व	**meteor** ulkā उल्का	**crescent moon** ardhchandr अर्धचंद्र

eclipse | grahaṇ | ग्रहण

space exploration • antarikṣ anveṣaṇ • अंतरिक्ष अन्वेषण

launch | prakṣepaṇ | प्रक्षेपण

astronaut | antarikṣ yātrī | अंतरिक्ष यात्री

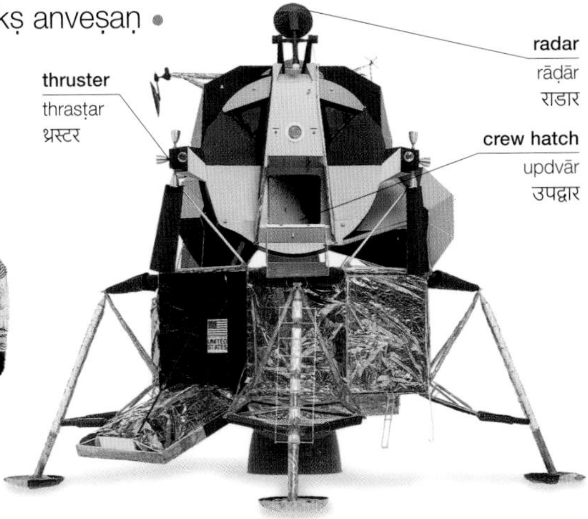

lunar module | chandryān | चंद्रयान

satellite | upgrah | उपग्रह

space station | antarikṣ kendr | अंतरिक्ष केंद्र

astronomy • khagol vijñān • खगोल विज्ञान

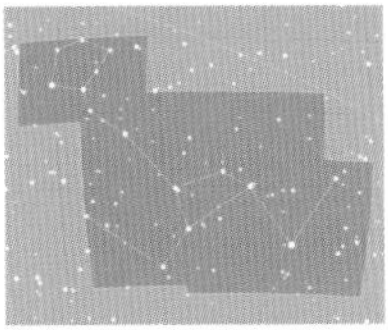

constellation | tārāmaṇḍal | तारामंडल

binoculars | dūrbīn | दूरबीन

Earth • pṛthvī • पृथ्वी

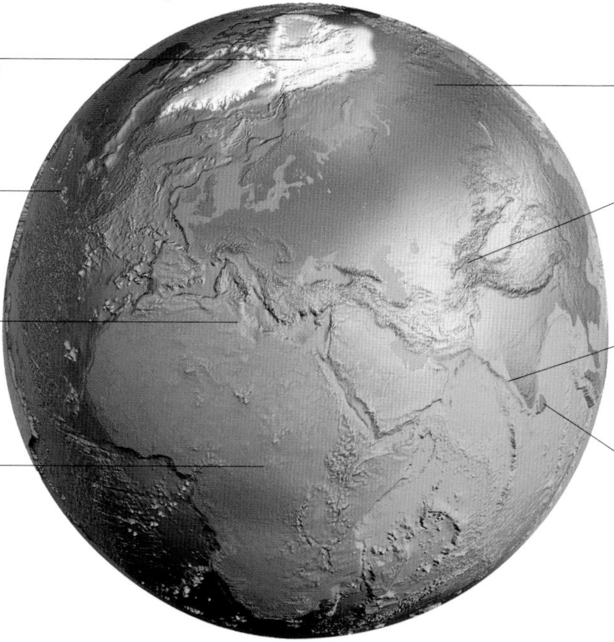

planet | grah | ग्रह

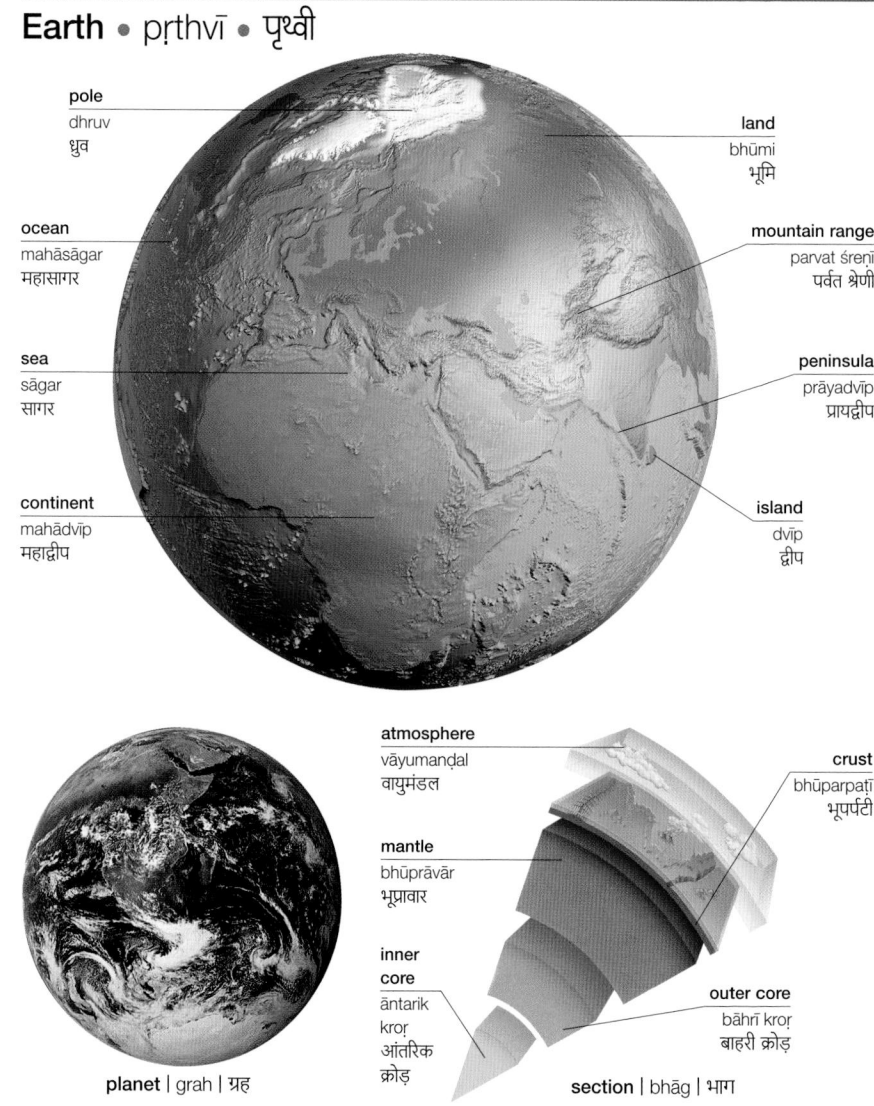

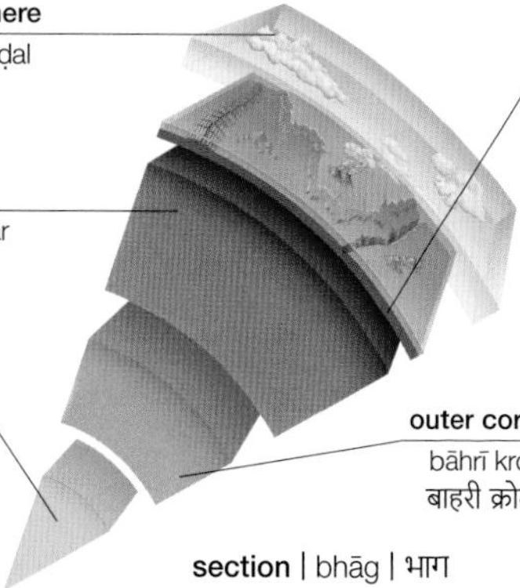

section | bhāg | भाग

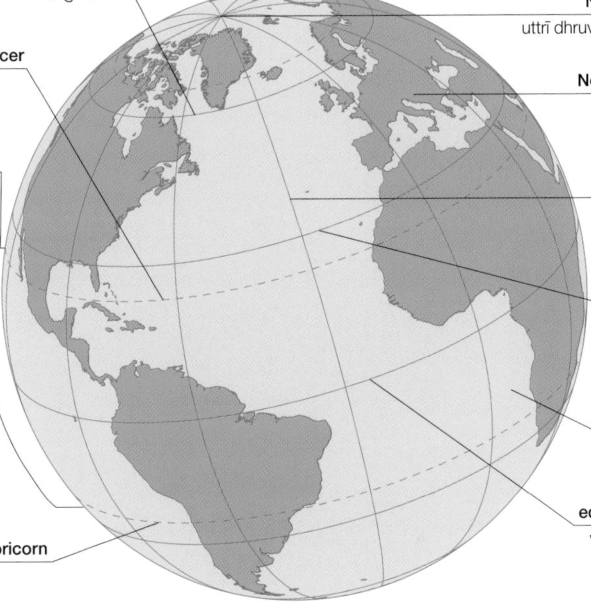

zones | kaṭibandh | कटिबंध

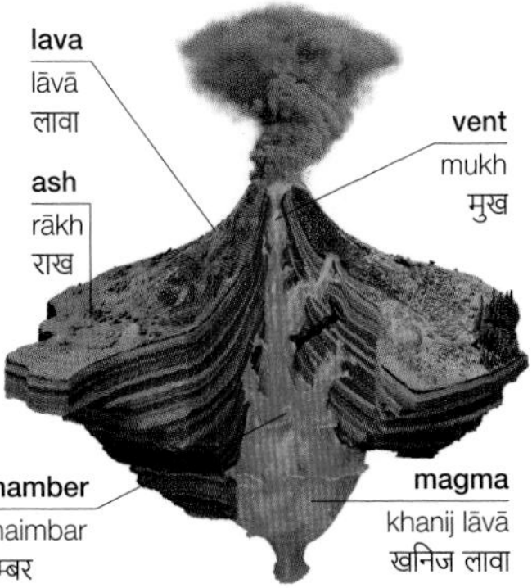

volcano | jvālāmukhī | ज्वालामुखी

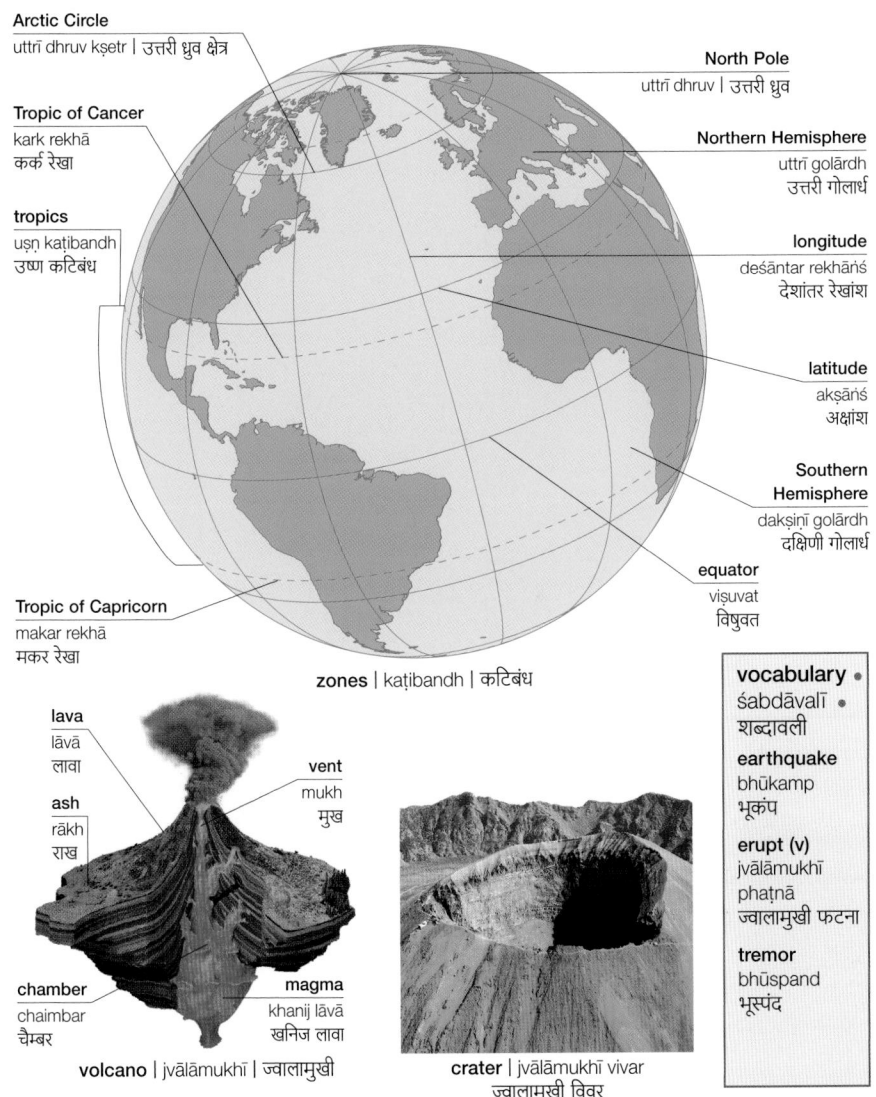

crater | jvālāmukhī vivar
ज्वालामुखी विवर

vocabulary • śabdāvalī • शब्दावली

earthquake
bhūkamp
भूकंप

erupt (v)
jvālāmukhī phaṭnā
ज्वालामुखी फटना

tremor
bhūspand
भूस्पंद

landscape • bhūdṛṣya • भूदृष्य

glacier
himnad | हिमनद

valley | ghāṭī | घाटी

hill
pahāṛī | पहाड़ी

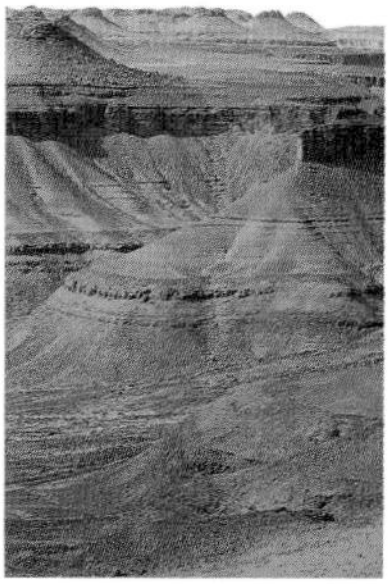

plateau
paṭhār | पठार

gorge
darrā | दर्रा

cave
guphā | गुफा

plain | maidān | मैदान

desert | registān
रेगिस्तान

forest | jaṅgal | जंगल

woods | van | वन

rain forest
varṣā van | वर्षा वन

swamp
daldal | दलदल

meadow
charāgāh | चरागाह

grassland | ghās kā
maidān | घास का मैदान

waterfall
jalprapāt | जलप्रपात

stream
dhārā | धारा

lake
jhīl | झील

geyser
garm jalsrot | गर्म जलस्रोत

coast
samudr taṭ | समुद्र तट

cliff | kharī chaṭṭān
खड़ी चट्टान

coral reef
pravāl dvīp | प्रवाल द्वीप

estuary | sāgar vilyan
सागर विलयन

weather • mausam • मौसम

exosphere
parāmaṇḍal
परामंडल

aurora
dhruvjyoti
ध्रुवज्योति

thermosphere
tāpmaṇḍal
तापमंडल

sunshine | dhūp | धूप

ionosphere
āyan maṇḍal
आयन मंडल

mesosphere
madhya maṇḍal
मध्य मंडल

ultraviolet rays
parābaiṅganī kirṇem
पराबैंगनी किरणें

stratosphere
samtāp maṇḍal
समताप मंडल

ozone layer
ozon parat
ओज़ोन परत

troposphere
nimntāp maṇḍal
निम्नताप मंडल

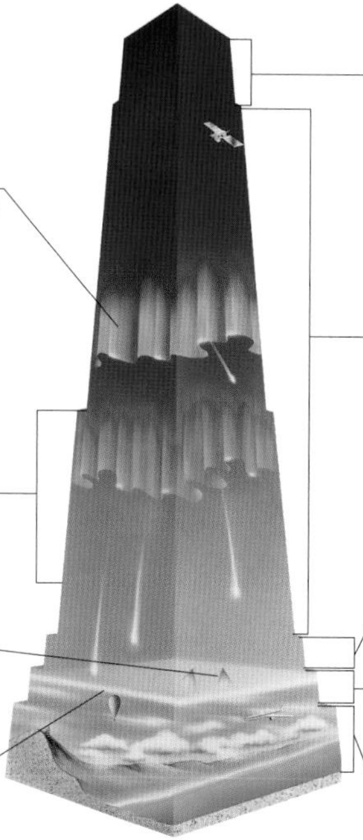

atmosphere | vayumaṇḍal | वायुमंडल

wind | pavan | पवन

vocabulary • śabdāvalī • शब्दावली

sleet himvarṣā हिमवर्षा	shower bauchhār बौछार	hot garm गर्म	dry sūkhā सूखा	windy tūfānī तूफ़ानी
hail ole ओले	sunny dhūpdār धूपदार	cold ṭhaṇḍā ठंडा	wet gīlā गीला	gale āndhī आंधी
thunder garaj गरज	cloudy meghācchann मेघाच्छन्न	warm gungunā गुनगुना	humid nam नम	temperature tāpmān तापमान

I'm hot/cold.
mujhe garmī/ṭhaṇḍ lag rahī hai
मुझे गर्मी/ठंड लग रही है।

It's raining.
bāriś ho rahī hai
बारिश हो रही है।

It's … degrees.
tāpmān … ḍigrī hai
तापमान... डिग्री है।

cloud | bādal | बादल

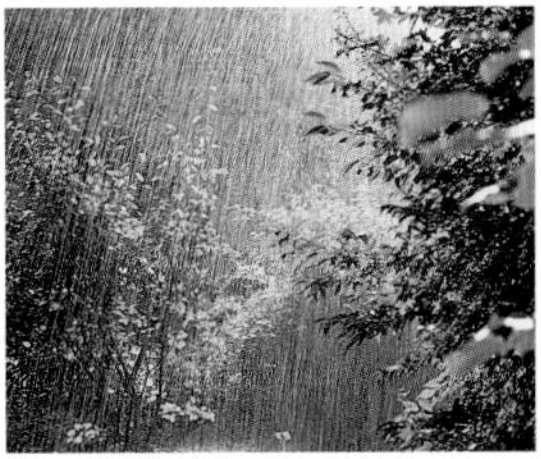

rain | bāriś | बारिश

storm | tūfān | तूफ़ान

mist | kohrā | कोहरा

fog | dhundh | धुंध

rainbow | indrdhanuṣ | इंद्रधनुष

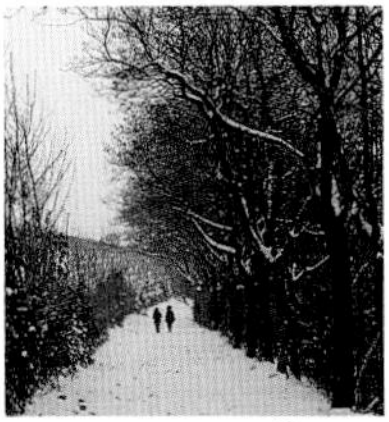

snow | him | हिम

frost | tuṣār | तुषार

ice | barf | बर्फ़

freeze | ṭhanḍ | ठंड

hurricane
chakrvāt | चक्रवात

tornado
bavanḍar | बवंडर

monsoon
varṣā | वर्षा

flood
bāṛh | बाढ़

rocks • pāṣāṇ • पाषाण

igneous • jvalāmukhīya śail • ज्वालामुखीय शैल

granite
grenāiṭ
ग्रेनाइट

obsidian
obsiḍiyan
ओबसिडियन

basalt
kālā patthar
काला पत्थर

pumice
jhāmak
झामक

sedimentary • avsādī śail • अवसादी शैल

sandstone
baluā patthar
बलुआ पत्थर

limestone
chūnā patthar
चूना पत्थर

chalk
khaṛiyā
खड़िया

flint
chakmak
चकमक

conglomerate
pāṣāṇit kaṅkaṛ
पाषाणित कंकड़

coal
koyalā
कोयला

metamorphic • rūpāntarit śail • रूपांतरित शैल

slate
sleṭ
स्लेट

schist
starit chaṭṭān
स्तरित चट्टान

gneiss
śail
शैल

marble
saṅgmarmar
संगमरमर

gems • ratan • रत्न

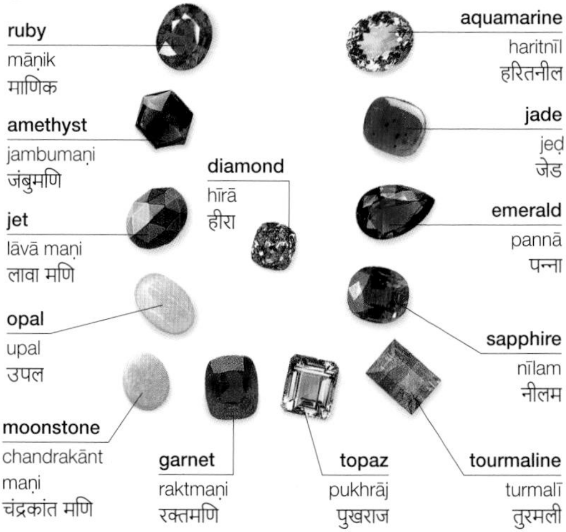

minerals • khanij • खनिज

quartz
sphaṭik
स्फटिक

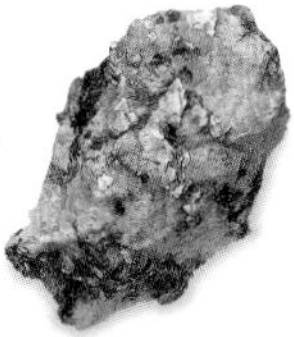

mica
abhrak
अभ्रक

sulfur
gandhak
गंधक

hematite
hemeṭāiṭ
हेमेटाइट

calcite
kailsāiṭ
कैल्साइट

malachite
melākāiṭ
मेलाकाइट

turquoise
fīrojā
फ़ीरोजा

onyx
sarpmaṇi
सर्पमणि

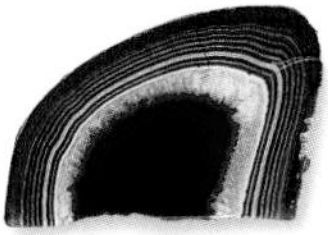

agate
akīk
अकीक

graphite
grefāiṭ
ग्रेफ़ाइट

metals • dhātu • धातु

gold
sonā | सोना

silver
chāndī
चांदी

platinum
pleṭinam
प्लेटिनम

nickel
nikal | निकल

iron
lohā | लोहा

copper
tāmbā | तांबा

tin
ṭin | टिन

aluminium
alyūminiyam
अल्यूमिनियम

mercury
pārā | पारा

zinc
jastā | जस्ता

animals 1 • paśu • पशु 1

mammals • standhārī jīv • स्तनधारी जीव

rabbit
ḳhargoś
ख़रगोश

hamster
haimsṭar | हैमस्टर

mouse
mūṣak | मूषक

rat
chūhā | चूहा

hedgehog
sāhī | साही

squirrel
gilahrī
गिलहरी

bat
chamgādaṛ
चमगादड़

raccoon
raikūn
रैकून

fox
lomṛī
लोमड़ी

wolf
bheṛiyā
भेड़िया

dog
kuttā | कुत्ता

cat
billī | बिल्ली

otter
ūdbilāv | ऊदबिलाव

seal
sīl | सील

sea lion
samudr siṅh
समुद्र सिंह

walrus
hāthī sīl
हाथी सील

whale
vhel | व्हेल

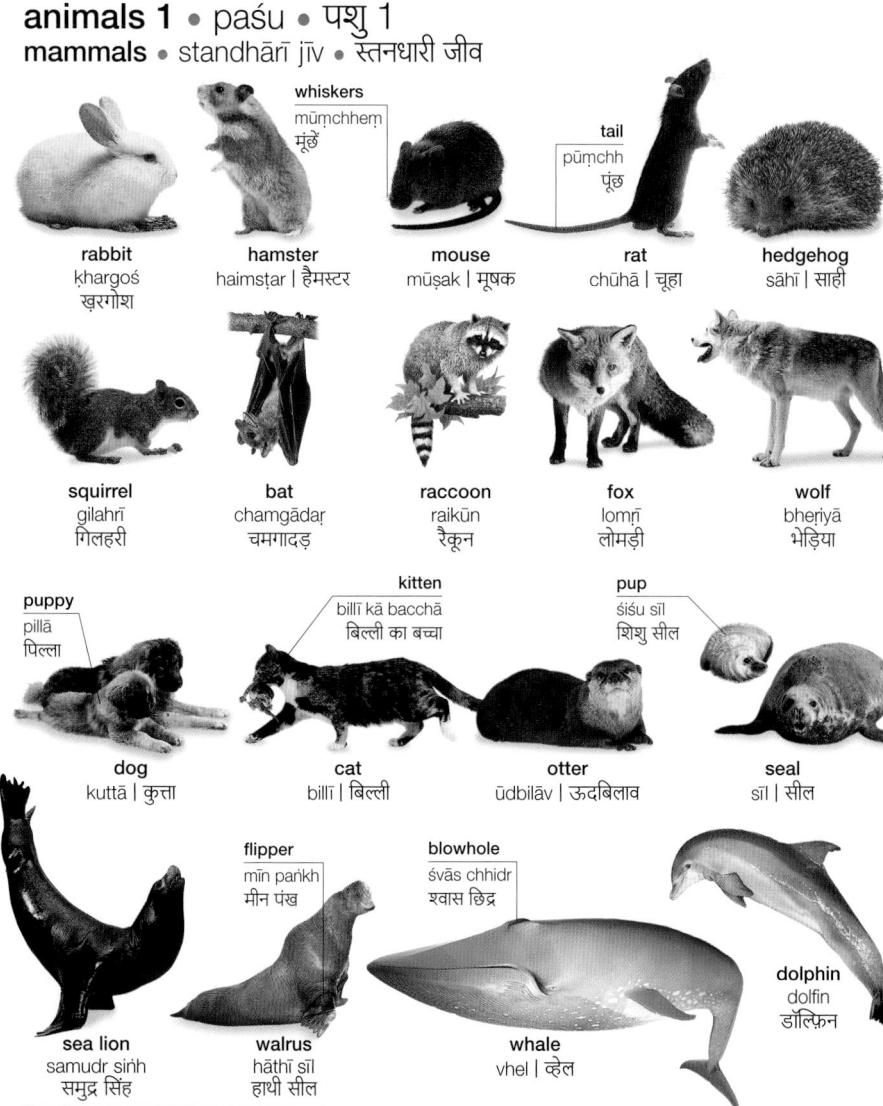

dolphin
dolfin
डॉल्फ़िन

deer
hiran | हिरन

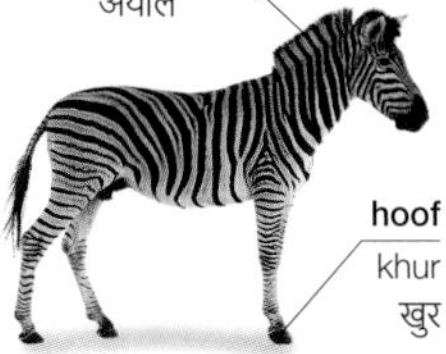

zebra
zebrā | ज़ेबरा

giraffe
jirāf | जिराफ़

camel
ūṃṭ | ऊंट

hippopotamus
dariyāī ghoṛā | दरियाई घोड़ा

elephant
hāthī | हाथी

rhinoceros
gaiṇḍā | गैंडा

tiger
bāgh | बाघ

lion
babbar śer | बब्बर शेर

monkey
bandar | बंदर

gorilla
gorillā | गोरिल्ला

koala
koālā | कोआला

kangaroo
kaṅgārū | कंगारू

bear
bhālū | भालू

polar bear
dhruvīya bhālū | ध्रुवीय भालू

animals 2 • paśu • पशु 2

birds • pakṣī • पक्षी

canary
chhoṭī pīlī chiṛiyā
छोटी पीली चिड़िया

sparrow
goraiyā | गोरैया

hummingbird | marmar pakṣī | मर्मर पक्षी

swallow
abābīl | अबाबील

crow
kauā | कौआ

pigeon
kabūtar | कबूतर

woodpecker
kaṭhphoṛvā
कठफोड़वा

falcon
bāz | बाज़

owl
ullū | उल्लू

gull
ghomrā | घोमरा

eagle
ukāb | उक़ाब

pelican
pelikan | पेलिकन

flamingo
rājhaṃs | राजहंस

stork
bagulā | बगुला

crane
sāras | सारस

penguin
peṅguin | पेंगुइन

ostrich
śuturmurg | शुतुरमुर्ग

goose
bataḳh | बतख़

swan
haṃs | हंस

peacock
mor | मोर

pheasant
tītar | तीतर

turkey
ṭarkī | टर्की

cockatoo
kākātū totā
काकातू तोता

beak
choṃch
चोंच

feather
far
फ़र

wing
paṅkh
पंख

claw
panjā
पंजा

parrot
totā | तोता

reptiles • sarīsṛp • सरीसृप

scales
sūkhī chamṛī
सूखी चमड़ी

alligator
ghaṛiyāl | घड़ियाल

lizard
chhipkalī | छिपकली

iguana
goh | गोह

shell
kavach
कवच

turtle | samudrī kachhuā | समुद्री कछुआ

tortoise
kachhuā | कछुआ

snake
sāṃp | सांप

snout
thūthnī
थूथनी

crocodile
magarmacchh | मगरमच्छ

animals 3 • paśu • पशु 3

amphibians • ubhayachar jīv • उभयचर जीव

frog
memḍhak | मेंढक

toad
thal memḍhak | थल मेंढक

tadpole
śiśu memḍhak | शिशु मेंढक

salamander
sarṭak | सरटक

fish • machhlī • मछली

eel
bām machhlī | बाम मछली

shark
śārk | शार्क

seahorse
aśvmīn | अश्वमीन

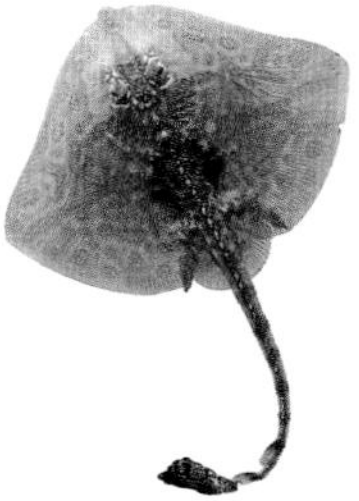

skate
skeṭ machhlī | स्केट मछली

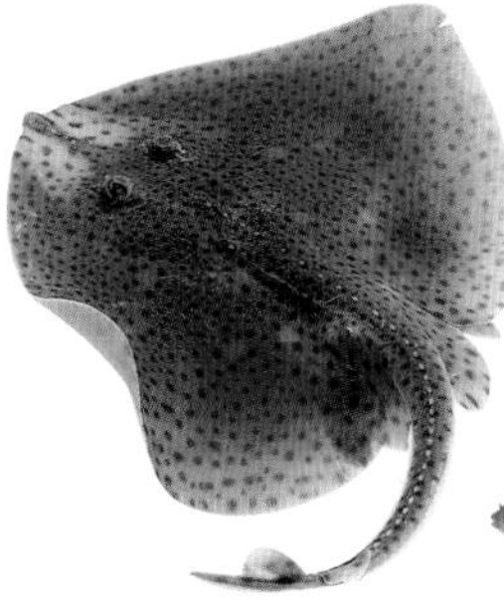

ray
re | रे

goldfish
sonmāchhī | सोनमाछी

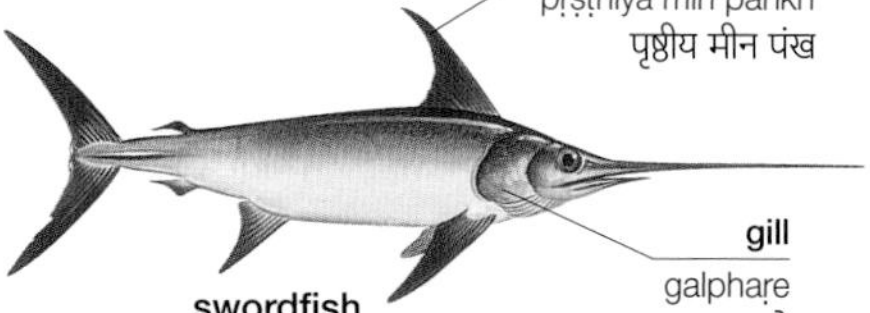

swordfish
khaṅg mīn | खंग मीन

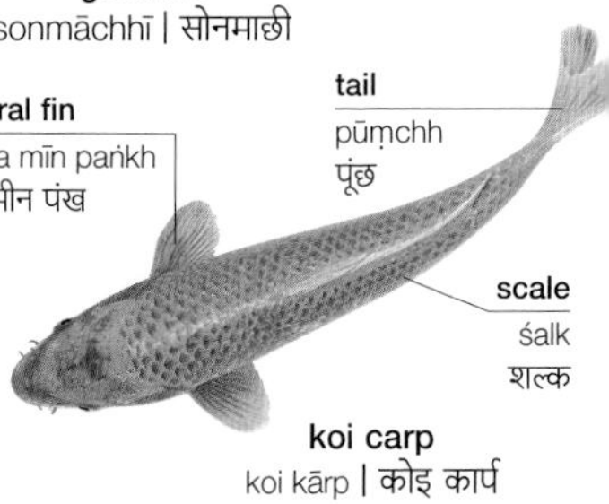

koi carp
koi kārp | कोइ कार्प

invertebrates • akaśerukī jīv • अकशेरुकी जीव

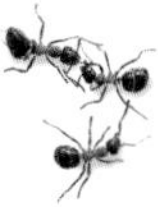

ant
chīṃṭī | चींटी

termite
dīmak | दीमक

bee
madhumakkhī | मधुमक्खी

wasp
barr | बर्र

beetle
phūṅgā | फूंगा

cockroach
tilchaṭṭā | तिलचट्टा

moth
pataṅgā | पतंगा

butterfly
titlī | तितली

cocoon
koyā | कोया

caterpillar
illī | इल्ली

cricket
jhīṅgur | झींगुर

grasshopper
ṭiḍḍā | टिड्डा

praying mantis
mantris | मंत्रिस

sting
ḍaṅk
डंक

scorpion
bicchhū | बिच्छू

centipede
kankhajūrā | कनखजूरा

dragonfly
ḍraigan flāī
ड्रैगन फ़्लाई

fly
makkhī | मक्खी

mosquito
macchhar | मच्छर

ladybug
leḍībarḍ | लेडीबर्ड

spider
makṛī | मकड़ी

slug
kambu | कंबु

snail
ghoṃghā | घोंघा

worm
kṛmi | कृमि

starfish
sṭār fiś | स्टार फ़िश

mussel
śambuk | शंबुक

crab
kekṛā | केकड़ा

lobster
lobsṭar | लॉबस्टर

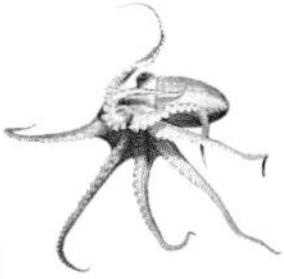

octopus
aṣṭbhuj | अष्टभुज

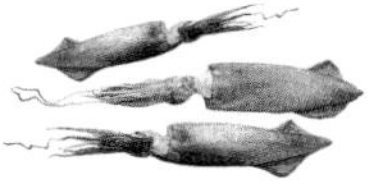

squid
skviḍ | स्क्विड

jellyfish
jelī fiś | जेली फ़िश

plants • vanaspati • वनस्पति

tree • peṛ • पेड़

oak | bāṃj | बांज

willow
śarpat | शरपत

poplar | vilāyatī
pīpal | विलायती पीपल

eucalyptus
nīlgiri | नीलगिरि

larch
śrīdāru | श्रीदारु

beech
bīch | बीच

birch
bhojvṛkṣ | भोजवृक्ष

pine
chīṛ | चीड़

cedar
devdār | देवदार

maple
mepal | मेपल

elm
chirābel | चिराबेल

lime | nīmbū kā
vṛkṣ | नींबू का वृक्ष

holly
śūlparṇī | शूलपर्णी

palm
tāṛ | ताड़

flowering plant • puṣpī paudhe • पुष्पी पौधे

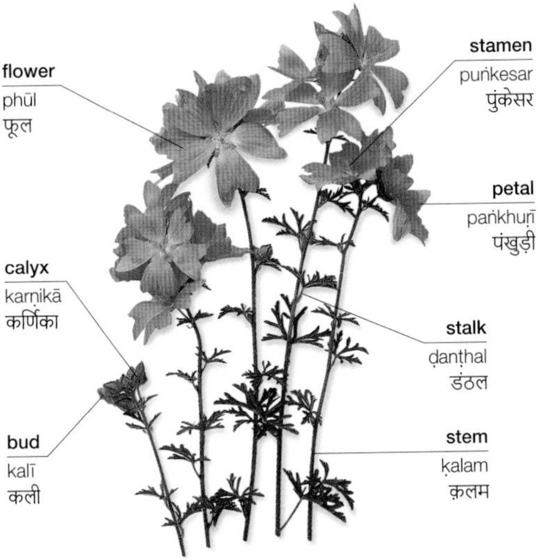

buttercup
baṭarkap | बटरकप

daisy
ḍezī | डेज़ी

thistle
ikṣugandhā
इक्षुगंधा

dandelion
kukrauṃdhā
कुकरौंधा

heather
haidar
हैदर

poppy
ahipuṣp
अहिपुष्प

foxglove
apsaroṅguli
अप्सरोंगुलि

honeysuckle
hanīsakal
हनीसकल

sunflower
sūryamukhī
सूर्यमुखी

clover
tinpatiyā
तिनपतिया

bluebells
jaṅglī gomed
जंगली गोमेद

primrose
primroz
प्रिमरोज़

lupines
lyūpin
ल्यूपिन

nettle
bicchhū-būṭī
बिच्छू-बूटी

city • śahar • शहर

street
saṛak
सड़क
curb
paṭrī
पटरी
street corner
galī kā nukkaṛ
गली का नुक्कड़
store
dukān
दुकान
intersection
caurāhā
चौराहा
one-way system
iktarfā rāstā
इकतरफ़ा रास्ता
sidewalk
fuṭpāth
फ़ुटपाथ
office building
kāryālaya khanḍ
कार्यालय खंड
apartment building
apārṭmenṭ khanḍ
अपार्टमेंट खंड
alley
galī
गली
parking lot
kār pārk
कार पार्क
street sign
mārg saṅketak
मार्ग संकेतक
barrier
khambhā
खंभा
street light
sṭrīṭ lāiṭ
स्ट्रीट लाइट

buildings • imārat • इमारत

town hall
ṭāun hol | टाउन हॉल

library
pustakālaya | पुस्तकालय

movie theater
sinemā | सिनेमा

theater
thieṭar | थिएटर

university
viśvvidyālaya | विश्वविद्यालय

school
vidyālaya | विद्यालय

skyscraper
gaganchumbī imārat
गगनचुंबी इमारत

areas • kṣetr • क्षेत्र

industrial park
audyogik kṣetr
औद्योगिक क्षेत्र

city
śahar | शहर

suburb
upnagar | उपनगर

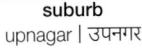

village
gāṃv | गांव

vocabulary • śabdāvalī • शब्दावली

pedestrian zone
paidal rāstā
पैदल रास्ता

avenue
rāstā
रास्ता

side street
galī
गली

square
chauk
चौक

manhole
mainhol
मैनहोल

bus stop
bas sṭop
बस स्टॉप

gutter
nālā
नाला

factory
kārḳhānā
कारख़ाना

church
charch
चर्च

drain
nālī
नाली

architecture • vāstuśilp • वास्तुशिल्प

buildings and structures • bhavan evam imārateṃ • भवन एवं इमारतें

skyscraper | gaganchumbī imārat | गगनचुंबी इमारत

turret
burj
बुर्ज

moat
khāī
खाई

castle
ḳilā | क़िला

church
girjāghar | गिरजाघर

dome
gumbad
गुम्बद

mosque
masjid | मस्जिद

temple
mandir | मंदिर

vault
mehrābdār chhat
मेहराबदार छत

synagogue | yahūdī pūjāsthal
यहूदी पूजास्थल

dam
bāndh | बांध

bridge
pul | पुल

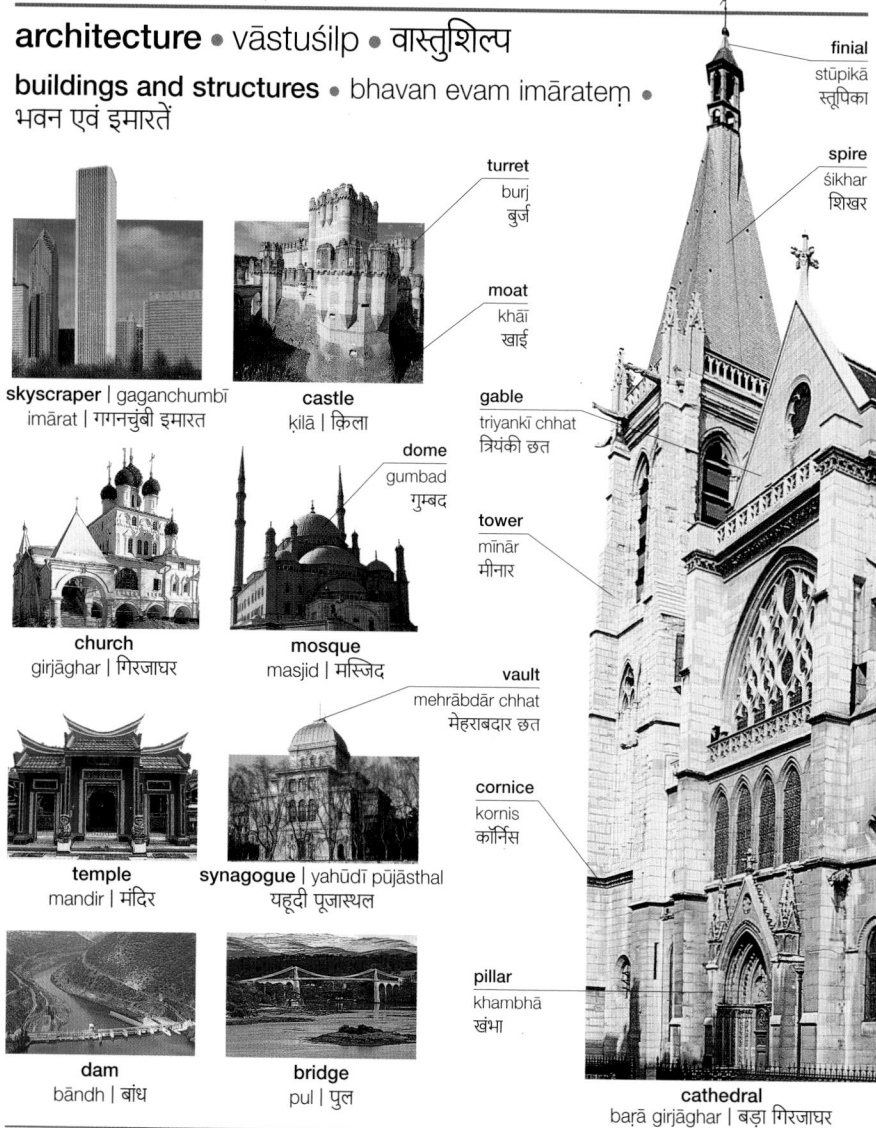

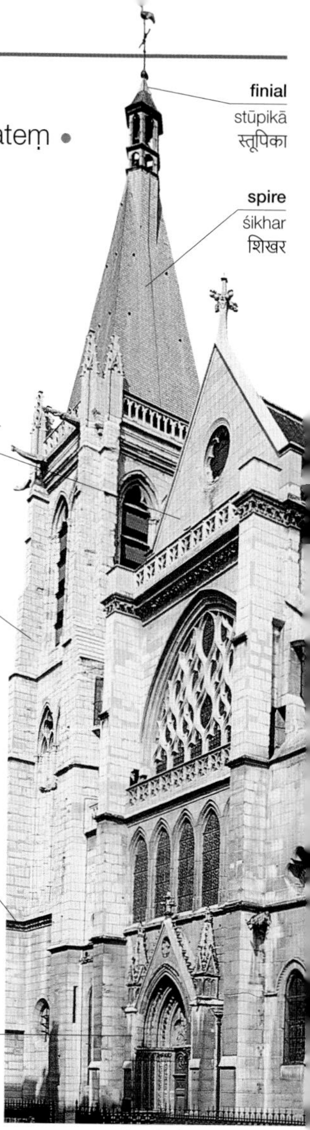

finial
stūpikā
स्तूपिका

spire
śikhar
शिखर

gable
triyankī chhat
त्रियंकी छत

tower
mīnār
मीनार

cornice
kornis
कॉर्निस

pillar
khambhā
खंभा

cathedral
baṛā girjāghar | बड़ा गिरजाघर

styles • śailī • शैली

Gothic
gothik | गॉथिक

architrave
prastarpād
प्रस्तरपाद

Renaissance
renesāns | रेनेसान्स

Baroque
bārok | बारोक

choir
gāyan sthal
गायन स्थल

Rococo
rokoko | रोकोको

arch
mehrāb
मेहराब

frieze
chitr vallarī
चित्र वल्लरी

buttress
puśtā
पुश्ता

pediment
trikonikā
त्रिकोनिका

Neoclassical
navśāstrīya | नवशास्त्रीय

Art Nouveau
ārṭ nūvo | आर्ट नूवो

Art Deco
ārṭ ḍeko | आर्ट डेको

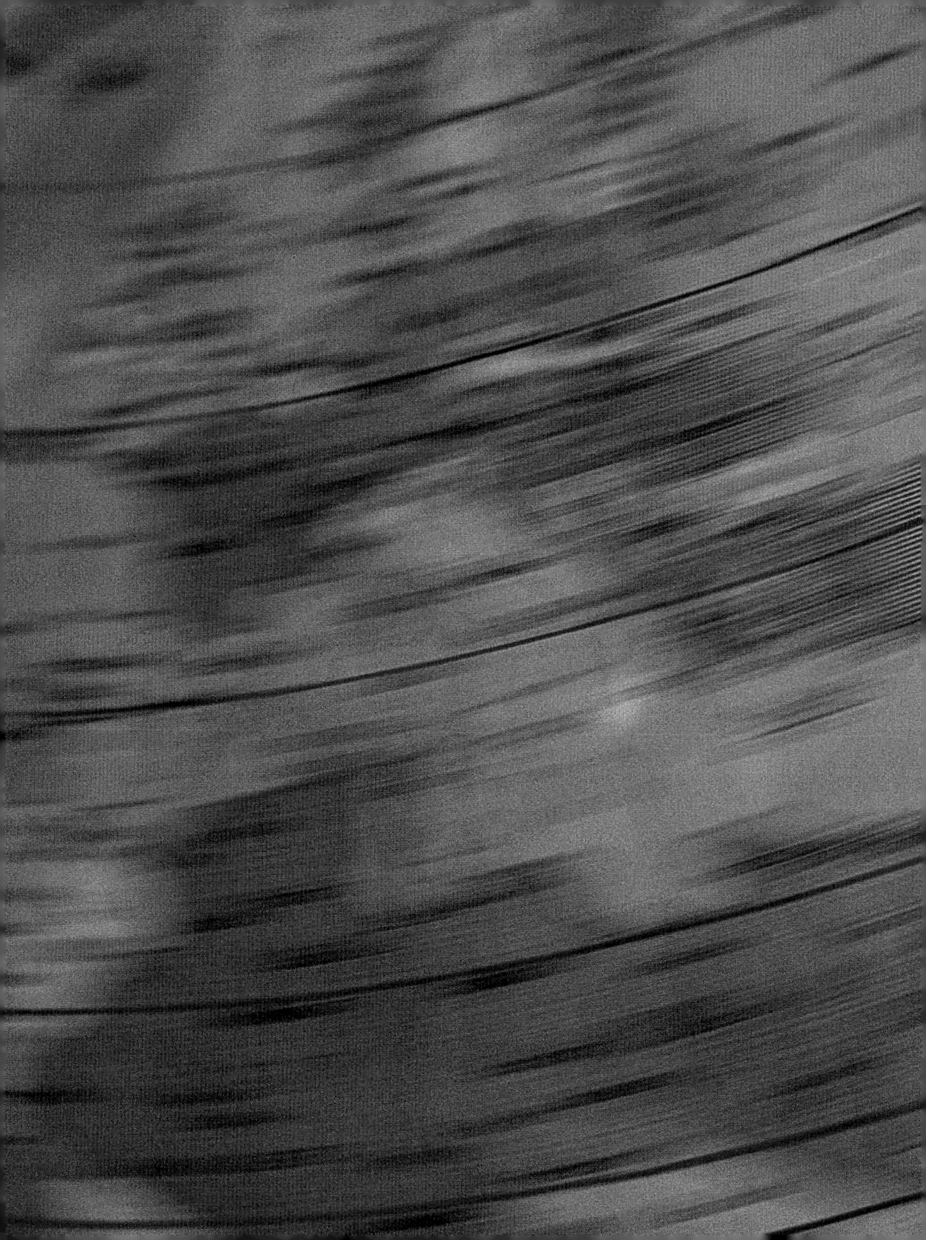

reference
sandarbh
संदर्भ

time • samaya • समय

minute hand
minaṭ kī suī
मिनट की सुई

hour hand
ghanṭe kī suī
घंटे की सुई

clock | ghaṛī | घड़ी

vocabulary • śabdāvalī • शब्दावली

second sekanḍ सेकंड	**now** abhī अभी	**a quarter of an hour** pandrah minaṭ पंद्रह मिनट
minute minaṭ मिनट	**later** bād meṃ बाद में	**twenty minutes** bīs minaṭ बीस मिनट
hour ghanṭā घंटा	**half an hour** ādhā ghanṭā आधा घंटा	**forty minutes** chālīs minaṭ चालीस मिनट

What time is it?
kyā samaya huā hai?
क्या समय हुआ है?

It's three o'clock.
tīn baj gae haiṃ
तीन बज गए हैं।

five past one
ek baj kar pāṃch minaṭ
एक बज कर पांच मिनट

ten past one
ek baj kar das minaṭ
एक बज कर दस मिनट

quarter past one
savā ek
सवा एक

twenty past one
ek baj kar bīs minaṭ
एक बज कर बीस मिनट

second hand
saikanḍ kī suī
सेकंड की सुई

twenty-five past one
ek baj kar pacchīs minaṭ
एक बज कर पच्चीस मिनट

one thirty
ḍeṛh
डेढ़

twenty-five to two
do bajne meṃ pacchīs minaṭ
दो बजने में पच्चीस मिनट

twenty to two
do bajne meṃ bīs mina
दो बजने में बीस मिनट

quarter to two
paune do
पौने दो

ten to two
do bajne meṃ das minaṭ
दो बजने में दस मिनट

five to two
do bajne meṃ pāṃch minaṭ
दो बजने में पांच मिनट

two o'clock
do baje
दो बजे

night and day • rāt aur din • रात और दिन

midnight
ardhrātri | अर्धरात्रि

sunrise
sūryodaya | सूर्योदय

dawn
bhor | भोर

morning
subah | सुबह

sunset
sūryāst | सूर्यास्त

noon
madhyāhn | मध्याह्न

dusk
sāyaṃkāl | सायंकाल

evening
sandhyā | संध्या

afternoon
dopahar | दोपहर

vocabulary • śabdāvalī • शब्दावली

early
jaldī
जल्दी

on time
samaya par
समय पर

late
der
देर

You're early.
āp jaldī ā gae haiṃ
आप जल्दी आ गए हैं।

You're late.
āp der se āe haiṃ
आप देर से आए हैं।

I'll be there soon.
maiṃ jaldī hī pahuṃch jāūṃgā
मैं जल्दी ही पहुंच जाऊंगा।

Please be on time.
kṛpyā samaya par pahuṃcheṃ
कृपया समय पर पहुंचें।

It's getting late.
der ho rahī hai
देर हो रही है।

I'll see you later.
maiṃ āpse bād meṃ milūṅgā
मैं आपसे बाद में मिलूंगा।

What time does it start?
yah kis samaya śurū hogā?
यह किस समय शुरू होगा?

How long will it last?
yah kab tak chalegā?
यह कब तक चलेगा?

What time does it end?
yah kab samāpt hogā?
यह कब समाप्त होगा?

calendar • kailenḍar • कैलेंडर

month
mās
मास

year
varṣ
वर्ष

January
janvarī
जनवरी

2010

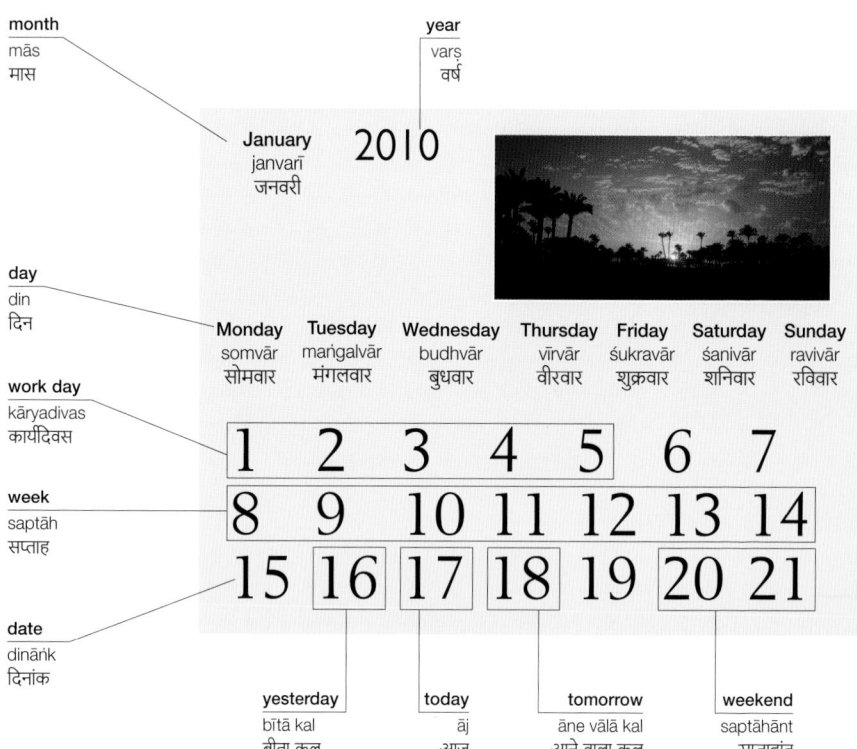

day
din
दिन

Monday	**Tuesday**	**Wednesday**	**Thursday**	**Friday**	**Saturday**	**Sunday**
somvār	maṅgalvār	budhvār	vīrvār	śukravār	śanivār	ravivār
सोमवार	मंगलवार	बुधवार	वीरवार	शुक्रवार	शनिवार	रविवार
1	2	3	4	5	6	7
8	9	10	11	12	13	14
15	16	17	18	19	20	21

work day
kāryadivas
कार्यदिवस

week
saptāh
सप्ताह

date
dināṅk
दिनांक

yesterday
bītā kal
बीता कल

today
āj
आज

tomorrow
āne vālā kal
आने वाला कल

weekend
saptāhānt
सप्ताहांत

vocabulary • śabdāvalī • शब्दावली

January
janvarī
जनवरी

February
farvarī
फ़रवरी

March
mārch
मार्च

April
aprail
अप्रैल

May
maī
मई

June
jūn
जून

July
julāī
जुलाई

August
agast
अगस्त

September
sitambar
सितंबर

October
akṭūbar
अक्टूबर

November
navambar
नवंबर

December
disambar
दिसंबर

years • varṣ • वर्ष

1900 nineteen hundred • unnīs sau • उन्नीस सौ

1901 nineteen hundred and one • unnīs sau ek • उन्नीस सौ एक

1910 nineteen ten • unnīs sau das • उन्नीस सौ दस

2000 two thousand • do hazār • दो हज़ार

2001 two thousand and one • do hazār ek • दो हज़ार एक

seasons • ṛtueṃ • ऋतुएं

spring
basant
बसंत

summer
grīṣm
ग्रीष्म

fall
patjhaṛ
पतझड़

winter
śarad
शरद

vocabulary • śabdāvalī • शब्दावली

century
śatābdī
शताब्दी

decade
daśak
दशक

two weeks
pakhvāṛā
पखवाड़ा

this week
is hafte
इस हफ़्ते

last week
pichhle hafte
पिछले हफ़्ते

the day before yesterday
bītā parsoṃ
बीता परसों

weekly
sāptāhik
साप्ताहिक

monthly
māsik
मासिक

annual
vārṣik
वार्षिक

millennium
sahsrābdī
सहस्राब्दी

next week
agle hafte
अगले हफ़्ते

the day after tomorrow
parsoṃ
परसों

What's the date today?
āj kyā tārīḳh hai?
आज क्या तारीख़ है?

It's February seventh, two thousand and seventeen.
āj 7 farvarī 2017 hai
आज 7 फ़रवरी, 2017 है।

numbers • aṃk • अंक

0 zero • śūnya • शून्य

1 one • ek • एक

2 two • do • दो

3 three • tīn • तीन

4 four • chār • चार

5 five • pāṃch • पांच

6 six • chhah • छह

7 seven • sāt • सात

8 eight • āṭh • आठ

9 nine • nau • नौ

10 ten • das • दस

11 eleven • gyārah • ग्यारह

12 twelve • bārah • बारह

13 thirteen • terah • तेरह

14 fourteen • chaudah • चौदह

15 fifteen • pandrah • पंद्रह

16 sixteen • solah • सोलह

17 seventeen • satrah • सत्रह

18 eighteen • aṭhārah • अठारह

19 nineteen • unnīs • उन्नीस

20 twenty • bīs • बीस

21 twenty-one • ikkīs • इक्कीस

22 twenty-two • bāīs • बाईस

30 thirty • tīs • तीस

40 forty • chālīs • चालीस

50 fifty • pachās • पचास

60 sixty • sāṭh • साठ

70 seventy • sattar • सत्तर

80 eighty • assī • अस्सी

90 ninety • nabbe • नब्बे

100 one hundred • sau • सौ

110 one hundred and ten • ek sau das • एक सौ दस

200 two hundred • do sau • दो सौ

300 three hundred • tīn sau • तीन सौ

400 four hundred • chār sau • चार सौ

500 five hundred • pāṃch sau • पांच सौ

600 six hundred • chhah sau • छह सौ

700 seven hundred • sāt sau • सात सौ

800 eight hundred • āṭh sau • आठ सौ

900 nine hundred • nau sau • नौ सौ

1,000 **one thousand** • ek hazār • एक हज़ार

10,000 **ten thousand** • das hazār • दस हज़ार

20,000 **twenty thousand** • bīs hazār • बीस हज़ार

50,000 **fifty thousand** • pachās hazār • पचास हज़ार

55,500 **fifty-five thousand five hundred** • pachpan hazār pāṃch sau • पचपन हज़ार पांच सौ

100,000 **one hundred thousand** • ek lākh • एक लाख

1,000,000 **one million** • das lākh • दस लाख

1,000,000,000 **one billion** • ek arab • एक अरब

fourth • chauthā • चौथा

fifth • pāṃchvāṃ • पांचवा

sixth • chhaṭhā • छठा

seventh • sātvāṃ • सातवां

eighth • āṭhvāṃ • आठवां

ninth • nauvāṃ • नौवां

tenth • dasvāṃ • दसवां

eleventh • gyārahavāṃ • ग्यारहवां

twelfth • bārhavāṃ • बारहवां

thirteenth • terhavāṃ • तेरहवां

fourteenth • chaudhavāṃ • चौदहवां

fifteenth • pandrahavāṃ • पंद्रहवां

sixteenth • solahavāṃ • सोलहवां

seventeenth • satrahavāṃ • सत्रहवां

eighteenth• aṭhārahavāṃ • अठारहवां

nineteenth • unnīsvāṃ • उन्नीसवां

twentieth • bīsvāṃ • बीसवां

twenty-first • ikkīsvāṃ • इक्कीसवां

twenty-second • bāisvāṃ • बाइसवां

twenty-third • teisvāṃ • तेइसवां

thirtieth • tīsvāṃ • तीसवां

fortieth • chālīsvāṃ • चालीसवां

fiftieth • pachāsvāṃ • पचासवां

sixtieth • sāṭhvāṃ • साठवां

seventieth • sattarvāṃ • सत्तरवां

eightieth • assīvāṃ • अस्सीवां

ninetieth • nabbevāṃ • नब्बेवां

(one) hundredth • sauvāṃ • सौवां

weights and measures • bhār aur māpak • भार और मापक

area • kṣetr • क्षेत्र

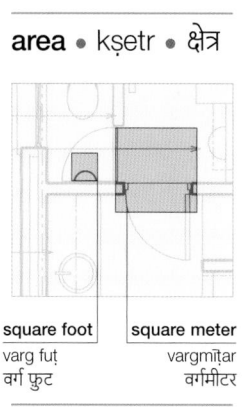

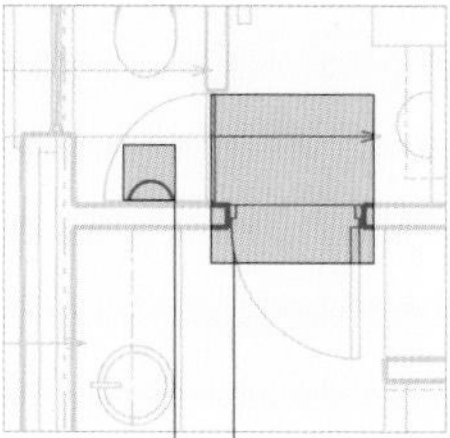

square foot
varg fuṭ
वर्ग फुट

square meter
vargmīṭar
वर्गमीटर

distance • dūrī • दूरी

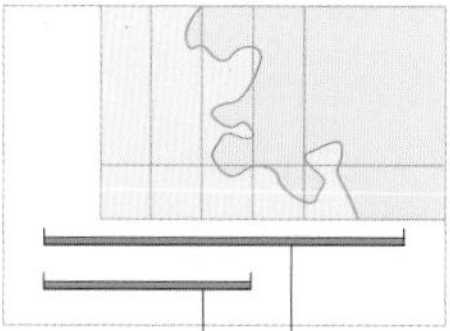

kilometer
kilomīṭar
किलोमीटर

mile
mīl
मील

pan
pain
पैन

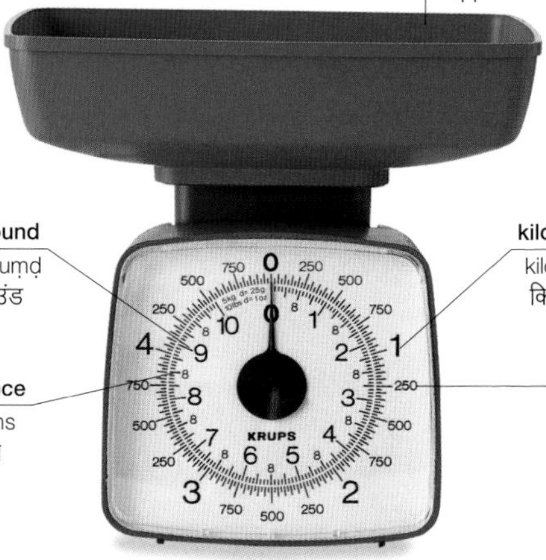

pound
pāuṃḍ
पाउंड

ounce
auṃs
औंस

kilogram
kilogrām
किलोग्राम

gram
grām
ग्राम

scale | tarāzū | तराजू

vocabulary • śabdāvalī • शब्दावली

yard
gaz
गज़

meter
mīṭar
मीटर

ton
ṭan
टन

milligram
milīgrām
मिलीग्राम

measure (v)
māpnā
मापना

weigh (v)
taulnā
तौलना

length • lambāī • लंबाई

foot
fuṭ
फुट

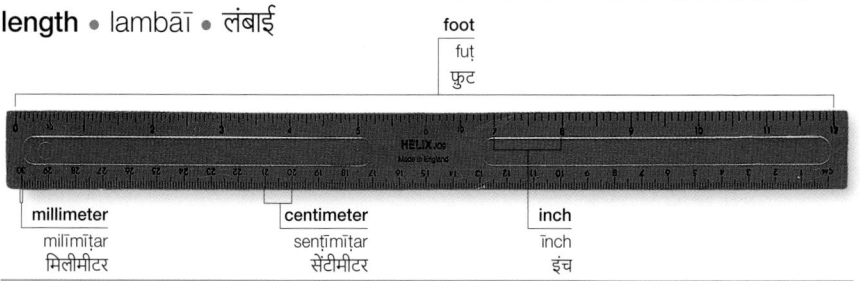

millimeter
milīmīṭar
मिलीमीटर

centimeter
senṭīmīṭar
सेंटीमीटर

inch
īnch
इंच

capacity • kṣamtā • क्षमता

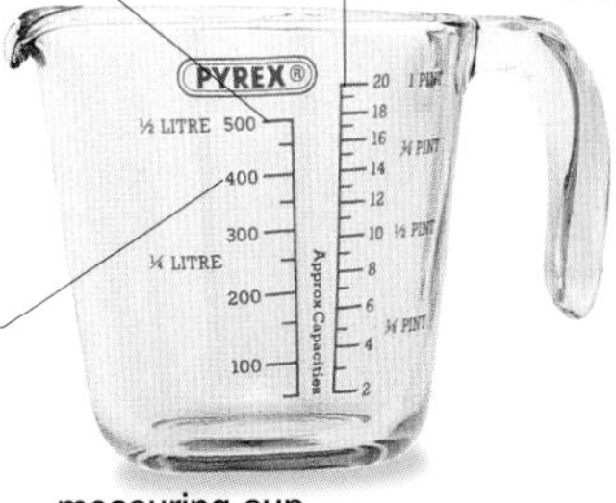

measuring cup
māpak jag | मापक जग

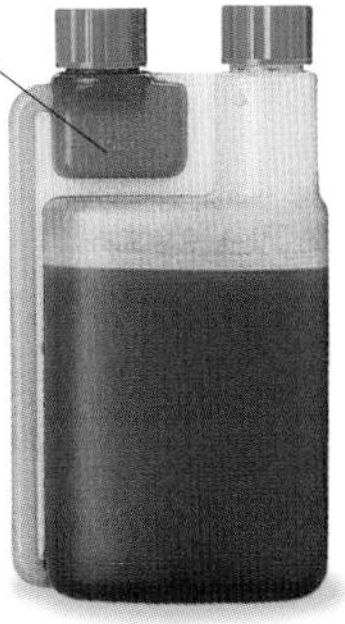

liquid measure
drav māp | द्रव माप

vocabulary • śabdāvalī • शब्दावली

gallon
gailan
गैलन

quart
kvārṭ
क्वार्ट

liter
līṭar
लीटर

container • kanṭenar • कंटेनर

carton
kārṭan | कार्टन

packet
paikeṭ | पैकेट

bottle
botal | बोतल

bag
thailā
थैला

tub | ṭab | टब

jar | jār | जार

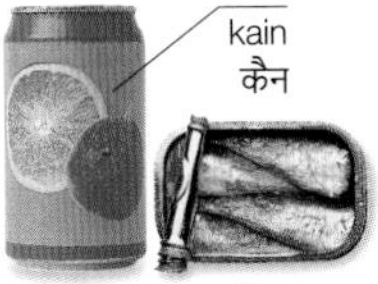

tin | ṭin | टिन

spray bottle
ḍispensar | डिस्पेंसर

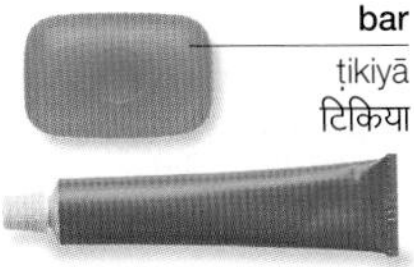

tube | ṭyūb | ट्यूब

roll | rol | रोल

pack | paik | पैक

spray can
spre kain | स्प्रे कैन

world map • viśv mānchitr • विश्व मानचित्र

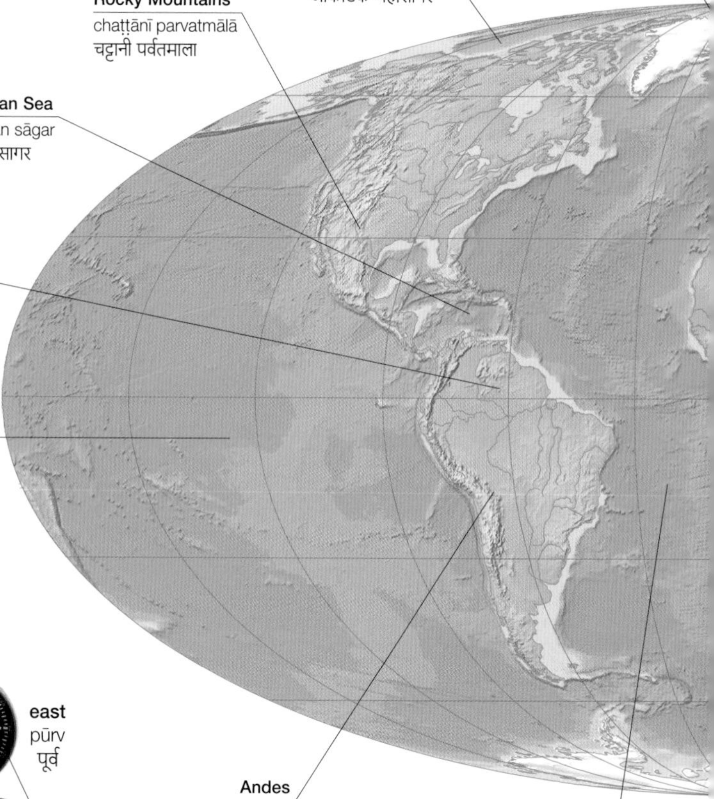

North Sea
uttarī sāgar
उत्तरी सागर

Arctic Ocean
ārkṭik mahāsāgar
आर्कटिक महासागर

Rocky Mountains
chaṭṭānī parvatmālā
चट्टानी पर्वतमाला

Caribbean Sea
kairebiyan sāgar
कैरेबियन सागर

Amazonia
amezoniyā
अमेज़ोनिया

Pacific Ocean
praśānt mahāsāgar
प्रशांत महासागर

Andes
aiṅḍīz
ऐंडीज़

Atlantic Ocean
atlāntik mahāsāgar
अतलांतिक महासागर

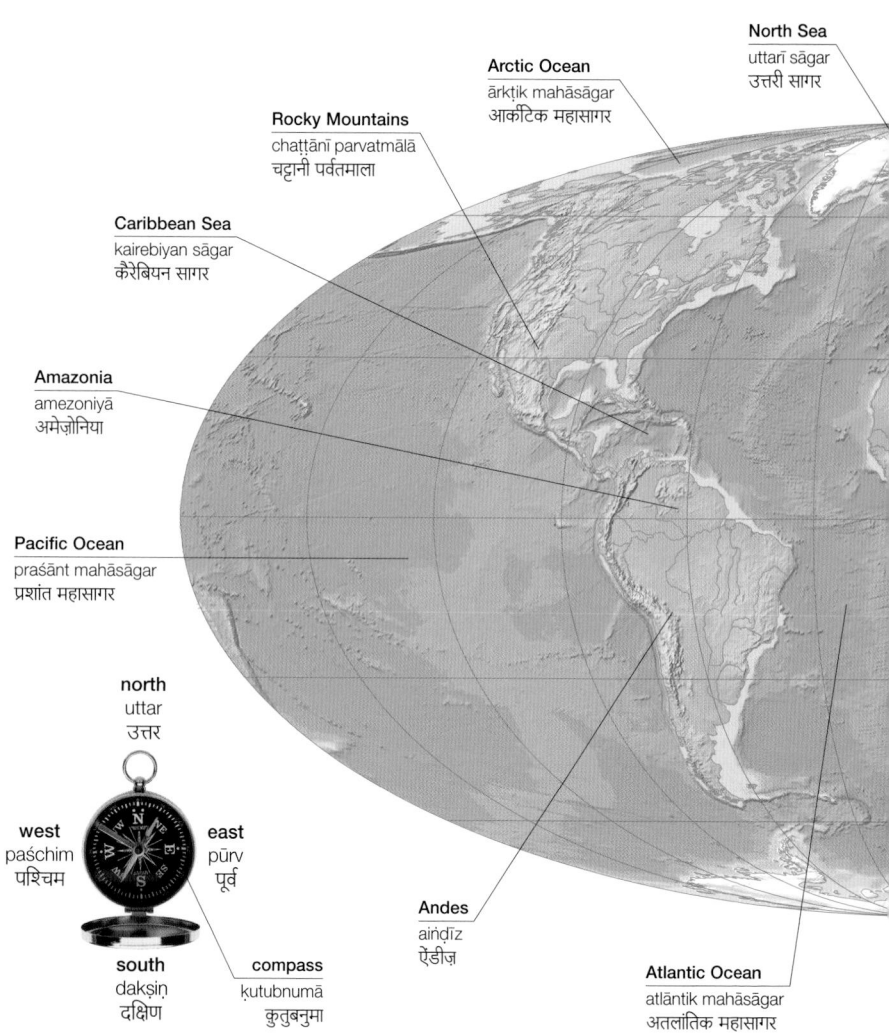

north
uttar
उत्तर

west
paśchim
पश्चिम

east
pūrv
पूर्व

south
dakṣiṇ
दक्षिण

compass
ḳutubnumā
क़ुतुबनुमा

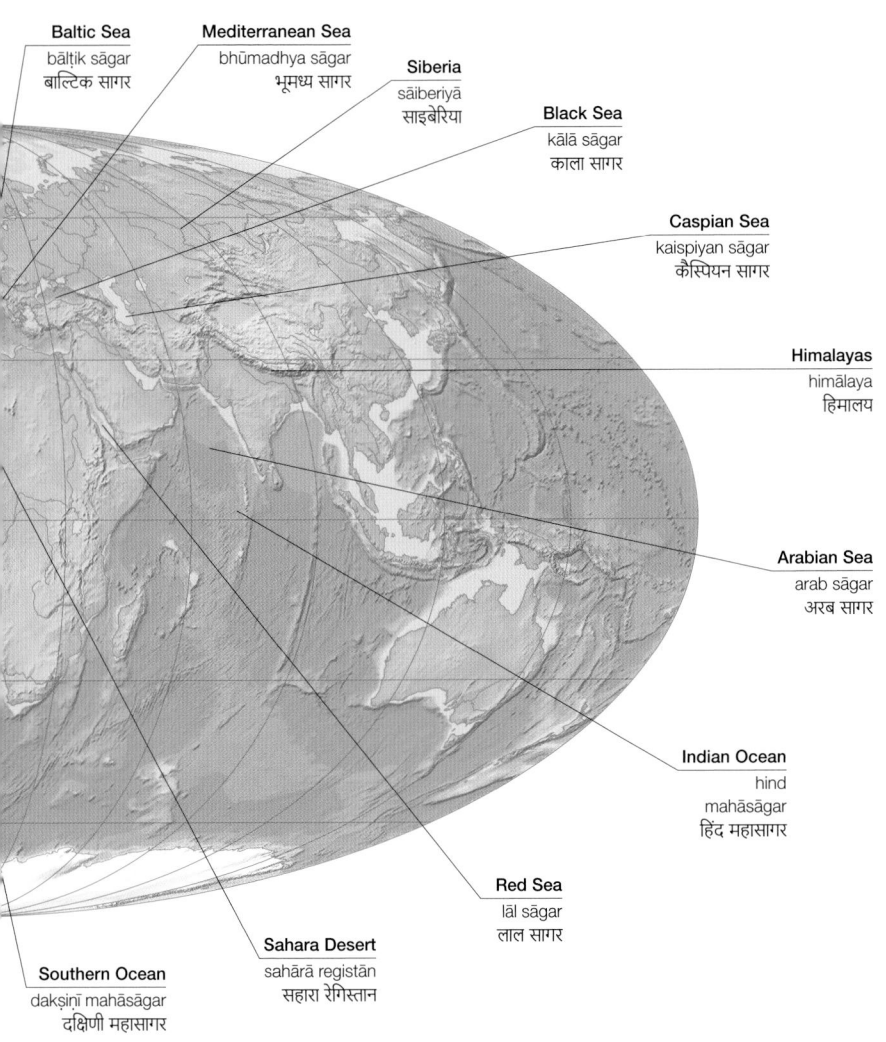

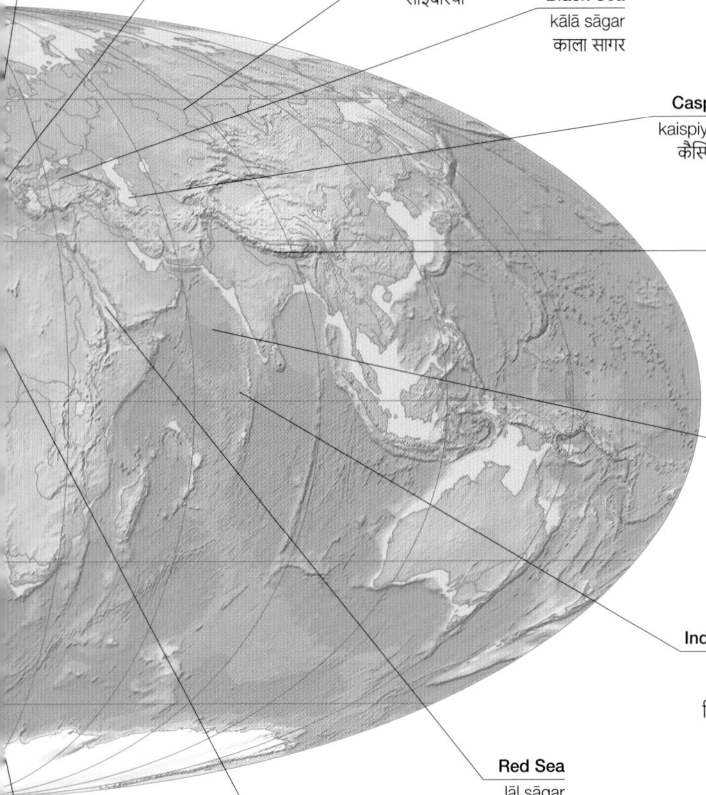

Baltic Sea
bālṭik sāgar
बाल्टिक सागर
Mediterranean Sea
bhūmadhya sāgar
भूमध्य सागर
Siberia
sāiberiyā
साइबेरिया
Black Sea
kālā sāgar
काला सागर
Caspian Sea
kaispiyan sāgar
कैस्पियन सागर
Himalayas
himālaya
हिमालय
Arabian Sea
arab sāgar
अरब सागर
Indian Ocean
hind mahāsāgar
हिंद महासागर
Red Sea
lāl sāgar
लाल सागर
Sahara Desert
sahārā registān
सहारा रेगिस्तान
Southern Ocean
dakṣiṇī mahāsāgar
दक्षिणी महासागर

North and Central America • uttar aur madhya amerikā • उत्तर और मध्य अमेरिका

Barbados • bārbāḍos • बारबाडोस

Canada • kanāḍā • कनाडा

Costa Rica • kosṭā rīkā • कोस्टा रीका

Cuba • kyūbā • क्यूबा

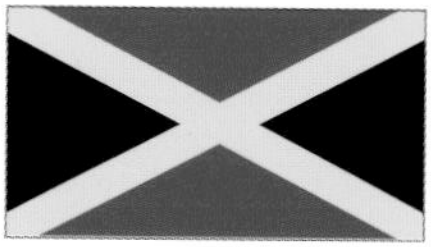

Jamaica • jamaikā • जमैका

Mexico • maiksiko • मैक्सिको

Panama • panāmā • पनामा

Trinidad and Tobago • trinidād aur ṭobāgo • त्रिनिदाद और टोबागो

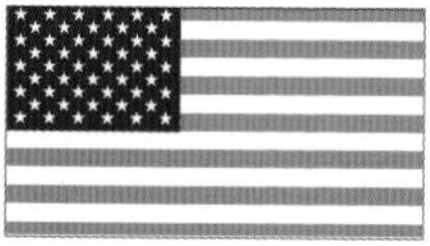

United States of America • saṃyūkt rājya amerikā • संयुक्त राज्य अमेरिका

Alaska • alāskā • अलास्का

Antigua and Barbuda • entīguā aur bārbuḍā • एंटीगुआ और बारबुडा

Bahamas • bahāmās • बहामास

Barbados • bārbāḍos • बारबाडोस

Belize • belīz • बेलीज़

Canada • kanāḍā • कनाडा

Costa Rica • kosṭā rīkā • कोस्टा रीका

Cuba • kyūbā • क्यूबा

Dominica • ḍominikā • डोमिनिका

Dominican Republic • ḍominik gaṇrājya • डोमिनिक गणराज्य

El Salvador • el selvāḍor • एल सेल्वाडोर

Greenland • grīnlainḍ • ग्रीनलैंड

Grenada • grenāḍā • ग्रेनाडा

Guatemala • gvāṭemālā • ग्वाटेमाला

Haiti • haitī • हैती

Hawaii • havāī • हवाई

Honduras • honḍurās • हॉन्डुरास

Jamaica • jamaikā • जमैका

Mexico • maiksiko • मैक्सिको

Nicaragua • nikārāguā • निकारागुआ

Panama • panāmā • पनामा

Puerto Rico • pyūrto rīko • प्यूर्तो रीको

St Kitts and Nevis • senṭ kiṭs aur nevis • सेंट किट्स और नेविस

St Lucia • senṭ lūśiyā • सेंट लूशिया

St Vincent and The Grenadines • senṭ vinsenṭ aur da grenāḍins • सेंट विन्सेंट और द ग्रेनाडिन्स

Trinidad and Tobago • trinidād aur ṭobāgo • त्रिनिदाद और टोबागो

United States of America • saṃyūkt rājya amerikā • संयुक्त राज्य अमेरिका

South America • dakṣiṇ amerikā • दक्षिण अमेरिका

Argentina • arjenṭīnā • अर्जेंटीना

Bolivia • bolīviyā • बोलीवयि

Brazil • brāzīl • ब्राज़ील

Chile • chilī • चलिी

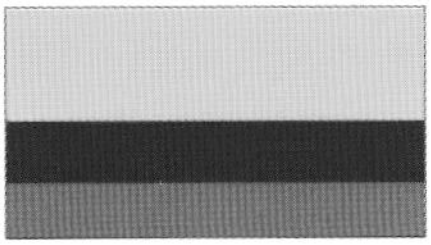

Colombia • kolambiyā • कोलम्बयि

Ecuador • ikveḍor • इक्वेडोर

Peru • perū • पेरू

Uruguay • urūgue • उरूगुए

Venezuela • venezuelā • वेनेजुएला

Argentina • arjenṭīnā • अर्जेंटीना
Bolivia • bolīviyā • बोलीवयि
Brazil • brāzīl • ब्राज़ील
Chile • chilī • चलिी
Colombia • kolambiyā • कोलम्बयि
Ecuador • ikveḍor • इक्वेडोर
Falkland Islands • foklaiṇḍ dvīp samūh • फ़ॉकलैंड द्वीप समूह
French Guiana • French gayānā • फ़्रेंच गयाना
Galápagos Islands • gālāpāgos dvip samūh • गालापागोस द्वीप समूह
Guyana • guyānā • गुयाना
Paraguay • pairāgue • पैरागुए
Peru • perū • पेरू
Suriname • sūrīnām • सूरीनाम
Uruguay • urūgue • उरूगुए
Venezuela • venezuelā • वेनेजुएला

vocabulary • śabdāvalī • शब्दावली

country deś देश	**province** prānt प्रांत	**zone** anchal अंचल
continent mahādvīp महाद्वीप	**territory** ilāḳā इलाक़ा	**district** zilā ज़िला
nation rāṣṭr राष्ट्र	**colony** kolonī कॉलोनी	**region** kṣetra क्षेत्र
state rājya राज्य	**principality** sāmrājya साम्राज्य	**capital** rājdhānī राजधानी

Europe • yūrop • यूरोप

France • frāṃs • फ़्रांस

Germany • jarmanī • जर्मनी

Italy • iṭlī • इटली

Poland • polainḍ • पोलैंड

Portugal • purtgāl • पुर्तगाल

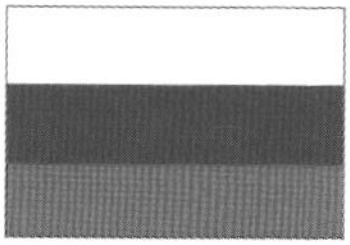

Russian Federation • rūs • रूस

Spain • spen • स्पेन

Albania • albāniyā • अल्बानिया

Andorra • anḍorā • अन्डोरा

Austria • osṭriyā • ऑस्ट्रिया

Balearic Islands • bailirik dvīp samūh • बैलिरिक द्वीप समूह

Belarus • belārūs • बेलारूस

Belgium • beljiyam • बेल्जियम

Bosnia and Herzogovina • bosniyā aur harzogovinā • बोस्निया और हर्ज़ोगोविना

Bulgaria • bulgāriyā • बुल्गारिया

Corsica • korsikā • कॉरसिका

Croatia • kroeśiyā • क्रोएशिया

Czech Republic • chek gaṇrājya • चेक गणराज्य

Denmark • ḍenmārk • डेनमार्क

Estonia • esṭoniyā • एस्टोनिया

Finland • finlainḍ • फ़िनलैंड

France • frāṃs • फ़्रांस

Germany • jarmanī • जर्मनी

Greece • grīs • ग्रीस

Hungary • haṅgarī • हंगरी

Iceland • aaislainḍ • आइसलैंड

Ireland • āyarlainḍ • आयरलैंड

Italy • iṭlī • इटली

Kaliningrad • kailinin grāḍ • कैलिनिनग्राड

Kosovo • kosovo • कोसोवो

Latvia • lātviyā • लातविया

Liechtenstein • likṭensṭāin • लिक्टेन्स्टाइन

Lithuania • lithuāniyā • लिथुआनिया

Luxembourg • lakzambarg • लक्ज़मबर्ग

Macedonia • meseḍoniyā • मेसेडोनिया

Malta • mālṭā • माल्टा

Moldova • molḍova • मॉल्डोवा

Monaco • monāko • मोनाको

Montenegro • monṭenegro • मोंटेनेग्रो

Netherlands • nīdarlainḍ • नीदरलैंड

Norway • nārve • नार्वे

Poland • polainḍ • पोलैंड

Portugal • purtgāl • पुर्तगाल

Romania • romāniyā • रोमानिया

Russian Federation • rūs • रूस

San Marino • sān marīno • सान मरीनो

Sardinia • sārḍīniyā • सार्डीनिया

Serbia • sarbiyā • सर्बिया

Sicily • sisilī • सिसिली

Slovakia • slovākiyā • स्लोवाकिया

Slovenia • sloveniyā • स्लोवेनिया

Spain • spen • स्पेन

Sweden • svīḍan • स्वीडन

Switzerland • sviṭzarlaind. • स्विटज़रलैंड

Ukraine • yūkren • यूक्रेन

United Kingdom • yūnāiṭeḍ kiṅ'gḍam • यूनाइटेड किंगडम

Vatican City • veṭikan siṭī • वेटिकन सिटी

Africa • afrīkā • अफ़्रीका

Egypt • misr • मिस्र

Ethiopia • ithiyopiyā • इथियोपिया

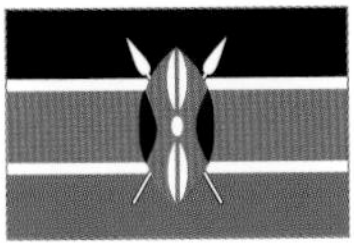

Kenya • kenyā • केन्या

Nigeria • nāijīriyā • नाइजीरिया

South Africa • dakṣiṇ afrīkā • दक्षिण अफ़्रीका

Uganda • yugāṇḍā • युगांडा

Algeria • aljīriyā • अल्जीरिया

Angola • aṅgolā • अंगोला

Benin • benin • बेनिन

Botswana • botsvānā • बोत्सवाना

Burkina Faso • burkinā fāso • बुर्किना फ़ासो

Burundi • burūṇḍī • बुरूंडी

Cabinda • kebindā • केबिंदा

Cameroon • kaimrūn • कैमरून

Central African Republic • madhya afrīkī gaṇrajya • मध्य अफ़्रीकी गणराज्य

Chad • chāḍ • चाड

Comoros • komoros • कोमोरॉस

Congo • koṅgo • कॉन्गो

Democratic Republic of the Congo • koṅgo loktāntrik gaṇrājya • कॉन्गो लोकतांत्रिक गणराज्य

Djibouti • jibūtī • जिबूती

Egypt • misr • मिस्र

Equatorial Guinea • ekveṭoriyal ginī • एक्वेटोरियल गिनी

Eritrea • eriṭriyā • एरिट्रिया

Ethiopia • ithiyopiyā • इथियोपिया

Gabon • gaibon • गैबोन

Gambia • gaimbiyā • गैंबिया

Ghana • ghānā • घाना

Guinea • ginī • गिनी

Guinea-Bissau • ginībissāū • गिनीबिस्साऊ

Ivory Coast • āivarī kosṭ • आइवरी कोस्ट

Kenya • kenyā • केन्या

Lesotho • lesotho • लेसोथो

Liberia • lāiberiyā • लाइबेरिया

Libya • lībiyā • लीबिया

Madagascar • maiḍāgāskar • मैडागास्कर

Malawi • malāvī • मलावी

Mali • mālī • माली

Mauritania • maurīteniā • मॉरीटेनिया

Mauritius • morīśas • मॉरीशस

Morocco • morokko • मोरोक्को

Mozambique • mozāmbīk. • मोज़ाम्बीक़

Namibia • nāmībiyā • नामीबिया

Niger • nāijar • नाइजर

Nigeria • nāijīriyā • नाइजीरिया

Rwanda • ruāṇḍā • रुआंडा

São Tomé and Principe • são ṭome aur prinsipe • साओ टोमे और प्रिंसिपे

Senegal • senegal • सेनेगल

Sierra Leone • sierā lione • सिएरा लिओने

Somalia • somāliyā • सोमालिया

South Africa • dakṣiṇ afrīkā • दक्षिण अफ़्रीका

South Sudan • dakṣiṇ sūḍān • दक्षिण सूडान

Sudan • sūḍān • सूडान

Swaziland • svāzīlaiṇḍ • स्वाज़ीलैंड

Tanzania • tanzāniyā • तंज़ानिया

Togo • ṭogo • टोगो

Tunisia • ṭyūnīśiyā • ट्यूनीशिया

Uganda • yugāṇḍā • युगांडा

Western Sahara • paśchim sahārā • पश्चिम सहारा

Zambia • zāmbiyā • ज़ाम्बिया

Zimbabwe • zimbābve • ज़िम्बाब्वे

Asia • eśiyā • एशिया

Bangladesh • bāṅglādeś • बांग्लादेश

China • chīn • चीन

India • bhārat • भारत

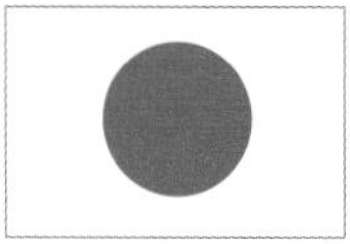

Japan • jāpān • जापान

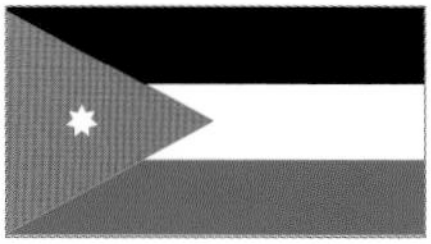

Jordan • jorḍan • जॉर्डन

Philippines • filīpīns • फ़िलीपीन्स

South Korea • dakṣiṇ koriyā • दक्षिण कोरिया

Thailand • thāilainḍ • थाइलैंड

Turkey • turkī • तुर्की

Afghanistan • afg̣ānistān • अफ़ग़ानिस्तान

Armenia • ārmeniyā • आर्मेनिया

Azerbaijan • azarbaijān • अज़रबैजान

Bahrain • bahareen • बहरीन

Bangladesh • bāṅglādeś • बांग्लादेश

Bhutan • bhūṭān • भूटान

Brunei • bruneī • ब्रुनेई

Cambodia • kamboḍiyā • कंबोडिया

China • chīn • चीन

Cyprus • sāipras • साइप्रस

East Timor • pūrvī timor • पूर्वी तिमोर

Fiji • fijī • फ़िजी

Georgia • jorjiyā • जॉर्जिया

India • bhārat • भारत

Indonesia • iṅḍoneśiyā • इंडोनेशिया

Iran • īrān • ईरान

Iraq • irāḳ • इराक़

Israel • izrāil • इज़राइल

Japan • jāpān • जापान

Jordan • jorḍan • जॉर्डन

Kazakhstan • kazākistān • कज़ाकिस्तान

Kuwait • ḳuvait • कुवैत

Kyrgyzstan • kirgistān • किर्गिस्तान

Laos • lāos • लाओस

Lebanon • lebnān • लेबनान

Malaysia • maleśiyā • मलेशिया

Maldives • māldīv • मालदीव

Mongolia • maṅgoliyā • मंगोलिया

Myanmar (Burma) • myānmār (barmā) • म्यांमार (बर्मा)

Nepal • nepāl • नेपाल

North Korea • uttar koriyā • उत्तर कोरिया

Oman • omān • ओमान

Pakistan • pākistān • पाकिस्तान

Papua New Guinea • papuā nyū ginī • पपुआ न्यू गिनी

Philippines • filīpīns • फ़िलीपीन्स

Qatar • ḳatar • क़तर

Saudi Arabia • saūdī arab • सऊदी अरब

Singapore • siṅgāpur • सिंगापुर

Solomon Islands • soloman dvip samūh • सोलोमन द्वीप समूह

South Korea • dakṣiṇ koriyā • दक्षिण कोरिया

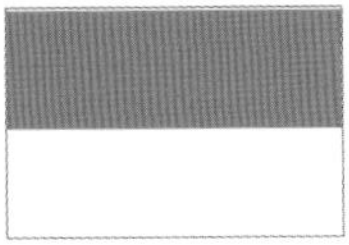

Indonesia • iṅḍoneśiyā • इंडोनेशिया

Saudi Arabia • saūdī arab • सऊदी अरब

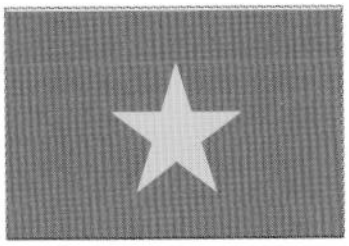

Vietnam • viyatnām • वियतनाम

Sri Lanka • śrīlaṅkā • श्रीलंका

Syria • sīriyā • सीरिया

Tajikistan • tajākistān • तजाकिस्तान

Thailand • thāilaiṇḍ • थाइलैंड

Turkey • turkī • तुर्की

Turkmenistan • turkmenistān • तुर्कमेनिस्तान

United Arab Emirates • sanyukt arab amīrāt • संयुक्त अरब अमीरात

Uzbekistan • uzbekistān • उज़्बेकिस्तान

Vanuatu • vanuātū • वनुआतू

Vietnam • viyatnām • वियतनाम

Yemen • yaman • यमन

Australasia • osṭreleśiyā • ऑस्ट्रेलेशिया

Australia • osṭreliā • ऑस्ट्रेलिया

New Zealand • nyūzīlaiṇḍ • न्यूज़ीलैंड

Australia • osṭreliā • ऑस्ट्रेलिया

New Zealand • nyūzīlaiṇḍ • न्यूज़ीलैंड

Tasmania • tasmāniyā • तस्मानिया

particles and antonyms • upsarg, pratyaya aur vilom śabd • उपसर्ग, प्रत्यय और विलोम शब्द

to
ko • को

from
se • से

for
ke lie • के लिए

toward
kī taraf • की तरफ़

over
ūpar • ऊपर

under
nīche • नीचे

with
sāth • साथ

without
bagair • बग़ैर

in front of
ke sāmne • के सामने

behind
pīchhe • पीछे

before
pahle • पहले

after
bād meṃ • बाद में

onto
ke ūpar • के ऊपर

into
ke andar • के अंदर

by
tab tak • तब तक

until
jab tak • जब तक

in
andar • अंदर

out
bāhar • बाहर

early
jaldī • जल्दी

late
der • देर

above
ūpar • ऊपर

below
nīche • नीचे

now
abhī • अभी

later
bād meṃ • बाद में

inside
andar • अंदर

outside
bāhar • बाहर

always
hameśā • हमेशा

never
kabhī nahīṃ • कभी नही

up
ūpar • ऊपर

down
nīche • नीचे

often
aksar • अक्सर

rarely
kabhī-kabhī • कभी-कभी

at
par • पर

beyond
pare • परे

yesterday
bītā kal • बीता कल

tomorrow
āgāmī kal • आगामी कल

on top of
ke ūpar • के ऊपर

beside
ke pās • के पास

first
pahlā • पहला

last
ākhrī • आख़री

between
ke bīch • के बीच

opposite
viprīt • विपरीत

every
pratyek • प्रत्येक

some
kuchh • कुछ

near
nikaṭ • निकट

far
dūr • दूर

about
lagbhag • लगभग

exactly
saṭīk • सटीक

here
yahāṃ • यहां

there
vahāṃ • वहां

a little
thoṛā sā • थोड़ा सा

a lot
bahut sā • बहुत सा

through
ārampār • आरम्पार

around
ghūm kar • घूम कर

along
sāth-sāth • साथ-साथ

across
ke pār • के पार

large
baṛā • बड़ा

small
chhoṭā • छोटा

wide
chauṛā • चौड़ा

narrow
saṅkrā • संकरा

tall
lambā • लंबा

short
chhoṭā • छोटा

high
ūṃchā • ऊंचा

low
nīchā • नीचा

thick
moṭā • मोटा

thin
patlā • पतला

light
halkā • हल्का

heavy
bhārī • भारी

hard
kaṭhor • कठोर

soft
mulāyam • मुलायम

wet
gīlā • गीला

dry
sūkhā • सूखा

good
acchhā • अच्छा

bad
burā • बुरा

fast
tez • तेज़

slow
dhīre • धीरे

correct
sahī • सही

wrong
galat • ग़लत

clean
sāf • साफ़

dirty
gandā • गंदा

beautiful
ḳhūbsūrat • ख़ूबसूरत

ugly
badsūrat • बदसूरत

expensive
mahaṅgā • महंगा

cheap
sastā • सस्ता

quiet
śānt • शांत

noisy • śor karne vālā
शोर करने वाला

hot
garm • गर्म

cold
ṭhanḍā • ठंडा

open
khulā • खुला

closed
band • बंद

full
bharā • भरा

empty
ḳhālī • ख़ाली

new
nayā • नया

old
purānā • पुराना

light
halkā • हल्का

dark
gahrā • गहरा

easy
āsān • आसान

difficult
kaṭhin • कठिन

free
ḳhālī • ख़ाली

occupied
vyast • व्यस्त

fat
moṭā • मोटा

thin
patlā • पतला

young
javān • जवान

old
būṛhā • बूढ़ा

better
behtar • बेहतर

worse
badtar • बदतर

black
kālā • काला

white
safed • सफ़ेद

interesting
rochak • रोचक

boring
ubāū • उबाऊ

sick
bīmār • बीमार

well
svasth • स्वस्थ

beginning
ārambh • आरंभ

end
ant • अंत

strong
mazbūt • मज़बूत

weak
kamzor • कमज़ोर

useful phrases • upyogī vākyāṅś • उपयोगी वाक्यांश

essential phrases
āvaśyak vākyāṅś
आवश्यक वाक्यांश

Yes • hāṃ • हां

No • nahīṃ • नही

Maybe • ho saktā hai
हो सकता है

Please • kṛpyā
कृपया

Thank you
dhanyavād
धन्यवाद

You're welcome.
āpkā svāgat hai
आपका स्वागत है।

Excuse me
māf kījiegā
माफ़ कीजिएगा।

I'm sorry.
māf karie
माफ़ करिए।

Don't
mat karo
मत करो।

OK • acchhā
अच्छा

That's fine
yah ṭhīk hai
यह ठीक है।

That's correct.
yah sahī hai
यह सही है।

That's wrong.
yah galat hai
यह ग़लत है।

greetings
abhivādan
अभिवादन

Hello
namaskār • नमस्कार

Goodbye
namaskār • नमस्कार

Good morning
suprabhāt • सुप्रभात

Good afternoon
namaskār • नमस्कार

Good evening
namaskār • नमस्कार

Good night
śubh rātri
शुभ रात्रि

How are you?
āp kaise haiṃ?
आप कैसे हैं?

My name is …
merā nām … hai
मेरा नाम ... है।

What is your name?
āpkā kyā nām hai?
आपका क्या नाम है?

What is his/her name?
unkā kyā nām hai?
उनका क्या नाम है?

May I introduce …
inse milie...
इनसे मिलिए...

This is …
ye … haiṃ
ये ... हैं।

Pleased to meet you
āpse milkar ḳhuśī huī
आपसे मिलकर खुशी हुई।

See you later
bād meṃ milte haiṃ
बाद में मिलते हैं।

signs • chihn • चिह्न

Tourist information
paryaṭak jānkārī
पर्यटक जानकारी

Entrance • praveś • प्रवेश

Exit • nikās • निकास

Emergency exit
saṅkaṭ dvār • संकट द्वार

Push • dhakeleṃ • धकेलें

Danger • ḳhatrā • ख़तरा

No smoking • dhūmrpān varjit • धूम्रपान वर्जित

Out of order
ḳharāb • ख़राब

Opening times
khulne kā samaya
खुलने का समय

Free admission • muft praveś • मुफ़्त प्रवेश

Reduced • kam mūlya par • कम मूल्य पर

Sale • sel • सेल

Knock before entering
praveś karne se pahle dastak deṃ • प्रवेश करने से पहले दस्तक लें

Keep off the grass
kṛpyā ghās par na chaleṃ
कृपया घास पर न चलें

help • sahāyatā • सहायता

Can you help me?
kyā āp merī sahāyatā kar sakte/saktī haiṃ?
क्या आप मेरी सहायता कर सकते/सकती हैं?

I don't understand.
samajh nahīṃ āyā
समझ नही आया।

I don't know.
mujhe patā nahīṃ hai
मुझे पता नही है।

Do you speak English?
kyā āp aṅgrezī bolte haiṃ?
क्या आप अंग्रेज़ी बोलते हैं?

I speak English.
maiṃ aṅgrezī boltā/boltī hūṃ
मैं अंग्रेज़ी बोलता/बोलती हूँ।

Please speak more slowly
kṛpyā aur dhīre boleṃ
कृपया और धीरे बोलें।

Please write it down for me.
kṛpyā ye mere lie likh deṃ
कृपया ये मेरे लिए लिख दें।

I have lost …
merā … kho gayā hai
मेरा ... खो गया है।

directions • nirdeś • निर्देश

I am lost • maiṃ bhaṭak gayā/gayī hūṃ • मैं भटक गया/गयी हूँ।

Where is the…?
… kahāṃ haiṃ?
... कहां हैं?

Where is the nearest ...?
nazdīkī ... kahāṃ hai?
नज़दीकी ... कहां है?

Where is the restroom?
śauchālaya kahāṃ hai?
शौचालय कहां है?

How do I get to ...?
maiṃ kaise pahuṃchū?
मैं कैसे पहुंचू?

To the right
dāīṃ taraf
दाईं तरफ़

To the left
bāīṃ taraf
बाईं तरफ़

Straight ahead
āge jākar sīdhā
आगे जाकर सीधा

How far is...?
... kitnī dūr hai?
... कितनी दूर है?

road signs • mārg chihn • मार्ग चिह्न

Caution • sāvdhānīt
सावधानी

Do not enter
praveś varjit
प्रवेश वर्जित

Slow down
raftār dhīmī kareṃ
रफ़्तार धीमी करें

Detour • parivartit mārg • परिवर्तित मार्ग

Keep right
dāīṃ taraf raheṃ
दाईं तरफ़ रहें

Freeway • hāīve
हाईवे

No parking
pārkiṅg niṣedh hai
पार्किंग निषेध है

Dead end
ām rāstā nahīṃ hai
आम रास्ता नही है

One-way street
iktarfā rāstā
इकतरफ़ा रास्ता

Residents only
keval nivāsiyoṃ ke lie
केवल निवासियों के लिए

Yield • rāstā denā
रास्ता देना

Roadwork
saṛak nirmāṇ kārya
सड़क निर्माण कार्य

Dangerous curve
ḳhatarnāk moṛ
ख़तरनाक मोड़

accommodation
āvās • आवास

I have a reservation.
mere pās ārakṣaṇ hai
मेरे पास आरक्षण है।

Where is the dining room?
bhojan kakṣ kahāṃ hai?
भोजन कक्ष कहां है?

What time is breakfast?
nāśte kā kyā samaya hai?
नाश्ते का क्या समय है?

I'll be back at... o'clock.
maiṃ ... baje lauṭūṅgā/lauṭūṅgī
मैं... बजे लौटूंगा/लौटूंगी।

I'm leaving tomorrow.
maiṃ kal jā rahā/rahī hūṃ
मैं कल जा रहा/रही हूं।

eating and drinking
khānā-pīnā
खाना-पीना

Cheers! • chiyars • चियर्स!

It's delicious/awful.
yah svādiṣṭ/besvād hai
यह स्वादिष्ट/बेस्वाद है।

I don't drink/smoke.
maiṃ śarāb/sigreṭ nahīṃ pītā/pītī
मैं शराब/सिगरेट नही पीता/पीती।

I don't eat meat.
maiṃ māṃs nahīṃ khātā
मैं मांस नहीं खाता।

No more for me, thank you.
mujhe aur nahīṃ chāhie, dhanyavād
मुझे और नहीं चाहिए, धन्यवाद।

May I have some more?
kyā mujhe thoṛā aur mil saktā hai?
क्या मुझे थोड़ा और मिल सकता है?

May we have the check? • kyā hameṃ bil mil saktā hai? • क्या हमें बिल मिल सकता है?

Can I have a receipt?
kyā mujhe rasīd mil saktī hai?
क्या मुझे रसीद मिल सकती है?

Smoking area
dhūmrapān kṣetr
धूम्रपान क्षेत्र

health • svāsthya
स्वास्थ्य

I don't feel well.
merī tabīyat ṭhīk nahīṃ hai
मेरी तबीयत ठीक नहीं है।

I feel sick.
maiṃ bīmār mahsūs kar rahā/rahī hūṃ
मैं बीमार महसूस कर रहा/रही हूं।

It hurts here.
yahāṃ dukhtā hai
यहां दुखता है।

I have a fever.
mujhe buḳhār hai
मुझे बुखार है।

I'm ... months pregnant.
mujhe ... mahīne kā garbh hai
मुझे ... महीने का गर्भ है।

I need a prescription for ...
mujhe ... ke lie ḍokṭarī nusḳhā chāhie
मुझे ... के लिए डॉक्टरी नुस्ख़ा चाहिए।

I normally take ...
sāmānyataḥ maiṃ ... letā/letī hūṃ
सामान्यत: मैं ... लेता/लेती हूं।

I'm allergic to ...
mujhe ... se elarjī hai
मुझे ... से एलर्जी है।

Will he/she be all right?
kyā vah ṭhīk ho jāegā/jāegī?
क्या वह ठीक हो जाएगा/जाएगी?

English index • aṅgrezi tālikā • अंग्रेज़ी तालिका

english

A

à la carte 152
abdomen 12
abdominals 16
above 320
acacia 110
accelerator 200
access road 216
accessories 36, 38
accident 46
account number 96
accountant 97, 190
accounting department 175
accused 180
ace 230, 273
Achilles tendon 16
acorn squash 125
acquaintance 24
acquitted 181
across 320
acrylic paints 274
actions 237, 229, 227, 233, 183
activities 263, 245, 162, 77
actor 254, 191
actors 179
actress 254
acupressure 55
acupuncture 55
Adam's apple 19
add *v* 165
addition 58
address 98
adhesive bandage 47
adhesive tape 47
adjustable wrench 80
admissions office 168
admitted 48
adult 23
advantage 230
adventure movie 255
advertisement 269
adzuki beans 131
aerate *v* 91
Afghanistan 318
Africa 317
after 320
afternoon 305
aftershave 73
aftersun lotion 108
agate 289
agenda 174
aikido 236
aileron 210
air bag 201
air-conditioning 200
air cylinder 239
air filter 202, 204
air letter 98
air mattress 267
air vent 210
aircraft 210
aircraft carrier 215
airliner 210, 212
airport 212
aisle 106, 168, 210, 254
alarm clock 70
Alaska 314
Albania 316
alcoholic drinks 145
alfalfa 184
Algeria 317
all meals included 101
all-purpose flour 139
Allen wrench 80
allergy 44
alley 298
alligator 293
alligator clip 167
allspice 132
almond 129
almond oil 134
almonds 151
along 320
alpine 87
alpine skiing 247
alternating current 60
alternative therapy 54
alternator 203
altitude 211
aluminium 289
Amazonia 312
ambulance 94
amethyst 288
amniocentesis 52
amniotic fluid 52
amount 96
amp 60
amphibians 294
amplifier 268
analog 179
anchor 179, 191, 214, 240
Andes 312
Andorra 316
anesthetist 48
angle 164
angler 244
Angola 317
angry 25
animals 292, 294
animated movie 255
ankle 13, 15
ankle length 34
anniversary 26
annual 86, 307
answer 163
answer *v* 99, 163
answering machine 99
ant 295
antenna 295
antifreeze 199, 203
Antigua and Barbuda 314
anti-inflammatory 109
antique store 114
antiseptic 47
antiseptic wipe 47
antiwrinkle 41
antler 291
apartment 59
apartment building 59, 298
apéritif 153
aperture dial 270
apex 165
app 99
appeal 181
appearance 30
appendix 18
appetizer 153
applaud *v* 255
apple 126
apple corer 68
apple juice 149
appliances 66
application 176
appointment 45, 175
apricot 126
April 306
apron 30, 50, 69, 212
aquamarine 288
Arabian Sea 313
arbor 84
arborio rice 130
arc 164
arch 15, 85, 301
archery 249
architect 190
architecture 300
architrave 301
Arctic Circle 283
Arctic Ocean 312
area 165, 310
areas 299
arena 243
Argentina 315
arithmetic 165
arm 13
armchair 63
Armenia 318
armpit 13
armrest 200, 210
aromatherapy 55
around 320
arrangements 111
arrest 94
arrivals 213
arrow 249
art 162
art college 169
Art Deco 301
art gallery 261
art history 169
Art Nouveau 301
art supply store 115
artery 19
artichoke 124
artist 274
arts and crafts 274, 276
arugula 123
ash 283
ashtray 150
Asia 318
asparagus 124
asphalt 187
assault 94
assistant 24
assisted delivery 53
asteroid 280
asthma 44
astigmatism 51
astronaut 281
astronomy 281
asymmetric bars 235
at 320
athlete 234
athletic shoes 31
Atlantic Ocean 312
ATM 97
atmosphere 282, 286
atrium 104
attachment 177
attack 220
attack zone 224
attend *v* 174
attic 58
attractions 261
auburn 39
audience 254
August 306
aunt 22
aurora 286
Australasia 319
Australia 319
Austria 316
auto racing 249
automatic 200
automatic door 196
automatic payment 96
avalanche 247
avenue 299
avocado 128
awning 148
ax 95
axle 205
ayurveda 55
Azerbaijan 318

B

baby 23, 30
baby bath 74
baby care 74
baby carriage 75
baby changing room 104
baby monitor 75
baby products 107
baby sling 75
back 13
back brush 73
backboard 226
backdrop 254
backgammon 272
backhand 231
backpack 31, 37, 267
backseat 200
backsplash 66
backstroke 239
backswing 233
bacon 118, 157
bacon strip 119
bad 321
badge 94, 189
badminton 231
bag 311
bag cart 233
bagel 139
baggage carousel 212
baggage claim 213
baggage trailer 212
bags 37
baguette 138
Bahamas 314
bail 181
bailiff 180
bait 244
bait *v* 245
bake *v* 67, 138
baked 159
baker 139
bakery 107, 114, 138
baking 69
balance wheel 276
balcony 59
balcony seats 254
bald 39
bale 184
Balearic Islands 316
ball 15, 75, 221, 224, 226, 228, 230
ball boy 231

ballet 255
balsamic vinegar 135
Baltic Sea 313
bamboo 86,122
banana 128
Bangladesh 318
banister 59
bank 96, 284
bank charge 96
bank transfer 96
bar 150, 152, 250, 256, 311
bar code 106
bar counter 150
bar mitzvah 26
bar snacks 151
bar stool 150
barb 244
Barbados 314
barbecue grill 267
barber 39, 188
bark 296
barley 130, 184
barn 182
Baroque 301
barrier 298
bars 74
bartender 150, 191
basalt 288
base 164, 229
base station 99
baseball 228
baseline 230
baseman 228
basement 58
basil 133
basket 95, 106, 207, 226
basket of fruit 126
basketball 226
basketball player 226
bass clarinet 257
bass clef 256
bass guitar 258
bassinet 74
bassoon 257
bat 225, 228, 290
bat *v* 225, 229
bath mat 72
bath towel 73
bathrobe 73
bathroom 72
bathtub 72
baton 235, 256
batsman 225
batter 228
batteries 260
battery 167, 202
battery pack 78
battleship 215
bay leaf 133
be born *v* 26
beach 264
beach bag 264
beach ball 265
beach hut 264
beach towel 265
beach umbrella 264
beak 293
beaker 167
beam 186, 235
bean sprout 122
beans 131, 144
bear 291
beat 259
beauty 40
beauty treatments 41
bed 70
bed and breakfast 101
bed linen 71
bedding 74
bedroom 70
bedside lamp 70
bedspread 70
bedspring 71
bee 295
beech 296
beef 118
beer 145,151
beer tap 150
beet 125
beetle 295
before 320
beginning 321
behind 320
Belarus 316
Belgium 316
Belize 314
bell 197
below 320
belt 32, 36, 236
bench 250, 262
Benin 317
berry 296
beside 320
bet 273
between 320
beyond 320
Bhutan 318
biathlon 247
bib 30
bicep curl 251
biceps 16
bicycle 206
bidet 72
biennial 86
bifocal 51
big toe 15
bike lane 207
bike rack 207
bikini 264
bill 97, 152
binder 173
binoculars 281
biology 162
biplane 211
birch 296
bird-watching 263
birds 292
birth 52
birth certificate 26
birth weight 53
birthday 27
birthday cake 141
birthday candles 141
birthday party 27
bishop 272
bit 242
bit brace 78
bite 46
bite *v* 245
bitter 124, 145
black 39, 272, 274
black belt 237
black coffee 148
black currant 127
black-eyed peas 131
black hole 280
black olive 143
black pudding 157
Black Sea 313
black tea 149
blackberry 127
bladder 20
blade 60, 66, 78, 89
blanket 71, 74
blazer 33
bleach 77
blender 66
blister 46
block 237
block *v* 227
blonde 39
blood pressure 44
blood test 48
blouse 34
blow-dry *v* 38
blow-dryer 38
blow out *v* 141
blowhole 290
blue 274
blue cheese 136
bluebells 297
blueberry 127
blues 259
blush 40
board 241
board *v* 217
board games 272
boarding pass 213
boardwalk 265
bob 39
bobbin 276
bobby pins 38
bobsled 247
body 12
body lotion 73
body systems 19
bodysuit 30
bodywork 202
boil *v* 67
bok choy 123
Bolivia 315
bolt 59
bomber 211
bone 17, 119, 121
bone meal 88
bongos 257
book 168
bookshelf 63, 168
bookstore 115
boom 95, 240
booster 281
boot 37
booties 30
bored 25
borrow *v* 168
Bosnia and Herzegovina 316
Botswana 317
bottle 61, 75, 135, 311
bottle opener 68, 150
bottled foods 134
bottled water 144
bottom tier 141
boundary line 225
bouquet 35, 111
bouquet garni 132
bout 237
boutique 115
bow 240, 249
bow tie 36
bowl 61, 65, 112
bowl *v* 225
bowler 225
bowling 249
bowling ball 249
box 254
box file 173
box of chocolates 113
box of tissues 70
box office 255
boxer shorts 33
boxercise 251
boxing 236
boxing gloves 237
boxing ring 237
boy 23
boyfriend 24
bra 35
bracelet 36
braces 50
braid 39
brain 19
brake 200, 204, 206
brake *v* 207
brake block 207
brake fluid reservoir 202
brake lever 207
brake pedal 205
bran 130
branch 296
branch manager 96
brandy 145
brass 256
Brazil 315
brazil nut 129
bread 157
bread flour 139
bread knife 68
bread roll 143
breadcrumbs 139
breadfruit 124
breads 138
break a record *v* 234
break water *v* 52
breakdown 203
breakfast 64, 156
breakfast buffet 156
breakfast cereals 107
breakfast table 156
breakfast tray 101
breast 12, 119
breastbone 17
breast pump 53
breastfeed *v* 53
breaststroke 239
breathing 47
breech birth 52
brick 187
bridge 15, 214, 258, 273, 300
bridle 242
bridle path 263
Brie 142
briefcase 37
briefs 33, 35
brioche 157
broadcast 179
broadcast *v* 178
broccoli 123
brochures 96
broil *v* 67
bronze 235
brooch 36
broom 77
broth 158
brother 22
brother-in-law 23
browband 242
brown 274
brown bread 139
brown flour 138
brown lentils 131
brown rice 130
browse *v* 177
browser 177
bruise 46
Brunei 319
brunette 39
brush 38, 40, 77, 83, 274
brush *v* 38, 50
brussels sprout 123
bubble bath 73
bucket 77, 82
buckle 36
bud 111, 297
buffet 152
build *v* 186

english

buildings 299
bulb 86
Bulgaria 316
bull 185
bull-nose pliers 80
bulldog clip 173
bullet train 209
bulletin board 173
bullseye 273
bumper 74, 198
bun 39, 139, 140, 155
bunch 111
bungalow 58
bungee jumping 248
bunker 232
bunsen burner 166
buoy 217
burger 154
burger bar 154
burger meal 154
burglar alarm 58
burglary 94
Burkina Faso 317
burn 46
burner 61, 67
Burundi 317
bus 196
bus driver 190
bus shelter 196
bus station 197
bus stop 197, 299
bus ticket 197
buses 196
business 175
business class 211
business deal 175
business lunch 175
business partner 24
business suit 32
business trip 175
businessman 175
businesswoman 175
bustier 35
busy 99
butcher 118, 188
butcher shop 114
butter 137, 156
butter beans 131
buttercup 297
butterfly 239, 295
buttermilk 137
butternut squash 125
buttock 13, 16
button 32
buttonhole 32
buttress 301
by 320
by airmail 98
bytes 176

C

cab 95
cabbage 123
cabin 210, 214
Cabinda 317
cabinet 66
cable 79, 207
cable car 246
cable television 269
cactus 87
caddy 233
caesarean section 52
café 148, 262
cafeteria 168
cake pan 69
cakes 140
calcite 289
calcium 109
calculator 165
calendar 306
calf 13, 16, 185
call button 48
calyx 297
cam belt 203
Cambodia 318
camcorder 260, 269
camel 291
Camembert 142
camera 178, 260, 270
camera case 271
camera crane 178
camera phone 270
camera store 115
cameraman 178
Cameroon 317
camisole 35
camp *v* 266
camp bed 266
Campari 145
camper 266
camper van 266
campfire 266
campground 266
camping 266
camping stove 267
campus 168
can 145, 311
can opener 68
Canada 314
canary 292
candied fruit 129
candies 113
candy 107, 113
candy store 113
cane 91
canes 89
canine 50
canned drink 154
canned food 107
canning jar 135
canoe 214
canola oil 135
canter 243
canvas 274
cap 36
capacity 311
Cape gooseberry 128
capers 143
capital 315
capoeira 237
cappuccino 148
capsize *v* 241
capsule 109
captain 94, 214
car 198, 200
car accident 203
car rental 213
car seat 198, 207
car stereo 201
car wash 198
caramel 113
caraway 131
card 27
card reader 97
cardamom 132
cardboard 275
cardigan 32
cardiology 49
cardiovascular 19
cards 273
cargo 216
Caribbean Sea 312
carnation 110
carnival 27
carpenter 188
carpentry bits 80
carpet 71
carriage 208
carriage race 243
carrier 75, 204
carrot 124
carry-on luggage 211, 213
cart 100, 208, 213
cartilage 17
carton 311
cartoon 178
cartwheel 235
carve *v* 79
carving fork 68
case 51
cash *v* 97
cash register 106, 150
cashew 129
cashews 151
casino 261
Caspian Sea 313
cassava 124
casserole dish 69
cassette player 269
cassette tape 269
cast 254
cast *v* 245
castle 300
casual 34
casual wear 33, 34
cat 290
catamaran 215
cataract 51
catch *v* 220, 227, 229, 245
catcher 229
caterpillar 295
cathedral 300
catheter 53
cattail 86
cauliflower 124
cave 284
CD 269
CD player 268
CEO 175
cedar 296
ceiling 62
celebration 140
celebration cakes 141
celebrations 27
celeriac 124
celery 122
cell 94, 181
cell phone 99
cello 256
cement 186
cement mixer 186
center 164
center circle 222, 224, 226
center field 228
centerboard 241
centerline 226
centimeter 310
centipede 295
Central African Republic 317
century 307
ceramic stovetop 66
cereal 130, 156
cervical cap 21
cervical vertebrae 17
cervix 20, 52
Chad 317
chain 36, 206
chair 64
chair *v* 174
chairlift 246
chalk 85, 162, 288
chamber 283
chamomile tea 149
champagne 145
championship 230
change a tire *v* 203
change channel *v* 269
change gears *v* 207
change purse 37
changing mat 74
channel 178
charcoal 266, 275
charge 94, 180
chart 48
chassis 203
check 96, 152
checkbook 96
checker 106
checkers 272
check-in *v* 212
check-in desk 213
checking account 96
checkout 106
checkup 50
cheddar 142
cheek 14
cheerleader 220
cheese 136, 156
chef 152, 190
chef's hat 190
chemistry 162
cherry 126
cherry tomato 124
chess 272
chessboard 272
chest 12
chest of drawers 70
chest press 251
chestnut 129
chewing gum 113
chick 185
chicken 119, 185
chicken burger 155
chicken coop 185
chicken nuggets 155
chicken pox 44
chickpeas 131
chicory 122
child 23, 31
child lock 75
child's meal 153
childbirth 53
children 23
children's clothing 30
children's department 104
children's ward 48
Chile 315
chili pepper 124, 143
chili powder 132
chill 44
chimney 58
chin 14
China 318
china 105
chip *v* 233
chiropractic 54
chisel 81, 275
chives 133
chocolate 113
chocolate bar 113
chocolate cake 140
chocolate chip 141
chocolate-covered 140
chocolate milkshake 149
chocolate spread 135
choir 301

choke *v* 47
chop 119, 237
chorizo 143
choux pastry 140
christening 26
Christmas 27
chrysanthemum 110
chuck 78
church 298, 300
chutney 134
cider vinegar 135
cigar 112
cigarettes 112
cilantro 133
cinder block 187
cinnamon 133
circle 165
circuit training 251
circular saw 78
circulation desk 168
circumference 164
citrus fruit 126
city 298, 299
clam 121
clamp 78, 166
clapper board 179
clarinet 257
clasp 36
classical music 255, 259
classroom 162
claw 291
clay 85, 275
clean *v* 77
clean clothes 76
cleaned 121
cleaner 188
cleaning equipment 77
cleaning fluid 51
cleanser 41
clear honey 134
cleat 220, 223, 240
cleaver 68
clementine 126
client 38, 175, 180
cliff 285
climber 87
climbing frame 263
clinic 48
clipboard 173
clitoris 20
clock radio 70
closed 260, 321
closet 71
cloth diaper 30
clothesline 76
clothespin 76
clothing 205
cloud 287
cloudy 286
clove 125
clover 297
cloves 133
club 273
club sandwich 155
clubhouse 232
clutch 200, 204
coal 288
coast 285
coast guard 217
coaster 150
coat 32
coat hanger 70
cockatoo 293
cockle 121
cockpit 210
cockroach 295
cocktail 151
cocktail shaker 150
cocoa powder 148
coconut 129
cocoon 295
cod 120
coffee 144, 148, 153, 156, 184
coffee cup 65
coffee machine 148, 150
coffee milkshake 149
coffee table 62
coffee with milk 148
cog 206
coin 97
coin return 99
cola 144
colander 68
cold 44, 286, 321
cold faucet 72
cold-pressed oil 135
collage 275
collar 32
collarbone 17
colleague 24
collect call 99
college 168
Colombia 315
colony 315
coloring pencil 163
colors 39, 274
comb 38
comb *v* 38
combat sports 236
combine 182
comedy 255
comet 280
comforter 71
comic book 112
commission 97
communications 98
commuter 208
Comoros 317
compact 40
company 175
compartment 209
compass 165, 312, 240
complaint 94
complexion 41
compliments slip 173
composite sketch 181
compost 88
compost pile 85
computer 176
concealer 40
conceive *v* 20
conception 52
concert 255, 258
concourse 209
concussion 46
condensed milk 136
conditioner 38
condom 21
conductor 256
cone 164, 187
confectioner 113
candy 107, 113
confident 25
confused 25
conglomerate 288
Congo 317
conifer 86
connect *v* 177
connection 212
conning tower 215
console 269
constellation 281
construction 186
construction site 186
construction worker 186, 188
consultation 45
contact lenses 51
container 216, 311
container port 216
container ship 215
continent 282, 315
contraception 21, 52
contraction 52
control tower 212
controller 269
controls 201, 204
convector heater 60
convertible 199
conveyer belt 106
cooked meat 118, 143
cookie sheet 69
cookies 113, 141
cooking 67
coolant reservoir 202
cooling rack 69
copilot 211
copper 289
copy *v* 172
coral reef 285
cordless drill 78
cordless phone 99
core 127
cork 134
corkscrew 150
corn 122, 130, 184
corn bread 139
corn oil 135
cornea 51
corner 223
corner flag 223
cornice 300
corset 35
Corsica 316
cosmetics 105
Costa Rica 314
costume 255
cottage cheese 136
cottage garden 84
cotton 184, 277
cotton balls 41
cough 44
cough medicine 108
counselor 55
count *v* 165
counter 96, 98, 100, 142, 272
countertop 66
country 259, 315
couple 24
courier 99
courses 153
court 226
court case 180
court clerk 180
court date 180
courtroom 180
courtyard 58, 84
couscous 130
cousin 22
coveralls 82
cow 185
cow's milk 136
crab 121, 295
cracked wheat 130
craft knife 81
crafts 275
cramp 239
cramps 44
cranberry 127
crane 187, 216, 292
crater 283
crayfish 121
cream 109, 137, 140
cream cheese 136
cream pie 141
crease 225
credit card 96
creel 245
creeper 87
crème caramel 141
crème pâtissière 140
crepes 155, 157
crescent moon 280
crew 241
crew hatch 281
crew neck 33
crib 74
cricket 225, 295
cricket ball 225
cricket player 225
crime 94
criminal 181
criminal record 181
crisp 127
crispbread 139, 156
crisper 67
Croatia 316
crochet 277
crochet hook 277
crockery 64
crockery 65
crocodile 293
croissant 156
crop 39, 183
crop farm 183
crops 184
crossbar 207, 222, 235
cross-country skiing 247
crosswalk 195
crow 292
crown 50
crucible 166
crushed 132
crust 139, 282
cry *v* 25
crystal healing 55
Cuba 314
cube 164
cucumber 125
cuff 32, 45
cuff links 36
cultivate *v* 91
cultivator 182
cumin 132
curb 298
cured 118, 159, 143
curling 247
curling iron 38
curly 39
currant 129
currency exchange 97
curry 158
curry powder 132
curtain 63, 254
curved 165
cushion 62
custard 140
customer 96, 104, 106, 152
customer service department 175
customer services 104
customs 212
customs house 216
cut 46
cut *v* 38, 79, 277
cuticle 15
cutlery 65
cuts 119

english

cutting 91
cutting board 68
cuttlefish 121
cycle *v* 207
cycling 263
cylinder 164
cylinder head 202
cymbals 257
Cyprus 318
Czech Republic 316

D

daffodil 111
dairy 107
dairy farm 183
dairy products 136
daisy 110, 297
dam 300
dance 259
dance academy 169
dancer 191
dandelion 123, 297
dandruff 39
dark 41, 321
dark chocolate 113
darkroom 271
darn *v* 277
dartboard 273
darts 273
dashboard 201
date 129, 306
daughter 22
daughter-in-law 22
dawn 305
day 305, 306
day planner 175
dead ball line 221
deadhead *v* 91
deal *v* 273
debit card 96
decade 307
decay 50
December 306
deciduous 86
decimal 165
deck 85, 214
deck chair 265
deck of cards 273
decorating 82
decoration 141
decorator 82
deep end 239
deep-fried 159
deep sea fishing 245
deer 291
defense 181, 220
defendant 181
defender 223
defending zone 224
defrost *v* 67
degree 169
delay 209
deli 107
delicatessen 142
delivery 52, 98
deltoid 16
Democratic Republic of the Congo 317
Denmark 316
denomination 97
denominator 165
dental care 108
dental floss 50, 72
dental hygiene 72
dental X-ray 50
dentist 50, 189
dentist's chair 50
dentures 50
deodorant 73
deodorants 108
department 169
department store 105
departments 49
departure lounge 213
departures 213
deposit *v* 96
deposit slips 96
depth 165
dermatology 49
desert 285
desiccated 129
designer 191, 277
desk 162, 172
desktop 177
desktop organizer 172
dessert 140, 153
dessert cart 152
destination 213
detective 94
detergent 77
detour 195
deuce 230
develop *v* 271
diabetes 44
diagonal 164
dial *v* 99
diameter 164
diamond 273, 288
diaper 75
diaper bag 75
diaphragm 19, 21
diarrhea 44, 109
dice 272
dictionary 163
die *v* 26
diesel 199
diesel train 208
difficult 321
dig *v* 90, 227
digestive 19
digital 179, 269
digital camera 270
digital projector 163
digital radio 268
dilation 52
dill 133
dimensions 165
dimple 15
dining car 209
dining room 64
dinner 64, 158
dinner menu 152
dinner plate 65
diopter 51
diploma 169
dipstick 202
direct current 60
directions 260
director 254
directory assistance 99
dirt bike 205
dirty laundry 76
disabled parking 195
discharged 48
disconnected 99
discus 234
discuss *v* 163
disembark *v* 217
dishwasher 66
disinfectant solution 51
dispenser 150
disposable 109
disposable camera 270
disposable diaper 30
disposable razor 73
dissertation 169
distance 310
distributor 203
district 315
dive 239
dive *v* 238
diver 238
divide *v* 165
divided by 165
divided highway 195
dividends 97
divider 173, 194
diving board 238
divorce 26
Diwali 27
DJ 179
Djibouti 317
do not bend *v* 98
do not enter 195
dock 214, 216
dock *v* 217
doctor 45, 189
doctor's office 45
doctorate 169
documentary 178
dog 290
dogsledding 247
doll 75
dollhouse 75
dolphin 290
dome 300
domestic flight 212
Dominica 314
Dominican Republic 314
dominoes 273
donkey 185
door 196, 198, 209
door chain 59
door knob 59
door knocker 59
door lock 200
doorbell 59
doormat 59
dormer 58
dorsal fin 294
dosage 109
double 151
double bass 256
double bassoon 257
double-decker bus 196
double room 100
doubles 230
dough 138
Dover sole 120
down 320
downhill skiing 247
download *v* 177
dragonfly 295
drain 61, 72, 299
drain valve 61
drainage 91
draining board 67
draw *v* 162
drawer 66, 70, 172
drawing 275
dress 31, 34
dress shoe 37
dressage 243
dressed 159
dressed chicken 119
dressing 47, 158
dressing table 71
dribble *v* 223, 227
dried flowers 111
dried fruit 156
drill 50
drill *v* 79
drill bit 78, 80
drinking cup 75
drinking fountain 262
drinks 107, 144, 156
drip 53
drive *v* 195, 233
driver 196
driver's seat 196
driveshaft 202
drop anchor *v* 217
drop cloth 83
dropper 109, 167
drops 109
dropshot 230
drown *v* 239
drugstore 108
drum 258
drum kit 258
drummer 258
dry 39, 41, 130, 145, 286, 321
dry *v* 76
dry cleaner 115
dry dock 217
DTV converter 269
duck 119, 185
duck egg 137
duckling 185
due date 168
duffel bag 37
duffel coat 31
dugout 229
dumbbell 251
dump truck 187
dunk *v* 227
duodenum 18
duplex 58
dusk 305
dust *v* 77
dust cloth 77
dust ruffle 71
dustpan 77
duty-free shop 213
DVD 269
DVD player 268
dyed 39
dynamo 207

E

eagle 292
ear 14
early 305, 320
earrings 36
Earth 280, 282
earthenware dish 69
earthquake 283
easel 174, 274
east 312
East Timor 319
Easter 27
easy 321
eat *v* 64
eat-in 154
eating 75
eau de toilette 41
eaves 58
éclair 140
eclipse 280
economics 169
economy class 211
Ecuador 315
eczema 44
Edam 142
edge 246
editor 191
eel 294
egg 20
egg white 137
eggcup 65, 137
eggplant 125
eggs 137

Egypt 317
eight 308
eight hundred 308
eighteen 308
eighteenth 309
eighth 309
eightieth 309
eighty 308
ejaculatory duct 21
El Salvador 314
elbow 13
electric blanket 71
electric blood pressure monitor 45
electric car 199
electric drill 78
electric guitar 258
electric kettle 66
electric meter 60
electric razor 73
electric shock 46
electric train 208
electrical goods 107
electrical tape 81
electrician 188
electricity 60
electronics 105
elephant 291
elevator 59, 100, 104
eleven 308
eleventh 309
elliptical trainer 250
elm 296
email 98, 177
email account 177
email address 177
embarrassed 25
embossed paper 83
embroidery 277
embryo 52
emerald 288
emergency 46
emergency exit 210
emergency lever 209
emergency phone 195
emergency room 48
emergency services 94
emigrate *v* 26
emotions 25
employee 24
employer 24
empty 321
enamel 50
encore 255
encyclopedia 163
end 321
end zone 220
endive 123
endline 226
endocrine 19
endocrinology 49
energy-saving bulb 60
engaged couple 24
engine 202, 204, 208, 210
engine room 214
engineer's cab 208
engineering 169
English breakfast 157
English horn 257
English mustard 135
engraving 275
enlarge *v* 172
enlargement 271
ENT 49
entrance 59
entrance fee 260
entrée 153
envelope 98, 173
environment 280
epidural 52
epiglottis 19
epilepsy 44
episiotomy 52
equals 165
equation 165
equator 283
equipment 165, 233, 238
Equitorial Guinea 317
equity 97
eraser 163
Eritrea 317
erupt *v* 283
escalator 104
esophagus 19
espresso 148
essay 163
essential oils 55
Estonia 316
estuary 285
Ethiopia 317
eucalyptus 296
Europe 316
evening 305
evening dress 34
events 243, 247
evergreen 86
evidence 181
excavator 187
excess baggage 212
exchange rate 97
excited 25
excuse me 322
executive 174
exercise bike 250
exercises 251
exfoliate *v* 41
exhaust pipe 203, 204
exhibit *v* 261
exhibition 261
exit 210
exosphere 286
expanding file 173
expecting 52
experiment 166
expiration date 109
exposure 271
express train 209
extend *v* 251
extension cord 78
exterior 198
external hard drive 176
extra time 223
extraction 50
eye 14, 51, 244, 276
eye shadow 40
eye test 51
eyebrow 14, 51
eyebrow brush 40
eyebrow pencil 40
eyecup 269
eyelash 14, 51
eyelet 37
eyelid 51
eyeliner 40
eyepiece 167

F

fabric 277
fabric conditioner 76
face 14
face cream 73
face mask 41, 225
face-off circle 224
face powder 40
facial 41
factory 299
faint *v* 25, 44
fair 41
fairground 262
fairway 232
falcon 292
Falkland Islands 315
fall 237
fall (autumn) 31, 307
fall in love *v* 26
fallopian tube 20
family 22
famous ruin 261
fan 60, 202
fan belt 203
fans 258
far 320
fare 197, 209
farm 182, 183, 184
farmer 182, 189
farmhouse 182
farmland 182
farmyard 182
farsighted 51
fashion 277
fast 321
fast food 154
fast-forward 269
fat 119, 321
fat-free 137
father 22
father-in-law 23
faucet 61, 66
fault 230
fava bean 122, 131
feather 293
feature film 269
February 306
feed *v* 183
feijoa 128
female 12, 20
feminine hygiene 108
femur 17
fence 85, 182, 243
fencing 249
feng shui 55
fennel 122, 133
fennel seeds 133
fenugreek 132
fern 86
ferry 215, 216
ferry terminal 216
fertilize *v* 91
fertilization 20
fertilizer 91
festivals 27
fetus 52
fever 44
fiancé 24
fiancée 24
fiber 127
fibula 17
field 182, 222, 228, 234
field *v* 225, 229
field hockey 224
fifteen 308
fifteenth 309
fifth 309
fiftieth 309
fifty 308
fifty five thousand, five hundred 309
fifty thousand 309
fig 129
fighter plane 211
figure skating 247
Fiji 319
file 81, 177
filing cabinet 172
fill *v* 82
filler 83
fillet 119, 121
filleted 121
filling 50, 140, 155
film 260, 271
film roll 271
filter 270
filter coffee 148
filter paper 167
fin 210, 239
finance 97
financial advisor 97
fingerprint 94
finial 300
finishing line 234
Finland 316
fire 95
fire alarm 95
fire department 95
fire engine 95
fire escape 95
fire extinguisher 95
fire station 95
firefighters 95, 189
firelighter 266
fireplace 63
firm 124
first 309
first-aid 47
first-aid kit 47
fish 107, 120, 294
fish and chips 155
fish counter 114, 120
fish farm 183
fish seller 120, 188
fisherman 189
fishhook 244
fishing 244, 245
fishing boat 217
fishing license 245
fishing port 217
fishing rod 244
fist 15, 237
fitness 250
fitting rooms 104
five 308
five hundred 308
flag 221, 232
flageolet beans 131
flakes 132
flamingo 292
flare 240
flash 270
flash gun 270
flashlight 267
flask 166
flat 256
flat bread 139
flat race 243
flat tyre 203, 207
flat wood bit 80
flatscreen TV 269
flavored oil 134
flax 184
fleece 74
flesh 124, 127, 129
flex *v* 251
flight attendant 190, 210
flight number 213
flint 288
flip chart 174
flip-flop 37
flipper 290
float ball 61
flock 183
flood 287

floor 58, 62, 71
floor exercises 235
floor plan 261
Florentine 141
floret 122
florist 110, 188
floss *v* 50
flours 138
flower 110, 297
flowerbed 85, 90
flowering plant 297
flowering shrub 87
flu 44
flute 139, 257
fly 244, 295
fly *v* 211
fly fishing 245
flysheet 266
foal 185
focus *v* 271
focusing knob 167
fog 287
foil 249
folder 177
foliage 110
folk music 259
follicle 20
font 177
food 118, 130, 149
food processor 66
foot 12, 15, 310
foot pedal 257
football 220, 222
football player 220
footboard 71
footpath 262
footstrap 241
for 320
forceps 53, 167
forearm 12
forecourt 199
forehand 231
forehead 14
foreign currency 97
foreskin 21
forest 285
fork 65, 88, 207
forklift 186, 216
formal 34
formal garden 84, 262
fortieth 309
forty 308
forty minutes 304
forward 222
foul 222, 226
foul ball 228
foul line 229
foundation 40
fountain 85
four 308
four-door 200
four hundred 308
four-wheel drive 199
fourteen 308
fourteenth 309
fourth 309
fox 290
foxglove 297
foyer 59
fraction 165
fracture 46
fragile 98
fragranced 130
frame 51, 62, 206, 267
frame counter 270
France 316
freckle 15
free 321
free kick 222
free range 118
free-throw line 226
free weights 250
freesia 110
freeway 194
freeze 287
freeze *v* 67
freezer 67
freight train 208
freighter 215
French bean 122
French fries 154
French Guiana 315
French horn 257
French mustard 135
French press 65
French toast 157
French twist 39
frequency 179
fresh 121, 127, 130
fresh cheese 136
fresh fruit 157
freshwater fishing 245
fret 258
fretsaw 81
Friday 306
fried 159
fried chicken 155
fried egg 157
friend 24
frieze 301
frog 294
from 320
front crawl 239
front door 58
front wheel 196
frontal 16
frost 287
frosting 141
froth 148
frown 25
frozen 121, 124
frozen food 107
frozen yogurt 137
fruit 107, 126, 128
fruit bread 139
fruit farm 183
fruit juice 127, 156
fruit tart 140
fruit yogurt 157
fruitcake 140
fry *v* 67
frying pan 69
fuel gauge 201
fuel tank 204
full 64, 266, 321
full bed 71
full moon 280
fumble 220
funeral 26
funnel 166, 214
furniture store 115
furrow 183
fuse 60
fuse box 60, 203
fuselage 210

G

gable 300
Gabon 317
Galápagos Islands 315
galaxy 280
gale 286
galley 214
gallon 311
gallop 243
galvanized 79
Gambia 317
game 119, 230, 273
game show 178
games 272
gangway 214
garage 58, 199
garbage can 67
garden 84, 261
garden center 115
garden features 84
garden plants 86
garden styles 84
garden tools 88
gardener 188
gardening 90
gardening basket 88
gardening gloves 89
garland 111
garlic 125, 132
garlic press 68
garnet 288
garter 35
garter straps 35
gas pump 199
gas station 199
gas tank 203
gasket 61
gasoline 199
gate 85, 182, 247
gate number 213
gauze 47, 167
gear lever 207
gearbox 202, 204
gears 206
gearshift 201
gel 38, 109
gems 288
generation 23
generator 60
genitals 12
geography 162
geometry 165
Georgia 318
gerbera 110
Germany 316
get a job *v* 26
get married *v* 26
get up *v* 71
geyser 285
Ghana 317
giant slalom 247
gifts shop 114
gill 294
gin 145
gin and tonic 151
ginger 125, 133
giraffe 291
girder 186
girl 23
girlfriend 24
girth 242
glacier 284
gladiolus 110
gland 19
glass 69, 152
glass bottle 166
glass rod 167
glasses 51, 150
glassware 64
glaze *v* 139
glider 211, 248
gliding 248
gloss 83, 271
glove 36, 224, 228, 233, 236, 246
glue 275
glue gun 78
gneiss 288
go to bed *v* 71
go to sleep *v* 71
goal 221, 223, 224
goal area 223
goal line 220, 223, 224
goalkeeper 222, 224
goalpost 220, 222
goat 185
goat cheese 142
goat's milk 136
goggles 238, 247
going out 75
gold 235, 289
goldfish 294
golf 232
golf bag 233
golf ball 233
golf cart 232
golf clubs 233
golf course 232
golf shoe 233
golf trolley 233
golfer 232
gong 257
good 321
good afternoon 322
good evening 322
good morning 322
good night 322
goodbye 322
goose 119, 293
goose egg 137
gooseberry 127
gorge 284
gorilla 291
Gothic 301
gown 169
grade 163
graduate 169
graduate *v* 26
graduation ceremony 169
graft *v* 91
grains 130
gram 310
grandchildren 23
granddaughter 22
grandfather 22
grandmother 22
grandparents 23
grandson 22
granite 288
grape juice 144
grapefruit 126
grapeseed oil 134
graphite 289
grass 86, 262
grass bag 88
grasshopper 295
grassland 285
grate *v* 67
grated cheese 136
grater 68
gratin dish 69
gravel 88
gravity 280
graze 46
greasy 39
Greece 316
green 129, 232, 274
green olive 143
green peas 131
green salad 158
green tea 149
greenhouse 85
Greenland 314
Grenada 314
gray 39, 274
grill pan 69
grilled 159
groceries 106
grocery cart 106
grocery store 114
groin 12

groom 243
ground 60, 132
ground coffee 144
ground cover 87
ground floor 104
ground meat 119
ground sheet 267
group therapy 55
grout 83
guard 236
guardrail 195
Guatemala 314
guava 128
guest 64, 100
guidebook 260
guided tour 260
guilty 181
Guinea 317
Guinea-Bissau 317
guitarist 258
gull 292
gum 50
gumdrop 113
gun 94
gurney 48
gutter 58, 299
guy rope 266
Guyana 315
gym 101, 250
gym machine 250
gymnast 235
gymnastics 235
gynecologist 52
gynecology 49
gypsophila 110

H

hacksaw 81
haddock 120
hemorrhage 46
hail 286
hair 14, 38
hair dye 40
hair straightener 38
hairdresser 38, 188
hairspray 38
Haiti 314
half an hour 304
half-and-half 137
half-liter 311
halftime 223
hallibut fillets 120
Halloween 27
halter 243
halter neck 35
ham 119, 143, 156
hammer 80
hammer *v* 79
hammock 266
hamper 263
hamster 290
hamstring 16
hand 13, 15
hand drill 81
hand fork 89
hand rail 59, 196
hand towel 73
handbag 37
handcuffs 94
handicap 233
handkerchief 36
handle 36, 88, 106, 187, 200, 230
handlebar 207
handles 37
handsaw 81, 89
handset 99
hang *v* 82
hang-glider 248
hang-gliding 248
hanging basket 84
hanging file 173
happy 25
harbor 217
harbor master 217
hard 129, 321
hard candy 113
hard cheese 136
hard cider 145
hard hat 186
hardboard 79
hardware 176
hardware store 114
hardwood 79
haricot beans 131
harness race 243
harp 256
harvest *v* 91, 183
hat 36
hatchback 199, 200
have a baby *v* 26
Hawaii 314
hay 184
hay fever 44
hazard 195
hazard lights 201
hazelnut 129
hazelnut oil 134
head 12, 19, 81, 230
head *v* 222
head injury 46
head office 175
headache 44
headband 39
headboard 70
headlight 198, 205, 207
headphones 268
headrest 200
headsail 240
health 44
health center 168
health food store 115
heart 18, 119, 122, 273
heart attack 44
heater controls 201
heather 297
heating element 61
heavy 321
heavy cream 137
heavy metal 259
hedge 85, 90, 182
hedgehog 290
heel 13, 15, 37
height 165
helicopter 211
hello 322
helmet 95, 204, 206, 220, 224, 228
help desk 168
hem 34
hematite 289
hen's egg 137
herb 55, 86
herb garden 84
herbaceous border 85
herbal remedies 108
herbal tea 149
herbalism 55
herbicide 183
herbs 133, 134
herbs and spices 132
herd 183
hexagon 164
high 321
high chair 75
high definition 269
high dive 239
high-heeled shoe 37
high jump 235
high speed train 208
highlights 39
hiking 263
hiking boot 37, 267
hill 284
Himalayas 313
hip 12
hippopotamus 291
historic building 261
history 162
hit *v* 224
hob 67
hockey 224
hockey stick 224
hoe 88
hold 215, 237
hole 232
hole in one 233
hole punch 173
holly 296
home 58
home delivery 154
home entertainment 268
home furnishings 105
home plate 228
homeopathy 55
homework 163
homogenized 137
Honduras 314
honeycomb 135
honeymoon 26
honeysuckle 297
hood 31, 75, 198
hoof 242, 291
hook 187, 276
hoop 226, 277
horizontal bar 235
hormone 20
horn 201, 204, 291
horror movie 255
horse 185, 235, 242
horse race 243
horseback riding 242, 263
horseradish 125
horseshoe 242
hose 89, 95
hose reel 89
hosepipe 89
hospital 48
host 64, 178
hostess 64
hot 124, 286, 321
hot-air balloon 211
hot chocolate 144, 156
hot dog 155
hot drinks 144
hot faucet 72
hot-water bottle 70
hotel 100, 264
hour 304
hour hand 304
house 58
household current 60
household products 107
hovercraft 215
hub 206
hubcap 202
hull 214, 240
human resources department 175
humerus 17
humid 286
hummingbird 292
hump 291
hundred 308
hundred and ten 308
hundred thousand 308
hundredth 309
Hungary 316
hungry 64
hurdles 235
hurricane 287
husband 22
husk 130
hydrant 95
hydrofoil 215
hydrotherapy 55
hypnotherapy 55
hypoallergenic 41
hypotenuse 164

I

ice 120, 287
ice and lemon 151
ice bucket 150
ice climbing 247
ice cream 137, 149
ice-cream scoop 68
ice cube 151
ice hockey 224
ice hockey player 224
ice hockey rink 224
ice maker 67
ice skate 224
ice-skating 247
iced coffee 148
iced tea 149
Iceland 316
icicle 287
icon 177
identity tag 53
igneous 288
ignition 200
iguana 293
illness 44
immigration 212
impotent 20
in 320
in brine 143
in front of 320
in oil 143
in sauce 159
in syrup 159
inbox 177
inch 310
incisor 50
incubator 53
index finger 15
India 318
Indian Ocean 312
indigo 274
Indonesia 319
induce labour *v* 53
industrial park 299
infection 44
infertile 20
infield 228
inflatable dinghy 215
inflatable ring 265
information 261
information screen 213
in-goal area 221
inhaler 44, 109
injection 48
injury 46
ink 275
ink pad 173
inlet 61
inline skating 249
inner core 282
inner tube 207
inning 228
innocent 181

english

insect repellent 108, 267
inside 320
insomnia 71
install *v* 177
instep 15
instructions 109
instruments 256, 258
insulation 61
insulin 109
insurance 203
intensive care unit 48
interchange 194
intercom 59
intercostal 16
intercourse 20
interest rate 96
interior 200
intermission 254
internal systems 60
international flight 212
internet 177
intersection 298
interviewer 179
into 320
in-tray 172
invertebrates 295
investigation 94
investment 97
ionosphere 286
Iran 318
Iraq 318
Ireland 316
iris 51, 110
iron 76, 109, 233, 289
iron *v* 76
ironing board 76
island 282
Israel 318
Italy 316
itinerary 260
IUD 21
Ivory Coast 317

J
jack 203, 273
jacket 32, 34
jackhammer 187
jade 288
jam 134, 156
Jamaica 314
January 306
Japan 318
jar 134, 311
javelin 234
jaw 14, 17
jazz 259
jeans 31, 33
jelly bean 113
jellyfish 295
Jerusalem artichoke 125
jet 288
jet skiing 241
jetty 217
jetway 212
jeweler 114, 188
jewelry 36
jewelry box 36
jewelry-making 275
jewelry store 114
jigsaw 78
jigsaw puzzle 273
jodhpurs 242
jog in place 251
jogging 251, 263
jogging suit 31
joint 17, 119
joker 273
Jordan 318
journal 168
journalist 190
judge 180
judo 236
juices and milkshakes 149
juicy 127
July 306
jump 237, 243
jump *v* 227
jump ball 226
jumping rope 251
June 306
Jupiter 280
jury 180
jury box 180

K
kale 123
Kaliningrad 316
kangaroo 291
karate 236
kayak 241
kayaking 241
Kazakhstan 318
kebab 155, 158
keel 214
keep net 244
kendo 236
Kenya 317
kernel 122, 129, 130
ketchup 135, 154
kettle 66
kettledrum 257
key 59, 176, 207
keyboard 176, 258
keypad 97, 99
kick 237, 239
kick *v* 221, 223
kickboard 238
kickboxing 236
kickstand 207
kid 185
kidney 18, 119
kilogram 310
kilometer 310
kimono 35
king 272, 273
king shrimp 121
kippers 157
kitchen 66, 152
kitchen knife 68
kitchenware 68, 105
kitten 290
kiwifruit 128
knead *v* 138
knee 12
knee length 34
knee pad 205
knee support 227
kneecap 17
knife 65
knife sharpener 68, 118
knight 272
knitting 277
knockout 237
knuckle 15
koala 291
kohlrabi 123
koi carp 294
Kosovo 316
kumquat 126
kung fu 236
Kuwait 318
Kyrgyzstan 318

L
labels 89
labia 20
laboratory 166
lace 35, 37
lace bobbin 277
lace making 277
lace-up 37
lacrosse 249
lactose 137
ladder 95, 186
ladle 68
ladybug 295
ladyfinger 141
lake 285
lamb 118, 185
lamp 62, 217
land 282
land *v* 211
landing 59
landing gear 210
landing net 244
landlord 58
landscape 271, 284
landscape *v* 91
lane 234, 238
languages 162
Laos 318
lapel 32
laptop 172, 176
larch 296
large 321
large intestine 18
larynx 19
last week 307
late 16, 305
later 304
latex paint 83
latitude 283
Latvia 316
laugh *v* 25
launch 281
launch pad 281
laundromat 115
laundry 76
laundry service 101
lava 283
law 169, 180
lawn 85, 90
lawn rake 88
lawnmower 88, 90
lawyer 180, 190
lawyer's office 180
laxative 109
lead singer 258
leaded 199
leaf 122, 296
league 223
lean meat 118
learn *v* 163
leather shoes 32
leathers 205
Lebanon 318
lecture hall 169
leek 125
left 260
left field 228
left-hand drive 201
left lane 194
leg 12, 119
leg pad 225
leg press 251
legal advice 180
legal department 175
leggings 31
legumes 130
leisure 258, 254, 264
lemon 126
lemon curd 134
lemon grass 133
lemon sole 120
lemonade 144
length 165, 310
lens 270
lens (eye) 51
lens (glasses) 51
lens cap 270
lens case 51
Lesotho 317
lesson 163
let! 231
letter 98
letter slot 58, 99
letterhead 173
lettuce 123
level 80, 187
lever 61, 150
Liberia 317
librarian 168, 190
library 168, 299
library card 168
Libya 317
license plate 198
licorice 113
liquor store 115
lid 61, 66
Liechtenstein 316
life buoy 240
life events 26
life jacket 240
life raft 240
lifeboat 214
lifeguard 239, 265
lifeguard tower 265
ligament 17
light 178, 321
light a fire *v* 266
light aircraft 211
light meter 270
light switch 201
lighter 112
lighthouse 217
lighting 105
lightning 287
lights 94
lily 110
lime 126, 296
limestone 288
limousine 199
line 244
line of play 233
linen 105, 277
lines 165
linesman 223, 230
lingerie 35, 105
lining 32
lining paper 83
link 36
lintel 186
lion 291
lip 14
lip brush 40
lip gloss 40
lip liner 40
lipstick 40
liqueur 145
liquid 77
liquid measure 311
literature 162, 169
Lithuania 316
liter 311
little finger 15
little toe 15
live 60, 178
live rail 209
liver 18, 118
livestock 183, 185
living room 62
lizard 293

load v 76
loaf 139
loan 96, 168
lob 230
lobby 100, 255
lobster 121, 295
lock 59, 207
lockers 239
log on v 177
loganberry 127
logo 31
loin 121
lollipop 113
long 32
long-distance bus 196
long-grain 130
long-handled shears 88
long jump 235
long wave 179
longitude 283
loom 277
loose-leaf tea 144
lose v 273
loser 273
love 230
low 321
lug nuts 203
luge 247
luggage 100, 198, 213
luggage department 104
luggage hold 196
luggage rack 209
lumbar vertebrae 17
lumber 187
lunar module 281
lunch 64
lung 18
lunge 251
lupines 297
lure 244
Luxembourg 316
lychee 128
lymphatic 19
lyrics 259

M

macadamia 129
mace 132
Macedonia 316
machine gun 189
machinery 187
mackerel 120
macramé 277
Madagascar 317
magazine 107, 112
magma 283
magnesium 109
magnet 167
maid service 101
mail carrier 98, 190
mailbag 98, 190
mailbox 58, 99
mainsail 240
make a will v 26
make friends v 26
make the bed v 71
makeup 40
making bread 138
malachite 288
Malawi 317
Malaysia 318
Maldives 318
male 12, 21
Mali 317
mallet 78, 275
Malta 316
malt vinegar 135
malted drink 144
mammals 290
man 23
manager 24, 174
Manchego 142
mane 242, 291
mango 128
manhole 299
manicure 41
mantle 282
manual 200
map 261
maple 296
maple syrup 134
maracas 257
marathon 234
marble 288
March 306
margarine 137
marina 217
marinated 143, 159
marine fishing 245
marjoram 133
mark v 227
market 115
marketing department 175
marmalade 134, 156
marrow squash 124
Mars 280
marshmallow 113
martial arts 237
martini 151
marzipan 141
mascara 40
mashed 159
masher 68
mask 189, 228, 236, 239, 249
masking tape 83
masonry bit 80
massage 54
mast 240
master's 169
mat 54, 235
match 230
material 79, 187, 276
maternity 49
maternity ward 48
math 162, 164
matte 83, 271
mattress 70, 74
Mauritiana 317
Mauritius 317
May 306
maybe 322
mayonnaise 135
MDF 79
meadow 285
meal 64
measles 44
measure 150, 151
measure v 310
measurements 165
measuring cup 69, 311
measuring spoon 109
meat 119
meat and poultry 106
meat tenderizer 68
meatballs 158
meathook 118
mechanic 188, 203
mechanics 202
medals 235
media 178
median stripe 194
medical examination 45
medication 109
medicine 109, 169
medicine cabinet 72
meditation 54
Mediterranean Sea 313
medium wave 179
meeting 174
meeting room 174
melody 259
melon 127
memory 176
memory stick 176
men's clothing 32
menstruation 20
menswear 105
menu 148, 153, 154
menubar 177
mercury 289
Mercury 280
meringue 140
mesophere 286
messages 100
metacarpal 17
metal 79, 289
metal bit 80
metamorphic 288
metatarsal 17
meteor 280
meter 310
Mexico 314
mezzanine 254
mica 289
microphone 179, 258
microscope 167
microwave oven 66
middle finger 15
middle lane 194
midnight 305
midwife 53
migraine 44
mile 310
milk 136, 156
milk v 183
milk carton 136
milk chocolate 113
milk shake 137
millennium 307
millet 130
milligram 310
milliliter 311
millimeter 310
mineral 144, 289
minibar 101
minibus 197
minivan 199
mint 113, 133
mint tea 149
minus 165
minute 304
minute hand 304
minutes 174
mirror 40, 71, 167
miscarriage 52
Miss/Ms. 23
missile 211
mist 287
miter block 81
mittens 30
mix v 67, 138
mixing bowl 66, 69
mixing desk 179
moat 300
mobile 74
model 169, 190
model-making 275
modeling tool 275
moisturizer 41
molar 50
molding 63
Moldova 316
mole 14
Monaco 316
Monday 306
money 97
money order 98
Mongolia 318
monitor 53, 172
monkey 291
monkfish 120
Monopoly 272
monorail 208
monsoon 287
Montenegro 316
month 306
monthly 307
monument 261
Moon 280
moonstone 288
moor v 217
mooring 217
mop 77
morning 305
Morocco 317
mortar 68, 167, 187
mortgage 96
mosque 300
mosquito 295
mosquito net 267
moth 295
mother 22
mother-in-law 23
motocross 249
motor 88
motorcycle 204
motorcycle racing 249
mountain 284
mountain bike 206
mountain range 282
mouse 176, 290
mousse 141
mouth 14
mouth guard 237
mouthwash 72
move 273
movie set 179
movie theater 255, 299
movies 255
mow v 90
Mozambique 317
mozzarella 142
Mr. 23
Mrs. 23
mudguard 205
muffin 140
muffin pan 69
muffler 203, 204
mug 65
mulch v 91
multigrain bread 139
multiply v 165
multivitamin tablets 109
mumps 44
mung beans 131
muscles 16
museum 261
mushroom 125
music 162
music school 169
musical 255
musical score 255
musical styles 259
musician 191
mussel 121, 295
mustard 155
mustard seed 131
Myanmar (Burma) 318

english

N

naan bread 139
nail 15, 80
nail clippers 41
nail file 41
nail scissors 41
nail polish 41
nail polish remover 41
Namibia 317
nape 13
napkin 65
napkin ring 65
nappy rash cream 74
narrow 321
nation 315
national park 261
natural 256
natural fiber 31
naturopathy 55
nausea 44
navel 12
navigate *v* 240
near 320
nearsighted 51
nebula 280
neck 12, 258
neck brace 46
necklace 36
nectarine 126
needle 109, 276
needle-nose pliers 80
needle plate 276
needlepoint 277
negative 271
negative electrode 167
neighbor 24
Neoclassical 301
Nepal 318
nephew 23
Neptune 280
nerve 19, 50
nervous 19, 25
net 217, 222, 226, 227, 231
net *v* 245
Netherlands 316
nettle 297
network 176
neurology 49
neutral 60
neutral zone 224
new 321
new moon 280
new potato 124
New Year 27
New Zealand 319
newborn baby 53
news 178
newsstand 112
newspaper 112
next week 306
nib 163
Nicaragua 314
nickel 289
niece 23
Niger 317
Nigeria 317
night 305
nightgown 31, 35
nightwear 31
nightstand 70
nightstick 94
nine 308
nine hundred 308
nineteen 308
nineteen hundred 307
nineteen hundred and one 307
nineteen ten 307
nineteenth 309
ninetieth 309
ninety 308
ninth 309
nipple 12, 75
no 322
no right turn 195
no stopping 195
nonstick 69
noodles 158
noon 305
normal 39
north 312
North and Central America 314
North Korea 318
North Pole 283
North Sea 312
Northern Hemisphere 283
Norway 316
nose 14, 210
nose clip 238
noseband 242
nosebleed 44
nosewheel 210
nostril 14
notation 256
note 256
notebook 163, 172
notepad 173
notes 191
notions 105
nougat 113
November 306
now 304
nozzle 89
number 226, 308
numerator 165
nurse 45, 48, 189
nursery 74
nursing 53
nursing bra 53
nursing pads 53
nut 80
nutmeg 132
nuts 151
nuts and dried fruit 129
nylon 277

O

oak 296
oar 241
oatmeal 157
oats 130
objective lens 167
oboe 257
obsidian 288
obstetrician 52
occupations 188, 190
occupied 321
ocean 282
ocean liner 215
octagon 164
October 306
octopus 121, 295
odometer 201
off-piste 247
off-ramp 194
office 24, 172, 174
office building 298
office equipment 172
office supplies 173
offside 223
oil 142, 199
oil paint 274
oil tank 204
oil tanker 215
oils 134
oily 41
ointment 47, 109
okra 122
old 321
olive oil 134
olives 151
Oman 318
omelet 158
on-ramp 194
on time 305
on top of 320
oncology 49
one 308
one billion 309
one million 309
one thousand 309
one-way street 194
one-way system 298
onesie 30
onion 124
online 177
onto 320
onyx 289
opal 288
open 260, 321
open-faced sandwich 155
open-top 260
opening night 254
opera 255
operating room 48
operation 48
operator 99
ophthalmology 49
opponent 236
opposite 320
optic nerve 51
optometrist 51, 189
orange 126, 274
orange juice 148
orangeade 144
orbit 280
orchestra 256
orchestra pit 254
orchestra seats 254
orchid 111
order *v* 153
oregano 133
organic 91, 118, 122
organic waste 61
origami 275
ornamental 87
orthopedics 49
osteopathy 54
ostrich 292
otter 290
ounce 310
out 225, 228, 320
out of bounds 226
out of focus 271
outboard motor 215
outbuilding 182
outdoor activities 262
outer core 282
outfield 229
outlet 60, 61
outpatient 48
outside 320
out-tray 172
oval 164
ovary 20
oven 66
oven mitt 69
ovenproof 69
over 320
over par 233
overalls 30
overdraft 96
overexposed 271
overflow pipe 61
overhead bin 210
overpass 194
overture 256
ovulation 20, 52
owl 292
oyster 121
ozone layer 286

P

Pacific Ocean 312
pack 311
pack of cigarettes 112
package 99
packet 311
pad 220, 224
paddle 231, 241
paddock 242
pail 265
painkillers 47, 109
paint 83
paint *v* 83
paint can 83
paint thinner 83
paint tray 83
painter 191
painting 62, 261, 274
paints 274
pajamas 33
Pakistan 318
palate 19
palette 274
pallet 186
palm 15, 86, 296
palm hearts 122
pan 310
pan fried 159
Panama 314
pancreas 18
panda 291
panties 35
pants 32, 34
panty hose 35, 251
panty liner 108
papaya 128
paper clip 173
paper napkin 154
paper tray 172
papier-maché 275
paprika 132
Papua New Guinea 319
par 233
parachute 248
parachuting 248
paragliding 248
Paraguay 315
parallel 165
parallel bars 235
parallelogram 164
paramedic 94
parents 23
park 262
park *v* 195
parka 31, 33
parking brake 203
parking lot 298
parking meter 195
Parmesan 142
parole 181
parrot 293
parsley 133

english

parsnip 125
particle board 79
partner 23
pass 226
pass *v* 195, 220, 223
passcode 99
passenger 216
passenger port 216
passenger seat 204
passion fruit 128
Passover 27
passport 213
passport control 213
pasta 158
pastels 274
pasteurized 137
pasting brush 82
pasting table 82
pastry 140, 149
pastry brush 69
pastry shop 114
pasture 182
patch 207
patchwork 277
pâté 142, 156
path 58, 85
pathology 49
patient 45
patio café 148
patio garden 85
pattern 276
pause 269
paving 85
pawn 272
pay *v* 153
pay-per-view channel 269
payment 96
payphone 99
payroll 175
pea 122, 131
peach 126, 128
peacock 293
peanut 129, 151
peanut butter 135
peanut oil 135
pear 127
pecan 129
pectoral 16
pectoral fin 294
pedal 61, 206
pedal *v* 207
pedestrian zone 299
pediatrics 49
pedicure 41
pediment 301
peel 128
peel *v* 67
peeled shrimp 120
peeler 68
pelican 292
pelvis 17
pen 163, 185
pen pal 24
penalty 222
penalty area 223
pencil 163, 275
pencil case 163
pencil sharpener 163
pendant 36
penguin 292
peninsula 282
penis 21
pentagon 164
peony 111
people 12, 16
pepper 64, 124, 152
peppercorn 132
pepperoni 142
percentage 165
percussion 257
perennial 86
perfume 41, 105
periodical 168
perm 39
perpendicular 165
persimmon 128
personal best 234
personal organizer 173, 175
personal trainer 250
Peru 315
pesticide 89, 183
pestle 68, 167
pet food 107
pet store 115
petal 297
petri dish 166
pharmacist 108, 189
pharmacy 108
pharynx 19
pheasant 119, 293
Phillips screwdriver 80
philosophy 169
Philippines 319
phone booth 99
photo album 271
photo finish 234
photograph 271
photograph *v* 271
photographer 191
photography 270
phyllo dough 140
physical education 162
physics 162, 169
physiotherapy 49
piano 256
piccolo 257
pick *v* 91
pick and mix 113
pickax 187
pickled 159
pickup 98, 258
picnic 263
picnic bench 266
picture frame 271
pie pan 69
piece 272
pier 217
pig 185
pig farm 183
pigeon 292
pigeonhole 100
piglet 185
pigsty 185
pigtails 39
Pilates 251
pill 21, 109
pillar 300
pillow 70
pillowcase 71
pilot 190, 211
PIN 96
pin 60, 237, 249, 276
pincushion 276
pine 296
pine nut 129
pineapple 128
pineapple juice 149
pink 274
pint 311
pinto beans 131
pipe 112, 202
pipe cutter 81
pipette 167
piping bag 69
pistachio 129
pita bread 139
pitch 225, 256, 266
pitch *v* 229
pitch a tent *v* 266
pitcher 65, 151, 229
pitcher's mound 228
pitches available 266
pith 126
pizza 154
pizzeria 154
place setting 65
placemat 64
placenta 52
plain 285
plane 81
plane *v* 79
planet 280, 282
plant *v* 183
plant pot 89
plants 86, 296
plaque 50
plaster 83
plaster *v* 82
plastic bag 122
plastic pants 30
plastic surgery 49
plate 65, 283
plateau 284
platform 208
platform number 208
platinum 289
play 254, 269
play *v* 229, 273
player 221, 231, 273
playground 263
playhouse 75
playing 75
playing field 168
playpen 75
plea 180
please 322
Plimsoll mark 214
plow *v* 183
plug 60, 72
plum 126
plumb line 82
plumber 188
plumbing 61
plunger 81
plus 165
Pluto 280
plywood 79
poach *v* 67
poached 159
pocket 32
pod 122
podium 235, 256
point 273
poisoning 46
poker 273
Poland 316
polar bear 291
Polaroid camera 270
pole 245, 282
pole vault 234
police 94
police car 94
police officer 94, 184
police station 94
polish 77
polish *v* 77
political science 169
polo 243
polyester 277
pomegranate 128
pommel 242
pommel horse 235
pond 85
ponytail 39
pool 249
pop 259
popcorn 255
poplar 296
poppy 297
poppy seeds 138
porch 58
porch light 58
pore 15
pork 118
port 145, 176, 214, 216
porter 100
portfolio 97
porthole 214
portion 64
portrait 271
Portugal 316
positive electrode 167
post office 98
postage 98
postal worker 98
postgraduate 169
poster 255
poster paint 274
postcard 112
postmark 98
pot *v* 91
potpourri 111
potato 124
potato chips 113, 151
potpie 143, 158
potted plant 87, 110
potter's wheel 275
pottery 275
potty 74
pouch 291
poultry 119
poultry farm 183
pound 310
pour *v* 67
powder 77, 109
powder puff 40
powdered milk 137
power 60
power cord 176
power outage 60
practice swing 233
praying mantis 295
pregnancy 52
pregnancy test 52
pregnant 52
premature 52
premolar 50
prenatal 52
prepared food 107
prerecorded 178
prescription 45
present 27
presentation 174
preservative 83
preserved fruit 134
press 178
press-up 251
presser foot 276
pressure valve 61
price 152, 199
price list 154
prickly pear 128
primer 83
primrose 297
principal 163
principality 315
print 271
print *v* 172
printer 172, 176
printing 275
prison 181
prison guard 181
private bathroom 100
private jet 211
private room 48
probe 50

problems 271
processed grains 130
procession 27
processor 176
produce seller 188
produce stand 114
producer 254
professor 169
program 176, 254, 269
programming 178
propagate *v* 91
propeller 211, 214
proposal 174
prosciutto 143
prosecution 180
prostate 21
protractor 165
proud 25
prove *v* 139
province 315
prow 215
prune 129
prune *v* 91
pruners 89
psychiatry 49
psychotherapy 55
public address system 209
puck 224
Puerto Rico 314
puff pastry 140
pull up *v* 251
pulp 127
pulse 47
pumice 288
pumice stone 73
pump 37, 207
pumpkin 125
pumpkin seed 131
punch 237
punching bag 237
pup 290
pupil 51
puppy 290
purple 274
push-up 251
putt *v* 233
putter 233
pyramid 164

Q

Qatar 318
quadriceps 16
quail 119
quail egg 137
quart 311
quarter of an hour 304
quarterdeck 214
quartz 289
quay 216
queen 272, 273
question 163
question *v* 163
quiche 142
quiche pan 69
quick cooking 130
quilt 71
quilting 277
quince 128
quinoa 130
quiver 249

R

rabbit 118, 290
raccoon 290
race 234
race-car driver 249
racecourse 243
racehorse 243
racing bike 205, 206
racing dive 239
rack 166
racket 230
racket games 231
racquetball 231
radar 214, 281
radiator 60, 202
radicchio 123
radio 179, 268
radio antenna 214
radio station 179
radiology 49
radish 124
radius 17, 164
rafter 186
rafting 241
rail 208
railcar 208
railroad network 209
rain 287
rain boots 31
rain forest 285
rain gear 245, 267
rainbow 287
rainbow trout 120
raincoat 31, 32
raisin 129
rake 88
rake *v* 90
rally 230
rally driving 249
RAM 176
Ramadan 26
ramekin 69
rap 259
rapeseed 184
rapids 240, 284
rappelling 248
rash 44
raspberry 127
raspberry jam 134
rat 290
rattle 74
raw 124, 129
ray 294
razor blade 73
razorshell clam 121
read *v* 162
reading light 210
reading list 168
reading room 168
real estate office 115
realtor 189
reamer 80
rear light 207
rear wheel 197
rearview mirror 198
receipt 152
receive *v* 177
receiver 99
reception 100
receptionist 100, 190
record 234, 269
record player 268
record store 115
recording studio 179
rectangle 164
rectum 21
recycling bin 61
red 274
red (wine) 145
red card 223
red currant 127
red eye 271
red kidney beans 131
red lentils 131
red meat 118
red mullet 120
Red Sea 313
reduce *v* 172
reduced-fat milk
reel 244
reel in *v* 245
referee 220, 222, 226
referral 49
reflector 50, 204, 207
reflector strap 205
reflexology 54
reggae 259
region 315
regional office 175
register 100
registered mail 98
regulator 239
reheat *v* 154
reiki 55
reins 242
relationships 24
relatives 23
relaxation 55
relay race 235
release *v* 245
remote control 269
Renaissance 301
renew *v* 168
rent 58
rent *v* 58
repair kit 207
report 174
reporter 179
reproduction 20
reproductive 19
reproductive organs 20
reptiles 293
research 169
reserve *v* 168
residence hall 168
respiratory 19
rest 256
restaurant 101, 152
restrooms 104, 266
result 49
resuscitation 47
retina 51
retire *v* 26
return 231
return address 98
reverse *v* 195
rewind 269
rhinoceros 291
rhombus 164
rhubarb 127
rhythmic gymnastics 235
rib 17, 119, 155
rib cage 17
ribbon 27, 39, 111, 141, 235
rice 130, 158, 184
rice pudding 140
rider 242
riding boot 242
riding crop 242
riding hat 242
rigging 215, 240
right 260
right field 229
right-hand drive 201
right lane 194
rim 206
rind 119, 127, 136, 142
ring 36
ring finger 15
ring ties 89
rings 235
rinse *v* 38, 76
ripe 129
rise *v* 139
river 284
road bike 206
road markings 194
road roller 83, 187
road signs 195
roads 194
roadwork 187, 195
roast 158
roast *v* 67
roasted 129
robe 31, 32, 35, 38
rock climbing 248
rock concert 258
rock garden 84
rocks 284, 288
Rocky Mountains 312
Rococo 301
rodeo 243
roll 139, 311
roll *v* 67
roller coaster 262
roller shade 63
rollerblading 263
rolling pin 69
romance 255
Romania 316
romper 30
roof 58, 203
roof garden 84
roof rack 198
roof tile 187
rook 272
room 58
room key 100
room number 100
room service 101
rooms 100
rooster 185
root 50, 124, 296
roots 39
rope 248
rose 89, 110
rosé 145
rosemary 133
rotor blade 211
rotten 127
rough 232
round 237
roundabout 195
route number 196
router 78
row 210, 254
row *v* 241
row boat 214
row house 58
rower 241
rowing machine 250
rubber band 173
rubber boots 89
rubber stamp 173
ruby 288
ruck 221
rudder 210, 241
rug 63
rugby 221
rugby field 221
ruler 163, 165
rum 145
rum and cola 151
rump steak 119
run 228
run *v* 228

runner bean 122
runway 212
Russian Federation 318
rutabaga 125
Rwanda 317
rye bread 138

S

sad 25
saddle 206, 242
safari park 262
safe 228
safety 75, 240
safety barrier 246
safety goggles 81, 167
safety pin 47
saffron 132
sage 133
Sahara Desert 313
sail 241
sailboat 215
sailing 240
sailor 189
salad 149
salamander 294
salami 142
salary 175
sales assistant 104
sales department 175
salesclerk 188
salmon 120
salon 115
salt 64, 152
salted 121, 129, 137, 143
San Marino 316
sand 85, 264
sand *v* 82
sandal 31, 37
sandbox 263
sandcastle 265
sander 78
sandpaper 81, 83
sandstone 288
sandwich 155
sandwich counter 143
sanitary napkin 108
São Tomé and Principe 317
sapphire 288
sardine 120
Sardinia 316
sashimi 121
satellite 281
satellite dish 269
satellite navigation (satnav) 195, 201
satsuma 126
Saturday 306
Saturn 280
sauce 134, 143, 155
saucepan 69
Saudi Arabia 318
sauna 250
sausage 118, 155, 157
sauté *v* 67
save *v* 177, 223
savings 96
savings account 97
savory 155
saw *v* 79
saxophone 257
scaffolding 186
scale 45, 69, 98, 118, 121, 166, 212, 256, 293, 294, 310
scaled 121
scallion 125
scallop 121
scalp 39
scalpel 167
scan 48, 52
scanner 106, 176
scarecrow 184
scared 25
scarf 31, 36
schedule 197, 209, 261
schist 288
scholarship 169
school 162, 169, 299
school bus 196
schoolbag 162
schoolboy 162
schoolgirl 162
science 162, 166
science fiction movie 255
scientist 190
scissors 38, 47, 82, 276
scoop 149
scooter 205
score 220, 256, 273
score a goal *v* 223
scoreboard 225
scorpion 295
scotch and water 151
Scrabble 272
scrambled eggs 157
scrape *v* 77
scraper 82
screen 97, 176, 255, 269
screw 80
screwdriver 80, 151
screwdriver bits 80
script 254
scrollbar 177
scrotum 21
scrub *v* 77
scrum 221
scuba diving 239
sculpting 275
sculptor 191
sea 264, 282
sea bass 120
sea bream 120
sea horse 294
sea lion 290
seafood 121
seal 290
sealant 83
seam 34
seamstress 191
seaplane 211
search *v* 177
seasonal 129
seasons 306
seat 61, 204, 209, 210, 242, 254
seat back 210
seat belt 198, 211
seat post 206
seating 254
second 304, 309
second floor 104
second hand 304
secondhand store 115
section 282
security 212
security bit 80
security guard 189
sedan 199
sedative 109
sedimentary 288
seed 122, 127, 128, 130
seed tray 89
seeded bread 139
seedless 127
seedling 91
seeds 88, 131
seesaw 263
segment 126
self defence 237
self-rising flour 139
self-tanning lotion 41
semi-hard cheese 136
semi-soft cheese 136
seminal vesicle 21
semolina 130
send *v* 177
send off *v* 223
Senegal 317
sensitive 41
sentence 181
September 306
Serbia 316
serve 231
serve *v* 64, 231
server 148,152, 176
service charge included 152
service charge not included 152
service line 230
service provider 177
service vehicle 212
serving spoon 68
sesame seed 131
sesame seed oil 134
set 178, 230, 254
set *v* 38
set honey 134
set sail *v* 217
set the alarm *v* 71
seven 308
seven hundred 308
seventeen 308
seventeenth 309
seventh 309
seventieth 309
seventy 308
sew *v* 277
sewing basket 276
sewing machine 276
sexually transmitted disease 20
shade 41
shade plant 87
shallot 125
shallow end 239
shampoo 38
shapes 164
share price 97
shares 97
shark 294
sharp 256
shaving 73
shaving foam 73
shears 89
shed 84
sheep 185
sheep farm 183
sheep's milk 137
sheer curtain 63
sheet 71, 74, 241
shelf 67, 106
shell 129, 137, 265, 293
shelled 129
shelves 66
sherbet 141
sherry 145
shiatsu 54
shield 88
shin 12
shingle 58
ship 214
shipyard 217
shirt 33
shock 47
shocked 25
shoe department 104
shoe store 114
shoes 34, 37
shoot *v* 223, 227
shopping 104
shopping bag 106
shopping center 104
shops 114
short 32, 321
short-grain 130
short wave 179
shorts 30, 33
shot 151
shotput 234
shoulder 13, 194
shoulder bag 37
shoulder blade 17
shoulder pad 35
shoulder strap 37
shout *v* 25
shovel 88, 187, 265
shower 72, 286
shower block 266
shower curtain 72
shower door 72
shower gel 73
shower head 72
showjumping 243
shredder 172
shuffle *v* 273
shutoff valve 61
shutter 58
shutter release 270
shuttle bus 197
shuttlecock 231
shy 25
Siberia 313
Sicily 316
side 164
side-by-side refrigerator 67
side effects 109
side mirror 198
side order 153
side plate 65
side saddle 242
side street 299
sidedeck 240
sideline 220, 226, 230
sidewalk 298
sidewalk café 148
Sierra Leone 317
sieve 68, 89
sift *v* 91, 138
sigh *v* 25
sightseeing 260
sign 104
signal 209
signature 96, 98
silk 277
silo 183
silt 85
silver 235, 289
simmer *v* 67
Singapore 319
singer 191
single 151

english

single-family 58
single room 100
singles 230
sink 38, 50, 61, 66, 72
sinker 244
sinus 19
siren 94
sirloin steak 119
sister 22
sister-in-law 23
site 266
site manager's office 266
sit-up 251
six 308
six hundred 308
sixteen 308
sixteenth 309
sixth 309
sixtieth 309
sixty 308
skate 120, 247, 294
skate *v* 224
skate wings 120
skateboard 249
skateboarding 249, 263
skein 277
skeleton 17
sketch 275
sketch pad 275
skewer 68
ski 241, 246
ski boot 246
ski jacket 246
ski jump 247
ski pole 246
ski run 246
ski slope 246
skier 246
skiing 246
skim milk 136
skin 14, 119
skin care 108
skinned 121
skirt 30, 34
skull 17
skydiving 248
skyscraper 299, 300
slalom 247
slate 288
sledding 247
sledgehammer 187
sleeper 30
sleeping 74
sleeping bag 267
sleeping compartment 209
sleeping mat 267
sleeping pill 109
sleet 286
sleeve 34
sleeveless 34
slice 119, 139, 140, 230
slice *v* 67
sliced bread 138
slicer 139
slide 167, 263
slide *v* 229
sling 46
slip 35
slip-on 37
slippers 31
slope 284
slotted spatula 68
slotted spoon 68
Slovakia 316
Slovenia 316
slow 321
slug 295
small 321
small intestine 18
small of back 13
smartphone 99, 176
smash 231
smile 25
smoke 95
smoke alarm 95
smoked 118, 121, 143, 159
smoked fish 143
smoking 112
snack bar 113, 148
snail 295
snake 293
snap 30
snare drum 257
sneaker 37, 251
sneeze 44
snooker 249
snore *v* 71
snorkel 239
snout 293
snow 287
snowboarding 247
snowmobile 247
snowsuit 30
soak *v* 130
soap 73
soap dish 73
soap opera 178
soccer 222
soccer ball 220
soccer field 220
soccer player 220, 222
soccer uniform 31, 222
socket 80
socket wrench 80
socks 33
sod *v* 90
soda bread 139
soda water 144
sofa 62
sofa bed 63
soft 129, 321
soft-boiled egg 137, 157
soft cheese 136
soft drink 144, 154
software 176
softwood 79
soil 85
solar system 280
solder 79, 80
solder *v* 79
soldering iron 81
soldier 189
sole 15, 37
solids 164
Soloman Islands 319
soluble 109
solvent 83
Somalia 317
some meals included 101
somersault 235
son 22
son-in-law 22
sonata 256
song 259
sorrel 123
sorting unit 61
soufflé 158
soufflé dish 69
sound boom 179
sound technician 179
soundtrack 255
soup 153, 158
soup bowl 65
soup spoon 65
sour 127
sour cream 137
sourdough bread 139
sous chef 152
south 312
South Africa 317
South Korea 318
South Sudan 317
Southern Hemisphere 283
Southern Ocean 313
souvenirs 260
sow *v* 90, 183
soybeans 131
space 280
space exploration 281
space heater 60
space shuttle 281
space station 281
space suit 281
spade 273
Spain 316
spare tire 203
spark plug 203
sparkling 144
sparring 237
sparrow 292
spatula 68, 167
speaker 174, 176, 258, 268
speaker stand 268
spearfishing 245
specialist 49
specials 106, 152
spectators 233
speed limit 195
speed skating 247
speedboat 214
speedboating 241
speedometer 201, 204
spell *v* 162
sperm 20
sphere 164
spices 132
spicy sausage 142
spider 295
spike *v* 90
spikes 233
spin 230
spin *v* 76
spin dryer 76
spinach 123
spine 17
spire 300
spleen 18
splint 47
splinter 46
split ends 39
split peas 131
spoke 207
sponge 73, 74, 83
sponge cake 140
spool 245
spool of thread 276
spoon 65
sport coat 33
sport fishing 245
sports 220, 236, 248
sports car 198
sportsman 191
sportswear 105
spotlight 259
sprain 46
spray 109
spray *v* 91
spray bottle 89, 311
spray can 311
spring 307
spring balance 166
spring greens 123
springboard 235
sprinkler 89
sprinter 234
sprocket 207
square 164, 272, 299
square foot 310
square meter 310
squash 231
squat 251
squid 121, 295
squirrel 290
Sri Lanka 318
St. Kitts and Nevis 314
St. Lucia 314
St. Vincent and the Grenadines 314
stable 185, 243
stadium 223
staff 175, 256
stage 167, 254
stages 23
stainless steel 79
stair gate 75
stair machine 250
staircase 59
stake 90
stake *v* 91
stalk 122, 297
stalls 254
stamen 297
stamp 98
stamp collecting 273
stamps 112
stance 232
stand 88, 205, 268
stapler 173
staples 173
star 280
star anise 133
star fruit 128
starfish 295
start school *v* 26
starting block 234, 238
starting line 234
state 315
statement 180
stationery 105
station wagon 199
steak 121
steam *v* 67
steam train 208
steamed 159
steel wool 81
steeplechase 243
steering wheel 201
stem 111, 112, 297
stencil 83
stenographer 181
step machine 250
stepdaughter 23
stepfather 23
stepladder 82
stepmother 23
stepson 23
stereo 269
stereo system 268
sterile 47
stern 240
stew 158
stick 224, 249
sticks 133
still 144
sting 46, 295
stir *v* 67
stir-fry 158
stirrer 150
stirrup 242

stitch 277
stitch selector 276
stitches 52
stock broker 97
stock exchange 97
stocking 35
stocks 97, 110
stomach 18
stomachache 44
stone 36, 275
stone fruit 126
stop 269
stop button 197
stopper 166
stopwatch 234
store 298
store directory 104
stork 292
storm 287
stout 145
stovetop 67
straight 39, 165
straight ahead 260
straighten *v* 39
strand of pearls 36
strap 35
strapless 34
stratosphere 286
straw 144, 154
strawberry 127
strawberry milkshake 149
stream 285
streaming 260
street 298
street corner 298
street sign 298
street vendor 154
streetcar 196
streetlight 298
stress 55
stretch 251
stretcher 94
strike 228, 237
string 230, 256, 258
strip *v* 82
stroke 44, 231, 233, 239
stroller 75
strong 321
stub 96
student 162
study 63, 162
stuffed 159
stuffed olive 143
stuffed toy 75
stump 225
styles 39, 239, 301
submarine 215
subsoil 91
substitute 223
substitution 223
subtract *v* 165
suburb 299
subway 208
subway map 209
succulent 87
suction cup 53
suction hose 77
Sudan 317
sugarcane 184
suit 273
sulfur 289
sultana 129
summer 31, 307
summons 180
sumo wrestling 237
Sun 280
sunbathe *v* 264
sunbed 41
sunblock 108, 265
sunburn 46
Sunday 306
sunflower 184, 297
sunflower oil 134
sunflower seed 131
sunglasses 51, 265
sun hat 30, 265
sunny 286
sunrise 305
sunroof 202
sunscreen 108
sunset 305
sunshine 286
suntan lotion 265
supermarket 106
supplement 55
supply pipe 61
support 187
suppository 109
surf 241
surfboard 241
surfcasting 245
surfer 241
surfing 241
surgeon 48
surgery 48
Suriname 315
surprised 25
sushi 121
suspect 94, 181
suspension 203, 205
swallow 292
swamp 285
swan 293
Swaziland 317
sweater 33
sweatshirt 33
Sweden 316
sweep *v* 77
sweet 124, 127, 155
sweet potato 125
sweet spreads 134
sweetcorn 124
sweets 113
swim *v* 238
swimmer 238
swimming 238
swimming cap 238
swimming pool 101, 238, 250
swimsuit 238, 265
swing *v* 232
swings 263
swiss chard 123
switch 60
Switzerland 316
swivel chair 172
sword 236
swordfish 120, 294
symphony 256
synagogue 300
synchronized swimming 239
synthetic fiber 31
Syria 318
syringe 109, 167
syrup 109
system 176

T

T-shirt 30, 33
tab 173
table 64, 148
table tennis 231
tablecloth 64
tablet 176
tachometer 201
tack *v* 241, 277
tackle 245
tackle *v* 220, 223
tackle box 244
tadpole 294
tae kwon do 236
tag *v* 229
tai chi 236
tail 121, 210, 242, 280, 290, 294
tailbone 17
tailgate 198
taillight 204
tailor 191
tailor shop 115
tailor's chalk 276
tailor's dummy 276
tailored 35
tailplane 210
Tajikstan 318
take a shower *v* 72
take notes *v* 163
take off *v* 211
talcum powder 73
tall 321
tamarillo 128
tambourine 257
tampon 108
tan 41
tandem 206
tangerine 126
tank 61
Tanzania 317
tap water 144
tape 173
tape dispenser 173
tape measure 80, 276
target 249
target shooting 249
taro root 124
tarragon 133
Tasmania 319
tattoo 41
tax 96
taxi driver 190
taxi stand 213
tea 144, 149, 184
tea with lemon 149
tea with milk 149
teabag 144
teacher 162, 190
teacup 65
team 220, 229
teapot 65
tear 51
teaspoon 65
techniques 79, 159
teddy bear 75
tee 233
tee-off *v* 233
teeing ground 232
teenager 23
telegram 98
telephone 99
teleprompter 179
telescope 281
television series 178
television studio 178
teller 96
temperature 286
temperature gauge 201
temple 14, 300
ten 308
ten thousand 309
tenant 58
tend *v* 91
tendon 17
tennis 230
tennis court 230
tennis shoes 231
tenon saw 81
tent 267
tent peg 266
tent pole 266
tenth 309
tequila 145
terminal 212
termite 295
territory 315
test 49, 163
test tube 166
testicle 21
text (SMS) 99
textbook 163
Thailand 318
thank you 322
Thanksgiving 27
the day after tomorrow 307
the day before yesterday 307
theater 254, 299
theme park 262
therapist 55
thermal underwear 35, 267
thermometer 45, 167
thermosphere 286
thermostat 61
thesis 169
thick 321
thigh 12, 119
thimble 276
thin 321
third 309
third floor 104
thirteen 308
thirteenth 309
thirtieth 309
thirty 308
this way up 98
this week 307
thistle 297
thoracic vertebrae 17
thread 276
thread *v* 277
thread guide 276
three 308
three hundred 308
three-point line 226
thriller 255
throat 19
throat lozenge109
throttle 204
through 320
throw 237
throw *v* 221, 227, 229
throw-in 223, 226
thruster 281
thumb 15
thumbtack 173
thunder 286
Thursday 306
thyme 133
thyroid gland 18
tibia 17
ticket 209, 213
ticket gates 209
ticket inspector 209
ticket office 209, 216
tie 32, 223
tiebreaker 230
tiepin 36
tiger 291
tile 272
tile *v* 82
tiller 240
time 234, 304
time out 220
timer 166
times 165, 261

english

timing 203
tin 289, 311
tip 36, 122, 246
tissue 108
title 23, 168
to 320
to go 154
toad 294
toast 157
toasted sandwich 149
toaster 66
tobacco 112, 184
today 306
toddler 30
toe 15
toe clip 207
toe strap 207
toenail 15
toffee 113
toggle 31
Togo 317
toilet 60, 72
toilet brush 72
toilet paper 72
toilet seat 72
toiletries 41, 107
toll booth 194
tomato 125, 157
tomato juice 144, 149
tomorrow 306
toner 41
tongs 150, 167
tongue 19, 37, 118
tonic water 144
tonne 310
tool rack 78
toolbar 177
toolbelt 186
toolbox 80
tools 187
tooth 50
toothache 50
toothbrush 72
toothpaste 72
top coat 83
top-dress *v* 90
top tier 141
topaz 288
topiary 87
topping 155
topsoil 85
tornado 287
tortoise 293
tossed salad 158
touch line 221
touchdown 221
tour bus 197, 260
tour guide 260
tourer 205
touring bike 206
tourist 260
tourist attraction 260
tourist information 261
tourmaline 288
tournament 233
tow away *v* 195
towards 320
tow truck 203
towel rack 72
towels 73
tower 300
town hall 299
townhouse 58
toy 75
toy basket 75
toys 105
track 208, 234
track and field 235
tracksuit 32
tractor 182
traffic 194
traffic jam 195
traffic light 194
traffic policeman 195
trail-riding 243
trailer 266
train 35, 208
train *v* 91, 251
train station 208
training wheels 207
tram 196, 208
transfer 223
transfer *v* 207
transformer 60
transmission 202
transplant *v* 91
transportation 194
trapezius 16
trapezoid 164
trash 177
trash can 61
travel agency 114, 190
travel brochure 212
travel-sickness pills 109
traveler's check 97
tray 152, 154
tray-table 210
tread 207
tread water *v* 239
treadmill 250
treble clef 256
tree 86, 296
trellis 84
tremor 283
triangle 165, 257
triceps 16
trifle 141
trim *v* 39, 90
trimester 52
trimmer 88
Trinidad and Tobago 314
tripod 166, 270, 281
trombone 257
Tropic of Cancer 283
Tropic of Capricorn 283
tropical fruit 128
tropics 283
troposphere 286
trot 243
trough 183
trout 120
trowel 89, 187
truck 194
truck driver 190
truffle 113, 125
trumpet 257
truncheon 94
trunk 198, 291, 296
trunks 238
try 221
tub 311
tuba 257
tube 311
Tuesday 306
tugboat 215
tulip 111
tumble dryer 76
tumbler 65
tuna 120
tune *v* 179
tune the radio *v* 269
tuning peg 258
Tunisia 317
turbocharger 203
Turkey 318
turkey 119, 185, 293
Turkmenistan 318
turmeric 132
turn 238
turn *v* 79
turn signal 198, 204
turn off the television *v* 269
turn on the television *v* 269
turnip 124
turpentine 83
turquoise 289
turret 300
turtle 293
tusk 291
tutu 191
tweezers 40, 47, 167
twelfth 309
twelve 308
twentieth 309
twenty 308
twenty-first 309
twenty minutes 304
twenty-one 308
twenty-second 309
twenty-third 309
twenty thousand 309
twenty-two 308
twig 296
twin bed 71
twin room 100
twine 89
twins 23
twist ties 89
two 308
two-door 200
two hundred 308
two o'clock 304
two thousand 307
two thousand and one 307
two weeks 307
tire 198, 205, 206
tire iron 203
tire lever 207
tire pressure 203

U

Uganda 317
ugli 126
Ukraine 316
ulna 17
ultralight 211
ultrasound 52
ultraviolet rays 286
umbilical cord 52
umbrella 36
umpire 225, 229, 230
uncle 22
unconscious 47
uncooked meat 142
under 320
under par 233
undercoat 83
underexposed 271
undergraduate 169
underpass 194
undershirt 33
underwear 32, 35
underwire 35
uniform 94, 189
United Arab Emirates 318
United Kingdom 316
United States of America 314
universe 280
university 299
unleaded 199
unpasteurised 137
unpick *v* 277
unsalted 137
until 320
up 320
upset 25
Uranus 280
ureter 21
urethra 20
urinary 19
urology 49
Uruguay 315
usher 255
uterus 20, 52
utility knife 80, 82
utility room 76
Uzbekistan 318

V

V-neck 33
vacation 212
vaccination 45
vacuum cleaner 77, 188
vacuum flask 267
vagina 20
valley 284
valve 207
vanilla 132
Vanuatu 319
variety meat 118
varnish 79, 83
vas deferens 21
vase 63, 111
Vatican City 316
vault 235, 300
veal 118
vegetable garden 85, 182
vegetable oil 135
vegetables 107, 122, 124
veggie burger 155
veil 35
vein 19
Venetian blind 63
Venezuela 315
venison 118
vent 283
ventilation hood 66
Venus 280
verdict 181
vest 33, 35
veterinarian 189
vibraphone 257
video game 269
video phone 99
video tape 269
Vietnam 318
viewfinder 271
village 299
vine 183
vinegar 135, 142
vineyard 183
vintage 199
viola 256
violin 256
virus 44
visa 213
vise 78
vision 51
visiting hours 48
visor 205
vitamins 108

vocal cords 19
vodka 145
voice message 99
volcano 283
volley 231
volleyball 227
voltage 60
volume 165, 179, 269, 311
vomit *v* 44

W
waders 244
wading pool 263
waffles 157
waist 12
waistband 35
waiting room 45
waitress 191
wake up *v* 71
walk 243
wall 58, 186, 222
wall light 62
wallet 37
wallpaper 82, 177
wallpaper *v* 82
wallpaper brush 82
wallpaper paste 82
walnut 129
walnut oil 134
walrus 290
ward 48
wardrobe 70
warehouse 216
warm 286
warm up *v* 251
warrant 180
wash *v* 38, 77
washer 80
washer-dryer 76
washer fluid reservoir 202
washing machine 76
wasp 295
waste disposal 61, 266
waste disposal unit 61
waste pipe 61
wastebasket 172
watch 36
watch television *v* 269
water 144, 238
water *v* 90, 183
water bottle 206, 267
water chamber 61
water chestnut 124
water closet 61
water garden 84
water hazard 232
water heater 61
water jet 95
water plant 86
water polo 239
water wings 238
watercolor paint 274
watercress 123
waterfall 285
watering 89
watering can 89
watermelon 127
waterskier 241
waterskiing 241
watersports 241
wave 241, 264
wavelength 179
wax 41
weak 321
weather 286
weaving 277
website 177
wedding 26, 35
wedding cake 141
wedding dress 35
wedding reception 26
wedge 37, 233
Wednesday 306
weed *v* 91
weed killer 91
weeds 86
week 306
weekend 306
weekly 307
weigh *v* 310
weight 166
weight bar 251
weight belt 239
weight training 251
west 312
Western 255
Western sahara 317
wet 286, 321
wet wipe 75, 108
wetsuit 239
whale 290
wheat 130, 184
wheel 198, 207
wheelbarrow 88
wheelchair 48
wheelchair access 197
whetstone 81
whiplash 46
whipped cream 137, 157
whisk 68
whisk *v* 67
whiskers 290
whiskey 145
white 39, 272, 274
white (wine) 145
white bread 139
white chocolate 113
white currant 127
white flour 138
white meat 118
white rice 130
whiteboard 162
whiting 120
whole 129, 132
whole-grain 131
whole-grain mustard 135
whole milk 136
whole-wheat bread 139, 149
whole-wheat flour 138
Wi-Fi 269
wicket 225
wicket-keeper 225
wide 321
width 165
wife 22
wig 39
wild rice 130
willow 296
win *v* 273
wind 241, 286
windbreak 265
windlass 214
window 58, 96, 98, 177, 186, 197, 209, 210
windpipe 18
windshield 198
windshield washer fluid 199
windshield wiper 198
windsurfer 241
windsurfing 241
windy 286
wine 145, 151
wine glass 65
wine list 152
wine vinegar 135
wing 119, 210, 293
wings 254
winner 273
winter 31, 307
winter sports 247
wipe *v* 77
wire 79
wire cutter 80
wire strippers 81
wires 60
with 320
withdrawal slip 96
without 320
witness 180
wok 69
wolf 290
woman 23
womb 52
women's clothing 34
womenswear 105
wood 79, 233, 275
wood glue 78
wood shavings 78
wood stain 79
wooden spoon 68
woodpecker 292
woods 285
woodwind 257
woodworking 275
work 172
workbench 78
workday 306
workshop 78
world map 312
worm 295
worried 25
wound 46
wrap 155
wrapping 111
wreath 111
wrench 81
wrestling 236
wrinkle 15
wrist 13, 15
wristband 230
writ 180
write *v* 162

X
X-ray 48
X-ray film 50
X-ray machine 212
X-ray viewer 45

Y
yacht 215, 240
yam 125
yard 310
yarn 277
yawn *v* 25
year 163, 306
yeast 138
yellow 274
yellow card 223
Yemen 318
yes 322
yesterday 306
yoga 54
yoga pose 54
yogurt 137
yolk 137, 157
you're welcome 322

Z
Zambia 317
zebra 291
zero 308
zest 126
Zimbabwe 317
zinc 289
zip 277
zip code 98
zone 315
zones 283
zoo 262
zoology 169
zoom lens 270
zucchini 125

Hindi index • hindī tālikā • हिन्दी तालकिा

अ

अंक *m* 308
अंकगणित *m* 165
अकशेरुकी जीव *m* 295
अकीक *m* 289
अंकुरित फली *f* 122
अक्टूबर *m* 306
अक्षांश *m* 283
अख़रोट *m* 129
अख़रोट का तेल *m* 134
अगला पाल 240
अगली फ़्रूट 126
अगले हफ़्ते 307
अगस्त *m* 306
अंगिया *f* 35
अंगुश्ताना *m* 276
अंगूठा *m* 15
अंगूठी *f* 36
अंगूर *m* 127
अंगूर का जूस *m* 144
अंगूर का बाग़ *m* 183
अंगूर के बीज का तेल *m* 134
अंगोला *m* 317
अग्र भाग *m* 210
अग्रिम पंक्ति का खिलाड़ी *m* 222
अंग्रेज़ी नाश्ता *m* 157
अंग्रेज़ी बीन 257
अंचल *m* 315
अचारित *m* 159
अज़रबैजान *m* 318
अजवायन *f* 133
अंजीर *m* 129
अटारी *f* 58
अटैचमेंट 177
अठारह *m* 308
अठारहवां *m* 309
अंडकोश *m* 21
अंडग्रंथि *f* 21
अंडरवायर्ड 35
अंडा *m* 20
अंडाकार 164
अंडाशय *m* 20
अड्की बीन 131
अंडे *m* 137
अंडे का कप *m* 65, 137
अंडे की भुर्जी *f* 157
अंतःप्रकोष्ठिका *f* 17
अंतर नगरीय रेलगाड़ी *f* 209
अंतरराष्ट्रीय उड़ान *f* 212
अंतराल *m* 254
अंतरिक्ष *m* 280
अंतरिक्ष अन्वेषण 281
अंतरिक्ष केंद्र *m* 281
अंतरिक्ष यान *m* 281
अंतरिक्ष यात्री *m* 281
अंतरिक्ष सूट *m* 281
अंतर्निर्मित अलमारी *f* 71
अतलांतिक महासागर *m* 312
अंतः वस्त्र *m* 32
अंतः संचार *m* 59
अतिरिक्त टायर *m* 203
अतिरिक्त तार *m* 78
अतिरिक्त भाग *m* 58
अतिरिक्त समय *m* 223
अतिरिक्त सामान *m* 212
अत्यधिक उद्भासित *m* 271
अंत्येष्टि *f* 26
अंतः स्राविकी 49
अंतः स्रावी 19
अदरक *m* 125, 133
अधोवस्त्र *m* 35, 105
अध्यक्षता करना *tr* 174
अध्ययन *m* 161
अध्ययन कक्ष *m* 168
अध्ययन सूची *f* 168
अध्यापक *m* 190
अध्यापिका *f* 162
अध्याय *m* 163
अनाज *m* 107, 130
अनाज एवं दालें 130
अनामिका *f* 15
अनार *m* 128
अनिद्रा *f* 71
अनिर्णित मैच *m* 223
अनुकूल स्थिति 230
अनुमानित तस्वीर *f* 181
अनुर्वर *m* 20
अनुसंधान *m* 169
अन्डोरा *m* 316
अन्य कलाएं *f* 275
अन्य खेलकूद *m* 248
अन्य जहाज़ *m* 215
अन्य दुकानें *f* 114
अनन्नास *m* 128
अनन्नास का जूस *m* 149
अपना विशेष प्रदर्शन 234
अपराधी *m* 181
अपर्चर नियंत्रक *m* 270
अंपायर *m* 225, 229, 230
अपारदर्शी टेप *m* 83
अपार्टमेंट *m* 59
अपार्टमेंट खंड *m* 298
अपास्चरीकृत 137
अपील *f* 181
अप्रैल *m* 306
अप्सरोंगुलि 297
अफ़ग़ानिस्तान *m* 318
अफ़्रीका *m* 317
अबाबील *m* 292
अभिनेता *m* 179, 254
अभिनेत्री *f* 191, 254
अभिमुक्त 181
अभियांत्रिकी *f* 169
अभियुक्त *m* 180
अभियोग *m* 180
अभियोजन *m* 180
अभी 304
अभ्यास करना *tr* 251
अभ्रक *m* 289
अमरूद *m* 128
अमेज़ोनिया *m* 312
अमेरिकन फुटबॉल *m* 220
अयाल *m* 242, 291
अरब सागर *m* 313
अर्जित अंक *m* 273
अर्जेंटीना *m* 315
अर्थशास्त्र *m* 169
अर्थिंग *f* 60
अर्धचंद्र *m* 280
अर्ध-मलाईरहित दूध *m* 136
अर्ध मुलायम चीज़ 136
अर्धरात्रि *f* 305
अर्ध सख़्त चीज़ 136
अलगनी *f* 76
अलमारी *f* 66, 70
अलसी *f* 184
अलार्म घड़ी *f* 70
अलार्म लगाना *tr* 71
अलाव *m* 266
अलास्का *m* 314
अल्जीरिया *m* 317
अल्ट्रासाउंड *m* 52
अल्प दृष्टि 51
अल्फ़ाल्फ़ा *m* 184
अल्बानिया *m* 316
अल्यूमिनियम *m* 289
अवमृदा *f* 91
अवसादी शैल *m* 288
अवस्थाएं 23
अविकसित भ्रूण *m* 52
अवोकाडो *m* 128
अंश *m* 165
अष्टभुज *m* 121, 164, 295
अंसच्छद पेशी *f* 16
अंसपेशी *f* 16
असमान छड़ें *m* 235
अस्तबल *m* 185, 243
अस्तर *m* 32
अस्थि *f* 17
अस्थि चिकित्सा 49, 54
अस्थि चूर्ण *m* 88
अस्थिपंजर *m* 17
अस्पताल *m* 48
अस्सी *m* 308
अस्सीवां *m* 309
अहाता *m* 182
अहिपुष्प *m* 297
अस्तर *m* 83
अग्निशामक उपकरण *m* 95
अग्निशामक कर्मी *m* 95
अग्नाशय *m* 18
अश्व मार्ग *m* 263
अश्वमीन 294

आ

आइकन *m* 177
आइवरी कोस्ट 317
आइसक्रीम *f* 137, 149
आइस क्लाइम्बिंग 247
आइस बकेट 150
आइसलैंड *m* 316
आइस स्केट 224
आइस स्केटिंग 247
आइस हॉकी *f* 224
आइस हॉकी का मैदान *m* 22
आइस हॉकी खिलाड़ी *m* 224
आइसिकल 287
आइसिंग 141
आइस्ड कॉफ़ी *f* 148
आई *f* 276
आई कप *m* 269
आई ब्रो पेंसिल *f* 40
आई ब्रो ब्रश *m* 40
आई लाइनर *m* 40
आई शैडो 40
आउट 225, 228
आउट-ट्रे 172
आउट फ़ील्ड 229
आउटबोर्ड मोटर *m* 215
आउटलेट *m* 61
आउट हाउस *m* 182
आकार देना *tr* 91
आकृतियां *f* 164
आक्रमण क्षेत्र *m* 224
आंख *f* 14, 51, 244
आँखों की जांच 51
आग *f* 95
आग जलाना *tr* 266
आग जलाने का उपकरण *m* 266
आंगन *m* 58, 84
आगमन 213
आगे का पहिया *m* 196
आगे की बत्ती *m* 198
आगे झुकना 251
आगे निकालना *tr* 195
आघात *m* 46
आज *m* 306
आटा *m* 138, 139
आटे की ब्रेड *f* 139
आठ *m* 308
आठवां *m* 309
आड़ी छड़ *f* 235
आड़ू *m* 126, 128
आंतरिक अंग *m* 18
आंतरिक क्रोड़ *m* 282
आत्मरक्षा *f* 237
आत्मविश्वासी *m* 25
आदमी *m* 23
आधा घंटा *m* 304
आधार *m* 164
आधार स्तंभ *m* 187
आधा लीटर 311
आधा वक़्त 223
आधासीसी 44
आंधी *f* 286
आने वाला कल *m* 306
आपराधिक रिकॉर्ड *m* 181
आपातकाल *m* 46
आपातकालीन कक्ष *m* 48
आपातकालीन दूरभाष *m* 195
आपातकालीन निकास *m* 210
आपातकालीन रक्षा मार्ग *m* 95
आपातकालीन लीवर *m* 209
आपातकालीन सेवाएं *f* 94
आपूर्ति नली *f* 61
आप्रवाससीमा शुल्क 212
आफ़्टरसन *m* 108
आभूषण निर्माण 275
आम *m* 128
आयत *m* 164
आयतन *m* 311
आयन मंडल *m* 286
आयरन *m* 109, 233
आयरलैंड *m* 316
आयरिस 110
आयाम *m* 165
आयुर्विज्ञान *m* 169
आयुर्वेद *m* 55
आरंभ पेय *m* 153
आरंभ रेखा *f* 234
आरंभ स्थल *m* 238
आरी *f* 81, 89
आरोप *m* 94
आर्कटिक महासागर *m* 312
आर्च 85
आर्ट डेको 301
आर्ट नूवो 301
आर्ट शॉप *f* 115
आर्टिचोक 124
आर्द्र पौध *f* 87
आर्मरेस्ट 200
आर्मेनिया *m* 318
आलंबन छड़ *m* 203, 205
आलू *m* 124
आलू बुख़ारा *m* 126
आवृत्ति *f* 179
आशुलिपिक *m* 181
आंसरिंग मशीन *f* 99
आंसू *m* 51
आस्तीन *f* 34
आस्तीन रहित पोशाक *f* 34
आह भरना *itr* 25
आहरण पर्ची *f* 96
आहार नली *f* 19
आंत्रपुच्छ *m* 18
आश्चर्यचकित 25
आफ़्टर शेव 73

इ

इकतरफ़ा रास्ता *m* 298
इक्का *m* 273
इक्कीसवां *m* 309
इक्षुगंधा *m* 297
इंगलिश मस्टर्ड *m* 135
इंच *m* 310
इंच टेप *m* 80, 276
इंजन *m* 202, 204, 208, 210
इंजन कक्ष *m* 214
इज़राइल *m* 318
इंटरनेट *m* 177
इटली *m* 316
इंटीरियर 200
इटेलियन हैम 143
इंडोनेशिया *m* 318
इतिहास *m* 162
इथियोपिया *m* 317
इंद्रधनुष *m* 287
इन-ट्रे 172
इन फ़ील्ड 228
इनबॉक्स *m* 177
इनलाइन स्केटिंग 249
इनलेट 61
इनस्टॉल करना *tr* 177
इनहेलर *m* 44
इमारत *f* 299
इमारती लकड़ी *f* 187
इमल्शन 83
इराक़ *m* 318
इलाक़ा *m* 315
इलायची *f* 132
इलेक्ट्रिक गिटार *m* 258
इलेक्ट्रिक रेज़र *m* 73
इलेक्ट्रिक हुक-अप *m* 266
इल्ली *f* 295
इंसुलिन 109
इंसुलेशन 61
इस्त्री *f* 76
इस्त्री करना *tr* 76
इस्त्री का तख़्ता *m* 76
इस्पात *m* 79
इत्र *m* 41
इत्र इत्यादि 105
इक्वेडोर *m* 315
इग्नीशन 200

ई

ईंट *f* 187, 273
ईंधन टैंक *m* 204
ईंधन मापी *m* 201
ई-मेल *m* 177
ई-मेल अकाउंट *m* 177
ई-मेल पता 177
ईरान *m* 318
ईस्टर *m* 27

उ

उक़ाब *m* 292
उंगलियों की छाप *f* 94
उंगली संधि *f* 15
उच्च पर्वतीय स्कीइंग 247
उच्च स्वर *m* 256
उच्चारण करना *tr* 162
उज़्बेकिस्तान *m* 318
उठना *itr* 71
उड़ना *itr* 211
उड़ान नंबर 212
उड़ान बुक करना *tr* 212
उड़ान भरना *tr/itr* 211
उड़ेलना *tr* 67
उतरना *tr* 211
उत्कीर्णन *m* 275
उत्कृष्ट खेल *m* 233
उत्तर 163, *m* 312
उत्तर और मध्य अमेरिका *m* 314
उत्तर कोरिया *m* 318
उत्तर देना *tr* 99, 163
उत्तरी गोलार्ध *m* 283
उत्तरी ध्रुव *m* 283
उत्तरी ध्रुव क्षेत्र *m* 283
उत्तरी सागर *m* 312
उत्सव *m* 27
उत्साहित 25
उथला छोर *m* 239
उदर *m* 18
उदरीय मांसपेशियां *f* 16
उद्यान *m* 85, 90, 262
उधार *m* 168
उधार लेना *tr* 168
उधेड़ना *tr* 277
उपकरण *m* 66, 165, 233, 238, 245
उपकरण द्वारा प्रसव 53
उपकरण बक्सा *m* 244
उपग्रह *m* 281
उपग्रह डिश 269
उपग्रह मार्गदर्शन 201
उपचार *m* 109
उपजंघिका *f* 17
उपतारा *m* 51
उपद्वार *m* 281
उपनगर *m* 299
उपरि दंत *m* 50
उपल *m* 288
उपवन *m* 84
उपस्थित रहना *tr* 174
उपहारों की दुकान *f* 114
उपाधि *f* 169
उपास्थि *f* 17
उबला अंडा *m* 137, 157
उबालना *tr* 67
उबासी लेना *itr* 25
उभयचर जीव *m* 294
उद्भासन *m* 271
उरुसंधि *f* 12
उरूगुए *m* 315
उरोस्थि *f* 17
उर्वर *m* 20
उर्वरक *m* 91
उर्वर बनाना *tr* 91
उल्का *m* 280
उल्टा भ्रूण *m* 52
उल्टी करना *tr/itr* 44
उल्लू *m* 292
उल्व द्रव *m* 52
उष्ण कटिबंध *m* 283
उष्णदेशीय फल *m* 129
उत्प्रवास करना *itr* 26
उन्नीसवां *m* 309
उन्नीस सौ 307

ऊ

ऊंचाई *f* 165, 211
ऊंची एड़ी के जूते *m* 37
ऊँची कुर्सी *f* 75
ऊंची कूद *f* 235
ऊंची डाइव *f* 239
ऊंट *m* 272, 291
ऊदबिलाव *m* 290
ऊन *m* 277
ऊनी चादर *f* 74
ऊपर उठना *tr* 139
ऊपरी चक्र *m* 141
ऊपरी दीर्घा *f* 254
ऊपरी परत *f* 83
ऊपरी मिट्टी *f* 85
ऊपरी लॉकर *m* 210
ऊपरी वस्त्र *m* 83
ऊब *f* 25
ऊबड़-खाबड़ *m* 232
ऊर्जा *f* 60
ऊष्मक *m* 53

ऋ

ऋण *m* 96
ऋतुएं *f* 307

ए

एक *m* 308
एक अरब 309
एक जगह जॉग करना *tr* 251
एक दिशा मार्ग *m* 194
एकपटरी रेलगाड़ी *f* 208
एक प्रकार का इटेलियन चीज़ 142
एक प्रकार का कंद *m* 124
एक प्रकार का फ़्रेंच चीज़ 142
एक प्रकार का समुद्री जीव 121
एकल 230
एकल घर *m* 58
एक लाख 309
एक शॉट 151
एक हज़ार 309
एकाइडो 236
एक्ज़ीक्यूटिव 174
एक्यूपंक्चर *m* 55
एक्यूप्रेशर *m* 55
एक्लेयर 140
एक्वेटोरियल गिनी 317
एक्स-रे *m* 48
एक्सरे देखने का बोर्ड 45
एक्सरे फ़िल्म *f* 50
एक्स-रे मशीन *f* 212
एटीएम *m* 97
एंटीगुआ और बारबुडा *m* 314
एंटी फ्रीज़ 199
एडाम चीज़ 142
एड़ी *f* 13, 15, 37
एथलीट *m* 234
एथलेटिक्स 234
एनडाइव पत्ती *f* 123
एनालॉग 179
एपिड्यूरल 52
एप्रन *m* 30, 50, 69 212
एप्लीकेशन *m* 176
एंबुलेंस *m* 94
एम डी एफ़ 79
एम्पियर *m* 60
एयर बैग *m* 201
एरिट्रिया 317
एलर्जी *f* 44
एलर्जी रोधक *m* 41
एल सेल्वाडोर *m* 314
एशिया *m* 318
एस एम एस 99
एस एल आर कैमरा *m* 270
एस्टोनिया 316
एस्प्रैसो 148
एम्बॉस्ड पेपर *m* 83

ऐ

ऐक्रेलिक रंग *m* 274
ऐक्सीलरेटर *m* 200
ऐंडीज़ 312
ऐतिहासिक इमारत *f* 261
ऐनिमेटेड फ़िल्म *f* 255
ऐम्प्लीफ़ायर *m* 268
ऐलन चाबी *f* 80
ऐशट्रे *f* 150

ऑ

ऑक्सीजन सिलेंडर *m* 239
ऑन लाइन 177
ऑपरेशन प्रसव *m* 52
ऑपेरा *m* 255
ऑफ़ साइड 223
ऑमलेट *m* 158
ऑरकिड *m* 111
ऑरिगानो 133
ऑरिगेमी 275
ऑर्केस्ट्रा *m* 254
ऑर्केस्ट्रा स्थल *m* 254
ऑर्डर देना *tr* 153
ऑल्टरनेटिंग करंट *m* 60
ऑस्ट्रिया *m* 316
ऑस्ट्रेलिया *m* 319
ऑस्ट्रेलेशिया 319
ऑप्टिक 150

ओ

ओज़ोन परत *f* 286
ओबसिडियन 288
ओबो 257
ओमान *m* 318
ओले *m* 286
ओवन *m* 66
ओवन के दस्ताने *m* 69
ओवन रोधी *m* 69
ओवर ड्राफ़्ट *m* 96
ओवर फ़्लो पाइप *m* 61

औ

औज़ार *m* 187
औज़ार पेटी *f* 80, 186
औज़ार रैक *m* 78
औद्योगिक क्षेत्र *m* 299
औपचारिक वस्त्र *m* 34
औरत *f* 23
औषधकारक *m* 189
औषध वितरक *m* 108
औषधि *f* 133
औषधि उद्यान *m* 84
औषधि एवं मसाले 132
औषधीय चाय *f* 149
औंस *m* 310
औसत खेलनिम्न खेल *m* 233

क

कक्ष *m* 48
कक्षा *f* 162, 280
कंक्रीट ब्लॉक *m* 187
कंगारू *m* 291
कंघा *m* 38
कंघी करना *tr* 38
कचालू *m* 124
कच्चा *m* 124, 129
कच्चा कोयला *m* 266
कच्चा मांस *m* 142
कछुआ *m* 293
कज़ाकिस्तान *m* 318
कटना 46
कटर *m* 89
कटल फ़िश 121
कटाई-छंटाई 87
कटाई मशीन *f* 182
कटिपरक कशेरुकाएं *f* 17
कटिपरक क्षेत्र *m* 13
कटिबंध *m* 283
कन्नी *f* 187
कंटेनर *m* 311
कटोरा *m* 65
कंट्री म्यूज़िक *m* 259
कंट्रोलर *m* 269
कंठ *m* 19
कठफोड़वा *m* 292
कंठमणि *f* 19
कठोर लकड़ी *f* 79
कंठच्छद *m* 19
कंडरा *m* 17
कड़वा *m* 124
कड़ा परिश्रम *m* 230
कड़ाही *f* 69
कंडिशनर *m* 38
कड़ी *f* 36
कड़ी/शहतीर *f* 186
कंडेंस्ड मिल्क *m* 136

हिन्दी

कंडोम *m* 21
कढ़ाई *f* 277
क़तर *m* 318
कतरने का औज़ार *m* 88
क़तला *m* 119, 121
क़तले किया हुआ 121
क़तार *f* 210, 254
कद्दू *m* 125
कद्दूकस *m* 68
कद्दूकस किया चीज़ *m* 136
कद्दू के बीज *m* 131
कंधा *m* 13
कनखजूरा *m* 295
कनपटी *f* 14
कनपेड़ा *m* 44
कनाडा *m* 314
कनिष्ठिका *f* 15
कन्फेक्शनर *m* 113
कन्फेक्शनरी *f* 113
कन्वर्टिबल 199
कपड़ा *m* 276, 277
कपड़ा दबाने वाला 276
कपड़े का कंडिशनर *m* 76
कपड़े धोने की मशीन *f* 76
कपड़े निचोड़ना *tr* 76
कपड़े निचोड़ने वाला 76
कपड़ेबदलने की गद्दी *f* 74
कपड़े मशीन में डालना *tr* 76
कपड़ों की टोकरी *f* 76
कंपनी *f* 175
कपाट *m* 58
कपाल *m* 17
कपास *m* 184
कंपास *m* 240
कपूर का पत्ता *m* 133
कप्तान *m* 214
कंप्यूटर *m* 176
कफ़ *m* 32
कफ़लिंक 36
कंबल *m* 71, 74
कबाब *m* 155, 158
कंबु *m* 295
कबूतर *m* 292
कंबोडिया *m* 318
क़ब्ज़कुशा 109
कम उद्भासित 271
कम तेल में पका 159
कम तेल में भुना 158
कमपारी 145
कमर *f* 12
कमर का मांस *m* 119
कमरख 128
कमरबंद *m* 35
कमरा *m* 58
कमरा नंबर *m* 100
कमरे *m* 100
कमरे की चाबी *f* 100
क़मीज़ *f* 33,34
कर *m* 96
करघा *m* 277
कराटे *m* 236
कर्क रेखा *f* 283
कर्ण 164 *m*
कर्णिका *f* 297
कर्त्तन दांत *m* 50
कर्मचारी *m* 24
कर्मचारी वर्ग *m* 175
कर्मीदल *m* 241
कर्लिंग खेल *m* 247
कर्लिंग चिमटा *m* 38
कर्ष नौका *f* 215
क़लईदार 79
कलछी *f* 68
क़लम *f* 297
क़लम बांधना *tr* 91
कला *f* 162
कलाई *f* 13, 15
कलाई पट्टी *f* 45
कला और शिल्प 274, 276
कला का इतिहास *m* 169
कला दीर्घा *f* 261
कलाबाज़ी 235
कला महाविद्यालय *m* 169
कली *f* 111, 125, 297
कलेजी *f* 118
कवच *m* 293
कवर *m* 51
कसनी *f* 37
क़साई *m* 118, 188
क़साई की दुकान *f* 114
कसावा *m* 124
कंसीलर *m* 40
कस्टर्ड *m* 140
काउंटर *m* 96, 98, 100, 142
काकातू तोता *m* 293
कांच *m* 69
कांच की छड़ *f* 167
कांच की बोतल *f* 166
कांच के गिलास *m* 65
काज *m* 32
काजू *m* 129, 151
काटना *tr* 67, 79, 91, 277
कांटा *m* 65, 244
कांटा *m* औज़ार 88
काटा हुआ 46
कांटे *m* 121
कान *m* 14
कान, नाक एवं गला चिकित्सा 49
क़ानून *m* 169, 180
कानूनी विभाग *m* 175
क़ानूनी सलाह 180
काबुली चने *m* 131
काम करने की मेज़ *f* 78
कार *f* 198, 200, 202
कार की छत *f* 202
कारखाना *m* 299
कार दुर्घटना 203
कार धुलाई 199
कार पार्क *m* 298
कारोबारी साझेदार *m* 24
कार्गो *m* 216
कार्टन *m* 311
कार्टून *m* 178
कार्ड *m* 27
कार्ड डालने की जगह 97
कार्डिगन *m* 32
कार्तिक शहद *m* 134
कार्निवल *m* 27
कार्नेशन 110
कार्मिक विभाग *m* 175
कार्य *m* 171
कार्यक्रम *m* 254, 269
कार्यदिवस *m* 306
कार्यवृत्त *m* 174
कार्यसूची *f* 174
कार्यशाला *f* 78
कार्यालय *m* 24, 172, 174
कार्यालय खंड *m* 298
कार्यालयी उपकरण *m* 172
कार्यालयी वस्तुएं *f* 173
काला *m* 39, 272, 274
काला ज़ैतून *m* 143
काला पत्थर 288
काला-भूरा *m* 39
काला सागर *m* 313
काली *f* 41
काली चाय *f* 149
कालीन *m* 71
काली मसूर *f* 131
काली मिर्च *f* 64, 132, 152
काष्ठ वाद्य यंत्र *m* 257
कांस्य *m* 235
कॉर्डलेस ड्रिल 78
काष्ठ-कला *f* 275
किक *f* 237, 239
किक बॉक्सिंग 236
किक मारना *tr* 221, 223
किकस्टैंड *m* 207
किटाणुनाशक रसद्रव्य *m* 51
किताबों की अलमारी *f* 63
किताबों की दुकान *f* 115
किनारा *m* 139, 246, 284
किनारी *f* 34
किनोया *m* 130
किपर्स *m* 157
किराए की कार *f* 213
किराएदार *m* 58
किराए पर लेना *tr* 58
किराना वस्तुएं *f* 106
किराया *m* 58, 197, 209
किर्गिस्तान *m* 318
क़िला *m* 300
किलोग्राम 310
किलोमीटर 310
किशमिश *f* 129
किशोरी *f* 23
किसान *m* 182, 189
की 176
कीटनाशक *m* 89, 183
कीटाणुनाशक 47
कीटाणुनाशक पट्टी *f* 47
कीन्स *m* 128
कीप *m* 166
की-पैड *m* 99
की बोर्ड *m* 258
क़ीमती पत्थर *m* 36
क़ीमा *m* 119
कील *f* 80
कीलक *m* 166
कीला *m* 50
कीलों वाले जूते *m* 233
कीवी *m* 128
कुकरौंधा *m* 297
कुंजी पटल *m* 97, 176
कुटा 132
कुटीर उद्यान *m* 84
कुठाली *f* 166
कुंडा *m* 59
कुतुबनुमा *m* 312
कुत्ता *m* 290
कुदाल *m* 187
कुमारी *f* 23
कुम्मकाट *m* 126
कुम्हार कर्म *m* 275
कुरकुरा *m* 127
कुरकुरा नमकीन 151
कुरकुरी ब्रेड *f* 139, 156
कुरेदनी *f* 89
कुर्सी *f* 63, 64
कुल्हाड़ी *f* 95
कुवैत *m* 318
कुश्ती *f* 236
कूंग-फू *m* 236
कूड़ा खींचने की नली *f* 77
कूड़ा निकास इकाई 61
कूड़े का निपटान 61
कूड़े का पंजा *m* 77
कूड़ेदान *m* 61, 67, 266
कूद *f* 243
कूदना *tr/itr* 227, 237
कूबड़ *m* 291
कूरियर *m* 99
कूलिंग रैक *m* 69
कूलेंट डिब्बा *m* 202
कूल्हा *m* 12
कृलिम मक्खन *m* 137
कृपया मोड़ें नहीं *tr* 98
कृमि *f* 295
कृषि भूमि *f* 182
कृत्रिम 31
कृत्रिम तालाब *m* 263
कृत्रिम प्रसव कराना *tr* 53
कृत्रिम मक्खी *f* 244
कृत्रिम श्वस 47
केक *m* 140
केक और मिष्टान्न *m* 140
केक की दुकान *f* 114
केकड़ा *m* 121, 295
केक बनाना 69
केक बनाने का सांचा *m* 69
केतली *f* 65, 66
केंद्र *m* 164
केंद्रित करना *tr* 271
केंद्रीय आरक्षण 194
केंद्रीय घेरा 222, 224, 226
केनडो *m* 236
केन्या *m* 317
केपोइरा 237
केप्पूचीनो 148
केबल *f* 79
केबल कार *f* 246
केबल टेलीविज़न *m* 269
केबिंदा 317
केबिन *f* 210
केम बेल्ट *f* 203
केल पत्ती *f* 123
केला *m* 128
केश प्रसाधक *m* 188
केश सज्जा *f* 39
केसर *m* 132
कैक्टस *m* 87
कैचर *m* 229
क़ैंची *f* 38, 47,82, 276
कैंडी *f* 113
कैन *m* 145, 311
कैन ओपनर *m* 68
कैनवस *m* 274
कैप *f* 21
कैपर्स 143
कैप्सूल *m* 109
कैफ़े *m* 148, 262
कैबिन *f* 214
कैमरा *m* 178, 260
कैमरा केस *m* 271
कैमरा क्रेन *m* 178
कैमराफ़ोन *m* 270
कैमरामैन *m* 178
कैमरून *m* 317
कैमरे की दुकान *f* 115
कैमरे के प्रकार 270
कैरामल *m* 113
कैरियर *m* 198
कैरेबियन सागर *m* 312
कैलिनिनग्राड *m* 316
कैलेंडर *m* 306
कैल्शियम *m* 109
कैल्साइट *m* 289
कैलक्युलेटर *m* 165
कैंसर विज्ञान *m* 49
कैसरोल *m* 69
कैसेट टेपकैसेट प्लेयर *m* 269
कैस्पियन सागर *m* 313
कॉकटेल *m* 151
कॉकटेल शेकर *m* 150
कॉकल सीपी *f* 121
कॉड मछली *f* 120
कॉर्डलेस फ़ोन *m* 99
कॉनसर्टीना फ़ाइल *f* 173
कॉन्गो *m* 317
कॉन्गो लोकतांत्रिक गणराज्य 317
कॉन्टेक्ट लेंस *m* 51
कॉन्सर्ट *m* 255, 258
कॉन्सोल *m* 269
कॉपर-टी *m* 21
कॉपी *f* 163, 172
कॉफ़ी *f* 144, 148, 148, 153, 156, 184
कॉफ़ी का प्याला *m* 65
कॉफ़ी की केतली *f* 65
कॉफ़ी के बीज *m* 144
कॉफ़ी टेबल *m* 62
कॉफ़ी मशीन *f* 148

कॉफ़ी मशीन *f* 150
कॉफ़ी मिल्कशेक *m* 149
कॉमेडी *f* 255
कॉम्पैक्ट डिस्क *f* 269
कॉरसिका 316
कॉर्कस्क्रू *m* 150
कॉर्नर *m* 223
कॉर्नर-झंडा *m* 223
कॉर्निस *m* 300
कॉल बटन *m* 48
कॉलर *m* 32
कॉलोनी *f* 315
कोआला *m* 291
कोइ कार्प 294
कोको पाउडर *m* 148
कोट *m* 32
कोट का हैंगर *m* 70
कोण *m* 164
कोणमापक/डी *m* 165
कोन *m* 187
कोफ़्ते *m* 158
कोमल सुर *m* 256
कोमोरॉस *m* 317
कोयला *m* 288
कोयला बत्ती *f* 275
कोया *m* 295
कोर्निया *m* 51
कोलम्बिया *m* 315
कोला *m* 144
कोलाज *m* 275
कोल्ड-प्रैस्ड तेल *m* 135
कोष्ठ *m* 100
कोसोवो *m* 316
कोस्टर *m* 150
कोस्टा रीका *m* 314
कोहनी *f* 13
कोहरा *m* 287
कौआ *m* 292
क्यारी *f* 85, 90
क्यूबा *m* 314
क्रिकेट *m* 225
क्रिकेट खिलाड़ी *m* 225
क्रिकेट गेंद *f* 225
क्रियाएं *f* 229
क्रिसमस *m* 27
क्रिस्टल चिकित्सा *f* 55
क्रिस्पर *m* 67
क्रिस्प्स 113
क्रीज़ *f* 225
क्रीड़ा नौका *f* 215, 240
क्रीम *f* 73, 109, 137, 140, 157
क्रीम कैरामल *m* 141
क्रीम चीज़ *m* 136
क्रीम पाई *f* 141
क्रीम पेस्ट्री *f* 140
क्रीम रहित दूध *m* 136
क्रेडिट कार्ड *m* 96
क्रेन *m* 186, 187, 216, 216
क्रेफ़िश 121
क्रैनबेरी 127
क्रॉप *f* 39
क्रॉस-कंट्री स्कीइंग 247
क्रॉस ट्रेनर *m* 250
क्रॉस बल्ले का खेल *m* 249
क्रॉसबार *m* 207, 222
क्रोएशिया *m* 316
क्रोशिया *m* 277
क्रोशिया हुक *m* 277
क्रोसां बन *m* 156
क्लच *m* 200, 204
क्लब सैंडविच *m* 155
क्लब हाउस *m* 232
क्लिप बोर्ड *m* 173
क्लीज़र *m* 41
क्लैपर बोर्ड *m* 179
क्लैरिनेट 257
क्वार्ट *m* 311
क्वार्टर डेक *m* 214
क्षमता *f* 311
क्षेत्र 299, *m* 310, 315
क्षेत्रफल *m* 165

ख

खंग मीन 120, 294
खंगालना *tr* 76
खगोल विज्ञान *m* 281
ख़ज़ांची *m* 106
ख़ज़ांची *m* 96
खजूर *m* 129
खटोला *m* 74
खट्टा *m* 126, 127
खट्टी क्रीम *f* 137
खट्टे फल *m* 126
खड़ंजा *m* 85
खड़िया *f* 85, 288
खड़ी चट्टान *f* 285
खतरा 195
खत्ती *f* 183
खदकना *tr/itr* 67
खनिज *m* 289
खनिज लावा *m* 283
खपच्ची *f* 46
खपची *f* 47
खंभा *m* 298, 300
खमीर *m* 138
खमीरी ब्रेड *m* 139
ख़रगोश *m* 118, 290
खरपतवार नाशक *m* 91
खरबूज़ *m* 127
खरल *m* 68, 16
खरादना *tr* 79
ख़राश की दवा *f* 109
ख़रीदारी 103
ख़रीदारी का थैला *m* 106
ख़रीदारी केंद्र *m* 104
खरोंच *f* 46
खरटि लेना *itr* 71
खलिहान *m* 182
खसखस *f* 130, 138
खसरा *m* 44
खाई *f* 300
ख़ाका *m* 275, 276
खाज *f* 44
खाता संख्या *f* 96
खाद *f* 88
खाद का ढेर *m* 85
खाद डालना *itr* 90
खाद्य पदार्थ *m* 117, 149
खाद्यान्न *m* 130
खाना *tr* 64, 75
ख़ाना *m* 67, 272
खाना पकाना *tr* 67
खाना बनाने की जगह 66
ख़ाने *m* 66
खाल *f* 119
खाल रहित 121
खांसी *f* 44
खांसी की दवाई *f* 108
खिड़की *f* 58, 96, 98, 186, 197, 209, 210
खिलाड़ियों का दल *m* 221
खिलाड़ी *m* 191, 221, 231, 273
खिलाड़ी को रोकना 230
खिलौना *m* 75
खिलौने *m* 105
खिलौने की टोकरी *f* 75
खीर *f* 140
खीरा *m* 125
खुबानी *m* 126
खुर *m* 242, 291
खुरचना *tr* 77, 82
खुरचनी *f* 82
खुरदरा *m* 271
खुरदरा स्टेंसिल *m* 83
खुरपा *m* 88
खुरपी *f* 89, 265
खुराक *f* 109
खुला 260
खुला कैफ़े *m* 148
खुला सैंडविच *m* 155
खुली चाय पत्ती *f* 144
खुली छत *f* 260
खुश 25
खुशबूदार 130
खूंटा *m* 90, 266
खूंटा ठोकना *tr* 90
खूंटी *f* 258
खूंटी से बांधना *tr* 91
खून की जांच 48
खेत *m* 182, 184
खेती करना *tr* 91
खेती योग्य भूमि *f* 183
खेतों के कामकाज *m* 183
खेतों के प्रकार 183
खेल *m* 230, 272, 273
खेल आरंभ करना *tr* 233
खेल का मैदान *m* 168, 243, 263
खेलकूद *f* 219
खेल घर *m* 75
खेलना *itr* 75, 229, 273
खेल प्रतियोगिता *f* 233
खेल बाड़ा *m* 75
खेल रेखा *f* 233
खोजना *tr* 177
खोदना *tr* 90
ख़ोल *f* 129

ग

गगनचुंबी इमारत *f* 299, 300
गज़ *m* 310
गंजा *m* 39
गटर *m* 58
गणित *m* 162, 164
गंतव्य स्थान *m* 213
गति नियंत्रक *m* 204
गतिमापक *m* 204
गतिविधियां *f* 77, 162, 227, 233, 245, 263
गति सीमा *f* 195
गत्ता *m* 275
गंदी दरी *f* 83
गंदे कपड़े *m* 76
गंदे कपड़ों की टोकरी *f* 76
गद्दा *m* 70, 267
गद्दी *f* 62, 206
गद्दे का स्प्रिंग *m* 71
गंधक *f* 289
गधा *m* 185
गमला *m* 89
गमले का पौधा *m* 110
गमले के पौधे *m* 87
गमले में डालना *tr* 91
गर्म पानी की थैली *f* 70
गरज 286
गर्डर 186
गर्दन का पट्टा *m* 46
गर्भद्वार *m* 20
गर्भधारण करना 20
गर्भनाल *m* 52
गर्भनिरोध *m* 21
गर्भ निरोधक गोलियां *f* 21
गर्भपात *m* 52
गर्भवती *m* 52
गर्भाधान *m* 52
गर्भावस्था *f* 52
गर्भावस्था जांच 52
गर्भाशय *m* 20, 52
गर्भाशय द्वार *m* 52
गर्म 286
गर्म कपड़े *m* 267
गर्म करने की धातु *f* 61
गर्म कोट *m* 31
गर्म जलस्रोत *m* 285
गर्म पजामी *f* 31
गर्म पानी का नल *m* 72
गर्म पेय *m* 144
गर्म सूट *m* 30
गर्म हवा का गुब्बारा *m* 211
गर्मी *f* 31
गर्वित 25
ग़लत प्रहार *m* 230
ग़लत शॉट *m* 230
गलफड़े *m* 294
गलही *f* 240
गला *m* 12, 19
गलियारा *m* 59, 106, 168, 210
गली *f* 298, 299
गली का नुक्कड़ *m* 298
गले की मोच *f* 46
गवाक्ष *m* 214
गवाह *m* 180
गहन चिकित्सा कक्ष *m* 48
गहराई *f* 165
गहरा छोर *m* 239
गहरे समुद्र में मछली पकड़ना 245
गाउन *m* 34
गाजर *f* 124
गांठ गोभी *f* 123
गाड़ी *f* 95, 266
गाड़ी चलाना *tr* 195
गाढ़ी क्रीम *f* 137
गाद *f* 85
गाना *m* 259
गाय *f* 185
गाय का दूध *m* 136
गायन स्थल *m* 301
गायिका *f* 191
गारा *m* 187
गाल *m* 14
गाल का गड्ढा *m* 15
गालापागोस द्वीप समूह *m* 315
गांव *m* 299
गिटार वादक *m* 258
गिनना *tr* 165
गिनी *f* 317
गिनीबिस्साऊ 317
गिफ़्ट पेपर *m* 111
गिरजाघर *m* 300
गिरना 237
गिरफ़्तार 94
गिराना 237
गिरी *f* 122, 129, 130
गिरी की चॉकलेट *f* 113
गिलहरी *f* 290
गिलाफ़ *m* 71
गिलास *m* 65, 150, 152
गीत *m* 259
गीला *m* 286
गुआर की फली *f* 122
गुच्छा *m* 111
गुच्छी *f* 125
गुठलीदार फल *m* 126
गुड़िया *f* 75
गुड़िया घर *m* 75
गुणा करना *tr* 165
गुदना *m* 41
गुदा 21
गुनगुना *m* 286
गुना 165
गुफा *f* 284
गुम्बद *m* 300
गुयाना *m* 315
गुरुत्व *m* 280
गुर्दा *m* 18, 119
गुलदस्ता *m* 35, 111
गुलदाऊदी 110

गुलदान *m* 62
गुलाब *m* 110
गुलाबी 145, 274
गुलाम *m* 273
गुलूबंद *m* 36
गुस्सा *m* 25
गुह्यवर्ति *f* 109
गूदा *m* 124, 127
गूंधना *tr* 138
गृहकार्य *m* 163
गृह साज-सज्जा *f* 105
गृह सज्जा *f* 82
गेट *m* 85
गेटिस *f* 35
गेंद *f* 75, 228, 230
गेंद धकेलना *tr* 222
गेंद पकड़ना 229
गेंद पर प्रहार करना *tr* 233
गेंद फेंकना *tr* 229
गेंदबाज़ *m* 225
गेंदबाज़ी करना *tr* 225
गेंद से ज़मीन छूना 220
गेम शो *m* 178
गेयर *m* 201, 206
गेयर बक्सा *m* 202, 204
गेयर बदलना *tr* 207
गेयर लीवर *m* 207
गेहूं *m* 184, 130
गेहूं का आटा *m* 138
गैंडा *m* 291
गैबिया 317
गैबोन 317
गैरेज *m* 58, 199
गैलन *m* 311
गैस बर्नर *m* 61
गैस्केट *m* 61
गॉज़ 47
गॉथिक 301
गोटी *f* 272
गोताख़ोर *m* 238
गोंद *m* 275
गोंद गन *m* 78
गोदी *f* 216
गो मांस *m* 118
गोरिल्ला *m* 291
गोरी *f* 41
गोरैया *f* 292
गोल *m* 221, 222, 223, 224
गोल आरी *f* 78
गोल का क्षेत्र *m* 221
गोलकीपर *m* 222, 224
गोल क्षेत्र *m* 223
गोल गला *m* 33
गोल चक्कर *m* 195
गोल दाग़ना *tr* 223
गोल पोस्ट 220, 222
गोल मारना *tr* 227
गोल रोकना *tr/itr* 223
गोल लाइन *f* 220, 224
गोल सीमा *f* 223
गोला *m* 164
गोला फेंक 234
गोलियां *f* 109
गोल्फ़ *m* 232
गोल्फ़ के जूते *m* 233
गोल्फ़ कोर्स *m* 232
गोल्फ़ क्लब *m* 233
गोल्फ़ खिलाड़ी *m* 232
गोल्फ़ ट्रॉली *f* 233
गोल्फ़ बैग *m* 233
गोल्फ़ बॉल *m* 233
गोल्फ़ सहायक 233 *m*
गोह *f* 293
ग्यारह *m* 308
ग्यारहवां *m* 309
ग्रंथि *f* 19
ग्रह *m* 280, 282
ग्रहण *m* 280
ग्रहिका *f* 280
ग्राउंड कवर *m* 87
ग्राटिन डिश *f* 69
ग्राम *m* 310
ग्राहक *m* 38, 96, 104, 106, 152, 175
ग्राहक सेवाएं 104
ग्राहक सेवा विभाग *m* 175
ग्रिल *f* 267
ग्रिल पैन *m* 69
ग्रीन 232
ग्रीनलैंड *m* 314
ग्रीवा कशेरुकाएं *f* 17
ग्रीवासंधि *f* 13
ग्रीष्म *m* 307
ग्रीस *f* 316
ग्रेनाइट *m* 288
ग्रेनाडा *m* 314
ग्रेफ़ाइट 289
ग्लाइडर *m* 211, 248
ग्लाइडिंग 248
ग्लेडियोलस 110
ग्वाटेमाला *m* 314
गट्ठा *m* 184
गद्दा *m* 74
गन्ना *m* 184

घ

घटा 165
घंटा *m* 257, 304
घटाना *tr* 165
घंटी *f* 197
घंटे की सुई *f* 304
घड़ियाल *m* 293
घड़ी *f* 36, 304
घन *m* 164
घनाकृतियां *f* 164
घबराया *m* 25
घर *m* 57
घरेलू उड़ानसंयोजन 212
घरेलू उपकरण *m* 60
घरेलू कार्य कक्ष *m* 76
घरेलू मनोरंजन 268
घरेलू वस्तुएं *f* 107
घाटी *f* 284
घाना *m* 317
घाव *m* 46
घास *f* 87, 262
घास काटना *tr* 90
घास काटने की मशीन *f* 88, 90
घास का थैला *m* 88
घास का मैदान *m* 285
घास-पात *f* 86
घास-पात से ढकना *tr* 91
घास बिछाना *tr* 90
घिसना *tr* 67, 77
घिसाई करना *tr* 82
घुंघराले 39
घुटना *m* 12
घुटने तक लंबी 34
घुड़दौड़ *f* 243
घुड़नाल *f* 242
घुड़सवार *m* 242
घुड़सवारी *f* 242, 263
घुड़सवारी के जूते *m* 242
घुड़सवारी खेल *m* 243
घुमाऊ कुर्सी *f* 172
घुमावदार कांटा *m* 68
घुलनशील 109
घेरे से बाहर 226
घोंघा *m* 295
घोड़ा *m* 185, 242, 272
घोड़ा गाड़ी दौड़ *f* 243
घोड़ा सधाना 243
घोड़े की तंग 242
घोड़े की मंद चाल 243
घोड़ों का बाड़ा *m* 243
घोमरा *m* 292

च

चकमक *m* 288
चकोतरा *m* 126
चक्का *m* 78
चक्का फेंक *m* 234
चक्रदंत *m* 207
चक्रवात *m* 287
चटख़नी *f* 59
चटनी *f* 135, 143
चटनी, सॉस इत्यादि 135
चटाई *f* 54, 235
चट्टान *f* 284
चट्टानी पर्वतमाला *f* 312
चड्डी *f* 33
चढ़ना *itr* 217
चतुः शिरस्क 16
चंद्रकांत मणि *m* 288
चंद्रयान *m* 281
चपटी ब्रेड 139
चप्पल *f* 31, 37
चप्पू *m* 241
चप्पू वाली नाव *f* 214
चबूतरा *m* 85
चमक आना *tr* 139
चमकाना *tr* 77
चमगादड़ *m* 290
चमचा *m* 68
चमड़े के जूते *m* 32, 37
चम्मच 65
चरखी *f* 214, 245
चरण *m* 237
चरना *tr* 183
चरपरा *m* 145
चरागाह *m* 182, 285
चर्च *m* 299
चल पट्टी *f* 106
चलाना *tr* 67
चश्मा *m* 51, 238, 247
चाक *m* 275
चाकू *m* 68, 80, 167
चाकू/छुरी तेज़ करने के उपकरण 118
चाकू तेज करने वाला 68
चाड 317
चांद *m* 280
चादर *f* 71, 74
चादर तकिया आदि *f* 105
चादर व तकिया गिलाफ़ आदि 71
चांदी *f* 289
चाप 15, 164
चांप 155
चापड़ *f* 68
चाबी *f* 59, 207
चाबुक 242
चाय *f* 144, 149, 156, 184
चाय का प्याला *m* 65
चार-दरवाज़ा *m* 200
चार सौ *m* 308
चारा *m* 244
चारा खाना *tr* 245
चारा लगाना *tr* 245
चार्ट *m* 48
चाल *f* 243, 273
चालक *m* 196
चालक कक्ष *m* 208, 210, 215
चालक यंत्र *m* 211, 214
चालक सीट *f* 196
चालीस *m* 308
चालीस मिनट *m* 304
चालीसवां *m* 309
चालू खाता *m* 96
चालू पटरी *f* 209
चावल *m* 130, 158
चिकन नगेट्स *m* 155
चिकन बर्गर *m* 155
चिकना 271
चिकनी मिट्टी *f* 275
चिकित्सक *m* 45, 55, 189
चिकित्सालय *m* 48
चिकोरी *f* 122
चिड़िया *f* 231
चिड़ियाघर *m* 262
चिड़ी *f* 273
चितरा राजमा *m* 131
चिंतित 25
चिपकने वाला टेप *m* 47
चिप बोर्ड *m* 79
चिप शॉट लेना *tr* 233
चिमटा 150, *m* 207
चिमटियां *f* 89
चिमटी *f* 40, 47, 53, 76
चिमनी *f* 58, 66, 214
चिराबेल 296
चिलगोज़ा *m* 129
चिली *m* 315
चिल्लाना *itr* 25
चित्र *m* 63, 274
चित्रकथा *f* 112
चित्रकार *m* 191, 274
चित्रकारी *f* 274
चित्रखंड पहेली *f* 273
चित्र बनाना *tr* 162
चित्र वल्लरी *f* 301
चित्राधार *m* 174, 274
चीज़ *m* 136, 156
चींटी *f* 295
चीड़ *m* 296
चीन *m* 318
चीनी मिट्टी के बर्तन *m* 64, 105
चीरना *tr* 79
चुकंदर *m* 125
चुनना/तोड़ना *tr* 91
चुंबक *m* 167
चुल आरा *m* 81
चूज़ा *m* 185
चूना पत्थर *m* 288
चूहा *m* 290
चेक *m* 96
चेक-इन डेस्क *m* 213
चेक इन *tr* 212
चेक गणराज्य *m* 316
चेक बुक *f* 96
चेंजिंग रूम *m* 104
चेडर चीज़ 142
चेन *f* 36, 206
चेयरलिफ़्ट *f* 246
चेरी *f* 126
चेलो 256
चेसिस 203
चेस्टनट *m* 129
चेस्ट प्रेस *m* 251
चेहरा *m* 14
चैनल *m* 178
चैनल बदलना *tr* 269
चैनल सेट करना *tr* 179
चैम्पियनशिप 230
चैम्बर *m* 283
चॉकलेट *m* 113
चॉकलेट की पट्टी *f* 113
चॉकलेट केक *m* 140
चॉकलेट चिप बिस्कुट *m* 141
चॉकलेट परत *f* 140
चॉकलेट बॉक्स *m* 113
चॉकलेट मिल्कशेक *m* 149
चॉकलेट स्प्रैड *m* 135
चॉप *m* 119
चोकर *m* 130
चोंगा *m* 169
चोंच *f* 293
चोट *f* 46

चोटी *f* 39
चोर घंटी *f* 58
चोरी *f* 94
चोली *f* 35
चौक *m* 299
चौखट *f* 186
चौड़ाई *f* 165
चौड़ी एड़ी के चप्पल 37
चौड़ी सीढ़ी *f* 59
चौथा *m* 309
चौदह *m* 308
चौदहवां *m* 309
चौराहा *m* 298
च्यूइंग गम *m* 113

छ

छज्जा *m* 58
छंटाई यूनिट *f* 61
छठा *m* 309
छड़ *f* 235, 250
छड़ी *f* 256
छत *f* 58, 62, 203
छत बग़ीची *f* 84
छतरी *f* 75
छत वाला *m* 58
छपाई *f* 275
छलना *m* 68
छलनी *m* 89
छलांग मारना 235
छल्ले *m* 89
छह सौ *m* 308
छाछ *f* 137
छांटना *tr* 39, 90, 91
छाता *m* 36, 148
छाती *f* 12, 119
छानना *tr* 91, 138
छायाकार *m* 191
छायादार पौधे *m* 87
छाल *f* 133, 296
छाला *m* 46
छात्र *m* 162
छात्रवृत्ति *f* 169
छात्रावास *m* 168
छिड़कना *tr* 91
छिपकली *f* 293
छिलका *m* 126, 127, 128, 137
छिलका रहित 129
छिले हुए झींगे *m* 120
छींक *f* 44
छीछड़े *m* 118
छीलना *tr* 67
छीलने वाला चाकू *f* 68
छुट्टियां *f* 212
छुट्टी देना 48
छुरी *f* 65, 81, 82
छुरी-कांटे *m* 64
छूट *f* 106
छेद *m* 37
छेद करना *tr* 50, 79
छेद करने की सुई *f* 78
छेनी *f* 81
छैनी *f* 275
छोटा *m* 32
छोटा आरा *m* 78
छोटा करना *tr* 172
छोटा चप्पू *m* 241
छोटा चम्मच *m* 65
छोटा ड्रम *m* 257
छोटा तौलिया *m* 73
छोटा दाना *m* 130
छोटा फूल *m* 122
छोटा बच्चा *m* 30
छोटी आंत *f* 18
छोटी आंत का अग्रभाग *m* 18
छोटी उंगली *f* 15
छोटी चिमटी *f* 167
छोटी चेचक *f* 44
छोटी दाढ़ *f* 50
छोटी पीली चिड़िया *f* 292
छोटी प्लेट *f* 65
छोटी मछली *f* 120
छोटी मूली *f* 124
छत्ता *m* 134
छन्नी *f* 68

ज

जई *f* 130
जंक्शन *m* 194
जग 65, *m* 151
जंगल *m* 285
जंगली *m* 118
जंगली *m* गोमेद 297
जंगली चावल *m* 130
जंगी जहाज़ *m* 215
जंघा का मांस *m* 119
जंघास्थि *f* 17
जज *m* 180
जड़ *f* 50, 124, 296
जड़ाऊ पिन *m* 36
जड़ी-बूटी *f* 55, 86, 134
जड़ी-बूटी औषध *f* 108
जड़ी-बूटी सेवन 55
जड़ें *f* 39
जननांग *m* 20
जननेंद्रिय *m* 12
जनवरी *f* 306
जन सूचना प्रणाली *f* 209
जन्म *m* 52
जन्मदिन *m* 27
जन्मदिन की पार्टी *f* 27
जन्म पूर्व 52
जन्म भार *m* 53
जंप बॉल *m* 226
जबड़ा *m* 14, 17
जंबुमणि *m* 288
जंबू *m* 133
जमा 165
जमा करना *tr* 96
ज़मानत *f* 181
जमाना *tr* 67
जमा पर्ची *f* 96
ज़मीनी व्यायाम *m* 235
जमैका *m* 314
जरबेरा *m* 110
ज़र्दी *f* 137, 157
जर्नल *m* 168
जर्मनी *m* 316
जल उद्यान *m* 84
जलक्रीड़ा *m* 241
जल चिकित्सा *f* 55
जलना 46
जलप्रपात *m* 285
जल पत्रक *m* 215
जल बाधक *m* 232
जलबेंत *f* 86
जलरोधक *m* 245
जलसह जूते *m* 244
जलीय पौध *f* 86
जल्दी 305
जल्दी पकने वाला 130
जस्ता *m* 289
जहाज़ *m* 214
जहाज़ घाट *m* 216
जहाज़ से उतरना *tr* 217
जागना *itr* 71
जांघ *f* 12, 119
जांघिया *m* 238
जांच *f* 49, 50, 94
जांचने की सलाई *f* 50
जानकारी *f* 261
जानुपृष्ठ पेशी *f* 16
जानुफलक *m* 17
जापान *m* 318
जापानी संतरा *m* 126
जामुन *m* 127
ज़ाम्बिया *m* 317
जायफल *m* 132
जार *m* 134, 166, 311
जाल *m* 217, 222, 227
जाल डालना *tr* 245
जाल से पकड़ना *tr* 245
जाली *f* 84, 226
जालीदार पर्दा *m* 63
जावित्री *f* 132
जासूस *m* 94
जिगर *m* 18
जिन *m* 145
जिन और टॉनिक 151
ज़िप *f* 277
जिप्सोफ़िला *m* 110
जिबूती *f* 317
जिम *m* 250
जिमनास्ट *m* 235
जिमनास्टिक *m* 235
जिम मशीन *f* 250
जिमीकंद *m* 125
ज़िम्बाब्वे *m* 317
जिराफ़ *m* 291
ज़िला *m* 315
जीतना *itr* 273
ज़ीन *m* 242
जीना 59
जीन्स 31, 33
जीपीएस *m* 195
जीभ *f* 19, 37, 118
ज़ीरा *m* 132
जीवन की ख़ास घटनाएं 26
जीवन रक्षक *m* 239, 265
जीवन रक्षक टावर *m* 265
जीवन रक्षा ट्यूब *m* 240
जीवन रक्षा नौका *f* 240
जीव विज्ञान *m* 162
जुआघर *m* 261
जुकाम *m* 44
जुड़वां *m* 23
जुर्म *m* 94
जुलाई *f* 306
जूड़ा *m* 39
जूडो *m* 236
जूता *m* 220, 223
जूता चप्पल विभाग *m* 104
जूतियां *f* 37
जूते *m* 34, 267
जूते की दुकान *f* 114
जूते-चप्पल *m* 37
जून *m* 306
ज़ूम 270 लेंस
जूरी *f* 180
जूरी बॉक्स *m* 180
जूस *m* 127
जूस एवं मिल्कशेक *m* 149
जेट स्कीइंग 241
जेटी 217
जेड *m* 288
जेनरेटर *m* 60
जेब *f* 32
ज़ेबरा *m* 291
जेल *f* 181
जेल का पहरेदार *m* 181
जेल की कोठरी *f* 181
ज़ेवर *m* 36
ज़ेवर पेटी *f* 36
जैक *m* 203
जैकेट *m* 32, 34
जैज़ 259
ज़ैतून *m* 151
ज़ैतून का तेल *m* 134
जैम *m* 156
जैम, शहद इत्यादि *m* 134
जैल *m* 38, 109
जेली फ़िश *f* 295
जैलीबीन 113
जैव *m* 91
जैविक 118, 122
जैविक कूड़ा *m* 61
जॉगिंग *m* 251, 263
जॉर्जिया *m* 318
जॉर्डन *m* 318
जोकर *m* 273
जोड़ *m* 17, 119
जोड़ना *tr* 165
जोतना *tr* 183
ज़ोर से मारना *tr/itr* 223, 231
जौ *m* 130, 184
ज्वार *m* 130
ज्वालामुखी *m* 283
ज्वालामुखी फटना *itr* 283
ज्वालामुखीय शैल *m* 288
ज्वालामुखी विवर *m* 283
जन्मदिन का केक 141 *m*
जन्म प्रमाणपत्र 26 *m*

झ

झंडा *m* 221, 232
झरबेरी *f* 127
झाईं 15
झाग *m* 148
झाड़न 77
झाड़ू *m* 77, 88
झाड़ू लगाना *tr/itr* 77
झामक *m* 73, 288
झालर *m* 71, 277
झिल्ली *f* 15
झींगा *m* 121
झींगुर *m* 295
झील *f* 285
झुकाना *tr* 251
झुंड *m* 183
झुनझुना *m* 74
झुर्रियां *f* 15
झुर्री-निवारक *m* 41
झूमर *m* 74
झूलती टोकरी *f* 84
झूला *m* 263, 266

ट

टंकी *f* 61
टकीला *m* 145
टक्कर अवरोध *m* 195
टख़ना *m* 13, 15
टन *m* 310
टप्पा मारना *tr* 227
टब *m* 311
टमाटर *m* 125, 157
टमाटर का जूस *m* 144, 149
टमाटर सॉस *m* 135, 154
टमिली-जुली गोलियां *f* 113
टर्की *m* 119, 185, 293
टर्बो चार्जर *m* 203
टर्मिनल *m* 212
टहनी *f* 296
टाइमर *m* 166
टाइमिंग *f* 203
टाइल *f* 58, 27
टाइल लगाना *tr* 82
टाई *f* 32
टाई-पिन *f* 36
टाउन हॉल *m* 299
टांकना *tr* 277
टांका लगाना 79
टांका लगाने का तार *m* 81
टांके *m* 52
टांके का उपकरण *m* 81
टांग *f* 12, 119
टायर *m* 198, 206
टायर के पेच *m* 203
टायर पर डिज़ाइन *f* 207
टायर प्रेशर 203
टायर बदलना *tr* 203
टायर लीवर *m* 207

टिकट *f* 209, 213
टिकट घर *m* 209, 216
टिकट निरीक्षक *m* 209
टिकट बैरियर *m* 209
टिकिया *f* 311
टिच बटन का सूट *m* 30
टिड्डा *m* 295
टिन *m* 289, 311
टिश्यू *m* 108
टिश्यू बॉक्स *m* 70
टी *f* 233
टीइंग ग्राउंड *m* 232
टीका *m* 45
टी बैग *m* 144
टीम *f* 229
टीम हमला 220
टीवी देखना *tr* 269
टी शर्ट *f* 30,33
टुकड़ा *m* 139, 140
टूथपेस्ट *m* 72
टूथब्रश *m* 72
टूरिंग बाइक *f* 206
टूलबार *m* 177
टेडी बियर *m* 75
टेनिस *m* 230
टेनिस कोर्ट 230
टेनिस जूते *m* 231
टेप *m* 173
टेप डिस्पेंसर *m* 173
टेबल टेनिस *m* 231
टेबल मैट *f* 64
टेम्पोन 108
टेली प्रॉम्प्टर *m* 179
टेलीफ़ोन बॉक्स *m* 99
टेलीविज़न चलाना *tr* 269
टेलीविज़न बंद करना *tr* 269
टेलीविज़न शृंखला *f* 178
टेलीविज़न स्टूडियो *m* 178
टेलीस्कोप *m* 281
टेल्कम पाउडर *m* 73
टोकरी *f* 88
टैक्सी-क़तार *f* 213
टैन करने की क्रीम *f* 41
टैब *m* 173
टैबलेट *f* 176
टैरागन *m* 133
टैरी नैपी *f* 30
टैक्सी चालक *m* 190
टॉनिक वॉटर *m* 144
टॉपिंग 155
टॉफ़ी *f* 113
टॉफ़ी की दुकान *f* 113
टॉयलेट *m* 72
टॉयलेट रोल *m* 72
टॉयलेट सीट *f* 72
टॉयलेट ब्रश *m* 72
टॉर्च *f* 267
टो करना *tr* 195
टोकरी *f* 82, 106, 207, 263, 265
टो क्लिप *f* 207
टोगो *m* 317
टोंटी *f* 89
टो ट्रक *m* 203
टोनर *m* 41
टोप *m* 36, 186
टोपी *f* 30, 31, 36, 238
टोल बूथ *m* 194
टोस्ट *m* 157
टोस्टर *m* 66
टोस्टेड सैंडविच *m* 149
टो स्ट्रेप *m* 207
ट्यूनीशिया *m* 317
ट्यूब *f* 311
ट्यूब चिप्पी *f* 207
ट्यूबा *m* 257
ट्यूलिप *m* 111
ट्रक *m* 194
ट्रक चालक *m* 190
ट्रफ़ल *m* 113
ट्रम्पेट *m* 257
ट्राइ *m* 221
ट्राइएंगल *m* 257
ट्राइफ़ल *m* 141
ट्राउट मछली *f* 120
ट्राम *m* 196, 208
ट्रांसफ़ॉर्मर *m* 60
ट्रांसमिशन *m* 202
ट्रॉली *f* 106
ट्रे *m* 152, 154
ट्रेक्टर *m* 182
ट्रे–टेबल *m* 210
ट्रे *f* 88
ट्रेडमिल *f* 250
ट्रेनर *m* 37
ट्रेनर्स *m* 31, 251
ट्रेबल क्लैफ़ *m* 256
ट्रेलर *m* 266
ट्रेवल एजेंसी *f* 114
ट्रैक सूट *m* 31, 32
ट्रैकिंग 243
ट्रैवल एजेंट *m* 190
ट्रैश *m* 177
ट्रॉमबोन *m* 257
ट्रॉली *f* 48, 100, 208, 213
ट्रॉली बस *m* 196

ठ

ठंड *f* 287
ठंडा 286*m*
ठंडा दही *m* 137
ठंडी चाय *f* 149
ठंडे पानी का नल *m* 72
ठेला गाड़ी *f* 88
ठोकना *tr* 79
ठोड़ी *f* 14
ठोस चीज़ 136
ठोस बर्फ़ पर स्कीइंग 247

ड

डंक *m* 46, 295
डग आउट 229
डट्टा *m* 81
डंठल *f* 122, 297
डंडी *f* 111, 235
डफली *f* 257
डंब बेल 251
डबल *m* 151
डबल कमरा *m* 100
डबल-डेकर बस *m* 196
डबल पलंग *m* 71
डबल बसून *m* 257
डबल बास *m* 256
डम्पर *m* 187
डरावनी फ़िल्म *f* 255
डर्ट बाइक *f* 205
डाइव *m* 239
डाइव मारना *tr* 238
डाउनलोड करना *tr* 177
डाउन हिल स्कीइंग 247
डाक कर्मी *m* 98
डाक कोड *m* 98
डाकघर *m* 98
डाक टिकट *f* 98, 112
डाक टिकट संग्रह 273
डाक थैला *m* 98, 190
डाकपेटी *f* 99
डाक व्यय *m* 98
डाकिया *m* 98, 190
डांगरी *f* 30
डाट *f* 72
डायनमो *m* 207
डायफ्राम *m* 21
डायरी *f* 175
डायरेक्ट करंट *m* 60
डायरेक्टरी *f* 99
डार्क रूम *m* 271
डार्टबोर्ड *m* 273
डार्ट्स *m* 273
डिक्की *f* 198
डिक्की का दरवाज़ा *m* 198
डिज़ाइनर 191, 277
डिजिटल 179, 269
डिजिटल प्रोजेक्टर *m* 163
डिजिटल बॉक्स *m* 269
डिजिटल रेडियो *m* 268
डिजिटल कैमरा *m* 270
डिटर्जेंट *m* 77
डिनर *m* 158
डिपस्टिक 202
डिपार्टमेंटल स्टोर *m* 105
डिप्लोमा *m* 169
डिंब वाहिनी *f* 20
डिब्बा *m* 209
डिब्बाबंद खाद्य पदार्थ *m* 107
डिब्बाबंद पेय *m* 154
डियोडरेंट *m* 73, 108
डिस्क *f* 224
डिस्पेंसर *m* 311
डिस्पोज़ेबल 109
डिस्पोज़ेबल कैमरा *m* 270
डिस्पोज़ेबल नैपी *f* 30
डिस्पोज़ेबल रेजर *m* 73
डीज़ल *m* 199
डीज़ल रेलगाड़ी *f* 208
डीजे *m* 179
डीवीडी *f* 268
डीवीडी प्लेयर *m* 268
डूबना *itr* 239
डेगची *f* 69
डेज़ी 110, 297
डेंटल फ़्लॉस *m* 50, 72
डेड बॉल लाइन 221
डेंडिलियन 123
डेढ़ *m* 304
डेनमार्क *m* 316
डेबिट कार्ड *m* 96
डेयरी उत्पाद *m* 136
डेयरी फ़ार्म *m* 183
डेली 107
डेस्कटॉप *m* 177
डेस्कटॉप ऑर्गेनाइज़र *m* 172
डेक *m* 214
डैक कुर्सी *f* 265
डैफ़ोडिल *m* 111
डैशबोर्ड *m* 201
डॉक 214
डॉक्ट्रेट *f* 169
डॉग स्लेजिंग 247
डॉल्फ़िन *f* 290
डोंगी *f* 214
डोमिनिक गणराज्य *m* 314
डोमिनिका *f* 314
डोमिनोस *m* 273
डोर्मर खिड़की *f* 58
डोरी *f* 89, 244
डोरी खींचना *tr* 245
डोरी वाला गला 35
डोले *m* 251
ड्रम *m* 258
ड्रम किट *f* 258
ड्रमर *m* 258
ड्राइव मारना *tr* 233
ड्राइव शाफ़्ट 202
ड्राई क्लीनर *m* 115
ड्रायर *m* 76
ड्रिप *f* 53
ड्रिलिंग मशीन के वज्र *m* 80
ड्रेनिंग बोर्ड *m* 67
ड्रेस *f* 31
ड्रेसिंग *f* 158
ड्रेसिंग किया हुआ 159
ड्रेसिंग गाउन *m* 31, 32, 35
ड्रैगन फ़्लाई 295
ड्रॉइंग पिन *f* 173
ड्रॉट्स *m* 272
ड्रॉपर *m* 109, 167
ड्रॉप शॉट 230
ड्रॉप्स *f* 109
ड्रेसिंग गाउन *m* 73

ढ

ढक्कन *m* 61, 66, 69, 134
ढलान *f* 284

त

तकिया *m* 70
तख़्ते *m* 186
तंग पजामी *f* 35, 242, 251
तजाकिस्तान *m* 318
तंज़ानिया *m* 317
तट *m* 264
तटरक्षक *m* 217
तटवर्ती क़स्बा *m* 217
तटस्थ क्षेत्र *m* 224
तटीय छाता *m* 264
तटीय झोपड़ी *f* 264
तंदूर में भूनना *tr* 67
तना *m* 258, 296
तनाव *m* 55
तनाव मुक्ति 55
तनियां 37
तनी 35
तंबाकू *m* 112, 184
तंबू का खंभा *m* 266
तंबू गाड़ना *tr* 266
तरकश *m* 249
तरणताल *m* 101, 238, 250
तरबूज़ *m* 127
तराजू *m* 69, 118, 166, 310
तर्जनी *f* 15
तल *m* 167
तिल का तेल *m* 134
तलना *tr* 67
तलमापी *m* 187
तल रेखा *f* 214
तलवा *m* 15
तलवार *f* 236, 249
तलवारबाज़ी 249
तला *m* 37
तलाक़ *m* 26
तला हुआ 159
तली मछली और चिप्स 155
तस्मानिया *m* 319
तस्मे/फ़ीते 37
तस्वीर *f* 271
तहख़ाना *m* 58
ताइक्वांडो *m* 236
ताई ची *m* 237
ताज़ा *m* 121, 127, 130
ताज़ा चीज़ *m* 136
ताज़े फल *m* 157
ताड़ *m* 86, 296
ताड़ की गांठें *f* 122
तापमंडल *m* 286
तापमान *m* 286
तापमान... डिग्री है। 286
तापमान मापक *m* 201
तांबा *m* 289
तार *m* 60, 79, 81, 98, 207, 258
तार कसना 50
तार काटने का यंत्र *m* 81
तारकोल *m* 187
तार छीलने का प्लास *m* 81
तारपीन *m* 83
तारा *m* 280
तारामंडल *m* 281
तारासमूह *m* 280
तालखंड *m* 256
ताल वाद्य *m* 257

ताला *m* 59, 207
तालाब *m* 85
ताली बजाना *tr* 255
तालू *m* 19
ताश *m* 273
ताश फेंटना *tr* 273
ताश रंग *m* 273
तिजोरी *f* 106, 150
तितली *f* 295
तिनपतिया *m* 297
तिपाई *f* 166
तिपाया स्टैंड *m* 270, 281
तिल *m* 14, 131
तिलचट्टा *m* 295
तिलहन का तेल *m* 135
तंत्रिका *f* 19
तीखा *m* 124
तीखी सॉसेजेस 142
तीतर *m* 119, 293
तीन-दरवाज़ा *m* 200
तीन सौ *m* 308
तीर *m* 249
तीली *f* 207
तीव्र धारा *m* 284
तीव्र नदी *f* 241
तीव्र प्रकाश संकेतक *m* 240
तीस *m* 308
तीसरा *m* 309
तीसवां *m* 309
तुरमली *m* 288
तुर्कमेनिस्तान *m* 318
तुर्कीसाइप्रस *m* 318
तुलसी *f* 133
तुषार *f* 287 *m*
तूना मछली *f* 120
तूफ़ान *m* 287
तूफ़ानी 286
तूलिका *f* 274
तेइसवां *m* 309
तेज़ गति रेलगाड़ी *f* 208
तेज़ धावक *m* 234
तेज़पत्ता 133*m*
तेंदू फल *m* 128
तेरह *m* 308
तेरहवां *m* 309
तेल *m* 134, 142, 199
तेल की टंकी *f* 204
तेल पोत *m* 215
तेल में पका 143
तैरना *itr* 238
तैराक *m* 238
तैराकी 238
तैराकी सूट *m* 265
तैल रंग *m* 274
तैलीय 39, 41
तोता *m* 293
तोरई *f* 125
तोहफ़ा *m* 27
तौलना *tr* 310
तौलिए *m* 73
तौलिया *m* 73
तौलिया हैंगर *m* 72
त्योरियाँ चढ़ना 25
त्योहार *m* 27
त्वचा *f* 14
त्वचा चिकित्सा *f* 49
त्वचा सुरक्षा 108
तंत्री वाद्य *m* 256

थ

थर्मामीटर *m* 45, 167
थर्मोस्टेट *m* 61
थल मेंढक *m* 294
थाइलैंड *m* 318
थाप *f* 259
थायरॉइड ग्रंथि *f* 18
थिएटर *m* 254
थिएटर *m* 29
थीम पार्क *m* 262
थूथनी *f* 293
थैंक्स गिविंग 27
थैला *m* 31
थैली *f* 291
थ्रस्टर *m* 281
थ्रिलर *m* 255
थ्री पॉइन्ट लाइन 226

द

दक्षिण *m* 312
दक्षिण अफ़्रीका *m* 317
दक्षिण अमेरिका *m* 315
दक्षिण कोरिया *m* 318
दक्षिणी गोलार्ध *m* 283
दक्षिणी महासागर *m* 313
दक्षिण सूडान *m* 317
दड़बा *m* 185
दंडादेश *m* 181
दंत चिकित्सक *m* 50, 189
दंत चिकित्सा-कुर्सी *f* 50
दंत वल्क *m* 50
दंत सुरक्षा 108
दमकल *m* 95
दमकल केंद्र *m* 95
दमकल दस्ता *m* 95
दम घुटना *tr/itr* 47
दमपुख़्त 158
दमा *m* 44
दरदरा *m* 132
दरबान *m* 100
दरवाज़ा *m* 182, 196, 198, 209
दरवाज़े का लॉक *m* 200
दरवाज़े की कड़ी *f* 59
दरवाज़े की घंटी *f* 59
दराज़ *f* 66, 70, 172
दराज़ों की अलमारी *f* 70
दरियाई घोड़ा *m* 291
दरी *f* 63, 267
दरोगा *m* 94
दर्ज़िन *f* 191
दर्ज़ी *m* 191
दर्ज़ी का चॉक *m* 276
दर्ज़ी की डमी *f* 276
दर्ज़ी की दुकान *f* 115
दर्दनाशक *m* 109
दर्दनाशक दवा *f* 47
दर्रा *m* 284
दर्शक *m* 233, 254
दर्शन शास्त्र *m* 169
दलदल *m* 285
दलाली *f* 97
दलिया *m* 130, 157
दवाई *f* 109
दवाई की अलमारी *f* 72
दवाई विक्रेता *m* 108
दवाख़ाना *m* 108
दशक *m* 307
दस *m* 308
दस लाख *m* 309
दसवां *m* 309
दस हज़ार *m* 309
दस्त *f* 44, 109
दस्ताना *m* 224, 228, 233, 236, 246
दस्ताने *m* 30, 36
दही *m* 137
दाई *f* 53
दाईं ओर की ड्राइव 201
दाएं मुड़ना निषेध 195
दाढ़ *f* 50
दांत *m* 50
दांत उखाड़ना 50
दांत का दर्द 50
दांता *m* 206
दांतेदार आरी *f* 81
दांतेदार चिमटी *f* 167
दांतों का एक्सरे *m* 50
दांतों की सफाई 72
दादा *m* 22
दादी *f* 22
दाम चुकाना *tr* 153
दामाद *m* 22
दायां *f* 260
दालचीनी *f* 133
दालान *m* 199
दालें *f* 131
दांवपेंच *m* 237
दिन *m* 306
दिनांक *m* 306
दिल *m* 119
दिल का दौरा 44
दिशा बदलना *tr* 241
दिसंबर *m* 306
दीमक *f* 295
दीर्घ दृष्टि *f* 51
दीर्घा *f* 254
दीवार *m* 58, 186
दीवाली 27
दुकान 298
दुकान सहायक *m* 188
दुखी 25
दुग्ध शर्करा *f* 137
दुपट्टा *m* 35
दुपट्टे का छोर *m* 35
दुबारा गर्म करना *tr* 154
दुंबाल *m* 240
दुर्घटना *f* 46
दुलकी *f* 243
दुग्ध उत्पाद *m* 107
दूध *m* 136, 156
दूध का डिब्बा *m* 136
दूध की चॉकलेट *m* 113
दूध दुहना *tr* 183
दूध वाली चाय *f* 149
दूरबीन *f* 281
दूरबीन का शीशा *m* 167
दूरभाष *m* 99
दूरी *f* 310
दूसरा *m* 309
दूसरी मंज़िल *f* 104
दृश्यदर्शी *m* 271
दृष्टि परीक्षक *m* 189
दृष्टि *f* 51
दृष्टि तंत्रिका *f* 51
दृष्टि पटल *m* 51
दृष्टि परीक्षक *m* 51
दृष्टि वैषम्य *m* 51
देखभाल करना *itr* 91
देय तिथि *f* 168
देर *f* 305
देवदार *m* 296
देश *m* 315
देशांतर रेखांश *m* 283
दो चोटी *f* 39
दोतीनचार 308
दो-दरवाज़ा *m* 200
दोनावा *m* 215
दोपहर *f* 305
दोपहर का भोजन *m* 64
दोपहर का मेनू *m* 152
दो बजे *m* 304
दोमुंहे बाल *m* 39
दोषी 181
दो सीटों वाली साइकिल *f* 206
दो सौ *m* 308
दोस्त *m* 24
दोस्त बनाना *tr* 26
दो हज़ार *m* 307
दो हज़ार एक *m* 307
दौड़ *f* 234
दौड़ का घोड़ा *m* 243
दौड़ का मैदान *m* 243
दौड़ना *tr/itr* 229
द्रव माप 311
द्रव्य *m* 77
द्वार पर्दा *m* 266
द्वारमंडप *m* 58
द्वारमंडप बत्ती *f* 58
द्वार संख्या *f* 213
द्विवार्षिक पौध *f* 86
द्विशिर पेशी *f* 16
द्वीप *m* 282
द्वय वाहन मार्ग *m* 195

ध

धन *m* 97
धनिया *m* 133
धनुर्विद्या *f* 249
धनुष *m* 249
धमनी *f* 19
धागा *m* 276
धागा डालना *tr* 277
धागे की रील *f* 276
धागे से सफ़ाई करना *tr* 50
धातु *f* 79, 289
धातु वज्र *m* 80
धान *m* 184
धारा *f* 285
धुआं *m* 95
धुआं निकास नली *f* 203, 204
धुंध *f* 287
धुरी *f* 205, 206
धुरी का ढक्कन *m* 202
धुले कपड़े *m* 76
धूप *f* 286
धूप का चश्मा *m* 51, 265
धूप घड़ी *f* 262
धूपदार 286
धूप से जलना 46
धूमकेतु *m* 280
धूमित मछली *f* 143
धूम्रपान *m* 112
धूम्रित 118, 121, 143, 159
धूल झाड़ना *tr* 77
धोना *tr* 77
ध्यान *m* 54
ध्रुव *m* 282
ध्रुवज्योति *f* 286
ध्रुवीय भालू *m* 291
ध्वनि पट्टी *f* 255
ध्वनिरोधक *m* 203, 204
ध्वनि संदेश *m* 99
ध्वनि स्तर *m* 179

न

नक़द निकालना *tr* 97
नक़ली बत्तीसी *f* 50
नकसीर *f* 44
नक़ाब *m* 189, 239, 249
नकेल *f* 242
नक़्शा *m* 261
नख क़ैंची *f* 41
नगाड़ा *m* 257
नथुना *m* 14
नदी *f* 284
नदी में मछली पकड़ना 245
नपुंसक *m* 20
नंबर *m* 273
नंबर प्लेट *f* 198
नंबर मिलाना *tr* 99
नब्बे *m* 308
नब्बेवां *m* 309
नम *m* 286
नमक *m* 64, 152
नमक रहित 137
नमकीन 137, 143, 155
नमकीन पानी में रखा 143
नम टिश्यु *m* 74
नमीयुक्त टिश्यू *m* 108
नमूना *m* 190

नया आलू *m* 124
नर्तकी *f* 191
नर्म 45, 48 129, 189
नर्सिंग ब्रा *f* 53
नल *m* 61, 66
नल का पानी *m* 144
नलसाज़ *m* 188
नलसाज़ी 61
नलिका *f* 53, 167
नली *f* 112
नवजात शिशु 53
नवंबर 306
नव वर्ष 27
नवशास्त्रीय 301
नवीकृत करवाना *tr* 168
नस *f* 19
नस चढ़ना 239
नहाना *itr* 72
नाइजर *m* 317
नाइजीरिया *m* 317
नाइटी *f* 31, 35
नाई *m* 39, 188
नाई की दुकान *f* 115
नाक *f* 14
नाख *m* 128
नाखून *m* 15
नागदौन साग *m* 124
नागरमोथा *m* 125
नाजुक वस्तु *f* 98
नाटक *m* 178, 254
नाड़ी *f* 47
नांद *m* 183
नान *m* 139
नाभि *f* 12
नाभि-रज्जु *m* 52
नाम *m* 104
नामकरण *m* 26
नामीबिया *m* 317
नायलोन *m* 277
नारंगी *m* 126, 274
नारियल *m* 129
नार्वे *m* 316
नाला *m* 299
नाली *f* 72, 299
नालीव्रण *m* 19
नाव उलटना *tr* 241
नाव खेना *tr* 241
नाव बांधना *tr* 217
नाविक *m* 189, 241
नाशपाती *m* 126
नाश्ता *m* 64
नाश्ते की ट्रे *f* 101
नाश्ते की मेज़ *f* 156
नासा पहिया *m* 210
निकर *m* 30, 33, 35
निकल *m* 289
निकारागुआ *m* 314
निकास *m* 61
निकास ढलान *f* 194
निकास द्वार *m* 210
निकास पाइप *f* 61
निकासी मार्ग *m* 61
निचला चक्र *m* 141
निजी ऑर्गेनाइज़र *m* 173
निजी कमरा *m* 48
निजी प्रशिक्षक *m* 250
निजी विमान *m* 211
निजी स्नानघर *m* 100
नितंब *m* 13, 16
निप्पल *m* 12, 75
निब *f* 163
निबंध *m* 163
नियंत्रण *m* 201
नियंत्रण टॉवर *m* 212
नियम उल्लंघन 223
नियंत्रण यंत्र *m* 204
निराना *tr* 91
निर्णायक अंक *m* 230
निर्देश *m* 109
निर्देशक *m* 254
निर्देशन 260
निर्देशिका *f* 260
निर्माण करना *tr* 186
निर्माण कार्य *m* 186
निर्माण स्थल *m* 186
निर्माता *m* 254
निवेश *m* 97
निवेश सूची *f* 97
निशाना *m* 249
निशानेबाज़ी *f* 249
निषेचन *m* 20
निहारिका *f* 280
निम्नताप मंडल *m* 286
निश्चेतन चिकित्सक *m* 48
नीचे वार करना 237
नीद की गोलियां *f* 109
नीदरलैंड *m* 316
नी पैड *m* 205
नीबू *m* 126
नीबू का वृक्ष *m* 296
नीबू वाली चाय *f* 149
नील *m* 274
नीलगिरि *m* 296
नीलम *m* 288
नीला *m* 274
नी सपोर्ट 227
नुकीला प्लास *m* 80
नुस्खा *m* 45
नूडल्स *m* 158
नृत्य *m* 259
नृत्य अकादमी *f* 169
नेगेटिव 271
नेगेटिव इलेक्ट्रोड *m* 167
नेट *m* 231
नेटवर्क *m* 176
नेपच्यून *m* 280
नेपाल *m* 318
नेल कटर *m* 41
नेल पॉलिश *f* 41
नेल पॉलिश रिमूवर *m* 41
नेल फ़ाइलर *m* 41
नेत्र चिकित्सा *f* 49
नैपकिन *f* 65
नैपकिन रिंग *f* 65
नैपी रैश क्रीम *f* 74
नॉनस्टिक *m* 69
नोक *f* 36, 122, 246
नोज़ क्लिप *f* 238
नोट *m* 97
नोट पैड *m* 173
नोट्स *m* 191
नोट्स लेना *tr* 163
नौ *m* 308
नौकरी पाना *tr* 26
नौका पाल *m* 241
नौकायन 241
नौका विमान *m* 211
नौका विहार 241
नौतल *m* 214
नौवां *m* 309
नौ सौ *m* 308
न्यायालय *m* 180
न्यायालय अधिकारी *m* 180
न्यायालय कर्मचारी *m* 180
न्यायालय की तारीख़ *f* 180
न्यूज़ीलैंड *m* 319
न्यूट्रल *m* 60
न्यूमैटिक ड्रिल *f* 187
नक़्क़ाशी करना *tr* 79

प

पंक *m* 259
पकड़ना *tr* 237, 245
पका *m* 129
पकाने के लिए तैयार मुर्ग़ 119
पका हुआ मांस *m* 118, 143
पके भोजन की दुकान *f* 142
पंक्चर 203, 207
पंक्ति *f* 234
पक्षाघात 44
पक्षी *m* 292
पक्षी निहारना 263
पक्षी-मांस *m* 119
पंख *m* 60, 119, 210, 293
पंखा *m* 60, 202
पंखा सीपी *f* 121
पंखुड़ी *f* 297
पगंडिका *f* 17
पगे फल *m* 129
पचपन हज़ार पांच सौ *m* 309
पंच बैग *m* 237
पंचभुज *m* 164
पचास *m* 308
पचासवां *m* 309
पचास हज़ार *m* 309
पंजा *m* 291, 293
पजामा सूट *m* 33
पंजे की अस्थि *f* 17
पटकथा *f* 254
पटकनी *f* 237
पटकनी देना 237
पटर *m* 233
पटरी *f* 208, 209, 298
पट्टी *f* 78
पटिया *f* 187
पट्टी *f* 47, 63
पठार *m* 284
पड़ोसी *m* 24
पढ़ना *tr* 162
पढ़ने का कमरा *m* 63
पढ़ने की बत्ती *f* 210
पर्णाङ्ग *m* 86
पतंगा *m* 295
पतझड़ *m* 307
पतली आरी *f* 81
पतली क्रीम *f* 137
पतवार *m* 241
पतवार हत्था *m* 240
पता *m* 98
पति *m* 22
पत्ती *f* 122, 296
पत्ते बांटना *tr* 273
पत्थर *m* 275
पथमापक यंत्र *m* 201
पथरीला बाग़ *m* 84
पदक *m* 235
पदयात्रा *f* 263
पंद्रह *m* 308
पंद्रह मिनट *m* 304
पंद्रहवां *m* 309
पनडुब्बी *f* 215
पनसुइया *f* 241
पनामा *m* 314
पनीर *m* 136
पंप *m* 207
पपड़ी *f* 136, 142
पंप शूज़ *m* 37
पपीता *m* 128
पपुआ न्यू गिनी *m* 318
पफ़ 40
पफ़ पेस्ट्री *f* 140
परकार *m* 165
परखनली *f* 166
परत लगाना 277
परफ़्यूम स्प्रे *m* 41
परसों *m* 307
परागज ज्वर *m* 44
पराचिकत्सक *m* 94
पराजित 273
पराबैंगनी किरणें *f* 286
परामंडल *m* 286
परामर्श 45
परामर्शदाता *m* 49, 55
परावर्तक *m* 204, 207
परावर्तक पट्टी *f* 205
परिक्रमण गणक *m* 201
परिचारिका *f* 191
परिचारिका सेवा 101
परिचित *m* 24
परिणाम *m* 49
परिधान *m* 34
परिधि *f* 164
परिमाण *m* 165
परिरक्षक *m* 83
परिवर्तनीय पाना 80
परिवर्तित मार्ग *m* 195
परिवहन *m* 193
परिवार *m* 22
परिसर *m* 168
परीक्षा *f* 163
परेशान 25
परोसना *tr* 64
परोसने का चम्मच *m* 68
पर्ची *f* 96
पर्णपाती *f* 86
पर्दा *m* 63, 254, 255
पर्म *m* 39
पर्यटक *m* 260
पर्यटक बस *f* 197
पर्यटक सूचना केंद्र *m* 261
पर्यटन-गाइड *m* 260
पर्यटन बस *f* 260
पर्यटन सूचना पुस्तिका *f* 212
पर्यटन स्थल *m* 260
पर्यावरण *m* 279
पर्वत *m* 284
पर्वत अवरोहण 248
पर्वत श्रेणी *f* 282
पर्वतारोहण 248
पर्वतीय पौधे *m* 87
पलक *f* 14, 51
पलंग *m* 70
पलंग का सिरहाना *m* 70
पलंगपोश *m* 70
पलटना 238
पलटा *m* 68
पलस्तर *m* 47, 83
पलस्तर करना *tr* 82
पवन *m* 286
पशु *m* 290, 292, 294
पशु आहार *m* 107
पशु चिकित्सक *m* 189
पशुधन *m* 182, 185
पश्चिम सहारा *m* 317
पसलियों के बीच का 16
पसली *f* 17, 119
पसली पंजर *m* 17
पंसारी की दुकान *f* 114
पहचान चिह्न *m* 53
पहचान बैज *m* 189
पहला *m* 309
पहली मंज़िल *f* 104
पहली सर्विस से बना अंक 230
पहाड़ी *f* 284
पहाड़ी बादाम *m* 129
पहिया *m* 198, 205, 207, 276
पाइंट *m* 311
पाइप *f* 112
पाइप कटर *m* 81
पाइपिंग बैग *m* 69
पाई *f* 143, 158
पाईप *f* 202
पाई बनाने का सांचा *m* 69
पाउंड *m* 310
पाउडर *m* 40, 77,109
पाउडर दूध *m* 137
पाक-चोई 123
पाकिस्तान *m* 318
पाचक *m* 19
पांचछहसात 308
पांचवा *m* 309
पांच सौ *m* 308

पांचा *m* 88
पाड़ *m* 186
पांडा *m* 291
पान *m* 273
पाना *m* 80, 203
पानी *m* 144, 238
पानी का नल *m* 95
पानी की धार *f* 95
पानी की नली *f* 95
पानी की बोतल *f* 206, 267
पानी के रंग *m* 274
पानी जाना *tr* 52
पानी में छोड़ना *tr* 24
पानी में पकाना *tr/itr* 67
पानी में पैर मारना *tr* 239
पायदान *m* 59, 71
पाया *m* 64
पारस्लि 133
पारा *m* 289
पारी *f* 228
पार्क करना *tr* 195
पार्किंग मीटर *m* 195
पार्सल *m* 99
पाल *m* 240, 241
पालक *m* 123
पालतू जानवरों की दुकान 115
पाल दंड *m* 95, 240
पालना *m* 75, 95
पाल नौका *f* 215
पाल नौकायन 240
पाषाण *m* 288
पाषाणित कंकड़ *m* 288
पास 226
पासकोड *m* 99
पास देना *tr/itr* 220, 223
पासपोर्ट *m* 213
पासपोर्ट कंट्रोल 213
पासा *m* 272
पासा फेंको 273
पास्चरीकृत 137
पास्ता *m* 158
पॉटी *f* 74
पात्र चयन 254
पार्श्व *m* 254
पार्श्व रेखा *f* 221
पाठ्य पुस्तक *f* 163
पिकअप 258
पिकनिक *f* 263
पिकनिक बेंच *f* 266
पिकॉलो *m* 257
पिघलाना *tr* 67
पिच *f* 225
पिचकारी *f* 89
पिचर *m* 229
पिचर का स्थान *m* 228
पिचिंडिका *f* 15
पिछला पहिया *m* 197
पिछला समतल पंख *m* 210
पिछली पतवार *f* 210
पिछली लाइट *f* 204
पिछली सीट *f* 200, 204
पिछले हफ़्ते *m* 307
पिज़्ज़ा *m* 154, 155
पिज़्ज़ा पार्लर *m* 154
पिट्ठू *m* 267
पिट्ठू बैग *m* 31, 37
पिंडली *f* 12, 13, 16
पिंडली की हड्डी *f* 17
पिता *m* 22
पिन *f* 60, 96, 249, 276
पिनकुशन *m* 276
पियानो *m* 256
पियानो का श्वेत पर्दा *m* 256
पियोनि *m* 111
पिरामिड *m* 164
पिलाटेज़ 251
पिल्ला *m* 290
पिसा 132
पिसी कॉफ़ी *f* 144
पिसी मिर्च *f* 132
पिस्ता *m* 129
पश्चिम *m* 312
पीकन *m* 129
पीछे करना *tr/itr* 195
पीछे की लाइट *f* 207
पीछे दौड़ना *tr* 229
पीटा ब्रेड 139
पीठ *f* 13, 64
पीठ का ब्रश *m* 73
पीठ की सबसे चौड़ी पेशी *f* 16
पीढ़ी *f* 23
पीतल के वाद्य *m* 257
पीनट बटर *m* 135
पीने का कप *m* 75
पीपुल कैरियर *m* 199
पीला *m* 274
पीला कार्ड *m* 223
पीली गाजर *f* 125
पी सी ओ फ़ोन *m* 99
पुंकेसर *m* 297
पुखराज *m* 288
पुच्छल *m* 280
पुच्छास्थि *f* 17
पुटक (झिल्लीदार छोटी थैली) *f* 20
पुडिंग राइस *m* 130
पुतली *f* 51
पुदीना *m* 133
पुदीने वाली चाय *f* 149
पुनः परत लगाना 187
पुन: प्रस्तुति 255
पुनर्चक्रण पात्र *m* 61
पुरःस्थ ग्रंथि *f* 21
पुरुष *m* 12, 13, 21
पुरुष परिधान *m* 32, 105
पुरुष मित्र *m* 24
पुर्ज़ा *m* 80
पुर्तगाल *m* 316
पुल *m* 300
पुल-अप करना *tr* 251
पुलिस *f* 94
पुलिस अधिकारी *m* 94
पुलिस कर्मी *m* 189
पुलिस कार *m* 94
पुलिस चौकी *f* 94
पुश्ता *m* 301
पुष्प चक्र *m* 111
पुष्पी पौधे *m* 297
पुस्तक *f* 168
पुस्तक प्राप्ति 168
पुस्तकालय *m* 168, 299
पुस्तकालय अध्यक्ष *m* 168, 190
पुस्तकालय कार्ड *m* 168
पुस्तकों की अलमारी *f* 168
पुट्ठे का मांस *m* 119
पूंछ *f* 121, 242, 290, 292, 294
पूछताछ 168
पूछताछ ऐप *m* 99
पूरक *m* 55
पूरा *m* 266
पूरा चांद *m* 280
पूर्व *m* 312
पूर्वरंग *m* 256
पूर्व रिकॉर्डेड *m* 178
पूर्वी तिमोर *m* 318
पूर्वस्नातक *m* 169
पूल बिलियर्ड *m* 249
पृथ्वी *f* 280, 282
पृष्ठपट *m* 254
पृष्ठीय मीन पंख *m* 294
पृष्ठच्छदा पेशी *f* 16
पेंगुइन *m* 292
पेच *m* 80
पेचकस *m* 80
पेचकस वज्र *m* 80
पेट *m* 12
पेंट *m* 83
पेंट का डिब्बा *m* 83
पेंट ट्रे *m* 83
पेट दर्द *m* 44
पेटा *m* 214, 240
पेंटिंग *f* 261
पेटी *f* 32, 36, 236
पेट्री डिश *f* 166
पेट्रोल *m* 199
पेट्रोल टंकी *f* 203
पेट्रोल पंप *m* 199
पेट्रोल स्टेशन *m* 199
पेठा *m* 125
पेड़ *m* 86, 296
पेन *m* 163
पेनल्टी क्षेत्र *m* 223
पेपर क्लिप *f* 173
पेपर ट्रे *m* 172
पेपर नैपकिन *f* 154
पेपर माशे *m* 275
पेय *m* 144
पेय पदार्थ *m* 107, 156
पेय हिलाने की डंडी *f* 150
पेरू *m* 315
पेलिकन *m* 292
पेशीबंध *m* 16
पेंसिल *f* 163, 275
पेंसिल केस 163 *m*
पेंसिल शार्पनर *m* 163
पेस्टिंग टेबल *f* 82
पेस्ट्री *f* 140, 149
पेस्ट्री ट्रॉली *f* 152
पेस्ट्री ब्रश *m* 69
पेस्टिंग ब्रश *m* 82
पैक *m* 311
पैक करवाके ले जाना 154
पैकेट *m* 311
पैंट *f* 32, 34
पैटी *f* 142
पैटी लाइनर *m* 108
पैड *m* 53, 220, 224, 225
पैडल *m* 61, 206
पैडल मारना *tr* 207
पैंतरेबाज़ी 237
पैदल पारपथ *m* 195
पैदल रास्ता *m* 262, 299
पैदा होना *itr* 26
पैन *m* 310
पैनकेक *m* 157
पैनल्टी *f* 223
पैबंद *m* 277
पैमाना *m* 163, 165
पैर *m* 12, 15
पैरवी *f* 180
पैरागुए *m* 315
पैराग्लाइडिंग 248
पैराशूट *m* 248
पैराशूट से उतरना 248
पैरों की सफ़ाई 41
पैरोल 181
पैशन फ्रूट *m* 128
पॉज़ 269
पॉज़ीटिव इलेक्ट्रोड *m* 167
पॉप *m* 259
पॉपकॉर्न *m* 255
पॉमेल हॉर्स *m* 235
पॉलिश *f* 77
पॉलीएस्टर *m* 277
पोकर 273
पोच्ड 159
पोंछना *tr* 77
पोछा *m* 77
पोडियम *m* 235, 256
पोत *m* 214
पोतघाट *m* 217
पोत निर्माण घाट *m* 217
पोता *m* 22
पोताग्र *m* 214
पोताधिकारी कक्ष *m* 214
पोती *f* 22
पोनी टेल *f* 39
पोर्ट *m* 145, 176
पोलरॉएड कैमरा *m* 270
पोलैंड *m* 316
पोलो *m* 243
पोस्ट कार्ड *m* 112
पोस्टर *m* 255
पोस्टर रंग *m* 274
पोस्टल ऑर्डर *m* 98
पौद *f* 91
पौध घर *m* 85
पौधों के प्रकार 86
पौने दो *m* 304
प्याज़ *f* 124, 125
प्यादा *m* 272
प्याली *f* 112
प्यूर्तो रीको 314
प्रकार 199, 205
प्रकाश स्तंभ *m* 217
प्रक्षेपण *m* 281
प्रक्षेपण स्थल *m* 281
प्रचालक *m* 99
प्रजनन *m* 19, 20
प्रति चैनल भुगतान 269
प्रतिद्वंद्वी *m* 236
प्रतिपदा का चांद *m* 280
प्रति बनाना *tr* 172
प्रतिरक्षक *m* 223
प्रतिरक्षक पंक्ति *f* 222
प्रतिरोध करना *tr* 220, 221, 223
प्रतिरोपित करना *tr* 91
प्रतिवादी *m* 181
प्रतिवेदन *m* 174
प्रतिशत 165
प्रतिस्पर्धा *f* 243
प्रतिस्पर्धाएं *f* 247
प्रतीक्षा कक्ष *m* 45
प्रत्यक्ष भुगतान 96
प्रत्यावर्तक *m* 203
प्रत्येक 320
प्रदर्शनी *f* 261
प्रदर्शित वस्तु *f* 261
प्रधान कार्यालय *m* 175
प्रपदास्थि *f* 17
प्रबंधक *m* 24, 174
प्रबंध निदेशक *m* 175
प्रमुख गायक *m* 258
प्रयोग *m* 166
प्रयोगशाला *f* 166
प्रवाल द्वीप *m* 285
प्रवेश *m* 168
प्रवेशक *m* 255
प्रवेश द्वार *m* 59
प्रवेश निषेध *m* 195
प्रवेश मार्ग *m* 216
प्रवेश शुल्क *m* 260
प्रशंसक *m* 258
प्रशांत महासागर *m* 312
प्रशामक *m* 109
प्रसव *m* 52
प्रसव में सहायक उपकरण *m* 53
प्रसव विशेषज्ञ *m* 52
प्रसाधक *m* 82
प्रसाधन *m* 104
प्रसारण *m* 179
प्रसारित करना *tr* 178
प्रसिद्ध खंडहर *m* 261
प्रसूति *f* 49
प्रसूति कक्ष *f* 48
प्रस्तरपाद *m* 301
प्रस्ताव *m* 174
प्रस्तुतकर्ता *m* 178
प्रस्तुतिकरण *m* 174
प्रस्थान *m* 213
प्रस्थान कक्ष *m* 213

प्रहार रोकना 237
प्राइमर m 83
प्राकृतिक चिकित्सा f 55
प्राकृतिक दृश्य m 271
प्राकृतिक रेशे m 31
प्रांगण m 104
प्राचीन वस्तुओं की दुकान f 114
प्राणी विज्ञान m 169
प्रांत m 315
प्राथमिक चिकित्सा f 47
प्राथमिक चिकित्सा पेटी f 47
प्राध्यापक m 169
प्राप्त करना tr 177
प्रायद्वीप m 282
प्रारंभ स्थान m 247
प्रिंटर m 172, 176
प्रिंट लेना tr 172
प्रिमरोज़ m 297
प्रीमियर m 254
प्रेम होना itr 26
प्रेशर वॉल्व m 61
प्रेषक पर्ची f 173
प्रेस m 178
प्रेस अप 251
प्रैक्टिस शॉट m 233
प्रॉपर्टी डीलर m 115
प्रोग्राम m 176
प्रोग्रामिंग 178
प्रोत्साहक टीम नेता m 220
प्रोसेसर m 176
प्रश्न m 163
प्रश्न पूछना tr 163
प्लग m 60
प्लाईवुड m 79
प्लाक m 50
प्लास्टिक की लंगोटी f 30
प्लास्टिक बैग m 122
प्लास्टिक सर्जरी f 49
प्लीहा m 18
प्लूटो m 280
प्ले m 269
प्लेट f 65, 88
प्लेटफ़ॉर्म m 208
प्लेटफ़ॉर्म संख्या f 208
प्लेटिनम m 289
पत्र m 98
पत्रिका f 112
पत्रिकाएं f 107
पत्रकार m 179, 191
पत्रपेटी f 99
पत्र मित्र m 24
पत्नी f 22
पन्ना m 288
पश्चिमी 255

फ

फ़र m 293
फ़रवरी f 306
फ़र्नीचर की दुकान f 115
फ़र्श m 62, 71
फल m 89, 107, 126, 128
फल एवं सब्ज़ियों की दुकान f 114
फली f 122
फलों का बाग m 183
फलों का रस m 156
फलों की टोकरी f 126
फ़ील्ड हॉकी f 224
फ़सल m 183, 184
फ़सल काटना tr 91, 183
फाइल f 177
फाइल-दराज़ f 172
फ़ाउंडेशन m 40
फ़ाउल m 226
फ़ाउल गेंद f 228
फ़ाउल लाइन f 229
फांक f 126
फ़ायर अलार्म m 95
फ़ायरप्लेस m 62
फ़ायरमैन m 189
फ़ार्म हाउस m 182
फाल m 182
फावड़ा m 88
फ़ास्ट फ़ूड m 154
फ़ास्ट फ़ॉरवर्ड m 269
फ़िगर स्केटिंग m 247
फ़िजी m 318
फ़िनलैंड m 316
फिरकी f 276
फ़िलर m 83
फ़िलिप्स पेचकस m 80
फ़िलीपीन्स m 318
फ़िलो पेस्ट्री f 140
फ़िल्टर m 270
फ़िल्टर कॉफ़ी f 148
फ़िल्टर पेपर m 167
फ़िल्म f 260, 271
फ़िल्म धोना tr 271
फ़िल्म रील f 271
फ़िल्म सेट m 179
फ़िशिंग परमिट m 245
फिसलना tr/itr 229
फिसल पट्टी f 263
फ़ीचर फ़िल्म f 269
फ़ीता m 235
फ़ीते वाले जूते m 37
फ़ीरोज़ा m 289
फ़ील्डिंग करना tr 225, 229
फुट m 310
फुटपाथ m 298
फुट पैडल f 257
फुटबॉल m 220, 222
फुटबॉल का मैदान m 220
फुटबॉल खिलाड़ी m 220
फुटबॉल मैदान m 222
फुटबॉलर m 222
फुटबॉल स्ट्रिप f 31, 222
फुट स्ट्रेप m 241
फुफेरा भाई m 22
फुल क्रीम दूध m 136
फुल बोर्ड m 101
फुंसी f 44
फुहारा m 72
फुहारे में नहाना tr/itr 72
फूंक से बुझाना tr 141
फूंगा m 295
फ़ूड प्रोसेसर m 66
फ़ूड हॉल m 105
फूफा m 22
फूल m 110, 297
फूलगोभी f 124
फूलदान m 111
फूलना itr 139
फूल-पत्ते m 110
फूलमाला f 111
फूल विक्रेता m 110, 188
फूलों की झाड़ी f 87
फ़ेंग शुई 55
फेंटना tr 67, 68
फेंटी हुई क्रीम f 137
फेफड़े m 18
फ़ेशियल m 41
फ़ेस ऑफ़ सर्कल m 224
फ़ेस पाउडर m 40
फ़ेस पैक m 41
फ़ेहोआ m 128
फ़ैक्स m 98
फ़ैन बेल्ट f 203
फैलाव m 52
फ़ैशन m 277
फ़ैसला m 181
फ़ॉकलैंड द्वीप समूह m 315
फ़ॉन्ट m 177
फ़ॉरसेप m 167
फ़ोकस नॉब 167
फ़ोकस से बाहर 271
फ़ोटो एल्बम m 271
फ़ोटो खींचना tr 271
फ़ोटोग्राफ़ी f 270
फ़ोटो प्रति 271
फ़ोटो फ़्रेम m 271
फ़ोटो बड़ी कराना 271
फ़ोन स्टैंड m 99
फ़ोर-व्हील ड्राइव m 199
फ़ोरहैंड m 231
फ़ोल्डर m 177
फ़्यूज़ m 60
फ़्यूज़ बॉक्स m 60, 203
फ़्यूज़िलेज m 210
फ़्राइंग पैन m 69
फ़्राइड अंडा m 157
फ़्राइड चिकन m 155
फ़्रांस m 316
फ़्रांसबीन m 122
फ़्रिज m 67
फ़्री किक 222
फ़्रीज़र m 67
फ़्रीज़िया m 110
फ़्री थ्रो लाइन f 226
फ़्रूट केक m 140
फ़्रूट गम m 113
फ़्रूट टार्ट m 140
फ़्रूट दही m 157
फ़्रूट ब्रेड m 139
फ़्रेंच गयाना m 315
फ़्रेंच जूड़ा m 39
फ़्रेंच टोस्ट m 157
फ़्रेंच फ़्राई f 154
फ़्रेंच ब्रेड f 138
फ़्रेंच मस्टर्ड m 135
फ़्रेंच हॉर्न m 257
फ़्रेट m 258
फ़्रेम m 51, 63, 206, 267
फ़्रोज़न m 124
फ़्रोज़न आहार m 107
फ़्रंट क्रॉल m 239
फ़्लाई ओवर m 194
फ़्लिप चार्ट m 174
फ़्लिपर m 239
फ़्लू m 44
फ़्लूट m 139
फ़्लैट m 59
फ़्लैटस्क्रीन टीवी f 269
फ़्लैन केक m 142
फ़्लैन बनाने का सांचा m 69
फ़्लैश m 270
फ़्लैश गन m 270
फ़्लोट m 238, 244
फ़्लोट बॉल m 61
फ़्लोरेन्टाइन 141
फ़व्वारा m 85
फन्नी f 24

ब

बंकर m 232
बकरी f 185
बकरी की दूध m 136
बकरी के दूध का चीज़ 142
बकसुआ m 36
बखिया f 277
बख़्शीश f 152
बग़ल f 13
बंगला m 58
बग़ीचा m 84, 262
बग़ीची f 84
बग़ीचे की रूप सज्जा f 84
बग़ीचे की शैलियां f 84
बगीचे के उपकरण m 88
बगीचे के पौधे m 86
बगुला m 292
बग्गी f 232
बग्गी दौड़ f 243
बग्घी f 75
बचत f 96
बचत खाता m 96
बचाव 220
बचाव पक्ष m 181
बच्चा m 23, 31
बच्चेदानी f 52
बच्चों का ताला m 75
बच्चों का थैला m 75
बच्चों का वॉर्ड m 48
बछड़ा m 185
बछड़े का मांस m 118
बजरी f 88
बंजी कूद f 248
बंजुफल m 125
बटन 32
बटरकप m 297
बटरफ़्लाई f 239
बटुआ m 37
बटेर f 119
बटेर का अंडा m 137
बड़ा करना tr 172
बड़ा गिरजाघर m 300
बड़ा दाना m 130
बड़ी आंत f 18
बड़ी क़ैंची f 89
बड़ी क्लिप f 173
बड़ी चिमटी f 167
बड़ी प्लेट f 65
बड़ी बर्फ़ानी दौड़ f 247
बड़ी सीपी f 121
बढ़ई m 188
बढ़ईगिरी के वज्र m 80
बढ़ाना tr 91, 251
बतख़ f 119, 185, 293
बतख़ का अंडा m 137
बित्तयां 94
बंद 260
बंदगोभी f 123
बंदर m 291
बंदरगाह m 214, 216, 217
बंदरगाह प्रमुख m 217
बंदरगाह में लाना tr 217
बदलना tr/itr 209
बंदूक़ f 94
बंधक m 96
बन 140, 155
बनसन बर्नर m 166
बनियान f 30, 33
बर्फ़ानी दौड़ f 247
बबूना की चाय f 149
बबूल m 110
बब्बर शेर m 291
बब्बल बाथ 73
बमवर्षक m 211
बीमा m 203
बम्पर 74, 198
बयान m 180
बरमा m 80
बरसाती 31, 32
बरसाती कोट m 31, 33
बराबर 165
बराबरी 230
बराबरी की दौड़ f 234
बरौनी f 51
बर्गर m 154
बर्गर बार m 154
बर्गर मील m 154
बर्तन m 105
बर्तन और छुरी-कांटे m 65
बर्तन धोने की मशीन f 66
बर्तन लगाने का तरीक़ा 65
बर्नर m 67
बर्फ़ f 120, 151, 287
बर्फ़ के साथ 151
बर्फ़ जमाने की जगह 67
बर्फ़ रहित 151

बर्फ़ व नीबू 151
बर्र *f* 295
बलुआ पत्थर *m* 288
बल्ब *m* 86
बल्ला *m* 225, 228
बल्लेबाज़ *m* 225, 228
बल्लेबाज़ी करना *tr* 225
बल्ले से खेलना *tr* 229
बवंडर *m* 287
बस *f* 196
बस अड्डा *m* 197
बस खड़ी करने की जगह 197
बस चालक *m* 190
बस टिकट *f* 197
बसंत *m* 307
बस स्टॉप *m* 197, 299
बसून 257
बसों के प्रकार 196
बहन *f* 22
बहरीन *m* 318
बहामास *m* 314
बहिः प्रकोष्ठिका *f* 17
बहु विटामिन *m* 109
बहू *f* 22
बाइक रैक *m* 207
बाइट्स *f* 176
बाइप्लेन 211
बाइसवां *m* 309
बाईं ओर की ड्राइव 201
बाईस 308
बाउल *m* 61
बाकला *m* 122, 131
बाग़ *m* 261
बाग़बानी *f* 90
बाग़बानी की दुकान *f* 115
बाग़बानी के दस्ताने *m* 89
बांग्लादेश *m* 318
बाघ *m* 291
बाज़ *m* 292
बांज *m* 296
बाज़ार *m* 115
बाजू *m* 13
बाजू पट्टी *f* 238
बाड़ *f* 85, 90, 182, 243
बाड़ *f* 85
बाड़ा *m* 84, 185
बाढ़ *f* 287
बाथ टब *m* 72
बाद में 304
बादल *m* 287
बादशाह *m* 273
बादाम *m* 129, 151
बादाम का तेल *m* 134
बादाम परत *f* 141
बांध *m* 300
बाधा दौड़ *f* 235, 243
बाबा सूट *m* 30
बाम मछली *f* 294
बायफ़ोकल 51
बायां *m* 260
बार *m* 150, 152
बार काउंटर *m* 150
बार कुर्सी *f* 150
बार कोड *m* 106
बारटेंडर 150, 191
बारबाडोस *m* 314
बारह *m* 308
बारहमासी 86
बारहवां *m* 309
बारिश *f* 287
बारीक *m* 301
बार स्नैक्स *m* 151
बाल *m* 14, 38
बाल-आहार *m* 153
बालकनी *f* 59, 254
शिशु सीट *f* 198, 207
बाल काटना *tr* 38
बाल चिकित्सा *f* 49
बाल धोना *tr* 38
बाल परिधान *m* 30
बाल विभाग *m* 104
बाल सीधा करने का उपकरण 38
बाल सुखाना *tr* 38
बाल-सुविधा केंद्र *m* 104
बाल सेट करना *tr* 38
बालों का फ़ीता *m* 39
बाल्टिक सागर *m* 313
बाल्टी *f* 77
बांस *m* 86, 122, 245
बांस-कूद *f* 234
बास क्लैफ़ 256
बास गिटार *m* 258
बांसुरी *f* 257
बास्केट *f* 226
बास्केट बॉल *m* 226
बास्केट बॉल खिलाड़ी *m* 226
बांह *f* 12
बाहर खाना 147
बाहर जाना 75
बाहरी क्रोड़ *m* 282
बाहरीगतिविधियां 262
बाहरी परत *f* 119
बाहरी लेन *f* 194
बाहरी स्वरूप 198
बाहरी हार्ड ड्राइव *f* 176
बाह्य रोगी *m* 48
बिकनी *f* 264
बिक्री विभाग *m* 175
बिक्री सहायक *m* 104
बिच्छू *m* 295
बिच्छू-बूटी *f* 297
बिछौना *m* 74
बिज़नेस ट्रिप *f* 175
बिज़नेस लंच *m* 175
बिज़नेस सूट *m* 32
बिजली *f* 60, 287
बिजली कटौती 60
बिजली का झटका 46
बिजली का टेप *m* 81
बिजली का मीटर *m* 60
बिजली का सामान *m* 105
बिजली की वस्तुएं *f* 107
बिजली बचाने वाला बल्ब *m* 60
बिजली मिस्त्री *m* 188
बिजली से चलने वाला रक्तचाप मापक *m* 45
बिजली से चलने वाली कार 199
बिजूका *m* 184
बिट ब्रेस 78
बिडे 72
बिना चर्बी का मांस 118
बिना सोचे किक मारना 220
बिब *m* 30
बिल *m* 152
बिल्ला *m* 94
बिल्ली *f* 290
बिल्ली का बच्चा 290
बिसात *f* 105, 272
बिस्कुट *m* 113, 141
बिस्तर बंद *m* 37
बिस्तर लगाना *tr* 71
बीकर 167
बीच 296
बीच तौलिया *m* 265
बीच थैला *m* 264
बीच बॉल *m* 265
बीज *m* 88, 122, 127, 128, 130, 131
बीजजनन 20, 52
बीज ट्रे *f* 89
बीज निकालने की सलाई 68
बीजयुक्त ब्रेड 139
बीज रहित 127
बीजरहित किशमिश *f* 129
बीता कल 306
बीता परसों 307
बीम *f* 235
बीमारी *f* 44
बीयर *f* 145, 151
बीयर टैप *m* 150
बीस 308
बीस मिनट 304
बीसवां *m* 309
बीस हज़ार 309
बुआ *f* 22
बुख़ार *m* 44
बुटीक *m* 115
बुंदे *f* 36
बुध *m* 280
बुधवार *m* 306
बुनना 277
बुनने की सलाई *f* 277
बुनाई *f* 277
बुफ़े *m* 152
बुरूंडी *m* 317
बुर्किना फ़ासो *m* 317
बुर्ज *m* 300
बुलबुलेदार 144
बुल्गारिया *m* 316
बुहारना *tr* 90
बूट *m* 37
बूस्टर *m* 281
बृहस्पति *m* 280
बेक करना *tr* 67, 138
बेक किया हुआ 159
बेकन *m* 118, 157
बेकर *m* 139
बेकरी *f* 107, 114, 138
बेक़सूर *m* 181
बेकिंग ट्रे *f* 69
बेगम *f* 273
बेगल बन 139
बेंच *f* 162, 250, 262
बेटा *m* 22
बेटी *f* 22
बेंत *f* 89, 91, 94
बेनिन 317
बेबी जूते *m* 30
बेबी टमाटर *m* 124
बेबी मॉनिटर 75
बेर और सर्दा 127
बेल *f* 87, 183
बेलचा *m* 187
बेलन *m* 69, 164
बेलना *tr* 67
बेलारूस *m* 316
बेलीज़ 314
बेल्जियम *m* 316
बेसबॉल *m* 228
बेसमैन *m* 228
बेस लाइन *f* 230
बेसिन *m* 38, 50
बेहोश 47
बेहोश होना *itr* 44
बैंक *m* 96
बैंक अंतरण 96
बैक गैमन 272
बैंक प्रबंधक *m* 96
बैंक प्रभार 96
बैक बोर्ड *m* 226
बैकस्ट्रोक 239
बैकस्विंग 233
बैकहैंड 231
बैग *m* 37
बैग की तनी 37
बैंगन *m* 125
बैंगनी 274
बैट *m* 231
बैटरियां *f* 260
बैटरी *f* 167, 202
बैटरी पैक *m* 78
बैठक *f* 62
बैठने की व्यवस्था 254
बैडमिंटन *m* 231
बैरा *m* 148, 152
बैल *m* 185
बैलिरिक द्वीप समूह *m* 316
बैले *m* 255
बैले स्कर्ट *f* 191
बॉक्स *m* 254
बॉक्स ऑफ़िस *m* 255
बॉक्स फ़ाइल *f* 173
बॉक्सर शॉर्ट्स 33
बॉक्सिंग दस्ताने *m* 237
बॉक्सिंग रिंग *f* 237
बॉक्सिंग व्यायाम *f* 251
बॉडी लोशन *m* 73
बॉडीवर्क 202
बॉब *m* 39
बॉयलर *m* 61
बॉल *m* 221, 224, 226
बॉल एक-दूसरे को देना *tr* 221
बॉल को घेरना 221
बॉल निशाने पर मारना *tr* 227
बॉल पकड़ना *tr* 227
बॉल फेंकना *tr* 221, 223, 226, 227, 229
बॉल बास्केट में डालना *tr* 227
बॉल ब्वॉय *m* 231
बॉल मारना *tr* 224
बॉल रोकना *tr* 227
बॉल लपकने को तैयार रहना *tr* 227
बॉल वापस आना 226
बॉल्सम सिरका *m* 135
बो-टाई *f* 36
बोतल *f* 61, 75, 135, 311
बोतल ओपनर *m* 68, 150
बोतलबंद खाद्य पदार्थ *m* 134
बोतलबंद पानी 144
बोत्सवाना *m* 317
बोनट *m* 198
बोना *tr* 90, 183
बोया 217
बोर्ड *m* 241
बोर्ड खेल *m* 272
बोर्डिंग पास *m* 213
बोलिंग *f* 249
बोलिंग बॉल *m* 249
बोलीविया *m* 315
बोस्निया और हर्ज़ेगोविना *m* 316
बोंगो *m* 257
बौछार *f* 286
ब्याज दर *f* 96
ब्रश *m* 38, 40, 77, 83, 274
ब्रश करना *tr* 38, 50
ब्रह्मांड *m* 280
ब्रा *f* 35
ब्राउज़ *itr* 177
ब्राउज़र *m* 177
ब्राउन ब्रेड *f* 139, 149
ब्राउन राइस *m* 130
ब्राज़ील *m* 315
ब्राज़ीलनट *m* 129
ब्रांडी *f* 145
ब्रिज *m* 258
ब्रिजताश की गड्डी *f* 273
ब्री चीज़ 142
ब्रीफ़केस *m* 37
ब्रुनेई *m* 318
ब्रेक 200, 204, 206
ब्रेक डाउन 203
ब्रेक द्रव्य डिब्बा *m* 202
ब्रेक पैडल *m* 205
ब्रेकफ़ास्ट बुफ़े *m* 156
ब्रेक ब्लॉक *m* 207
ब्रेक लीवर *m* 207
ब्रेड *f* 157

ब्रेड एवं आटा 138
ब्रेड का चूरा *m* 139
ब्रेड काटने की छुरी *f* 68
ब्रेड फ्रूट *m* 124
ब्रेड बनाना 138
ब्रेड रोल *m* 143
ब्रेड स्लाइस 138
ब्रेसलेट *m* 36
ब्रेस्टस्ट्रोक 239
ब्रोकली *f* 123
ब्लशर *m* 40
ब्लीच 77
ब्लू चीज़ *m* 136
ब्लूज़ *m* 259
ब्लेज़र *m* 33
ब्लेड *m* 66, 78
ब्लेंडर *m* 66
ब्लैक करंट 127
ब्लैक कॉफ़ी *f* 148
ब्लैक पुडिंग 157
ब्लैकबेरी *f* 127
ब्लैक बेल्ट *f* 237
ब्लैक होल *m* 280
ब्लोअर *m* 60

भ

भगच्छेदन 52
भगशिश्निका *f* 20
भगोष्ठ *m* 20
भयभीत 25
भरना *tr* 82
भरवां *m* 159
भरवां ज़ैतून *m* 143
भराव 140
भरावन 50, 155
भरा हुआ 64
भर्ती 48
भवन एवं इमारतें 300
भवन नक़्शा *m* 261
भाई *m* 22
भाग *m* 282
भाग देना *tr* 165
भाजक *m* 165
भानजा *m* 23
भानजी *f* 23
भाप चालित
रेलगाड़ी *f* 208
भाप में पका 159
भाप से पकाना *tr/itr* 67
भार *m* 244
भार और मापक *m* 310
भारत *m* 318
भारोत्तोलन *m* 251
भाला फेंक *m* 234
भालू *m* 291
भाले से मछली पकड़ना 245
भावनाएं *f* 25
भावी वर-वधू 24
भाषाएं *f* 162
भिगोना *tr* 130
भिंडी *f* 122
भिन्न 165
भीतरी गांठ *f* 122
भीतरी छिलका *m* 126
भीतरी परत *f* 83
भीतरी लेन *f* 194
भीतरी ट्यूब *f* 207
भुगतान *m* 96
भुगतान स्थल *m* 106
भुजा *f* 164
भुना *m* 129, 158
भुना हुआ 159
भूकंप *m* 283
भूखा *m* 64
भूगोल *m* 162
भूटान *m* 318
भूतल *m* 104
भूदृष्य *m* 284
भूनना *tr* 67
भूपर्पटी *f* 282
भूप्रावार *m* 282
भूमध्य सागर *m* 313
भूमि *f* 282
भूमिगत नक़्शा *m* 209
भूमिगत मार्ग *m* 194
भूमिगत रेलगाड़ी *f* 208
भूरा *m* 274
भूरे रंग का होना 41
भूसंपत्ति दलाल *m* 189
भूसी *f* 130
भूस्पंद *m* 283
भेजना *tr* 177
भेड़ *f* 185
भेड़ का दूध 137
भेड़िया *m* 290
भेड़ों का बाड़ा *m* 183
भोजन *m* 64
भोजन कक्ष *m* 64, 168
भोजन के दौर 153
भोजनयान *m* 209
भोजवृक्ष *m* 296
भोर *f* 305
भौतिकी *f* 162, 169
भौंह *f* 14, 51
भ्रमित 25
भ्रूण *m* 52

म

मई *f* 306
मकई *f* 184
मकई का तेल *m* 135
मकई ब्रेड *f* 139
मकड़ी *f* 295
मंक फ़िश *f* 120
मकर रेखा *f* 283
मकान *m* 58
मकान मालिक *m* 58
मक्का *m* 130
मक्खन *m* 137, 156
मक्खी *f* 295
मक्खी से मछली पकड़ना *m* 245
मग *m* 65
मगरमच्छ *m* 293
मंगल *m* 280
मंगलवार *m* 306
मंगुष्ठ *m* 128
मंगेतर *m* 24
मंगोलिया 318
मिर्च *m* 132
मंच *f* 254
मच्छर *m* 295
मच्छर अवरोधक *m* 267
मच्छरदानी *m* 267
मछली *f* 107, 120, 294
मछली का टुकड़ा *m* 119
मछली की टोकरी *f* 245
मछली की दुकान *f* 114, 120
मछली चारा *m* 244
मछली पकड़ना 244
मछली पकड़ने का कांटा 244
मछली पकड़ने का जाल 244
मछली पकड़ने के प्रकार 245
मछली पकड़ने वाला 244
मछली पालन क्षेत्र *m* 183
मछली रखने का जाल *m* 244
मछली विक्रेता *m* 188
मछली हुक *m* 244
मछुआरा *m* 189
मछुआरी नाव *f* 217
मंज़िल *f* 58
मंजीरा *m* 257
मटन 118
मटर *f* 122, 131
मटरा *m* 131
मत्स्य बंदरगाह *m* 217
मंदिर *m* 300
मद्य पेय *m* 145
मंद्र क्लैरिनेट 257
मधुमक्खी *f* 295
मधुमेह *m* 44
मधुर संगीत *m* 259
मध्य अफ़्रीकी गणराज्य *m* 317
मध्यपट *m* 19
मध्य मंडल *m* 286
मध्यमिका *f* 15
मध्य रेखा *f* 226
मध्य लेन *f* 194
मध्याह्न *m* 305
मनचेगो चीज़ 142
मनोचिकित्सा *f* 49, 55
मनोरंजन *m* 253
मफ़िन 140
मफ़िन ट्रे *m* 69
मरना *itr* 26
मरम्मत का सामान 207
मरहम *m* 47, 109
मरहम पट्टी *f* 47
मराकस 257
मरीज़ *m* 45
मरोड़ *f* 44
मर्मर पक्षी *f* 292
मलावी *m* 317
मलेशिया *m* 318
मल्ल क्रीड़ा *m* 236
मशरूम *m* 125
मशीन गन *f* 189
मशीनरी *f* 187
मसला हुआ 159
मसाला *m* 83
मसाले *m* 132
मसालेदार सॉसेज 142
मसाले में लिपटा 143, 159
मसालों की पोटली 132
मसूड़ा *m* 50
मस्कारा *m* 40
मस्जिद *f* 300
मस्टर्ड *m* 155
मस्तिष्क *m* 19
मस्तूल *m* 240
महिला मेज़बान *m* 64
महाद्वीप 282, *m* 315
महाविद्यालय *m* 168
महासागर *m* 282
महिला परिधान *m* 34, 105
महिला मित्र 24
महिला व्यवसायी 175
महीन आटा 139
माइक्रोफ़ोन *m* 179, 258
माइक्रोलाइट *f* 211
माइक्रोवेव ओवन *m* 66
माउंटेन बाइक *f* 206
माउथ गार्ड *m* 237
माउथवॉश *m* 72
माउस *m* 176
माणिक *m* 288
माता *f* 22
माथा 14 *m*
मानव-चालित 200
माप 151 *f*
मापक *m* 150, 165
मापक चम्मच 109
मापक जग *m* 69, 311
मापना *tr* 310
मार्ग *m* 212
मार्ग चिह्न *m* 194
मार्गदर्शित पर्यटन *m* 260
मार्ग निर्देशन करना *tr* 240
मार्ग निर्देशिका *f* 260
मार्ग संकेतक *m* 298
मार्गिका *f* 214
मार्च *m* 306
मार्टिनी 151
मार्मलेड *m* 134, 156
मार्शमैलो *m* 113
मार्शल आर्ट्स *m* 237
माल कक्ष *m* 215
मालगाड़ी *f* 208
मालगोदाम *m* 216
माल डिब्बा *m* 216
मालदीव *m* 318
माल पोत *m* 215
मालवाहक *m* 215
माल वाहक बंदरगाह *m* 216
मालिक *m* 24
मालिश *f* 54
माली *m* 188, 317
माल्ट का सिरका *m* 135
माल्टा *m* 126, 316
मास *m* 306
मांस *m* 118
मांस कूटने का औज़ार 68
मांस के टुकड़े 119
मांसपेशियां *f* 16
मांसपेशियां गरमाना *tr* 251
मांसाहारी खाद्य पदार्थ 107
मासिक 307
माहवारी *f* 20
माल्ट वाला पेय 144
मिक्सिंग डेस्क 179
मिक्सिंग बाउल 66, 69
मिंट टॉफ़ी 113
मिट्टी *f* 85
मिट्टी का बर्तन *m* 69
मिट्टी रोधक *m* 205
मितली *f* 44
मितली की दवा *f* 109
मिनट *m* 304
मिनट की सुई *f* 304
मिनरल वॉटर *m* 144
मिनी बस *f* 197
मिनी बार 101
मिरगी *f* 44
मिरैंग 140
मिर्च *f* 143
मिलने का समय 45, 48, 175
मिलाना *tr* 67,138
मिलीग्राम 310
मिलीमीटर 310
मिलीलीटर 311
मिल्कशेक *m* 137
मिश्रित अनाज ब्रेड 139
मिश्रित सलाद *m* 158
मिसाइल *f* 211
मिस्र 317
मिष्ठान्न *m* 153
मिस्त्री *m* 188
मीट का पेस्ट *m* 156
मीटर *m* 310
मीटर ब्लॉक 81
मीट हुक *m* 118
मीटिंग *f* 174
मीठा *m* 124, 127, 155
मीठी गोलियां *f* 113
मीठी मकई *f* 122, 124
मीठे खाद्य *m* 107
मीठे बन 157
मीडियम वेव *m* 179
मीडिया *m* 178
मीन पंख *m* 290
मीन शल्क *m* 121
मीनार *f* 300
मील *m* 310
मुक़द्दमा *m* 180
मुक्का *m* 237
मुक्का मारना 237
मुक्केबाज़ी *f* 236
मुख *m* 283
मुखौटा *m* 228, 236
मुख्यद्वार *m* 58
मुख्याध्यापक *m* 163
मुख्याध्यापिका *f* 163

मुंगरा *m* 275
मुट्ठी *f* 15, 237
मुद्रा *f* 97
मुनक़्क़ा *m* 129
मुर्ग़ *m* 119
मुर्गा *m* 185
मुर्गी *f* 185
मुर्ग़ी का अंडा *m* 137
मुर्गी पालन केंद्र *m* 183
मुलायम खिलौने *m* 75
मुलायम चीज़ 136
मुलायम लकड़ी *f* 79
मुलेठी कैंडी *f* 113
मुवक्किल *m* 180
मुस्कान *f* 25
मुंह *m* 14
मूंगफली *f* 129, 151
मूंगफली का तेल *m* 135
मूंछें *f* 290
मूर्तिकार *m* 191
मूर्ति शिल्प *m* 275
मूल्य *m* 152, 199
मूल्यवर्ग *m* 97
मूल्य सूची *f* 154
मूषक *m* 290
मूस पुडिंग 141
मूसल 68, *m* 167
मूत्र *m* 19
मूत्रनली *f* 20, 21
मूत्र विज्ञान *m* 49
मूत्राशय *m* 20
मृग मांस *m* 118
मृत त्वचा उतारना *tr* 41
मेघाच्छन्न 286
मेज़ *f* 64, 148, 172
मेज़पोश *m* 64
मेज़बान *m* 64
मेज़ लगाना *tr* 64
मेज़ सज्जा *f* 152
मेड़ *f* 85, 182
मेंढक *m* 294
मेढ़ा *m* 185
मेथी *f* 132
मेन कोर्स *m* 153
मेन सप्लाई *f* 60
मेनू के अनुसार 152
मेनू बार *m* 177
मेपल *m* 296
मेपल सिरप *m* 134
मेमना *m* 185
मेमोरी *f* 176
मेमोरी स्टिक *f* 176
मेरुदंड *m* 17
मेरुदंड उपचार *m* 54
मेलाकाइट *f* 289
मेला स्थल *m* 262
मेवे *m* 151, 156
मेवे और गिरी 129
मेशर 68
मेसेडोनिया *m* 316
मेहमान *m* 64, 100
मेहराब *m* 301
मेहराबदार छत *m* 300
मैकरल मछली *f* 120
मैकाडेमिया *m* 129
मैकेनिक *m* 203
मैक्सिको *m* 314
मैग्नीशियम *m* 109
मैच *m* 230
मैडागास्कर *m* 317
मैदा *m* 138
मैदान *m* 226, 227, 228, 234, 285
मैदा ब्रेड *f* 139
मैदे का चीला *m* 155
मैनहोल *m* 299
मैराथन *m* 234
मॉइश्चराइज़र *m* 41
मॉडल *m* 169
मॉडल बनाना 275
मॉनिटर *m* 53, 172
मॉरीटेनिया 317
मॉरीशस *m* 317
मॉल्डोवा *m* 316
मोच *f* 46
मोज़स बास्केट 74
मोज़ाम्बीक़ *m* 317
मोज़े *m* 33
मोज़ेरेला 142
मोटर *f* 88
मोटर क्रॉस 249
मोटर नौका *f* 214
मोटरबाइक *f* 204
मोटरबाइक रेस *f* 249
मोटर रेस *f* 249
मोटर साइकिल *f* 205
मोटा आटा *m* 139
मोटा प्लास *m* 80
मोटी सौंफ़ *f* 133
मोंटेनेग्रो *m* 316
मोतियाबिंद *m* 51
मोतियों की माला *f* 36
मोनाको *m* 316
मोनोपोली *f* 272
मोबाइल फ़ोन *m* 99
मोमबत्ती *f* 141
मोर *m* 293
मोरी *f* 91
मोरोक्को *m* 317
मोहर *f* 98
मोहरा *m* 272
मौसम *m* 286
मौसमी 129
म्यांमार (बर्मा) *m* 318
म्यूज़िकल 255
म्योनीज़ 135
मंत्रिस 295
मरूआ *m* 133
मच्छर अवरोधक *m* 108

य

यमन *m* 318
यहूदी उपनयन *m* 26
यहूदी पर्व *m* 27
यहूदी पूजास्थल *m* 300
यातायात *m* 194
यातायात जाम 195
यातायात पुलिसकर्मी *m* 195
यातायात बत्ती *f* 194
यातायात संकेत *m* 195
यांत्रिकी *f* 202
यात्री *m* 208
यात्री चेक 97
यात्री विमान *m* 210
यात्रा आरंभ करना *tr/itr* 217
यात्री *m* 216
यात्री जहाज़ *m* 215, 216
टर्मिनल *m* 216
यात्री बंदरगाह *m* 216
यात्री वाहक जहाज़ *m* 215
युगल *m* 24, 230
युगांडा *m* 317
यूक्रेन *m* 316
यूनाइटेड किंगडम *m* 316
यूरेनस *m* 280
यूरोप *m* 316
येरुशलम आर्टिचोक *m* 125
योग *m* 54
योग आसन *m* 54
योनि *f* 20
यौन रोग *m* 20

र

रक़म *f* 96
रकाब *m* 242
रक्तचाप *m* 44
रक्तमणि *f* 288
रक्तस्राव *m* 46
रक्षा क्षेत्र *m* 224
रक्षा जैकेट *f* 240
रक्षा नौका *f* 214
रक्षा-स्तंभ *m* 214
रंग *m* 39, 42, 274
रगड़ 46
रंगना *tr* 83
रंग-रूप *m* 41
रंगीन खड़िया *f* 274
रंगीन पेंसिल *f* 163
रंगे हुए 39
रग्बी 221
रग्बी का मैदान 221
रग्बी स्ट्रिप 221
रजत *m* 235
रज़ाई *f* 71
रजिस्टर *m* 100
रजिस्टर्ड डाक *m* 98
रडर *m* 210
रंदा *m* 81
रंदा करना *tr* 79
रद्दी की टोकरी *f* 172
रन *m* 228
रफ़ू करना *tr* 277
रबड़ *f* 163
रबड़ की मोहर 173
रबड़ की ट्यूब 265
रबड़ के जूते *m* 89
रबड़ नली *f* 89
रबड़ बैंड *m* 173
रम *f* 145
रम और कोक 151
रमज़ान *m* 27
रमणीय स्थल *m* 261
रविवार *m* 306
रसभरी *f* 127, 128
रसभरी जैम *m* 134
रसायन शास्त्र *m* 162
रसीद *f* 152
रसीला *m* 127
रसेदार *m* 158
रसोइए की टोपी *f* 190
रसोइया *m* 152, 190
रसोई *f* 66, 152
रसोई उपकरण *m* 68
रस्सी *f* 243, 248. 266
रस्सी कूद *f* 251
रस्से *m* 240
रहना और नाश्ता 101
राइट फ़ील्ड 229
राई *f* 131
राई ब्रेड *f* 138
राख *f* 283
राजगिरी के वज्र *m* 80
राजगीर *m* 186, 188
राजधानी *f* 315
राजनीति *f* 169
राजमा *m* 131
राजहंस *m* 292
राजा *m* 272
राज्य *m* 315
राडार *m* 214, 281
रात और दिन 305
रात का भोजन *m* 64
राष्ट्र *m* 315
राष्ट्रीय उद्यान *m* 261
रास्ता *m* 58, 85, 299
रात्रि पोशाक *f* 31
रिकॉर्ड *m* 234, 269
रिकॉर्ड की दुकान *f* 115
रिकॉर्ड तोड़ना *tr* 234
रिकॉर्ड प्लेयर *m* 268
रिकॉर्डिंग स्टूडियो *m* 179
रिंग *f* 226, 235
रिंच *f* 81
रिट *f* 180
रिटर्न 231
रिफ़्लेक्सोलॉजी 54
रिबन *m* 27, 111, 141
रिम 206
रिमोट कंट्रोल *m* 269
रियरव्यू मिरर *m* 198
रिले दौड़ 235 *f*
रिवर्स चार्ज कॉल 99
रिवाइंड 269
रिश्तेदार 23 *m*
रिसीवर 99 *m*
रिस्ट बैंड 230 *f*
रिफ़्लेक्टर 50 *m*
रील *f* 244
रुआंडा *m* 317
रुई के फाहे *f* 41
रुकना मना है 195
रुखी *f* 41
रुट नंबर *m* 196
रुमाल *f* 36
रुसी *f* 39
रूखे *m* 39
रूटर *m* 78
रूपांतरित शैल *m* 288
रूम सर्विस *f* 101
रूस *m* 318
रे 294
रेकी *f* 55
रेखाएं *f* 165
रेखांकन *m* 275
रेखांकन पटल *m* 275
रेखागणित *m* 165
रेगमाल *m* 81, 83
रेगिस्तान *m* 285
रेग्यूलेटर *m* 239
रेज़र ब्लेड *f* 73
रेड आई 271
रेड करंट *m* 127
रेडिएटर *m* 60, 202
रेडियो *m* 179, 268
रेडियो एंटीना *m* 214
रेडियो घड़ी *f* 70
रेडियो सैट करना *tr* 269
रेडियो स्टेशन *m* 179
रेत *f* 85, 264
रेत का अखाड़ा *m* 263
रेत का महल *m* 265
रेती *f* 81
रेनबो ट्राउट मछली *f* 120
रेनेसान्स 301
रेफ़री *m* 220, 222, 226, 227
रेफ़्रीजरेटर *m* 67
रेमिकीन *m* 69
रेलगाड़ी *f* 208
रेलगाड़ी के प्रकार 208
रेलगाड़ी डिब्बा *m* 208
रेल नेटवर्क *m* 209
रेलवे परिसर *m* 209
रेलवे स्टेशन *m* 208
रेलिंग *f* 59
रेवाचीनी *f* 127
रेशम *m* 277
रेशेदार *m* 127
रेसिंग डाइव 239
रेसिंग ड्राइवर *m* 249
रेसिंग बाइक *f* 205, 206
रेस्तरां *m* 101, 152
रेस्तरां में खाना 154
रैक *m* 166
रैकून *m* 290
रैकेट *m* 230
रैकेट के खेल *m* 231
रैकेट बॉल *m* 231
रैगे 259
रैप 259
रैम 176
रैली ड्राइविंग 249
रॉक *m* 259

रॉक कॉन्सर्ट *m* 258
रॉकेट सलाद *m* 123
रोइंग मशीन *f* 250
रोएं से बनी रज़ाई *f* 71
रोकना *tr* 207
रोकोको 301
रोग़न *m* 79, 83
रोग निदान *m* 49
रोज़मर्रा के वस्त्र *m* 33, 34
रोज़मेरी 133
रोटर ब्लेड *f* 211
रोड बाइक *f* 206
रोड रोलर *m* 187
रोड साइड कैफ़े *m* 148
रोना *itr* 25
रोपना *tr* 183
रोमछिद्र *m* 15
रोमांच कथा *f* 255
रोमानिया *m* 316
रोमांस *m* 255
रोम्पर सूट *m* 30
रोल *m* 139, 155, 311
रोलर *m* 83
रोलर कोस्टर *m* 262
रोलर ब्लाइंड 63
रोलर ब्लेडिंग 263
रत्न 288

ल

लकड़ी *f* 79, 275
लकड़ी का गोंद 78
लकड़ी का चम्मच 68
लकड़ी की छीलन 78
लकड़ी के दाग़ 79
लक्ज़मबर्ग *m* 316
लक्ष्य *m* 273
लंगर *m* 214, 240
लंगरगाह *m* 217
लंगर डालना *tr* 217
लगाम *f* 242
लगाम की मुखरी *f* 242
लंगोटी *f* 75
लघु-प्रतिमा *f* 260
लच्छी *f* 277
लज्जित 25
लटकाना *tr* 82
लड़का *m* 23
लड़की *f* 23
लड़ाकू विमान *m* 211
लता *f* 87
लतामंडप *m* 84
लपकना *tr* 220
लंब 165
लंबा *m* 32
लंबाई *f* 165, 310
लंबा बटन *m* 31
लंबी कूद *f* 235
लंबी पोशाक *f* 34
लंबे मोज़े *m* 35
लंबे हत्थे की क़ैंची *f* 88
ललाट *m* 16
लवंग बदर *m* 132
लवणित 121, 129
लसिका *f* 19
लहर *f* 241, 264
लहसुन *m* 125, 132
लहसुन कूटने वाला 68
लाइट *f* 62, 178
लाइट बटन *m* 201
लाइटमीटर *m* 270
लाइटर *m* 112
लाइटिंग 105
लाइन्स मैन *m* 223, 230
लाइबेरिया *m* 317
लाइव 60
लाओस *m* 318
लातविया *m* 316
लाभांश *m* 97
लाल 145, 274
लाल कार्ड *m* 223
लाल पत्तागोभी *f* 123
लाल भूरा 39
लाल मसूर *m* 131
लाल मांस *m* 118
लाल मिर्च *f* 124
लाल सागर *m* 313
लावा *m* 283
लावा मणि *f* 288
लिकर *m* 145
लिक्टेन्स्टाइन 316
लिखना *tr* 162
लिथुआनिया *m* 316
लिनेन *m* 277
लिप ग्लॉस *m* 40
लिप ब्रश *m* 40
लिपस्टिक *f* 40
लिफ़ाफ़ा *m* 98, 173
लिफ्ट *f* 59, 100, 104
लिब लाइनर *m* 40
लिमोज़ीन 199
लिली *f* 110
लीक *f* 125
लीग *f* 223
लीची *f* 128
लीटर *m* 311
लीबिया *m* 317
लीवर *m* 61, 150
लीवर आर्च फ़ाइल 173
लेक्चर थियेटर *m* 169
लेखन सामग्री *f* 105
लेखाकार *m* 97, 190
लेखा विभाग *m* 175
लेग प्रेस *m* 251
लेडीबर्ड *f* 295
लेन *f* 234, 238
लेप *m* 83
लेबनान *m* 318
लेबल *m* 89
लेमन कर्ड *m* 134
लेमन ग्रास *m* 133
लेस 35
लेंस *m* 51, 167, 270
लेंस कैप *m* 270
लेस बनाना 277
लेस बॉबिन 277
लेसोथो 317
लेफ़्ट फ़ील्ड 228
लैटर बॉक्स *m* 58
लैटर हैड *m* 173
लैदर वस्त्र *m* 205
लैंप *m* 62, 217
लैपटॉप *m* 172, 176
लैंप स्टैंड *m* 166
लैमन सोल *m* 120
लेंस कवर *m* 51
लेंस साफ़ करने का
द्रव्य 51
लॉकर *m* 239
लॉकेट *m* 36
लॉग ऑन करना *tr* 177
लॉन्ग वेव *m* 179
लॉन्ड्री *f* 115
लॉन्ड्री सेवा 101
लॉबस्टर *m* 295
लॉबी *f* 100, 255
लॉलीपॉप *m* 113
लॉन्ड्री *f* 76
लोई *f* 138
लोक संगीत *m* 259
लोग *m* 11
लोगनबेरी 127
लोगो *m* 31
लोब 231
लोबिया *m* 131
लोमड़ी *f* 290
लोहा *m* 289
लौंग *f* 133
ल्यूपिन 297
लैंडिंग गियर 210
लैंप *m* 207

व

वकील *m* 180, 190
वकील का कार्यालय *m* 180
वक्ता *m* 174
वक्र *m* 165
वक्षीय कशेरुकाएं *f* 17
वक्षीय मीन पंख *m* 294
वज़न *m* 166, 250
वज़न छड़ *f* 251
वज़न-मापी *m* 45, 98
वज़नी पेटी *f* 239
वज़ीर *m* 272
वन *m* 285
ट्विन कमरा *m* 100
वनस्पति *f* 296
वनस्पति तेल *m* 135
वनस्पति नाशक *m* 183
वनुआतू 318
वयस्क *m* 23
वर्ग *m* 164
वर्ग फ़ुट *m* 310
वर्गमीटर *m* 310
वर्दी *f* 94, 189
वर्ष *m* 163, 306, 307
वर्षा *f* 287
वर्षा वन *m* 285
वसा *f* 119
वसा रहित 137
वसीयत बनाना *tr* 26
वाइन *f* 145, 151
वाइन गिलास *m* 65
वाइन सिरका *m* 135
वाइब्राफ़ोन *m* 257
वाइस सूची *f* 152
वाईटबोर्ड *m* 162
वाई फ़ाई *m* 269
वातानुकूलन *m* 200
वाद्य यंत्र *m* 256, 258
वाद्यवृंद *m* 256
वापस अपने स्थान पर पहुंचना
228
वापसी का पता 98
वायलिन *m* 256
वायु छलनी *f* 202, 204
वायु छिद्र *m* 210
वायुमंडल *m* 282, 286
वायुयान *m* 210, 212
वायुयान वाहक *m* 215
वायोला *m* 256
वारंट *m* 180
वार्षिक 307
वार्षिकी पौध *f* 86
वाल्व *m* 207
वाशर *m* 80
वाष्प स्नान *m* 250
वास्कट *m* 33
वास्तुशिल्प *m* 300
वास्तुकार *m* 190
विकर्ण रेखा *f* 164
विकलांग पार्किंग स्थल *m* 195
विकल्प बुलाना 223
विकिरण चिकित्सा *f* 49
विकेट *m* 225
विकेट कीपर *m* 225
विग *m* 39
विंग मिरर *m* 198
विचार-विमर्श करना 163 *tr*
विजेता *m* 273
विज्ञान *m* 162, 166
विज्ञान कथा फ़िल्म *f* 255
विज्ञापन *m* 269
विटामिन *m* 108
विटींग 120
विंटेज कार *f* 199
विंडशील्ड 205
विंड सर्फ़र 241
विंड सर्फ़िंग 241
विंडस्क्रीन *f* 198
विंडस्क्रीन वाइपर *m* 198
विंडो *f* 177
वितरक *m* 203
वितरण *m* 98
वित्त *m* 97
वित्तीय सलाहकार *m* 97
विनिमय केंद्र 97 *m*
विद्यालय *m* 162, 169,
299
विद्युत कंबल *m* 71
विद्युत ड्रिल *f* 78
विद्युत तार *m* 176
विद्युत रेलगाड़ी *f* 208
विधियां *f* 79, 159
विनिमय दर *f* 97
विपणन विभाग *m* 175
विपरीत प्रभाव 109
विभाग *m* 49, 169
विभाजक *m* 173, 194
विमान चालक *m* 190, 211
विमान परिचारिका *f* 190, 210
वियतनाम *m* 318
विराम *m* 256
विराम घड़ी *f* 234
विलंब *m* 209
विलायती पीपल *m* 296
विवाह *m* 26, 35
विवाह की पोशाक *f* 35
विवाह भोज *m* 26
विशारद *m* 169
विशेष 152
विषपान 46
विषाणु *m* 44
विषुवत *m* 283
विहार स्थल *m* 265
विश्वकोश *m* 163
विश्व मानचित्र *m* 312
विश्वविद्यालय *m* 299
वी गला 33
वीज़ा *m* 213
वीडियो गेम *m* 269
वीडियो फ़ोन *m* 99
वीथिका *f* 254
वीरवार *m* 306
वुड 233
वृत्त *m* 164
वृत्तचित्र *m* 178
वॉटर पोलो *m* 239
वेज 233
वेज बर्गर *m* 155
वेट सूट *m* 239
वेटिकन सिटी *m* 316
वेतन *m* 175
वेतनसूची *f* 175
वेधनी *f* 78
वेनेज़ुएला *m* 315
वेनेशियन ब्लाइंड 63
वेबसाइट *f* 177
वेलिंगटन बूट *m* 31
वेवलैंथ *m* 179
वेशभूषा *f* 29, 255
वेक्यूम क्लीनर *m* 77, 188
वैकल्पिक खिलाड़ी *m* 223
वैकल्पिक चिकित्सा *f* 54
वैक्यूम फ़्लास्क *m* 267
वैक्स *m* 41
वैगन *m* 199
वैज्ञानिक *m* 190
वैनिला (पौधा) *m* 132
वॉटरक्रेस *m* 123
वॉटर चेम्बर *m* 61
वॉटरप्रूफ़ 267
वॉटर स्कीअर *m* 241
वॉटर स्कीइंग 241

वॉफ़ल्स 157
वॉलपेपर m 82, 177
वॉलपेपर पेस्ट m 82
वॉलपेपर ब्रश m 82
वॉलपेपर लगाना tr 82
वॉली 231
वॉलीबॉल m 227
वॉलेट m 37
वॉल्यूम स्तर 269
वॉशबेसिन 72
वॉशर-ड्रायर m 76
वोदका m 145
वोदका और संतरा 151
वोल्टेज 60
व्यक्ति चित्र m 271
व्यंजन सूची f 148, 153, 154
व्यवसाय m 175, 188, 190
व्यवसायी m 175
व्यस्त 99
व्यस्त समय 209
व्यायाम m 251
व्यायाम चिकित्सा f 49
व्यायामशाला f 101
व्यायाम शिक्षा f 162
व्यायाम साइकिल f 250
व्यावसायिक श्रेणी f 211
व्यावसायिक सौदा m 175
व्यास 164
व्हाइट करंट 127
व्हिस्की 1 f 45
व्हीलचेयर f 48
व्हीलचेयर सुविधा 197
व्हेल f 290
वस्त्र m 38, 205

श, ष

शकरकंदी f 125
शंकु m 164
शंकुचि मछली f 120
शंकुवृक्ष m 86
शक्ति परीक्षा f 237
शटऑफ़ वॉल्व m 61
शटर रिलीज़ 270
शटल बस f 197
शतपुष्पिका f 133
शतरंज m 272
शताब्दी f 307
शनि m 280
शनिवार m 306
शफ़तालू m 126
शंबुक m 121, 295
शमीज़ f 35
शयन कक्ष m 70
शयन यान m 209
शरद f 307
शरद ऋतु f 31
शरदीय क्रीड़ाएं f 247
शरपत m 296
शराब की दुकान f 115
शरीर m 12
शरीर तंत्र m 19
शर्त f 273
शर्माना 25
शलग़म m 123, 124
शल्क m 294
शल्य कक्ष m 48
शल्य चिकित्सक m 48
शल्य चिकित्सा f 45, 48, 49
शहतीर f 186
शहद m 134
शहर m 298, 299
शहरी मकान m 58
शाखा f 175, 296
शादी करना itr 26
शादी का केक m 141
शारीरिक जांच f 45
शार्क f 294
शास्त्रीय संगीत m 255, 259
शिकंजा m 78
शिकंजी f 144
शिकायत f 94
शिकार m 119
शिखर m 300
शिमला मिर्च f 124
शियात्सु 54
शिरोवल्क m 39
शिविर m 267
शिविर लगाना tr 266
शिविर वाहन m 266
शिविर स्थल m 266
शिशु m 23, 30
शिशु अश्व 185
शिशु उत्पाद m 107
शिशुगृह m 74
शिशु जन्म m 53
शिशु देखभाल 74
शिशु पट्टा m 75
शिशु बतख़ f 185
शिशु मेंढक m 294
शिशु सील f 290
शिशु सूअर m 185
शिशु स्नान m 74
शिश्न m 21
शिश्नच्छद m 21
शीतल पेय m 144, 154
शीर्ष m 164
शीर्षक m 168
शीशा m 40, 71, 167
शीशा परखने की इकाई f 51
शुक्र m 280
शुक्रवार m 306
शुक्रवाहिनी f 21
शुक्राणु m 20
शुक्राशय m 21
शुतुरमुर्ग m 292
शुरुआत अवरोध 234
शुल्क मुक्त दुकान f 213
शूज़ पेस्ट्री f 140
शून्य m 230, 308
शूलपर्णी f 296
शेड m 85
शेयर m 97
शेयर दलाल m 97
शेयर पूंजी f 97
शेयर बाज़ार m 97
शेयर मूल्य m 97
शेरी 145
शेविंग फ़ोम m 73
शेल्फ़ f 106
शैम्पू m 38
शैम्पेन m 145
शैल 288
शैलियां f 239
शैली f 301
शॉट मारना tr 232
शॉट मारने का तरीक़ा 232
शॉर्ट वेव m 179
शॉवर m 72
शॉवर का पर्दा m 72
शॉवर जैल m 73
शॉवर दरवाज़ा m 72
शो जंपिंग 243
शोध निबंध m 169
शोध प्रबंध m 169
शोभायात्रा f 27
शोरबा m 158
शोरबे का मसाला m 132
शोल्डर पैड m 35
शोल्डर बैग m 37
शौक़िया मछली पकड़ना f 245
शौचालय m 61, 266
श्री f 23
श्रीदारु 296
श्रीमती f 23
श्रीलंका m 318
श्रृंगार मेज़ f 71
श्रेणी f 163
श्रेडर 172
श्रोणि f 17
श्रोणिक मांस m 121
श्वास छिद्र m 290
श्वास नली f 18, 19, 239
श्वास यंत्र m 109
श्वसन 19
षड्भुज m 164

स

सऊदी अरब m 318
संकट सूचक बत्ती f 201
संकुचन m 52
संकेतक m 198, 204
संक्रमण m 44
संक्रमण रहित 47
सख़्त 124, 129
संख्या f 226
संगमरमर m 288
संगीत m 162
संगीतकार m 191
संगीतमय जिमनास्टिक m 235
संगीत विद्यालय m 169
संगीत शैलियां f 259
संग्रह m 98
संग्रहालय m 261
संचार m 98
संचालक m 256
सजावट f 111, 141
सजावटी 87
सटा हुआ घर m 58
सड़क f 298
सड़क का किनारा m 194
सड़क निर्माण कार्य m 187, 195
सड़कें f 194
सड़न f 50
सड़ा हुआ 127
संतरा m 126
संतरे का जूस m 144, 149
संतान होना tr 26
सत्तर m 308
सत्तरवां m 309
सदमा m 47
सदमा लगना 25
संदर्भ m 303
सदाबहार m 86
संदिग्ध 94, 181
संदेश m 100
संध्या f 305
संध्याकालीन मेनू m 152
सनटैन लोशन m 265
सन बेड m 41
सन ब्लॉक m 108, 265
सनस्क्रीन 108
संपर्क करना tr 177
संपर्क टूटना 99
संपादक m 191
सप्तक m 256
सप्ताह m 306
सप्ताहांत 306
सफ़री पलंग f 266
सफ़री स्टोव m 267
सफ़ाई उपकरण m 77
सफ़ाई करना tr 77
सफ़ाई कर्मी m 188
सफ़ारी पार्क m 262
सफ़ेद m 39, 145, 272, 274
सफ़ेद चावल m 130
सफ़ेद चॉकलेट m 113
सफ़ेद ज़ीरा m 131
सफ़ेद बन 139
सफ़ेद भाग m 137
सफ़ेद मांस m 118
सफ़ेद राजमा m 131
सफ़ेद सरसों f 184
सफ़ेद स्पिरिट f 83
संबंध m 24
सबूत m 181
संबोधन m 23
सब्ज़ियां f 122, 124
सब्ज़ियों का बग़ीचा m 85
सब्ज़ियों के खेत m 182
सब्ज़ी काटने का तख़्ता m 68
सब्ज़ी विक्रेता m 188
सभा कक्ष m 174
सभा f 174
संभोग m 20
समकोणक m 165
समचतुर्भुज m 164
समतल तख़्ता वज्र m 80
समताप मंडल m 286
समन 180
समय m 234, 261, 304
समय पर 305
समय पूर्व 52
समय समाप्त 220
समय-सारणी f 209, 261
समय सूची f 197
समलंब m 164
समस्याएं f 271
समांगीकृत दूध m 137
समाचार m 178
समाचार पत्र विक्रेता m 112
समाचार पत्र m 112
समाचार वाचक m 179, 191
समानांतर m 165
समानांतर चतुर्भुज m 164
समानांतर छड़ें f 235
समाप्ति क्षेत्र m 220
समाप्ति तिथि f 109
समाप्ति रेखा f 226, 234
समारोह m 140
समारोह केक m 141
समीकरण m 165
समुद्र m 264
समुद्र किनारे मछली पकड़ना 245
समुद्र तट m 285
समुद्र में मछली पकड़ना 245
समुद्र सिंह m 290
समुद्री कछुआ m 293
समुद्री जहाज़ m 214
समुद्री झींगा m 121
समुद्री भोजन m 121
समुद्री लहरें f 241
समूह चिकित्सा f 55
सम्मोहन चिकित्सा f 55
संयुक्त अरब अमीरात m 318
संयुक्त राज्य अमेरिका m 314
संरक्षित 118, 143, 159
संरक्षित फल m 135
सरटक 294
सरपट चाल f 243
सरस फल m 296
सरीसृप m 293
सर्किट ट्रेनिंग 251
सर्दी f 31, 44
सर्पमणि f 289
सर्फ़ बोर्ड m 241
सर्फ़र m 241
सर्फ़िंग 241
सर्बिया m 316
सर्व 231
सर्वर m 176
सर्विस करना tr 231
सर्विस लाइन 230
सलाद f 149
सलाद पत्ता m 123
सलामी 142
सलून m 199

सवा एक 304
संवाहक *m* 204
संवेदनशील *m* 41
संशीतित 121
संसाधित अनाज *m* 130
ससुर *m* 23
सहयोगी *m* 24
सह-विमान चालक *m* 211
सहस्राब्दी *f* 307
सहायक *m* 24
सहायक रसोइया *m* 152
सहायक वस्तुएं *f* 36
सहारा रेगिस्तान *m* 313
सहेजना *tr* 177
सत्रहवां *m* 309
साइकिल *f* 206
साइकिल चलाना *tr* 207, 263
साइकिल लेन 206 *f*
साइट प्रबंधक कार्यालय *m* 266
साइड ऑर्डर 153
साइड की सड़क *f* 194
साइड ज़ीन *f* 242
साइड टेबल *f* 70
साइड डेक *m* 240
साइड लाइन 220, 226, 230
साइड लैम्प *m* 70
साइबेरिया *m* 313
साईस 243
साउंड तकनीशियन *m* 179
साउंड बूम *m* 179
साओ टोमे और प्रिंसिपे 317
साक्षात्कारकर्ता *m* 179
सागर *m* 282
सागर विलयन *m* 285
साग-सब्ज़ी *f* 107
साज-श्रृंगार *m* 40
साज सामान *m* 215
साठ *m* 308
साठवां *m* 309
सादू *m* 23
सातवां *m* 309
साथी *m* 23
सादी 145
सादी चॉकलेट 113
सान 81
सान मरीनो 316
सांप *m* 293
साप्ताहिक *m* 307
साफ़ रास्ता *m* 232
साबुत 129, 130, 132
साबुत ब्रेड *f* 139
साबुत मूंग *f* 131
साबुत सरसों *f* 135
साबुन *m* 73
साबुनदानी *f* 73
सामने की लाइट *f* 205
सामान *m* 79, 100, 187, 198, 213
सामान कक्ष *m* 196
सामान की चल पट्टी *f* 212
सामान की जगह *f* 209
सामान गाड़ी *f* 212
सामान वापसी 213
सामान विभाग *m* 104
सामान्य 39
सामान्य श्रेणी *f* 211
साम्राज्य *m* 315
सायंकाल *m* 305
सायबान *m* 148
सायरन *m* 94
सारस *m* 292
सार्डिन 120
सामन मछली *f* 120
सार्डीनिया *m* 316
सालगिरह *f* 26
साली *f* 23
सास *f* 23
सांस *f* 47
साहित्य *m* 162, 169
साही *f* 290
साहुल डोरी *f* 82
सिएरा लिओने *m* 317
सिंक *f* 61, 66
सिक्का *m* 97
सिक्का वापसी 99
सिंक्रोनाइज़्ड तैराकी *f* 239
सिगरेट *f* 112
सिगरेट की डिब्बी *f* 112
सिंगल 151
सिंगल कमरा *m* 100
सिंगल पलंग *f* 71
सिंगापुर *m* 318
सिगार *f* 112
सिंघाड़ा *m* 124
सिट-अप 251
सितंबर *m* 306
सिनेमा *m* 255, 299
सिनेमा हॉल *m* 255
सिफ़ारिश *f* 49
सिर *m* 12, 19
सिरका *m* 135, 142
सिर की चोट *f* 46
सिरदर्द *m* 44
सिरप *m* 109
सिर-पट्टा *m* 242
सिरप में बना 159
सिर से मारना *tr* 222
सिरहाना *m* 200
सिरा *m* 80, 210
सिरिंज *f* 109, 167
सिलना *tr* 277
सिलाई की टोकरी *f* 276
सिलाई चयन बटन *m* 276
सिलाई मशीन *m* 276
सिलेंडर *m* 202
सिले वस्त्र *m* 35 *m*
सिसिली *m* 316
सिस्टम 176
सिग्नल *m* 209 *m*
सीख *f* 68
सीख़चे *m* 74
सीखना *tr* 163
सीग *f* 291 *f*
सींचना *tr* 89, 90, 183
सीट *f* 61, 64, 204, 209, 210, 242, 254
सीट की पीठ *f* 210
सीट पोस्ट 206
सीट बेल्ट *f* 198, 211
सीडी प्लेयर *m* 268
सीढ़ियों का जंगला *m* 59
सीढ़ियों के गेट *m* 75
सीढ़ी *f* 82, 95, 186
सीढ़ीनुमा झूला *m* 263
सीध में 260
सीधा करना *tr/itr* 39
सीधा प्रसारण 178
सीधी *f* 165
सीधी दौड़ *f* 243
सीधे बाल *m* 39
सीप *f* 265
सीपी *f* 121
सी बास 120
सी ब्रीम 120
सीमा रेखा *f* 225
सीमा शुल्क चौकी *f* 216
सीमेंट *f* 186
सीमेंट मिक्सर *m* 186
सीरिंज से उल्व- द्रव निकालना 52
सीरियल *m* 156
सीरिया *m* 318
सील *f* 290
सीलबंद जार *m* 135
सीलेंट 83
सीवन 34
सीसा युक्त 199
सीसा रहित 199
सीसॉ 263
सुई लगाना 48
सुखाना *tr* 76
सुखाया हुआ 129
सुगंध चिकित्सा *f* 55
सुगंधित तेल *m* 55, 134 *m*
सुनहरा *m* 39
सुनहरा-भूरा *m* 39
सुनार *m* 188
सुनार की दुकान *f* 114
सुपर बाज़ार *m* 106
सुबह *f* 305
सुबह का नाश्ता *m* 156
सुरक्षा *f* 75, 212, 240
सुरक्षा कर्मी *m* 189
सुरक्षा चश्मा *m* 81, 167
सुरक्षा बैरियर *m* 246
सुरक्षा वज्र *m* 80
सुरक्षित 228
सुरक्षित करना *tr* 168
सुविधाजनक भोजन *m* 107
सूअर *m* 185
सूअर का मांस *m* 118
सूअर पालन केंद्र *m* 183
सूअरबाड़ा *m* 185
सूई *f* 109, 276
सूई की नोक *f* 277
सूई के नीचे की पत्ती *f* 276
सूक्ष्मदर्शी *m* 167
सूखा *m* 130, 286
सूखा अलूचा *m* 129
सूखा बंदरगाह *m* 217
सूखी घास *f* 184
सूखी चमड़ी *f* 293
सूखी फ्रांसबीन 131
सूखे पत्ते निकालना *tr* 91
सूखे फूल *m* 111
सूचना पट्ट *m* 173
सूचना स्क्रीन *f* 213
सूजन रोधी 109
सूजी *f* 130
सूंड़ *f* 291
सूडान *m* 317
सूती कपड़ा *m* 277
सूप *m* 153, 158
सूप का चम्मच *m* 65
सूप की प्लेट *f* 65
सूफ़ले *m* 158
सूफ़ले बर्तन *m* 69
सूमो कुश्ती *f* 237
सूरजमुखी *m* 184
सूरजमुखी का तेल *m* 134
सूरजमुखी के बीज *m* 131
सूरीनाम *m* 315
सूर्य *m* 280
सूर्यमुखी *m* 297
सूर्यास्त *m* 305
सूर्योदय *m* 305
सूर्य स्नान करना *tr* 264
सेकंड 304
सेकंड की सुई 304
सेट *m* 178, 254
सेंट किट्स और नेविस 314
सेंटर फ़ील्ड 228
सेंटर बोर्ड *m* 241
सेंट लूशिया 314
सेंट विन्सेंट और द ग्रेनाडिन्स 314
सेंटीमीटर *m* 310
सेंड ऑफ़ 223
सेनेगल 317
सेब *m* 126
सेब का जूस *m* 149
सेब की वाइन *f* 145
सेब सिरका *m* 135
सेम *f* 131
सेलेरी *f* 122
सेवाएं *f* 93, 101
सेवा प्रदाता *m* 177
सेवा वाहन *m* 212
सेवा सम्मिलित 152
सेवा सम्मिलित नहीं 152
सेवानिवृत्त होना *itr* 26
सेफ़्टी पिन *f* 47
सैकंड हैंड शॉप 115
सैक्सोफ़ोन *m* 257
सैट *m* 230
सैंडर *m* 78
सैंडविच *f* 155
सैंडविच काउंटर *m* 143
सैंडिल *f* 31, 37
सैनिक *m* 189
सैर-सपाटा *m* 260
सैनिटरी पैड *m* 108
सॉकर *m* 222
सॉकेट *m* 60, 80
सॉकेट रिंच *f* 80
सॉरेल पत्ती *f* 123
सॉर्बेट 141
सॉलवेंट *m* 83
सॉस *f* 135, 155
सॉस में 159
सॉसेज 155, 157
सॉसेजेस 118
सॉफ़्टवेयर *m* 176
सोआ *m* 122, 133
सोडा ब्रेड *f* 139
सोडा वॉटर *m* 144
सोनमाछी 294
सोना *itr* 71, 74
सोना *m* 289
सोनाटा *m* 256
सोने जाना *itr* 71
सोफ़ा *m* 62
सोफ़ा-कम-बेड 63
सोमवार *m* 306
सोमालिया *m* 317
सोयाबीन *m* 131
सोल मछली *f* 120
सोलहसत्रह 308
सोलोमन द्वीप समूह *m* 318
सोल्डर करने का तार *tr/itr* 79
सौ 308
सौतेला बेटा *m* 23
सौतेली बेटी *f* 23
सौतेले पिता *m* 23
सौतेली माता *f* 23
सौंदर्य प्रसाधन *m* 107
सौंदर्य *m* 40, 105
सौंदर्य उपचार *m* 41
सौंदर्य प्रसाधन *m* 38, 41
सौर मंडल *m* 280
सौवां *m* 309
स्कंधास्थि *f* 17
स्कर्ट *f* 30, 34
स्काइडाइविंग 248
स्कार्फ़ *m* 31
स्क्विड 121, 295
स्की 241, 246
स्कीइंग 246
स्कीइंग प्रतियोगिता 247
स्की कूद *f* 247
स्की जैकेट *f* 246
स्की पोल 246
स्की बूट *m* 246
स्की मार्ग *m* 246
स्कीयर *m* 246
स्की स्लोप 246
स्कूटर *m* 205
स्कूप *m* 68, 149
स्कूबा डाइविंग 239
स्कूल आरम्भ करना *tr* 26
स्कूलछात्र *m* 162

स्कूल छात्रा f 162
स्कूल बस f 196
स्कूल बस्ता m 162
स्केट 247
स्केट बोर्ड m 249
स्केट बोर्डिंग 249, 263
स्केट मछली f 120, 294
स्केटिंग करना tr 224
स्कैन m 48, 52
स्कैनर m 106, 176
स्क्रैबल m 272
स्क्वैश m 231
स्कॉच और पानी 151
स्कोर m 220
स्कोर बोर्ड m 225
स्क्रीन f 97, 176, 269
स्क्रीनवॉश m 199
स्क्रीन वॉश डिब्बा m 202
स्क्रोलबार m 177
स्क्वॉट m 251
स्खलनीय नली f 21
स्टंप m 225
स्टाउट m 145
स्टाफ़ m 256
स्टार एनीस 133
स्टार फ़िश f 295
स्टार्टर m 153
स्टिक f 224, 249
स्टीयरिंग f 201
स्टीरियो m 201, 269
स्टेडियम m 223
स्टेप मशीन f 250
स्टेपल्स m 173
स्टेप्लर m 173
स्टेबलाइज़र्स m 207
स्टैंड m 88, 205, 268
स्टॉक m 97
स्टॉक्स m 110
स्टॉप m 269
स्टॉप बटन m 197
स्टॉपर m 166
स्टॉल f 254
स्टोर निर्देशिका f 104
स्टोव m 66, 67
स्ट्राइक f 228
स्ट्रिंग f 230
स्ट्रीट लाइट f 298
स्ट्रीट स्टॉल m 154
स्ट्रीमिंग f 269
स्ट्रेच 251
स्ट्रेचर m 94
स्ट्रैप m 35
स्ट्रैप रहित पोशाक f 34
स्ट्रॉ 144, 154
स्ट्रॉबेरी f 127
स्ट्रॉबेरी मिल्कशेक 149
स्ट्रोक m 233, 239
स्ट्रोक्स m 231
स्तन m 12
स्तनधारी जीव m 290
स्तन पंप m 53
स्तनपान m 53
स्तनपान कराना tr/itr 53
स्तरित चट्टान m 288
स्तूपिका f 300
स्थान m 266
स्थान उपलब्ध 266
स्थिर 144
स्नातक m 169
स्नातक समारोह m 169
स्नातक होना itr 26
स्नातकोत्तर m 169
स्नान की चटाई f 72
स्नानघर m 72
स्नान स्थल m 266
स्नायु m 19, 50
स्नायु जाल m 17
स्नायु विज्ञान m 49
स्नूकर m 249
स्नैक बार m 148
स्नैक्स बार m 113
स्नो बोर्डिंग 247
स्नो मोबाइल m 247
स्पंज m 73, 74, 83
स्पंज केक m 140
स्पंज फ़िंगर 141
स्पार्क प्लग m 203
स्पिन f 230
स्पिरिट लेवल 80
स्पीकर m 176, 258, 268
स्पीकर स्टैंड m 268
स्पीड बोटिंग 241
स्पीड मीटर m 201
स्पीड स्केटिंग 247
स्पेन m 316
स्पेनिश सॉसेज 143
स्पैचुला m 68, 167
स्पॉट लाइट f 259
स्पोर्ट्स m 105
स्पोर्ट्स कार f 199
स्पोर्ट्स जैकेट f 33
स्पोर्ट्स ब्रा f 35
स्प्रिंग तुला f 166
स्प्रिंगबोर्ड m 235, 238
स्प्रे m 109
स्प्रे कैन m 311
स्फटिक m 289
स्मारक m 261
स्मार्टफ़ोन m 99, 176
स्मृति चिह्न m 260
स्मोक अलार्म m 95
स्प्लैशबैक m 66
स्याही f 275
स्याही पैड m 173
स्लाइड f 167
स्लाइसर m 139
स्लिंग पट्टी f 46
स्लिप f 35
स्लीप सूट m 30
स्लीपिंग बैग m 267
स्लेज गाड़ी f 247
स्लेज पर फिसलना 247
स्लेट f 288
स्लेटी f 39, 274
स्लोवाकिया m 316
स्लोवेनिया m 316
स्वचालित 200
स्वचालित दरवाज़ा m 196
स्वचालित सीढ़ियां f 104
स्वच्छ m 121
स्वर m 256
स्वर तंत्र m 19
स्वरमान m 256
स्वरलिपि f 255, 256
स्वर संगति f 256
स्वर्ण m 235
स्वस्थता f 250
स्वागत m 100
स्वागत अधिकारी m 100
स्वागतकर्ता m 190
स्वाज़ीलैंड m 317
स्वास्थ्य m 43
स्वास्थ्य आहार की
दुकान f 115
स्वास्थ्य केंद्र m 168
स्विच f 60
स्विट्ज़रलैंड m 316
स्विमसूट m 238
स्विस चार्ड m 123
स्वीडन m 316
स्वीडन का शलग़म m 125
स्वेटर m 33
स्वेट शर्ट 33
स्त्री f 12, 13, 20
स्त्री-रोग चिकित्सा f 49
स्त्री-रोग विशेषज्ञ m 52
स्त्री-स्वच्छता सामान m 108

ह

हंगरी m 316
हजामत f 73
हज़ारा m 89
हड्डी f 119
हड्डी टूटना 46
हत्था m 36, 88 187, 210
हथकड़ी f 94
हथेली f 15
हथौड़ा m 80, 187
हनीमून m 26
हनीसकल 297
हमला m 94
हर 165
हरा m 129, 274
हरा कद्दू m 124
हरा ज़ैतून m 143
हरा प्याज़ m 125
हरा सलाद m 158
हरा सलाद पत्ता m 123
हरितनील m 288
हरी चाय f 149
हरे-भरे पौधों से बना घेरा 85
हल रेखा f 183
हल्का भूनना tr 67
हल्का वायुयान m 211
हल्दी f 132
हवा f 241
हवाई 314
हवाई अड्डा m 212
हवाई डाक द्वारा 98
हवाई पट्टी f 212
हवा भरा गद्दा m 267
हवा भरी डोंगी f 215
हवा रोधक m 265
हवा लगाना tr 91
हवालात f 94
हंस m 119, 293
हंस का अंडा m 137
हंसना itr 25
हंसली f 17
हस्तकला उपकरण m 275
हस्ताक्षर m 96, 98
हाइ डेफ़िनिशन 269
हाई-फ़ाई सिस्टम m 268
हाईलाइट 39
हाईवे m 194
हाथ m 13, 15
हाथ का सामान m 211,
213
हाथ गाड़ी f 75
हाथी m 272, 291
हाथी दांत m 291
हाथी सील 290
हाथों की सफ़ाई 41
हाफ़ बोर्ड m 101
हार m 36
हारना itr 273
हारमोन m 20
हार्ड बोर्ड m 79
हार्डवेयर m 176
हार्डवेयर शॉप f 114
हार्प 256
हिंद महासागर m 313
हिम m 287
हिमनद m 284
हिमवर्षा f 286
हिम वाहन m 247
हिम स्खलन m 247
हिमालय m 313
हिरन m 291
हिस्सा m 64
हीटर m 60
हीटर कंट्रोल m 201
हीरा m 288
हुक m 187, 276
हुकुम 273
हुचका 89
हृदय m 18
हृदय एवं रक्तवाहिनी f 19
हृदय चिकित्सा f 49
हेज़लनट तेल m 134
हेमेटाइट m 289
हेयर डाई 40
हेयर ड्रायर m 38
हेयर ड्रेसर m 38
हेयर पिन f 38
हेयर बैंड m 38
हेयर-स्प्रे m 38
हेलमेट m 95
हैंग-ग्लाइडर m 248
हैंग-ग्लाइडिंग 248
हैंगिंग फाइल f 173
हैचबैक 199
हैट m 242, 265
हैड m 230
हैंड ड्रिल f 81
हैडफ़ोन m 268
हैंड बैग m 37
हैंड ब्रेक m 203
हैंडरेल 196
हैंडल m 106, 207, 230,
242
हैंडसेट 99 m
हैंडिल 200 m
हैंडीकैप 233 m
हैंडीकैम 260, 269 m
हैडॉक 120 m
हैती 314 m
हैदर 297 m
हैम 119, 143, 156 m
हैम बर्गर 155 m
हैमस्टर 290 m
हैलमेट 204, 206, 220,
225, 228, 236 m
हैलमेट का शीशा 205 m
हैलिबट क़तली 120 f
हैलीकॉप्टर 211 m
हैलोवीन 27
हॉकी 224 f
हॉकी स्टिक 224 f
हॉट चॉकलेट 144, 156 m
हॉट डॉग 155 m
हॉन्डुरास 314 m
हॉर्न 201, 204 m
हॉर्स 235 m
होटल 100, 264 m
होंठ 14 m
होम डिलीवरी 154 f
होम्योपैथी 55 f
होल 232 m
होल इन वन 233
होल पंच 173 m
होवर क्राफ़्ट 215 m
होश में लाना 47

त्र

त्रिकोणीय गरेबान m 32
त्रिकोनिका f 301
त्रिज्या f 164
त्रिनिदाद और टोबागो m 314
त्रिभुज m 164
त्रिमास m 52
त्रियंकी छत f 300
त्रिशिर पेशी f 16

acknowledgments • ābhār • आभार

DORLING KINDERSLEY would like to thank Christine Lacey for design assistance, Georgina Garner for editorial and administrative help, Kopal Agarwal, Polly Boyd, Sonia Gavira, Cathy Meeus, and Sant Sameer for editorial help, Claire Bowers for compiling the DK picture credits, Nishwan Rasool for picture research, and Suruchi Bhatia, Miguel Cunha, Mohit Sharma, and Alex Valizadeh for app development and creation.

The publisher would like to thank the following for their kind permission to reproduce their photographs:
Abbreviations key: (a-above; b-below/bottom; c-center; f-far; l-left; r-right; t-top)

123RF.com: Andrey Popov / andreypopov 23bc; Andriy Popov 34tl; Brad Wynnyk 172bc; Daniel Ernst 179tc; Hongqi Zhang 24cla, 175cr; Ingvar Bjork 60c; Kobby Dagan 259c; leonardo255 269c; Liubov Vadimovna (Luba) Nel 39cla; Ljupco Smokovski 75crb; Oleksandr Marynchenko 60bl; Olga Popova 33c; oneblink 49bc; Robert Churchill 94c; Roman Gorielov 33bc; Ruslan Kudrin 35bc, 35br; Subbotina 39cra; Sutichak Yachaingkham 39tc; Tarzhanova 37tc; Vitaly Valua 39tl; Wavebreak Media Ltd 188bl; Wilawan Khasawong 75cb; **Action Plus:** 224bc; **Alamy Images:** 154t; A.T. Willett 287bcl; Alex Segre 105ca, 195cl; Ambrophoto 24cra; Blend Images 168cr; Cultura RM 33r; Doug Houghton 107fbr; Hugh Threlfall 35tl; 176tr; Ian Allenden 48br; Ian Dagnall 270t; Levgen Chepil 250bc; Imagebroker 199tl, 249c; Keith Morris 178c; Martyn Evans 210b; MBI 175tl; Michael Burrell 213cra; Michael Foyle 184bl; Oleksiy Maksymenko 105tc; Paul Weston 168br; Prisma Bildagentur AG 246b; Radharc Images 197tr; RBtravel 112tl; Ruslan Kudrin 176tl; Sasa Huzjak 258t; Sergey Kravchenko 37ca; Sergio Azenha 270bc; Stanca Sanda (iPad is a trademark of Apple Inc., registered in the U.S. and other countries) 176bc; Stock Connection 287bcr; tarczas 35cr; Vitaly Suprun 176cl; Wavebreak Media ltd 39cl, 174b, 175tr; **Allsport/Getty Images:** 238cl; **Alvey and Towers:** 209 acr, 215bcl, 215bcr, 241cr; **Peter Anderson:** 188cbr, 271br. **Anthony Blake Photo Library:** Charlie Stebbings 114cl; John Sims 114tcl; **Andyalte:** 98tl; **Arcaid:** John Edward Linden 301bl; Martine Hamilton Knight, Architects: Chapman Taylor Partners, 213cl; Richard Bryant 301br; **Argos:** 41tcl, 66cbl, 66cl, 66br, 66bcl, 69cl, 70bcl, 71t, 77tl, 269tc, 270tl; **Axiom:** Eitan Simanor 105bcr; Ian Cumming 104; Vicki Couchman 148cr; **Beken Of Cowes Ltd:** 215cbc; **Bosch:** 76tcr, 76tc, 76tcl; **Camera Press:** 38tr, 256t, 257cr; Barry J. Holmes 148tr; Jane Hanger 159cr; Mary Germanou 259bc; **Corbis:** 78b; Anna Clopet 247tr; Ariel Skelley / Blend Images 52l; Bettmann 181tl, 181tr; Blue Jean Images 48bl; Bo Zauders 156t; Bob Rowan 152bl; Bob Winsett 247cbl; Brian Bailey 247br; Chris Rainer 247ctl; Craig Aurness 215bl; David H.Wells 249cbr; Dennis Marsico 274bl; Dimitri Lundt 236bc; Duomo 211tl; Gail Mooney 277ctcr; George Lepp 248c; Gerald Nowak 239b; Gunter Marx 248cr; Jack Hollingsworth 231bl; Jacqui Hurst 277cbr; James L. Amos 247bl, 191ctr, 220bcr; Jan Butchofsky 277cbc; Johnathan Blair 243cr; Jose F. Poblete 191br; Jose Luis Pelaez.Inc 153tc; Karl Weatherly 220bl, 247tcr; Kelly Mooney Photography 259tl; Kevin Fleming 249bc; Kevin R. Morris 105tr, 243tl, 243tc; Kim Sayer 249tcr; Lynn Goldsmith 258t; Macduff Everton 231bcl; Mark Gibson 249bl; Mark L. Stephenson 249tcl; Michael Pole 115tr; Michael S. Yamashita 247ctcl; Mike King 247cbl; Neil Rabinowitz 214br; Pablo Corral 115bc; Paul A. Sounders 169br, 249ctcl; Paul J. Sutton 224c, 224br; Phil Schermeister 227b, 248tr; R. W Jones 309; Richard Morrell 189bc; Rick Doyle 241ctr; Robert Holmes 97br, 277ctc; Roger Ressmeyer 169tr; Russ Schleipman 229; The Purcell Team 211ctr; Vince Streano 194t; Wally McNamee 220br, 220bcl, 224bl; Wavebreak Media LTD 191bc; Yann Arhus-Bertrand 249tl; **Demetrio Carrasco / Dorling Kindersley (c) Herge / Les Editions Casterman:** 112ccl; **Dorling Kindersley:** Banbury Museum 35c; Five Napkin Burger 152t; **Dixons:** 270cl, 270cr, 270bl, 270bcl, 270bcr, 270ccr; **Dreamstime.com:** Alexander Podshivalov 179tr, 191cr; Alexxl66 268tl; Andersastphoto 176tc; Andrey Popov 191bl; Arne9001 190tl; Chaoss 26c; Designsstock 269cl; Monkey Business Images 26clb; Paul Michael Hughes 162tr; Serghei Starus 190bc; **Education Photos:** John Walmsley 26tl; **Empics Ltd:** Adam Day 236br; Andy Heading 243c; Steve White 249cbc; **Getty Images:** 48bcl, 94tr, 100t, 114bcr, 154bl, 287tr; George Doyle & Ciaran Griffin 22cr; David Leahy 162tl; Don Farrall / Digital Vision 176c; Ethan Miller 270bl; Inti St Clair 179bl; Liam Norris 188br; Sean Justice / Digital Vision 24br; **Dennis Gilbert:** 106tc; **Hulsta:** 70t; **Ideal Standard Ltd:** 72r; **The Image Bank/ Getty Images:** 58; **Impact Photos:** Eliza Armstrong 115cr; Philip Achache 246t; **The Interior Archive:** Henry Wilson, Alfie's Market 114bl; Luke White, Architect: David Mikhail, 59tl; Simon Upton, Architect: Phillippe Starck, St Martins Lane Hotel 100bcr, 100br; **iStockphoto.com:** asterix0597 163tl; EdStock 190br; RichLegg 26bc; SorinVidis 27cr; **Jason Hawkes Aerial Photography:** 216t; **Dan Johnson:** 35r; **Kos Pictures Source:** 215cbl, 240tc, 240tr; David Williams 216b; **Lebrecht Collection:** Kate Mount 169bc; **MP Visual.com:** Mark Swallow 202t; **NASA:** 280cr, 280ccl, 281tl; **P&O Princess Cruises:** 214bl; **P A Photos:** 181br; **The Photographers' Library:** 186bl, 186bc, 186t; **Plain and Simple Kitchens:** 66t; **Powerstock Photolibrary:** 169tl, 256t, 287tc; **PunchStock:** Image Source 195tr; **Rail Images:** 208c, 208 cbl, 209br; **Red Consultancy:** Odeon cinemas 257br; **Redferns:** 259br; Nigel Crane 259c; **Rex Features:** 106br, 259tc, 259tr, 259bl, 280b; Charles Ommaney 114tcr; J.F.F Whitehead 243cl; Patrick Barth 101tl; Patrick Frilet 189cbl; Scott Wiseman 287bl; **Royalty Free Images:** Getty Images/Eyewire 154bl; **Science & Society Picture Library:** Science Museum 202b; **Science Photo Library:** IBM Research 190cla; NASA 281cr; **SuperStock:** Ingram Publishing 62; Juanma Aparicio / age fotostock 172t; Nordic Photos 269tl; **Skyscan:** 168t, 182c, 298; Quick UK Ltd 212; **Sony:** 268bc; **Robert Streeter:** 154br; **Neil Sutherland:** 82tr, 83tl, 90t, 118c, 188ctr, 196tl, 196tr, 299cl, 299bl; **The Travel Library:** Stuart Black 264t; **Travelex:** 97cl; **Vauxhall:** Technik 198t, 199tl, 199tr, 199cl, 199cr, 199ctcl, 199ctcr, 199tcl, 199tcr, 200; **View Pictures:** Dennis Gilbert, Architects: ACDP Consulting, 106t; Dennis Gilbert, Chris Wilkinson Architects, 209tr; Peter Cook, Architects: Nicholas Crimshaw and partners, 208t; **Betty Walton:** 185br; **Colin Walton:** 2, 4, 7, 9, 10, 28, 40l, 42, 56, 92, 95c, 99tl, 99tcl, 102, 116, 120t, 138t, 146, 150t, 160, 170, 191ctcl, 192, 218, 252, 260br, 260l, 261tr, 261c, 261cr, 271cbl, 271cbr, 271ctl, 278, 287br, 302.

DK PICTURE LIBRARY:
Akhil Bahkshi; Patrick Baldwin; Geoff Brightling; British Museum; John Bulmer; Andrew Butler; Joe Cornish; Brian Cosgrove; Andy Crawford and Kit Hougton; Philip Dowell; Alistair Duncan; Gables; Bob Gathany; Norman Hollands; Kew Gardens; Peter James Kindersley; Vladimir Kozlik; Sam Lloyd; London Northern Bus Company Ltd; Tracy Morgan; David Murray and Jules Selmes; Musée Vivant du Cheval, France; Museum of Broadcast Communications; Museum of Natural History; NASA; National History Museum; Norfolk Rural Life Museum; Stephen Oliver; RNLI; Royal Ballet School; Guy Ryecart; Science Museum; Neil Setchfield; Ross Simms and the Winchcombe Folk Police Museum; Singapore Symphony Orchestra; Smart Museum of Art; Tony Souter; Erik Svensson and Jeppe Wikstrom; Sam Tree of Keygrove Marketing Ltd; Barrie Watts; Alan Williams; Jerry Young.

Additional photography by Colin Walton.

Colin Walton would like to thank:
A&A News, Uckfield; Abbey Music, Tunbridge Wells; Arena Mens Clothing, Tunbridge Wells; Burrells of Tunbridge Wells; Gary at Di Marco's; Jeremy's Home Store, Tunbridge Wells; Noakes of Tunbridge Wells; Ottakar's, Tunbridge Wells; Selby's of Uckfield; Sevenoaks Sound and Vision; Westfield, Royal Victoria Place, Tunbridge Wells.

Restructuring Schools with Technology

Linda Roehrig Knapp

Allen D. Glenn
University of Washington

Allyn and Bacon
Boston • London • Toronto • Sydney • Tokyo • Singapore

For all those teachers who are trying to restructure their classrooms with technology—it's worth the many extra hours of work.
For Michael, Justin, Molly, and Abby—thanks for your help and your patience.

Vice President, Education: Nancy Forsyth
Marketing Manager: Kathy Hunter
Production Administrator: Marjorie Payne
Editorial Assistant: Kate Wagstaffe
Cover Administrator: Linda Knowles
Composition Prepress/Buyer: Linda Cox
Manufacturing Buyer: Aloka Rathnam
Editorial-Production Service: Chestnut Hill Enterprises

Library of Congress Cataloging-in-Publication Data

Knapp, Linda Roehrig.
Restructuring schools with technology / Linda Roehrig Knapp, Allen D. Glenn.
p. cm.
Contents: Includes bibliographical references and index.
ISBN 0-205-15799-8
1. Educational technology—United States. 2. Educational change—United States. I. Glenn, Allen D. II. Title.
LB1028.3.K63 1996
371.3'078—dc20 95-5118
CIP

Printed in the United States of America

10 9 8 7 6 5 4 3 2 00 99 98 97 96

CONTENTS

Preface vii

PART I *Theory & Practice: REVIEW, RETHINK, RESTRUCTURE Conventional Beliefs and Practices in Education* 1

1 **Thinking About Instruction in a Different Way** 3
Skills and Understandings for Tomorrow's Graduates 4
Restructuring Schools 6
Technology's Role in Restructuring Classrooms 12
Summary 13
References 13

2 **Technologies for Restructured Classrooms** 14
Role of Technology in Restructuring Classrooms 15
General Role of Technology 15 • Implications of Using Technology for the Teacher 17
Creating an Environment for Effective Use of Technology 20
Why Be an Innovative Teacher in a Restructured Classroom? 21
References 22

3 **Foundations for Change: Student Performance and Classroom Structure** 24
Power of Computer Technology 25
Student Attitudes 25 • Student Performance 26
A Case for Using Computer Technology in Restructured Classrooms 27
Communication Support and Skill Building 28 • Developing Research Skills 28 • Increasing Problem-Solving Abilities 29 • Learning through Simulated Environments 29 • Distance Learning 30 • A Comment about the Teacher's Role 30

How Many Computers are Enough? 31
The Power of Using Video 33
Communicates Information 33 • Influences Attitudes and Behaviors 34
The Case for Including TV and Video in the School Curriculum 36
Teaching Critical Viewing Skills and Visual Literacy 36 • Television and Video as Educational Resources 37
Interactive Video 39
Concluding Thoughts 40
References 40

PART II *Implementation: REVIEW, RETHINK, RESTRUCTURE Curriculum & Instruction* 43

4 Instructional Approaches across the Curriculum 45
Teaching Students How to Write for All Disciplines 45
Teaching Students How to Critique and Revise Their Work 47
Teaching Multimedia Composing and Editing Skills 49
Composing a Multimedia Presentation 49 • Editing a Multimedia Presentation 51
Effective Use of Student Collaborative Groups 52
Team Teaching Using Interdisciplinary Curricula 57
Distance Learning: Using Technology to Teach Students in Distant Locations 58
Using Videotapes in the Classroom 60
Using Television: Channel One, CNN Newsroom, or Other Specialized Programming 61
Using Alternative Assessments 62
Outcome-Based Education 62 • Performance-Based Assessment 63 • Authentic Assessment 63 • Exhibitions 64 • Portfolios 65 • Video Assessment 65
References 67

5 Communication 68
Rationale 68
Communication Skills 68 • The Importance of Teaching Communication Skills 69 • The Added Value of Using Technology for Communication 69
Classroom Scenarios and Other Suggestions for Implementation 71
Elementary School Newspaper 71 • High School Newspaper 74 • Video Yearbook 76 • Writing Academy 77 • An Elementary Cross-Disciplinary Communication Program 78 • Communication and Critical Thinking 81 • Videotape Projects: Middle School 82 • Videotape Projects: High School 83 • Interactive Video Projects: Middle School 86 • Interactive Video Projects:

High School 87 • Communication Through Visual Arts and Music 88
References 90

6 **Problem Solving 97**
Rationale 97
Problem-Solving Skills 98 • The Importance of Teaching Problem-Solving Skills 98 • The Added Value of Using Technology for Solving Problems 99
Classroom Scenarios and Other Suggestions for Implementation 99
Teaching Problem-Solving with Specialized Software 100 • Tool Software for More General Use 105 • Comprehensive Interdisciplinary Projects not Associated with any Particular Type of Software 109

7 **Inquiry 111**
Rationale 111
The Process of Inquiry 112 • The Importance of Teaching Structured Inquiry 113 • The Added Value of Using Technology for Inquiry 114
Classroom Scenarios and Other Suggestions for Implementation 114
Generic Technology 115 • Research Tools: Inquiry and the Modern School Library 121 • Specialized Curriculum Software 126
References 127

8 **Critical Thinking 128**
Rationale 128
Critical Thinking Skills 129 • The Importance of Teaching Critical Thinking Skills 129 • The Added Value of Using Technology for Critical Thinking 130
Classroom Scenarios and Other Suggestions for Implementation 132
Emotive Language 132 • Responsible Persuasive Writing and Critical Analysis of Persuasive Arguments 135 • Teaching Film Techniques and Critical Thinking Through Television 138 • Current Events as an Approach to Teaching Critical Thinking 140 • An Interdisciplinary Study of 19th Century America 142 • Critical Thinking and the Use of Statistics 144 • Critical Analysis of Visual Perspectives 145
References 146

9 **Basic Skills 147**
Rationale 147
Basic Skills 147 • The Importance of Teaching Basic Skills while Involving Children in Doing Real Work that Requires Those Skills 148 • The Added Value of Using Technology to Teach Basic Skills 149
Classroom Scenarios and Other Suggestions for Implementation 150
Reading 151 • Integrated Reading and Writing 151 • Writing Stories: Basic Plot Structure 152 • Writing Essays:

Topic Sentences and Coherent Paragraphs 154 • Writers' Tools 156 • English as a Second Language (ESL) 156 • Mathematics 157 • Specialized Technology for Mathematics and Language Skills: Integrated Learning Systems 159

10 Beyond the Classroom: Implementation in the school, district, state 162
Rationale 162
Restructuring a School 162
Restructuring a District 166
Restructuring State Policies 171
How Educators Can Influence Politicians and Their School Reform Policies 174

PART III *Reflection: REVIEW & RETHINK Restructured Beliefs and Practices 177*

11 National Issues and the Role of Technology 179
Standards and Assessment 179
America 2000 180 • The New Standards Project 184 • Critical Issues 187 • Standards and Assessments in a Restructured School with Technology 189
Teacher Preparation, Continued Staff Development, and the Professionalization of Teaching 191
A Vision for Schools of the 21st Century 191 • Preparing Professionals to Teach in Today's and Tomorrow's Schools 198 • Continuing Education for Working Professionals 202
Decentralization/Site-Based Management 203
School Choice 206
Ability Grouping/Tracking 210
Multicultural Education 213
References 215

12 The Process of Change 216
Teaching and Learning in Restructured, Technology-Rich Classrooms 216
What We Have Learned about the Change Process 217 • Moving Ahead . . . Ready, Set, Go! 221
References 224

Index 225

PREFACE

The United States is in the midst of restructuring its education system. Politicians, business men and women, and parents are calling for change. They contend that educators must rethink how children are educated, if all children are to be successful learners and be prepared for life in a global, technological society.

The federal government has taken an active role in the education reform movement. Former President Bush and President Clinton both introduced major educational initiatives to set national standards, clarify student performance, and support innovative models. Federal financial support for innovative districts has been provided, and legislation has been passed in Congress. In the coming decade national government policies will continue to shape the school reform movement.

At the state level, all fifty states are involved in educational reform. Governors have lead the way in these efforts by pushing for the specification of student learning outcomes, different methods of assessment, different school organization, and other initiatives to insure that U.S. students are better prepared than ever before. For example, in the state of Washington, a Governor's Council on Education Reform and Funding introduced a broad-based plan to reform all of K–12 education and teacher education. Whether it be Washington, Florida, Maine, Kentucky, or Hawaii, legislators, educators, and citizens are debating issues of education reform.

Locally, school districts are introducing district level initiatives focusing on site-based management, integrated curriculum, and multimedia technologies as ways to assist all educators in rethinking school structure, instruction, and student learning. All are clarifying student learning outcomes and examining the curriculum to insure that each outcome is integrated into the curriculum across grade levels.

An integral component of restructuring schools is technology. Almost all schools now have computers, printers, VCRs, CD-ROMs, videodiscs, and cable network links. While not creating the revolution in learning once predicted, emerging technologies are steadily increasing their presence in classrooms and reshaping what and how students learn and the way teachers think about teaching, learning, and organizing the classroom.

As educators move through the 1990s, it will be the combination of the rethinking of the structure of the schools and the merging of technologies into this restructured environment that will offer the best hope for the renewal of our schools. This book is about the role technology plays in creating the classroom of today and tomorrow. It is for those who are interested in changing the way students learn. It is a practical book for educators who are interested in infusing technology into learning. It is about rethinking the way we educate our children and youth.

ACKNOWLEDGMENTS

A sincere thank you to the individuals and publishers who granted permission for us to use information from their published works in our book. Thank you to Apple Computer's Learning Technologies Group for allowing us to paraphrase from research reports Linda previously wrote while working there, and Apple Computer, Inc., for permitting us to include interview information she previously reported for publication in Apple's *Curriculum Software Guides* and in *Apple Education News*. Thanks to Shoreline Public School District in Washington State for letting us reuse information Linda gathered and reported in a series of public reports about the district's use of educational technology. Thank you to The Puget Sound Educational Consortium (PSEC) for allowing us to use information Linda collected and wrote in a pamphlet published for their membership. Thank you University of Washington College of Education for letting us use information from your guiding assumptions, program principles, and specific objectives of the new teacher education program. Thanks to *Education Week* for permission to use information from their special report, "A Matter of Choice: The Debate Over Schools and the Marketplace." And thanks to Simon & Schuster for granting permission for us to use material from Linda's book, *The Word Processor and the Writing Teacher.*

Thank you to: Houghton Mifflin for permission to use excerpts from *Horaces' School* by Theodore Sizer. Copyright © 1992 by Theodore R. Sizer. Reprinted by permission of Houghton Mifflin Company. All rights reserved; Carnegie Foundation for permission to reprint the scenario of an ideal classroom in their report, "A Nation Prepared: Teachers for the 21st Century," 1986. The Carnegie Foundation for the Advancement of Teaching. Reprinted with permission; Yale University Press for permission to use information from *Keeping Track: How Schools Structure Inequality,* by Jeannie Oakes. Copyright © 1985 by Yale University; Harvard University Press for permission to paraphrase information from *Mind and Media: The Effects of Television, Video Games, and Computers,* by Patricia Marks Greenfield. Copyright (c) 1984 by Patricia Marks Greenfield. Reprinted by permission of Harvard University Press; Teachers College Press for permission to paraphrase information from *Designing Groupwork: Strategies for the Heterogeneous Classroom, Third Edition,* by Elizabeth G. Cohen. Copyright © 1994 by Elizabeth G. Cohen.

PART I

THEORY & PRACTICE REVIEW, RETHINK, RESTRUCTURE

Conventional Beliefs and Practices in Education

All across the United States there appears to be a growing consensus among educators and the public that we need to seriously examine our public schools. The question most often being asked is, "Are today's schools preparing students for tomorrow's changing world?" Some vocal critics suggest they are not and massive changes must take place immediately if the United States is to remain a leading nation. Others contend that the majority of the schools are doing a good job. The truth, as always, lies somewhere in between those two positions. Most educators would contend, however, that schools do need to seriously rethink the current system because of the many changes that are taking place in society. Restructuring education therefore is in the public spotlight.

The restructuring movement, like any other, has many different interpretations and implementations. This book illustrates the movement as seen by those educators who advocate major changes in *what* students learn (how to find information, think about it, and synthesize it, rather than how to memorize it), and *how* students learn (through exploration, collaborative groupwork, and critical examination, rather than acquiring information primarily from teachers and textbooks). They also believe that technology plays an important role in this new approach to teaching and learning. The following three chapters introduce a restructured approach to schooling that addresses the needs of today's learners and describes how technology can significantly improve teaching and learning as well as the institutions that support them.

1

THINKING ABOUT INSTRUCTION IN A DIFFERENT WAY

Americans have high expectations for their schools. They expect schools to teach students basic skills, prepare them for the world of work or higher education, and teach them to be responsible citizens in a democracy. Such beliefs in intellectual, vocational, personal and social values were present in the early days of the country and remain true today. As noted educator John Goodlad (1984) says, when Americans think about schools, they "want it all." They want schools to prepare young people for the future, and when the future becomes threatened, citizens believe schools should provide the answers. If they do not, they believe schools ought to change.

Americans, again, are looking to education for meeting the challenges facing the United States. The decade of the 1990s appears to be quite unsettling. Where jobs once seemed secure and abundant, downsizing and scarcity are common. National trade agreements and emerging foreign economies eliminate jobs held by family members for generations. Old political foes have collapsed and have been replaced by internal conflicts in places not familiar to many. And, increasing diversity and social upheavals create tensions in an already tense society. To make matters worse, some critics contend that U.S. students do not measure up to their peers in other countries. How can the United States remain a leader, critics ask, if our schools are failing? Some of these critical statements are overgeneralizations and a vigorous debate has taken place between critics and educators about the overall quality of the schools. The truth is that some schools are doing an outstanding job of preparing some students for the 21st Century; however, a growing number of schools are not preparing students and, in far too many cases, students of color appear to be falling father behind. See the comments on foundations for change in Box 1-1.

Whether one believes that U.S. schools are in crisis, education reform is at the heart of the debate about the future. Some critics are calling for dramatic changes that would do away with schools as we now know them and provide new educational alternatives. Others seek a renewed educational system as the means of addressing U.S. problems and leading its citizens to a more productive future. Throughout this debate, schools continue to grapple with the real issues of trying to prepare citizens for the rapidly-changing world in which they live. Many are exploring new and exciting ways to help students learn. Others continue as they have in the past, perpetuating a view of schooling quite comfortable to someone who graduated many, many years ago. Whether a "friend or foe" of education, everyone believes a well-educated citizenry is the key to the future and these future citizens need different essential learning outcomes.

SKILLS AND UNDERSTANDINGS FOR TOMORROW'S GRADUATES

The story is told that when John Dewey was establishing his laboratory school at the University of Chicago he had a great deal of difficulty in finding the appropriate furniture for the school. He wanted multipurpose furniture—furniture that could be moved around and used for a variety of purposes. What he found was school furniture designed for listening. Dewey did not want his students just to sit and listen, because listening meant passivity and absorption (Ginger, 1958). He wanted active learners. His view of how students learned and what they were to learn differed dramatically from many educators of the time.

So it is today. Educators and citizens are once again examining the curriculum and the way the school is organized. Proponents of educational change contend that schools must change from an emphasis on the recall of knowledge to enabling students to think abstractly, problem-solve, collaborate with others, and seek out creative solutions. Educators, according to critics, must stop teaching facts, skills, and concepts as if they were furniture of the mind to be acquired, occasionally dusted, and used for a lifetime. Instead, educators need to help students learn to think for themselves and be able to create knowledge. Teachers must get out of the "information-providing" business and into the "question-asking" business, prompting students to seek information

BOX 1-1 Foundations for Change

The Need to Restructure Education

The traditional school system was designed for a time when broken families were unusual unless a parent had died. Parents pushed their children to excel; mothers stayed at home; commercial television didn't exist; drugs were practically unknown.

> *The traditional model of education is dependent for its success on at least three conditions: a cohesive family and social structure; a willingness to accept educating the vast majority of children to only a low level [in 1940 only 20% of students graduated from high school].*
>
> *In the 1940s and 1950s dropouts dropped into a different world. Decent-paying jobs were available to unskilled workers . . . a grade school dropout could still work his way up, and a high school dropout could almost count on being able to afford a house . . . Times have changed.*
>
> [Albert Shanker, *Phi Delta Kappan*]

> *Critics argue that powerful institutional forces have combined to reinforce a very limited model of teaching and learning in most schools. This model has come to be characterized as "Teaching is telling, knowledge is facts, and learning is recall" (Cohen, 1988). For most advocates of restructured schools this model is obsolete . . . in terms of the kind of knowledge required to participate in an advanced post-industrial economy.*
>
> [Richard Elmore, *Restructuring Schools*]

What Students Need to Learn

> *We should want every student to know how mountains are made, and that for most actions there is an equal and opposite reaction. They should know who said 'I am the state' and who said 'I have a dream.' They should know about subjects and predicates, about isosceles triangles and ellipses. They should know where the Amazon flows and what the First Amendment means. They should know about the Donner Party and slavery, and Shylock, Hercules, and Abigail Adams, where Ethiopia is, and why there is a Berlin Wall. . . .*
>
> [William J. Bennett speaking as U.S. Secretary of Education, in an address to the National Press Club]

> *The information explosion changes the nature of knowing from the ability to recall information to the ability to define problems, retrieve information selectively, and solve problems flexibly. Rapid advance changes the nature of learning from the need to master topics in class to the need to learn autonomously. Educated citizens need to know how to revise their ideas and how to locate and synthesize information.*
>
> [Marcia Linn, *Establishing a Research Base for Science Education*]

and learn to process it. Education goals must shift from facts and formulae to assisting young people to *find* facts and *develop* strategies to solve problems they will confront in the future. Table 1-1 summarizes some of the changes expected in schools.

The majority of today's classroom teachers do not oppose the changes presented in Table 1-1. In fact, many teachers have been moving in these directions for a number of years. For example, the 1960s also witnessed a major emphasis in discovery learning and inquiry teaching. New curriculum materials, based on the key concepts and generalizations of the disciplines, were introduced into the schools. Consequently, many teachers across the nation would find comfort in these goals. The question is "How do we restructure?"

As Americans consider restructuring the educational system, it is critical to remember that there is no simple answer or quick fix. To assume so is to not understand the complexity of the problem. In 1991, for example, there were 45 million students enrolled in the schools in the United States. These students attended 80,000 schools in 15,512 school districts scattered across fifty states. Over 2,550,000 teachers were involved in providing the education to these students. Bringing about change in such a complex system is a daunting task.

To achieve these revitalized educational goals, educators must think carefully about how schools are structured, the manner in which teachers teach, the organization of the curriculum, classroom organization, assessment techniques, and the use of technology. Educators must (1) redesign curriculum and instruction to promote problem solving and deeper understanding, (2) empower schools to design their own structure and decision-making processes, and (3) assist schools in becoming more accountable to parents and the community. Schools must become intellectual environments for students and staff—places where teachers are knowledgeable and work with students in the learning process; places where students are helped to learn as much as they possibly can, and if they fall behind or have difficulty learning, they can get help; and places filled with adults who care, mentor and support learning. These schools must be new organizations whether housed in old buildings or in new creative structures where architecture and learning create an integrated, community learning environment.

RESTRUCTURING SCHOOLS

It is important to remember that today's schools are organized the way they are because society has shaped them over the years. For example,

TABLE 1-1 Renewing American Education: Recommended Changes

	Conventional Schools	Restructured Schools
Learning	Students learn by absorbing information and skills presented through listening to teachers' lectures and reading textbooks.	Students learn by constructing their own knowledge through inquiry, experience, teachers, textbooks, and other resources.
Teaching	Teachers introduce information and skills, provide exercises to practice skills and memorize information, and check students' ability to remember these lessons.	Teachers engage students in activities that require them to think critically, solve problems, and seek answers to their own questions. Teachers serve as model learners, mentors, coaches, and resources.
Curriculum	Curriculum emphasizes mastery of skills and concepts through a curriculum divided into subject areas. Students are sometimes assigned to upper and lower tracks according to how well they do on specific tests.	Curriculum promotes student inquiry, and is designed to engage students in solving real problems that extend into all subject areas. In-depth knowledge of important concepts is emphasized.
Classrooms	Classrooms are primarily isolated settings where teachers deliver information, and students practice skills and answer questions. The focus is on the individual and competition.	Classrooms are multipurpose rooms where learners engage in research and problem-solving activities related to specific topics of study. The focus is on cooperation and team building.
Assessment	Assessment focuses on short answer and essay tests that emphasize the ability to recall information, rather than understand it or apply it in some meaningful way.	Assessment focuses on student demonstrations of their ability to express, apply and defend knowledge and skills. Students also have opportunities for self-assessment, and the overall attitude is one of continual improvement and in-depth learning.
Technology	Educational "technologies" have traditionally included pencils and paper, chalkboards, textbooks, manipulatives, and other resources that help students develop basic skills, concepts, and generalizations.	A variety of technologies are now available to assist learners in the creation of knowledge and skills. Many of the these new technologies can support research, analysis, problem-solving, and communication processes more effectively than the traditional resources.

after World War II, schools were asked to prepare young persons for careers in the industrial world. They responded by creating schools based on factory models where students were often known as products and were sorted into various categories, such as vocational and college preparatory. Over the years, schools were reshaped by a baby boom that brought thousands of young people into the school system, a civil rights movement that integrated the classroom, and a science and mathematics reform effort created by the 1957 launching of the Soviet Sputnik satellite. Schools responded to these societal changes by adapting to the calls for reform.

Once again, schools are being asked to change to meet the immediate and future needs of tomorrow's graduates. Schools are being asked to rethink the way they are structured, the curriculum, and instructional strategies. Critics suggest that far too often educators start with a set of givens—school-day organization, standard curriculum, and length of school year—and let those shape how and what students learn. Schools must focus more on the skills and understandings students need for the information age, including higher level thinking, collaborative problem-solving, and fostering an ability to create new knowledge.

Many school systems across the country are adopting an *outcome-based education* (OBE) model as the basis for their restructuring efforts. This model involves first identifying desired learning outcomes for students and then determining the most appropriate instructional organization. The organization then shapes what students need to do and the time needed to achieve these outcomes. In shaping these programs, OBE proponents contend that all students can learn, success influences self-concept which in turn influences learning, instruction can be directly related to improved learning, and specific conditions can be established to enhance the learning process.

The outcome-based philosophy is the driving force for much of the current reform effort across the nation. Federal and state educational organizations are using the concepts to determine policy decisions, and local school districts are redefining curriculum to represent essential student performance goals. It is too early to determine the impact of this movement on learning and organization. As more schools restructure, more data will be available to judge the efficaciousness of such a model.

What is evident is that the organizational structure of U.S. schools is currently being questioned. Whether or not one views the current system as effective, those who look to the future are asking if schools are organized properly, whether or not all schools should be organized in the same manner, and whether or not schools should have more control over their organization and decision-making policies. Restructuring the way schools are organized will influence the teaching and learning that occurs there.

Educators are also being asked to rethink the manner in which students are taught and learn. As noted in Table 1-1, teaching and learning in tomorrow's classrooms must focus on engaging students in activities to help them construct their own knowledge. A shift must take place from acquiring to constructing knowledge. Outstanding teachers understand the complexity of teaching and continually seek to find more effective methods of assisting students to learn. Often they are frustrated in this process by their own lack of knowledge and experience with such methods, the manner in which schools are organized, and societal factors that impact the lives of their students.

A careful study of schools by John Goodlad (1984) found that in far too many schools teachers focus on having students recall facts, concepts, and formulae through lectures, technology, and textbooks. Students' knowledge base is equal to the amount of information they have accumulated and their ability to recall and communicate it. The teacher's primary roles are that of presenting information, providing exercises for students to practice skills and memorize facts, concepts or generalizations, and then evaluating the students' ability to remember the information.

Recently research by cognitive psychologists has brought into question this traditional instructional strategy. Studies suggest that learners develop their own understandings based on their own experiences and observations. Students learn, not by listening to information presented by others, but by actively manipulating and synthesizing information in such a way that it complements and expands existing understandings. Learners constantly interpret new information based on their own knowledge base; consequently, a student's failure to learn may be more due to their own misunderstandings rather than a failure to absorb new information. (See Box 1-2, Foundations for Change.)

This newly acquired information on how students learn clearly indicates that the teacher's role must change. The conventional lecture-practice-recall instructional model needs to be replaced by one that assists students to find and put information together in unique and different ways, to critically analyze it, and to relate the information to their own knowledge and skills. The industrial age has been replaced by the information age. A knowledge of facts is no longer as essential as the ability to creatively solve problems and continue learning throughout life. Tomorrow's citizens must be able to take raw data, continually search for new ways to represent reality and solve problems. To achieve

BOX 1-2 Foundations for Change

How Children Learn

> *Recent research on learning by cognitive scientists has demonstrated quite convincingly that individuals learn by constructing their own understandings based on personal observation and experience, rather than by remembering what others tell them. When teachers present information, learners modify it to fit their existing perceptions. If their perceptions are not realistic, as is often the case, their knowledge continues to grow, but distorted by their fundamental misconceptions. Students' problems arise, therefore, not from failure to absorb information, but from inability to detect and correct fundamental misconceptions. Consequently, teaching involves helping students analyze and restructure their own understandings, rather than simply providing correct information and appropriate concepts.*
> [Marcia Linn, *Establishing a Research Base for Science Education*]

> *Some students need more time to complete a task than others, and most learn better through one method than another. Some learn best by reading chapters in a book, others by watching and listening to a videotape, and still others by direct experience. Some children comprehend new material most readily when they analyze it in a teacher-led seminar, others when they teach it to younger students or when they grapple with it alone. Some students can master a concept the first time around because they have prior knowledge that has established a context for the unfamiliar material. Others need two tries or three or more and opportunities to see that beliefs they have acquired—say, about the flatness of the earth—are wrong. Some children shine in large groups; others are too insecure to participate. Some students can pace their efforts over a semester or a year, while others need the sharper incentives provided by shorter time periods.*
> [Albert Shanker, *Phi Delta Kappan*]

these goals students need to learn how to assess and revise their own learning. They must manipulate their knowledge and continually refine their own understanding of the world.

Instead of presenting information for students to remember, teachers must increase the amount of time that students are engaged in learning activities that prompt them to seek information, process it, and expand their own understandings. Teachers need to serve as models, mentors, coaches, and resources for students. These changes also mean that educators need to identify the critical skills and understandings students should be able to demonstrate upon the completion of instruction, and to create new curricula to help students learn them.

In most U.S. secondary schools students spend their days studying specific topics in one-hour blocks. During a typical hour of instruction about 70 percent of the time is devoted to instructional activities. Involvement is primarily verbal interaction between the teacher and the students with the teacher doing most of the talking. Students often listen to the teacher lecture or explain, answer the teacher's questions, and work on written assignments. Instruction is mostly directed toward the whole class with some time allotted for discussion, group activities, individual reading, or using technology. Each class session is usually organized around a specific topic within a subject area; classes contain a specific age group, and the textbook provides the basis for most of the work. The goal for the student is to acquire a set body of knowledge and skills.

All of these planned activities for students compose the formal curriculum and are designed to achieve the overall goals of the school. The formal curriculum centers on *what* is taught and *when* it is taught. Most schools, especially at the secondary level, center their curriculum around the academic disciplines with national organizations and local educators determining what should be included in the curriculum. Over the decades almost all academic disciplines have established national organizational structures to shape the school's curriculum. Today these organizations are developing new sets of skills and understandings for students to learn which will reshape the content of the new curriculum.

Common elements among the current issues being discussed include the continuing controversy over in-depth coverage versus broad coverage of content; interdisciplinary teaching versus a subject-specific approach; project-based student work versus practice exercises; and collaborative work versus individual work. These topics have been points of contention for decades. Questions confronting teachers include:

- Is the in-depth study of a few topics more beneficial for learning than the broad coverage of a number of topics?
- Is integrated or interdisciplinary study of a topic more beneficial to the learner than focusing on a single discipline?
- Do students gain a more sophisticated understanding of an area through project-based activities or practice exercises?
- Is it possible to assess student performance at a different level than the recall of information?

Research on learning supports affirmative answers to each of these questions. Students tend to gain a greater understanding of a problem if it is approached from an in-depth, interdisciplinary perspective and when they are engaged in project-based activities related to real problem-solving. Students who are actively involved in the learning process retain the knowledge and are able to apply their new knowledge to new situations. Cooperative groups lead to more creative solutions to complex problems, engage more students in the learning process, and permit learners to assist each other while learning. New assessment approaches such as performance tests and student portfolios examine learning from a perspective different than that of recalling factual information. And, emerging technology is permitting educators to create assessments to measure more complex thinking.

Effective classrooms, whether at the elementary or secondary level, engage students in these kinds of active learning experiences. Curriculum and organization are structured differently to allow such learning to occur, teacher behavior changes from dispenser to facilitator, and student behavior from receptor of information to creator of new knowledge. Such changes can occur in all classrooms.

TECHNOLOGY'S ROLE IN RESTRUCTURING CLASSROOMS

One of the most dramatic changes of the last twenty years has been the incredible advance in technology. Information and communication technologies such as personal computers, video products such as videocassettes and videodiscs, and communication devices such as modems and facsimile machines, have changed the world. Increased performance and speed have been matched by declining costs, thus enabling more and more schools to have access to these new technologies.

With the increase in access to these advanced technologies, educators have had opportunities to explore different ways to teach and design instruction. Where once drill and practice exercises dominated computer use in classrooms, word processing and databases have become the most-used software applications. Where once computer programming was considered an essential skill for all serious students of technology, software controlled by icons allows students to access multiple levels of information. New technologies continue to evolve into more powerful and sophisticated applications.

What do these advances mean for the classroom? Emerging technologies provide the opportunity for educators to move forward with the assumptions listed in Table 1-1. Technology, used appropriately, can help the teacher and student restructure how the classroom is organized, what topics are studied, and how students learn and are assessed. To suggest that simply using technology will bring about all the needed changes is simplistic. The presence of new technologies will not change schools. But, technology, if integrated into effective teaching and learning practices, can help restructure the classroom. Chapter 2 focuses on the general principles of technology that can be utilized in the classroom.

SUMMARY

Americans have high expectations for their schools. Throughout history, schools have helped citizens prepare for the future. As the United States moves into the 21st Century, schools are once again being asked to prepare the next generation of citizens for a more technological, global world. New skills and understandings have been identified that call for students to be able to problem-solve, utilize technology, collaborate, and create knowledge. The citizen of tomorrow will be able to develop strategies to solve problems and will be able to utilize a variety of technologies. Bringing about these changes will not be easy. Schools are complex organizations, and schools have been the subject of reform efforts throughout their history. Important changes can, however, begin in classrooms, the most critical location of change.

REFERENCES

Elmore, Richard F., and Associates (1990). *Restructuring Schools: The Next Generation of Educational Reform.* San Francisco: Jossey-Bass Publishers.

Ginger, R. (1958). *Altgeld's America: The Lincoln Ideal Versus Changing Realities.* Chicago: Quadrangle Books.

Goodlad, John I. (1984). *A Place Called School.* New York: McGraw-Hill.

Linn, Marcia C. (1986). *Establishing a Research Base for Science Education: Challenges, Trends, and Recommendations.* (Report of a national conference held January 16–19, 1986.) Berkeley, CA: Lawrence Hall of Science and the Graduate School of Education at University of California, Berkeley, 1986.

Shanker, Albert (1990). "The End of the Traditional Model of Schooling—and a Proposal for Using Incentives to Restructure Our Public Schools." *Phi Delta Kappan.* January 1990, pp. 345–357.

2

TECHNOLOGIES FOR RESTRUCTURED CLASSROOMS

Schools seeking to provide the type of education students need for the future are involving students in interdisciplinary projects that call for collaboration over extended periods of time and the development of products that demonstrate their knowledge. Teachers in these schools do more coaching than telling and spend a considerable amount of time working with individual students or groups of students. Within these information-rich learning environments, students and teachers utilize a variety of technologies to support the design of materials, communication of knowledge, and storage and retrieval of information.

Indeed, electronic technology is an essential ingredient in these restructured classrooms. Barbara Means and Kerry Olson (1993), after reviewing research related to school reform and technology, contend that technology:

- Often stimulates teachers to present more complex tasks and material
- Tends to support teachers in becoming coaches rather than dispensers of knowledge
- Provides a safe context for teachers to become learners again and to share their ideas about curriculum and method
- Can motivate students to attempt harder tasks and to take more care in crafting their work
- Adds significance and cultural value to school tasks

Means and Olson (1993) conclude their review by noting that "technology is supporting kinds of activities that students might have done before, but it is making portions of them easier to accomplish and adding cultural value to the task by making it possible for students to produce products in the same way adults would to approximate real-world standards of quality."

ROLE OF TECHNOLOGY IN RESTRUCTURING CLASSROOMS

Today almost every school has a set of computers, at least one VCR, and access to some form of television. Students spend some time working each week using computers for a variety of tasks. Of these tasks, word processing is the most widely used computer software. Each year school districts continue to invest significant amounts of dollars in new technologies (Becker, 1993).

It is important when thinking about electronic technologies not to focus only on computers. When we speak of electronic technologies we include computers, CD-ROMs, telephones, facsimile machines, modems, and video technologies such as television sets, video recorders, videodisc players, cable and satellite connections, and camcorders. All of these technologies are available in more and more schools as a means to assist teachers and students in the learning process. The most common technologies are video and TV; however, more and more schools are increasing the availability of computer and computer-related technologies.

As one thinks about the possible uses of this wide variety of technology in the classroom, it can become overpowering. The teacher is confronted with a variety of questions such as: (1) What general role do these technologies play in the classroom? (2) What are the implications of using technology for me as a teacher? (3) Will the use of technology help my students learn? and, (4) How do I integrate them into my teaching? Let us first look at the first two questions. Chapter 3 and Part III focus on the last two questions.

General Role of Technology

Generally speaking, electronic technologies provide one or more of three general roles. They may:

- *Provide information.* The technology serves as a repository of information that can be accessed usually in linear form and via one-way communication. Examples include videotape players, videodiscs, CD-ROMs, and computer databases. Information may also be presented via television, cable TV, and satellite transmissions. The essential characteristic of these technologies is as a storehouse of data to be accessed by the user.

- *Develop knowledge and skills.* Interactive computer programs are the best example of such a technology. Programs, developed by commercial companies, assist students in learning content and developing problem-solving and data-analysis skills. These technologies respond to inputs from the learner and may be accessed in a nonlinear fashion.
- *Link different locations.* Two-way communication via telephones, electronic networks and satellite devices are examples of technologies that allow parties to communicate with each other. Here individuals in one site are able to communicate directly with persons in another. Such communication may be live or real-time or it may be delayed such as when one uses an electronic network.

Given these different roles, the teacher then must make choices about the appropriateness of the technology to meet specific learning outcomes. In addition to these broad differences, technologies also differ on four other attributes:

- *The depth and quality of the information provided may vary.* For example, a videotape may present only the most general information about a topic in a linear fashion, while a videodisc may offer detailed information about the same subject and the ability to easily access the data on any part of the disk.
- *Different technologies and their applications have direct implications on the manner in which the classroom is organized.* For example, by using a cable television show pre-recorded earlier, the organization of the classroom would very likely be teacher-directed and whole-class oriented. Using computer and CD-ROM materials in learning stations would mean a different, more student-directed, classroom.
- *Technologies differ on cost and amount of integration needed to use them.* Showing a videotape in a VCR is quite simple today because most schools have VCR players. Playing the material usually involves pushing two or three buttons. The cost of the equipment is reasonable and it is fairly simple to run. Using a computer software program to access a videodisc is more complex and costly. Most schools do not own integrated multimedia packages at this time; thereby, requiring the teacher to "put things together" prior to using the technologies in the classroom. The cost is also higher.
- *Technologies vary in the flexibility of use.* Using a computer program for whole-class instruction is much more flexible than being tied to a particular time and location for a satellite transmission on a specific topic. The ability to use a particular piece of technology on a more flexible schedule directly impacts teacher selection and use.

As teachers begin to think about using technology in the classroom it is important to keep these general differences in mind because they impact instruction in a number of ways.

Implications of Using Technology for the Teacher

Using technology effectively in the classroom will enable teachers to be more successful and will assist students in learning what they need to be effective citizens (Means and Olson, 1993; Cotton, 1991; Bialo and Sivin, 1990; and Sheingold and Hadley, 1990). Research on the effect of integrating technology into classroom instruction effectively suggests the following direct impact on the teacher. Teachers teaching with technology say they:

- Expect more from their students and expect their students to take more care in preparing their work
- Can present more complex material
- Believe students understand more difficult concepts
- Can meet the needs of individual students better
- Can be more student-centered in their teaching
- Are more open to multiple perspectives on problems
- Are more willing to experiment
- Feel more professional because, among other things, they spend less time dispensing information and more time helping students learn

Are these results that most teachers want? Yes, they are. Research in classrooms across the nation suggests that such conclusions are not unique to or isolated in one or two sites. Such changes are happening in markedly different schools and at different grade levels. But, these results are not achieved without effort and without having met some prior conditions.

As teachers begin restructuring their classrooms, a number of questions enter their minds when they begin to think about how technology can be infused. Key among these questions are the following:

- *How will students react to technology?* This question is often asked by teachers. A common myth is that all students love technology and have little trouble adapting to using technology in the classroom. Generally this conclusion is true. Interactive technologies are a part of young people's world; however, students differ in their attitudes toward technologies and how they view them as learning tools. A study by Alvestad and Wigfield (1994), for example, found the following differences among children as they approach a learning task in a computer lab. They found that students who (1) prefer challenging work achieve more; (2) are motivated by curiosity and interest do better than those who merely sought to please the teacher; (3) have an internal criteria for success or failure achieve higher than those with external criteria.

Different learning styles apply to the use of technology, and teachers need to assume that not all students will find the same type of experience with technology rewarding. It is also evident that there are still differences between boys and girls. Boys tend to have more experience with interactive technologies than girls. Boys, for example, are the highest users of video games, and use technology at home more than girls. Children from different socioeconomic backgrounds also have different technology experiences. Caucasian students tend to have more experience using technology than do African American and Hispanic students (Becker, 1993). Turkel (1984) long ago suggested that using technology should lead the student to a clear understanding of him or herself and their relationship with others, but it is clear that differences between boys and girls and social classes exist.

- *How will technologies affect our concept of knowledge?* The recall of knowledge has been the mainstay of the educational system for decades. As access to vast quantities of information becomes easier, the emphasis on remembering that information will shift to being able to manage the sources, ask pertinent questions, and draw conclusions. These are the new skills of tomorrow. Data-rich environments will cause us to shift away from simply attempting to recall the facts to attempting to put these facts together in a meaningful way to solve problems and make value judgments about what ought to be.
- *How will technology change the location for teaching and learning?* For years educators have been talking about the fact that soon people will be learning in a number of locations besides the traditional classroom. In fact, this is indeed the trend in restructured classrooms. As students become more independent learners and teachers become facilitators of learning, learning related to a particular area of study begins to occur in a number of places in and outside the school. Students collect data for a science project by using technology in the field to measure water samples, downloading information from a national database using the networked computer in the media center, and using word processing to finish the final report in the technology laboratory. Small groups of students are working at technology stations around the room and conferencing with students in another city via satellite. Learning is taking place in a variety of locations.

- *What type of new skills will students need to learn?* In describing the use of databases in social studies classrooms, Hunter (1987) provides wise counsel by noting, "We cannot expect tools to teach the skills, any more than we expect a pencil to teach a child to write." While many students today have little fear of the technology, they still may lack the skills needed to effectively learn by using the technology. A database, no matter how easy to access, is not a video game. Prior instruction on how to use some technologies will be important.
- *How will the technology change my classroom and my relationship with my students?* New highly interactive technologies motivate students, focus student attention, and teach important facts, concepts, and skills. Teachers notice that students enjoy using the technology and can get more information from the technology than they can from the teacher. For some teachers this changed relationship between them and their students is uncomfortable. If you see your role as an information provider, emerging technologies and restructured classrooms will alter that role.
- *How will technology impact the accountability for achievement in the classroom?* Technology makes it easier to evaluate achievement. For example, if a school is using a set of structured learning programs designed to teach and monitor mathematics skills through a networked computer system, it will be possible to check each student's progress. This progress then can be used to determine the effectiveness of the program and the teacher's instructional efforts. On a more positive side, the same technology will allow the teacher and student to monitor the student's learning and to make adjustments in instructional strategies. Whichever side of the issue, increased accountability will come with technology.
- *How does this technology work?* An important part of being a teacher is being ready to assist students in achieving the learning outcomes for the lesson. No one wants to have a lesson fail because the technology does not work or because you don't know how to operate the technology. That is why the overhead projector is so popular; everyone can "run" one. What this means is that prior preparation is needed to gain familiarity with the technology. The more complicated the technology the more the need to gain competence in using the technology.
- *How much time is needed to get ready to use the technology in the classroom?* Research findings based on actual classroom practices suggest that effective technology teachers spend time learning about the technology and the software programs, and planning on how to infuse the technology into the lessons (Sheingold and Hadley, 1990; White, 1987). The more comfortable one is with instructional issues

and knowledgeable about the content, the easier it will be to explore exciting ways to use the technology.

- *How will the use of technology change my teaching style?* Teachers have very specific beliefs about how best to teach. The introduction of technology into the classroom will begin to bring these beliefs into question. In-depth studies by Dwyer, Ringstaff, and Sandholtz (1990) suggest that teachers go through an "instructional evolution in technology" which moves from adoption of technology to common instructional practices to adaptation of technology to experiment with different instructional practices to appropriation of technology into new strategies to invention where technology is used to create learning experiences by the student. Familiarity, confidence, and success lead to changed perceptions of how technology can be used to achieve different student learning outcomes.
- *What kind of classroom management problems may occur if I use technology?* Classroom management is one of the most important issues for the teacher. This means prior planning and thinking about the type of technology and support materials that are to be used. For example, selecting a computer program that must be individually used means a different kind of management issue than a program that is designed for use by a group of students. Selecting a videotape that runs 90 minutes poses problems in most secondary classrooms where periods tend to run only 50 minutes. Classroom management issues can be handled if considered as a part of the planning process. We will return to these issues in Part II of the text.

While there are undoubtedly many other questions to be considered, those noted above are worthy of careful thought prior to restructuring your classroom. They are not intended to discourage, but to help you understand more clearly the implications of the strategies discussed in Part II of the book. While one can never be completely prepared for the unexpected that occurs when a group of students enter the classroom, the thoughtful teacher has considered many alternative strategies and is ready to adjust.

CREATING AN ENVIRONMENT FOR EFFECTIVE USE OF TECHNOLOGY

As the amount of technology has increased in schools, more attention has been paid to creating an environment that is conducive to its effective use. Teachers simply cannot be expected to acquire the needed skills to incorporate technology into instruction with a supportive environment and the availability of some technical assistance. Sheingold and Hadley (1990) and Means and Olson (1993) have examined some of the conditions needed for a technologically favorable teaching and learning environment. Here are the essentials:

- *Appropriate technology must be available.* You use the technology that is most readily available. That is why the VCR is the most commonly used piece of technology in schools. It is there; it is easy to use; and it can be used on your time schedule. Planning to use technology means you will need to have access to it for use when and where you need. This will take some planning.
- *It will take time and practice to integrate technology into the instructional program.* Effective use of technology usually occurs in classrooms of teachers who have had a number of years of experience using the technology. This is especially true for teachers who want to use computers and computer-related technologies. This does not mean novice teachers cannot begin to restructure their classrooms by incorporating technology. In fact, in Part II we present a number of alternatives that are appropriate for the beginning teacher as well as the more experienced teacher. Both persons must realize however that time and experience will be needed.
- *Support is needed.* Someplace, either in the building or the school district, there needs to be someone to assist the teacher trying innovative uses of technology. Our suggestion is to find another teacher in the building or in the district who is exploring new ways to use technology. Other teachers are often the best source of information and encouragement.
- *Colleagues and administrators need to support innovation.* This is so obvious that we often forget it, but innovative teachers teach in innovative schools that support their exciting ideas.

The innovative teacher always seeks out colleagues who are interested in change and new ways of thinking about teaching and learning. In fact, the research suggests that teachers involved in using technology think more about these issues and are more reflective of their teaching methods.

WHY BE AN INNOVATIVE TEACHER IN A RESTRUCTURED CLASSROOM?

All teachers want their students to learn and succeed. Often the challenges appear so great and the conditions so difficult that the teacher has difficulty keeping this goal uppermost in his or her mind. Technology will not work miracles for teachers, but restructuring the classroom along the lines recommended in Part II may have some profound effects. As Sheingold and Hadley (1990) concluded about the experienced teachers they studied:

> *They seem to take a flexible, even experimental, approach to their teaching with technology. In their emphasis on students' making their own products, and in their structuring of project-based learning activities for their students, they appear to be helping students engage actively and expansively with the technology and, more important, with the material and topics they are learning. Indeed, some of these teachers appear to be creating, through their use of technology, the conditions for deep, engaged, and meaningful learning.*

Those are powerful conclusions. They are conclusions that are supported by emerging research on the impact of technology on students learning and attitudes. Let us turn our attention to this area.

REFERENCES

Alvestad, K. and Wigfield, A. (1994). "A Matter of Motivation," in *Computers in Education,* Sixth Edition, John J. Hirschbuhl, ed. Sluice Dock, Guilford, Connecticut: Dushkin Publishing Group, Inc.

Becker, H. (1993). "Analysis and Trends of School Use of New Information Technologies." Available by sending $15 payable to VC Regents, C/O Cheryl Craft, Dept of Education, University of California at Irvine, Irvine, CA 92717-5500

Bialo, E. and Sivin, J. (1990). "Report on the Effectiveness of Microcomputers in Schools." Software Publishers Association, Washington D.C.

Cotton, K. (1991). "Computer-Assisted Instruction." School Improvement Research Series, Close-up #10. Portland, OR: Northwest Regional Educational Laboratory, May.

Dwyer, D. C.; Ringstaff, C. and Sandholtz, J. (1990). "The Evolution of Teachers' Instructional Beliefs and Practices in High-Access-to-Technology Classrooms." A paper presented at the American Education Research Association, Boston, Massachusetts.

Hunter, B. (1987). "Knowledge-Creative Learning with Data Bases." *Social Education,* 51 (January): 38–43.

Means, B. and Olson, K. (1993). "Supporting School Reform with Educational Technology." A paper presented at the American Educational Research Association, Atlanta, Georgia.

Sheingold, K. and Hadley, M. (1990). "Accomplished Teachers: Integrating Computers into Classroom Practice." Center for Technology in Education: Bank Street College of Education, September.

Turkel, S. (1984). *The Second Self: Computers and the Human Spirit.* New York: Simon and Schuster, Inc.

White, C. (1987). "Teachers Using Technology." *Social Education 51* (January): 44–47.

3

FOUNDATIONS FOR CHANGE: STUDENT PERFORMANCE AND CLASSROOM STRUCTURE

The introduction of a new technology often leads to exaggerated claims about the effectiveness of the new technology in enhancing student performance. Such claims were made for radio, television, computers, and videodiscs. This new technology is better than textbooks! This new technology is more effective than lectures! Or, this new technology will replace the teacher! We have all seen these similar headlines; headlines often written to sell the technology rather than to describe how it might be part of a learning environment. Knowledgeable teachers know there is no quick and single solution to the diversity of learning styles that exist among students. So before bringing a new technology into their classrooms, knowledgeable teachers want to know that if they commit the time and energy to integrate it into their classrooms, the efforts will be rewarded with improved student achievement. The bottom line, as it has always been, is "Will it improve students' learning?"

During the last decade a growing body of research has begun to provide evidence of the impact of technology on student performance and classroom structure. For example, Cotton (1991) reviewed fifty-nine studies directly related to computer-assisted instruction and student outcomes. Researchers have moved away from studies that simply focused on this-technology-is-better-than studies to examine more carefully the impact of technology on the total learning environment and on specific learner outcomes. For those who are seeking the straightforward unequivocal answer to student learning problems, the answers are still disappointing, But, for the educator who understands the complexity of teaching and learning, the findings are encouraging and provide evidence of the effectiveness of these new technologies. Let's begin by examining computer technology.

POWER OF COMPUTER TECHNOLOGY[1]

Computer technology has received the most attention during the last decade. Schools have made significant commitments to the purchasing of computers with the expectation that student performance would improve. School board members, superintendents, principals, and teachers often ask, "Are computers worth the money?" The research in two general areas provides some powerful indicators that indeed the cost is worth it.

Student Attitudes

Children favor computers over television. They say, "TV does what it wants to do. A computer does what you want it to." They prefer an interactive participatory role to a passive one. As a result students enjoy using computers and like coming to classes where computers are being used. Why? There are a number of reasons.

Effective computer software programs actively engage the student and provide considerable learner control. Feedback is immediate, helpful, and without embarrassment. Active participation tends to keep the student motivated to remain on task, and graphics and engaging formats peak student interest.

Incorporating computer technologies into instruction also increases the positive attitude students have toward coming to school, the class, and learning in general. Attitudes also improved toward writing, reading, mathematics, science, and business as a result of using computers as part of instruction. These attitude changes are of particular importance in subjects such as mathematics where "math anxiety" often detracts from learning basic concepts and skills.

Because attitudes toward learning improve, self-esteem and feelings of empowerment also improve. Students who are in control of more of their learning begin to feel better about their ability to do the work. In

---

[1]The generalizations about the effectiveness of computers are based on the synthesis of the research presented by Kathleen Cotton, by Ellen Bialo and Jay Sivin, and by Robert Tierney. Over 120 research studies were reviewed by these authors.

fact, technology can motivate students to attempt harder tasks and to take more care in crafting their work.

Interaction among and between students is also impacted when students use computers. Cooperative learning centered around a computer activity, for example, leads to increased content-related student talk and an increase in the number of ideas presented for consideration. These structured groups also permitted students with different academic abilities to interact in a more positive and helpful manner.

Student Performance

More and more studies suggest that educational computer applications have a direct impact on student performance. Cotton (1991)[2] concludes the research on computer assisted instruction suggests the following:

- When incorporated as a part of instruction, computer-assisted instruction leads to higher academic gains.
- The use of word processors in writing programs leads to better writing outcomes than the use of paper and pencil or conventional writing.
- Student learning rate is faster with computer-assisted instruction than with conventional instruction.
- The retention of content is superior.
- Computer-assisted instruction appears to be most effective in the areas of science, foreign languages, mathematics, reading, and language arts.
- The amount of structure depends on the students' prior knowledge and the complexity of the task. Students with prior knowledge want more control over the program while students with little prior knowledge want more structure. The use of sophisticated databases by younger students requires more structure in the lesson (Ehman and Glenn, 1987).
- Lower-achieving students, younger students, and economically disadvantaged students tend to benefit more from computer-assisted instruction.
- Computer-assisted instruction is more effective teaching lower-cognitive material than higher-cognitive material. (Authors' note: There are new simulation programs on the market now that teach far more sophisticated cognitive skills.)

---

[2]This research focuses on computer-assisted instruction, CAI, which refers to drill-and-practice, tutorial, or simulations activities offered either by themselves or as a supplement to traditional, teacher-directed instruction.

Research related to higher-level learning is emerging. Studies examining the use of databases incorporated into an instructional system suggest that students are able to generate sophisticated generalizations, draw out more inferences, and synthesize their conclusions into positions.

Generally speaking the results related to the impact of the use of computer technologies upon student attitudes and performance are quite positive. It is clear that computer applications alone do not achieve the results teachers and learners want. If used as part of a total teaching and learning experience, computer applications are effective. Some additional discussion provides further insights.

A CASE FOR USING COMPUTER TECHNOLOGY IN RESTRUCTURED CLASSROOMS

Before microcomputers were developed for educational use in schools, educators and students managed with textbooks, workbooks, motion video, and other such resources. When computers were introduced to schools in the 80s, some educators instantly recognized their value as "interactive" learning resources. This interactive quality caused many educators to see computers as instrumental in confronting some of the educational problems such as poor communication skills, lack of research skills, and lack of problem-solving ability. Computer advocates believed the technology could help solve these problems. Let's examine examples of how computer technology can contribute to each of these areas.

Communication Support and Skill Building

Innovative teachers use computer technologies to support instruction in all kinds of communication. Word processing capabilities, for example, emphasize the process approach to writing by permitting students to revise drafts several times without having to copy them over. Moreover, there is software available that directly supports the processes of brainstorming, organizing ideas and outlining, drafting, receiving peer and teacher comments, checking for spelling and grammatical errors, and finally printing a perfected, clean copy. If the ultimate goal is to publish students' writing in a newspaper or magazine format, there is software that enables young editors to design page layouts with columns, hairline rules, graphics, and other special features; transfer copy into the design; and then print out high-quality master pages. If the goal is to make an oral presentation, there is software that enables presenters to create text and graphic slides for projection (via slide projector, overhead projector, or electronic projection system) during their presentations. Multimedia presentations are also possible with text, graphics, video, music, and whatever else the student and the available equipment can provide. The purpose of all of these electronic features is to help communicators make their points more clearly and completely, more accurately, and more dynamically.

Developing Research Skills

Technology is being used by teachers to support a wide range of student research activities. When students seek information not available in the classroom they need to go elsewhere, and computers make it possible to search other sources without leaving school. Electronic databases, for example, contain massive amounts of text, audio, and visual information that can be made available to student researchers. Such databases include anything from encyclopedias and bibliographies, to videodisc collections of slides and motion video from museums, science institutions, and other archives. In the process of learning to search electronic databases—CD-ROMs, videodiscs, online services, and other formats—students learn to think about information in a more organized way, by selecting key words that pinpoint information they want, and then reorganizing it for comparison and analysis. Alternatively, students can create their own databases that they and others may continue to build over time.

Another example of computer technology that helps students develop research skills is computer "probeware." Probeware transforms the computer into a mini science lab. It consists of little wire-like probes that extend from the computer to measure physical properties such as light and heat, and software that displays the measurements on a computer screen. This microcomputer-based laboratory (MBL) permits learners to do hands-on experiments with equipment that is generally easier to use, safer, and more precise than traditional laboratory equipment.

For example, in an experiment that compares the speed of falling objects—a basketball, a tennis ball, and a golf ball—students use the computer's timer to determine which lands first, second, and third. When the balls land at exactly the same time, students are able to test hypotheses, run several experiments, and develop conclusions related to the experiment. Or, in an experiment that compares the temperatures of boiling liquids, water and vegetable oil, for instance, students watch the liquid temperatures rise on the computer screen and identify the moment and temperature that each begins to boil. The advantage of computer technology in both experiments is that it redirects the students' attention from fussing with lab equipment and fudging inaccurate measurements, to observing process and analyzing results.

Increasing Problem-Solving Abilities

Teachers also employ computer technology to help their students develop problem-solving strategies. There is considerable software that has already gained popularity among elementary teachers because of its ability to engage youngsters in developing problem-solving skills. Most of the earlier programs were designed to build and practice problem-solving skills within a fixed set of experiences, rather than provide tools to help students solve problems of their own design. Increasingly, however, more software is being developed that does provide more generic tools for exploring ideas when solving a variety of problems. For example, there is software that converts numerical data to graphs and charts, permitting learners to visualize numerical relationships and how they change when the numbers change. Another kind of tool enables learners to electronically draw geometric shapes on the computer screen and measure any angle, length, and area within the shapes. With electronic accuracy and speed, students can replicate and alter their constructions to test out theories, form generalizations, and prove hypotheses.

At the secondary level, databases either on purchased computer discs or accessed through electronic networks are being used in social studies, science, and English. Linked with word processing programs these databases have become powerful sources of information for students.

Learning through Simulated Environments

Computer simulations offer students the opportunity to confront problems and make decisions in an imaginary environment that is realistic enough to provide meaningful issues and appropriate consequences. In such practice situations, students hypothetically experience consequences of their actions. Then they can analyze the whole process afterwards and try again. In essence, simulations provide an effective, safe way for students to learn to make intelligent decisions when they really count.

For example, in a simulation of a state park students design the public areas, including boat launches, picnic areas, hiking trails, and so forth, in whatever configuration they wish. They are given information about the park's size, animal population, water sources, climate, and other data to help them determine what facilities the park can handle without damaging the ecological balance. The goal is to maintain a balance between citizen use of the park and the need for plants and animals to flourish. When students have completed their plans for the park, the simulation analyzes their data and calculates its impact on the environment over time so that students can see the short- and long-term effects of their decisions.

Distance Learning

Telecommunications capabilities make it possible for students and teachers to share information—personal messages, reports, data, graphics, and so on—across cities, states or continents, thus ending the isolation of the classroom. Many teachers get their students involved in collaborative projects in which students from different regions contribute data they have collected locally. Some projects, for example, have examined water quality, air pollution, or other environmental concerns, by comparing samples from all over the country. Others have compared local customs, surveyed immigrant populations, or collected opinions about issues such as youth suicide. Most projects produce some kind of joint report or newsletter.

Educators also are getting involved in collegial networking through telecommunications. Using a network utility (such as CompuServe or Prodigy) for storing and distributing the electronic mail, they share experiences and advice, as well as trade curricula, reports, and other such information. The advantage is that teachers, who have been left alone in their classrooms with few opportunities to attend professional conferences, can now meet and share ideas with distant colleagues. It is hardly a replacement for face-to-face communication, but telecommunications can be an effective medium for trading printed information and maintaining long-term relationships.

A Comment about the Teacher's Role

Teachers want to develop independent learners. But, this does not happen by simply telling students to go off and teach themselves how to read, solve math problems, or write research reports. If we have done our job right, they will be able to teach themselves new skills and concepts in time, after we have taught them a number of fundamental processes including how to pursue and manage their own learning. In the meanwhile, teachers need to provide a good deal of help.

When students are about to learn a new process, such as writing a news story, teachers should model the entire process, from doing interviews and collecting factual information, to writing paragraphs in an appropriate style. Often it makes sense to introduce new skills and processes to the whole class in a teacher-led lesson. A computer with a large-screen projection system can be an extremely effective teaching tool in this kind of situation. Using the computer and large screen as an "electronic chalkboard," the teacher can demonstrate how to write a news story by entering students' suggested sentences and guiding the story's language and development as the students watch and contribute. At the end of such a lesson, the teacher can print and duplicate copies of the story to provide students with a realistic model of a news story they can refer to when writing their own.

HOW MANY COMPUTERS ARE "ENOUGH"?

Seasoned computer-using educators can often be heard advising school administrators and other education budget managers, "If you can afford only a few computers, give them to teachers." Teachers must personally experience the computer advantage and become comfortable users before they can effectively implement computer-supported activities in the classroom. When teachers are confident and convinced that the computer offers significant advantages to learning, they will begin inventing ways to include that one computer, or several, in their curriculum activities.

In the one-computer classroom, teachers soon discover they can use the computer as a smart chalkboard, mini laboratory, or demonstration tool. For example, in a lesson on how to edit a composition, the teacher can display a student's first draft on the screen and involve students in a guided discussion of how to improve its structure and mechanics, by implementing student-proposed changes. In this way, the students can observe how well their suggestions work. Teachers can usually type faster than they can write with chalk, and with this electronic chalkboard all kinds of changes can be made and observed instantly. With access to an overhead projection system, the entire class can view one screen. Alternatively, two (or more) video monitors can be connected to a computer, enabling students to view the screen that is located closest to them.

Using a variety of software, the electronic chalkboard can be used to demonstrate any number of complex processes. With simulation software, for example, the whole class can participate in political negotiations concerning a hypothetical crisis between two powerful nations and its threat to the international balance of power. Selected representatives from several consulting countries will need to be successful diplomats or face economic and/or military disaster. Such a simulated experience can involve the entire class and only one computer. With interactive video capabilities, teachers can show objects and processes that expand and strengthen students' understanding of the natural world, processes such as how trees sprout from seeds, how whales have babies, or bees make honey.

Aside from being an effective tool for class demonstrations and whole class learning experiences, the single classroom computer can also be used as a student resource, like the resident fish, encyclopedia, or globe, albeit the computer is more versatile and responsive. After teachers have demonstrated how to use the software that governs each resource, students may be invited to go to the computer when they need to in the process of completing certain projects and activities. For instance, young historians may need to look up information in a database containing information about a country they are studying; researchers may need to create handouts for a presentation; editors may use it to design a class publication; and small groups may use it to perform experiments.

Many teachers express extreme joy and satisfaction with their single classroom computer. Yet there are few who refuse more computers when they are offered. Classroom inventories range from one, to one per student. When there are "enough" computers readily available, say enough so that students can use a computer whenever they need to, then teachers can realistically think about computers as significantly effective writing and thinking tools for students. In writing, for example, for the learning process to be most effective, students need to use the computer for almost all phases of writing, from keyboarding first drafts, to revising and printing perfected copies.

For computers to be truly effective in helping students learn to think analytically and solve complex problems, the computer tools—databases, simulations, graphics, videodiscs, and so on—need to be available when students are engaged in the processes, not a half hour or a day later. Research shows that computers do help students learn to be more competent writers, researchers, and problem-solvers when they use computers on a daily basis. When they use computers occasionally, students can indeed experience more effective practice environments for learning basic skills, and they can also benefit from the teacher's use of technology for demonstration purposes. But if they use computers only occasionally, they will not be empowered to adopt the computer as a personal tool that is as fully integrated into their lives as other technology tools like telephones, calculators, cameras, photocopy machines, VCRs, and televisions.

THE POWER OF USING VIDEO

The use of video in schools has a very mixed history. Films and videotape form the core of instructional uses of technology in schools. Elementary teachers and secondary science and social studies teachers are the most common users of video, with mathematics teachers at either level being the least likely to use video in their classrooms. In fact, roughly 80 percent of science and social studies teachers in a recent study reported using "video, film, or filmstrips" once or twice a month or more (Ingels, 1992).

Television, film, and video are strikingly different from earlier visual aids and more powerful because they involve constant movement of sophisticated images, accompanied by words and sound effects that reinforce and extend the visual information communicated. Considerable research shows that when video presentations are compared to single medium audio or visual presentations of the same material, the combined use of media results in more recall of information than viewing pictures, reading, or listening to the material by itself (Kozma, 1991). Motion video captivates the viewer and creates a lasting impression as it entertains, conveys information, molds attitudes, and influences behavior.

Communicates Information

Research shows that children remember video-based information longer than information they read or hear. When information is communicated by dynamic images, speech, and sound effects, the result is a far greater learning experience than if the same information is read or presented by a teacher. Research also shows that if the video presentation is accompanied by class discussion and/or related reading, the learning is significantly greater than if any one medium is used by itself.

On the other hand, Kozma (1991) reports that people who are very knowledgeable about a particular subject can process text information faster and more strategically than they can with audiotape or video, suggesting that text would suffice for these learners. Further, novice learners may fail at comprehending some video presentations if their pace of processing new information is slower than the pace of the presentation. Learners with some familiarity of the subject are most likely to benefit from the pace and combination of audio and visual material presented in video.

Greenfield (1984) reports that motion video can be extremely effective in teaching children about the natural world and current events. Motion video has unique power in its ability to present unfamiliar environments and events that are difficult to conceptualize when explained in words. Video footage of exotic places and foreign cultural events as well as the effects of natural disasters and war, create a deeper impression on individuals than reading or hearing the same information. In the classroom, viewing motion video of a volcano erupting, a butterfly emerging from its cocoon, or an astronaut walking on the moon is a far more effective way of explaining these events than trying to describe them in words.

Current events are also increasingly being taught by motion video. Network news programs, for instance, are often used for this purpose. CNN news is the most widely used cable news source in schools. Other commercial education channels remain in their infancy and little data are available about their effectiveness and use. What information is available suggests that television's impact on students is increased when:

- The teacher is committed to using news in the classroom.
- Expanding student knowledge of national and worldwide events is a school goal.
- The program is shown during appropriate classes.
- The news is relevant and newsworthy.

Influences Attitudes and Behaviors

In addition to conveying information, the visual and emotional impact of motion video images can have a significant influence on viewers' attitudes and behaviors. Viewer perception of global conflicts, for example, has been shown to be influenced by television news coverage. Greenfield (1984) reports that TV programming can also perpetuate sex-role and ethnic stereotypes or be used to break down existing sex-role stereotypes and build more broadminded attitudes. In a research study of a public television series (*Freestyle*) designed to change sex-role attitudes in pre-teens, girls learned to be more independent and career-oriented and boys learned to be more nurturing and expressive of feelings. Findings showed that the show had the greatest change effect when viewed in class, accompanied by discussion, rather than when children viewed it at home. Watching the show at home without discussion, for example, convinced girls that it is appropriate for boys to do housework and child care; but only with follow-up class discussion were the boys convinced as well. And, studies of *Sesame Street* have shown that television can also strengthen the self-respect of individuals in these groups as well as change the attitudes of young viewers towards them. Studies of programs that are designed to expand ethnocentric attitudes also have positive results as young viewers learn that peers in other countries are just as interesting, intelligent, and fun as peers in their own country.

Not only are viewers' attitudes influenced by video-based media, so are their behaviors. Children often imitate popular television characters' ways of dressing, speaking, and even their social behaviors. Research confirms that watching anti-social behavior on television can influence the viewers' behavior negatively, just as watching positive social behavior can have a favorable effect (Greenfield, 1984).

Research also shows that children sometimes have difficulty distinguishing between fiction and reality on television "because fictional stories are often recorded in realistic settings with convincing actors and because both fiction and news stories are seen on the same screen, often during the same viewing period" (Greenfield, 1984). Greenfield also notes that accepting as reality the eccentric personalities, lifestyles, and daily events presented in TV's melodramas causes children to develop misconceptions of reality. Further, some speculate that when young viewers confuse news stories with action scenes in TV dramas, it can ultimately desensitize them toward violence and human suffering. Again, class discussion and parental involvement can do much to help children learn to distinguish fiction from reality and encourage them to criticize shows that promote violence, prejudice, sex-role stereotypes, and other anti-social or narrow-minded attitudes and behaviors. Research affirms the learning value of adult intervention while the child is watchning or immediately afterwards.

Another popular criticism of video-based media is that it tends to be fast-paced, which contributes to its ability to captivate children and make them less interested in reading books, building models, and others lower-paced activities. Greenfield (1984) explains that the accelerated nature of motion video means that viewers do not have time to reflect on what they are seeing, and in the long term can transform young viewers into restless and impatient learners in slower-paced classroom environments. Indeed, research does suggest that extensive television watching can lead to an impulsive style of thinking and lack of persistence in intellectual tasks. Print, on the other hand, allows time for reflective thought, and it can present individuals' thoughts more effectively than video-based media. TV and video are limited to communicating people's thoughts through faceless narration or other such techniques. As a result, children do not observe TV characters thinking very often; what they see is fast-paced, often impulsive behavior that may influence their own behavior over time (Greenfield, 1984).

In sum, the widespread criticism of television is misfocused on the medium itself. It is not the television that is at fault. Indeed, television is an extremely effective teaching tool. What's at fault is how television has been used. However, if used wisely, motion video can be a positive and powerful teaching and learning resource. Video-based media are more effective than the printed word for conveying certain types of information, and they make learning available to those who are unsuccessful with traditional school approaches, cannot read, or are unable to attend school.

THE CASE FOR INCLUDING TV AND VIDEO IN THE SCHOOL CURRICULUM

Teaching Critical Viewing Skills and Visual Literacy

Imagery is the language of the information age, argue an increasing number of educators. With the current predominance of video-based media outside school, the evidence points out that we all learn from TV and video whether we like it or not. For this reason, if for none other, it is imperative that children and adults learn the language of imagery. Its symbols, vocabulary, structure, and conventions are distinctly different from print media. Printed words are static and processed in sequence; motion picture images are fluid and dynamic, and must be processed simultaneously and rapidly, before they change.

Learning to process images on a screen is in some ways comparable to learning to read. Greenfield (1984) explains that a viewer must learn to decode visual symbols (e.g. cutting from one shot to another, panning from one side of a scene to the other, zooming from a long shot to a close-up and the reverse), audio symbols (e.g., faceless narrators, background music). These symbols/techniques are used to represent certain ideas. For example, when a visual sequence cuts from one character to another it indicates a particular relationship between them, perhaps one notices the other in a crowd, or is thinking about the other person. A person's ability to understand these symbols depends on the individual's viewing experience as well as stage of development. (Very young children typically are confused by some symbolic techniques.) In general, the more one watches motion video, the more adept one becomes in processing the symbols, recognizing popular formats, and anticipating outcomes. Thus, video-based media has a distinct advantage as a learning resource because all individuals need to do to learn from visual media is to watch it; to learn from print media they must learn to read.

Teaching children to be critical receivers of this visual information, however, is quite another matter. According to Greenfield (1984), today's youngsters are experienced image viewers, but they do not understand the power of images—how they are created and how they influence attitudes and behaviors on purpose or inadvertently. Children are particularly vulnerable viewers because they do not have the analytical skills to realize they are being manipulated. Given that so much of what children see on television is biased and simplistic, it is essential that they learn to be critical viewers. Children need to learn to evaluate the quality of information and analyze the techniques used in production. Parents can help by watching television with their children and openly discussing the techniques as they are used, as well as their purpose.

Educators can be extremely effective in teaching visual literacy by having students watch shows in class and then critically analyzing what they have seen. For example, one curriculum activity might include watching a TV news show or documentary and then evaluating the content in terms of its relevance, accuracy, point of view, sources used, and so forth. The discussion would also examine the camera techniques (close-ups, panning, etc.) and their purpose as well as the editing techniques (what points are highlighted by the clips and what has been left out).

Another way to develop visual literacy is to have students produce their own video shows. Through the experience of creating a five-minute news story, for instance, students would be called upon to research a newsworthy event, select and interview sources on video, gather on-the-scene footage, and edit the material to support the complete news story presented by a young TV news anchor. Then, the whole class would identify and analyze the point of view conveyed by the video clips and the anchor's presentation. Following this, the producers might be asked to re-edit the video material to present a different point of view. This kind of productive, teacher-guided activity can be extremely effective in teaching youngsters to be intelligent consumers (and creators) of visual information.

Television and Video as Educational Resources

During the 70s and 80s, while most educators and parents were busy admonishing commercial TV and banishing it from the classroom, innovative others were busy developing Educational Television (ETV) from the dull, mugshot, lecture approach of its origin, to the more engaging educational approaches used in producing shows such as Sesame Street, Square One, DeGrassi Junior High, The Voyage of the Mimi, and

CNN Kid's News, not to mention the increasing number of high-quality documentaries, news specials, historical dramas, etc., currently being produced.

Now that over 90 percent of the nation's schools have VCRs and most teachers also have them at home, teachers are beginning to record selected TV shows when they're broadcast and show them to the class when they fit the curriculum. The greatly increased convenience of using this media has certainly contributed to its growing popularity as a teaching tool. Research in the area of instructional use indicates that when students view video with a purpose (e.g. for a follow-up discussion or assignment), they pay greater attention and are able to respond with a deeper level of understanding, than when they watch for entertainment (Kozma, 1991).

Recognizing that there are now a fair number of high-quality video and TV shows available to the public, some educators have begun to use motion video to teach reading, literature, and writing. Not only do video stories facilitate better comprehension and memory of the story itself, they also stimulate a desire to read similar stories. Indeed, popular movies and TV shows have generated interest in reading related books, and some teachers have taken advantage of this interest by making the books readily available, and/or including them in the course of study. Some teachers also include study and critique of TV scripts in the reading curriculum. Literature-based reading programs often study both a printed version of classic stories as well as a video version.

Alternatively, some teach high-quality movies as literature, examining such elements as plot structure, character development, and point of view. This approach has a particular advantage with poor or unmotivated readers because the medium is available to all students regardless of their reading level; they are more highly motivated to participate; and many can approach the analysis at a higher level of expertise than they can in the print medium. Given the interest and motivation inspired by motion video, some teachers use it to teach writing structures as well. Once the plot structure of a television drama is pointed out to the children (who have little trouble recognizing the plot structure in TV shows), it is easier to apply that same structure—introduction, conflict development, climax, resolution—to writing a story of their own.

Besides providing entertainment at home and enrichment in the schools, motion video technology has significantly increased the educational possibilities for students who are unable to attend school or live in remote areas without opportunities for specialized instruction. Instructional television via satellite, for instance, can bring lessons in foreign languages, calculus, chemistry, and other advanced or specialized subjects to individual students or small schools that do not have the resources. The decreasing cost of technology and increasing availability make this kind of distance learning more feasible for both individuals and groups of students.

INTERACTIVE VIDEO

The popularizing of videotape made it easy for teachers to extend their curriculum use of motion video by recording selected TV programs or choosing from a vast array of pre-recorded titles. As a result, teachers use motion video to support their lessons more often than before, but not as often as they might if they could conveniently show just a minute of tape here or a few seconds there to illustrate particular points. Sometimes teachers want to show a specific process, such as how hummingbirds fly and eagles soar, and, in this case, it makes sense to show the sequences step-by-step and then repeat them several times over. Sometimes teachers want to freeze the video on a single image to point out a specific moment in the process. Videotape does not fulfill these needs very well, but when the video images are stored on a videodisc that is controlled by a computer, it introduces a whole new world of possibilities.

Unlike videotape, a videodisc can contain any combination of slides, diagrams, maps, text, and motion video sequences. It can play forward and backward at variable speeds and can freeze a single frame indefinitely. The user can quickly and easily locate any frame on the disc, simply by keying the frame number. When the videodisc is controlled by a computer, the information on the disc becomes a visual database that can be accessed and manipulated in any number of ways for all kinds of purposes. This computer-based capability is called "interactive video," as it combines the interactive and information processing features of the computer with the visual information and appeal of motion video. For example, if a teacher wants to show students how the hummingbird's method of flight differs from the eagle's, with a keystroke he or she could access videodisc sequences that picture each of these birds in flight and then show them in slow motion or one frame at a time. If the disc does not contain diagrams of the birds' wing structures, the teacher could locate those diagrams elsewhere, scan them (to make a digitized computer image), and display them on the computer screen, beside the video screen.

Alternatively, let's say that students have been asked to examine the causes of earthquakes and prepare an interactive video presentation. To do this, they search an earth science videodisc for diagrams of fault movement and video clips of earthquakes in action; they read books, and consult other resources as well. Then they create the presentation combining the information they have written from texts and visual information they have selected to illustrate certain points. The completed presentation begins with a dramatic video clip of a massive earthquake, followed by a text explanation of the earth's crust and its patterns of movement. Illustrations of the earth's surface layers and fault movement leading up to a major earthquake appear on the computer screen when the right arrow key is pressed. With another keystroke, further video sequences appear that show close-ups of the earth's surface as the quake occurs. The presentation concludes with an image of a rail fence that has been separated by an earthquake; one section of the fence standing several yards away from the other.

Videodiscs are currently available that contain the highest quality slide and motion video collections from the nation's best museums and scientific institutes. For example, there is an encyclopedia that presents history of the 20th century through news clips or film; video and slide collections from the Smithsonian National Air and Space Museum, the National Gallery, and the NASA space program, as well as subject area collections covering earth science, life science, physical science, and astronomy.

CONCLUDING THOUGHTS

In this chapter we have discussed the role that educational technology can play in restructuring the classroom to enable students to better prepare for the coming century. We've presented both research findings and detailed discussion to help educators think about the role of technology in changing the way teachers teach and students learn in the classroom. The following chapters provide more concrete discussion and examples of how educators can go about restructuring curriculum and instruction to create more effective learning environments.

REFERENCES

Baker, Eva L.; Gearhart, M.; and Herman, J. L. (1990). *Assessment: Apple Classrooms of Tomorrow (ACOT) Evaluation Study, First- and Second-Year Findings.* Alexandria, VA: ERIC Document Reproduction Service.

Bialo, E. and Sivin, J. (1990). "Report on the Effectiveness of Microcomputers in Schools." Software Publishers Association, Washington, D.C.

Cotton, K. (1991). "Computer-Assisted Instruction," School Improvement Research Series, Close-up #10, Portland, OR: Northwest Regional Educational Laboratory, May.

Dwyer, D. C.; Ringstaff, C.; and Sandholtz, J. H. (1990). *Teacher Beliefs and Practices, Part I and Part II.* Alexandria, VA: ERIC Document Reproduction Service.

Ehman, L. H. and Glenn, A. D. (1987). *Computer Based Education in the Social Studies.* Bloomington, IN: ERIC Clearinghouse for Social Studies/Social Science Education.

Ehman, L. H.; Glenn, A. D.; Johnson, V.; and White, C. S. (1990). "Using Computer Databases in Student Problem Solving: A Study of Eight Social Studies Teachers' Classes." A paper presented at the Annual Meeting of the National Council for the Social Studies, College and University Faculty Assembly, Anaheim CA, November.

Fisher, C. W. (1989). *Student Empowerment: The Influence of High Computer Access on Student Empowerment.* Alexandria, VA: ERIC Document Reproduction Service.

Greenfield, P. M. (1984). *Mind and Media: The Effects of Television, Video Games, and Computers.* Cambridge: Harvard University Press.

Hiebert, E. H.; Quellmalz, E. S.; and Vogel, P. (1989). *Writing: A Research-Based Writing Program for Students with High Access to Computers.* Alexandria, VA: ERIC Document Reproduction Service.

Ingels, S. J., et al. (1992). "National Education Longitudinal Study of 1988: First Follow-up Student Component Data File User's Manual," Volumes 1 and 2. Washington DC: National Center for Educational Statistics, April.

Johnson, J. and Ettema, J. (1982). *Positive Images: Breaking Stereotypes with Children's Television.* Beverly Hills, CA: Sage.

Kelly, H. and Gardner, H., Eds. (1981). *Viewing Children through Television.* San Francisco: Jossey-Bass.

Kozma, R. B. (1991). "Learning with Media," *Review of Educational Research,* Summer, Vol, 61, No. 2, pp. 179–211.

Means, B. and Olson, K. (1993). "Supporting School Reform with Educational Technology." A paper presented at the American Educational Research Association, Atlanta, Georgia.

Sandholtz, J. H.; Ringstaff, C.; and Dwyer, D. C. (1990). *Classroom Management: Teaching in High-Tech Environments—Classroom Management Revisited, First-Fourth Year Findings.* Alexandria, VA: ERIC Document Reproduction Service.

Sheingold, K. and Hadley, M. (1990). "Accomplished Teachers: Integrating Computers into Classroom Practice," Center for Technology in Education: Bank Street College of Education, September.

Tiemey, R. J. (1989). *Student Thinking Processes: The Influence of Immediate Computer Access on Students' Thinking.* Alexandria, VA: ERIC Document Reproduction Service.

U.S. Office of Technology Assessment (1988). *Power On! New Tools for Teaching and Learning.* Washington D.C.: U.S. Government Printing Office.

PART II

IMPLEMENTATION

Review, Rethink, Restructure Curriculum & Instruction

The curriculum chapters that follow present practical applications of the research-based pedagogical framework and rationale for technology use presented in Part I. Rather than organizing curriculum chapters by traditional subject area (e.g., English, history, math, science), they are organized by type of learning experience, which may include several traditional subject areas or focus on one. Chapters 5–9 each present a restructured curriculum area, its pedagogical rationale, classroom scenarios, and suggestions for implementation. Curriculum areas include: communication, problem solving, inquiry, critical thinking, and basic skills. The scenarios and suggestions for implementation are derived from research in teaching and technology and from the real experiences of teachers. All of them integrate the use of technology at some level.

Many of the implementation chapters present scenarios that involve common instructional approaches, such as using collaborative groups, teaching multimedia composition, and applying alternative assessments. Rather than repeat how these across-the-curriculum approaches can be implemented every time they come up in the examples, the book presents these approaches in this section's introductory Chapter 4.

Following the restructured curriculum Chapters 5–9, Chapter 10 focuses on restructuring at the school, district, and state levels, including the processes of planning and implementation.

4

INSTRUCTIONAL APPROACHES ACROSS THE CURRICULUM

TEACHING STUDENTS HOW TO WRITE FOR ALL DISCIPLINES

In any strong writing program, the teacher provides direct instruction and modeling of how to write a narrative or expository essay, followed by ample student writing activities. The teacher models good writing practices by demonstrating the processes of generating ideas, organizing them, and composing a first draft. Editing and revising skills also need to be demonstrated after students have composed the first draft.

In an elementary classroom, for instance, the teacher would begin by modeling the processes of generating ideas, organizing and drafting them for (and with) the whole class. Below is an example of how a fourth grade teacher models how to write a persuasive essay for her students.

> With students seated in a semicircle around her, the teacher asks them, "What's your favorite place to go on a Saturday or Sunday?"
>
> Students spontaneously respond, "The zoo," "A baseball game," "My friend's house," "Skating," and so forth.
>
> The teacher records their suggestions on her keyboard and displays the list on a large display screen.
>
> They select a favorite place by popular vote—the zoo—and the process continues. "How can we convince readers that visiting the zoo is the best possible thing to do to do this weekend?" she asks.

Once again, students' answers appear on the overhead screen, and soon students are arguing about which arguments are the most persuasive. "If I tell my parents the zoo is *educational,* they'll take me!" claims one contributor.

"But that's no reason for a kid to go," points out another.

"How about if we say that both kids and grown-ups will like the zoo because they can pretend they're traveling all around the world to see different animals!" adds another.

After the group selects the most persuasive reasons for visiting the zoo, the teacher guides them in formulating a topic sentence and opening paragraph that present the favorite place and why a reader should go there.

Then she asks, "What happens after we convince the reader to go to our favorite place?" guiding them forward to the process of gathering information about the chosen place.

Using the same instructional approach, she models how to read and take notes from different sources. In this case, she records facts such as admission fee, hours the zoo is open, whether food is available, if there are facilities, public transportation to the zoo, and so forth.

Finally, using the same group suggestion process, she guides the children through the experience of synthesizing the information and expressing it in their own words. She does this by having them compose sentences out loud, while she records them on the word processor and displays them on the large screen. Then, as they develop paragraphs, they also suggest sentence revisions to make the paragraphs more organized and coherent. This process continues until the students (and teacher) are happy with the completed essay.

When the lesson is over, students go away with a model of how to write a persuasive essay and they also have a printed copy. They are then ready to work independently or in pairs to repeat the writing process modeled by their teacher.

By the time students reach secondary school, teachers would like to expect that the students already know how to write basic narrative and expository forms of writing. However, for whatever reason, many students enter junior high and even high school with little prior experience and/or expertise in writing. Consequently, secondary teachers must also demonstrate the processes of writing basic narrative and expository prose, as well as how to compose more complex documents, including research reports, short stories, and multimedia presentations.

To demonstrate the processes involved in composing any of these documents, teachers can develop a simple example assignment and go through all the steps of gathering information, organizing it into the appropriate format, and creating a rough draft. The demonstration process is similar to the one modeled for elementary students (above), but presented at a more appropriate level for older students.

The curriculum chapters that follow include further examples of teaching the writing process to elementary and secondary students.

TEACHING STUDENTS HOW TO CRITIQUE AND REVISE THEIR WORK

One of the most important skills all writers need to acquire in order to improve their own writing is the facility to recognize what is wrong with it, so that they can attempt to make it better. The ability to critique a piece of writing constructively is a skill that doesn't come automatically to most people, however. Writers have to learn it and practice it in order to help themselves (and others) become better writers.

One way to help students learn critiquing skills is by arranging them in small peer groups of three or four students, and having them regularly critique one another's writing assignments. But first the teacher must put considerable effort into teaching students critiquing skills, so they can begin working independently in these groups, reading one another's papers, critiquing them, and making suggestions for improvements.

The most effective way to teach the editing process is to demonstrate it, while involving students in the process. To prepare for such a demonstration, select a student-written paper that lies somewhere within the class's normal range of writing competency, duplicate copies for everyone, and be prepared to display the text on a large overhead display screen.

[Note: Students are advised in the beginning that their papers will be shared with classmates and therefore, they should not select experiences and topics to write about that are private. Initially, they will be uncomfortable sharing their work, and especially with having their papers critiqued in front of the class. Explain that every writer's work can be improved, but that the long-range benefits of the experience are well worth the brief discomfort. The teacher should also make sure that even the best writers in the class have their papers critiqued in the same manner. It's also important to frequently read aloud and praise successful papers written by all students.]

When you are ready to begin the demonstration, display the essay to be critiqued on a large display screen and follow these steps (which can be modified for elementary students):

1. Review with the students what the assignment was, and list on the chalkboard the specific suggestions or advice you made when the assign-

ment was given (e.g., use concrete details rather than vague, sweeping statements; do not use words that express a direct opinion, such as good, evil, smart, pretty, etc.).

2. Read the paper aloud to the class. Explain that reading a paper out loud is an important step because it helps the writer (and reviewers) hear how it "sounds." Many common writing problems—such as awkward sentences, weak transitions, and poor organization—can be detected simply by reading a paper aloud. Advise students to go through this simple process themselves, just before completing any draft they write.

3. Ask students to comment on the positive aspects of the paper (e.g., the transitions between ideas are smooth; the general organization is logical; the ending is effective). Then point out a few general areas that are less successful (e.g., the paper is a bit too general—it needs more specific examples; the tense keeps switching between past and present).

4. Then go back and reread the first paragraph, sentence by sentence, asking students if each sentence is appropriate in its context. Guide them to recognize where the problems occur and discuss what's wrong. Ask for suggestions on how to reword the sentences to make them work better.

5. Continue critiquing the paper in this manner until the end. Students probably will not remedy all the problems, but it is likely they will identify the most important ones and make suggestions to the writer for improvements in the next draft. When critiquing papers longer than two or three pages, students can be guided to focus their comments on the larger organizational problems, rather than on pointing out every mechanical error. Students whose papers are being critiqued are instructed to make corrections on their copy when possible and write notes in the margins concerning suggestions on structure, style, or other, more complex changes.

6. Conclude the critique with a summary of the areas that need the most revision. If there are an overwhelming number of problems, pick out a few important ones for the writer to work on improving for the next draft.

[Note: Elementary students cannot be expected to develop highly sophisticated critiquing skills, but they can become quite proficient at recognizing what "makes sense" or does not, and what "sounds right" or does not. Learning to figure out what to do to make their writing better, helps students improve their fundamental skills such as spelling and punctuation, as well as higher-level skills such as organization and style.]

After one or two demonstrations of the critiquing process, students can meet in small editing groups and begin critiquing one another's papers, following the steps outlined above. The teacher should continue working closely with the groups—especially in the beginning—helping them focus on working together to identify problems and to offer suggestions for improvement.

At some point, the teacher should help the students discover that even the best writers in the class can benefit from having others critique their work. This is easily accomplished by guiding the class through a critique of the best paper. No matter how skillful a person is at writing, it is beneficial to have someone else read an early draft and provide constructive criticism, because most writers cannot effectively be their own objective audience. All writers—even professionals—can improve their work by having a second reader critique their work.

When the editing groups have finished their work, writers take the suggestions made about their papers and use them to write a second draft. The teacher reads the second drafts and makes further suggestions for the third and (perhaps) final draft.

A positive way to end the cycle is to share some of the particularly successful final drafts with the class, so that students can enjoy praise and feel a sense of accomplishment at least as often as they are directed to focus on the less successful aspects of their work. It also helps if teachers save some of these final papers to present as models for students in future classes when they attempt a similar assignment for the first time.

In sum, learning to critique and revise a piece of writing is a skill that is different from learning to compose. Yet it has not been widely taught in school, mostly because until recently, teachers have chosen not to require students to recopy or retype second and third drafts of their papers. With word processing, however, the time-consuming and boring job of recopying disappears. What is left is the more thought-provoking work of identifying problems in one's writing and devising solutions to improve it, a process that's not unlike solving problems in math and science. It is challenging work, but often captivating, and certainly the benefits for students—significantly improved writing—makes it well worth the effort.

TEACHING MULTIMEDIA COMPOSING AND EDITING SKILLS

Composing a Multimedia Presentation

The instructional process of teaching students to compose and edit multimedia presentations is fundamentally the same as teaching students to write and edit written compositions. However, communicating in multiple media calls for further skills, including the ability to select the appropriate media for communicating to a particular audience for a specific purpose. Visual communication has its own unique vocabulary and techniques, as do music and speech. When communicating in multiple media, the designer/composer must understand the languages and techniques of all these media as well as how to integrate them such that the results convey the intended ideas more effectively than would be possible in a single medium.

Many teachers begin by involving students in the creation of videotape productions that focus on a visual component, with narration and music or other sound effects to complete the presentation. When students become experienced at managing these components to build a coherent videotape presentation, they are ready to tackle an interactive video project that combines video footage with computer displays (of text, diagrams, and graphics) and audiotaped sound. The process of developing an interactive video project is far more complex than creating a videotape because it involves integrating media from laserdisc, computer, and audiotape technologies.

To approach the task of teaching students to compose multimedia documents—videotape and/or interactive video—teachers can use the suggested modeling process for teaching written communication, extending the steps to include composition with other media. Additional steps include how to create a storyboard to complete the overall design process, and how to piece together the individual media segments to create an integrated document. The teacher would select a simple example topic for a multimedia document and then demonstrate the steps for production. Let's say the task is to create an interactive video presentation about the organization and functioning of a bee colony. The demonstration might include the following steps:

1. Students, together with the teacher, would outline the information they wanted to cover, such as the different types of bees in the colony and their specific functions, the organization of labor, methods of communication, mating activities, and process of honey production.
2. They would discuss what medium would communicate each of these pieces of information most effectively. For example, a graphic diagram of the bees' different jobs might best present the organization of labor, video footage might best communicate how bees produce honey and their mating activities, and background narration might be used most effectively to explain the overall patterns of behavior and activities of the colony.
3. They would then create a "storyboard," which is an organizing device that separates the multimedia production into individual infor-

mation segments. Initially, the storyboard looks like a grid of large, empty blocks. Students then fill in each block by writing down the information they want to cover and what media they want to use to cover it. For instance, the first block could be labeled "Introduction to the Bee Colony" and would indicate the need for video footage of the bee hive and its inhabitants, and for narration that explains the purpose and focus of the presentation. The narrator's script could be included in the storyboard or written on a separate piece of paper. Each consecutive block would also be filled in with the text, visuals, sound, and other components needed to make the next point in the presentation.

4. When the storyboard is finished, the more technical work begins. Participants need to identify the exact film footage to be included in each storyboard block; create the text, diagrams, photos, and other computer-based elements to be included; and record the scripted narration for each block.

5. Finally, each of the media segments must be integrated to create a unified whole. This may be a single videotape that includes all the segments, or it may involve a more complex interactive video set-up that includes a computer, monitor, laserdisc player, and tape recorder.

Obviously, the entire process can't possibly be demonstrated in a single day. The suggested approach is for the teacher to employ students as team members in the production of this initial demonstration presentation. When producing interactive video projects, students often develop particular expertise and take on the production jobs that use their expertise. For example, some become technology experts and are used by production groups to piece together the different media segments. Others have just the right voices to do the narration. Others are good at creating computer graphics and diagrams. And others are best at writing scripts or selecting background music and sound effects. Because these composition projects can be quite complex, it may take a while to develop expertise in any of the areas of production. Some teachers allow students to take on the same job for several presentations, before attempting to switch jobs and develop another expertise.

Editing a Multimedia Presentation

The process of critiquing and revising a multimedia presentation "draft" is also more complex than reviewing a written draft because it requires reviewers to address all media components. Creators must have sufficient technical skills to alter video clips, narration and other sound effects, as well as the text. To approach the task of teaching students to edit multimedia documents, teachers can use the suggested process described previously for revising written compositions as a base, while extending the details to include a review of the creator's use of individual media and the relative success of the overall design. The effectiveness of the presentation would depend not only on the quality of the text, diagrams, footage, narration, and music, but just as importantly on the way it was put together. Does the film footage successfully engage the audience such that they are motivated to learn the details? Are the detailed explanations easily understandable to the audience and are they presented in such a way as to keep the viewers'/listeners' attention? Do the visuals strengthen the text presentation? Does the sound track enhance the production? Do each of the media mesh together and enhance one another so that the total production is better and more effective than any of its parts?

The whole class would be called upon to critique the production, providing feedback on the use of the visual, text, and audio elements of the work, as well as on how effectively the overall message was communicated to the intended audience. Following this kind of critique, the creator(s) would then go back and revise the individual components in an effort to improve the final production.

Chapters that follow include several other examples of these multiple media composing and editing processes at work.

EFFECTIVE USE OF STUDENT COLLABORATIVE GROUPS

Having students work in small groups has become a popular teaching strategy in the last decade—a positive trend because accumulated research now affirms that students learn more when they explain and defend their ideas with others. Research shows that group interaction has a favorable effect on understanding mathematical concepts as well as reading comprehension. It helps students develop understandings that transfer to other areas. It helps them learn to solve complex problems, improves language proficiency, and increases social skills. Further, groupwork helps participants learn to be active participants in democratic processes, conduct rational and orderly discussions, plan and carry out simple and complex tasks, and make decisions independently. In sum, working in small groups enables more students to actively communicate, think, and learn, and thus is a more effective strategy than having students simply listen to a teacher's explanation.

However, even though the use of student groups has been increasing in recent years, in many cases groupwork has been ineffective because students have not been taught how to work cooperatively. Without prior training, student groups typically end up with one person doing most of the work, or the members spend much of their time arguing about who should do what, or the students can't stay focused on the task and the discussion evolves into social chatter.

Teachers simply cannot place students into peer groups, present the assignment, and expect the participants to work together successfully. Group assignments and group processes must be carefully thought out by the teacher beforehand, and students must be taught how to work within groups, because groupwork involves very different skills and processes compared to individual work.

As defined in Dr. Elizabeth Cohen's (1994) book, *Designing Groupwork: Strategies for the Heterogeneous Classroom,* groupwork is an instructional approach in which students work together, without direct supervision, to complete a well-defined task. Delegating authority to student groups gives them responsibility for planning and allocating the work. It makes them free to complete the group task the way they choose, while still remaining accountable to the teacher for a final product.

According to Cohen, students can benefit from working collaboratively on routine tasks, but groupwork yields the greatest gains when the learning goals include understanding concepts, solving problems creatively, and improving oral language skills. Groupwork can be an extremely effective learning approach when groups are asked to solve complex problems, interpret literary works, complete construction projects, develop historical or political points of view, and so forth.

Depending on the task at hand, groups may operate in a couple of different ways. One type of assignment calls for a single group product or solution. For example, the group may be asked to interpret a poem or prepare arguments for one side of a political debate. Since the group has a single collaborative goal, it must reach a consensus of opinion and method of process, and work closely together while completing the entire assignment. This approach can be problematic if group members have difficulty reaching consensus and working as a tightly integrated group. The approach can also be modified to enable members to divide up the initial work, while still facing the ultimate task of reaching group consensus and producing a unified product or solution.

Another type of group assignment calls for group members to produce individual products, but use the group to share ideas and the overall workload. For example, a group may be assigned a certain period of history and given responsibility to prepare a report containing separate chapters on government, social life, scientific developments, and so on. They then take an essay test on the entire period. Students would divide up the work, giving each member responsibility for a chapter; yet they would still need to share information and ideas to make their pieces fit together into a coherent report, and they would depend on one another's work to gain a full understanding of all aspects of the period.

Any type of groupwork must be carefully planned and structured if it is to succeed. The group task must be carefully defined with clear instructions that include suggested or assigned activities, discussion questions, products, available resources, and so forth. The group's tasks should call upon members to think critically, seek information, solve problems, and create products that include the artistic, physical, intellectual and other skills/talents of group members. Designing groupwork that is carefully structured to enlist every member in some capacity can also be a particularly effective way to work with students who have extremely diverse academic skills.

As outlined in Cohen's book, to insure successful collaboration within student working groups, teachers must:

- Purposefully compose groups that reflect a cross-section of the classroom, including gender, racial/ethnic orientation, academic ability, and so on, rather than permit students to form their own groups.
- Prepare activity cards for each group that include instructions for what the group is to discuss and what kind of group product they should turn out. Members also receive report sheets to answer discussion questions individually, or in some form express their own ideas on the topic. This assures both group and individual accountability.
- Assign students specific roles within the group, such as facilitator, reporter, summarizer, resource manager, technician, and so on, and rotate the roles after each group activity.
- Teach students how to work in groups before they begin. They must understand: (1) how to do each of the assigned group jobs; (2) how to help other group members without doing the work for them; and (3) how to check on what other members are doing by listening, encouraging, and suggesting rather than criticizing or taking over.

  Prepare students for these jobs by discussing them with the entire class, so members know what to expect of each person who takes on a job, and so they will be willing to accept the person in that role. The facilitator's job is often the most complex and challenging, so that job should be assigned carefully to set a good model. A job that requires advanced technology expertise (e.g., using interactive video equipment or a video editing machine) may have to remain with a few students who have been specially trained to use the equipment.
- Convince students that many different abilities are needed to complete the groupwork, not just traditional academic abilities. Students

with talent for keen observation, visualization, spatial problem-solving, organization, and careful listening, as well as drawing, playing a musical instrument, acting, or building can make significant contributions. Convince them that no one person is good at all the abilities and everyone is good in at least one ability.
- Intervene only if a group cannot get started, or gets stuck along the way. Resist the urge to step in and tell them what to do; insist that they play the roles and use the new behaviors they have learned to make the group work.
- Observe each group, looking for opportunities to recognize "low-status" kids for positive contributions. Compliment these students for competently performing some intellectual skill. The more frequently a teacher finds ways to point out intellectual contributions of low-status students, the more the status problem is removed and the "high-status" peers begin to revise their perceptions of their classmates.

Evaluating and assigning grades to groupwork is a complex and delicate endeavor. Some teachers choose to assess the group's work as a whole, awarding every member the same grade. However, this approach can cause some students to take over others' work (the work of those members perceived to be less able) in an effort to insure a good grade for themselves. Evaluating each group member's contribution separately can also have negative effects in that students tend to focus less on the quality of the group product and more on their own contributions. The problem with awarding individual grades is that individuals who appear to contribute little in terms of product, may be contributing much with regard to making suggestions, or arbitrating compromise. Those who appear to have contributed greatly to the final product, however, may have bullied their way into the spotlight with little regard for their teammates' ideas or efforts. It is extremely difficult to fairly evaluate the contributions or each member, or to attribute a concrete grade to such a complex process.

To address potential problems such as non-contributing members and members who tend to take over, teachers can hold periodic peer feedback sessions for students to discuss their grievances and work toward collaborative solutions. Such feedback sessions are arranged while the groupwork is in process, so problems can be addressed when the group is still functioning, and members can then resume their work with better results.

In sum, traditional methods of evaluating the group as one or as individuals, do not seem to work particularly well. Teachers who have tried these methods of evaluation and found them deficient are now attempting to explore other means of assessment. One viable solution is to provide feedback on group products rather than assign grades. Teachers who use this approach typically involve students in a process of self-evaluation that focuses on both their individual contributions and the work of the entire group. This evaluation/feedback process includes discussion of how effectively the group managed to integrate everyone's ideas and reach solutions agreeable to the majority, and what kinds of contributions individual members made to easing the process as well as developing a product. This method of assessment does not appeal to teachers who feel a strong need to assign concrete grades for groupwork, but many who formerly felt this way, are now beginning to discover that providing comprehensive feedback to groups and individuals can be more effective than assigning grades in helping kids learn and improve.

Groupwork is now being used extensively for completing projects that involve technology. It can be debated whether groupwork is employed because there aren't enough computers or video cameras for every student, or because the learning is enhanced by groupwork, but teachers who use both groupwork and technology seem to agree that they both significantly improve student learning.

In the chapters that follow readers will find numerous examples of how groupwork and technology are effectively integrated as student groups conduct research via telecommunications, explore distant cultures through visual technologies, create multimedia products, and participate in other such collaborative learning experiences.

TEAM TEACHING USING INTERDISCIPLINARY CURRICULA

Interdisciplinary learning can occur through a variety of teaching approaches, ranging from situations in which teachers of different subject areas cover similar topics simultaneously, to situations in which subject area teachers completely integrate their curricula.

The first approach is the easiest because subject disciplines remain distinct, secondary school schedules don't have to be changed, or curricula rewritten. An example of this approach is when the English and history teachers decide to cover 19th-century literature (in English class) and history (in history class) during the same semester. The advantage is that history learning is strengthened by experiencing human thought and experiences of the period through literature. The students' study of literature is likewise enriched by understanding the historic period in which the literature takes place. Elementary teachers can integrate English and history curricula quite easily within their own classrooms. For example, elementary students could read selections such as *Sing Down the Moon, The Lone Hunt, Oregon at Last!, Caddie Woodlawn,* and the *Little House in the Big Woods* series, while studying relations with the Native Americans and the Westward expansion, and *Rifles for Watie, Red Badge of Courage, By Secret Railway,* and *The Perilous Road,* while studying the Civil War.

Science and history can be taught simultaneously by demonstrating how periods of history are influenced by scientific discovery or invention such as Darwin's scientific theory of the Origin of the Species, the invention of the cotton gin, the combustible engine, and electricity.

History and English easily combine with a number of other subjects, including music, art, health, physical education, astronomy, and geology. Almost any subject can inspire a need to communicate and thus tie in with English, and most subjects enjoy a rich history of evolution and human experience. Imaginative teachers can find infinite ways to link up to their colleagues' curriculum plans.

A more ambitious approach is for teacher teams to create interdisciplinary units that link two or more subject areas. This approach involves more teacher planning time and a secondary school schedule that's flexible enough to combine class periods as well as subjects. Interdisciplinary units can involve students in comprehensive projects such as building a scaled model of the local city. This project would call for students to learn new math, geometry, and drafting skills; study local history and government; review the environmental choices made by the city concerning how waste, water, air, and energy sources are dealt with; study the roads and public transportation systems; and countless other issues. Interdisciplinary units can also address complex problems such as the causes of the Civil War, which would involve considerable study of 17th-, 18th-, and early 19th-century U.S. history, including the origins of the slave trade and political movements, scientific inventions that increased the differences between the North and South, sociological study of the Northern and Southern cultures, literature of the period, and so on.

The most complete interdisciplinary approach occurs when teachers integrate their curricula such that all disciplines are woven into one coherent and comprehensive curriculum. This approach involves huge amounts of teacher planning and coordination, a school schedule that has no period divisions, and parents who are willing to depart from traditional education. It is showcased nationally through many schools within the Coalition of Essential Schools, as well as individual schools, and a number of alternative programs within school systems. Examples of integrated instruction include semester or year-long programs that address broad topics such as the 19th century around the world, how inventions have influenced civilization, art as a reflection of human history; or tasks such as design a tax system that is fair, design an ideal educational system, or a national health care system.

Many educators favor some level of subject integration for several reasons. They argue that it mirrors the real world more accurately than discipline-based instruction, making it easier to understand complex ideas, and infinitely more sensible. Students more readily see the interconnections between subjects and how their learning connects to real life. Although it is easier and more efficient to cover subject-related learning objectives in the separate discipline approach (at least until new curricula are developed), the integrated approach enables students to gain a deeper understanding of what they are learning.

In many cases, teachers still have discipline-based objectives, such as understanding the U.S. political structure and processes, demonstrating proficiency in using mathematical formulas, or writing well-organized and grammatically correct essays. Indeed, while teaching an interdisciplinary unit, teachers may frequently focus on subject-related skills and understandings, and use the disciplines to organize some lessons/activities, without losing focus on the larger, integrated objectives.

Educators teaching in secondary schools that have not yet adopted any integrated approach, or who are just venturing into integrated territory, would be wise to begin with the simultaneous teaching approach, and then move on to increasingly more integrated learning experiences as success and confidence grow.

Elementary teachers have a much easier job of creating and implementing integrated curricula because they can do it on their own, without having to spend extensive planning time with another teacher (though this is certainly a valuable option) or deal with an inflexible, fragmented school schedule.

Curriculum chapters that follow provide examples of various levels of subject integration and demonstrate how integrated curricula can work for individual classroom teachers, as well as teams of teachers from all subject areas. The examples also show how the use of technology can strengthen and expand the nature and value of interdisciplinary learning.

DISTANCE LEARNING: USING TECHNOLOGY TO TEACH STUDENTS IN DISTANT LOCATIONS

Distance learning has become popular in recent years with the emerging financial difficulties experienced by many school districts and the development of new technologies that enable districts to employ one teacher to instruct students in multiple schools. For example, if only a few students in a district want to take advanced calculus, and they attend different schools, the district can hire one calculus teacher to teach them all, by using distance learning technologies to reach all locations.

Technically, distance learning is the use of telecommunications equipment such as the telephone, television, computer, video, fiber optics, cable broadcast, and satellites to send instructional programming to students at various locations. Distance learning is currently used to provide instruction for students of all ages, from elementary level courses to professional development workshops.

A typical distance learning class might look like this:

- At 10:00 am students at several different schools enter their distance learning classrooms, each equipped with TVs, telephones, and keypads.
- An adult facilitator (not necessarily a certified teacher) greets them, collects homework, and makes sure the equipment is up and running.
- At 10:05 the instructor appears on the TV screen (another screen displays the white board the instructor uses frequently, and another displays the computer and video monitor the instructor uses for video and text support).
- For the next 50 minutes, the instructor presents an information-rich lesson that includes white board notes, video clips, and computer-generated charts and diagrams. Individual students are able to ask or respond to the instructor's questions by using the classroom telephone, and all students use classroom keypads to respond to questions the teacher asks them during class. The instructor is able to quickly tally their responses which helps her determine how well the students are understanding the lesson.

Currently, distance learning is most cost-effectively used in districts that have small numbers of students in different schools who enroll in courses such as physics, calculus, statistics, Latin, German, and other specialized courses. However, the technology and the concept of delivering instruction in this manner are yet young, and many educators are exploring a wide variety of possible applications.

Little research has been completed on the educational impact of distance learning; however, the Office of Technology Assessment indicated in its 1989 report *Linking for Learning: A New Course for Education,* that distance learning appears to be as effective as on-site, face-to-face instruction in the classroom. The report states further that students claim they benefit from exposure to a greater range of ideas, peers, and teachers made possible by the system's expanded educational community. However, they add that distance learning can be frustrating when the learning group is large and it becomes difficult to ask questions and get help during class.

The current model for distance learning involves one teacher delivering a lecture—sometimes accompanied by video footage, lab demonstrations, or other supplements to the direct lecture method—with students able to ask questions and/or receive help when they need it. This model does not lend itself to much class discussion, groupwork, or other such teaching approaches advanced in this book. However, as suggested above, the concept and the technologies are new and there's a good deal of potential for innovative educators to design new and more interactive ways to use the technologies for alternative instructional approaches.

USING VIDEOTAPES IN THE CLASSROOM

The use of video technology in the classroom has increased faster than any other new technology in decades. Currently almost all schools in the country have videotape players, and in many schools, every classroom is equipped to show videos to students. But how is this equipment used? The typical use of videos is to provide supplementary, visual information to a curriculum unit being covered by the class. That's fine, but what generally happens is the teacher brings the tape into class (often without having viewed it first) and plays the entire tape. The teacher may ask a few questions afterwards and generate a short class discussion, but generally the video viewing experience is passive, much like the students' viewing of television programs at home. Typically watching a video is perceived by students as an entertaining diversion; they often don't relate the video to what they are studying in class, and the experience has little educational value.

In order to elevate video watching to an effective educational experience, it must become an interactive experience. The students must be actively involved in watching, and integrating what they see with what they're learning in class. The teacher plays a vital role in this transformation by actively engaging students in discussing what they see and processing the new information. There are a variety of ways to do this. Some things the teacher can do are:

1. Preview the tape and devise questions to ask the class before viewing the tape. Mention some of the issues that are raised in the tape and discuss what students think about them beforehand. Perhaps their ideas/opinions will change when they watch the tape.

2. Stop the tape periodically to emphasize and discuss points that have just been made. Freeze frames to examine particular visual images and their influence on what viewers may think.

3. Discuss the tape after viewing it, including its major points, point of view, and authenticity. Relate what students learned from the tape to what they're learning in class through lectures, discussion, textbooks, and other sources.

4. Show brief video clips rather than the entire video. Often the lessons teachers want to emphasize through visual example don't require the showing of an entire video. Viewing quickly becomes passive and major points are lost if students are presented with additional video information that moves far from the lesson at hand.

Few educators would argue against the value of video to provide visual context and real-world information to the printed and lecture-based information students most commonly receive in the classroom. However, the true value of video can only be obtained when the visual information is effectively integrated into the classroom learning. Research affirms the positive relationship between learning through video and the degree of interactivity involved. Research also indicates that students' attitudes improve when they're actively involved in the video presentations. It is time for teachers to take on a more active role when showing videos to their students—ultimately the process will be more fun and more educational.

USING TELEVISION: CHANNEL ONE, CNN NEWSROOM, OR OTHER SPECIALIZED PROGRAMMING

In 1990, Whittle Communications brought children's television news programming into the spotlight, when it offered schools the opportunity to receive free television and video equipment if they agreed to require all students to watch a 12-minute news program every school day. The news program parallels the format of major network news programs. News anchors and reporters are young adults who cover a range of topics from highlights of U.S. and world news from a teenager's perspective, to feature stories designed for junior high and high school students such as coping with stress or how to find a summer job.

Research done on this program's impact on students' education (Ehman, 1991), indicated that students' interest in and knowledge of geography and current events improved. Social studies teachers reported that they used the news broadcast to supplement information in regular lessons and to stimulate discussions of current events issues. And a strong majority of all subject area teachers reported that the program was a positive addition to the school curriculum. However, a controversy arose over a 2-minute portion of the broadcast that included advertisements for sponsors' products which caused some states and school districts to prohibit their schools' involvement with the network.

An alternative to Channel One programming is Turner Broadcasting Company's CNN Newsroom. Their daily program offers 15 minutes of commercial-free news and features designed for junior high and high school students. The program's advantage is that it contains no advertising. The disadvantage is that Turner does not offer participating schools free equipment and programming. Both networks offer similar news programming for teens; and both offer printed supplementary materials, newsletters, and an additional library of videotapes that range from special reports on recent and historic events, historic movies, and documentaries, to teacher training workshops.

For many teachers who are interested in using video to strengthen classroom teaching, these school-network partnerships offer a wealth of resources. Social studies teachers especially, can use the daily broadcasts as a springboard for discussions on current events, and other subject area teachers can use the supplementary videos to strengthen lessons in history, science, health, economics, art, literature, creative writing, and other areas. As demonstrated in the above section on using video in the classroom, it is essential to keep the video and TV viewing interactive. Teachers can engage students in discussions about what they see and should not hesitate to stop a video to discuss a point or raise an issue related to what is presented on the tape.

USING ALTERNATIVE ASSESSMENTS

The current movement to restructure schools introduces the need for new forms of assessments to measure students' progress toward new educational goals, such as the ability to solve complex problems, think analytically, work collaboratively, and learn autonomously.

This section defines some of the popular new assessment approaches and suggests how to go about applying one or two of them.

Outcome-Based Education

Outcome-based Education has become a popular buzzword across the nation and consequently is used to refer to any number of assessment strategies. Basically, an outcome-based educational system has clear learning goals for students, detailed outcomes that identify progress toward those goals, and standards for those outcomes. For example, if the goal is to communicate effectively in a variety of settings, outcomes would demonstrate the learner's ability to: (1) gather information from multiple sources; (2) organize, analyze, and apply such information; (3) express information, ideas, and emotions in a variety of ways; (4) use technology to gather, process, and express information and ideas.

Districts and states that adopt an outcome-based approach to education set out to systematically change the entire system. It is a complex process that first involves defining educational goals, standards, and expected outcomes for students. Then, assessment strategies and measures must be designed to assess student outcomes against the standard. Typically, these assessments include performance-based tests such as writing essays, constructing models, solving complex problems, and developing portfolios. A number of states have been working on this process in recent years and Chapter 10 reports on the progress some of them have made.

Performance-Based Assessment

Performance-based assessment is often the term used to describe the methods of assessment used in the outcome-based educational approach. These assessment methods require students to create answers or products that demonstrate their knowledge or skills in particular areas. Performance tests include writing essays, solving complex problems, conducting experiments, presenting oral arguments, constructing working models, or assembling portfolios of representative work. Representing a broader set of educational objectives, performances can also include baseball games, driving tests, music recitals, and cooking demonstrations.

One example of a performance-based task involves fourth-grade students in making decisions about purchasing fish for a school aquarium. Considerations include how many fish will fit in a certain size tank, the cost of the fish, what types of fish get along together and what ones don't. Students are given a chart that pictures several kinds of fish with information on each: the name, cost, length, color, special needs, and so on. The students' task is to select as many different kinds of fish as possible to fit in a 30-gallon aquarium, without spending more than $25. Then they write a letter to the principal presenting their recommendation for purchasing these fish for the school's fish tank.

Authentic Assessment

Assessment is authentic when the tasks used in testing are equal or similar to the best tasks found in instruction. Ideally, assessment tasks are part of the classroom curriculum and would include writing samples, projects, performances, portfolios, and exhibitions. Authentic assessments engage students in using knowledge and skills to solve the kinds of problems and do the kinds of things students will face in the world outside school.

Exhibitions

Exhibitions are comprehensive demonstrations of skills or competence. Students typically spend a good deal of time acquiring information and learning new skills in preparation for their exhibitions. The exhibition itself is usually a public gathering in which a student demonstrates mastery in the areas defined by the original assignment. Students are often expected to perform, explain, and defend their work when questioned by members of the audience. A well-designed assessment calls for both proof of the student's understanding of the content and the student's ability to think independently and imaginatively.

The most widespread use of exhibitions in their fullest sense is in schools that participate in the Coalition of Essential Schools. Founder and co-director of the coalition, Theodore Sizer, offers some example exhibition assessments in his book, *Horace's School.*

1. *Mathematics and Social Studies*

   Your group of five classmates is to complete accurately the federal Internal Revenue Service Form 1040 for each of five families. Each member of your group will prepare the 1040 for one of the families. You may work in concert, helping one another. "Your" particular family's form must be completed by you personally, however.

   Attached are complete financial records of the family assigned to you, including the return filed by that family last year. In addition, you will find a blank copy of the current 1040, including related schedules, and explanatory material provided by the Internal Revenue Service.

   You will have a month to complete this work. Your result will be "audited" by an outside expert and one of your classmates after you turn it in. You will have to explain the financial situation of "your" family and to defend the 1040 return for it which you have presented.

   Each of you will serve as "co-auditor" on the return filed by a student from another group. You will be asked to comment on that return.

Good luck. Getting your tax amount wrong—or the tax for any of the five families in your group—could end you in legal soup! (p. 48)

2. *Arts and Sciences*

   Assemble from metal pipes a wind instrument. Write a piece of music that uses it and perform this piece for us.

   Present to us design drawings for the instrument and be prepared to explain precisely how and why it works. (p. 118)

3. *Engineering, Science, and Mechanics*

   The engine and drive train of the 1983 Chevette before you has been "sabotaged" by us in a number of ways. Please troubleshoot the problems and repair them in the shortest amount of time and with as few new parts as possible. Draw up a description both of the problems and of your specific remedies; include a bill for the owner. (You should assign your labor time at the rate of $28 per hour.) Be prepared to defend your troubleshooting strategy, to explain why the sabotage caused flaws in the engine's functioning; and to tell us whether there were remedies you considered and then discarded. (p. 118)

Portfolios

Portfolios contain collections of a student's work over time. They may include anything from essays and reports, to multimedia presentations and videotaped performances.

Portfolios are perhaps the most widely used alternative assessment, and though they became popularized by English teachers who had students collect their best narrative and expository essays, portfolios are now used in all subject areas. Art teachers have their students prepare video portfolios that display their artwork and describe the student's artistic development across the year. Science teachers have their students develop portfolios that include research reports, videos of students doing experiments and other projects, and photographs of insect collections, inventions, community projects, and so forth.

Teachers with experience in using portfolios as a means of assessment suggest that others interested in initiating portfolio work keep in mind the following advice:

- Over time, the portfolio must contain evidence that the student has engaged in self-reflection.

- During the course of developing the portfolio, the student may include all work in the portfolio for purposes of reflection, self-evaluation, and revision. However, at the end of the year, the student, guided by the teacher, would select the pieces that best demonstrate growth and achievement, and those pieces that the student is willing to make public.
- An effective portfolio is not just a collection of all the student's work, it is a selective accumulation of characteristic work that demonstrates the student's development in skills, creativity, thinking, ability to assess and revise his or her own work. It showcases the achievements and the potential of the student.
- The process of assessing and scoring portfolio entries must be made clear to the student and must be articulated in the portfolio for others who might review the portfolio. Assessment should include both teacher assessment and student assessment.
- Students should have many opportunities to view examples of model portfolios.

School districts and states that adopt portfolio assessment as an integral part of the system's assessment strategy have to develop a systematic set of standards and measures so that all students in the system are compared fairly to the same standard. The process of standardizing portfolio assessment is complex and time-consuming, yet many educators and administrators believe it is necessary, and worth the effort.

Video Assessment

The use of video recording has become a popular assessment device as it enables teachers to videotape and then review individual student and group performances as well as their work in progress. The tape can later be used for student self-evaluation, class review, teacher evaluation, and outside evaluation.

For example, student groups can work collaboratively in class to design a product (e.g., a school building) and then present their designs to peers, and/or outside observers. The teacher would tape the groups in action, interviews with students (asking them to explain what they are learning and why), and the final presentation. The completed videotape presents a record of the students' thinking, work processes, organization, and final presentation. Each of these processes can then be critically reviewed by the students, their peers, the teacher, and/or outside evaluators.

The chapters that follow include several examples of how teachers are using video as an effective review and assessment tool.

REFERENCES

Cohen, Elizabeth G. (1994). *Designing Groupwork: Strategies for the Heterogeneous Classroom, Second Edition.* New York: Teachers College Press.

Ehman, L. (1991). "Using Channel One in Social Studies Classrooms: A First Look." A paper presented at the annual meeting of the National Council for the Social Studies, Washington D.C., November.

Sizer, Theodore R. (1992). *Horace's School: Redesigning the American High School.* New York: Houghton Mifflin Company.

U.S. Office of Technology Assessment (1989). Linking for Learning: A New Course for Education. Washington, D.C.: U.S. Government Printing Office.

5

COMMUNICATION

RATIONALE

Communication for a variety of purposes and audiences may include the processes of writing, speaking, drawing, composing music, designing multimedia presentations, and so forth. Sharing one's ideas in any of these media involves the critical task of organizing and presenting ideas in a manner that ensures others will grasp the intended meanings.

In all of the learning experiences described in subsequent chapters, students are asked to communicate their ideas in many different forms, including discussions, formal presentations, written and multimedia reports. When called upon to articulate and defend their ideas, the process compels students to reassess their own understandings, which often influences them to revise and/or expand their own knowledge. Although communication is an essential element in most of the book's curriculum activities, this chapter focuses on communication as a learning experience in itself.

Communication Skills

Fundamental skills include the ability to organize ideas logically and express them clearly to the intended audience. When writing, this includes the use of standard punctuation, grammar, and sentence structure. More advanced skills include the ability to write in different genres for different purposes and audiences, using a greater variety of writing techniques.

Speakers call upon the same organizational skills as writers, but speakers must also consider the unique characteristics of oral presentation, including how one captures and keeps the audience's attention, use of visual aids, physical gestures, and voice intonation.

When communicating in multiple media, the writer/speaker/artist/producer must employ additional skills, including the ability to select the appropriate media for communicating to a particular audience for a specific purpose. The creator must understand how to use audio and visual media to communicate effectively, and how to integrate text and speech with these media so that the multimedia production conveys the intended ideas more effectively than would any single medium.

The Importance of Teaching Communication Skills

To determine the value of teaching communication skills, it makes sense to reflect on one's fundamental learning goals. Our goals are to teach young people to be intelligent, independent thinkers as well as contributing team members—to be able to find information and learn new skills when they need to, and be able to think critically, solve problems, and understand complex ideas. Just as important, we believe it is essential for citizens to be able to communicate—explain what they know and understand, defend their ideas, and listen with an open mind to others. Learning to express thoughts and ideas is necessary for survival; learning to express them accurately, coherently, and thoughtfully, can elevate a person who is perceived as ignorant to one recognized as intelligent.

The processes of learning and applying communication skills involves several, if not all of the learning goals advocated in this book. The very process of learning to communicate involves acquiring new skills, thinking analytically, solving related problems as they arise, and developing an understanding of several media language styles and techniques. For all of these reasons, learning to communicate effectively through speech and writing, as well as through visual and other media, is perhaps the most fundamental of all learning experiences. In this book, it is the first and most expansive goal.

The Added Value of Using Technology for Communication

Written Communication

Long before there was research to support them, teachers claimed their students' writing dramatically improved with the use of computers. Indeed, the computer with word processing software has probably convinced more individuals to become technology users than any other computer application. Now research demonstrates that when students edit and revise their papers, the results tend to be better, and with word processing, they often revise many times because it's easier and they do not have to recopy drafts.

Computer-printed papers inspire greater pride in student writers because their papers look better without crossed out mistakes and smudged eraser marks, and printed papers look more "grown up." From the teacher's perspective, computer-printed papers are easier to read, and poorly handwritten papers often inadvertently influence readers to judge them more critically.

When students' work is visible on a computer screen, it is more publicly accessible to classmates, which encourages spontaneous sharing and further involvement in collaborative writing projects. It is also easy to print multiple copies for sharing and peer editing activities. Students tend to be more highly motivated to rework and revise their papers when the results will be computer "published" and distributed for others to read.

However, in spite of all the computer can do, it cannot teach students to be effective writers who can write clear and coherent paragraphs for a variety of purposes and genres. Students need to learn to write through direct instruction, modeling of the writing processes, guidance, and positive criticism. High quality instruction is the most essential ingredient in learning to write. Only teachers can provide that.

Oral Communication

To date, little research has been completed to affirm the value of using technology to teach oral communication. However, forward-thinking teachers have found that video technology can significantly strengthen the speech curriculum. They find that by videotaping students' oral presentations and then guiding them through a review of their performances, students can more readily understand their strengths and weaknesses and more easily improve.

Multimedia Communication

Again, there is little research to document the positive experiences teachers are having with integrating written, oral, and visual media into the extremely powerful form called multimedia communication. Studies do show, however, that learning is strengthened when a variety of media are used, rather than just one. Each medium emphasizes particular kinds of information and when combined they support each other, so that the results convey more and richer information.

CLASSROOM SCENARIOS AND OTHER SUGGESTIONS FOR IMPLEMENTATION

Elementary School Newspaper

Classroom projects that focus on communication as a learning objective typically address issues such as purpose of communication, audience, point of view, appropriate media and format, and so forth. Perhaps the most popular of these projects in both elementary and secondary classrooms is the student newspaper or literary publication.

Our exemplary elementary class participated in a newspaper publication project in which students interviewed other students across the country via telecommunications, wrote and edited articles, designed the layout, desktop published the newspaper, and delivered it electronically. The student-run project called for considerable collaborative planning and commitment, development of basic writing and editorial skills, and proficiency at designing computer graphics and page layout. At the end of the project, students critically evaluated the final publication in an effort to learn from their experience and share their knowledge with the next newspaper staff.

Let's take a closer look at the process. The project began as a pen-pal program which involved students in sending and receiving letters via telecommunications to classrooms in Alaska, California, Hawaii, Florida, and Maine. It was fun for students to learn about their peers' favorite rock singers, movies, and hobbies, as well as what they were studying in school, their ideas on foreign relations, environmental issues, local cultural traditions, and family background. One drawback of the program, however, was that students' letters sometimes weren't answered promptly, or not at all. A drawback from the teacher's point of view was that he wanted students to view friendly letter-writing as informal, and therefore did not use the letters as a means of teaching editing skills or enforcing high standards of writing.

Within a year, the pen-pal program evolved into a national newspaper project, enabling the teacher to use the experience to teach writing skills and insist on high standards, while retaining the students' interest in communicating with peers around the country. Further, the publication project enabled students to write for a larger audience; experience the adult roles of reporter, editor, layout artist, and production manager; and see their finished product as a nearly professional newspaper. The classroom sites rotated the job of collecting articles and producing the newspaper. This enabled each classroom teacher to go through the entire process once or twice a year with their class, while still contributing and receiving issues throughout the year.

The process of newspaper production works something like this. The teacher "sets the stage" by establishing the classroom as a newspaper office, assigning students roles such as reporters, editorial board members, copy editors, and layout artists.

Students then learn about the different styles of writing appropriate for newspapers, such as news articles, features, and reviews. They brainstorm article ideas and divide up the proposed stories, and set out to interview, research, observe, or do whatever is necessary to complete their assigned stories. Some interviews involve telecommunications, enabling the journalist to gather information from sources at the other school sites, or interview experts in distant places. Students from the other sites also contribute articles.

Once all stories have been collected from the production site as well as other sites, the editorial board meets to select articles for the issue. After stories are selected, they go to the copy editors for revision. Meanwhile, student artists read the copy in an effort to locate and/or create graphics and other artwork that will complement the stories. When the edited stories are ready, the layout process begins.

The layout artists, who have been learning to use a page layout program, begin formatting the copy into columns and arranging it in the newspapers' established format. (At the elementary level, teachers often design the publication layout and provide students with a template so they do not have to learn all the features of a highly sophisticated layout program.) Artwork may be scanned and entered into the layout, and computer graphics may also be entered into the layout, or they may be cut and pasted on the master sheets after the text is printed.

When the master copy is completed, it may be printed at a local quick-print shop and mailed (or faxed) to all sites. If the layout contains no cut and paste material, the master copy can be sent via telecommunications to the other sites.

After congratulations are enjoyed—praise from parents as well as peers and adults in the school—the newspaper staff sits down to critically review their finished product. They discuss the strengths and weaknesses of its content and its ability to keep readers interested; and they assess the quality of writing (organization, mechanics, and style) and the quality of the art, graphics, and layout (whether these visually enhance the text and overall presentation of the stories)—all the important elements of total communication. A summary of their self-evaluation is shared with other sites, and others send along their group evaluations of the issue.

The process of producing a newspaper is educationally valuable for more reasons than learning writing skills and production procedures.

Through the editorial board experience, for example, students learn how to evaluate good writing and to articulate what elements make it good. Here's how.

During board meetings, the editor who is assigned responsibility for a given story, reads it and recommends it for acceptance or rejection. A specific reason for the decision must be given because the goal is to help writers improve on future articles. A statement such as "It's not good enough" or "It doesn't say much" are unacceptable because they are not helpful to the writer. "The story doesn't give enough details to understand the game," is a more helpful response. So is "The writer clearly explains the experience of scuba diving, an experience that most of the kids in our school have never had." The teacher plays a minor role in these meetings. He or she simply determines whether the reasons given are acceptable and records the results. The final decision about each piece is based on a majority vote of the board.

Using this process, the board members gradually select articles that will definitely be included, ones that may be included but need a lot of editing first, and fillers that will be included only if there is space. Articles that have been rejected are often revised by the authors and resubmitted for a future issue. Through this selection experience, students also learn about what is newsworthy and what is not. They also learn that clear and complete explanations are imperative if written communication is to be successful.

An example of this process occurred at a board meeting in which two young authors who had jointly written a movie review listened to the board reject several similar articles because they lacked supportive details. Just before their own article was to be discussed, the boys withdrew it, knowing it would not be accepted for the same reason. They were motivated to rework the story, however, because they knew what it needed—more supportive details. They revised the piece, resubmitted it, and the article was accepted.

Still another benefit comes when students edit stories that come off the student "newswire." Under these circumstances, an editor must learn to perfect the copy and retain the writer's intended meaning without having him or her right there to answer questions. This makes the editing process both more objective and difficult, as well as more realistic. When an editor makes significant changes, it is customary to e-mail the article back to the writer to make certain the original ideas are intact. Sometimes another byline is added giving credit to both the writer and editor.

A number of newswire contributors do not speak English as their first language, and they find the newspaper experience helps improve their English. They gain practice in writing English when they write articles, and practice in reading when they read others' stories. Indeed, these students often discover that they are able to edit and improve articles written by other children who are having similar difficulty learning the English language. This situation helps struggling students see that they have some skills their counterparts find difficult, and provides them with a new sense of accomplishment.

Participation in the national newspaper project also helps young people understand the role that newspapers play in society and how newswire networks function. They learn what makes a story newsworthy, and what is appropriate for a given audience and medium. They also begin to understand why people write things and what makes a story interesting to others. This latter point becomes abundantly clear each time they read other editions of the newspaper and discover which of their stories have been published. But the most important benefit for writing teachers is that students who work on the newspaper discover what adult writers know well: Writing is a process of working out ideas through a series of drafts with the purpose of communicating to a particular audience.

Over time, this project has become international and interdisciplinary. Participating classrooms are now located in Mexico, Canada, Japan, and England, as well as in the original sites in the United States. In secondary schools, social studies teachers have teamed with the English teachers to research and report on current political issues, participate in collaborative geographical projects, and explore regional histories of participating sites. Science teachers have also gotten into the act by involving students at several sites in collecting and analyzing scientific data such as weather, water quality, and soil composition, and reporting results in the international newspaper.

High School Newspaper

There are not many high schools that publish a newspaper so often that members of the press face extreme pressure to meet deadlines. But whenever there are tight deadlines, word processing helps produce copy fast. Professional newspaper journalists typically work under continual pressure, and sometimes they are expected to complete several writing assignments within a single day.

Young journalists would do well to practice drafting newspaper articles on the computer keyboard, rather than taking time to write a draft by hand before entering it on a word processor. At journalism school, students typically compose on the keyboard and are pressed to complete assignments before leaving the classroom. The ability to plan, write, and revise on the spot is a valuable skill, and one that is appropriate to practice in a high school journalism class. The word processor, of course, helps facilitate this activity.

Teachers in schools that have word processing equipment and access to a typesetting machine or other means to produce master copies of full-size newspaper pages, might adopt a "professional" approach to creating a student newspaper. The following paragraphs provide a glimpse of how one class of very diligent journalists put together a rather sophisticated high school publication.

The *Eagle* is a biweekly newspaper published by specially selected high school sophomores, juniors, and seniors. To be admitted into the journalism class that meets daily to produce this eight-page paper, students must be recommended by their English teacher. The recommendation process is as follows: Every spring the journalism teacher sends a form to all English teachers asking them to indicate students in their classes who are: (1) excellent writers, (2) responsible, (3) able to accept criticism, (4) able to work well with other students, and (5) willing to put in a lot of time after school and on weekends. Using these and other references, the journalism teacher (who is also the *Eagle*'s faculty advisor) builds a class list for the following year.

The advisor appoints an editor-in-chief just before school closes in June, and she or he takes over the paper in September. The other editors are selected in the fall, when it becomes clear who's good at what.

When the course begins in the fall, students learn to use the word processing system right away, because they are expected to turn in all copy on disks. They learn basic newspaper terminology as well as the typesetting commands necessary to give appropriate printing directions to the typesetter. Editors and staff writers also learn standard editing symbols and use the Associated Press stylebook as a reference.

The first issue does not come out until October, so during the first few weeks of class the advisor teaches common writing styles used by journalists for news articles, features, reviews, and editorials. However, the advisor mentioned that in reality, the students primarily teach one another; editors have high standards and they insist that writers meet those standards. At first, the advisor read the copy herself, intending to point out undetected problems, but soon discovered that her corrections were almost identical to the copy editor's.

The *Eagle* is run completely by the students. One staff member commented that if it wasn't that way it would not be a good paper—there would be nobody there after school and nobody on weekends. The editors give the article assignments and establish the deadlines. Reporters enter copy on a word processor, and then the appropriate editor reviews it and returns it to the writer for corrections. Next it goes to the copy editor, who corrects the grammar and mechanics. Finally the disk is turned over to the typesetter. (This school has a typesetting machine and one or two students learn the skills involved and become the official typesetters.) When the copy is unusually late, it can be edited right on the typesetting machine.

The typesetting machine converts the copy into standard columns, which are then cut, waxed, and pasted on the layout sheets. Photos and ads are half-toned, sized, waxed, and put on the layout sheets as well. Then the hairlines and heads are added, and this camera-ready copy gets a final proofreading before it is delivered to the print shop.

During second period, every other Friday, the paper is distributed to everyone in the school. Then, during the class session following its publication, the staff critiques the strengths and weaknesses of the issue and makes assignments for the next. After each issue, staff members also complete a self-evaluation form on which they itemize everything they did for the issue and give themselves a grade (optional). The advisor and editors meet to review the evaluations and determine staff members' grades for the issue. Individual students may be present during the discussion of their grade. According to the advisor, this evaluation process provides an excellent opportunity for students to learn to communicate more effectively with peers.

Except for the cost of hardware and software, the *Eagle* is supported entirely by student-raised funds. The newspaper staff, led by their business manager, raise money through ads solicited from the student body and the local community. Indeed, it is not uncommon for the newspaper to finish the year with one or two thousand dollars in the bank!

Video Yearbook

In recent years, video yearbooks have become popular among high school students as a supplement, or even replacement for the much-cherished printed memorial to the graduating class. Video yearbooks can be produced by the students themselves, by professional companies, or some combination of student and professional groups.

Student-produced video yearbooks are becoming increasingly more popular as more schools and individuals obtain and become skillful at using video cameras and editing equipment. There are several advantages to having students produce their own video yearbook: (1) the medium seems to foster greater student creativity than traditional yearbooks; (2) it encourages a broader range of student participation; (3) video is more effective at capturing the action and emotional energy of a moment than text and still photos; and (4) student-produced video yearbooks can be less expensive than printed yearbooks.

The disadvantages of such a project can be discouraging, however. Some disadvantages include: (1) It is easy to record an event on video, but difficult to achieve high technical quality and to capture the complete story of the event clearly and accurately in just a few seconds or minutes of footage. Consequently, amateur video yearbooks often lack the polish of professionally created video or print yearbooks; (2) someone, with appropriate equipment, has to be available to record all the memorable events of the year; (3) care must be taken to include everyone in the graduating class, or some students and important activities could be left out of the final product; (4) the school must own the equipment needed to edit the hours of videotape that students submit.

Some professional video yearbook companies will assist students in producing a video yearbook that combines professional and student-shot videos, special effects, and music. These companies generally do the editing and production of the final tape. This alternative may work best for some schools, as it enables students to participate (though their participation is far less) in the process while providing the professional skill that can transform a ho-hum home video into a meaningful and entertaining reflection of the students' senior year. Because video yearbooks are paid for by the students who purchase them, no significant cost is incurred by a school. However, a professionally produced video yearbook is likely to cost two to three times more than a student-produced yearbook.

If the idea of creating a student-produced yearbook is intriguing, the safest route to take would be to hire a professional company the first year and then study the process carefully before attempting to take on the task next year. It would also be wise to encourage next year's graduating class to begin learning the art and craft of videography. They could practice creating video stories by shooting and editing footage of the junior prom or school sports events.

Writing Academy

The need for improving students' communication skills is emphasized in many school and district curriculum agendas. Yet very few districts have gone so far as to transform schools into "writing academies" that stress communication skills—especially writing—in all subject areas. In such an academy, every subject teacher receives extended professional development geared to help them teach writing skills appropriate for their subject areas. In math, students are asked to explain mathematical concepts in writing; science students learn that if they articulate scientific principles clearly to others, they understand them better themselves; social studies teachers pay more attention to their students' ability to present ideas on paper as well as in class discussions, and find that students who learn to write effectively are better able to organize their thoughts in class discussions as well. Further, students who formerly lacked confidence in their ability to contribute to class discussions discover that with better writing skills they have more confidence in their ability to articulate their ideas and consequently contribute more in class.

Of course, not all schools will become writing academies. However, asking students to write frequently—and insisting on a high standard of work—in all subject areas is a practice that should be adopted by all schools.

The role of technology—especially word processing—in such a school would be critical. Students should have ready access to computers with word processing so they can complete assignments for all their subjects. (See "The Added Value of Using Technology for Communication: Written Communication" on pages 69–70, for a rationale of the benefits of writing with word processing.)

An Elementary Cross-Disciplinary Communication Program

At this exemplary elementary school, students start writing with computers in kindergarten, and begin lessons in keyboarding in second grade. After that, some teachers continue formal keyboarding practice, and others just have students regularly write with computers. The second/third grade teacher we'll focus on here, has her students write and revise much of their written work on computers. Since there is only one computer in her classroom, she permits students to go to the computer lab or another classroom because she believes it's important to be able to use writing tools when they're needed and she doesn't want kids to have to postpone writing until it's their turn to go to the lab.

This teacher has developed an extensive curriculum that integrates communication lessons with science, math, social studies, and art. At the time of observation, her focus was on a study of the desert. The study began with a brainstorming session in which the class created a "word map" of the desert that included all the information about plants, animals, climate, and terrain the children already knew. Students then selected plants and animals for further individual study. They went to the library for information on their topic, took notes, and developed more detailed word maps for their chosen animals and plants.

As their research progressed, the teacher introduced them to the "field guides" that are often distributed at national parks. They discussed how a field guide describes the park's plants and animals briefly, while still conveying the essential characteristics. The class then decided to create their own field guide, and students composed entries that described their particular plants and animals. The final, computer-published field guide included illustrated descriptions of the desert terrain and its inhabitants.

Thorough these initial desert activities, students practiced oral communication skills informally through class discussions, and written communication skills while taking notes on their research, developing word maps, and drafting and revising their field guide entries.

Students then set out to build a three-dimensional replica of the desert that would reside in an adjacent hallway alcove. This project enabled them to communicate what they had learned in a visual format. To accomplish this, they had to construct scaled models of their plants and animals and figure out how to set them up in an authentic desert terrain. After a few weeks and considerable effort, the colorful and extremely realistic 20′ × 6′ desert was complete. Students then acted as "park rangers" while they guided younger children on instructional tours through the mini desert. The teacher videotaped students' oral presentations of their plants and animals so they could review their own performances. She believes this process helps them gain self-confidence. When they see themselves on videotape, they discover that they really do know the material.

Some students explored another kind of visual communication that involved creating animations with a still-video camera. For one of these animations, the children drew step-by-step pictures of a snake capturing and eating a dove. They used the school's still-video camera to photograph each drawing, and then transferred the images to a computer program that permitted them to view the images in a smoothly animated series on the computer screen. Other animations included a desert sunset, sunrise, and a lizard regenerating its tail. The teacher reported that this activity was extremely effective. Kids had to think through all the steps, as well as visualize the completed animation. They could have made a flip book with their pictures, but creating a real animation was so much more powerful for them because they felt like young animation professionals.

With a stronger understanding of the desert and what it might be like to live there, students were ready to write poetry. They watched a video that communicated images and desert life entirely without sound. Then they brainstormed words and phrases that described what they saw and felt. As a class, they put these together into freestyle poetry that captured a moment in the desert and created a mental picture of it for readers. Success with free verse led to a study of Cinquain, Diamonte, Haiku, and Tanka forms of poetry, and the kids were off and writing. After experimenting with all of these forms, students selected one or two of their best poems to "publish" in a computer-printed and hand-illustrated class poetry collection.

All-in-all, the range of communication skills these students learned and practiced while studying the desert is impressive. By contributing to class discussions, making oral presentations, creating visual representations, and writing research notes, reports, and poetry, the students gained an understanding of how to communicate to different types of audiences through a variety of visual, oral, and written forms. They used computer technology for all of their writing activities, and photographic and video technologies to strengthen and assess their visual and oral communication activities.

Parents still might ask if the technology actually helps their kids learn more or better. This teacher responded with an example: When you first start teaching kids how to write paragraphs, they have a lot of difficulty creating logical sequences of sentences. The most effective way to teach them how to write coherent paragraphs is to cut up a disorganized paragraph and rearrange the sentences into a more logical order. It's a laborious process, and you have to go over it several times before they can do it in their own writing. But, when you use a computer to cut and paste the sentences and make other revisions, the instructional process is much easier and more effective, and it's also easier for the kids to rearrange their own sentences.

She also said that some kids write more willingly with computers. Before, when they wrote by hand, they used to be so self-conscious about poor spelling that they didn't want to write. With electronic spelling tools available, such as the computer's spell checker and the Franklin speller, these kids have relaxed much more about their writing, mostly because they know the teacher will now pay attention to their ideas rather than focus on their spelling mistakes. She hastened to add that she does think that students need to work on spelling, but she also thinks that poor spellers need to learn to recognize when words are misspelled and find out how to spell them. The electronic tools help students learn this skill.

Concerning the use of technology for oral and visual communication, the teacher mentioned again that using a video camera to record students' oral presentations was extremely helpful in providing them with feedback, and using photographic technology to support their animations was far more effective than making hand-held flip books.

Communication and Critical Thinking

Our exemplary teacher in this scenario teaches English in a suburban middle school. Her classes do a lot of writing and publishing of their work, and all of it is closely tied to a carefully thought out communication curriculum. One element of this curriculum is an ongoing focus on critical thinking, and to achieve this, she has the kids explore ways that different people think and communicate. At the time of this observation, students had just finished examining how artists think and were beginning a study of how inventors think—how they approach a problem, attempt to solve it, and communicate their solution to others.

Students began by choosing specific inventions and writing imaginative essays describing how the inventions might have been invented. Humor prevailed as writers told tall tales about the invention of the waffle iron, water bed, and lawn mower, for instance. These essays were computer published into a booklet that was made available to other students in the school. The class also evaluated these essays and developed a set of criteria for good writing that they could refer to when writing future assignments.

To continue their study of inventors and their communication strategies, student groups selected a technological invention (e.g., the television, computer, robot, laser) and conducted research on how the technology works and how it was actually invented. Groups prepared computer-printed reports, posters, and other materials to support their oral presentations. The teacher videotaped these presentations for students to evaluate their own performances, and for the whole class to review and identify criteria for a successful oral presentation. For example, they identified one presentation as outstanding because the group engaged the audience by asking questions, and they used effective models to describe their invention.

Students were then ready to try out the inventor's problem-solving and communication strategies by creating their own inventions and "selling" them to a critical audience. They each wrote a statement describing a problem that needed to be solved and an invention they proposed would solve the problem. Students kept notebooks of their plans and their progress. They created charts, sketches, diagrams, and finally a detailed drawing or model of the finished invention, which they presented to their classmates, the "potential customers." The array of newly invented technologies included a laser alarm clock that would keep a sleepyhead from going back to bed; a robot that could make one's bed; and a computer-driven light system that would help customers locate specific rental videos amid hundreds on the shelves.

By that point, students had explored the processes inventors use to create new technologies that will solve problems. Simultaneously, the students had also confronted problems of their own concerning how to communicate the inventors' thought processes. In each case, the students used computer technology to help them communicate what they'd learned or imagined, and in each case they had to decide how to communicate the information most effectively to a specific audience, through writing, oral presentations, and visual representations.

After examining the thinking and communication strategies of inventors, the teacher guided the class to observe inventors and their inventions from a more critical, outsider's perspective. From this perspective, students would learn how critics think and communicate, and they would also have opportunities to take on the critical reviewer's role themselves.

To pursue this perspective, the class viewed videotapes and read essays that point out negative consequences of new technologies (their use in demolishing rainforests, their invasion of privacy, for example), and the class debated the pros and cons of their adoption. The focus here was on critical thinking and oral communication. Students had to think analytically, form their own opinions, communicate them, and defend them in the face of opposition.

All of the teacher's communication activities included technology to help students communicate more effectively. Students used computers consistently for all of the writing assignments, and according to their teacher, the computer has helped them improve their writing. The teacher used video technology to communicate critical perspectives of technology, and to provide an alternative opportunity for learning through this powerful visual communication tool. She also used video technology to record students' oral presentations for review purposes, which could not have been done without the technology.

Videotape Projects: Middle School

In this exemplary middle school classroom, students study the use of video as a effective medium for communication. As a way to discover for themselves its relative effectiveness, the teacher asks student groups to create a videotape that answers a specific question. In this case the question was: Which make better pets, dogs or cats? Groups were arranged such that pro-cat people were placed together and pro-dog people were together. Those who were undecided were dispersed among the groups.

Within these groups, students brainstormed the arguments they would use to defend their group's position, and tried to imagine what video clips would portray dogs or cats as the better pet. Students who had these pets at home were asked to do most of the videotaping, but they had a lot of help from other group members. Some used their family videocameras and others checked out a school camera.

For the next week or so, students planned what kinds of shots they wanted to get to support their arguments, and the young videographers attempted to get the footage as best they could. Every day or two the groups met to review the video clips and make suggestions for further taping.

After a few such review sessions, groups began to discuss the thread of their arguments and how they would piece together their video clips to create a coherent argument. At that point, the teacher reminded students that pro-cat people should consider including footage of dog behaviors that render them inferior pets, and pro-dog people might also select compromising clips of cats that would further their own arguments.

Then, the teacher introduced the scriptwriter's practice of storyboarding, and showed the class how to make their own. Using this new organizing tool, groups begin to design how they would edit and piece together their video clips. The storyboard also helped them plan what the narrator would say as each clip appeared on the screen. In each group, one or two members drafted the scripts, making sure to include all the important arguments, and placing the arguments on the storyboard squares that went with the video clip on that square.

After a group had identified and labeled all the video clips it wanted to include in the final video and what the narrator would say during each clip, the teacher took the group to the high school editing lab and helped them assemble the final video (after school and on weekends). When all groups were finished, the class viewed one another's final products and then assembled for group analysis and assessment of their work.

Videotape Projects: High School

Our exemplary high school teacher spent several years integrating computers into his writing program so that student writers were comfortable drafting and revising their work on computers. Then one day, he heard about a multimedia workshop being offered by the district and got permission to take some of his students along. That experience proved to be a major turning point for him and his students. He explained that when he watched those kids creating multimedia presentations, he discovered how images and sound energize what writers can do with a flat piece of paper.

Since then, this teacher's English classes have never been the same. He introduced students to multimedia communication by having them develop poetry presentations that involved reading poems aloud while supportive images flashed in the background. Students then created stand-alone presentations by videotaping their own performances. The next step was to write scripts for more extensive videos that included information about the selected poets—what was characteristic about their work, general themes covered in their poems, and reading of exemplary poems.

According to the teacher, adding visual images to their oral reports gave the words more life and made the presentations more powerful. In fact, the visual images provided additional information that made the results more informative as well. Having grown up with television and video, these students were already experienced visual learners, and that experience made it easier for them to learn multimedia composition.

With some fundamental multimedia skills in place, the teacher wanted to challenge students to move to a more sophisticated level of multimedia communication. He collaborated with the tenth-grade history teacher to get students involved in creating projects for the 1992 National History Day Competition.

One multimedia project examined America's impact on the native culture of Micronesia. After conducting extensive research, the group used the school's video editing lab to integrate images, voice, music, and text into a video presentation. The editing lab includes all the equipment needed to create multimedia products: a computer and monitor, laserdisc player and monitor, VCR and monitor, CD player, scanner, still-video camera, printer, video editing machine, and stereo mixer.

According to the teacher, the students went through many, many drafts. Early on, they became infatuated with images and lost track of what they wanted to say. Then, suddenly they realized that the images and sound meant nothing without a strong, coherent message. At that point, they understood that what they really were doing was composing an essay—a multimedia essay. And from then on the organizational process was clear and they moved forward to support their message with appropriate words, images, and sound. According to the teacher, the result was far more powerful and informative than a written report, or oral presentation could be by itself. The group entered their completed video in the regional competition and won first place in the multimedia category.

Some teachers and parents may wonder whether spending so much time creating multimedia presentations will hamper students' writing development, which they believe is most essential. There are a couple of ways to answer this question. One is to argue that multimedia is quickly becoming a primary means of communication (many claim it already is, exemplified by television), and that learning to communicate with multiple media while in school gives these students a significant advantage.

Another way to address this concern is to examine what students are actually doing when they're composing with multimedia. After spending time playing around with all the images they can find, students discover that they cannot communicate very effectively with images alone. They learn that they need to organize their ideas and carefully plan out what can be most appropriately said by words, by images, and by sound. They develop storyboards to outline exactly what they want to accomplish with each medium. Then they write a script for the verbal communication, a list of frame numbers for the visuals, and identification numbers for each sound section before integrating the media onto one videotape in the editing lab.

The success of the whole piece lies in the composer's ability to communicate the central idea clearly and coherently. It's like writing an essay, only more difficult, and more effective because the message is communicated through words, images, and sounds, with each supporting and enriching the other. Because of this need to organize, outline, and write the fundamental ideas of a multimedia presentation, it is unlikely that students' written communication skills will suffer by working with multiple media. In fact, it is far more likely that their writing will improve.

Since their early experiments with multimedia, this teacher's students have grown much more knowledgeable in their use of the technology. He admitted that they know more than he does—he has been able to offer feedback and resources for them to get help, but they have pretty much taught themselves.

Opportunities for using technology in the communication curriculum arise continually. For example, students recently produced a documentary video that demonstrated progress made on a community environmental improvement project. The goal of the project was to restore the area as a valuable wetland and public park. The young producers integrated video footage, still-video photos, text, music, and voice into a videotape that won a district grant for the project.

In sum, the teacher emphasized that this is only the beginning of what educators can do with technology. The students are advancing rapidly in production skills and in their ability to communicate with people. As they grow more capable—and they are very rapidly doing so—they'll need more technology to support their abilities and there will be an increasing demand for the equipment they already have.

More and more teachers are encouraging their students to use multiple media to complete their "writing" assignments. Some final products are in the form of videotape presentations, as described above, and others integrate media into computer-based presentations such as the projects described below.

Interactive Video Projects: Middle School

One middle school teacher in a multicultural urban community presented a lesson to his class on how to write a descriptive essay that portrays a student's family members (their appearance, interests, skills, and shortcomings), by asking the students to create multimedia "essays" that portray family members and their activities more clearly and effectively than text can by itself. To do this, students searched their family photo albums for pictures that captured favorite family activities, members' individual interests, and relationships within the family. Students used audiocassette recorders to interview family members about their interests and ideas, and also candidly captured family gatherings (e.g., dinner table conversations) that further expressed family interactions.

Students then drafted the text of their essays using multimedia composing software, while applying the principles they'd learned about how to write a clear and concise descriptive essay with concrete details that enable a reader to "picture" the people and events, and form their own opinions about them. They selected, scanned, and placed the digitized photos into the document. Then, they selected appropriate excerpts of their audiotapes and used audio translating devices to digitize and place these excerpts into the presentation wherever they wanted them to be heard.

Students presented their completed multimedia documents on classroom computers. For each presentation, a title card displaying the name of the presentation and its creator first appeared on the screen. Then, when the viewer pressed the right arrow button, another card appeared containing introductory text and a photo of the family. Each time the reader pushed the right arrow button another text card appeared, with accompanying photos or other artwork. Some cards also had a button labeled "push me," and when the reader did so, an audio sound track played a segment of taped family conversation or a personal interview.

The class enjoyed listening/reading/viewing all of them, and then assembled for a class discussion to assess their work. They discussed which presentations were most effective and tried to explain specifically why. They discussed whether the visual and/or audio supplements to the text made the whole presentation more or less effective. And they discussed whether they could portray their families as successfully if they had used text alone rather than additional media.

The teacher—being an English teacher dedicated to teaching students how to write effectively—then asked them to write another draft of the text, attempting to convey the important details that the photos and audiotaped voices captured and their previous text drafts had not. The results produced more effective essays than the students usually produce because they paid closer attention to describing visual images, including quotes, and providing other concrete details. But, the students agreed that the multimedia documents still portrayed their families more completely and effectively.

Interactive Video Projects: High School

In a high school English class, student groups were asked to select the piece of literature they thought best depicts the conditions of the Industrial Revolution in the 20th-Century United States, and defend their choice in a multimedia presentation.

Student groups first had to propose and discuss members' individual suggestions for the most representative piece of literature, make a democratic decision, and then begin planning the presentation, grappling with issues such as: What arguments could they use to defend their choice? What expert resources could they use to strengthen their defense? How much and what information would they include about the Industrial Revolution and the economic/political/social conditions that prevailed? What kinds of counter arguments could they expect, and how would they defeat them?

Then, group members informally assessed the expertise of each member concerning things like, which member knows most about the Industrial Revolution or would be most interested in researching the topic? Who will look for artwork of that period that most effectively illustrates the perspective of the selected literature? Who will take the time to search for relevant video footage from the school's *Video Encyclopedia of the 20th Century* and other sources? Who's willing to organize an audio or videotaped interview with the school's American History teacher? Who has good technology skills and could take primary responsibility for putting the pieces together once the group creates a master design?

These and other tasks were assigned and members began working independently or in pairs to complete their initial tasks. The group continued to meet daily to check on progress and to help one another solve problems.

When all members were ready with their contributions, they met together to share what they had learned. Then they began to design a multimedia document that would present and defend their selection most effectively. Together, they discussed and/or reviewed selected video footage, scanned photos, taped interviews, and other contributions, and selected the most powerful pieces that neither duplicate nor contradict each other, but strengthen the total argument.

The groups then created storyboards by dividing the presentation into many sections represented by squares on large sheets of paper. Each square represented a single screen display within the total presentation. Together, they designed each screen, outlining what points the text should make and what artwork, photos, audio or video clips should accompany the information on the card. When the storyboard was completed, two members drafted the text for each screen, and two technicians begin importing the different media selections into the multimedia composing software. The group reviewed a first draft and determined what revisions were necessary in each of the media components. Several drafts followed before everyone was satisfied with the final presentation. Luckily, the class had enough computers available so that each group's presentation could be loaded on a separate computer and operated independently, enabling everyone in the class to move around and see/read/hear each group's work.

After congratulations and a production party, the class convened to assess each group's work. First they discussed whether any of the presentations caused them to change their minds about which piece of literature best represents the Industrial Revolution. Then, as in the previous multimedia project example, they discussed each presentation's strengths and weaknesses, including the relative effectiveness of the different media used.

Finally, they discussed whether (and how) they could have used audio and visual media to misrepresent what they perceived as a truthful interpretation of the historic period. Just as printed words are sometimes used to present a single, slanted point of view, so can audio and video media—usually far more powerfully because people more readily believe what they hear from the mouths of experts and what they see with their own eyes.

Communication Through Visual Arts and Music

Many parents and educators advocate high academic standards that include not only subject area competencies, but the ability to learn independently, think analytically, solve problems, and work collaboratively. Yet many do not understand how a strong visual arts program can promote high academic standards, advance intellectual growth, and be useful in further education, the workforce, and throughout life.

Evidence shows that the arts do support high educational standards. Research indicates that students who study the arts perform significantly better in standardized reading and math tests, and demonstrate greater creativity and better communication skills.

Years of observation also show that when students become involved in the arts they develop self-discipline; they learn to teach themselves new skills, think analytically, solve problems, and work collaboratively. Another feature of the arts is that the learning process is extremely active, and research demonstrates that learning is far more effective when students are mentally and physically involved in the process.

Because artistic creativity is often limited in other areas of education, many highly intelligent students with the need to express their own ideas discover that the arts are the most effective way to do this. Indeed, some students who have been unsuccessful in academics are able to find success in the arts, which helps them build self-esteem and determination that they can then transfer to academic areas.

When people think of the arts, they usually think of paints and pastels, clay and plaster, or violins and trumpets. They seldom picture computers, video cameras, and TV monitors. But as art teachers and their students are beginning to discover, these technology tools enable artists to create new kinds of art forms, and to express themselves in new media that communicate effectively in today's culture.

The technology also provides powerful instructional tools for the teacher. For example, in music, technology enables the teacher to provide private instruction within a class of students, and to invite beginners to join an electronic band. It also enables students to compose music and print it out as sheet music. In art, teachers use technology to help students learn to draw, to see and perceive in new ways, and to help them assess their own progress. Students use the same tools to draw pictures, enhance photographs, create video sequences, and produce multimedia presentations.

These are only a few examples of what technology can do to strengthen a school's visual arts and music programs. The following classroom examples describe how three high school teachers use technology to help students develop essential concepts and competencies in their art and music classes.

Art

Our exemplary art teacher had little use for technology until she won a Fulbright fellowship to China and decided to bring a video camera. After returning, she created a video for her Fulbright project, and within a couple of years produced a series of videos that attracted considerable interest within the community and with art educators nationally. This prompted her to get students involved in artistic video projects, and before long they produced a video that convinced the teacher (and the school district) that she was moving in the right direction.

The students' six-minute video entitled *Imagine* began with a series of concrete images that presented how people live in other cultures and students' artistic responses to those conditions. The sound track featured John Lennon's "Imagine All the People" in the background. Gradually, the concrete images gave way to more abstract impressions that evolved from the original images. The musical background also gave way to a new song that was written as a response to Lennon's original piece.

Students did the artistic composition and planning for the video, but the actual production work had to be done in the teacher's home studio, because at that time the school didn't have video editing equipment. The success of the video did, however, provide enough interest and support for the school to acquire the technology students would need to begin producing videos at school.

Now this teacher uses video as an integral part of her art program both as an instructional tool and as a creative tool for producing art. As an instructional tool, she uses it to help students learn to draw. For example, when students are attempting to draw from a model, she takes a video picture of the model and transfers the image to a computer for display on a large screen. The process flattens the three-dimensional model to a two-dimensional picture. Some students find it easier to draw from a picture than a model, so the technology offers them a choice.

The teacher also uses video technology to record and access students' progress by developing video portfolios. Beyond just displaying a collection of their best work, she uses the technology to record formal presentations in which students discuss the most important things they have learned about the artistic process, their conceptual and skill development, and how their images evolved from sketchbook sketches to final products. The teacher noted that the students' ability to reflect on their progress and make aesthetic judgments about what they've done is now exceptional.

In addition to its use as an instructional tool, video technology is also a powerful artistic tool. Students in these art classes use it to produce an alternative to the traditional self portrait, for example. They take a video picture of a student and transfer it to a computer that displays the image on a screen. Then they use a drawing program to artistically alter the portrait by changing colors, shapes, and lines, as well as stretching, shrinking, and applying other techniques to create a new image that conveys the artist's personal interpretation.

Students in the video technology class use video as an artistic tool for expressing themselves in multiple media. First, they learn to use film, still-, and motion-video cameras, and the devices that enable them to alter and enhance images. Then, they use the cameras and enhancement devices to produce images and create new images from them. Finally, students combine these images with narration, music, and sound effects to produce a final product on videotape. To accomplish this, however, they need to plan what they want to communicate to the audience, and develop a detailed technical script for integrating the different media. Finally, they use the video editing studio to integrate all the components onto a single videotape.

A student in this class commented that, by taking the class, he had discovered that video technology can help an artist express himself in more holistic ways, such as enhancing images, adding special effects, or creating a sound track. The project he was working on at the time was a short video that pictures a sculpture he made that's been dramatically altered by special effects (smoke emerging from the eyes and mouth), and the audio track includes a poem he wrote. He said the video medium enabled him to express his ideas much more fully than either the sculpture or the poem could by itself.

One would think that this kind of complex production work would require honor students to complete the task, but according to the teacher, the arts attract a number of students who are unsuccessful in other aspects of school. She explained that there are many highly intelligent kids who are academically at-risk because they resist repetitive and mechanical work. These students are incredibly intuitive and creative; they can solve problems; and they can see the relationship of parts to the whole in a powerful way. She added that students should be free to think and act creatively, and to express themselves in ways that don't always conform to a text format. Many of these students are attracted to technology because it inherently encourages exploration, problem solving, and the creation of new products. They like to use the technology tools to create new art forms that enable them to communicate more effectively than traditional media.

Parents and educators might still wonder if art is really essential for all students, especially if they're already successful in academics. This teacher's immediate response was to remark that responsible citizens of the 21st century must be aware of and respect their cultural heritage and the heritage of other cultures. One of the best ways to do this is to study the art forms of different cultures. If kids can appreciate these, they are bound to develop a respect for themselves and for others. It's a great multicultural experience that helps broaden their understanding and sensitivity to others who are different.

Another reason art is important for everyone is that by attempting to create their own art forms, students begin to look at the world differently. They observe things more acutely and are more aware of the influence of lighting, lines, patterns, perspective, and so forth, when observing the world around them. Also, much of art involves problem solving and developing creative approaches to solving them. The teacher commented that to teach a student that there is only one right answer to a problem is to misteach a student. To let them discover there are many ways to solve a problem is very important. So, yes, art is essential.

And how essential is it to include technology in art education? Art programs that include technology enable students to explore the media that are most widespread and popular in today's culture. The teacher remarked that today's kids are the biggest visual consumers ever, and it's a disservice to them if they're not encouraged to develop skills in this area. They also need to develop a critical eye for what they are seeing. When kids begin producing their own videos, they learn how video techniques such as camera angle, lighting, cut shots, and so on, communicate particular emotions, and points-of-view. When they begin to understand these techniques they more readily evaluate what they see and discount what's low quality. The bad stuff is really insulting to them as videographers and as aware consumers. So, yes, technology is essential too.

In another high school, an art teacher helps photography students understand how modern technology can be used to alter photographs, and how that impacts the belief people have concerning how photographs consistently tell "the truth."

Students learn to understand the power of these manipulation techniques by using them to alter their own photographs in artistic ways. Unlike those trying to alter photographs in subtle ways that will not be noticed by the observer, art students create bold reinterpretations of the original images. To do this, they take a still video photograph, transfer it to a computer, and use a drawing program to alter it. They can draw over it, stretch or shrink it, change the original lines, apply spray paint or other painting techniques, and come up with a new image that is usually recognizable, but conveys the creator's own interpretation of the images.

Photography students use still-video technology to create sequences of photographs for documentaries, visual stories, and instructional aids. For example, one sequence teaches beginning photographers how to develop film. Each photograph in the series illustrates a single step in the process that can be projected on the classroom TV screen. It's like a slide show, except the production process is faster and cheaper because no film development is required and it's easier to manage. Other example projects include an animated story of a Coke can and a Pepsi can, and a documentary that observes children interacting in a primary school classroom.

Students in this teacher's regular art classes use the computer drawing program as an artistic tool to create original art forms that combine images and text. One such project involves students in designing a new kind of sandwich or ice cream sundae, drawing a picture of it with a computer drawing program and labeling each part. These kinds of techniques are used regularly in various forms of commercial art, and this class provides an introduction to the techniques used by professionals.

These examples of current uses of technology tools in photography, commercial art, education, and entertainment, are only a small sampling of how widespread technology has already become in the workforce. The teacher believes that most jobs in the future will involve computers, and therefore it's important to provide young people with some exposure to technology while in school. That is one of the reasons she includes technology in her art program. Another is that she believes technology is an effective motivator for many art students. Of course, a few students hate to use computers, she admitted, but others work endlessly at the computer. She also believes technology provides valuable alternative media for art students to use in expressing their ideas. She said that many of them really enjoy creating new interpretations from original images, and others like to produce video sequences as a means of expressing themselves in both visual and audio media.

Music

Our exemplary high school music teacher became interested in technology in the 1980s, when the music industry was undergoing a technological revolution. At the same time, he realized that technology could revolutionize music education, and since then he's created a unique music program that uses technology to help students learn to play instruments, compose music, and record their work in a classroom recording studio. Here is how he does it.

In the beginning piano classes, the teacher uses technology primarily as an instructional tool. Students enter a classroom full of keyboards with earphones, which are connected together and to the teacher's central computer system. This set-up enables him to teach a class of beginners who are learning at different rates, and to provide them with private or small group instruction while the rest practice other pieces. The teacher can play for them; and they can talk through the microphone connected to their earphones. According to the teacher, their progress is as good as if they were taking private lessons, only the technology enables him to teach twenty at a time, which is a far more cost-effective for students, and the public school system. Further, this program enables the school to serve students who otherwise would be excluded from music at the secondary level because the regular instrumental program focuses on musicians who have been playing since the program began in fifth grade.

With technology at his fingertips, the teacher can offer these students a new approach. The beginning students can play in a great sounding band on the very first day when they've learned just two chords. The teacher simply directs the computer to play one of many songs he has written in the system, and in seconds a drum, base guitar, and keyboard begin to play the Beatles song "Let It Be." Students can then accompany the band with notes and chords that are appropriate for their level of competence. When they reach a difficult section, he can stop the band and direct it to repeat that part very slowly, allowing students to practice until they're ready to play it at the regular tempo.

Another advantage of the technology as an instructional tool is that the teacher can use it for practice exercises and testing. He directs the computer to play certain musical sequences and asks students to write down the rhythm notation or melody line, for instance. Since the technology can play the sequences, it frees him to walk around the class and help students in their efforts.

The teacher said that music class is the one place where students who are not very successful in other aspects of school can really excel. When they learn to play an instrument, they discover that they're capable of things they never dreamed of before. All they need is to learn to play the instrument. He also commented that studying music is one of the fastest ways kids can accomplish so many of the things we want for them—self-esteem, good study habits, and the ability to concentrate. He claimed that music is really making a positive impact on his students' lives.

Once students have mastered the basics, they begin to use technology as an artistic tool for musical composition. They do not need to be musical virtuosos to compose, all they need is a desire to be creative, some musical ideas, and a basic ability to play the keyboard. Of course, talent is still important, he hastened to add, because if the student doesn't have interesting musical ideas, the results won't be very satisfying. But the point is, they don't have to be accomplished musicians, or be able to write musical notation.

For example, a composer can sit at a keyboard that's connected to a computer with appropriate software, invent a new melody and attempt to play it on the keyboard at any speed. The computer will record the notes, rests, and other musical elements, and play them back, permitting the composer to hear how they sound and make alterations. Measure-by-measure, students can compose and revise the melody, and then add layers in the form of harmony and additional instruments. The piece can include a single instrument playing a melody, or several instruments playing the same or accompanying melodies. The computer can also translate what is played on the keyboard into musical notation and print out sheet music for an entire band or orchestra.

Students who want to get more deeply involved in music technology and use it to compose and record their own work are welcome to take the music technology course, which provides an opportunity to learn how to use the artistic tools of today's high-tech recording industry.

What makes the industry so different now is that many recordings are no longer based on performance, but on the expertise of technicians who piece together musical sounds, voices, and other elements, to create a finished piece of music that would be difficult or impossible to perform on stage. Many students are interested in learning more about or even entering the recording business, and this course gives them a good introduction.

In the class, students first learn about the recording equipment—what is there, what it can do, and how to operate it. Then they use the equipment to compose music and produce projects. According to their teacher, some of the finished products have approached professional quality.

One student in that class noted that his group had just used multitrack recording equipment to record "Bad Moon Rising." He said that he thinks the class gives students a great opportunity to learn about modern music technology, especially for those (including himself) who want to become involved in music professionally. He added that everything is being done with computers now, so it's good that they have a chance to learn how to use them to write and record music.

Commenting on his extensive experience teaching music, the teacher said that music engages kids in a highly active style of learning. Nothing is less passive than music. It's interesting that educators today are calling for more active, group learning situations in academic areas, and these approaches are at the core of music education. It's also interesting that students who have studied music are typically successful in their other classes. He emphasized that everybody can be a winner in music, and when they learn success in one area, it shows them a path for success in other areas as well.

As for the value of technology in music education, this teacher's entire program is based on the technology tools that permit him to teach beginning musicians so effectively, and enable more advanced students to compose and record their work.

REFERENCES

Knapp, Linda. (1993). "Learning to Communicate in Written, Oral, and Multimedia Formats." Report written for the Shoreline School District, Seattle, Washington.

Knapp, Linda. (1993). "New Media, New Recognition for Visual and Performing Arts." Report written for the Shoreline School District, Seattle, Washington.

6

SOLVING PROBLEMS

RATIONALE

Problem-solving skills are critical when individuals confront complex problems, dilemmas, or tasks to complete. A "problem" situation can include anything from solving a math problem to designing a local sports arena or keeping peace between two conflicting nations.

The teaching/learning process involves guiding students through the processes of (1) defining the problem (dilemma, task, etc.); (2) developing strategies to solve the problem or complete the task; (3) planning steps for completion; (5) implementing the plan, which often includes gathering information, learning new skills, trying out possible solutions, and so on, and (6) evaluating the finished product as well as the process. During this process, the teacher fosters development of higher order thinking skills as students devise strategies, anticipate possible consequences, and analyze their results.

When students work collaboratively, the learning process also includes development of certain social skills such as dealing with members' diverse ideas and proposed strategies, appropriating the workload, and presenting the results.

Learning to solve problems is a vital skill that students cannot learn by memorizing facts and formulas and then recalling them for use in essays and tests. Teachers first need to help students learn to use fundamental problem-solving strategies and then learn to develop and experiment with other strategies of their own. The ability to solve problems creatively and effectively is a skill today's students will need for further education, for jobs, and for life in the coming years.

Problem-Solving Skills

As outlined above, fundamental problem-solving skills include the ability to define the problem, pick an appropriate strategy to solve the problem, plan steps for completion, implement those steps, and finally reflect on the process when it is finished. In addition to following a straightforward process for solving problems, effective problem-solvers need to be able to:

- Apply a variety of problem-solving strategies
- Develop new strategies to solve particular problems when necessary
- Remain open-minded during the process, maintaining a willingness to explore alternative strategies and solutions, and an acceptance of mistakes as part of the process

More sophisticated skills include an ability to:

- Apply problem-solving strategies in all subject areas
- Work collaboratively to solve problems (which includes development of social skills such as dealing with members' diverse suggestions, delegating the workload, and presenting the results)
- Work through problems embedded in complex contexts, verify and interpret their results, reason logically, and communicate clearly
- Use problem-solving tools to implement strategies (e.g., calculators, computer spreadsheets, databases, graphs, and charts)
- Use higher order thinking skills while devising strategies, anticipating possible consequences, and analyzing results

The Importance of Teaching Problem-Solving Skills

Helping students learn to identify problems of all kinds and develop strategies for solving them successfully is one of our primary educational goals. Why? Because we cannot teach children enough answers, facts, and formulas to help them function ten years from now. The world will be different, the workplace will be different, and a person's greatest educational asset will be his or her ability to learn new skills, facts, and strategies for solving problems or completing unfamiliar tasks. Learning to solve problems is a life skill that's increasingly more critical as the world grows more interdependent and as individuals confront new and more complex problems in their jobs and in their lives.

The Added Value of Using Technology for Solving Problems

Many modern electronic technologies are designed as tools for helping people gather information, organize it, analyze it, and use it to help solve difficult problems. Calculators, graphing calculators, databases, spreadsheets, graph and chartmaking software, geometric construction software, simulations, and many other kinds of tools provide unprecedented help for student and professional problem-solvers.

Indeed, many educators suggest that it was the introduction of these technologies in schools that enabled teachers to incorporate problem-solving into their curricula, or if it was already there, to spend a good deal more time on it. Previously, such tools were not available to students. The introduction of calculators enabled students to spend less time doing calculations and more time developing strategies for solving complex problems. Database and spreadsheet software enabled students to spend less time collecting factual information and more time analyzing it and coming up with generalizations and/or theories to test out. Geometric construction tools enabled students to spend less time measuring and constructing geometric figures and more time devising formulas and developing a deeper understanding of mathematical functions.

The rest of this chapter provides more specific examples of how these and other technology tools can be used to help students learn to solve problems more effectively.

CLASSROOM SCENARIOS AND OTHER SUGGESTIONS FOR IMPLEMENTATION

Since problem-solving is part of the process of designing and completing any complex task, all of the major projects described in this implementation section—before and after this chapter—involve problem-solving to some degree. This chapter, however, focuses on the art/craft of solving problems, and the examples selected for description emphasize the initial and continued development of a student's ability to solve unfamiliar and sometimes frustratingly complicated problems that are very much a part of the real world.

Years ago, when computers first became popular among "some" teachers, the one thing many of them raved about most was the computer's ability to help students learn to solve problems. Many teachers taught their students how to program computers using BASIC or LOGO programming languages, and were delighted by their students' increasing ability to solve the logic problems that constantly arose during the process. Programming reached its height of popularity when many believed that being able to program a computer would be useful, if not essential in their students' future. Few believe that anymore, though of course we'll always need talented programmers. Some teachers still teach programming as a useful approach to learning to solve problems (and of course, future programmers still need to learn), but since those days, a whole range of other software tools have become available to help students learn to develop problem-solving skills in a variety of contexts.

In 1989, The National Council of Teachers of Mathematics (NCTM) developed content standards for mathematics learning, which have become the unofficial national standards for K–12 mathematics. NCTM's proposed changes for curriculum and assessment in math stress problem-solving as they reflect a contemporary view of what it means to be mathematically literate in an information society. They call for the use of calculators and computers in helping students develop the ability to apply mathematical ideas to problem situations, and work with others to develop strategies and solutions. With a well-articulated new standard, school districts across the country have increased their emphasis on problem-solving in the curriculum. Technology developers also have begun producing more and better products that address the NCTM standards while continuing to motivate kids.

As other subject area authorities devise content standards for their disciplines, the need for students to learn to solve problems comes up again and again, such that when all disciplines have finished developing standards, we'll see some kinds of problem-solving skills included in all of them.

Teaching Problem-Solving with Specialized Software

Skill-Building Software

A third grade teacher who believes that problem-solving is the most important thing she teaches, begins by using specialized software to introduce students to a variety of problem-solving strategies. In one program, for instance, the screen presents a grid of 25 squares with an animal (or two) concealed behind a particular square(s). Using the arrow keys, a player moves around the grid in search of the hidden animal(s). The first game offers no clues as to the animal's whereabouts, leaving the player with only the primitive guess and check strategy. Each game after that offers clues that aid the player in using progressively more sophisticated strategies for finding the animals. (Basic strategies include: gather more data, keep a record, use the data you have, and so on.)

This teacher introduces the program to the whole class using one computer and two monitors so that everyone can see the screen display. During the demonstration, she leads them through the process of identifying and describing various strategies they can use for locating the animal(s). Then she sends them off to continue working in pairs.

Back as a whole group once again, she questions them: What did you do? How did you do it? What methods (strategies) did you come up with? She lists these strategies on the chalkboard. As the kids learn to think about what they're doing and to articulate their thought processes, a simple realization such as, "If I have no information, I'll use guess and check, but if I do have information, I can use a more powerful strategy," is a significant turning point. With this ability to analyze the process and seek the most suitable approach, students are well on their way to effective problem-solving.

According to this teacher, such programs have an additional advantage in that children who are poor readers often do extremely well in a visual environment that depends on logical thinking for success, rather than reading ability or recall of facts.

As to whether students take these skills and apply them when confronted with problems in other situations, the teacher suggests that they do, but only when she reminds them with a comment such as, "Who has a strategy?" at the appropriate moment. However, she believes that over time, students will begin to apply their strategies independently, they just need more opportunities to develop new strategies and practice them in a variety of situations. Still, one teacher can't embed a lifetime of problem-solving skills and the ability to use them all by herself in one year. Students need guided and independent problem-solving experiences throughout their schooling.

Problem-Solving in Mathematics

Another elementary teacher discovered that presenting mystery adventures that also require students to solve complex math problems, works extremely well in his class, so he began using a specialized product that employs both a video format and a computer format.

In the video-based adventure, a couple of bears race to the scene of a fire, face threatening gang members, and attempt to establish a rock band. While watching the video, students take notes. At certain points, the teacher stops the video for class discussion and for student groups to solve math problems that allow the bears to continue. According to the teacher, the individual groups have very different approaches, and soon discover there's often more than one way to solve a problem. The kids also discover how closely related these math problems are to their lives outside school. In addition, the teacher (and the software) emphasize language development and group processing skills. For example, students must explain (without using numbers) how they figured out answers. They must also explain how knowing the answers will benefit the bears.

The computer-based mysteries this teacher also used take place in a hotel, a toy store, a museum, and a seaside town. In each case, the young sleuths meet and interview various people who provide clues, after the detective helps them solve their own problems. As students progress, they accumulate many facts and must determine which ones are relevant and which are not. The facts they think are relevant they record in an electronic notebook. When faced with a problem to solve, detectives must determine what mathematical operation they will use to solve the problem and what data they need to calculate the answer. The notebook includes a calculator which enables students to concentrate on strategy rather than on computation. When students successfully solve a problem they advance to the next. If their answer is incorrect, they are given a hint and another try. Problems within each level of the program grow progressively more challenging.

Both of the video- and computer-based activities are accompanied by ample support material for the teacher that explains how to use the technology, how to guide students in group work, and how to coach them in developing problem-solving strategies.

Interdisciplinary Problem-Solving

Some specialized technology packages are interdisciplinary, multimedia, and extraordinarily comprehensive. The *Voyage of the Mimi* (and its sequel) is a well-known example that has been popularized by broadcasting the video component on public television. The complete package includes a video series, computer software, laboratory peripherals, and text support materials. It integrates math and science primarily, but also includes opportunities for language development. The video is divided into 13 story episodes. Each 15-minute episode is followed by a 15-minute documentary that provides further information about topics/issues only touched on in the video (e.g., what it really means to be deaf as shown by one of the deaf crew members in the story, how whales communicate, how ecological systems are balanced). The video component tells a very engaging story about a young boy and how his relationship with his grandfather (who is the skipper of the *Mimi*) changes over the summer voyage. The crew is composed of a cross-section of U.S. students, and together they experience a series of academic and extra-curricular adventures that keeps students glued to the story until the *Mimi* finally reaches home port.

The computer component is designed to help kids explore scientific concepts as well as develop specific skills. Curriculum areas covered include maps and navigation, ecological systems, and whales and their environment. After watching the *Mimi* crew study charts and plot a course for the whale search, students begin their own adventures with maps and navigation. First, they learn about latitude and longitude through a software game; then, through another game they learn the time/rate/distance formula commonly used in navigation. After developing other navigation skills, students attempt to rescue a whale caught in a fishing net by locating their own position on the chart, locating the position of the fishing trawler, plotting a course, and calculating how fast they'll have to go to get there in time.

In the eco systems module, students play a simulation game that places them on an island where they have to figure out how to survive for a whole year. But before they begin, they have to create an ecologically balanced island. While on the island, they can hunt, fish, gather firewood, and so on, but the ultimate goal is to leave the island a year later with the island in as good a state as when they arrived.

According to a fifth grade teacher who has been using this curriculum unit for several years, the purpose of these activities isn't necessarily to teach kids to navigate or balance the ecology of an island, but to teach them the underlying math and science concepts, and to develop their abilities to solve problems.

Simulations in Social Studies

Computer-based simulations are another approach teachers are increasingly using to help their students learn to develop problem-solving strategies in almost any subject area. One teacher remarked that he can teach kids how to solve problems and make responsible decisions without computer simulations, but with them, he can do a better job. The true value of simulations is that they enable learners to grapple with real-life problems in an environment that allows them to see the consequences of their decisions, without causing harm to themselves or others. In such practice situations, it's okay to make mistakes, even beneficial, because people learn by making poor choices, experiencing the results, and then analyzing the whole process later.

In our example classroom, the teacher uses a simulation that places students in the advertising department of a company that manufactures children's snacks. The company plans to sponsor a television drama that portrays the lives of children following a nuclear war. The show is extremely graphic and includes violence. Many film critics claim the show is excellent and that the violent scenes are well done and essential to the message. Other critics claim the violence is unnecessary and sickening. Anti-violence and parent groups threaten to boycott the snack food company if the show is not edited. You (the company's advertising department) are responsible for handling this crisis. What are you going to do?

First, students are directed to prioritize their goals and then they have to act before the show is scheduled to air. This department (group of students) decides that maintaining the integrity of the show is their top priority, and they also decide to meet with the anti-violence and parent groups. At that meeting, the groups demand to know why a company that sells children's snacks also supports violence. . . . Each time the department makes a decision, new consequences and a new set of choices arise. Periodically, a "personal consultant" appears to offer counsel and suggest specific readings (included in an accompanying reference book) that provide information to help them make an intelligent decision. The book includes briefs such as historical references to similar incidents and opinions of well-known and respected individuals. On the last day before airing, the department has to make its final decision. Let's say the show goes on in its original form. What happens? . . . .

When it is over, a computer printout indicates how close the students came to successfully supporting their established priorities, and which decisions led them astray. According to the teacher, it's possible to maintain your number-one priority, but impossible to have them all. He added, "You have to compromise somewhere, just like in real life."

Another example simulation used primarily with high school students, enables them to design a city. As city planners, students plan for parks, industry, residential areas, retail stores, schools, public utilities, city government, and so forth. If their city contains many green spaces, the cost of public utilities will rise. If they place factories beside residential neighborhoods, the crime rate goes up and the property value goes down. According to one teacher who uses it, the program contains the factual information students need and the power to alter their plans, but it's up to the young designers to balance the needs of residents, corporations, environmentalists, and the government.

Simulations in Science

In another school, an eighth grade teacher uses a computer simulation to teach problem-solving in science. In this simulation, students become the powerful managers of fictitious energy-producing companies. In the beginning, these companies produce only animal power. Then, as the managers learn more about how energy is produced—from water, wood, coal, oil, atoms, and the sun—they begin utilizing a variety of sources. The goal of the companies is to keep solvent. To accomplish this, managers have to make certain decisions concerning which energy source to use and what impact it will have on the company and on the environment.

According to the teacher, the simulation introduces students to several different science concepts. They learn that energy can be produced in many ways and they learn how various forms of energy are produced. They learn about the similarities, differences, advantages, and disadvantages of producing each type of energy. And they also learn how such natural forces as drought and pollution affect energy production.

Tool Software for More General Use

Graphing Tools

Some elementary teachers have begun using graphing software to help their students understand such abstract notions as percentages and variables. These teachers say that using graphs helps their students visualize numerical relationships and how they change when the numbers change.

One teacher explained that the graphs provide a natural bridge between concrete manipulatives and abstract numbers. She remarked that kids are not able to visualize numbers very well, so when they compare numbers it is important for them to be able to actually see the relationship. She said that graphs give kids something to look at that is both concrete and representational. When they are looking at a graph, the teacher can talk about the abstract comparison of numbers.

In this teacher's classroom students begin by comparing things that are very real to kids, like their favorite foods or their physical characteristics. Later they move on to curriculum-related comparisons in all subject areas. In one of the initial activities they collect data on every child's eye color. Then they enter the data and convert it into a bar graph. The software can also produce pie graphs and pictographs, so they view the data in those forms too. The students' motivation increases when they can see comparisons so clearly in the graphs, and soon they are comparing data on bedtimes, pets, favorite books, and TV shows.

The teacher remarked that once kids learn to use the tool, they use it whenever making a graph seems appropriate, which is often. For example, they periodically graph the weather data they've collected, and one student group graphed the number of soldiers who fought in each battle during the Revolutionary War. The latter graph revealed startling information that prompted them to discuss how the Americans managed to win battles with so few soldiers.

At the secondary level, a high school teacher uses graphs to teach students to derive algebraic formulas from real-life numerical relationships. During class, students plot the data they are given on a scatter plot. In this case, the data is the average monthly rainfall in their city. They notice that the shape of the graph (over the course of a year) closely resembles a parabola. After identifying the shape, students write an equation that they think best describes the relationship. When they enter the equation into the graphing program, the computer draws a graph of the equation that approximates the pattern of the data. According to the teacher, graphing activities such as this help students visualize the algebraic equations they are learning and provide a link to realistic applications.

[Note: There are now graphing calculators available that can handle most if not all the functions performed by graphing software.]

Geometric Construction Tools

A geometric construction tool enables students and teachers to electronically draw geometric shapes and measure any angle, length, and areas within the shapes. They can also replicate constructions, which is essential for forming generalizations and developing hypotheses.

Because this tool enables one to construct geometric shapes faster and more accurately than by hand, it means that teachers and students can spend less time constructing shapes and more time examining relationships, developing theories, and testing them out. The tool fosters logical thinking rather than recall of math facts and formulas. It can be used by a teacher as an electronic chalkboard for demonstrating and developing geometric concepts with the whole class, and it can be used as a personal geometry calculator and constructor for working on specific problems.

In our example classroom, a high school teacher uses it to introduce geometry concepts beginning with triangle midsegments. He asks students to use the tool to draw a triangle, label the midpoints of the three sides, and connect the points with line segments. Students look at their screen drawings (which are all different) and the teacher poses the question: What do you think is true? One student offers that the line segments form a smaller triangle inside, which is 1/3 or maybe 1/4 the size of the original triangle. The tool can measure area, so they quickly discover that all of their inner triangles are exactly 1/4 the size of the original triangle. What else is true? A student suggests that the line segments of the inner triangle are equal to half the length of the line segments of the original triangle. The tool can measure length, so they do it and discover that this is true for all of their triangles.

The lesson continues in this manner, with the teacher guiding students toward forming certain generalizations about triangles. They might come up with as many as 10 conjectures, the teacher noted. They write them down and then for homework write arguments for why these conjectures would be true, or provide counter examples to show why they would be false. The next day, students discuss their arguments and ultimately come up with geometric proofs that support their assumptions.

According to the teacher, using this kind of tool provides a much richer learning experience because students have more control over the direction of their learning and more power to follow through. But it is sometimes harder for the teacher, because students inevitably come up with results the teacher doesn't expect. One has to be willing to be put on the spot and willing to learn along with the students.

Spreadsheets in Elementary School

In addition to graphs, some elementary teachers also use spreadsheets to help their students visualize mathematical relationships. In our sample classroom, students established their own economic system by forming a government that set up a federal reserve, which printed currency that financed banks. The banks loaned money to entrepreneurs who chose to start up companies. The banks then had to keep records of the loans, interest on the loans, payments, and so forth, on a spreadsheet.

One group of students set up a miniature telephone company. They borrowed telephones from the local phone company, built a switchboard, and connected clusters of students between two classrooms. Company employees had to bill customers, record payments, and balance the books. This they accomplished with the help of a spreadsheet the teacher set up for them.

Another enterprise was a refreshment business, which provided lots of jobs and ample revenue. Some employees went to a local apple orchard to collect apples and cider, others made popcorn, others packaged the food. Salespeople took orders from students in other classrooms and later delivered the goods. Bookkeepers kept track of the daily financial transactions on a spreadsheet, and the net income was enough to send the class on a whale-watching trip.

According to the teacher, spreadsheets provide an excellent format for keeping track of finances. A spreadsheet keeps everything neatly organized and consistent. It also displays the information visually, in a way that helps kids understand the relationships between the numbers. He added that seeing the numerical relationships in the spreadsheet format helps kids understand percentages and how they work when calculating interest. The spreadsheet helps kids learn about place, value, decimals, making calculations, seeing relationships, understanding variables, and working with large numbers.

Spreadsheets in High School

At the high school level, spreadsheets are sometimes used as tools for teaching algebra. One teacher, for example begins the year by setting up a simple spreadsheet for students to use as a calculator, with variables and relationships already built into it. Then he poses problems for them to solve using the spreadsheet.

One such spreadsheet is set up to analyze the amount of money students can make by organizing a car wash. They manipulate variables such as the amount of money they charge, the number of people in each working group, the cost of materials, and the number of cars they expect to wash. Each time they change one of the variables, it affects everything else.

After working with a few such spreadsheets to solve different types of problems, students become familiar with how the variables work. Since the spreadsheets involve realistic situations that students can relate to, it's easier for them to see the relationships between the numbers and how they change.

The next step is to present students with a spreadsheet that already has tables set up and labeled, but the formulas have not yet been entered. After playing around for a while with the data that is included, students attempt to complete the tables. To do this, they have to identify how one variable is related to another and what has to be done with the numbers in order to compute a third value. For example, one such spreadsheet is set up to analyze the costs involved in remodeling an apartment. Carpeting is one of the costs, so students have to calculate the area of the floor and then multiply that by the cost of each square yard of carpeting to estimate the total cost. Next, students have to describe the relationship between the variables. During this step, they are essentially building their own formulas. In the carpeting example, the relationship they describe would be: the carpet cost equals the length of the floor, times the width, times the cost per yard of carpet. Finally, they attempt to translate their descriptions into algebraic formulas that are appropriate for the spreadsheet.

The culminating activity for these students occurs when the teacher presents them with a problem and challenges them to develop a suitable spreadsheet themselves. He demonstrates the process during a whole class lesson, and then they venture off to try it on their own.

Comprehensive Interdisciplinary Projects not Associated with any Particular Type of Software

As mentioned earlier, any major project that students take on will cause them to confront hurdles along the way that prompt them to apply whatever problem-solving skills they possess. Further, the whole approach to designing and completing a project parallels the processes used when solving a problem. In some cases, teachers—or teams of teachers—have involved themselves and their students in comprehensive, interdisciplinary projects that provided academic and other adventures they will never forget.

Students and teachers in an alternative high school program that had integrated disciplines and included advanced technology of all descriptions, decided to join forces in the construction of a scaled model of their city. The 20 × 20-foot model included operable cars, cranes, traffic lights, city lights, railway crossing, elevators, pile drivers, and other devices controlled by eleven computers. (Picture a collector's highly sophisticated model train set with complete paraphernalia.) The project's success depended upon students learning new science and civics concepts as well as math, language, and technology skills. All subjects were meshed together in the design, problem-solving, and construction processes, and through these processes students developed new knowledge and skills in their subject areas as well as new understandings about how to work collaboratively in groups and how competencies in one subject area helped them in another and another.

One adventurous elementary teacher tried something similar, though slightly less ambitious, in her own classroom. In this case, the idea of planning and building a model city evolved from a series of activities that focused on students' ethnic backgrounds. Students came from many different ethnic groups and the teacher wanted to get them working on a project that would interest everyone and also place value on their separate origins and cultures. One activity involved writing autobiographies, and another involved building physical monuments to commemorate things of great family importance that they thought needed to be remembered in the year 2100. Following these activities, they decided to build a multiethnic city.

In their first city-building experience they spent one day planning the city, and the next day they built the whole city with hundreds of items brought from home, including tin cans, boxes, hairpins, elastics, and so forth. According to the teachers, their "instant city" was total chaos. The kids disregarded their plans and built an entire city with no roads, no water, no electricity. . . . It was a wonderful experience for them, the teacher remarked. If they hadn't done it that way, they never would have believed how important it is to plan first.

The second attempt involved considerably more planning. They developed deeds for each parcel of land, designed buildings in varying geometric shapes (so all wouldn't look like shoeboxes), and they had lessons in scale. They mapped the school neighborhood—its bus routes, city buildings, water table, ethnic groupings, energy sources, and so on. They chose a form of city government with a city mayor and city council, and elected classmates for those offices. When the planning was finished, they sculpted the landforms from foam strips that created a surface of about 15 × 6 feet, and then they constructed buildings with assorted materials. The city they finally built did have roads, water, electricity, and everything else the students had planned.

After everything was built and they "lived in their city for a while" they decided to form a committee to expand the public transportation system so that students could visit classmates across town more easily. When the city council heard how much that project would cost they. . . .

7

INQUIRY

RATIONALE

To inquire means to ask questions, to investigate, to examine closely. Pre-school children do it quite naturally as they struggle to understand things that appear so mysterious to them, such as why it rains or how flowers grow. In their view, the world is controlled by all-powerful, all-knowing grown-ups, and whatever the adults do not know or cannot control, monsters and fairies do. As they gather experiences and a few answers to their questions, they begin to see the world as more rational, or at least more comprehensible, and they begin to discover their own power to explore and find answers for themselves.

When they enter school, however, they receive many more answers to questions they did not ask and fewer opportunities to ask their own questions and seek answers. School has an orderly curriculum that determines what the children must learn and when. Children are given answers to remember, and then teachers ask them the questions, confounding the natural process of inquiry. Soon students learn not to ask questions in school unless they are directly related to the topic being covered.

This book's restructured curriculum attempts to regenerate the learner's natural inclination to ask questions and seek answers. Inquiry within a school setting, however, cannot revisit the preschooler's tendency to ask a steady stream of unrelated questions, or foster the pursuit of answers in scattered directions. We suggest a process of guided inquiry that involves learners in asking questions and seeking answers within a broad curriculum area, and using common research strategies to seek answers for themselves.

For example, let's say that an eighth grade class is studying state government. The overall learning objectives are that the students learn how their state government functions, what kinds of issues and legislation are handled by the state government, and which issues are currently most prominent. Within these general guidelines, students come up with their own questions and favored topics to pursue. Whatever students don't choose to cover is left to the teacher to present so that students will end up with a balanced understanding of the state government.

When students have selected topics for inquiry, they begin to explore all the available resources in an effort to collect as much information as they can. Then they examine the information with an objective, analytical eye (using critical thinking skills). They synthesize ideas as they discover relationships between ideas and often come up with new interpretations or theories concerning their topic. Then, they design an appropriate format to share their new understandings with classmates (using communication skills). This sharing process in turn encourages others to ask questions that compel the presenter to promote, defend, and reflect on his or her own ideas. Through this process of presenting, discussing, and reflecting on their ideas, all participants gain a deeper and more personal understanding of the concepts under discussion. It is a far more effective approach to learning than when information is simply presented to students and they are expected to remember it.

The Process of Inquiry

A thorough inquiry, such as the ones proposed in this book, involves the student in the processes of exploration, analysis, synthesis, reflection, and communication. Students collect information, analyze it, discover relationships, and build new knowledge that is personally meaningful. They share their understandings with others, thus providing opportunities to promote, defend, reflect, and revise their own ideas. The process yields a deeper and more integrated understanding of the concepts being studied; it also provides meaningful opportunities to learn and practice basic skills related to the particular subject of inquiry.

Our emphasis on student inquiry is based on a growing research base which asserts that learners "construct" their own understandings/knowledge from the information they acquire. This is referred to as the *constructivist* approach to learning, and it differs from the traditional approach which assumes a teacher can "deliver" knowledge to a learner.

In the traditional curriculum, structured inquiry is usually limited to science experiments (where the outcomes are usually known anyway), and occasional research reports (that seldom challenge traditional perspectives or present original ideas). In this restructured curriculum, the process of inquiry is encouraged daily. It may be employed in class to re-explore the causes of the Civil War, in groups to examine the cultural implications of *Huckleberry Finn,* or to predict the winner of the next presidential election. The process is repeatedly modeled by the teacher, and students are encouraged to apply it whenever they have questions or new topics to explore. The goal is to emphasize exploration and analysis of topics rather than (but not excluding) memorization of facts.

The Importance of Teaching Structured Inquiry

Outside of school, asking questions, seeking answers, and integrating the newly acquired information into one's knowledge base is a common occurrence. After graduation, it is the most common way of learning. So why teach a structured approach to inquiry if we already know how to ask questions and assimilate answers? Well, let's see. If a child asks about who leaves presents on Christmas Day and the parent answers Santa Claus; the very young child is likely to believe it as truth. However, an older child begins to ask further questions, such as why did Santa use the same wrapping paper as you, Mommy; or why is Santa's handwriting just like Daddy's? If a twelve-year old reads in an historical novel that General Custer was a brave soldier who fought savage Indians to make the country safe for American settlers, he is likely to believe it. The reader might also begin to develop a negative opinion of Native Americans, as well as certain attitudes concerning aggression and violence in the pursuit of personal or national goals. If, on the other hand, we encourage that student to ask questions about what he read and seek further information from other sources (conveying the Native American's point-of-view, for example), share his information, and reflect on his own and others' comments, the reader may develop a more informed and balanced understanding of Custer and that period of U.S. history.

Teaching learners to question what they hear, see, and read (critical thinking), and to seek further information that they analyze and synthesize with what they already know (inquiry) are critical learning goals of this book—because we want to teach youngsters to develop in-depth and balanced understandings of complex ideas.

Most of today's adults never received this kind of encouragement to pursue alternative points of view other than the teachers' or the textbooks', and consequently, many adults all too easily believe what they read, see, and hear as the truth. The teaching/learning approach in this book, and its restructured curriculum are an attempt to prepare children to become adults who question information, seek alternative points of view, think critically, and develop thorough and balanced understandings of the world around them.

The Added Value of Using Technology for Inquiry

The use of technology in the process of inquiry is immensely valuable, as modern technology offers a wide range of information resources and tools for seeking and analyzing information. For example, modern research tools such as electronic encyclopedias, card catalogs, periodical indexes, and full-text resources (e.g., indexed newspapers and magazines that also include the full text of their articles), provide immediate information from near and distant libraries. Video-based resources such as the *Video Encyclopedia of the 20th Century,* taped television programs, video documentaries, and others provide additional visual information that offer an additional perspective. Microcomputer-based laboratories offer inquiring students extremely accurate tools for conducting scientific experiments independently, because the tools are safe, economical, and easy to use.

The classroom examples that follow demonstrate how teachers and students are currently using these and other such tools to collect information, analyze it, synthesize the new information with what they already know, reflect on what they've discovered, and communicate their new understandings with others.

CLASSROOM SCENARIOS AND OTHER SUGGESTIONS FOR IMPLEMENTATION

Once again, we note that an increasing number of schools and districts are now shifting their emphasis from having students learn facts, to having them learn to solve problems, explore information, and think critically. In sync with this trend, technology developers are increasingly producing video, software, and multimedia products that foster this new teaching/learning approach.

This section provides examples of teachers who use a wide range of technologies to teach inquiry. Some use generic technologies such as databases, telecommunications, VCRs, television, and so on to create activities and curricula that inspire and support student inquiry. Some teachers use more specific research tools such as electronic encyclopedias, online database services, and video databases to support inquiry. Others use specialized products that range from computer simulations to complete multimedia curricula that are designed to engage students personally in the inquiry process.

Generic Technology

Database Software in Elementary Science

Our first exemplary classroom is located by the ocean in a warm region of the country. For years, the classroom teacher took her fifth graders out to explore and learn about the ocean environment, yet she became frustrated because every year they would gather and study a wonderful assortment of specimens, and then the next year a new class would gather and study many of the same things all over again. Rather than being able to build on what other classes had already learned, each class repeated the same process.

Finally (after a professional development workshop on computers), the teacher decided to have her students begin developing an ongoing database of information on their collections so they could learn from others' work as well as add new information to it. That original database still continues to grow every year. Here's how the whole process works.

First, the teacher takes students on snorkeling field trips in search of interesting marine life. As they collect various plants and animals, they take field notes that describe the exact location of the organism. They record data such as air temperature, water temperature, depth, distance from the shore, type of shore bottom, and so forth. To gather this data, students have to learn to use the scientific instruments that help them test water salinity, capture a sample of the ocean bottom, chart the location, and measure temperature.

Back in the classroom, students consult the database to discover which of their specimen are already entered in the database and which ones are new. For those already entered, the student tries to find new information to add. Sometimes they find information in the database that contradicts their own data, and in that case they do further research to learn which student's data is correct, or if they both are. The collected specimens that have not yet been entered in the database become the collector's responsibility. The student enters his or her field trip data in the database. Then the student does further research on the collected specimens and adds information that he or she thinks is particularly interesting. Finally, the student takes pictures of the specimens, scans them, and enters them into the database as well. This stored information is then readily accessible to anyone else who wants or needs it. To date, there are over 1,000 species entered.

According to the teacher, the database activities have given new meaning and purpose to the field trips. The kids are motivated to find specimens that aren't in the database so they can add to it, and they also enjoy reading—and checking—what others have contributed. Also, because they now have that handy resource of information, the teacher has created additional activities that prompt students to go to the database (as well as other sources) to seek the information they need.

Electronic Laboratories in Elementary Science

In another elementary school far from the seashore, a teacher was interested in having his fourth grade students do scientific experiments in the classroom, but his school had no science lab, and the district curriculum offered no suggestions for classroom experiments. A colleague brought him a box of strange computer cables and other paraphernalia accompanied by a book of suggested experiments, and then left, promising that the equipment would plug into the classroom computer and that he would have a lot of fun with it. That box of computer "probeware" effectively changed the teacher's science program forever.

Computer probeware, more formally referred to as a Microcomputer-Based Laboratory (MBL), consists of computer peripherals or "probes" that are used to measure physical properties such as heat and light. The accompanying software records, analyzes, and displays these measurements on the computer screen. In practice, this means that students can do hands-on experiments with equipment that is often easier to use, safer, and more precise than traditional laboratory equipment. They can observe their initial measurements and the resulting changes on the display screen as they occur, which makes the results more distinctive and easier to understand.

After spending a Saturday figuring out how to use the equipment (and trying out some experiments with his family), this teacher introduced his class to discovery science by reenacting Galileo's observation of fallen objects. The purpose of the experiment is to determine if larger and heavier objects fall faster than smaller and lighter ones. Being somewhat of a ham, the teacher arrived at school dressed as Galileo and invited students to assist in the experiment as Galileo might have done it back in the 16th century. They took three balls of different sizes and weights—a basketball, tennis ball, and golf ball—and went up to the head of the staircase on the second floor. From there, three students dropped the balls simultaneously, and three students observed their landing from below. The observers were confused by what they saw. They expected the basketball to land way before the others, so they claimed the basketball landed first, tennis ball second, and golf ball last, but admitted that the results were so close they couldn't be certain. According to the teacher, the students assumed the heavier and bigger balls would land before the smaller and lighter ones, and that this assumption influenced their observations.

Then they repeated the experiment using the computer light probe that serves as an extremely accurate timer. The results showed (on the computer screen) that all three balls landed at the same time. Students trusted that the computer equipment can measure more accurately than their eyes, so were willing to accept the computer-proven theory. (One wonders what Galileo's students saw without these precise tools.)

The experiment was finished, but the class discussion was not. Students wondered why a feather or a piece of paper would not hit the ground at the same time as the balls. Someone suggested that they flutter . . . something holds them up. What is it? . . . air, they realize. Air resistance can significantly delay the fall of a feather, but not a golf ball. And a new idea is introduced.

This experiment showed them that the computer's ability to measure accurately is significant. Yet, if they had looked only at the experimental data, they could have assumed that a feather would land along with the balls. From this teacher-guided experience, they learned that a human's ability to think about things, make comparisons, and come up with revised theories is crucial. Both accurate instruments and critical thinking are essential for the inquiry process in science to be successful.

Video Production for Interdisciplinary Learning

Another approach some teachers use to get their students involved in the inquiry process is to have them produce a daily news broadcast. Admittedly, this is a major commitment for teachers as well as students, but those who do it claim the educational rewards are well worth the effort.

Our example case involves a sixth grade class that has been producing daily shows for half a year. A group of students (who were interested in learning to use a video camera and computer-based editing tool, and could spend time outside school acquiring the skills) handles the equipment. The other jobs—news anchor, reporters, and weatherpeople—rotate on a biweekly basis. Each morning, the show is "broadcast" for 10 minutes in every classroom. It includes national, local, and school news, sports news, announcements, entertainment reviews, lost and found information, and a weather report.

News features are researched, developed, and videotaped in class and are often directly related to social studies issues covered in the curriculum, but with an up-to-date and analytical twist. For instance, when the national news was filled with stories of a food crisis in Somalia, the teacher linked this news event to the sixth grade curriculum in social studies (African studies), science (nutrition), and mathematics (percentages). The result was that student reporters developed more informed and interesting news stories.

Sports news not only covers school and popular professional games, it adds further information such as graphs of previous team and player records, which students developed by gathering data and entering it in a computer-based graphing tool. Book, movie, and video reviews are linked to the language arts curriculum, and they often add depth and breadth to the news stories as well. For instance, students reviewed "The Gods Must Be Crazy" (a movie about Africans that takes place in Africa) and *Things Fall Apart* (a book about Africa by a native African) when broadcasting news stories on Somalia. Students tape an up-to-date weather report minutes before the morning broadcast, by capturing the weatherperson's personal reactions to the weather while standing outside. Even this spontaneous activity is often followed up by weather maps and data that were collected and taped the previous day. As in adult TV, the weatherperson frequently has to admit that yesterday's prediction is today's best joke.

Since the school already owned video equipment and was wired for video in every classroom, the daily news broadcast hasn't incurred any additional expenses. It's been going on for a couple of years now and the teacher who initiated the project is now doing it as a team project with the other sixth grade class.

Database Software in Middle School

Our exemplary eighth grade class experienced the process of inquiry through their study of U.S. immigration. First they explored 19th century immigration to the United States by "adopting" hypothetical immigrant families and then making housing and employment decisions for the family based on historical facts they got from an available database. This assignment concluded the planned curriculum unit, but the students wanted to explore immigration further. Their motivation was based on the fact that many of their parents were immigrants; indeed, half the students spoke another language besides English at home, and the immigrant families represented at least five different countries.

They decided to build another database that would contain information on U.S. immigration in the 20th century. The research began in their community, but quickly extended across the country. They used telecommunications to link with schools in California, Texas, Florida, and Michigan. The numbers of 20th century immigrants where so large they decided to do a substudy of students who had immigrated within the past 10 years. In this study, students asked their recently immigrated peers to answer survey questions concerning what difficulties they have experienced here; what they like and dislike about the United States; what education and/or jobs their parents had before and after immigration.

After entering the survey information in the database, the students began analyzing data from both the 19th and 20th century databases in an effort to answer their research questions. The questions included: Do recent immigrants have some of the same problems that immigrants had a century ago? What conditions are the same now? What's different? According to their teacher, the inquiry process helped students develop a far greater understanding of immigration in the United States than the approach they had used previously.

Seventh graders in the same district studied third world countries as part of their social studies curriculum. In the past, they had been asked to memorize facts about third world countries and then recall them in a test. According to the teacher, many of the students didn't even understand what "mortality rate" meant, even if they did memorize it. Then, the librarian introduced this teacher to computer databases and offered to team up with him in an effort to transform the study of the third world into an inquiry. They spent a semester planning, and then tried out their new curriculum with the next group of students.

Students began the study by watching videos, slides, and photographs of several Third World countries. They went to the library media center to search a database for countries with a per capita income of less than $5,000. Then, each selected a country. They began collecting information on their chosen countries, writing down facts such as literacy rate, mortality rate, per capita income, and so forth. From there, they continued their research by searching online databases and the CD-ROM encyclopedia, as well as numerous print materials.

They each entered their country's population growth rate in a spreadsheet along with the World Bank formula for determining how many years it would take for the population to double. With this information, they tried to come up with ideas about how their countries could avoid disaster from overpopulation, improper land use, government instability, poor health, inadequate education, and other problems that intensify as the population grows.

Finally, students wrote fictional autobiographies that included personal descriptions of their lifestyles, as well as proposals suggesting how their countries could survive and even grow stronger in the future. According to the English teacher (who joined the social studies teacher and librarian for this project), the kids were so excited that many rewrote their papers half a dozen times. The social studies teacher was happy because the students had a much better understanding of the content area than in the old approach. The librarian was also happy because she had a couple more converts for her media center.

Multiple Resources in High School English and History

Moving out of the middle school environment and on to high school, let's take a look at a situation in which the 10th grade English and history teachers have teamed up to offer an integrated unit on U.S. history, culture, and literature during the period between World War I and World War II. During the summer, these two teachers designed the inquiry-based curriculum and then scoured the local libraries for sources, begged their principal for money to purchase technology-based resources, and finally won a district grant that enabled them to buy some software and resource materials.

They began by showing the class film footage from that period. (They were most fortunate that the district owned the *Video Encyclopedia of the 20th Century.*) Footage included clips of soldiers fighting in WWI, speeches by Churchill, Roosevelt, Hitler, and other world leaders of that period, and finally clips of WWII battles. This visual imagery piqued the students' curiosity and motivated them to ask further questions. In an effort to answer their questions as well as cover the subject matter in a somewhat chronological manner, the teachers recorded the questions and provided some time for students to try to answer one another's questions based on the understandings they currently had. This gave the teachers an idea of what students already knew and what major misunderstandings they shared. The teachers took notes on the discussion and then put these notes and the students' questions aside for future reference.

The class began a rather systematic exploration of the period. They were given a comprehensive list of resources—print, electronic, human, and so on—that represented many points of view, including wealthy white male American, poor white male American, recent immigrant, African American, female American, German American, Jewish American, Japanese American, American child, American politician, and so forth. The list also included resources that presented German, English, French, and Japanese points of view.

Individually, their task was to take on a persona representing one of these points of view, and then to study the historic period from that fictional person's perspective.

In small groups, they had a second research task, which was to select one of the subject matter areas—politics, social environment, economy, entertainment, literature, art, and so on—and develop a multimedia presentation to share with the class. Group members would maintain their personas to enrich the presentation with a variety of perspectives.

Before students set out to do the research independently and in groups, the teachers modeled the structured process of inquiry they wanted students to follow. From then on, students were free to come and go from the classroom in search of resources or a quiet space to work. Teachers remained in the classroom to help when needed, and they also made themselves available by phone in the evenings and on weekends. Twice a week, the class met as a whole to discuss their progress, and groups met more frequently to accomplish their collaborative tasks.

When student research was completed, the class met for a series of events. One was a television talk show in which the moderator (teacher) asked various guests (students representing their persona) to comment on issues such as what caused WWII, why the United States entered the war, what life was like for their persona in between the wars, and so forth. The second event was actually a series of class discussions on issues such as who prospered during the period directly following WWI, who didn't, and why; how successful was the New Deal; what happened to women during that period; what were the effects of the war on new immigrants, on African Americans, on children, and so on. The third event was a panel discussion on what the nation learned from this period in history and what lessons ought to have been learned that were not. The final event consisted of a re-run of the questions students had discussed at the beginning of the semester. It proved entertaining as well as thought-provoking as students realized how freely they had voiced opinions that were without any factual base.

The semester's final examination included a research report (text or multimedia) that each student prepared regarding his or her persona, a written essay exam on the period, and the groups' presentations. After the presentations, the students and their teachers were ready for a party.

Research Tools: Inquiry and the Modern School Library

Examples of students engaging in inquiry presented so far have taken place in the classroom. However, in many schools the rapidly emerging place for learning these skills is in the library, or the Library Media Center (LMC) as it is often called. Now a model for change and adaptation to the needs of students in the information age, the traditional library as we know it is becoming the information heartbeat of a modern school.

An LMC continues the traditional library's function of warehousing and lending a full selection of fiction and non-fiction books and periodicals, including abundant resources for student research. What's different is that the LMC has expanded its collection to include a variety of technology-based resources. Many of these electronic resources enable students to strengthen their print-based learning by watching visual examples and by listening to explanations. Others, such as multimedia encyclopedias and the electronic card catalog, enable young researchers to locate the information they need faster and more effectively than they can from print resources.

The role of the librarian has changed so dramatically that in many cases she is now called the Library Media Specialist (LMS). An LMS does more than just provide access to printed information, she helps students learn to locate and process information from a vast array of print and electronic resources. The LMS teaches students the strengths and weaknesses of each media resource, the appropriate use of each, and how to gather information in each medium. The LMS also provides staff development by helping teachers understand the effectiveness of each media resource and how they can use various media to make their teaching more effective.

Elementary School

Our exemplary elementary school librarian began acquiring multimedia resources as soon as she took over the library in 1990, because she is a strong advocate of helping children learn through a combination of paper and electronic media. As a former classroom teacher, she has always taught with a variety of print, visual, and audio resources because she believes that kids deserve alternative learning opportunities. Not surprisingly, she is in accord with research in the area that suggests students learn more effectively with a variety of media. She believes that we owe it to students to teach them to be competent users of information from any resource, in print and electronic formats.

To teach students to be competent users of information, this LMS employs a teaching approach that progresses from direct instruction to empowering students to be independent users and thinkers. First she teaches the children (and their teachers) how to use each media resource and provides easy-to-follow direction cards they can use later to refresh their memories. Next, she breaks the class into small groups and has them move around to each station where they use the resources to answer specific research questions she has given them. These questions prompt students to try each of the resource functions, so they will discover the full range of what's possible with that particular resource. Finally, students are ready to use the resources independently, and indeed they do, including at lunchtime and after school.

While teaching students how to use the print and electronic resources, the librarian is also teaching them research strategies they can use now, at university, and in the workplace. The skills and concepts she teaches focus on process—how to locate information and evaluate its usefulness; how to digest information in an encyclopedia article or video clip, for instance; how to integrate it with other information; and finally, how to communicate the learner's new knowledge of the topic under research.

Let's observe an example of this whole process in action. Fourth graders at this school study Early American history from 1680–1800. Long before the unit is scheduled to begin, the LMS and the fourth grade teachers searched the district's media catalogs and other materials to find a variety of relevant resources to strengthen the course curricula.

One fourth-grade teacher created a curriculum unit that involved small groups of students doing library research and then organizing their notes into both a written report and an oral presentation. Her goals were to get students to become more independent learners and to work effectively in groups. She commented that the experience has been the most exciting thing she's ever done with a class. She added that by learning to use the tools for finding information, the kids have become more curious, more independent, and more self-confident in their ability to figure things out for themselves.

Before starting this adventure, the teacher spent a couple of days coaching her students on how to work cooperatively in small groups. They talked about the need to help each other by listening to and respecting one another's ideas, finding tasks for members that fit their interests and abilities, handling disagreements, and so forth. According to the teacher, these preliminary lessons turned out to be the key to successful small groups.

Before beginning their research, the class went to the LMC to learn how to use each of the resources they would be using for their projects. Then, during their two weeks of research (45 minutes per day) in the LMC, each group worked at six different resource stations that included an electronic encyclopedia, a video series on that historic period, a laserdisc, the electronic card catalog, film strips, and a variety of print references.

The teacher had written out lessons and objectives for each group to help them structure their inquiry as they moved from resource to resource taking notes. Halfway through the process, the class spent a week outside the library learning how to process the information they were gathering. To help them learn to organize their notes, she had each group transform the written lessons she had given them into a detailed outline and then transfer their notes into the outline. She taught them how to avoid copying from an encyclopedia and other sources—how to paraphrase the information in their own words, and how to quote and credit printed excerpts they did want to include. Then they continued their research with these fundamentals in mind.

When the research was finished, groups proceeded to expand and develop their outlines into written reports, and they also created oral reports to teach the rest of the class what they had learned about their particular topic.

What is different or better about the electronic resources? The LMS and the teacher agree that when students can see pictures and listen to the historical context while watching, it makes their learning of history much richer, and they're more likely to remember what they've learned. The librarian added that the electronic encyclopedia helps teach kids inquiry and problem-solving strategies. When they go to this resource they have to know some key words to search for the information they want. They need to think for themselves. She added that too many of us just give them the information rather than giving them the opportunity to be self-sufficient and learn to get the information or solve the problem for themselves. These kids are building research and problem-solving strategies that will help them throughout life.

Secondary School

Our exemplary LMS at the secondary level has been working as a librarian in the district for 20 years. During recent years, technology has emerged as a major factor in modernizing the library program. As she noted, changes in the library reflect changes in the workplace in our society, and she sees her job as helping students adjust to new technologies in the workplace.

In 1989, her high school library acquired computers and software that enabled students to search electronic indexes for books and magazine articles as well as use electronic dictionaries and encyclopedias. According to the librarian, it was becoming apparent that learning to use electronic resources is a skill that students will need throughout high school, college, and the rest of their lives. She and other librarians also realized that it was their job to help students learn to use the electronic resources effectively. In addition to learning how to access information, students must learn to analyze and organize it, and communicate it through written papers, oral reports, and multimedia presentations. To this end, the LMS purchased six computers with word processing software to reside in the library for students to use at any time to help them record, organize, and create their own written reports. The LMC also has a fully equipped video editing room that some teachers and students use to create multimedia presentations.

The school has just introduced a new course for freshman that includes the three components necessary for learning to access information electronically, process it, and organize it into an appropriate format. Students will first learn keyboarding skills; then they'll learn to search and select relevant information from a variety of resources; then they'll combine keyboarding and searching skills as they take notes, analyze, and organize their information, draft written reports, edit them, and finally produce a polished research paper.

This high school currently has nineteen computer-based resources in addition to the six computers used for word processing. Seven support the card catalog system, two contain the magazine index, one is for the electronic dictionary, two are for the electronic encyclopedias, one contains a timeline of history, another has the complete works of Shakespeare and index, another has summaries of important news articles, another has a CIA factbook, one manages circulation, one is used for telecommunications, and the most recent one contains the full text of the local city newspaper.

Some of these electronic resources are just indexes (e.g., the card catalog and magazine index) that refer students to printed books and magazine articles for complete information, and others include complete information (e.g., the encyclopedia, dictionary, and the full text of the newspaper). The LMS emphasized that technology doesn't make print material obsolete. In some cases it just makes it easier and faster to access the print information.

In addition to computer-based resources, the LMC also has a fax machine which enables individuals to receive full text articles from other schools, libraries, and government offices. This speedy method of getting printed material has some unique advantages. For example, classes studying the state's government can get recent bills and other documents directly from the legislative offices, and classes studying particular foreign countries can fax interview questions to individuals in those countries and get answers almost as quickly as if they were doing the interview in person.

This librarian has also championed the use of telecommunication at the high school, and her efforts have inspired some teachers to involve their students in international projects through telecommunications networks such as PeaceNet, Learning Link, and Internet. One English class, for example, communicated directly with students in Israel during the Persian Gulf War, a Spanish class linked up with peers in Argentina and Spain, and another class interviewed German students while the Berlin Wall was coming down.

According to this LMC, in the future, telecommunications will be the common means for getting information in school, libraries, the workplace, and in our homes. She claims that learning to use electronic resources and having them readily available for student use, is increasingly more critical in our children's education. She believes that students who don't have these resources available are educationally handicapped. She emphasized that schools need to provide all students with information processing skills and ready access to computers at school. It's an equity issue for public education. This high school's new freshman course will teach students these essential skills, and that's a good start, she noted. After that, the challenge will be to provide easy access to these resources once students have learned the skills.

Specialized Curriculum Software

Technology developers have finally gained respect and been accepted by educational administrators, and are already in heavy competition with textbook companies to win state adoptions, especially since a few influential big-money states have permitted schools to spend their textbook money on technology-based curriculum materials. To date, most of the curriculum products that use an inquiry-based approach are in the area of science. These kinds of products are quite new, so the examples below describe only the technology, rather than its use in a particular classroom. Specific products are not named because the intention here is to describe the range of products currently available.

One such product is an interactive videodisc series designed for middle school classrooms. It uses an inquiry-based approach to the exploration of basic physics principles with the help of a roller coaster and sports activities. In the roller coaster module, students explore Newton's laws of motion as they try to design a roller coaster that provides a thrilling ride without derailing the coaster. When they make modifications to the design, they also observe the effects as the coaster speeds up or slows down. In the sports module, students begin to understand parabolic flight when throwing water balloons at the coach, and conservation of momentum when playing baseball. Students can get advice from experts—a physicist, police officer, engineer, and grandmother—or consult an embedded reference that explains physics terms with text and visuals.

Another product that is designed for grades three and up, focuses on our solar system. It features a film documentary that introduces the sun, planets, and asteroids, the astronomical forces that act among them, and theories of the solar system's origin. The product is primarily a visual and factual resource, but the software interface makes it so easy for kids to explore on their own that some teachers claim its more than just a resource.

There are also complete multimedia curriculum packages available for specific grade levels. One such example presents a seventh grade science curriculum that includes units on life science, physical science, ecology, and earth science. Using a hands-on approach, there are computer simulations to play, databases to consult, video clips to watch, texts to read, and written work to complete. Each unit begins with a question that creates the context for the scientific inquiry. For instance, the first unit begins with the question: How do heredity and the environment affect our health and our lives? Each unit is divided into smaller sections that also have organizing questions such as: How does the nervous system work in the human body? A comprehensive curriculum guide helps the teacher lead and assist students through their individual and group explorations.

REFERENCES

Knapp, Linda. (1993). "Information Access and the Modern School Library." Report written for the Shoreline School District, Seattle, Washington.

8

CRITICAL THINKING

RATIONALE

Critical thinking involves analysis of ideas or opinions, comparison of opposing views, thoughtful decision-making, and other such analytical processes. Learners develop and practice critical thinking skills when they are provided with guided opportunities to critically examine the work, thoughts, and opinions of others as well as their own.

The learning process may include guided experiences in analyzing completed works such as plays, books, speeches, editorials, TV programs, and paintings; evaluating one's own or classmates' work; and participating in formal debates. The process also may include learning to analyze available information while developing one's own work, such as learning to assess points of view in opposing editorials; or learning to examine information from several sources before determining who to vote for, what issues to support, or what product to buy.

The process of critical thinking helps students learn to identify bias (including their own), examine alternative points of view, and analyze the merit of each before drawing conclusions or making decisions. These critical thinking skills can be applied in almost any traditional subject area in school; they are also essential skills outside of school where individuals are constantly bombarded with shallow and biased thinking that is presented through clever persuasive techniques. It is essential in this emerging information age for individuals to learn to form opinions and make decisions based on their own ability to think critically and analytically.

Critical Thinking Skills

Critical thinking skills include the ability to:

- Distinguish between facts and opinions
- Understand language differences between words that are "neutral" and convey no bias (e.g., house, woman, food, thin), and "loaded" words that convey bias (e.g., shack, broad, delicacy, skinny, etc.)
- Understand body language and speech patterns that convey neutral and biased meanings, and the persuasive techniques used to influence people's thoughts and feelings through music and art. In other words, learn to identify bias in all media, including newspapers, magazines, television, public speeches, TV commercials, and printed advertisements.
- Be able to analyze the presenter's arguments and determine which ideas are supported by evidence and which are supported by emotional appeal without evidence
- Seek and analyze the other side of a speaker/writer's arguments and explore all perspectives before choosing a side or making a decision
- Develop research and analytical skills for gathering information about a topic and determining the accuracy and truth of the information
- Form reasoned opinions (based on facts and evidence), build arguments, and then share and defend these opinions before others

The Importance of Teaching Critical Thinking Skills

One of our most fundamental learning goals is to teach young citizens to be intelligent, independent thinkers, which also means critical and analytical thinkers. Traditionally, students have been encouraged to absorb the information presented to them by teachers and textbooks. They have been encouraged to accept this information as the truth, remember it, and repeat it in their essays and tests. Students have learned to accept teachers, books, newspapers, TV news, and other adult-produced media as unquestionable authorities that present "the truth." Consequently, students continue to believe these authorities after they leave school, producing an adult population that can often be fooled by the underlying point of view or bias that exists in most forms of communication.

To be fair, many traditional school curricula do include some opportunities for learning critical thinking skills. Some English courses include analysis of literature. Good writing programs cover various forms of analytical writing from compare and contrast to critical essays; some study editorials and reviews, propaganda, and advertising; and some teach students to constructively critique one another's papers. Some social studies programs critically analyze historical and political issues; science programs promote scientific inquiry; and so forth.

In fact, since teaching critical thinking skills has gained popularity in recent years, more disciplines are including it in their curricula. However, as long as the instructional approach consists of primarily teacher lectures and teacher-led discussions, supported by a class textbook, students will have little opportunity to challenge information given to them and/or become responsible for seeking and presenting points of view other than the teacher's or textbook's. Even if students are encouraged to challenge information-giving "authorities" during the units involving critical thinking, once the unit is completed, students are usually expected to return to their customary practice of accepting what they see, hear, and read in class as the truth.

If we really want children to become intelligent, independent thinkers we must encourage them to do so consistently, not just when we tell them to. Of course, this does not mean that students have permission to be rude or disrespectful. In an earnest effort to learn, the process of challenging information involves questioning and analyzing it, seeking further information, and proposing alternatives. But this should not be interpreted as disrespect for the information or authority being challenged. In a true learning environment, information from many sources is freely questioned and analyzed in an effort to develop greater understanding of important issues. In the process, learners also begin to realize the complexity of "truth." Critical thinking skills and the ability to understand complicated issues may not have been essential for citizens of the 19th and early 20th centuries, when so many people worked in factories and other labor jobs (including the military) that called for unquestioned obedience to authority in a strict hierarchical system. But today, most young people can look forward to jobs that call upon them to work in teams, solve problems, and think critically to make important decisions. Further, many of their jobs will change such that they'll need to learn new skills or be re-educated for new jobs. For all of these reasons, today's children need to become intelligent, critical, and independent thinkers.

The Added Value of Using Technology for Critical Thinking

Some of our modern technologies, such as the television, video, and musical recordings have heightened the need to teach children critical thinking skills. In addition to periodicals, these media seem to be the most popular and effective vehicles for spreading opinions and influencing people's thoughts and feelings. On the other hand, these media can also be extremely effective tools for teaching students to think critically. In addition, computer-based tools, such as online information resources and interactive video, are effective in helping critical thinkers seek information with alternative points of view. Let's briefly look at how each of these media can be used to teach critical thinking skills.

Television

Rather than serving as a tool to foster critical thinking, this technological invention has greatly intensified the need to help viewers become critical thinkers. Of course, it is not the technology that creates superficial and often narrow-minded programming and advertising as well as political and cultural propaganda. It is the producers who are well aware of the public's inability to think critically, or their tolerance of such practices (or perhaps people believe they can do little to change it).

As an instructional tool for teaching critical thinking, television can be used as a primary source of information to be challenged. Students can view programs and analyze the spoken language, ideas, body language, sound effects, context, and other elements in pursuit of the show's bias, followed by exploration of other points of view. Students can survey a range of shows in an effort to identify those that present multiple perspectives and do not attempt to oversimplify complex issues.

Video

Videocassette recorders (VCRs) have rapidly become more popular for school use than televisions. Virtually all U.S. schools now have VCRs. This is because VCRs enable teachers (and students) to record selected television shows for viewing in the classroom, and teachers can select from a rapidly growing collection of educational videos that support particular topics they are covering.

One of the most valuable features of video technology is that it enables students to create videos with a video camera. Using this tool, students can produce and review their own news broadcasts, documentaries, dramas, and so forth. It is with this tool that they can apply critical thinking skills in an effort to produce shows that offer more than one perspective and seek deeper understanding of complex issues. In addition, teachers can use a video camera to record students' presentations and then guide them through a critical thinking session in which they analyze which aspects of the presentation are successful and which can use some improvement.

Interactive video

Interactive video takes video capabilities one giant step further. When analyzing visual material (e.g., news clips and documentaries) that is stored on videodisc, students can search for specific information and access it instantly, just as they can search a text database. For example, if they are analyzing a news clip that was broadcast on television during the Vietnam War, they might search for and collect all the frames that show happy soldier faces and all those that reveal pain. The comparison might yield some insights about the network's view of the war.

Students can also use the capabilities of interactive video to present the results of their analysis to others. The technology enables them to store and organize audio, visual, and textual information into a multimedia presentation. For example, the presentation could display text that explains the analysis as well as film clips that appear on the screen to support the points made. Further research might include analysis of additional news broadcasts over time in an effort to verify hunches and determine if the network's point of view changed over time.

Electronic information resources

Online information resources such as news retrieval services, bibliographical databases, encyclopedias, and other such electronic resources assist critical thinkers in their quest for alternative perspectives and in-depth understanding. News retrieval services, for instance, can help young analysts search hundreds of national and international periodicals by topic, date, event, or any keyword they choose. In some cases, they can retrieve full text articles, synopses, or at least bibliographical information for accessing the articles in a library. Electronic encyclopedias, almanacs, and a host of more specialized resources are also available via telecommunications, videodisc, or CD-ROM.

CLASSROOM SCENARIOS AND OTHER SUGGESTIONS FOR IMPLEMENTATION

Emotive Language

A careful examination of emotion-filled language helps students learn to recognize biased, emotional words and phrases that are commonly used in written and spoken language, and to understand how they distort the truth. The following is an example lesson on the topic that could be used with elementary or secondary students.

Before class, the teacher locates a couple of periodical articles that contain numerous slanted words that attempt to appeal to the readers' emotions and prejudices. Advertisements, reviews, and letters to the editor are good sources for this kind of language. Duplicate at least one for the class discussion and save another on a disk for a classroom writing activity.

In class, the teacher draws a picture of a fat woman on the chalkboard—a rough sketch will suffice. Then she asks the class for words to describe the shape of this lady—a neighbor who always complains about the loud music coming from your upstairs window or the bike you sometimes leave on the sidewalk in front of her house. Examples might include: obese, fat, gross, immense, flabby, dense, two-ton, gluttonous, pig, tub, hippo, and so on.

Next, the teacher tells them that this lady is your most beloved aunt, who always defends you in the face of parental criticism, takes you to lunch, and buys you expensive birthday presents. Examples might include: plump, full-figured, robust, round, heavy-set, big boned, solid, large-framed, muscular, portly, ample-bodied, and so on.

The teacher then draws three columns on the board and labels them Positive, Neutral, and Negative; and discusses *denotation* (the literal, explicit meaning of a word, the dictionary definition) and *connotation* (the feelings and attitudes associated with the word). She scatters a few words or phrases under the appropriate headings on the board, and asks the class to fill in the rest of the columns for each word. Here is an example of what could result:

Neutral
difficult to move
Positive
firm, solid, stable, secure, rooted, loyal, settled, established
Negative
rigid, stubborn, stiff, unpliant, inflexible, stern, unyielding

Neutral
reluctant to spend money
Positive
thrifty, economical, careful, frugal, sparing
Negative
tightwad, stingy, skinflint, cheap, close-fisted, miserly

Neutral
house, abode, residence, dwelling
Positive
home, cottage, nest, chalet, castle, hideaway, mansion
Negative
shack, dump, hut, hole, hovel, pigpen, white elephant

To make the point clear and for an entertaining aside, the teacher reads to the class the following example of emotive language. The speaker is a politician delivering a speech. [from "The Prohibitions' Last Stand" by Kenneth Vinson, in *The New Republic*, October 16, 1965.]

> *If when you say whiskey you mean the devil's brew, the poison scourge, the bloody monster, that defiles innocence, dethrones reason, destroys the home, creates misery and poverty, yea, literally takes the bread from the mouths of little children; if you mean the evil drink that topples the Christian man and woman from the pinnacle of righteous, gracious living into the bottomless pit of degradation and despair, and shame, and helplessness, and hopelessness, then certainly I am against it.*
>
> *But, if when you say whiskey you mean the oil of conversation, the philosophic wine, the ale that puts a song in their hearts and laughter on their lips, and the warm glow of contentment in their eyes; if you mean Christmas cheer; if you mean the stimulating drink that puts the spring into the old gentleman's step on a frosty crispy morning; if you mean the drink which enables a man to magnify his joy, and his happiness, and to forget, if only for a little while, life's great tragedies, and heartaches, and sorrows; if you mean that drink, the sale of which pours into our treasuries untold millions of dollars, which are used to provide tender care for our little crippled children, our blind, our deaf, our dumb, our pitiful aged and infirm; to build highways and hospitals and schools, then certainly I am for it.*
>
> *This is my stand, I will not retreat from it. I will not compromise.*

The teacher then passes out one of the duplicated articles that contains emotive language and reads it to the class. Students are asked to underline all the loaded words they can find.

What effect does using this biased, emotional language have on the reader? The class discusses this question, and the need to be clear, honest, and logical when trying to persuade an audience to accept your way of thinking. Some persuasive writing deviates from the truth in order to appeal to the prejudices and/or special interests of an audience (most political speeches), but writers and speakers who use too much slanted language eventually lose credibility with their audience. Many respected writers and speakers do use an emotional appeal successfully to persuade others, but they use it moderately, and not without objective facts to back up their feelings. Logical arguments and factual evidence are the most effective techniques of argument.

As a classroom writing activity, students meet in small groups to work on a biased article that has already been entered on a word processor and saved on a disk. Groups read the article on the screen and revise it, conveying the opposite bias (or, write it with neutral words that contain no bias). They save the rewrites using a different file name, leaving both versions on the disk.

An alternative classroom writing activity would be to divide the class into groups of four. One student pair in each group collaboratively composes a letter or speech on the word processor that advocates something they feel strongly about. The second pair composes a letter or speech that severely criticizes the same thing. They then save these entries on the disk. The following day, the group members trade disks and rewrite the pieces with the opposite bias, saving their rewrite under a separate file name, leaving all versions on the disk.

The teacher picks a few to read aloud and then discusses how the arguments would be stronger if the writers used logical and factual information to support their positions, instead of an emotional appeal. If students did slip into some sound logical arguments, the teacher points them out, and uses them as leads into the next writing activity.

Groups of four students compose a speech or letter on the same general topic as before, but this time they all take the same position and support it with logical arguments and examples rather than emotional language. They print out the final versions, and the teacher reads them that evening to check whether students have, in fact, learned to make the distinction between emotional appeal and logical persuasion.

As a final assignment, students find an article that uses a considerable amount of slanted language to persuade. They underline the biased words and phrases, and rewrite the article, changing the words to convey the opposite bias (as in the whiskey speech). Finally, they attach the original article to the rewrite and hand in both articles. The teacher reads them and selects the most effective combinations to read to the class.

Responsible Persuasive Writing and Critical Analysis of Persuasive Arguments

Persuasive writing may well be the writing style that readers are exposed to more than any other. It is used in advertising, campaigning, marketing, and public relations, as well as for presenting proposals, defending positions, and advocating causes. Being able to persuade an audience to adopt a particular opinion, idea, point of view, or proposal is a powerful skill and an important goal, but difficult to accomplish responsibly. The following activities can help secondary school students learn to compose persuasive essays that use logical arguments, and will also help students learn to critically analyze others' persuasive arguments.

Before class, the teacher locates one or two persuasive essays that use logical arguments, supported by factual information and examples, in order to persuade an audience to adopt the writer's point of view on the subject. "A Modest Proposal" by Jonathan Swift, is a dramatic example of a persuasive essay that uses logical arguments, while omitting the obvious emotional underpinnings that would naturally prohibit the proposal's acceptance. A political speech is another possible choice for an example, an editorial from a newspaper or an opinion piece from a national magazine would also serve. The selected essay should be duplicated and passed out to students to begin the activity.

In class, the teacher passes out and reads the example essay aloud. He asks the class to identify the writer's thesis statement or paraphrase the position being advocated. Then he asks them to identify the specific arguments presented in the essay. How effective are the arguments? What arguments could be made against the proposed system? Does the writer anticipate those arguments and present counter arguments? Does the writer use emotive language and if so, does it weaken or strengthen the argument? Even if blatant emotive language is not used, does the writer appeal to the audience's emotions or attitudes in some way and if so, how does it contribute to the argument?

The class then brainstorms possible topics for a persuasive paper. Examples might include:

- Working while attending school
- The credit card system of buying
- The value of a liberal arts education
- Treatment of the elderly
- What to do about alcoholism
- Police protection
- Why the United States hasn't yet had a woman president
- Cheating in the classroom
- Ethics in U.S. business
- Pre-marriage contracts

The class picks a topic for this exercise and then discusses how a writer would go about gathering information pertaining to the subject.

The teacher explains that to be convincing, a writer should present a logical argument which includes a coherent collection of facts and examples that are arranged to lead to a particular conclusion. There are two methods of argumentation that are commonly used in persuasive writing—inductive arguments and deductive arguments. Inductive arguments begin with a series of statements that include factual information and/or examples that lead up to and conclude with the writer's position on the topic. Deductive arguments begin with a statement that expresses the writer's position, followed by supportive, factual information and examples. This deductive form of argumentation is the one most student writers tend to use in persuasive essays.

The example essay the teacher passed out earlier used the [deductive/inductive] approach. The class discusses which approach would be most appropriate for the topic chosen for this exercise, and how writers would go about organizing notes taken on the topic.

The teacher explains that although a persuasive paper should be soundly based upon logical arguments and factual supportive information, a writer must also consider the emotional impact of the presentation on the audience. Even though writers are advised not to rely on emotive, slanted writing that appeals to the emotional attitudes of an audience, an occasional emotional plea can be effective. (Readers, beware of these tactics!) An ethical writer will refrain from reinforcing people's prejudices or other immoral or unworthy attitudes.

When the planning exercise is finished, the teacher lists the preparation steps on the board, as a reminder for them as they complete their assignments.

Steps to follow when planning and writing a persuasive essay:

1. Choose a controversial topic that you feel strongly about and know something about.
2. Brainstorm ideas and gather facts, examples, and other information pertaining to the topic.
3. Plan the method of argument (e.g., an inductive or deductive approach).
4. Organize notes into a rough outline by grouping them in categories and arranging them in the order of presentation.
5. Compose the first draft.

Students choose their own topic for a persuasive paper and begin doing the research for it right away. This assignment may be expanded so that it invites groups of students to do research and prepare major proposals involving larger-scale topics, such as designing an improved city government, school system, or health care system. Groups could then present their proposals to the class as panel presentations. Alternatively, students could organize debates on various topics that would involve teams in preparing arguments that defend opposite sides of the issue (e.g., which is a more affective approach to accomplishing reform: civil disobedience or violence?). Groups who present in this manner still need to produce a written paper that articulates and defends the arguments.

After first drafts are entered on a word processor, they are critiqued by members of a peer editing group. The topics chosen for this assignment are typically interesting and provocative, and therefore students usually do an effective job of identifying the strong and weak arguments in classmate's papers. Final drafts are passed in (or presented), shared among classmates, and assessed by the students and teacher.

This writing-based approach to teaching persuasive writing and critical thinking provides a foundation from which teachers and students can move on to extended activities involving critical examination of televised persuasive speeches, advertisements, and so forth, followed by persuasive multimedia presentations that are designed and produced by students.

Teaching Film Techniques and Critical Thinking Through Television

According to Professor Patricia Greenfield (1984) , children tend to approach television as an "easy" medium, expend little mental effort on watching it, and therefore learn rather superficially from it. In contrast, they view print as more difficult, invest more mental effort, and learn more deeply from it. However, if children are told to look carefully and try to learn from television, the depth of learning becomes greater. Television viewing comes to resemble reading in this respect. If television were part of school assignments, teachers would very naturally give just this type of instructional message.

In our exemplary elementary classroom, television is treated as a serious object of study. As a class in English literature might talk about the techniques and style of Shakespeare and Dickens, these children talk about the techniques and style of television programs.

The curriculum is divided into different areas of television techniques, such as light and shadow, color, forms, motion, and time/space. For example, in the area of motion, children learn to distinguish camera movement from person movement and to find times when both camera and person move together. In the area of time/space, they discuss the differences among objective time (clock time of the program), the illusion of time created by editing, and subjective time (whether time moves quickly or slowly for the viewer.) Whereas the techniques of print literature, based on verbal forms, are difficult for younger children to perceive and analyze, the forms of television make use of children's well-developed visual abilities—abilities which television both exploits and fosters.

Greenfield reported that this curriculum was tested for a school year with eight- and nine-year-old children. These children were compared at the end of the year with another class taught by the same teacher without the television curriculum. In writing about a short television sequence, the children who had studied the forms and aesthetics of television commented on formal features such as color and composition. Children in the other group wrote only about story line. The year of studying television also caused a shift in the children's television-viewing tastes, action and formula programs dropped from their lists of favorite shows and were replaced by more challenging programs. No such change took place in the other class.

These results show that elementary school children can analyze the forms of television, much as we might expect older children to analyze the forms of literature. In so doing, children take a more active approach to the medium, becoming aware not only of content but of how television's forms and techniques create that content. In short, they become aware of the message of their medium.

Equally important, treating television as a serious object of study makes children expend more effort in viewing television, so that they choose more challenging programs. Greenfield speculated that if this type of television course could be widely taught in schools, the level of popular taste might increase greatly and there might therefore be a public demand for higher-quality programming. This could have a tremendous impact on television in the United States, where audience ratings determine a program's fate on the commercial networks.

Note that this type of course does not depend upon the overall quality of program content that is available. It depends only on having a range of techniques on the air. Thus, it is a positive approach to television, and one that can make use of formula comedies, commercials, and action shows, as well as of more educational programming.

Another, more direct approach to teaching about television in school focuses specifically on teaching children critical reviewing skills. Greenfield explained that this approach is designed to counteract the negative effects of U.S. commercial television, and consequently, camera techniques tend to be treated as devices for deception rather than for art. In fact, the techniques have both sides to them depending on how they are used by the filmmaker. Both approaches to the study of television have distinctive contributions to make, and an effective teacher can integrate a critical reviewing approach with the more artistic, analytical approach that focuses on techniques.

Current Events as an Approach to Teaching Critical Thinking

With television bringing global events into our living rooms—in some cases, as they happen—it's a pity that more teachers don't take advantage of these history-in-the-making opportunities to teach social studies, geography, communication, history, sometimes math and/or science, and just about every other discipline including critical thinking.

The Persian Gulf War in 1991, provided just such an opportunity, and in this extraordinary case many teachers did take advantage of it. Some teachers have dubbed the process a "living curriculum" because there are no established objectives or lesson plans to follow; teachers have to develop them as they go along. Certainly, it's the current technologies—television, VCR, telecommunications, CD-ROM, online news services—that make these kinds of news-breaking studies possible.

A wise teacher can build a living curriculum by using students' natural interest in certain current events, and connect these studies to the subject area's curriculum objectives, thus adding breadth and depth to students' understanding.

For example, high school English and history teachers in one school teamed up to study the Persian Gulf War by creating and producing two videotaped programs that were broadcast to students and faculty in the school. To complete the project (which evolved and expanded as the war progressed), students collected newspaper clippings and taped evening news coverage as homework. Then, in class, they critically reviewed the articles and video footage in an effort to select clips that were most "objective," meaning they excluded emotional interviews and/or views of dead bodies or other scenes that influence viewers' opinions by making them angry or sympathetic with one side, without providing balanced coverage or enough factual information.

Through various personal connections, they were able to locate an individual who was extremely familiar with Iraqi culture and style of government, and another who thoroughly understood Israeli culture and government. Two volunteer students then interviewed these individuals (interview questions were developed by the class). One interview was done over the phone (the Iraqi expert was currently living in the United States) with an audiotape recorder hooked up to tape the interview. The other interview was done via telecommunications, as the Israeli expert lived in Israel. Information from these interviews were added to the students' growing collection of information.

The school's CD-ROM encyclopedia enabled them to get further information on the history, culture, and politics of the Middle East; the online news service provided news stories from foreign newspapers; and teachers and parents provided additional books and other resources with more information than the students could possibly read, critically review, and synthesize. So they divided the resources among students and skimmed most of it to sort out what would be useful to read carefully and what was either too biased, duplicated other sources, or was otherwise unsuitable.

Assembled as a whole class, they discussed how to organize their presentations. They decided to produce a video of news clips collected from several networks. It would be a collage of clips that presented several points of view, including the Iraqi's (using excerpts of the taped interview as a sound track), the Israeli's (information from the interview spoken by a narrator), the American (interview with a social studies teacher), and so forth. The video would be narrated by one of the students, enabling them to include additional information gathered from other sources. One student group took on the task of storyboarding the videotape and bringing a draft for the class to review.

Simultaneously, another group decided to organize a panel discussion that would include two student experts (one representing the Iraqi side, and another representing the Allies), two teacher experts (the social studies teacher and another teacher who had lived for a while in Saudi Arabia), a local TV news anchor, and a state senator. The group then took on the task of planning what questions the moderator should ask, including questions such as: What were the "real" causes that led to the outbreak of war? Could the conflict have been solved without going to war? Is it appropriate to publish detailed battle plans that include aircraft launch sites and potential targets? How will the results of the war (the Allies won) affect the United States, Iraq, Israel, Kuwait, and others?

While these groups planned the video and panel discussion, the rest of the class acted as research staff, continuing to read and critically examine the information collected so far, marking essential pieces of information and delivering them to the video or panel group for later use.

When the video group finished drafting their storyboard, the whole class reviewed and revised it until it was ready for production. A technical staff was formed of those students most proficient at using the video editing equipment and those who wanted to learn. Others in the group continued to work on the project during production, helping to locate video clips and making last minute revisions if better clips were discovered. One student drafted the narrator's script and others reviewed and helped revise it. When the whole video was finished, the class critiqued it, sent it back for a few minor revisions, reviewed it again, and then approved it.

When the panel group finished its work, they presented their proposed format and questions to the others, who suggested a few changes before sending the questions, rules, and format to the invited participants. The panel discussion was presented live to the school, and was also taped for a post-panel critical analysis.

Both projects were so successful that the local cable network offered to broadcast the tapes for the entire community to see.

Study of 19th Century America

For this interdisciplinary semester of study, secondary level English, social studies, science, math, art, and music teachers teamed up to explore the 19th century.

Social studies objectives were met by critically analyzing the economic, social, and political conditions leading up to the Civil War, the war itself, and the long period of adjustment following the war; multicultural, regional, and political perspectives of the century; westward expansion, the beginning of the Industrial Revolution, the impact and issues related to immigration, and so forth. (One primary source was Howard Zinn's *A People's History of the United States,* with its non-traditional, multiple perspectives and inclusion of many original sources.)

English objectives were met by a variety of reading, writing, and oral activities. Students read and critically analyzed literature of the 19th century including selections by Cooper, Poe, Twain, Stowe, Douglass, Stone, Garrison, and Fuller. They wrote critical essays related to the literature, and political issues of the period, as well as to the diverse cultural, regional, and political perspectives of the times. They debated critical issues, and prepared multimedia and other kinds of presentations related to the century under study.

Science objectives were met by exploring the scientific discoveries and inventions of the 19th century and examining their impact on future science discoveries and inventions (e.g., the cotton gin, steam engine, typewriter, sewing machine, electric light, telegraph system, photography) as well as their impact on cultural, political, and other conditions that followed.

Mathematics objectives were met by teaching grade level mathematical concepts and applying them to problems of the 19th century. For example, students developed formulas and graphs to record and predict population changes through the century, including native Americans, American-born whites, white immigrants, American-born blacks, blacks who were transported here, and so on. They studied economic conditions in the North (industrial) and South (agricultural) before the Civil War, and developed what they thought were fair export/import trade agreements and pricing for internally produced goods. They explored cost-of-living issues including wages, rent, food costs, and developed family budgets and a post-Civil War tax system they thought was fair for everyone—factory owners and their workers, plantation owners, merchants, and others.

Art objectives were met through examining and critically evaluating art produced in the 19th century, including Matthew Brady's photographs of the Civil War, Whistler's portraits, and Remington's scenes of life in the west. They examined how 19th century artists reflected their times and they, in turn, attempted to reflect the 1990s through their own artwork.

Music objectives were met by studying/playing/singing music of the 20th century, such as "Dixie," "Oh Canaan, Sweet Canaan, I am Bound for the Land of Canaan," "Many Thousand Go," "Oh! Susanna," and "Camptown Races," and attempting to compose music in a style of that period.

The individual subject objectives were definitely present, but they were thrown into a common curriculum pot and blended together to produce an integrated course of study that was uninterrupted by 45-minute period bells. All subject teachers were available to students during the school day and all teachers worked toward helping their own discipline's objectives blend in with the others. Indeed, they spent a month during the summer designing the integrated curriculum, and since some of them had already been using computers and multimedia production in their courses, the curriculum planning was infused with production ideas that quite naturally integrated subject areas.

For example, one of the major curriculum projects involved students in designing and producing multimedia presentations that critically examined social, economic, and political causes of the Civil War, including influences from literature such as *Uncle Tom's Cabin, Time on the Cross, Narrative of the Life of Frederick Douglass* and *The Bonds of Womanhood;* original newspapers such as *The Liberator* and *North Star;* propaganda leaflets such as *Walker's Appeal;* and speeches by notables such as Abraham Lincoln and Shawnee Indian Chief Tecumseh. Students' multimedia presentations also included information about scientific inventions (e.g. cotton gin, steam engine), art (political cartoons, paintings, photographs), and music (e.g., Negro spirituals and songs of Stephen Foster). Although the presentations couldn't include original film footage because that medium hadn't yet been invented, students could choose to do video interviews of 19th century experts and include those.

The students' school day typically included times when they concentrated on science while learning about a new invention or attempting to redesign or perfect something invented back then, for instance. They might need basic math lessons on how to calculate and graph population trends, or how to develop a formula for equitable post-Civil War factory wages, for example. In any case, the period-free schedule was so flexible that teachers could call students together for lessons whenever needed. Basically, however, the flexible school day enabled students to spend large amounts of time doing research, meeting in groups, designing and producing documents and presentations, or leaving the school to do interviews, seek information from a museum, or whatever.

Later in the semester, students began preparing for their final examination, which included a research paper (or multimedia document) on a selected topic, followed by an oral defense of the research; a creative writing piece, work of art, or musical composition; and finally, a written essay examination.

Critical Thinking and the Use of Statistics

During a summer school session that included junior high students and some teachers in training, a professor of education taught participants how to think critically about statistical data through the use of database and spreadsheet applications. In the unit, the professor demonstrated that the selection and interpretation of data is subjective, and how individuals can—and do—manipulate it to suit their needs. His goal was to help students to become more critical consumers of information.

First, he passed out a list of 12 cities in the United States and asked the students to rank them in order of preference. (Students were asked to imagine that a parent has been offered employment in all 12 cities and that they were to have a part in choosing where the family will live.) After identifying Honolulu, Miami, and San Diego as the top three choices, the class discussed why they ranked cities high or low. It turned out that they rated recreational facilities and climate as most important overall.

Next, they took a look at the Rand McNally ranking of U.S. cities, published in *Places Rated Almanac: Your Guide to Finding the Best Places to Live in America*. Students discovered that their favorites ranked rather low and that Pittsburgh, Pennsylvania, which was number one on the Rand McNally list, ranked very low on the class list. Then the students began analyzing why the ratings were so different. It became obvious that both were subjective, and that the students and the people at Rand

McNally believed that very different things were important in choosing a place to live.

At that point, the professor showed them how ratings can be altered by changing the assumptions about what's important and thereby re-weighting the data. Student groups then created spreadsheets of the cities to practice manipulating data.

The next activity was a simulation game. Students formed teams, and each team picked a city out of a hat. The task for each team was to convince a panel of judges that its city was the ideal location for construction of a huge computer research facility, which would bring great economic growth to the community. Each team was required to collect valid data and to create a spreadsheet that included similar data on all six cities. (Data included average temperature, population, number of movie theaters, and other such categories.) Teams could then develop formulas that involved identifying certain "ideal" characteristics about a city, and then weighting these characteristics more heavily in the spreadsheet. By selectively weighting certain characteristics, students were able to manipulate the data to favor their particular city.

The winning team was Philadelphia, as that team presented the strongest arguments, backed up by valid data. Following the victory, the professor proceeded to demonstrate how Philadelphia could easily be dropped to the bottom of the ranking, simply by changing the basic assumptions. For example, if you assume that small is better, Philadelphia is not so great.

The point here, the professor explained, is not that weighting data is bad; we all do it often. (Look at our grading systems, for example; we weight certain tests and assignments more than others, and that dramatically affects students' grades.) The point is that it's important to look critically at the data—to understand where it comes from and how it is being used.

Critical Analysis of Visual Perspectives

In some cases, multimedia technologies have made it possible to teach concepts that have previously been extremely difficult to teach, sometimes because our eyes deceive us when we observe objects from a single, visual perspective.

For example, a physics activity that is included in an experimentally developed videodisc pictures children spinning on a playground merry-go-round. A ball is rolled across the merry-go-round while it spins. Viewed from the perspective of someone on the merry-go-round, the ball moves in a pronounced arc as it travels across the moving surface.

When viewed from above, however, it travels in a straight line. Observers on the ground would swear the ball curved while rolling, until they saw the same sequence from above. The physics concept of relative motion is further demonstrated by a computerized component that allows students to plot the ball's path on a computer screen, while watching it move across the merry-go-round on the video screen.

There are numerous other examples of critical observation and thinking that are made possible (or certainly easier to understand) by video technology. One can now watch a video of a horse (or other animal) running, and then slow down the process to a frame-by-frame analysis of movement in an effort to learn how the legs move—which are on the ground when, and so forth. One can videotape magic tricks being performed and then slow the video to a frame-by-frame analysis in hopes of discovering the "trick" maneuver that the eye can't see at regular speed. One can observe in very slow motion, how a curve ball moves to fool a batter, how flowers blossom, a butterfly emerges from a cocoon, a calf is born, and so forth. These experiences may not all involve direct critical thinking, but they do help the learner begin to understand that what they "think they see" may not be the full truth, and that critical observation, just like critical thinking, involves a careful analysis of all the components before the full truth is known.

REFERENCES

Vinson, K. (1965). "The Prohibitions' Last Stand." The *New Republic,* October 16.

Greenfield, Patricia M. (1984). *Mind and Media: The Effects of Television, Video Games, and Computers.* Cambridge: Harvard University Press.

9

BASIC SKILLS

RATIONALE

The need for students to learn fundamental language and computational skills (as well as basic skills within any subject area) is heartily supported by the pedagogical tenets of this book. The issue that distinguishes the pedagogical approach in this book from more conventional approaches is not whether to teach basic skills to students; it is *how* to teach these skills. Reflecting on our fundamental understanding that learning is an active process that involves students in assessing new information and integrating it into their evolving knowledge base, it is critical that new concepts and skills be taught and learned within the context of larger learning experiences that are meaningful to students.

For example, attempting to learn basic skills—such as punctuation and capitalization—by simply memorizing rules and completing worksheets offers students little opportunity to relate these skills to their existing knowledge and experience with written communication. However, if the same skills are taught and practiced in the context of larger writing projects, such as a class publication (for which the editorial standard is high and a critical audience of peers and adults will review their work), the acquisition of these basic skills becomes a relevant and important task for the students. In this context, the skills are more likely to be incorporated into the students' knowledge base and applied when doing other written work.

Basic Skills

Basic skills are defined in this book as the fundamental construction tools of a discipline. Students handle these tools and learn how to use them more expertly as they build academic experiences that grow more complex as their skills develop. In writing, the construction skills include spelling, punctuation, sentence structure, paragraph development, and so forth; reading skills include pronunciation, work recognition, and intonation; mathematics skills include addition, subtraction, multiplication, and division. And every other domain from music and art to baseball and farming comes with a toolkit of essential construction tools.

We need to teach basic construction skills to our students, but let us teach them in context—in situations where children will understand the underlying linguistic/mathematical concepts and their relevance to life. A carpenter asks an apprentice to hammer a nail or saw a board with a project in mind; a basketball coach asks players to practice dribble and shoot drills, to prepare for a scrimmage or game (unfortunately, some coaches do drill their players to boredom and lose potentially good players that way).

Actually, some children do enjoy practicing certain basic skills out of context. They like practicing the skills they happen to be good at (some look forward to that spelling test at the end of the week because they usually get 100 percent), or if they are intrinsically interested in the skill itself (some children think adding up long lists of numbers is fun, and computer games have made practicing certain skills fun). But few children enjoy practicing all the basic skills they need to learn. Further, there are untold numbers of children who do extremely well in those spelling tests, but when it is time to write an essay, they misspell many words, even those they got right in the spelling tests. And there are young computational wizards who cannot begin to solve a word problem.

We need a balance. A balance between teaching kids to use fundamental tools and letting them use these tools to create meaningful products.

The Importance of Teaching Basic Skills while Involving Children in Doing Real Work that Requires Those Skills

Few adults would dispute the need to learn fundamental language and mathematical skills. In fact, those adults who lack competence in these skills are often the most avid supporters of teaching them in school.

Our argument lies in a slightly different area, prompting a shift in the heading of this section from "The importance of teaching basic skills" to "The importance of teaching basic skills while involving children in doing real work that requires those skills." We do *not* advocate teaching basic skills *first,* before letting the child write an essay or solve a word problem. Instead, we advocate giving the child an essay to write *first,* and then raising the issue of punctuation or sentence structure to help the child make the essay better, in fact, good enough so that other children and adults will enjoy reading it. This does not mean no worksheets whatsoever, but it does mean setting the context and making the need for learning and practicing the skills clear to the child. First, you motivate the students by giving them real projects that are meaningful to them; then, as they discover the need for basic skills to complete their projects successfully, you help them acquire the basic skills they need.

The Added Value of Using Technology to Teach Basic Skills

There are a number of computer-based products available that will help children practice and improve basic language and math skills. The most prominent and popular are the game-format programs that typically place the learner in an environment where practice exercises are presented and the child produces correct answers as rapidly as possible, before being eaten by a monster or otherwise losing to the computer.

Some products offer tutorials that attempt to both teach the learner basic skills and to provide practice sessions. Keyboarding tutorial software is a good example of this approach. A number of multimedia products have also become available that appeal to learners who learn better with ample visual and audio support. Some products that were designed as professional tools, such as spelling and grammar checkers, are now being used to help children identify problems in those areas so they can correct their mistakes. And some schools use a much more comprehensive approach by purchasing Integrated Learning Systems (ILS) for their computer labs. An ILS covers basic skills systematically in an effort to make sure all students are taught all skills and that each student's progress is accurately monitored.

Any of these technology tools can be an asset in helping children learn fundamental skills, if they are used appropriately. The benefits are that game programs can make practice fun, tutorials can provide an alternative way of learning new skills, multimedia approaches can engage more of the senses, and skill checkers can help students become more effective reviewers. The drawbacks are that these same products can be used to isolate basic skills as a separate subject and cause the learner to learn them out of context, and thus be less skilled at applying them successfully in the context of real work. Another hazard is that teachers sometimes assume that these aids can remove the burden of teaching basic skills from their shoulders and this increases the risk of isolating them from the context of what they consider more meaningful classroom work.

The section below presents examples of how these and other approaches to teaching basic skills are successfully applied in the classroom.

CLASSROOM SCENARIOS AND OTHER SUGGESTIONS FOR IMPLEMENTATION

Examples in this section focus on fundamental language and computational skills. Other basic skills—from playing musical scales to keyboarding—can be taught using the same approaches outlined in the examples below, and there are software programs available that can help teach those basic skills as well.

Reading

Not all children have parents available to sit on the couch with them and help as they struggle with words, sentences, and finally paragraphs. In overflowing classrooms, teachers also don't have time to provide the individual attention most children need when they begin reading. So many young learners who could be good readers get off to a slow start.

New technology advances in speech synthesis, however, are now making it possible for children to learn to read with the aid of a computer (a poor substitute for help that comes with a hug and words of encouragement, but certainly far better than no help). Some teachers use the computer technology as supplemental support for young readers who benefit from additional practice. For illiterate adults, it is a blessing to be able to learn to read privately, without having to experience the embarrassment of their situation in front of others.

Our exemplary teacher uses a CD-ROM series of children's literature complete with sound, pictures, and text. This teacher does not use textbooks or phonics workbooks to teach first graders to read; his whole reading curriculum is based on involving kids in reading classic children's stories. Stories in this series include *Cinderella, The Tale of Peter Rabbit, Thomas' Snowsuit,* and others. The technology can display the story text with illustrations and read it aloud at various speeds. At the simplest level, the technology enables the reader to see a word, hear it pronounced, and then see an illustration of what the word names.

The teacher introduces a story by bringing a beautifully illustrated hardcover edition to class, and reading it while everyone sits in a circle around him. He gives dramatic voices to each character and physically transforms the story into theater for them. Copies of the book remain in the classroom for children to take whenever they want to curl up in a corner to read.

Next, the teacher introduces the technology version of the story by first showing them how it works, and then explaining what he wants them to do with it. In this case, he asks them to go through the story as often as they need to until they can read it aloud without help from the computer voice. With several networked computers available, readers can work independently, which he says is a tremendous benefit, because they are already at very different reading levels.

Most children will have the computer read the whole story through first, while they enjoy the illustrations and the computer's voice. Then, they will attempt to read it by themselves, get stuck (some on the third word, others on the third page), and ask the computer to read that word or words for them. Some children only need to read the story through a couple of times before they can read it to the teacher without help. Some will work through it many times. These are the children the teacher spends much of his time with, both standing by the computer and sitting down with the actual book. The rapidly advancing students get chances to read with the teacher too, and while they read, he quickly assesses their proficiency and guides them on to more advanced stories.

Integrated Reading and Writing

Some technologies enable a teacher to integrate reading and writing activities so that students learn both skills simultaneously; the teacher does this by having students write and then read their own and their classmates' writings.

In one classroom, for example, the teacher uses a "talking word processor" to teach basic reading and writing skills. At the very elementary level, children type simple words and ask the computer to read them back. For instance, say two students want to write the word *boat.* If they don't know how to spell it, they might type it incorrectly as *b-o-t.* But when they hear the computer read it back, they will know it's not right because the computer will correctly pronounce *bot* not *boat.* When they finally do type *b-o-a-t,* they will know it is right because the computer will correctly pronounce the word *boat.* If they write a sentence that is actually a fragment, such as *Running very fast,* it won't sound right when the computer reads it back. A complete sentence, *The dragon was running very fast,* will sound correct when read aloud.

The teacher has students work in pairs for these beginning activities so that they have one another to help problem-solve when they confront problems such as the *bot* example. She actively monitors the pairs at work, checking to make sure one student isn't dominating the activity such that the other is either intimidated or otherwise unable to learn. And she changes student groupings often so that they frequently get a chance to be the "more able" reader or writer. She also coaches them concerning how to work collaboratively in groups so that both members are respected and both are continually learning.

As students progress, they begin to write complete stories. They keyboard their stories, read them, have classmates read them, and ask the computer to read them too. This computer reading also helps them proofread the entire story.

Writing Stories: Basic Plot Structure

Some teachers use a standard, silent word processor to teach students to write. Our exemplary teacher here favors a group writing approach to introduce the basic structure of a story and teach fundamental writing skills in an informal and nonthreatening manner.

In this second/third grade classroom, the teacher prompts and assists in the creation of a coherent and grammatically correct narrative that, when printed out, can serve as a model for students as they write their own stories. In addition, students generally feel more confident in attempting to write a story independently after first participating in the story-making process with their classmates.

The teacher begins with a class discussion about the kinds of things even the simplest story has to include: A beginning (Once upon a time, Mary . . .), a middle (something has to happen involving Mary), and an ending (. . . so, Mary outwitted the fox and got home safely). At least one character has to do something, or something has to happen to the character.

The teacher then asks students to think about what happened this morning while they were eating breakfast, on their way to school, or outside during recess. Any one of these experiences could become a tiny story. The teacher offers an example:

> Sunday morning, when everybody over 10 years old was still asleep, Annabell decided to get her own breakfast. She climbed up on the kitchen counter and reached high for the cereal box. But, as she tried to pull it off the top shelf, out fell bags of pretzels, chocolate chips, and marshmallows, instead.
>
> Now, Annabell, being a very well-behaved girl who naturally didn't want to create a mess in the kitchen by spilling any more food, decided to make do with what she had. Wearing a grin that

made her ears wiggle, Annabell munched a bowl of pretzels with chocolate chips and marshmallows on top.

The teacher suggests that inventing a story, like she just did, might be more interesting than describing what actually did happen that morning, but that some of their real life experiences will make excellent story material.

Next she explains that the class is going to write a group story on the word processor about what happened to them this morning, and that everyone will help. The story will be fiction, she explains, because it will include everybody's suggestions, and they may choose to exaggerate or make up something that happened to them, as long as it is believable.

As the teacher opens up a new file for this story (she's sitting at the keyboard and there is an oversized screen that all students can see), she asks them what name they want to give the major character. She enters: Once upon a time there was a boy named Jonah. Then she prompts, "Okay, Sarah, what shall we say next?" and so the story grows. . . .

The teacher seldom has trouble getting a lot of action in the story. The tricky part is to help the storytellers see that they need to provide descriptive information about the characters, setting, and so forth, and to help them understand the importance of building a climax and creating an appropriate conclusion.

The advantage of using a word processor in this activity is that she can enter and revise the storytellers' contributions quickly and easily. As the story progresses, the class may decide to alter certain facts, incidents, or other elements, and individual students will surely want to change the wording of their segments as they compose them orally. When the first draft is completed, the whole class participates in suggesting further additions and revisions.

When the story is just the way they want it, the teacher prints copies for everyone. This story serves as a model for them when writing their own stories later. (The teacher also duplicates her own example story, if the class story is so long it might intimidate beginning writers.) The children are invited to illustrate these stories.

The next day, two things happen. Some of the students begin drafting their own stories individually or in pairs. Others, who are not ready to write yet, dictate story beginnings to the teacher and work with her until they are ready to continue alone or in a group.

When drafts are done, students read their stories in groups of four or five and try to help one another make corrections—whatever help they can offer, from correcting spelling to smoothing awkward sentences or suggesting a better conclusion. The teacher participates in these primary editing sessions to get a head start on helping them learn to coach one another in a positive and helpful manner. From these editing groups, the teacher develops a list of basic skills problems that showed up in several stories (e.g., capitalization or sentence fragments).

Later, she tells them about her plan to "publish" their personal stories in a class book (they like that idea). Yet, to publish a book that other students and grown-ups will read means that maybe they ought to make their stories perfect, like professional authors (they agree). So, with this hook, she introduces the common problems they have with capitalization, for instance, and explains when it is appropriate to capitalize a word. Then, together and individually they do some practice exercises. Right after that, they read their own stories over and capitalize the words that need to be capitalized. The next day she might introduce another common problem, followed by practice and revisions in their own papers. She helps with the rest of the story editing without formal lessons, realizing that in a full year of writing she can squeeze in a lot of basic skills lessons, while keeping that work interesting and meaningful.

At the conclusion of this activity, students each have their own printed and illustrated story. The teacher duplicates their stories and binds them together into anthologies for everyone in the class.

Writing Essays: Topic Sentences and Coherent Paragraphs

As students begin to compose paragraphs and short essays, one of the common problems that arises in their work is lack of sequence and coherent organization of sentences in their paragraphs. At that point, it is time to teach them about topic sentences and supportive sentences. Our exemplary elementary school teacher uses the following lessons.

First she locates some well-written paragraphs with effective topic sentences and duplicates them for students to use as models. (When possible, she uses student-written paragraphs.) She also duplicates some paragraphs that are poorly organized with weak topic sentences or none at all.

Following is an example of a well-organized paragraph:

> *When Dad went food shopping today he brought home five bunches of asparagus. He didn't buy any other vegetables, so you can imagine what we'll be having for dinner every night until Sunday. I figure we'll have boiled asparagus tonight, creamed asparagus on Wednesday, asparagus soufflé on Thursday, asparagus nut muffins on Friday, and asparagus soup on Saturday. And, if there's any left over, you can guess what's for breakfast on Sunday—asparagus pancakes. Next week I think I'll go along and help Dad with the shopping.*

Next is an example of a poorly organized paragraph:

Dad likes asparagus. He even brought five bunches of it today at the market. Next week I guess I'll go along with him and help him out with the shopping. This week we'll probably have to eat asparagus every night for supper—would you believe boiled asparagus, creamed asparagus, asparagus soup, and asparagus soufflé? We'll probably even get asparagus pancakes on the last day, if we're unlucky. I wish Dad didn't like asparagus so much.

In class, the teacher begins by asking students to define *topic sentence.* She helps them along if necessary, by explaining that its function is to state the main idea of a paragraph, and that it often presents an attitude or opinion about the main idea. She explains that a good topic sentence makes a meaningful generalization that is broad enough to cover all the supportive information presented in the paragraph, and specific enough to be interesting. She then writes a few example topic sentences on the chalkboard or word processor, and asks students to propose some as well.

Next, she hands out the duplicated examples of well-written paragraphs with effective topic sentences and displays them on the large screen. She discusses how the rest of the sentences support the topic sentence with details such as additional facts and/or examples. Then she passes out (and displays) the example paragraphs that are not so well organized, with weak topic sentences, or none at all. She helps the class revise these paragraphs by strengthening the structure; devising an appropriate topic sentence, rearranging the order of sentences, and adding supportive information whenever necessary.

The teacher then writes a few weak topic sentences on the word processor and asks volunteers to help improve them. For example:

Weak	Strong
Dad likes asparagus.	When Dad went shopping today, he brought home five bunches of asparagus.
Sometimes it gets very hot in the summertime.	There's Aunt Betsy over on the porch; today she's just sitting, sweating, and sipping lemonade.
You shouldn't hit people when you're angry; to let off steam you should exercise instead.	Next time you feel like smashing someone in the face, try running a mile instead.

Finally, she asks each student to compose a paragraph on a word processor using one of the revised topic sentences. After students have finished, she has them meet in peer editing groups for help in revising and editing their work.

Writers' Tools

Some teachers invite their students to use additional writer's tools, such as spelling checkers, grammar checkers, prompts, and so on, and some devise their own methods of assisting writers electronically. Spelling and grammar checkers can help students identify mistakes that they didn't realize they had made, and some teachers take advantage of this editing help. For example, a teacher might ask students to use a spelling checker to list the words they misspelled (spelling them correctly) for further practice, or use a grammar checker in a whole-class session to point out common problems for the class to discuss.

Prompts are little cues that are embedded in a word processor to help students organize their writing in particular formats, such as book reports, news stories, narrative essays, and so forth. Teachers can create prompts by writing them in a word processor file and making that file available to students. For example, a prompt file for a book report might begin with requests for specific information such as name, date, or type of book. Other prompts would ask for thematic information including: What major problems do the main characters face in the story? How are the problems solved? Explain why you liked (or didn't like) the story. For students who have particular problems with writer's block, this tool can work miracles. But, don't forget to remove the "training wheels" before the writer becomes too dependent.

Teachers can invent other kinds of electronic helpers as well. One helper might be the addition of a "structure checker" that students use after writing a first draft. Created like a prompt file, it would ask the student questions concerning the organization of their essays, thus prompting them to revise in ways they might not think about otherwise. For instance, such questions might include: What is the most important idea expressed in this essay, and is it expressed clearly? What major points are made, and are they coherent? Are there specific examples and details to support the main points? Is your conclusion strong and conclusive? and so on.

*English as a Second Language (ESL)**

Whether teachers use a primary language approach or an immersion approach to teaching English to non-native speakers, technology can be helpful. For example, in an elementary ESL classroom where the primary

*Many of the instructional approaches and technology aids mentioned in this and other chapters are also effective when used with ESL students. ESL teachers should review all of the chapters in the implementation section of the book and select those they think will most effectively support their particular instructional approaches.

language approach is used, students first learn basic subjects (reading, writing, science, and math) in their primary language. Then they move to a transitional program where they receive instruction entirely in English. In this exemplary class, students use computers with word processing and drawing software to write and illustrate stories. According to their teacher, they often work in pairs so that the more proficient students can help those less skilled. One particular benefit of using a computer to write and illustrate their stories is that the children will experiment with new ideas and techniques much more freely than they will with pencil and paper.

ESL classes that contain students who speak several different native languages most likely use the immersion approach and begin speaking English in the classroom right away. (The teacher might use this approach because she or he believes it's more effective, or because it's not an option to teach such a diverse group of language speakers in their own native languages.) For those who concentrate on teaching English, there is a variety of specialized software available to help.

One multimedia product, for example contains a visual database of more than a thousand photographs, and uses speech, stories, and skill-building software to help beginning students improve their English proficiency. Students identify words and sentences in the context of topics such as the weather, shopping, reading maps, and other real-world activities. They see a photo, hear the word pronounced, and then hear it used in a conversational context. Each word is then followed by a pictorial story that dramatizes the word under study. Students also use the computer's microphone to record their pronunciation of the word and hear it played back. The program's audio capabilities enable students to practice independently by speaking into the microphone and comparing their words and sentences to the models provided in the program. Additional vocabulary games such as word scrambles and spelling games help make practicing more fun. The program's visual capabilities enable a teacher to import additional pictures and create new vocabulary lists. The product also has record-keeping capabilities that permit teachers to track each individual student's progress over time.

Mathematics

Our approach to teaching basic computational skills is essentially the same as in language—give the children context and meaning for what they are learning. Before handing out worksheets with addition and subtraction problems, initiate a class bake sale so that students have to count cookies, add up the money they collect, and subtract sold cookies from the inventory. Let them make change for customers; let them hold the quarters and trade them with classmates for two dimes and a nickel. Then let them eat what's left over. Have them bring in pumpkins and measure them; divide them in half, in quarters, eighths, and so on. Invite children to establish business enterprises for which they must keep careful records of inventory, profits, and expenses, as well as write checks for materials and give credit to customers who forgot to bring their money. When the bookkeeping records do not balance, it's time for some lessons in the appropriate basic skills so the business won't go bankrupt.

Of course, teachers cannot be expected to invent adventures for every math concept they need to teach, but the idea is to attach their lessons and practice sessions to real-life purposes that are more immediate and convincing than saying "you'll need this when you grow up."

There is a lot of technology available to help. Several examples have already been introduced in the problem-solving and inquiry chapters, others are included below.

In our classroom example, a fourth grade teacher integrates language and mathematics learning by having his students run an entire publishing business. He claims that, through this enterprise, students learn a host of basic math skills used in bookkeeping, in addition to the array of language skills they develop by writing for the publication.

The purpose of the company is to publish a newspaper. But to accomplish this the company must employ a variety of "professionals" who write, edit, take photographs, design layout, handle sales, pay employees, balance the books, and perform whatever other jobs must be done. Students develop basic math skills primarily through the business management aspect of the enterprise. The company's business department uses checks (produced by the classroom bank) to purchase paper and other supplies from the school; and to pay employees, taxes, employee benefits, and other expenses. And they keep careful records of these expenditures as well as the money that comes in for the issues sold. They also have to figure out how much the company owes in taxes and how much should be deducted for company employees' social security (all of this based on fourth-grade level tax codes written by the teacher). Balancing the books is a major challenge for them, so he breaks down the process into steps with mini tutorials for each step. Evidently, the students stay motivated throughout the school year and sometimes the company makes a profit.

The only technology tools these students use to perform their business management tasks is a word processor for correspondence and keeping records, and a calculator for performing mathematical functions. He reports that the kids have become whizzes at using a calculator, and he's making progress at trying to design a simple spreadsheet that they can use for bookkeeping.

For teachers who do not want to organize such an elaborate enterprise themselves, there are computer simulations available to do it for you. There are simple ones that enable students to operate a lemonade stand for which they must determine how much to charge for a glass of lemonade, given certain variables such as the weather, expenses, and so forth. If they charge too much, they won't sell much lemonade, nor will they sell much on a cold and rainy day. But, on a hot and sunny day, they can sell many glasses if the price is right and they have enough supplies. More sophisticated simulations can involve students in brokering Wall Street investments in a world market that depends on constantly changing international conditions and the broker's ability to estimate, predict, and make quick decisions.

Some teachers like to use technology that supports basic skills instruction by providing practice environments that are fun for kids. There is a lot of software available for that. For instance, there are games that challenge the player to type answers for simple addition, subtraction, or multiplication problems before being caught by a monster. Others ask the player to identify prime numbers, select factors of a given number, find numbers that are greater than or less than the given number, and so forth. Still others test the player's understanding of place value, associativity, inverses, and order of operations in mathematics. There are probably software programs available to entertain students while they practice almost any basic skill in mathematics.

Specialized Technology for Mathematics and Language Skills: Integrated Learning Systems

Integrated Learning Systems (ILSs) are touted by enthusiastic supporters as the complete solution to teaching basic language and mathematics skills to students. Essentially, an ILS is a comprehensive, computer-based K–8 basic skills curriculum, accompanied by a management system that can link learning objectives with particular lessons, as well as track students' progress throughout the system. It is most commonly used in computer labs where numerous computers are networked together so that teachers can bring whole classes in to work on basic skills.

The advantages of the ILS are that students can work independently at their own rates, receive immediate feedback, avoid the embarrassment that comes with being slow or making mistakes in public, and experience success as they progress. Students with poor reading skills have opportunities to learn in other modalities, as the system provides graphics, sound, and animation to help them learn. The advantages for the teacher are that record-keeping is done by the computer; they can have their students progress through the ILS systematically and be assured that all skills are covered; or they can locate and use ILS lessons that match their own lessons in the classroom.

Its primary drawback is that in actual practice, teachers tend to send their students into the lab to "do basic skills." Then they go back to the classroom to do reading, writing, and mathematics. Basic skills remain isolated from the rest of their work and thus the critical goal of linking basic skills to meaningful work is lost in the process. Research supports this concern, as test scores of these students' basic skills are highly variable. It seems that the vendors report high gains in test scores, while independent sources show modest or negligible gains.

Some educators claim the drawbacks can be alleviated if the computers reside in classrooms and teachers use the ILS to support the project work and lessons they are doing in class. Indeed, some studies suggest that students whose teachers are more involved with their ILS work are more likely to produce greater learning gains.

One teacher who is highly supportive of the ILS in her school, says that practicing basic skills the old way (with worksheets) was like getting kids to practice housekeeping chores or table manners, but that now it's akin to honing their cooking or jump rope skills—they want to! She says that the computer tutorials and practice sessions come with sound, graphics, animation, and games that make it fun for children, and since the approach is supportive, with lots of positive feedback, the kids feel good about themselves and are motivated to keep going.

This teacher brings her third grade students to the school's ILS lab every day. They key in their ID numbers and the software automatically presents each child with the material the teacher has specifically assigned. As the student progresses, the computer periodically assesses how fast to push ahead. A score of 80 percent (or whatever standard the teacher sets) enables them to proceed to the next objective. A lower score indicates the need for a tutorial, and students who continue to perform poorly are directed to seek help from a teacher.

The teacher keeps track of students' progress by checking the tally of individual scores. These reports enable her to identify exactly which skill areas students need to work on and which ones they don't. This teacher selects the learning objectives she wants students to cover and plans individual sequences for each student. The sequences can be revised at any time and within each assignment students can progress independently, including skipping over practice sessions that they do not need. However, the software does not permit students to move beyond the assigned area of study without permission.

This teacher and other avid supporters of ILSs argue that the system covers all the fundamental skill areas so that students' individual weaknesses can be identified and remedied. They also argue that because the software takes the basic skills worry off their desks (and the time it takes to correct exercises and record grades), it frees them to plan educational adventures that complement their (and their students') personal interests and talents.

It is encouraging that many students enjoy these activities and feel successful in their efforts to learn basic skills. However, experience and research have documented two important assumptions: (1) if basic skills are highly emphasized with ample practice exercises and individual help, students' basic skills performance will improve significantly more than when basic skills are not stressed; but, (2) students who have mastered basic skills in isolation are frequently not able to apply those skills to realistic situations such as solving word problems or writing essays.

How can educators solve this dilemma? Some claim that the best, most recent ILS software addresses the new NCTM standards for mathematics that calls for the application of basic math skills in problem-solving contexts. They claim the new ILS software also includes meaningful applications of basic language skills. Even so, the jury is still out and debating about these systematic approaches, and probably will stay out indefinitely, because it's dangerous to judge whether any packaged system or approach can provide a complete solution to the elusive "basic skills problem."

10

BEYOND THE CLASSROOM: IMPLEMENTATION IN THE SCHOOL, DISTRICT, STATE

RATIONALE

Some schools restructure as a result of being told by the district that they must adopt a restructured curriculum, convert to a school-based management model, become technology users, replace academic tracking with total integration, or whatever. If the motivation to change originates outside the school, it is difficult to predict a successful transition for those schools, unless there are also strong advocates within the school. On the other hand, some schools want to restructure themselves, but face resistance from a centrally managed district that will not budge. These schools may have a better chance for success, if they can build considerable community support. The most successful restructuring approach—though research hasn't yet documented what experience is already demonstrating—involves a collaboration among teachers, school, and district-level leaders who share a similar vision for change.

This chapter offers some examples of how various institutions have, or are in the process of, restructuring. Examples represent institutional change at the school, district, and state levels.

RESTRUCTURING A SCHOOL

Restructuring not only involves changing curriculum and instructional practices in the classroom, it also involves changing the way schools are organized. Restructuring the way schools are organized involves redefining the roles of teachers, school administrators, parents, and students. Many believe that for long-term success, the most effective way to do this is to bring together all stakeholders to talk—share their pedagogical visions, and reach an agreement concerning goals for student learning, standards, curriculum, instructional approaches, and how they will manage themselves. These kinds of conversations are currently happening in schools all over the country. The "Restructuring Movement" has prompted such efforts and motivated educators to press forward. But how far schools will go in their efforts is up to the schools.

Many of the schools that have successfully restructured adopted features that are consistent with the principles and applications presented in this book. For instance, a representative from one restructured school explained that two principles underlie their school's commitment to restructuring: (1) learning is best achieved by doing, and (2) technology supports this kind of active learning better than anything else so far. Another shared principle is that learning is best accomplished when subjects are integrated and activities are meaningful. This principle often leads to school-community partnerships of all kinds—with businesses, social service institutions, senior citizen groups, other schools and universities, and with individuals and organizations around the globe. Other common restructuring principles include the need for independent learning, collaborative learning, and life-long learning. Plus, restructured schools share the need for new forms of assessment, increased connectivity among educators nationally, more professional time to develop new curricula and instructional approaches as well as to learn to use new technologies and other resources.

The actual steps for how a school moves from wanting to restructure, to planning and implementation, are extremely varied. Some begin with broad-based school/community meetings, some begin with meetings of school leaders, and some begin when a team of advocates draw up a plan and then manage (or don't manage) to sell it to the school and community. One comprehensive example of this process is documented in Theodore Sizer's book, *Horace's School.* The book is fiction, but quite realistic in its portrayal of the complexities of such a process, the time commitment, risk of failure, and rewards of accomplishment.

Many school districts have "alternative" schools that are often established because a group of particularly active and vocal parents are not completely satisfied with the available public schools in the district and take it upon themselves to create a school that will satisfy them. With support from the district, these parents sit down with interested teachers and administrators from the district and design a new structure and curriculum for their school. If the design is acceptable to district administrators and the group can solicit enough interest and students to make the school financially feasible, a new school with a uniquely different structure and curriculum is established. Alternative schools had been in existence (and later dissolved if the interest and parental advocacy waned) for many years before the Restructuring Movement appeared on the horizon. Yet many of the principles that commonly underlie these schools are similar to the principles of the Restructuring Movement.

Some restructured schools are established as "model schools" that offer the public a model of what the designer's ideal school would be like. An example of this kind of school is the Saturn School in St. Paul, Minnesota, which was established in the latter 1980s, and is funded by the local teacher's union, university, and technology consortium. The Saturn School has abundant technology and a dramatically different educational structure. There are no textbooks. Students help construct their own Personal Growth Plans (PGP), and learning takes place in the local community as well as inside the classroom. Evidently, this school has retained a conventional curriculum, but has added to it "new skills for a changing world," including global communications, apprenticeships, community service activities, cooperative learning, project-based work, and videography. The school contains discourse rooms (with a central multimedia station, large-screen projection system, and response terminals), work areas, a writing and desktop publishing center, a LEGO Logo robotics area, an ILS (integrated learning system) lab, and areas for small-group activities. The pedagogical emphasis is on developing student responsibility for designing their PGPs (with parents and teachers) and fulfilling their contracted commitments.

An example of a school that redesigned itself is Seven Oaks Elementary School in Lacey, Washington. This school spent a year planning its restructuring process. Committees composed of the principal, parents, teachers, and district administrators developed a design that includes mixed grade clusters (two grades in each) in which a teacher keeps the same children for two years. Teachers meet every week to discuss student outcomes, assessments, and interdisciplinary projects, and they continue to communicate via the school's electronic mail system. Technology is abundant in this school (it's funded by IBM and gets additional inservice training through the state's Schools for the 21st Century program). The classrooms, library, and science lab are networked together, and each classroom has five computers and a printer. Language Arts lessons and materials are neatly integrated into other subject curricula. Math instruction focuses on problem-solving and relevant application of math concepts to other subject areas. Instructional approaches emphasize collaborative learning in small groups. Integrated projects include challenges such as designing a model of an energy-efficient house out of a cardboard box. Assessment of such projects includes videotaping students' presentations so that both teachers and students can review and assess progress from year to year. Students use the library to search for information on electronic resources, they organize and draft information on word processing software, and then desktop-publish final publications for dissemination, and/or they integrate information into multimedia presentations using text, audio, and video media.

Willison Central School, a K–8 school in Vermont, has been gradually restructuring since 1984. After defining what they thought students should know and be able to do as a result of schooling, this school developed a curriculum and assessment strategy based on their defined "Essential Behaviors for Learners." Students are organized into multigrade houses with 80–100 students and four adult "facilitators." Students are taught to be independent learners who seek and process information in information-rich, interactive environments. Students are responsible for their own learning, and they have ready access to a vast array of resources, including the teacher-facilitator. Subjects are frequently integrated, and often students spend bell-free mornings working on projects that call for skills and concepts from several subject areas. Students in one of the more experimental high-tech houses, are learning to produce sophisticated multimedia reports which they present on the school's 100-inch display screen. These students are also developing electronic portfolios that include reports, visuals, and videos that demonstrate their work and progress in all subject areas.

University Terrace Elementary School, in Baton Rouge, Louisiana, is restructuring itself into a community-based service center. The idea for this restructured approach came from the school's need to get community support for learning. The school is composed primarily of economically disadvantaged students whose parents had been demonstrating little interest in the school or their children's education. In an effort to gain parental support by getting parents to come to the school and to become involved in positive learning experiences themselves, the school opened its doors weekday evenings and Saturday mornings, and offered programs and services for parents and their children. They offered classes that focused on single-parent issues, financial planning, job training, adult education, child care, and parent-child activities. They offered classes in first aid and babysitting, they offered tutoring, computer classes, sports activities, and they served as a clearing house for local resources and family counseling. Evidently, the computers are the big draw for both kids and their parents. Interest is picking up, and the principal is hopeful that growing parental support will lead to other kinds of academic programs and restructuring efforts in the long term. The underlying principle here is that if you can get parents to develop positive attitudes about school (many of them had poor school experiences in their youth), then they will help their kids develop positive attitudes about school.

RESTRUCTURING A DISTRICT

There are many different approaches for district restructuring as well. Some districts have a strong central power base and approach reform systematically, maintaining control over the restructuring of student learning objectives, standards, and assessments, while in some cases permitting individual schools to develop curricula and instructional strategies to reach the district's objectives. On the other hand, some districts are so decentralized that individual schools are free to implement their own visions.

One district in Florida tried a unique approach in sending out a national request for proposals for restructured school designs. The district's long-range goal is to select plans for restructuring 49 schools over seven years. Nine proposals were selected the first year, and eight of them were developed by teacher/principal teams from inside the district, and the ninth was proposed by a private, out-of-state organization. The first of these restructured schools features ample technology and a shared decision-making approach. This first school is still in the developmental stage, so it remains to be seen how a "proposal/contract" approach to school restructuring works.

A suburban district in Washington state began the restructuring process by developing an overall plan for restructuring student learning goals, standards, and assessments; shifting to school-based management; providing extended inservice opportunities; and integrating technology into the entire system. The task was monumental, and further complicated (enriched) by an irresistible opportunity to join a national restructuring program that has its own reform agenda.

With a master plan in place, this district set out to conduct research in the community to learn what the residents liked and did not like about the current system. At the same time, a planning committee composed of teachers, administrators, school board members, and parents was formed to develop the student learning goals and standards. School-based design teams (composed of the principal, 2 teachers, and 2 parents) were also formed to begin creating a plan for the implementation of the new learning goals and standards. This district had a headstart on technology infusion in so far as all schools had been equipped with advanced technologies (computer labs, and at least one computer and VCR in each classroom) during previous building remodeling efforts. However, many of the teachers were still not integrating technology into their curricula or instructional approaches. Consequently, the district planned to provide staff development incentives to help them achieve full integration of technology.

With all of these plans set in motion, the district now faces two major problems that will undoubtedly determine the success or failure of this restructuring effort. First, the community was not pushing for these kinds of reforms, and neither were the teachers. The master plan was developed by the administration, before the teachers and community were invited to join the effort. What remains to be seen is how effective a sell job the administration can manage. It's possible they will be successful, because teachers in this district are dedicated to helping children learn and flexible enough to change; and parents are vocal, highly involved, and anxious to improve their children's education. Both groups are cautious, however, and somewhat fearful of taking risks concerning the children's education.

The second potential problem the district faces is that teachers may or may not be willing or able to replace their current curriculum and instructional approaches with new and very different ones. The plan calls for significant revisions in what teachers teach and how they teach, based on a new set of goals, expected outcomes, and assessment strategies. Plus, the plan calls for school-based management, which places additional management responsibilities on teachers who already feel they have a heavy workload.

It is too soon to predict what will happen to this district's restructuring plans. There are not yet enough models or research findings to predict its chances for success.

The Restructuring Movement has been active at the school and district levels for at least a decade, so considerable advice is available to schools and districts concerning how to go about restructuring. One popular source of advice is to hire an expert consultant who is familiar with how schools and other organizations work (e.g., businesses, hospitals, the military), and has experience in successfully implementing change in these institutions. One such consultant, whom we will use here as our example, works with school districts and their constituents as they plan and implement reform designs. According to this consultant, the restructuring process involves breaking familiar habits and hierarchies of authority, shifting management responsibility, and increasing the flow of information among parents, teachers, and school administrators. To successfully restructure, a district needs to first find out where it is now, and then decide where it wants to be. There needs to be a clearly designed management model and a map of specific goals to move toward.

In his presentations to parents and educators, this consultant clarifies the need for restructuring by describing the traditional system as a top-down management model that was appropriate for a factory-based society and the military, but not for today. He proposes a shared-management model, which is far more appropriate for a society that depends upon sharing and cooperation among colleagues and nations.

The traditional management model he describes is represented by a triangle of authority that places most of the information, policy development, and decision-making power with a few leaders at the top (the school board and district administrators). Those at the middle level (principals and other school-based administrators) develop procedures to carry out decisions handed down from above. The labor force at the bottom (teachers) implements decisions and procedures developed by the upper two authorities. In this model, the quality of the product (student learning) is tested and assigned numbers for easy comparison.

This authoritarian system has little room for collaboration. Its management does not know how to listen and learn, work as a team, go for long-term qualitative goals, or give responsibility to those on the bottom. In the top-down system, when something goes wrong, the top tells the middle what to do with the bottom (see Figure 10-1).

The consultant then notes that if people want to change this deeply rooted model, they have to realize that it is centuries old and extremely

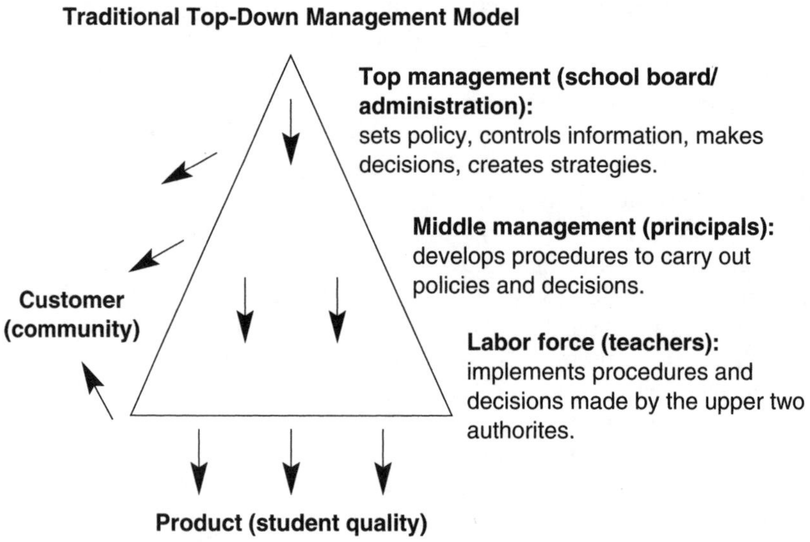
Traditional Top-Down Management Model
Top management (school board/ administration):
sets policy, controls information, makes decisions, creates strategies.
Middle management (principals):
develops procedures to carry out policies and decisions.
Labor force (teachers):
implements procedures and decisions made by the upper two authorites.
Customer (community)
Product (student quality)

FIGURE 10-1

difficult to budge. It is also a unified system, every part of it affects every other part, so the entire system has to be changed. If you touch any part of it, you have to change all of it.

This extremely rigid management model may still be evident in business today, but school districts are generally not as centralized or authoritarian as corporations. Still, school districts bear some resemblance to this ancient model and much can be learned by examining its limitations.

After clearly illustrating this rather extreme model, he describes a new management system that is both stable and flexible, and has proven successful in other school districts (see Figure 10-2). Characteristics of this model include the following:

- It asks for the truth about how the school system is doing, and listens openly to responses from all levels of the system and the community. The results—good and bad—are published with an attitude of openness, because learning from mistakes is genuinely supported.
- The community is involved, and individuals come with enormous needs and demands that are extremely diverse. But according to the consultant, you can't have a world class system without the customer/parent to help you understand quality and how well you're doing.
- The community participates in designing the system's vision, goals, and measures. This participation also gives them a share of responsibility for the results.

A Shared-Management Model

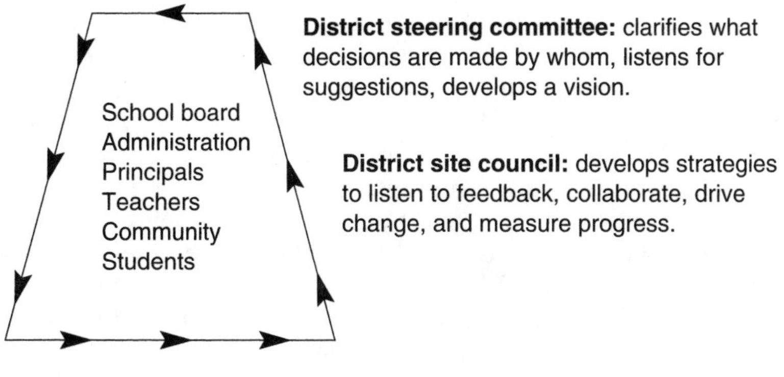

FIGURE 10-2

- Management is driven from needs and issues that come from below, not above. Thus, many administrators spend time in schools and classrooms listening to and dealing with their needs and issues.
- A team of educators and community representatives clarifies what decisions are to be made by whom and why. The consultant offers the family as a comparable model in that some decisions are made by parents (family, budget, insurance coverage), some by children (what they wear, what activities to join), and some jointly (what subjects to take, how to spend vacations), and so forth. Further, the decision-making process evolves as the participants are more able to manage bigger decisions.
- The product of this system is student effort. Learners are empowered to make more decisions as they mature, and become more responsible for their own learning. They participate in determining measures for their effort, productivity, and quality of work. And they take greater responsibility for their progress.

The consultant also proposes how districts can best implement the restructuring process. He outlines the steps as follows:

1. First of all, everyone involved in the change process must want to work together to improve the system as well as the product (students' effort and productivity).
2. Set up a district steering committee (representing the community and all levels of the system) to give others permission to make decisions, and to set the parameters.
3. Send the steering committee out to listen and learn from all levels of the system and community about how the system is doing. Publish a written report that includes failures as well as strengths. This consultant noted that if you tell the truth, it shifts the relationship to one of mutual honesty rather than deceit. Develop an attitude that fosters learning from mistakes; this is no longer a punitive system. Develop a vision of the ways you want the system to work.
4. Establish a district site council to develop strategies that will change relationships between different levels, with emphasis on listening, collaborating, and measuring progress.
5. Encourage administrators to spend time in schools. Their expertise is needed there and they are also needed to establish channels of communication between the school community and the administration.
6. Set goals that are realistic. Change one thing at a time, with a map and a timeline for the whole system at hand. Listen to what others say, measure your progress, and publish results.

Districts that do not choose to hire a consultant can also get help in their restructuring efforts from the multitude of handbooks and other support materials that suggest strategies and procedures for planning and implementing reform designs. Basically, the planning strategies proposed by most resources are similar to the ones suggested by our example consultant. This basic framework for the process of restructuring also allows for individual schools to do their own planning and implementation of the district's overall vision, or establish their own visions if the district plan allows for that level of diversity.

RESTRUCTURING STATE POLICIES

Several states in the United States have taken bold steps to restructure education within the entire state. Washington, for example, was prompted to redesign its educational system after a teachers' strike shut down schools for a week in 1991 and won citizen support for reform. The governor established a council to design a performance-based educational system that would improve student performance by establishing new educational goals, setting high standards, defining expected outcomes, and designing a better system of assessment and accountability.

The resulting design that was passed into law in 1993 articulates four student learning goals:

1. Read with comprehension, write with skill, and communicate effectively and responsibly in a variety of ways and settings.
2. Know and apply the core concepts and principles of mathematics; social, physical, and life sciences; civics and history; geography; arts; and health and fitness.
3. Think analytically, logically, and creatively, and be able to integrate experience and knowledge to form reasoned judgments and solve problems.
4. Understand the importance of work and how performance, effort, and decisions directly affect future career and educational opportunities.

The law in Washington calls for a Commission on Student Learning to identify the knowledge and skills all public school students need to know and be able to do based on the student learning goals, to develop student assessment and school accountability systems, and to take other steps necessary to develop a performance-based education system. With the help of advisory committees, the Commission must also develop essential academic learning requirements for each of the learning goals. The Commission is also mandated to construct a statewide assessment system designed to determine if each student has mastered the essential academic learning requirements. This assessment system will also be used to evaluate instructional practices and to initiate support for students who have not mastered the learning requirements at the appropriate periods in each student's educational development.

Successful completion of the high school assessment will lead to a certificate of mastery. For most students this will be at about age 16. Upon achieving mastery, students will be able to continue to pursue career and educational objectives through integration of academic and vocational education, such as work-based learning, school-to-work transition programs, tech prep, and preparation for technical college, community college, or university education. Participation in this assessment system is optional until the year 2000–2001.

Regarding accountability for schools, the Commission must develop a statewide accountability system to monitor and evaluate the level of learning in individual schools and school districts. The accountability system will include an assistance program to help schools and districts having difficulty in helping students meet the essential academic learning requirements, a system to intervene in schools with students who persistently fail to reach the standard, and an awards program for schools whose students improve.

The law also calls for the Superintendent of Public Instruction to develop and implement a Washington State K–12 education technology plan. The plan will be designed to expand the use of education technology in the schools by providing technical assistance to schools, developing a network to connect educational institutions, and establishing a grant program for schools to acquire new technology.

Soon after this education reform law was passed, certain groups of citizens representing fundamental Christian groups and other conservative points of view, began voicing disapproval of the reforms and gathering support for a referendum to overturn the law. One of their major criticisms was the inclusion of critical thinking in the school curriculum. They believed that teaching students to think critically meant teaching them to reject the values and religious beliefs that they had been taught at home and in church. Unfortunately, many people assume that *critical* means *criticize* rather than *think about, analyze,* and *examine other points of view.* Rather than trust that home and church values can withstand such analysis, they fear a breakdown in home-taught values and blame it on the school system's practice of teaching students to think carefully and completely.

It remains to be seen how Washington's reform law plays itself out in the years to come. Many other states will be watching.

Kentucky is a few years ahead of Washington in terms of establishing statewide reforms. Kentucky passed The Kentucky Education Reform Act of 1990 after the state supreme court ruled the state's entire system of public education was unconstitutional. Financed by a $1.4 billion tax increase, the educational system has been redesigned to an outcome-based approach. The approach is based on the beliefs that all children can learn at high levels and that schools are the center of change. What follows is that schools must be given the resources to help children succeed, and that they are also accountable for students' progress. Schools that do well are rewarded and those that do poorly are punished (e.g., the school's educators might be put on probation or fired). Schools have considerable control over how they operate and are governed by school-based decision-making councils. The plan also calls for increasing technology equipment and use in the state schools as well as increasing inservice training for educators.

The designers articulated six learning goals and then identified 75 expected outcomes. The law called for the state to develop a new system of performance assessments including portfolios and appropriate tests. The law also required elementary schools to adopt ungraded programs, to establish pre-school programs for at-risk children, and make available family-resource and youth-service centers as well as tutoring services to at-risk students and their families.

Results? A couple of years after the law passed, some administrators were complaining that the reforms were not moving fast enough. On the other hand, teachers were overwhelmed as they struggled with totally different learning environments (e.g., ungraded classrooms), and tried to adapt to radically different instructional approaches (e.g., team teaching, group learning), and curricula (e.g., whole language approach, problem-solving, critical thinking).

Although performance-based assessment measures were still under development, baseline assessments were made on all students in grades 4, 8, and 12. Contrary to tradition, students were not compared against one another but against identified standards of what students should know and be able to do. Scores were assigned to levels of performance labeled: novice, apprentice, proficient, and distinguished. Evidently, 90 percent of the state's students fell below the proficient level. Many were surprised, and the interpretations ranged from a realization that student's performance hasn't been as good as parents and teachers thought, to total denial and the assumption that the tests were invalid. What is particularly frightening to educators in the state is that although they have 20 years to raise all students to the proficient level, they are expected to improve by a certain percentage every year. Schools that raise their level by 1 percent will receive monetary rewards. Those that don't will be required to develop a school-improvement plan and be given funds and assistance to improve. Schools that decline by more than 5 percent will be put on probation.

Yet, the biggest challenge the state's reform law faces is the need to build expertise and leadership in support of the reforms. There is money for increased teacher development, and teachers affirm that they are getting more and better training than before. Still, resistance to change is common among both school people and parents, and this barrier has to be overcome in order to achieve success over the long term.

How Educators Can Influence Politicians and Their School Reform Policies

State and national politicians have tremendous power to totally restructure education, and yet very few of them know much about what is going on in classrooms now, what works and doesn't work, and how public schools operate. Who can they best learn from? Teachers. And yet, teachers are characteristically unpolitical beings. They tend to focus on their work in the classroom and school, and seldom get involved in political advocacy to promote reforms that reflect what they've learned about how children learn most successfully. Consequently, legislators make decisions on the basis of what they learn from other politicians, educational consultants (usually far removed from the classroom), committees of business leaders and other sources with their own special interests concerning public education.

Educators must become actively involved in informing policymakers about the school reforms they have learned are most advantageous for kids and will work most effectively. One way to insure that information will flow to policymakers is for schools to develop an overall strategy for the process. For example, school staff could make a list of appropriate state and national legislators and the reporters from local newspapers who cover education. Systematically send them descriptions of particularly innovative curricula being taught and what days would be good to visit and observe. If reporters do not come, take pictures anyway (that include students and politicians, if any of them come) and deliver them to the local newspaper. Send them copies of reform proposals initiated at the school. Assign a staff member to keep tabs on what the legislature is doing and when school-related issues are debated, activate others to write, call, and volunteer to testify. All of these approaches will prompt school staff to become more involved in educational concerns outside the school; it will help teachers and schools become less isolated; and will help teachers learn to become leaders among adults as well as within their own classrooms. These are empowering experiences, and empowering teachers will help them develop professionally, just as effectively as empowering students helps them develop academically.

Another way teachers and schools can affect the policymaking process is to initiate or join existing coalitions for reform. This effort can be as simple as joining an education forum/conference on a telecommunications network, attending an educator's conference and linking on to one of the advocacy groups offered there, joining an organization such as the Foxfire Teacher Outreach Network, the Urban Mathematics Collaborative, the Coalition of Essential Schools, the Accelerated Schools Network, the Success for All Schools program, and a host of others. Coalitions that are politically active and can demonstrate that their approaches work, can have a significant influence on state and national education policy.

Without adequate information directly from educators, state and national policymakers tend to develop policy that serves the needs of politicians, business leaders, and other advocacy groups, and what they do design may be far from what educators feel is workable or good for kids. Educators need to get involved, not only to promote their own interests, but to improve education for kids and for the future of this country.

PART III

REFLECTION

REVIEW AND RETHINK RESTRUCTURED BELIEFS AND PRACTICES

In Part I, we presented our vision of what a restructured approach to education would look like and why including technology in that vision is so important. In Part II, we offered examples and suggestions of how educators can (and do) make that vision a reality. Part III, then, reviews and rethinks our vision for restructuring education by examining how other initiatives could impact the vision, and by reviewing what research can tell us about the process of change.

Chapter 11 reflects on the vision and its implementation by examining national initiatives and issues that are currently catching the public eye, and consequently impacting educational policy and practice in many (positive and negative) ways. These initiatives/issues do not directly involve the educational use of technology; however, any major initiative that impacts educational systems also impacts our technology-enriched vision and thus can't be ignored.

Chapter 12 reflects on the simple truth that changing one's familiar attitudes and behaviors about schooling is not easy. Starting at the age of six, most of us experienced the traditional mode of instruction in which teachers and textbooks delivered information that was sliced into separate subject areas, and students recited it back by voice or on paper. This lecture, practice, and recitation method of instruction has prevailed for generations. Consequently, it takes commitment and courage for educators to adopt new instructional approaches that cross subject boundaries and engage students in active, collaborative work that may be viewed by others as disruptive and noisy. But, those who have weathered the change and witnessed the unusual growth in students' motivation, skills, and understandings, are joining the growing number of revisionists who are now making successful change more readily attainable for others.

11

National Issues and the Role of Technology

The 1980s certainly stirred things up in education. Following *A Nation at Risk* and other diatribes against the nation's schools, public scrutiny of public education set the stage for radical reform. Yet, everyone has different ideas about what those reforms should be, so it has taken years for individuals and coalitions to build regional and national support for their designs. The pedagogical vision presented in this book, for instance, has attracted a large and growing number of supporters, demonstrated by the fairly widespread implementation of its principles.

This chapter discusses the progress made by popular national movements that directly impact or are in some way related to our vision.

STANDARDS AND ASSESSMENT

This movement is probably the loudest in terms of public voice, and the most volatile in that it directly affects so many people. The public is shouting for higher educational standards because they are convinced that U.S. students know less and are less academically competent than their counterparts in other industrialized nations. The general public does not concern itself much with *how* students should reach those standards (that's left to educators), but emphasizes that they must reach them. The public also wants national examinations to make sure students reach those high standards, *and* so they can make educators accountable for student performance. *High stakes* assessment it's called, because if the students do well, teachers and schools are rewarded (usually with bonuses); but if students do poorly, teachers and schools are punished (e.g., with pay cuts, loss of grant money, probation). Inevitably, economically disadvantaged schools are at a further disadvantage in this approach unless they receive a tremendous amount of direct support to make them equal, so they may compete fairly.

Some educational leaders (e.g., Theodore Sizer, director of the Coalition of Essential Schools) do not believe that national exams are necessary. They propose that students, educators, and schools be held accountable to the local community. His answer to assessment and accountability is for schools to hold student "exhibitions" at the end of the year that are open to the public. In this way, students are assessed by peers, educators, parents, and the public; and accountability is local, direct, and a natural outcome of the educational process.

Other educational leaders accept the public's demand for national assessments, and put their efforts into supporting the design that best matches their values and educational goals. The rest of this section outlines two of the most prominent national initiatives, followed by comments made by nationally known standards and assessment experts. The most critical issues in the area of standards and assessment are also summarized at the end.

America 2000

Description

America 2000 is a long-term strategy to achieve national learning goals that originated from a governors' summit which included then Governor Bill Clinton and was championed by then President George Bush in 1990–92.

The strategy puts forward national education goals for the year 2000, which include the following:

- All children will start school ready to learn.
- The high school graduation rate will increase to at least 90 percent.
- All students will leave grades 4, 8, and 12 having demonstrated competency in English, mathematics, science, history, and geography.
- U.S. students will be first in the world in science and mathematics achievement.
- Every adult American will be literate and will have the knowledge and skills necessary to compete in a global economy as well as exercise the rights and responsibilities of citizenship.
- Every school will be free of drugs and violence and will offer a safe, disciplined environment conducive to learning.

The strategy proposes that the National Education Goals Panel (NEGP), established in 1990, oversee development of "world class standards" that will incorporate the knowledge and skills U.S. students need to be prepared for further study and for the work force. The strategy further proposes that the Panel oversee development of a set of American Achievement Tests based on the five core subjects listed in the goals. America 2000 recommends that colleges use these tests in admissions and employers pay attention to them in hiring. The strategy further proposes that scholarships be awarded to students who do well on these tests and that national "report cards" provide comparable public information on how schools, districts, and states are doing, as well as the entire nation.

The strategy suggests that Congress authorize a National Assessment of Educational Progress to collect state-level data in grades 4, 8, and 12 beginning in 1994, and proposes that these tests may also be used by districts and schools.

The plan suggests that with standards, tests, and report cards to tell parents and voters how their schools are doing, parents should also be able to act on those judgments by choosing which school their child will attend. Such choices would include both public and private schools. It proposes that incentives be provided to states and localities to adopt comprehensive choice policies, and that dollars from federal aid programs follow the child.

The plan proposes that teachers, principals, and parents at each school be given authority and responsibility to make decisions about how the school will operate and that rewards be given to schools that make notable progress toward the national goals. Congress will be asked to enact a new program that provides federal funds to states that can be used as rewards. Differential pay will be encouraged for those who teach well, who teach core subjects, who teach in dangerous and challenging settings, or who serve as mentors for new teachers.

America 2000 also calls for business leaders to establish a New American Schools Development Corporation (NASDC) to fund design teams that will create "break-the-mold" model schools. NASDC was established as a private foundation in 1991 and in 1992 it awarded contracts to support eleven design teams in their development of model schools and school systems designed to reach the national goals and standards.

In conjunction with the America 2000 strategy, the U.S. Secretary of Labor established the Secretary's Commission on Achieving Necessary Skills (SCANS) to identify the skills young people need to enter the workplace, and to propose levels of proficiency and methods of assessment that can be incorporated into school programs. The Commission has now identified particular personal qualities, thinking skills, and basic skills that it considers important in the workplace and has recommended these skills be addressed in national assessments for grades 8 and 12. SCANS has also proposed a high school credential that certifies mastery of these skills.

In response to the America 2000 proposals, Congress established the National Council on Education Standards and Testing (NCEST) to study the feasibility and desirability of national standards and testing in education—whether standards and exams would promote improvement; whether they were appropriate with such wide variations of school conditions; and whether such exams can be valid, reliable, fair, and cost-effective.

The council's 1992 report did recommend a national system of educational standards and assessments, claiming that they are needed to promote educational equity, preserve democracy, improve economic competitiveness, and provide shared knowledge and values in an increasingly diverse and mobile population.

The council proposed there be standards for students that address both content and level of performance, and standards for schools that ensure the tools, opportunities, and conditions for success are available to all children. Standards must reflect high expectations and provide focus and direction; they must be dynamic and they must be voluntary.

The council recommended a set of examinations that would include components to assess individual students as well as large-scale samples. The exams would include multiple measures that are aligned to high national standards and produce comparable results. The report also indicated that issues of validity, reliability, and fairness must be addressed in developing such tests. Exams should be voluntary, and developmental. The report also proposed that exams become "high-stakes" assessments that could be used for graduation, college admission, and employment as well as accountability for schools and teachers.

Reflective Comments

Congress did not put any of the America 2000 components into law while George Bush was president, though Congress did pass legislation in 1994 that formally adopts the national goals. National polls indicate public support for national standards and examinations, but many highly esteemed educators are vigorously opposed to the plan. They argue that the public is not well informed about the damage that high-stakes testing has done to this country's educational system. A large accumulation of research now suggests that high-stakes national examinations with serious consequences will be even more harmful to disadvantaged students who are already victimized by inequities among schools. They argue that when schools are awarded more money for high achievement and less for low achievement, the rich get richer and the poor get poorer. When students are tracked into high and low groups, the best teachers and resources generally go to the top groups and the children who need them most get what's left. Further, experience shows that such high-stakes examinations cause teachers, schools, and communities to focus on the exams rather than the broader and deeper learning goals of a complete curriculum.

Aside from the content issues, many predict that national tests would cost tens of millions of dollars to develop and at least $3 billion a year to administer. Finally, even those educators who do not oppose the concept of national standards and assessments worry that the process is moving too fast for careful thought when the risks for our children are far too great.

The following are comments from specific standards and assessment experts:

> *For years test scores have been used to place students in different curricular and instructional tracks, to retain them in grade, and to assign them to remediation, readiness, and special education programs. The potential benefits of using tests to place students in these treatments have been taken for granted. The associated harms went unnoticed for a long time. Evidence is now accumulating that many educa-tional treatments involving testing for placement are not efficacious for many students, have harmful side effects, and reduce opportunities to learn.*—George F. Madaus, Director of the Center for the Study of Testing, Evaluation, and Educational Policy at Boston College

> *Proposals to use the test results as a basis for awarding federal funds, far from stimulating school improvement, would create perverse incentives for schools to exclude low-scoring students and for talented staff to avoid teaching in challenging schools.*—Linda Darling-Hammond, Co-director of the National Center for Restructuring Education, Schools, and Testing (NCREST)

> *Simply imposing a national test on schools to jump-start reform will aggravate even further the general feeling of teachers that educational reform is something being done to them and their students rather than for them. Private enterprise has learned the hard way that competitive productivity requires involving the workhorse rather than dictating to it. Better student achievement must be developed in the*

classroom, and only the teacher can do it. Teachers should have a central role in reform if we are to benefit from their dedication and commitment. To date, this hasn't happened; a national test would represent another step in the wrong direction.

If we start tagging a single test on a single day to such high stakes as promotion, graduation, and in some states financial incentives and penalties on teachers and schools, then we are putting a very important human decision on a very thin reed. That's bad policy. If we need accountability to help us judge how our schools are doing, then let's get information, not simply scores from a single test.—Gregory R. Anrig, President of Educational Testing Services

We need high standards, but those standards must be adapted to local needs. They must be flexible, situational, and multicultural, rather than national, mandated, and standardized. They must be tied to instructional decisions that teachers have helped to make and for which they can be held accountable.—Ann Lieberman, Co-director of NCREST

The New Standards Project

Description

The New Standards Project (NSP) was established in 1990 to develop a national system of assessing student performance. It is co-directed by Lauren Resnick, of the Learning Research and Development Center at University of Pittsburgh, and Marc Tucker, of the National Center on Education and the Economy. The project is developing a system of national examinations built on the assumption that all students can achieve at high levels and that it is effort rather than native ability or family background that enables students to succeed.

The exam system includes a detailed set of goals for students and instruments to assess student progress toward those objectives. It may take some students longer than others, but the assumption is that all students can reach high standards of performance. School staffs are provided with the resources and incentives they need to help all students meet the standard. Decisions about how best to assist students to reach those objectives are made by adults in the school and those professionals are held accountable for the results of their efforts. The project is opposed to a national curriculum, believing that there are many approaches and outcomes that can lead students to the same level of mastery.

This widespread project supports a national agenda that calls for three types of national standards:

- Content standards—what students should know and be able to do in various subject areas
- Performance standards—levels of quality of student work on tasks that reflect the content standards
- School delivery standards—criteria for assessing whether schools are providing students the opportunity to learn material reflected in the content standards

The National Council of Teachers of Mathematics has already published content standards for mathematics, and standards for other subject areas are being developed.

NSP is developing model examinations that will emphasize thinking, problem-solving, and a capacity to apply knowledge to real-world problems. Assessments include live performances assessed by teacher judges, projects, and portfolios of students' best work collected over time. According to the designers, these "curriculum-embedded" assessments change the nature of testing by making it an integral part of the instructional process.

The plan calls for teacher involvement in the process of developing tasks as well as assessing the results. This involvement promotes development of common standards and scoring. The idea is to have a single system of standards that allows for any number of instructional approaches and assessments to get there. The assumption is that one can make valid comparisons among districts and states without destroying the individuality of authentic assessment within a classroom.

States and districts could adopt model exams designed by the project, or create their own, calibrated to the national standards. The project proposes there can be considerable variability among exams that are still calibrated at some judgmental level. This point distinguishes the project from other national exam initiatives that favor a uniform set of standardized tests. There is no specified date when all students are assessed with the result determining their future. In this system, it does not matter when a child succeeds because ultimately all children will.

The co-directors suggest that the initial exams would be ones that students take during a specified period of time. But their goal is to get to the point where most students' assessments are built on their accomplishments over time. The initial exams will be centrally designed, but the goal is for most assessments to be designed by classroom teachers for their own students. At that point, teachers will have internalized the standards of the teaching profession. Finally, the co-directors add that this ideal cannot be realized without a commitment to provide schools in which every kid has a fair shot at achieving the standard and teachers are prepared and treated as professionals.

Reflective Comments

Similar in its acceptance of national standards and examinations with comparable results, the New Standards Project differs from America 2000 in approach. Many educators support the ideas put forth by the Project, but object to the national standardization of testing because of the high cost of standardizing such tests and the high-stakes consequences that would inevitably follow comparisons among students, teachers, and schools. They argue that any assessment that is standardized, no matter how authentic, will eventually be misused.

The following are comments from specific standards and assessment experts:

> *Scores on high-stakes tests tend to be regarded by parents and students as the main if not the sole objective of education.*
>
> *High-stakes tests can force students to leave school before they have to take the examination, or after failing it.*
>
> *Fear of a low score on a certification test is intended to motivate students to work hard, but that's likely only if students believe that they have a good chance of achieving the rewards attached to high test performance. For students who are not likely to do well, the possible negative effects are of serious concern. Research suggests that competency tests for graduation and test-based retention policies are linked to increasing the dropout rate.*—George F. Madaus, Director of the Center for the Study of Testing, Evaluation, and Educational Policy

> *I don't see any political initiatives to reduce the load for English teachers from 120–175 students. It's all very well to change the writing assessment, but it's something else to make it possible for teachers to teach writing properly. That costs money; that means changing the insides of schools; that's not happening.*
>
> *Do we know how to assess those qualities of mind and spirit that we most value well enough to build them now into a national examination system that has high stakes? I suggest no.*
>
> *How can we set up a high-stakes system before guaranteeing to some reasonable level the elimination of the grotesque inequities in states?*
>
> *The New Standards Project is going in the right direction, but standardizing authentic assessment is taking a very fragile, very pow-*

erful notion and trying to hook it into something of an essentially political nature.—Theodore R. Sizer, Director of the Coalition of Essential Schools

[Counter response:] We have to get rid of the current system of standardized tests because it is so bad, and there is no political chance that the country will give up its current national testing system without a replacement for it.—Lauren Resnick, Co-director of the New Standards Project

Critical Issues

Following is a summary of the most salient concerns that educational leaders have with regard to the national standards and assessment initiatives. Each issue listed includes a summary of arguments from both sides of the issue. Generally, the issues focus more on proposed approaches to assessment rather than standards. The critical issues include cost, equity, high-stakes consequences, accountability, and compatibility of local, state, and national programs.

Cost

Critics of proposals to develop national/state exams predict that to develop and administer such tests would cost 6 to 20 times more than the current practices. They argue that the price tags on proposals for new educational systems are so high that the public will refuse to pay for entire programs, resulting in piecemeal approaches that could be more harmful than helpful (e.g., providing money for new assessments, but not for equalizing school conditions or educating teachers).

Those who support national and/or state assessments counter that the assessments are not so expensive if teachers develop and score them. The only additional expense would come from extending the teachers' work year and expanding their professional expertise. To address the issue of high price tags on complete programs, they respond that partial implementation of reforms is better than nothing, and that if it takes more time to get full programs into place, it's worth the wait.

Equity

Many educators worry that establishing high standards that all students are expected to meet will create a larger gulf between those schools that are already successful and those that are not. They say that impoverished schools with many disadvantaged students and few resources would be far behind the starting line in a race to achieve high standards.

Supporters of national/state standards and assessment programs agree that current inequities need to be addressed and claim that special efforts will be made to bring disadvantaged schools and students to a higher, competitive level.

High-Stakes Consequences

This is perhaps the most critical issue as it also impacts issues of equity, curriculum and instruction, tracking, and accountability. Educational researchers report findings that indicate examinations with high-stakes consequences (e.g., rewards for schools and teachers who raise test scores and consequences for those who don't; and placement of students in instructional tracts) are harmful to all students, but especially disadvantaged students and schools that already suffer from low self-esteem and failure when compared to others. Research further shows that when exam scores have high-stakes consequences, then curriculum and instructional practices inevitably focus on the examinations themselves rather than on the broader and deeper goals of a complete curriculum. In addition, some evidence suggests that mastery exams prompt students to leave school before they have to take the test, or after failing it.

Supporters of high-stakes exams argue that the new, alternative forms of assessment are the products of a broad and challenging curriculum, so that "teaching to the test" is a positive practice. They note that when teachers and schools are involved in developing curriculum and assessments, they can legitimately be expected to be responsible for improving results. They agree that disadvantaged schools and children need special assistance to ensure they have an equal chance to improve and ultimately meet high standards. Concerning the issue of mastery tests, they argue that results of those tests help schools and families make informed decisions concerning a student's future in an academic or career program.

Accountability

Some educators believe that accountability need not depend upon comparisons among students, schools, or nations. They believe that schools should be accountable to the local community, and that schools be assessed by the community through student performances and exhibitions that are public and that reflect the values of the community. Some suggest that accountability should focus on making sure that disadvantaged children get a better education, that all children have opportunities to reach high standards, and that the best teachers work in places where learners are hardest to teach.

Counter arguments reflect the public's demand for comparisons among schools and nations, and accountability for tax dollars invested in education. Some note that the current system of standardized testing is so bad it has to go, but, there is no political chance the public will give up the current testing system without a replacement for it. They propose the newly designed assessment systems are a vast improvement over existing practices.

Proposal Compatibility

If the U.S. Congress supports the development of national standards and assessments, and individual states also put state-level standards and assessments into law, what will happen? Will the states' programs be in violation of the national program? Or, will the federal government encourage individual states to establish their own standards and assessments? Further, what will happen to the standards and assessment programs that individual school districts have established? These are some of the unanswered questions that many are asking, while educators around the nation continue to debate the issues, as they work toward improving standards and assessment practices.

Standards and Assessment in a Restructured School with Technology

Changes in how teachers assess students and how students assess themselves are vital to the restructuring movement and vital to the integration of technology into education.

In order for students to learn to educate themselves and to become autonomous, life-long learners who continually acquire new knowledge and skills, they must learn to critically evaluate their current skills and understandings so they can determine how to expand and improve them. Some of the new approaches to assessment include methods for student self-assessment as well as teacher assessment approaches that include the students' reflections/critiques of their own work.

The restructuring movement calls for greater emphasis on problem-solving, critical thinking, inquiry, communication, collaboration, and integration of traditional subject areas. Inclusion of these elements in the school curriculum necessitates changes in conventional assessment approaches in order to fairly evaluate students' progress in learning these newly emphasized skills. If the curriculum and instructional emphases are changed, then it's also essential to reform standards and assessment practices at the same time one is restructuring the curriculum and instruction.

BOX 11-1 Alternative Assessment Terms

Outcome-Based Education

An outcome-based educational system has clear learning goals for students, detailed outcomes that identify progress toward those goals, and standards for those outcomes. For example, if the goal is to communicate effectively in a variety of settings, outcomes would demonstrate the learner's (1) ability to gather information from multiple sources; (2) organize, analyze, and apply it; (3) express information, ideas, and emotions in a variety of ways; and (4) use technology to gather, process, and express information and ideas.

Authentic Assessment

Assessment is authentic when the tasks used in testing are equal or similar to the best tasks found in instruction. Ideally, assessment tasks are part of the classroom curriculum and would include writing samples, projects, performances, portfolios, and exhibitions.

Performance-Based Assessment

Performance-based tests require students to create answers or products that demonstrate their knowledge or skills in a particular area. Performance tests could include writing essays, doing mathematical computations, baking bread, conducting experiments, presenting oral arguments, repairing electric appliances, constructing working models, or assembling portfolios of representative work.

Exhibitions

Exhibitions are comprehensive demonstrations of skills or competence. They may call for a student to create a new, equitable national tax system, for example, demonstrate a personal invention, perform in a student-written play, or present original research on the causes and effects of the violent conflicts in Northern Ireland.

Portfolios

Portfolios contain collections of a student's work over time. They may include anything from essays and reports to hypermedia presentations and videotaped performances.

Changes in standards and assessment approaches are also critical for the full integration of technology. Studies have shown that thorough integration of technology often naturally leads to greater student collaboration, fusion of subject areas, and autonomous learning, as well as inquiry, critical thinking, and problem-solving skills. And as we have previously noted, new emphasis on these areas necessitates new standards and methods of assessment.

TEACHER PREPARATION, CONTINUED STAFF DEVELOPMENT, AND THE PROFESSIONALIZATION OF TEACHING

A Vision for Schools of the 21st Century

In the mid-1980s, the Carnegie Foundation sponsored a Task Force on Teaching as a Profession to develop a vision of teaching and learning in the 21st century and a plan for implementing that vision. The final report in 1986 featured a scenario of the task force's visionary school, which included many of the characteristics presented in this book. Though the vision was published nearly a decade ago, it is still relevant today, showing that the movement to restructure has been present for a while. The Carnegie vision did not articulate how technology would be integrated into classrooms of the future, instead it focused on how lead teachers and other adults would interact with students in such classrooms. Our own vision of how technology could be used in classrooms such as these has been outlined in previous chapters. The point of recalling this vision here is to spotlight the need to elevate the teacher's job—to make teaching equal to other professions that command public respect, are compensated appropriately, demonstrate clear expertise in the field, and have comprehensive professional preparation programs with high standards.

The following is the task force's vision of a high school in the year 2000.

> *It is the year 2000. We are in a high school in a midwestern city serving children in a low income community. Most of the professional teaching staff have been Board certified. Many hold the Advanced Certificate issued by the Board. The professional teachers run the school with an Executive Committee of Lead Teachers in overall charge. There are many other people available to help the teachers, including paid teachers aides, technicians and clerical help; interns and residents working in the school as part of their professional teacher preparation programs; student tutors from the university, a few people on loan from nearby firms, and a retired person working as a volunteer tutor.*
>
> *We begin our visit by talking with several eleventh graders about their work in history and government. Last year, the history teachers had the students study the muckrakers and the "good government" movement in the Progressive Era. They got a good grasp of the central issues at stake in those days. Earlier this year, many of those students served as interns in local government agencies. They prepared reports*

on their work that included some rather interesting analyses of the role of local government and the conflicts that arise. When they sat for their exam in government at the end of the semester, they evidently surprised some of the readers with their ability to bring a strong historical perspective to the way they framed and defended their views on the exam questions. They were asked to describe the advantages and disadvantages for various groups in the city of the bill now before the legislature to convert from the current strong mayor form of local government to a city manager form.

Most of these students did very well on the local government part of the state exams the next year even though some of the questions on the exam were on subjects they had not studied. With their strong historical perspective and firm understanding of the dynamics of city government and politics, they could figure out what kinds of information they needed to answer the exam questions. They picked out the relevant facts very quickly from the data the examiners had supplied for the students. Because their analytical skills were pretty sharp they could sift through and interpret the information to come to a defensible—and often rather original—answer to the exam questions.

What was really exciting to these youngsters' point of view was what happened this morning when the political columnist in the major daily paper came over for a seminar. They were evidently able to convince him that he had misunderstood the real nature of a key issue in the recent election, and he had gone off saying that he was going to write a column on that point that would acknowledge their contribution. They could not wait until the column appeared in the paper. One of the students said with determination that he was going to study journalism in college and become a columnist, too. Another said she would not be content with reporting on politics, but was going to study political science and become a politician herself.

We decide to visit with these youngsters' social studies teacher, Dave Oxton, in his office. A Phi Beta Kappa graduate of the University of Chicago, he is full of pride in his students. Most come, he says, from low-income families. Their parents are not well educated and few expected their children to do well in school or go to college.

Dave, who is Black, grew up in a community very like the one he now teaches in. He describes how he and two other teachers have worked with these students and their families over the past 15 years. When they started out at the school, they sought out the leaders of several community based organizations and city agencies, and put together a plan for helping the teachers in the school to see the world as the students saw it, and to help the community based organizations and city agencies coordinate their programs more closely with one another and with the school.

Eventually, the local business community was drawn in. They made it clear to the school staff and the students what skills the students needed to get entry level jobs and promised that jobs would in fact be available to those students who met the standards, and wanted to go to work right out of high school.

Three nearby colleges and one university joined in, providing college students to tutor the youngsters, advisors to help them understand what was needed to go to college, an intensive summer enrichment program to help them keep up with the school's demanding curriculum. As these youngsters began to believe in themselves and their ability to succeed academically, they found they could do as well as any students in the community. Their own success made believers out of the students in the lower schools.

One effort that made a surprisingly big difference—both for high school students and the younger students—was the program in which the older students were trained to tutor the younger ones. When many of the older youngsters discovered how superficial their knowledge was when they tried to teach something they thought they knew, they made a real effort to master the material. They developed a real pride in their ability to help the younger students and many are going on to become teachers.

All of this, says Dave, is much easier to describe than it was to do. His background, and that of his colleagues, helped a lot. Dave's degree is in history. The two other teachers with whom he has worked closely have degrees in economics and psychology. Together, they had the skills they needed to analyze what was really going on in the community and in the lives of these students and their parents. They were able to draw on their undergraduate and graduate studies to get a perspective on the problems these students faced and on the techniques that might work to address those problems that would otherwise have been very hard to come by.

We have an hour before our appointment with Maria Lopez, the Lead Teacher elected by her peers as the head of the executive committee of the school. We duck into a lab room where 10 students are working, a few alone, others in small groups. Computer work stations are scattered about. A lab technician is working with some of the students.

One small group of students is developing a strategy for their full-time, three-week project to assess the toxicity of the pollutants in an open sewer. They have to analyze the chemical and biological composition of the effluent, locate its source, and bring their results to the attention of the appropriate authorities. They are working on the project with the city's environmental agency, a local firm that specializes in the analysis of toxic materials, and their teachers of chemistry, biology, and social studies. They know that all this work is intended to help them prepare for their statewide test in science, but they know also that their social studies teacher has designed the project so they will be well prepared for that part of the social students examination that deals with students' grasp of conflicts in public policy.

Sarena Welsh, one of the students, does a computer search and comes up with some articles that might be used to build a candidate list of pollutants, and a second that lists standard computer-based analysis techniques for determining the presence of these pollutants in the effluent. Another student, Jim Howard, whose interests run more toward policy issues, searches the city data base to find the names of companies that have been cited over the last few years for violations of the state and local environmental laws. They know that their teachers can help them interpret the more technical language in these sources, but they want to go as far as they can on their own. Bill remembers that one of their instructors, who works part time at the local firm that is involved in the project, offered to loan some analysis equipment that the group can use with their school computers. He calls him to arrange for the use of the equipment next week. Sarena calls an assistant director of the environmental agency who agrees to give the team a briefing on the legal procedures involved in resolving environmental issues. Together they put together a work plan, knowing that their teachers will take it apart ruthlessly when they make their presentation in two days.

We cannot help but be impressed with the mastery of subjects displayed by these students, subjects that, until only a few years ago, were not typically taught until college or even later. What is even more impressive is that these students exhibit the healthy skepticism of inquiring minds, genuine creativity, and a real understanding of the conceptual underpinning of the subjects they have studied which they are able to apply to solving real problems.

There is half an hour before our appointment with Maria Lopez. We drop in on a class in which there is a spirited debate going on. The teachers asked the students to speculate about how Mark Twain would have written A Connecticut Yankee in King Arthur's Court *if he had written it toward the end of the 20th Century. The assignment called for some knowledge of the critical literature on the book itself, a good feel for the spirit of the times in which Mark Twain lived, and an analysis of the current American character and outlook. Each of the students has written a critical essay on the topic, and six have been selected to defend their positions before the rest of the class.*

The students know that their test in this course will be based not just on the knowledge of what others have said about the major work of literature, but also on their ability to come up with original analyses that make use of the critical methods they have studied, as well as what they know about American culture and technological development.

Sally Hubby, the teacher, majored as an undergraduate in American literature. She is supported in this course by an instructor who graduated with honors from Ball State University with a degree in American history. The instructor is working on his Master in Teaching degree at the university. This particular class is being conducted by the instructor, while the teacher works with a small group of students engaged in a special project. The two work really well together. Sally, who has an Advanced Certificate from the Board and holds down important leadership responsibilities in the school, has started to look for opportunities to involve the young instructor on several teachers' committees to give him an opportunity to take on additional responsibilities in stages.

On the way to Maria Lopez' office we pass the computer graphics lab. It is presided over by Martin Southworth, an engineer on the staff of Applied Infometrics, a local software engineering firm. Martin, we are told, is a specialist on the uses of computer based graphics and design tools. We learned that most of the students in the class are planning to go into various technical support roles in the local machine tool industry, but Martin takes particular pride in the fact that several young women in the school, after working in his lab, decided on pursuing engineering careers in college. He got them hooked on design work and then worked with the Lead Teachers in the math and science areas to make the courses in that area build on their enthusiasm for design.

The conversation with the chair of the executive committee gets off to a fast start. A question about the goals of the school produces an animated monologue that lasts almost half an hour. Maria Lopez describes how the professional teachers in the schools met with the parents over six months to come to an understanding about what they wanted for their children, how they then discussed state and local standards and objectives, and then came up with a plan for their school.

It was a tricky process. The teachers' plan had to address the state and local objectives for these students, and take into account what the parents wanted as well. But in the end, the objectives had to reflect what the teachers themselves thought they could and should accomplish for the students. If they set the objectives too low, they might be easily accomplished, but the teachers' bonuses would be commensurately low. Achievement of ambitious objectives would bring substantial rewards under their bonus plan, but none at all if they were not met. After long discussions with the district administrators, some objectives were set lower than the district had in mind, but others were set higher. Needless to say, the teachers were very interested in the year-end results that would be made public four weeks after the end of the spring term.

Other districts and other states, she said, used different methods to provide incentives to teachers for producing real gains for students. This method had been worked out through a process in which the teachers had been fully involved and with which they were comfortable, and that had produced real commitment on their part to the system. But it would not work at all, she observed, were it not for the fact that the teachers had the resources they need to provide an effective instructional environment for the students and the freedom to decide how those resources were used.

We have to break off the conversation to go to the weekly teachers' meeting.

The teachers' committee working on restructuring the school day gives a progress report. The Lead Teacher who chairs the committee, one of the most respected teachers in the school, begins by reminding everyone that the committee was created because the teachers needed more time to coach individual students, and thought too much time was being spent in lecture style classes. The committee lays out an approach that relies more heavily on the use of small seminar sessions run by instructors whose work is supervised by the professional teachers, freeing teachers for more time to work with individual students. The meeting gives its approval to the general approach, points out some problems, and sets a date for the next report.

Members of another committee bring in a plan for introducing advanced mathematics concepts at an earlier level than they now appear in the curriculum. They have been following a debate about the evolving techniques of mathematical modeling closely and are convinced that high school students can grasp the fundamentals of these techniques if they can be taught in the context of real applications. They have been working with some local firms that use the new approaches in their business, and offer an approach to instruction that involves seminar work at the school closely integrated with field work in the firms. Their report includes an incisive analysis of the conceptual problems students typically have in grasping the techniques and the pedagogical methods that can be used to overcome them. They note in passing that some recent immigrants seem to have particular difficulty in dealing with this material. One of the Lead Teachers who has become a recognized expert in the cultural background of these immigrant children points out that the native language of these students does not include words for key concepts. He suggests some journal articles that the committee might read to help them overcome the problem.

A Lead Teacher who heads a committee attempting to develop a curriculum to stimulate creative problem-solving behavior in students reports on the success of a trial approach based on the combined efforts of a poet from the community arts center and a science teacher. The students have come to see that there are many ways to frame problems and many ways to approach the solution of those problems. Their search for right answers has yielded to the insight that intuition plays a major role in science and structure plays an equally important role in poetry. It is too early to draw firm conclusions, she says, but the first round for student scores on the new state examinations in science and English seems to indicate that this approach might pay handsome dividends. The teachers agree to extend the experiment to other areas of the curriculum.

The meeting closes with a report from the school administrator hired by the teachers' executive committee last year. She has worked up a specification for specialized testing services, based on the technical information provided by the teachers with advanced training in psychometrics. The school district central office and the local office of a national firm have both submitted bids. After a short but heated debate, the teachers decide to award the contract to the school district, based on the great improvement in the district's technical staff and their ability to respond quickly to changing requirements.

After the meeting, we get another few minutes with Maria Lopez. In response to our questions, she acknowledges that the professional teachers on her staff spend more time deciding how the school is to run than they used to. But, despite this, they have no less time to devote to instruction than before, because there are many more people around to take care of all the things which used to occupy teachers that had nothing to do with instruction.

She leans across the table to make the main point. This school, she says, could never have accomplished what it has in the last few years without the Board-certified teachers it has. Their skill, commitment and drive are the school's biggest asset. When the state revised its education code 10 years ago to focus on holding teachers accountable for student performance, leaving them free to decide how the objectives were going to be achieved, she saw an enormous improvement in the morale of her best teachers and a rededication to teaching. The reorganization of the school soon followed, creating a very flexible approach to the use of all kinds of people now available to support the professional teachers. Over the years, the Lead Teachers have worked out subtle ways of guiding the development of the school without recreating the old bureaucratic methods. There is nothing she would rather do, Maria says, than teach.

But what matters most, she says, are the students. The improvement in their performance over the years has been nothing short of spectacular. Dropouts have all but disappeared. Using the state tests as a measure, the academic skills of those not going on to college right away are nearly as strong as those of the most able students in this inner city school a decade ago. The best students are performing at a level that is close to that of the top students in the state. The pride in her voice as she says all this is unmistakable.

[From: *A Nation Prepared: Teachers for the 21st Century,* May 1986]

Preparing Professionals to Teach in Today's and Tomorrow's Schools

To prepare teachers for taking over the role of lead teacher in a high school such as the one described above, requires a teacher preparation program that is very different from what is the norm today. A number of national coalitions have taken on the task of designing up-to-date professional preparation programs, among the most prominent are the Holmes Group, the Center for Educational Renewal, and Re:Learning. These and other such design groups seem to share some fundamental objectives concerning program organization and common goals for teacher professionals.

For example, they believe that teacher preparation can best take place within or closely tied to public schools. These are often called *Professional Development Schools* or *Partner Schools,* and they serve to integrate teaching and administrative practices with professional preparation of new teachers and administrators, continual education for experienced educators, and school-based research for university professors and school practitioners.

They believe that teachers need to be prepared to take on leadership roles in managing the school, and in managing the instructors, trainees, and aids who work with them in the classroom. Teacher professionals need to be prepared to work in schools that are designed as "communities of learning" which actively involve children in realistic, project-based learning that includes seeking information and resources from the local community and the global community. These communities of learning may also include a wide range of age groups from toddlers to seniors, as well as a range of guest experts that extend from bricklayers to physicists.

Teacher professionals must acquire a high level of knowledge in the subject matter they will be teaching, and in instructional methodology appropriate for schools of the 21st century. They must know how to design and teach interdisciplinary curricula and to work collaboratively with colleagues to implement these curricula. Teacher professionals must also be highly capable of responding to the needs of diverse learners, and integrating them into the real work of the classroom. And they must personally model inquiry-based learning, critical thinking, use of technology tools, and other such approaches highly valued by educators today.

Using guidelines and models offered by the leading experts in professional preparation programs, individual colleges of education still need to take on the task of redesigning their professional development programs in order to prepare teachers and school administrators for the schools of the 21st century.

The University of Washington College of Education, for example, recently spent two years designing a new preparation program for elementary and secondary teachers. The guiding assumptions and program principles are presented below.

Guiding Assumptions and Program Principles

- The process of educating teachers for a democratic and inclusive society implies the responsibility for ensuring that our graduates hold high standards for themselves as teachers and for their students as learners. We are committed to the preparation of ethical, caring teachers who understand and accept their responsibility to educate all students and to believe in each student's ability to learn and grow.
- The process of educating teachers must include both academic preparation grounded in the best available research, theory, and practice, and the practical knowledge and skill gained only by working in actual schools and classrooms with experienced educators. Therefore, teacher preparation must involve collaboration between the two sites of the university and the school. While there may always be a tension between these two sites for teacher preparation, we must work to make this a productive tension for prospective teachers.
- As our society grows increasingly diverse, we must prepare teachers to work effectively with a diverse student population. The entire program must emphasize the needs of diverse learners and help prospective teachers acquire the knowledge and skills to work with all students. Because of the focus on diversity, pedagogical issues

related to culture, ethnicity, language, race, social class, exceptionalities, and gender must be integrated across the curriculum.

- The process of educating teachers must take into consideration the prior knowledge, experiences, and beliefs of prospective teachers, just as we want our graduates to take seriously the prior knowledge and experiences their students bring with them to the classroom. Early experiences in the teacher education program should help students articulate and reflect upon their prior conceptions of teaching, learning, students, subject matter, and schools and examine the implications of these assumptions.
- Modeling is an essential part of the process of educating teachers. Teachers in the teacher education program must model the characteristics of effective and caring teachers in their relationships with students. Teachers must model respect for diversity, high academic standards, teaching excellence, collaboration and cooperation, reflection and continuing professional development, fair evaluation practices, adaptation of curriculum and instruction for diverse learners, and strong, school-community linkages.
- Classroom management is a primary concern of prospective teachers. Yet, issues of classroom management are not easily detachable from issues about the purposes of schools, ethics, learning and instruction, cultural differences, and adolescent development. Therefore, there must be multiple and repeated opportunities across curricular blocks to investigate and reflect upon strategies used in schools to create positive learning environments for students and to respond to student misbehavior. Learning about classroom management must take place both in field experiences and in university coursework.
- Reasonable people disagree about the nature of "effective" teaching. While we want the program to be conceptually coherent with regard to issues involved with teaching and learning, we cannot expect that all instructors who teach in the program will agree on significant issues. However, students should not be left to make sense of contradictory information on their own. Instructors must acknowledge and discuss contrasting or conflicting theoretical frameworks and their implications for classroom teaching. Reflective seminars also offer an opportunity to sort out and discuss contrasting theories.
- Research universities hold research as a primary mission, in addition to teaching. For this reason, a teacher education program housed within a research university must include an emphasis on current research and must be connected with the research programs of faculty and doctoral students. Prospective students, as well as coop-

erating schools and departments, must understand the research mission of the College of Education and should be encouraged to work with faculty and doctoral students in developing research questions and in conducting studies.

These guiding assumptions and principles provide the frameworks for more specific objectives, including the following:

- All teachers need a firm understanding of subject matter, pedagogy, the ways the subject matter influences teaching, and the social contexts of teaching. These elements are integrated throughout the program.
- Issues of classroom management, assessment, technology, motivation, and lesson planning are best taught within the context of subject matter instruction and field experiences.
- Multicultural issues and an understanding of the needs of all elementary/secondary students should be addressed through the content blocks, field experiences, and reflective seminars.
- Teachers should be reflective practitioners, reflecting on their own learning and that of their students. They should engage in problem-solving and professional exploration as they continually refine their abilities as educators. Reflective seminars provide the time and support that is needed for teacher interns to develop in these areas.
- Coursework and reflective seminars must provide an environment which encourages teacher interns to integrate what they read, hear, and observe. This approach provides models for interns which will enable them to provide such opportunities to their future students.
- There should be coordination and coherence across course blocks and between coursework and field experiences. Tensions between theory and practice should be minimized by coordination between field and university, and by direct discussion of these issues in professional reflective seminars with teacher interns, supervisors, and cooperating teachers.
- Collaboration is an essential component of an effective program and a characteristic of an effective professional. It begins with the collaboration between schools and the university and is continued in the collaboration inherent in teaching in an integrated program. It should be evident in the collaboration among teacher interns and among the diverse professionals who work with children in schools. This emphasis on collaboration reflects the changing contexts of teaching, in which teachers are increasingly asked to work with special educators, parents, and health and social service professionals to meet the needs of all students.

- Teacher interns must be placed in exemplary sites, where educators are interested in professional development and mentoring of emerging teachers.
- Teacher interns need experiences working with diverse students and working in different school contexts. They should participate in field placements which provide them with experiences at both primary and intermediate grades, and in urban and suburban settings.
- Supervision of teacher interns in the field should be a shared responsibility among university supervisors, site supervisors, and cooperating teachers. Supervisors must be knowledgeable about content studied in the course blocks.
- Evaluation should be a shared responsibility, with input from course instructors, site supervisors, university supervisors, cooperating teachers, and the teacher interns themselves. The evaluation should be consistent with coursework and best practice.

These principles are integrated into a program that is more interdisciplinary in nature, closely linked with practice, involves practitioners in the teaching, and emphasizes reflection on the teaching/learning process. Emphasis is on the development of reflective practitioners who are able to create a knowledge base for teaching.

Integration of Technology in a Restructured Teacher Education Program

Integration of technology in any restructured approach to teacher education involves consistent modeling of effective uses of technology in the classroom and in the curriculum. Instruction must demonstrate appropriate uses of a variety of technology tools for both teaching and learning.

Technology needs to be readily accessible for prospective teachers to learn to use it in ways that are directly related to both teaching and learning situations. The key here is for program instructors to model appropriate technology use in restructured classrooms and curricula, and for prospective teachers to have frequent opportunities to practice using technologies as learning tools and also as teaching tools.

Continuing Education for Working Professionals

Although inservice staff development is now clearly recognized as a critical need in most school districts—training in new instructional approaches, use of technology, and school management skills, for instance—the current paucity of funding for public school education prohibits any significant increase in staff development programs. Districts and states are developing ambitious designs for restructuring their schools, but there is little money available to help teachers learn to update their instructional practices to fit with these totally new learning goals and instructional approaches.

The alternative, and what seems to be happening at a grass roots level, is that a growing number of teachers are picking up new instructional approaches from their colleagues, reading books such as this, taking evening and summer courses from other educational institutions, and inventing their own new teaching strategies. Over the past decade, more and more innovative and forward-thinking teachers have adopted the notion of autonomous, life-long learning and applied it to their own professional development. The result is that a growing, perhaps nearly a critical mass of educators are now experimenting with and/or practicing new learning goals and instructional approaches similar to the ones advocated in this book.

DECENTRALIZATION / SITE-BASED MANAGEMENT

Public education in the United States is managed by individual states. It is their responsibility to determine how to run their educational systems, including how much control the state government has over the learning goals, curriculum, organization, and financing of local districts and schools. In some states, the government maintains tight control over these areas, and others leave curriculum and management up to the districts. School districts also vary according to how much central control they wield over individual schools. The traditional model has been quite centralized, with district offices controlling curriculum, hiring, purchasing of textbooks, school budgets, and school management.

Currently, the trend is toward greater control at the school-building level, popularly termed *site-based management*. The idea is that teachers, principals, and parents will be happier and more productive if they have greater control over making decisions concerning their own school. The concerns and conflicts now lie in determining how much control, and what kinds of control should the schools have. Should they be totally self-governing, with control over their own learning goals, curriculum, standards and assessments, instructional approaches, textbooks, budgets, hiring and firing, organization and management style, and so forth. Or, should the district/state maintain control over learning goals, standards and assessments, and curriculum, but leave the rest, including managing the school and its budget, up to the school?

States and districts that are experimenting with more decentralized management plans are now discovering the advantages, disadvantages, and implementation problems associated with transferring authority and responsibility to diverse constituencies, and especially those with little or no experience in managing themselves. (Chapter 10 gives some examples of school, district, and state-level implementation processes.)

At the national level, countries such as England and New Zealand have initiated reform policies in which greater authority has been awarded to individual schools. England, for example, maintains national control over the school curriculum as well as standards and assessments. However, individual schools now have the authority (and responsibility) to manage funds for salaries, building costs, inservice activities, and so forth. Funds are allocated to schools according to the age and number of students in the school. These funds are then managed by the school's governors and headteacher.

New Zealand's decentralization plan gives schools the authority for full decision-making and management of such areas as: curriculum management, financial management, personnel management, school evaluation and review, parental and community involvement, and school improvement. The school is responsible for staff appointments, teacher supervision, and building maintenance. Each school develops a charter with considerable community consultation. A school sets its own local goals and objectives within overall national curriculum guidelines. The school develops and is responsible for meeting the responsibilities defined in a contract between the community, the institution, and the national minister of education.

According to research completed after the first year of New Zealand's decentralized plan, the change was too rapid. Principals and school management teams were suffering from a flood of paperwork, and the amount of learning required to assume these new roles and responsibilities was too much for many participants. But then, who could expect that such monumental changes could be accomplished easily or effortlessly within one year. The plan deserves careful observation of its implementation over a greater period of time.

Several states in the United States have adopted ambitious reform plans that give varying degrees of self-governing authority to schools. Washington State, for instance, has established state-level learning goals, and is in the process of establishing standards and assessment measures. Schools will be held accountable for students' progress and a system of rewards and punishments will be implemented. After using a state-level formula for allotting funds to districts and schools, the state encourages districts to allow individual schools to be self-managed in terms of deciding how to design and implement the state's learning goals, standards, and assessments, as well as manage building funds.

This design retains centralized state power for determining most of the important educational decisions, such as establishing learning goals, standards, and assessments. Designing specific curricula to implement these goals, and managing funds and personnel are about what's left for the districts and schools to control. Since the design and implementation of this plan will continue through the decade, its effectiveness will be determined later.

Some school districts are designing their own plans for restructuring that include delegating decision-making power to individual schools. Chicago, for example, has given complete budgetary control to the schools. Through local school committees, parents, teachers, and principals have control over budget and personnel decisions. The central district office has cut 1,000 of its positions in two years. The short-term effects of these changes have caused some unintended results, however, namely that student achievement scores have gone down each year for the past four years.

The Dade County schools in Florida tried a similar plan for granting decision-making authority to schools. In addition to management of finances and personnel, this plan gave schools power to reform their own curricula. However, after four years, administrators noted that student achievement was not improving and that site-based management had focused on the work environment for teachers, rather than on curriculum reform. Consequently, the district decided to centralize all curriculum functions.

Examples of problems with implementing site-based management plans abound. However, many of these problems arise and are reported during the school's transition period from no power to considerable power. It is not surprising that such a transition process is not easy. Few teachers have had any preparation for taking over school management, parents are not accustomed to being asked for their opinions or being included in the decision-making process, and school administrators are not used to giving up their traditional decision-making authority. It's no wonder that problems arise during the transition. Before hasty judgment is passed in favor of giving up site-based management and recentralizing power to the district office, these plans need a good deal more time to work out the problems and revise and refine their management designs. Districts also need to realize that individuals involved in management need opportunities to acquire the appropriate skills. It is also critical to remember that the school, whether managed at the district level or at the local site, cannot control all the conditions that influence a student's success in learning. If students are to improve their academic and social skills, the community must be responsible.

The advantage of site-based management for schools that want to move ahead with technology infusion is that they can do it more rapidly with less interference from district bureaucratic procedures. However, the disadvantage is that because technology infusion costs so much money, it typically requires full district support to raise and allocate funds for purchasing equipment and providing staff development for learning to use the technology.

SCHOOL CHOICE

The school choice movement involves allowing parents to freely choose which school they want their children to attend. Variations to the movement range from allowing parents to choose any public school within their local school district, to permitting them to attend a school in another district, to providing them with tuition vouchers to enable them to choose either a public or private school.

The theory behind the choice movement is that the public school system is so bad that it should be transformed into a private, market-driven system. The belief is that government-run programs are hopelessly inefficient and produce inferior quality products, and that private, market-driven businesses are more efficient and produce better results.

Advocates of school choice believe that if we adopt a market-driven educational system, good schools will thrive, bureaucracies will diminish, and bad schools will either improve or be pushed out by the forces of the free market. Opponents of school choice contend that the long-cherished idea of offering every child equal access to high-quality public education will be seriously threatened if schools become competitive, for-profit businesses rather public service institutions. They prefer to address the public school system's problems by restructuring the system from within. Those in the middle are willing to experiment with innovative choice programs at a local level. They want to examine the relative successes that districts and states have in their efforts, and observe what happens to the private enterprises that already exist (e.g., Edison Project and Educational Alternatives) over the next few years.

Professor James W. Guthrie (1992), of the Graduate School of Education at University of California at Berkeley, has thought deeply about school choice and suggested in a forum that certain criteria must be met before choice can become a viable option:

- Common standards: There needs to be some clarification of what schools are expected to accomplish. Schools that accept vouchers must be accountable to some public agency at the local, state, or national level.

- Adequate information: Parents must be provided with sufficient information for making informed choices.
- Fair admissions: There cannot be racial, religious, or former-behavior qualifications for admission to schools that accept public funds.
- Regulations: Both public and private schools must play by the same rules.
- Transportation: There's no real choice unless transportation is provided within a reasonable geographic area.
- Fair voucher plan: A voucher plan should provide incentives for racial and socioeconomic integration (e.g., schools would reserve a certain percentage of places for low-income students).
- Handicapped students: Schools must not be permitted to exclude handicapped students.
- Tuition restrictions: Schools accepting vouchers must not be able to increase tuition above the amount of the voucher unless tuition is based on the family's ability to pay.

Another choice expert, Professor Willis Hawley, at Vanderbilt University's Peabody College, pointed out in the same forum that those who support school choice hold certain assumptions that simply are not true. For example, many believe that private schools outperform public schools, that private schools are more innovative, that a market for education would function like the market for cars and breakfast cereals, that sufficient entrepreneurs would jump into the education market, that private school tuitions would not rise, and that people of different social classes would be equally effective customers. According to Hawley, none of these assumptions are true. He believes that a better choice is to reform the public school system that we already have.

Other bits of information collected by educational researchers who follow the choice movement include the fact that magnet schools—free choice schools that have been specifically designed to attract parents through special programs, the promise of integration, and other incentives—are selected by parents for one primary reason . . . location. Another interesting note is that one major company that has been in the privatized "public" school business for five years (Educational Alternatives, Inc.) has not yet made a profit.

Why are parochial schools successful, one might ask? The answer, according to Guthrie, is that they can demand a considerable amount of contributed time from parents, they hold a large number of fund-raising activities, they receive services from religious orders, they run large class sizes, and most importantly, they are not required by law to take care of disabled children and have few minority programs.

In 1992, the Carnegie Foundation for the Advancement of Teaching completed a one-year study on school choice, revealing that the claims about the benefits of school choice greatly outnumber the evidence. According to the report, most public school parents have little desire for such a system. Indeed, the push for choice is coming more from politicians than from parents. The study reported that in states where school choice has been adopted, fewer than 2 percent of eligible parents participate in the programs. Parents who do transfer their children to another school do so mostly for non-academic reasons. More than half of the respondents said that the best way to improve public education is to strengthen all neighborhood schools by giving them the resources needed to achieve excellence. Only 15 percent believe that the best way to improve schools is by letting them compete for students. In response to other studies (often funded by private school organizations) that show more favorable parental attitudes toward school choice, the Carnegie study found that public opinion polls about choice are notoriously tricky, and that respondents' answers vary depending on how the questions are worded.

Well-known educator and writer, Jonathan Kozol, is adamantly opposed to public-private school choice. He says that choice enthusiasts believe that if people can choose, everybody will get the school they want. Kozol retorts that this simply isn't so. He explains that many inner city parents are illiterate and have no way of learning about the choices available to them. Consequently, what almost always happens is that children of the rich and well-educated get the best schools. Poor kids and those with poorly-educated parents end up in schools that no one chooses except by default. And, what happens when cross-district choice programs are established to encourage integration between poor cities and wealthy suburbs? Many kids transfer from poor city schools to rich suburban schools, but no one from the suburbs opts to go to a poor city school. So what happens is that the poor city schools get even worse.

The voucher plan, he argues is just as ineffective. If you live in a poor city, for instance, your voucher might be for about $2,500, because that's what's spent per pupil in your district. If you live in a rich suburb, your voucher might be for $15,000 or $19,000, because that's what's spent per pupil in that district. Will a $2,500 voucher buy you a place in a private school, or even a suburban school? Kozol explains that vouchers would increase fragmentation, which is already responsible for the inequality in the public school system. Instead, he proposes that we provide equal, high quality, innovative, and humane schools for all our children. This, he believes, is the best possible solution, and the only really democratic one.

Alternative Schools Within the Public School System

"Alternative" school choices within public school districts have been around for some time, and this kind of school provides parents with an alternative to the district's typical neighborhood school. Alternative schools are usually established by a group of active parents and teachers who are not happy with the "regular" schools in the district. These schools often are designed around a particular philosophy or set of learning goals that differ from the norm. Many offer programs designed for students who have not been successful in the regular schools. Often the schools are characterized by less structure; they mix students of different ages and abilities, they do not assign grades, they build curricula and projects around students' voiced interests, and so forth. Other alternative schools are characteristically more rigorous, maintaining higher standards, more academic work, more requirements, and more competitive grading. These kinds of public school "choices" provide parents with true alternatives without destroying the democratic nature of the public school system.

One example of this system at work on a slightly larger scale is the Minnesota "Charter Schools" program that was voted into law in 1991. The law permits licensed teachers to create independent public schools under a contract with the local school board. The school board maintains control by negotiating the outcomes a charter must meet, but cannot interfere with its daily practices. The schools must meet the performance standards specified in their charters to keep their contracts. Otherwise, they are free of most other state and local regulations. Students who attend these schools bring with them the same funds that would be allotted for them in their home schools.

The initial years of the program, however, reveal that the charter schools tend to serve a special population of students that has not been well served by the public school system. One school, for instance, enrolls students who are not enrolled in any other educational program—essentially students who dropped out or were otherwise alienated by the system. Another charter school is designed to serve the district's deaf students. One of the reasons for this result is that the law as originally passed, gives school boards sole authority to grant charters, with no appeal for those charters that are rejected. Further, teachers in charter schools cannot be part of the district's collective bargaining unit.

These and other kinds of problems still need to be sorted out for the charter schools program to last. However, based on the sound idea of providing alternative choices within the public school system, several other states have adopted similar laws, including California, Connecticut, Florida, and Wisconsin, as well as many individual school districts within other states.

The most shining example of alternative public school choices is probably East Harlem. The movement there began back in the late 1960s when parents and teachers fought the teachers' union and education bureaucracy for greater control over schools. By the early 1970s, East Harlem had a new school board and an activist superintendent who managed to recruit top-notch educators to take a risk by joining—and having an opportunity to totally redesign—East Harlem's schools.

Several alternative schools emerged, including a school for the performing arts, another for students who were essentially rejected by other schools, and another that featured less structure and more creative inquiry. Over the next decade many new schools were established with distinctive identities: a school of science and humanities, a school for gifted children, a school for young children with troubled histories, a school for environmental science, a maritime school, a career academy, and so forth.

By 1982, there were 22 alternative schools. The district attracted so much attention it was able to procure ample federal funds from various agencies and foundations. This attention also caused the schools to be greatly sought after by families outside the district and consequently, admission to the most highly regarded schools became highly competitive. Thus, the free-choice schools ended up choosing the students rather than the parents and children choosing the schools.

Still, the model of providing parents with alternative public schools that feature distinctly different educational philosophies and goals, is one that is certainly worthy of serious consideration. The goal in this case would also have to be that all the available choices (not just the showcase alternative schools) offer high-quality education, enabling all children to get a good education regardless of what school they end up attending.

Technology Integration and School Choice

As previously mentioned in the site-based management section, the advantage of empowering schools to operate independently is that if the local support for technology is strong, a school can move more rapidly toward complete technology integration. However, since funding for technology is often a big issue for schools, it may be more difficult for an individual school to acquire funds to purchase technology and pay for staff development so that teachers can learn to use it and to integrate it into their curricula.

ABILITY GROUPING / TRACKING

Ability grouping or "tracking" is the common practice of sorting students by ability, achievement, and/or future potential. Tracked students are often sorted into advanced, standard, and slow classes; academic, general, and vocational programs. In some schools, students are sorted separately for different subject areas, such that an individual may be placed in advanced English and standard math, and the sorting may change from year to year. In other schools, students are sorted into academic/general/vocational programs that determine the level of all their classes, and the initial placement is maintained throughout high school.

Sorting is commonly done by evaluating each student's standardized test scores to determine placement. Often teachers' recommendations are also used to make placement decisions, and in some cases special tests help determine placement (e.g., essay samples for English and problem-solving and/or computational exercises for math).

Once students are sorted into these groups/tracks, the results become public, and inadvertently students are labeled in the eyes of their peers and teachers. The groups are not equally valued in the school; teachers tend to view them differently and teach them differently. Teachers' and students' expectations are different for each group and over time, students tend to live up to the expectations of them within their assigned group.

Why do schools track/group students? They believe it is in the best interests of the students and also because it is a good deal easier for teachers to teach and manage (at least using traditional methods) homogeneous groups.

However accumulated research over time has shown that tracking/ability grouping is *not* in the best interests of children. Professor Jeannie Oakes, at the University of Colorado, who has spent years examining the effects of tracking, reports in her book, *Keeping Track: How Schools Structure Inequality,* several commonly held assumptions about tracking that have clearly been proven wrong. Those assumptions are:

- Bright students will be held back if placed in mixed groups.

  Research shows this is not true. No group of students has been found to benefit consistently from being in a homogeneous group.
- Slower students develop more positive attitudes about themselves and school when they are not placed in groups with others who are far more capable.

  Research shows that students placed in average and low-track classes do *not* develop positive attitudes. The tracking process fosters lowered self-esteem among these students. Students placed in lower classes are usually seen by teachers and students as dumb, and students in low-tracks tend to develop lower aspirations. Further, student behaviors have been found to be influenced by track placement. Low-track students participate less in extra-curricular activities, exhibit more misconduct in school, and are involved more often in delinquent behavior outside of school. Low-track students are more alienated from school and have higher drop-out rates.

- The placement process used to sort students is accurate and fair in its assessment of past achievements and native abilities. The most common criteria for determining placement are standardized tests, teacher and counselor recommendations (including grades), and students and parental choice. However . . .

  Standardized tests tend to measure a student's general ability rather than achievement in school. It has also been shown that current standardized tests favor middle-class white children and that lower-class minority children are less likely to do well because of their language and experience differences.

  Teacher and counselor recommendations are also biased. Oakes reported that it is unlikely that these educators—who often have over 150 students to recommend (many more for counselors)—can make fair decisions for all students. At least one study has indicated that students are often placed into groups on the basis of educators' assessment of their language, dress, and behavior, as well as their test-determined academic potential.

  Parent choice is typically heavily influenced by the school guidance process. Students and parents are given the student's test scores and often made aware of the teachers' or counselor's recommendation. Confronted with this information, many parents and students feel powerless to fight the will of the school and the tests.

- It is easier for teachers to address individual needs in homogeneous groups than in extremely diverse groups.

  This assumption may well be true, if one assumes that the only, or the best way to teach students is through the traditional lecture/whole class methods of "delivering" information to all students, and then expecting them to recite it back in tests and essays. Oakes argued that even if tracking students makes the teacher's work easier, it is not worth the educational and social price we pay for it.

Educators should be aware that there are other, more effective methods of teaching any groups of students. Indeed, many of the instructional approaches advocated in this book are far more appropriate to use with diverse groups of students than the old methods.

Another thing to keep in mind when trying to imagine dealing with untracked, diverse groups of children is that modern technology can be a marvelous aid in dealing with very different abilities, achievement levels, rates-of learning, learning styles, and so forth. Chapter 3 illustrates characteristics of computer and video technologies that can help very different students learn effectively while working in the same classroom. These characteristics include the computer's ability to tutor and provide exercises for students at their individual levels and rates of progress. The computer's capacity to provide immediate feedback, encouragement, and privacy also helps foster the learner's self-esteem and promotes greater motivation and progress. If video is added to this classroom environment, students have an even broader set of resources for their diverse learning styles. Students who learn more effectively from visual information and audio information can experience greater academic success when these tools are used.

Further, when teachers involve diverse student groups in project work, there are a lot more jobs to do that attract different skills and interests when technology-based resources are available to the groups. Oftentimes, students who are not strong readers or writers, turn out to be talented computer users, problem-solvers, or artists, and can thus be valuable contributors to the group. Teachers who work effectively with diverse students often design group projects that involve a broad range of tasks that call upon different kinds of skills and interests. This kind of activity shifts the focus from achieving excellence only through traditional academic skills, and offers those students who are often bright, but with less academic experience, opportunities to demonstrate their abilities in other areas. Such opportunities help these students build self-esteem, and also help their peers break stereotypical attitudes while developing respect for their strengths. Over time, the students with less academic experience will have built enough self-confidence and determination to meet the challenge of improving their academic skills, and they will have earned the respect of their peers—who can also be effective tutors.

MULTICULTURAL EDUCATION

Prior to the 1960s, most immigrants to the United States came from European countries. Since then, the majority of immigrants have come from Asia, Hispanic countries, and the Caribbean. Demographers calculate that by the year 2050, the U.S. population will be 60 percent non-white. Traditionally, our country has placed great value on diversity, claiming that the wide range of experiences, skills, knowledge, and values these different groups bring, contributes greatly to our nation's strength and rich national culture.

However, this diversity, especially its rapid growth in the past ten years, presents an extreme challenge to the nation and its schools.

Americans need to exercise greater tolerance, understanding, and appreciation of different cultures, and educators need to learn how to deal with the influx of students who do not know the language, customs, behavior patterns, and mores of U.S. culture. Right now, there is a tremendous need for multicultural education in the schools.

What is multicultural education? Many educators interpret it to mean simply teaching students about different minority groups, celebrating minority heroes, participating in Black History Month, singing Hanukkah songs at Christmastime, recognizing the Chinese New Year, Cinco de Mayo, and so forth. Some teach multiculturism through their social studies curriculum by covering international issues and perspectives, rather than teaching it as a separate curriculum focused on ethnic, racial, and other cultural groups in this country. Unfortunately, few teachers truly integrate multicultural education into their daily activities, pointing out and discussing differences as they arise in class (e.g., students' ways of gesturing, addressing the teacher or another student; by celebrating students' birthdays according to their cultural traditions; playing different country's traditional sports in P.E. or during recess).

The major challenge of multicultural education is helping educators and students learn to deal with a wide diversity of language backgrounds, academic skills and abilities, attitudes about education, study habits, ability to concentrate, work styles, support from home, ability to get along with classmates, and so forth. Educators today are constantly trying to figure out how to cope with this extreme level of diversity, and trying to design curriculum and instructional approaches that will engage all these children, challenge them at their own levels, and help them experience academic growth and success. It is a major challenge, and one that leads some educators to experiment with restructuring their curriculum and instructional approaches in ways that are similar to the ones suggested in this book.

For instance, these innovative teachers often find that well-structured groupwork can help students with diverse interests and skills learn more effectively than when the class is taught as one group. They find that supporting their lessons with ample visual information helps students from different language and cultural backgrounds learn more effectively. Computer technology can also play a major role in providing multicultural education. While textbook companies struggle to produce thicker texts with a wider range of content and perspectives as well original-source examples of these perspectives, computer technology already has the capacity to store huge amounts of this kind of information and make it available to students at the appropriate moment. Another example is the use of telecommunications networks to connect students from affluent suburban and poor inner-city schools, and get them talking to one another. School children can also communicate with peers from Asian, Hispanic, and European countries in an effort to enrich their knowledge and widen their perspectives, and also to gain greater respect and understanding of other people's points of view.

The goal here is for teachers to strive for both academic excellence and a greater understanding/appreciation of other cultures in their multicultural education programs, not just the latter. In the future, classrooms will grow even more academically and culturally diverse, and it's critical that we develop appropriate curricula and instructional approaches to deal with student differences—not by separating them into little homogeneous learning ghettos—but by helping them learn together, by sharing their differences, their knowledge, special talents, and personal interests.

REFERENCES

"A Matter of Choice: The Debate Over Schools and the Marketplace." A Special Report published by Education *Week.,* December 6, 1992.

Carnegie Foundation Task Force on Teaching as a Profession. (1986). *A Nation Prepared: Teachers for the 21st Century.* The Report of the Task Force on Teaching as a Profession, Carnegie Foundation for the Advancement of Teaching.

Knapp, Linda. (1992). *Standards and Assessments.* A report prepared for the Puget Sound Educational Consortium, University of Washington, Seattle, WA.

Oakes, Jeannie (1985). Keeping *Track: How Schools Structure Inequality.* New Haven: Yale University Press.

12

THE PROCESS OF CHANGE

This chapter reflects on the theory and practice presented in the first three chapters and the subsequent applications of those approaches in the implementation chapters. It reports research on teachers who work in technology-rich classrooms, and chronicles the process they experience while attempting to change their own practices. The chapter also offers some insights, perspectives, and suggestions for successful long-term change.

TEACHING AND LEARNING IN RESTRUCTURED, TECHNOLOGY-RICH CLASSROOMS

Changing the way one teaches is a challenge. Over the years most of us become comfortable with a certain style of managing instruction and students. Each new group of students influences the way we teach, but generally this year's classroom feels and looks a lot like last year's. When we listen to what students say about teachers, we hear comments like "She makes you work with other kids," "He uses a lot of films," "You have to write a lot in her class," and, "You get to use computers in his class." Even though the students don't mention the names of the teachers, it's possible to know who they are because teachers have reputations that characterize their teaching. As we gain more experience, our teaching style continues to slowly evolve. Our core teaching style, however, is based on the way we were taught, a strong belief in helping students learn, and by what is acceptable practice in the building. But, teaching style does change. A number of factors influence this evolution. Key among these are:

- Observing effective teaching strategies being used by other teachers
- Incorporating new instructional approaches that become popular among teachers
- Applying what is learned from continuing professional studies
- Utilizing new technologies

Most teachers use a variation of the teacher-centered model of instruction (See Chapter 2) in which the emphasis is on assisting students to learn a body of knowledge and skills. This approach is comfortable because there is a great deal of predictability—it gives teachers control of the process, and allows them to plan ahead, test student achievement, and cover a breadth of content.

On the other hand, some teachers use discovery modes of instruction that are more process-oriented, and place the responsibility for learning more on the student. These experiences help students acquire knowledge by becoming deeply involved in manipulating information and thinking about it—through inquiry, problem-solving, critical thinking, and communication processes—and then integrating what they have learned into their own knowledge base. A number of teachers currently use these restructured approaches to teaching and learning—some with the added benefit of technology, and others without. The chapters in Part II focus on ways of shifting one's instructional approach toward this style of teaching and learning.

In a restructured classroom there is a much greater emphasis on the individual student, autonomous learning, and the exploration of real-life problems and issues. This makes it much more difficult for teachers to maintain control of what happens in the classroom because students are busy doing research, discussing issues with classmates, going to the library, and working with technology.

How then does the teacher "teach" the students anything? In fact, the teacher's role changes from one who delivers information to one who assists students in their quest for information and helps them learn to process the information they acquire. The teacher's role is to help students become independent learners, and to think about what they learn in rational ways. Restructured classrooms are a more accurate mirror of real-life working environments in which people work on projects, collaborate with colleagues, assume responsibility for products, and use a variety of technology tools.

What We Have Learned about the Change Process

Using technology effectively can help teachers restructure their classrooms and move from a teacher-centered lecture approach to a more learner-centered inquiry approach. As Sheingold and Hadley (1990) noted, when technology is used extensively in the learning process, the teacher begins to expect more of students, present more complex material, and assume a greater role as learning coach.

Technology also helps students become more independent learners and develop products that are more sophisticated. It helps facilitate collaborative group work, provides access to a vast amount of information for inquiry (in audio, visual, and textual forms), provides access to alternative perspectives for analysis and critical thinking, and offers a variety of ways for learners to communicate their new understandings. Teachers also adopt technology because it offers them powerful instructional tools. Not only can they use a computer as an "electronic blackboard" when they want to provide information for students, they can also use it to model learning skills they are trying to teach students, such as how to search for information from a variety of sources, how to brainstorm and draft an essay, and how to edit and revise essay drafts. (See Chapter 2 for a more detailed description of how technology can improve teaching and learning.)

In sum, teachers choose to use technology because they can employ it to make their own teaching more effective and because they can offer students a variety of extremely useful learning tools. This is what entices many teachers to spend the time to learn how to use and integrate technology into their curricula and their instructional practices.

What happens to teachers, students, and classrooms once major steps have been taken? One research study (Dwyer, Ringstaff, & Sandholtz, 1990a, 1990b) examined the process of change over a four-year period. The results of this study are consistent with comments of many other teachers concerning their experiences in learning to use technology and integrating it into their curriculum and instructional practices.

The research report emphasized that most teachers bring to the classroom a common set of beliefs about schooling, built upon years of participating in the traditional system as former students and then as teachers. It is this long-standing view of schooling—based on the lecture, recitation, and seatwork model of instruction—that persists despite the best efforts of activists in the school restructuring movement. Consequently, when teachers move into high-technology classrooms with ambitious goals of restructuring, they still experience intense inner conflict as they explore alternative approaches which sharply contrast their beliefs about classroom management, curriculum, and instruction.

The research findings revealed that teachers spent the first year learning to use the technology and then figuring out how to make it fit into their traditional curricula and instructional approaches. By the end of the first year, teachers reported that students' motivation and self-esteem had improved and their standardized test scores had remained stable.

During the second year, teachers discovered they could cover the traditional curriculum in less time with technology, leaving more time for critical analysis, inquiry, and problem-solving activities. (Once they had covered the standard curriculum, they were comfortable experimenting with restructuring ideas.) They reported students were doing more independent research, writing more, revising more, and ending up with better quality work. Teachers were pleased with the changes, and began experimenting with new instructional strategies as well as new curricular goals and activities.

By the third year, most teachers were experiencing a major turning point. They understood technology well enough to use it naturally as a tool to accomplish real work; they were more confident in applying more innovative approaches such as team teaching, collaborative learning, and interdisciplinary projects. Students were more actively involved in both teaching and learning the new lessons they and the teachers designed.

(Note: This study focused on classrooms that had enough computer-based technology readily available for students to use whenever they wanted. Further, the study reported that after the first group of teachers progressed through these development stages, other teachers who joined them took less time because they had abundant support from more experienced teachers and students.)

At the end of the four-year study, teachers were just entering the final development stage. They were beginning to build entirely new learning environments that utilize technology as a flexible learning tool. At that point they had come to view learning as an active, creative, and interactive process, and they saw knowledge as something learners must construct rather than receive from someone else.

(Note: Interestingly, using the technology actually helped these teachers adopt restructured beliefs and practices. Without it, they might have continued their traditional practices indefinitely.)

The teachers in this study developed technology skills, pedagogical attitudes, and behaviors at different rates, and not all the teachers chose to change their attitudes and behaviors beyond using the technology to strengthen and enrich traditional curriculum and instructional methods. Some teachers (and schools) in this study still continue to favor traditional curriculum and instructional approaches, and have developed these approaches so successfully that they've gained state and national recognition.

Furthermore, not all teachers in the study survived their experiences with technology. One teacher chronicled in the study, fought a continuous inner battle between her need for a quiet, orderly classroom and her desire to foster the more dynamic learning experiences that emerged in her high-tech classroom. The result was vacillation: at one point she would encourage collaborative learning and innovative projects, but then she would become frustrated with the commotion and switch back to a lecture and seatwork mode. Lacking support for her efforts from colleagues or family, this teacher could not resolve her inner conflict and ultimately left the high-tech classroom.

Many other teachers also experienced similar frustrations as they struggled to replace what was familiar and successful, with what was unfamiliar, but they believed was better for their students. They wondered if they were losing their authority, if student groups were wasting time, and if the students were actually learning without their lectures. Gradually, with support from colleagues, administrators, family, and friends, these teachers were able to overcome their doubts and become experts at developing more effective learning experiences for their students, and more relevant beliefs to guide further professional growth.

A second study, based on the same research data as the above study (Sandholtz, Ringstaff, & Dwyer, 1990), examined the evolution of classroom management in these high-tech classrooms. The results of this study suggest that when experienced teachers begin teaching in technology-rich classrooms, the changes the technology brings are so great that teachers re-experience the novice teacher's struggles with classroom management. Because these teachers are focused on controlling the classroom in the early stages, they have no time to develop new instructional approaches. Instructional innovation begins when teachers have mastered the management issues.

During the first year, the infusion of computers introduced a whole new realm of student misbehaviors, including copying software illegally, stealing work from others' disks, tampering with network systems, resisting transitions to non-computer activities, and so on. The technology also created physical problems in the classrooms such as window glare, chalk dust, and power outages. Frustration peaked as teachers had to deal with computer breakdowns, network jams, software incompatibilities, and distribution hassles. Since instruction was often dependent upon the technology, problems upset both daily and long-range plans. Classroom dynamics created additional problems. Many teachers were bothered by the increased noise and movement that emerged in their high-tech classrooms. Some felt threatened by the students' technology expertise and their new power to learn independently with technology.

By the second year, however, teachers had developed strategies for dealing with many of the problems. They treated misbehavior with appropriate consequences, and cheating with class discussions and grading penalties. They designed new physical arrangements to optimize classroom space and organizational systems for software and other paraphernalia. Technical problems continued, but were less disruptive, and teachers were more able to avoid them. Teachers developed expertise with the technology, resulting in greater confidence and increased tolerance of noise and movement. Students' engagement increased and discipline problems decreased.

By the third year, teachers were using technology to help manage the classroom. They used it to keep records, grade tests, develop materials, and individualize instruction. They devised ways to cover the standard curriculum faster with computers, leaving time for analytical thinking and problem-solving. They also began to employ student experts as peer teachers, and generally their teaching approach shifted from instruction-centered to learner-centered. This shift resulted in greater student interest and motivation, causing students to be more confident and competent learners.

(Note: As mentioned earlier, the teachers under study entered high-tech classrooms without mentors to help them adapt. As additional teachers entered these same classrooms in later years, their development occurred much faster, indicating that having expertise and support available makes a considerable difference in speed of development as well as success or failure.)

Moving Ahead . . . Ready, Set, Go!

As we have seen, learning to use new technology tools, and taking major steps to change one's instructional practices can be a difficult task for many teachers. However, a rapidly growing number of teachers are undaunted by the reports of those who have struggled; they are eager to try anyway, have confidence they will find the change easier, and believe it is well worth the effort. What often ignites the final fires of enthusiasm and commitment to change is when teachers see their colleagues integrating technology tools successfully, when they see students enthusiastically using them, and when they see the sophisticated products that these students create.

How do teachers who want to restructure their classrooms with technology begin the process? Here are some suggestions:

- Learn to use the technology for yourself. . . . Use computers for word processing, locating information relevant to your curriculum, communicating electronically with colleagues, conducting experiments, exploring simulations, or creating multimedia documents;

and use video equipment for making your own videos. Have fun with technology, explore its potential, and imagine how it might fit in with your learning goals and curriculum.

- Re-examine your current learning goals for students and see how they match the ones put forth in the restructured approach offered in this book. Consider revising your goals and how that will affect your curriculum and instructional practices.
- Visit as many restructured classrooms as possible, both those that include technology tools and those that do not. The point is to see how other teachers have managed to change from lecture-based instruction, to inquiry-based learning approaches that include collaborative work; interdisciplinary curricula; and projects that help students learn to seek information and think about it critically, solve real-world problems, and develop new skills and understandings.
- Read books and articles about restructuring with technology and discuss your ideas with colleagues. Take workshops and attend conferences whenever possible. Seek mentors, especially in your own school or district, if possible. Find out what resources are available through the school and/or district (e. g., what video and computer technologies are available for classroom use; does the district have a library of videos or catalogs of videos available on loan; will the district provide or pay for teachers to learn to use technology and to integrate it into their curricula).
- Begin to invent ways you can change your current instructional approaches to include new, restructured approaches. Re-design your curriculum to include new leaning goals and instructional approaches, one unit at a time. Experiment with single units for the first six months or a year before revamping a whole year's curriculum plans.
- Treat yourself to a summer vacation of playing with technology and dreaming up ways to use it with students, while you update your learning goals, curriculum, and instructional approaches. Then design new technology-rich curricula based on these goals and approaches. Whenever possible, borrow ideas and curriculum lessons that others have used successfully.

How do school principals and district superintendents who want to restructure with technology proceed?

First, provide teachers with technology tools and time to learn how to use them for personal and instructional purposes. Encourage teachers to follow the suggestions listed above and see that they get lots of support for learning how to use the technology tools. Then, provide incentives for teachers to begin integrating technology into their classrooms, and re-designing curriculum and instructional practices to incorporate restructured learning goals. Send teachers to conferences, link them to mentors, provide release time to visit restructured classrooms, and planning time to collaborate and create interdisciplinary units. Schedule staff development workshops and faculty meetings that focus on restructuring, and place considerable creative effort in helping teachers understand what students need to learn to live in the 21st century and how essential it is to re-design student learning goals, curricula, and instructional practices. Try whatever means you can devise to inspire teachers to change, and then support them well throughout the transition.

Students also need to be willing to change. Students are accustomed to being given information (by the teacher and textbook), and told what to do and how to do it. They are dependent on teachers to carefully guide their learning and make choices for them concerning how they think about new information, and how they communicate with others. Many students are not accustomed to seeking information independently, thinking about it in new and critical ways, and reporting their own thoughts about it in original formats. Nor are they accustomed to working collaboratively on projects that have meaning beyond the classroom (e.g., doing research or service projects for the community); becoming immersed in an interdisciplinary curriculum; or working in active classrooms where group discussions, independent research, construction work, and other activities might be going on at the same time.

Teachers need to help students make the transition by clarifying the new learning goals, why they are important, and how students' learning will change from absorbing information delivered in lectures and textbooks to seeking new information on their own. They need to understand the fundamental structure and purpose of the new curriculum and their new responsibilities within it. The new approach is not without structure and discipline, it is simply different and more like an adult professional working environment.

Teachers who have restructured successfully report that their students much prefer working in the new learning environment because it allows them more flexibility, more opportunities to be creative, pursue their own interests, think for themselves, work independently, or work with peers. It's much more fun for them and students also report that they learn more when they have to get the information, think about it, and communicate it to others.

Still, this process of change is not easy. Both teachers and students have to struggle to avoid falling into old habits. Motivation for change tends to go in spurts and there are bound to be times when teachers and students lack the energy to be creative or analytical. Be patient with yourselves. It takes time, and keep in mind that it gets easier the longer you do it, and that it is definitely worth the effort.

REFERENCES

Dwyer, D. C., Ringstaff, C., & Sandholtz, J. H. (1990a). *Teacher Beliefs and Practices Part I: Patterns of Change*. Cupertino, CA: Apple Classrooms of Tomorrow, Apple Computer, Inc.

Dwyer, D. C., Ringstaff, C., & Sandholtz, J. H. (1990b). *Teacher Beliefs and Practices Part II: Support for Change*. Cupertino, CA: Apple Classrooms of Tomorrow, Apple Computer, Inc.

Sandholtz, J. H., Ringstaff, C., & Dwyer, D. C. (1990). *Teaching in High-Tech Environments: Classroom Management Revisited, First-Fourth Year Findings*. Cupertino, CA: Apple Classrooms of Tomorrow, Apple Computer, Inc.

Sheingold, K. and Hadley, M. (1990). "Accomplished Teachers: Integrating Computers into Classroom Practice." Center for Technology in Education: Bank Street College of Education, September.

INDEX

Ability grouping, 210–213
Accelerated Schools Network, 175
Accountability, 19, 172, 180, 188–189
Active learning, 4, 163
African American students, 18
Alternative schools, 109, 163–164, 209–210
Alvestad, K., 17
America 2000, 180–184, 186
Anrig, Gregory R., 183–184
Arts programs
  communication through, 88–95
  critical thinking and, 143
Assessment, 12, 62–66, 179–190
  America 2000, 180–184, 186
  authentic, 63–64, 190
  in conventional versus restructured schools, 7, 189–190
  exhibitions, 64–65, 190
  high stakes, 179–180, 188
  issues concerning, 187–189
  New Standards Project, 184–187
  outcome-based education, 8, 62–63, 190
  performance-based, 63, 190
  portfolios, 65–66, 190
  state-level restructuring and, 172, 173–174
  video, 66
At-risk students, 91
Authentic assessment, 63–64, 190

Basic skills, 147–161
  in communication, 68–69
  in critical thinking, 129
  defined, 147–148
  in English as a Second Language (ESL), 156–157
  importance of teaching, 148–149
  Integrated Learning Systems (ILS) for, 149, 159–161
  in mathematics, 157–159
  in reading, 150–152
  technology and, 149–150
  in writing, 151–156
Becker, H., 15, 18
Bennett, William J., 5
Bialo, Ellen, 17, 25*n.*
Bush, George, 180, 182

Cable and satellite connections, 15, 34, 61, 62
Camcorders, 15
Carnegie Foundation for the Advancement of Teaching, 191–198, 208
Caucasian students, 18
CD-ROMs, 15, 150–151
Center for Educational Renewal, 198

Change process, 216–224
  challenges of, 216–217
  research on, 217–221
Channel One, 61, 62
Chicago, site-based management in, 205
Classroom management, 19, 20, 200, 201
  change process and, 217–221
  computers and, 24–32
  video technology and, 33–40
Classrooms
  in conventional versus restructured schools, 7
  impact of technology in, 17–20
  management of. *See* Classroom management
  organization of, 16
Clinton, Bill, 180
CNN news, 34, 38, 62
Coalition of Essential Schools, 57, 64–65, 175, 180
Cognitive psychology, 9, 10
Cohen, Elizabeth, 53–55
Collaborative groups
  in classroom, 52–56
  multimedia presentations and, 49–52
Collaborative teaching, 201
Communication, 68–96
  basic skills in, 68–69
  computers and, 27–28
  critical thinking and, 81–82
  cross-disciplinary approach to, 78–81
  importance of teaching, 69
  interactive video projects in, 86–88
  school newspapers in, 71–76
  technology in, 69–70
  through music, 93–95
  through visual arts, 88–93
  video technology and, 33–34, 76–77, 82–86
  video yearbooks in, 76–77
  writing academies in, 77–78
Communities of learning, 198
CompuServe, 30
Computer-assisted instruction. *See* Computers
Computers, 12, 15, 24–32
  communication support and, 27–28
  distance learning and, 18, 30, 58–60
  inquiry and, 28–29, 111–127
  number of, 31–32
  problem-solving skills and, 29, 99
  skill building and, 27–29, 100–101
  student attitudes toward, 25–26
  student performance and, 24–25, 26–27
  teacher's role with, 30–31
Computer software
  database, 99, 115–116, 118–120
  geometric construction tools, 106–107
  graphing tools, 105–106
  for problem solving, 100–110
  simulation, 29–30, 31–32, 103–105, 145, 159
  skill-building, 27–29, 100–101
  spreadsheets, 99, 107–109
Constructivist approach, 9–11, 112–113
Cooperative learning, 12, 26
Cotton, Kathleen, 17, 24, 25*n.*, 26
Critical thinking, 128–146
  analysis of persuasive arguments, 138
  basic skills in, 129
  communication and, 81–82
  current events in teaching, 140–142
  emotive language and, 132–135
  in English, 140–142
  importance of teaching, 129–130
  in mathematics, 142–143, 144–145
  in music, 143
  persuasive writing and, 135–138
  in science, 142, 145–146
  in social studies, 140–142
  and statistics, 144–145
  technology and, 36–37, 130–132
  television and, 36–37, 131, 138–140
  in visual arts, 143
  visual perspectives and, 145–146

Current events, in living curriculum, 140–142
Curriculum areas, 43

Dade County (Fla.) schools, 205
Darling-Hammond, Linda, 183
Databases, 27, 28
Database software, 99, 115–116, 118–120
Decentralization, 203–206
DeGrassi Junior High, 38
Designing Groupwork: Strategies for the Heterogeneous Classroom (Cohen), 53–55
Dewey, John, 4
Disadvantaged students, 182–183, 188
Discovery learning, 6
Distance learning, 18, 30, 58–60
District-level restructuring, 63, 166–171, 204, 222–223
Drill-and-practice approach, 5, 26
Dwyer, D. C., 20, 218, 220

East Harlem (N.Y.), alternative schools in, 210
Educational Alternatives, Inc., 207
Educational Television (ETV), 37–38
Effective classrooms, 12
Effective teaching, 200
Ehman, L. H., 26, 61–62
Electronic chalkboards, 31–32, 218
Electronic information resources, 30, 132
Elementary school classrooms
  critical thinking in, 138–140
  database software in, 115–116
  electronic laboratories in, 28–29, 117–118
  graphing tools for, 105–106
  inquiry in, 115–118
  Integrated Learning Systems (ILS) and, 149, 159–161
  interdisciplinary approach in, 58, 78–81, 102–103, 109–110
  Library Media Center (LMC) and, 122–124
  mathematics in, 101–102, 157–159
  problem solving in, 100–103
  reading in, 150–152
  school newspapers in, 71–74
  science in, 28–29, 115–118
  skill-building software in, 100–101
  specialized curriculum software in, 126–127
  spreadsheets in, 107–108
  video production in, 117–118
  writing instruction in, 45–46, 48, 152–156
Elmore, Richard, 5
Emotive language, 132–135
England, site-based management in, 204
English
  critical thinking in, 140–142
  multiple resources in high school, 120–121
  See also Reading; Writing
English as a Second Language (ESL), 156–157
Equity, 187–188
Exhibitions, 64–65, 190
Expectations, for schools, 3–4, 5

Facsimile machines, 12, 15
Factory model of education, 8
Florida
  district-level restructuring in, 166
  site-based management in, 205
Foxfire Teacher Outreach Network, 175
Freestyle, 34

Geometric construction tools, 106–107
Ginger, R., 4
Glenn, A. D., 26
Goodlad, John I., 3, 9
Grammar checkers, 156
Graphing tools, 105–106
Greenfield, Patricia M., 33–34, 35, 36, 37, 138–140
Guthrie, James W., 206–207

Hadley, M., 17, 19, 21, 22, 218
Hawley, Willis, 207
High school classrooms
  critical thinking in, 140–144
  English in, 120–121, 140–142
  geometric construction tools, 106–107
  graphing tools for, 106
  inquiry in, 120–121
  interactive video in, 87–88
  interdisciplinary approach in, 58, 109, 140–144
  Library Media Center (LMC) and, 124–126
  mathematics in, 142–143
  music in, 93–95, 143
  problem solving in, 103–105
  school newspapers in, 74–76
  science in, 142
  simulations in, 103–104
  social studies in, 103–104, 120–121, 140–142
  spreadsheets in, 108–109
  videotape projects in, 83–86, 140–142
  visual arts in, 89–93, 143
  in the year 2000, 191–198
High stakes assessment, 179–180, 188
Hispanic students, 18
Holmes Group, 198
Horace's School (Sizer), 64–65, 163
Hunter, B., 19

Ingels, S. J., 33
Inquiry, 6, 28–29, 111–127
  database software in, 99, 115–116, 118–120
  defined, 111
  electronic laboratories for, 28–29, 116–117
  in English, 120–121
  importance of teaching, 113–114
  multiple resources in, 120–121
  process of, 112–113
  school library and, 121–126
  in science, 115–117
  in social studies, 120–121
  specialized curriculum software for, 126–127
  technology for, 114, 117–118
  video production and, 117–118
Integrated Learning Systems (ILS), 149, 159–161
Interactive computer programs, 16
Interactive video, 39–40, 86–88
  critical thinking and, 132
  high school projects in, 87–88
  middle school projects in, 86–87, 126, 127
  and specialized curriculum software, 126–127
Interdisciplinary learning
  critical thinking in, 140–144
  elementary school, 58, 78–81, 102–103, 109–110
  high school, 58, 109, 140–144
  problem solving in, 102–103, 109–110
  team teaching in, 56–58

Keeping Track: How Schools Structure Inequality (Oakes), 211–212
Kentucky, state-level restructuring in, 173–174
Kozma, R. B., 33, 38
Kozol, Jonathan, 208

Learning
  constructivist approach to, 9–11, 112–113
  in conventional versus restructured schools, 7, 9
  distance, 18, 30, 58–60
  interdisciplinary. *See* Interdisciplinary learning
  new approaches to, 9–11
  in technology-rich classrooms, 216–223
  See also specific subject areas and schooling levels
Learning styles, 18

Library Media Center (LMC), 121–126
  described, 121–122
  elementary school, 122–124
  high school, 124–126
Lieberman, Ann, 184
Linking for Learning: A New Course for Education, 59–60
Linn, Marcia C., 5, 10
Living curriculum, 140–142
Location for teaching and learning, 18, 30
Louisiana, school-level restructuring in, 165–166

Madaus, George F., 183, 186
Mathematics
  basic skills in, 157–159
  critical thinking in, 142–143, 144–145
  Integrated Learning Systems (ILS) and, 159–161
  problem solving in, 101–102
  standards in, 100, 161, 185
Means, Barbara, 14–15, 17, 21
Microcomputer-Based Laboratories (MBLs), 28–29, 116–117
Middle school classrooms
  critical thinking skills in, 81–82, 144–145
  database software in, 118–120
  inquiry in, 112, 118–120
  interactive video in, 86–87, 126, 127
  problem solving in, 104–105
  science simulations in, 104–105
  social studies in, 118–120
  videotape projects in, 82–83
Minnesota
  "Charter Schools" program, 209
  school-level restructuring in, 164
Modeling, 200
Model schools, 164
Modems, 12, 15
Multicultural education, 201, 213–215
Multimedia presentations, 28, 49–52
  composing, 49–51, 84–86
  critical thinking and, 145–146
  editing, 51–52
  in high school videotape projects, 83–86
  value of, 70
  Voyage of the Mimi, The, 38, 102–103
  See also Interactive video
Music
  communication through, 93–95
  critical thinking and, 143

National Assessment of Educational Progress (NAEP), 181
National Council of Teachers of Mathematics (NCTM), 100, 161, 185
National Council on Education Standards and Testing (NCEST), 182
National Education Goals Panel (NEGP), 181
Nation at Risk, A, 179
Nation Prepared, A, 191–198
Networking, 30
New American Schools Development Corporation (NASDC), 181
Newspapers, school, 71–76
New Standards Project (NSP), 184–187
"Newswires," 73–74
New Zealand, site-based management in, 204

Oakes, Jeannie, 211–212
Olson, K., 14–15, 17, 21
Online information resources, 30, 132
Oral communication
  panel discussions in, 141–142
  technology in, 70
Outcome-based education (OBE), 8, 62–63, 190

Page layout software, 72
Panel discussions, 141–142
Parents
  expectations for schools, 3–4, 5
  school choice and, 206–210
Partner schools, 198–202
Pen-pal programs, 71

Performance-based assessment, 63, 190
Persuasive writing
  composition in, 135–138
  critical analysis of, 138
Photography, 92–93
Portfolios, 65–66, 190
Pre-school children, inquiry and, 111
Primary school classrooms. *See* Elementary school classrooms
Probeware, 28–29
Problem solving, 97–110
  computers and, 29, 99
  geometric construction tools for, 106–107
  graphing tools for, 105–106
  importance of teaching, 98
  interdisciplinary approach to, 102–103, 109–110
  in mathematics, 101–102
  nature of, 97–98
  in science, 104–105
  simulations in, 103–105
  skill-building software and, 100–101
  in social studies, 103–104
  spreadsheets and, 99, 107–109
Prodigy, 30
Professional development schools, 198–202
Prompts, 156

Reading
  basic skills in, 150–152
  integration of writing and, 151–152
  See also English; Writing
Reflective practice, 201
Re:Learning, 198
Research skills. *See* Inquiry
Resnick, Lauren, 184, 187
Restructuring movement, 1, 6–12, 162–175
  district-level, 63, 166–171, 204, 222–223
  innovative teaching in, 21–22
  organizational structure of schools and, 8–9, 11
  outcome-based education (OBE) model and, 8, 62–63, 190
  recommended change in, 7
  school-level, 162–166
  standards and assessment in, 189–190
  state-level, 63, 171–175, 204
  technology role in, 12–13, 15–20
  traditional instructional strategy versus, 5, 9–12, 18
Ringstaff, C., 20, 218, 220

Sandholtz, J. H., 20, 218, 220
Saturn School (St. Paul, Minn.), 164
School choice, 206–210
School districts. *See* District-level restructuring
School-level restructuring, 162–166
School newspapers, 71–76
  elementary school, 71–74
  high school, 74–76
Science
  critical thinking in, 142, 145–146
  database software in elementary school, 115–116
  electronic laboratories in elementary school, 28–29, 116–117
  simulation in middle school, 104–105
  specialized curriculum software in, 126–127
Secondary school classrooms. *See* High school classrooms
Secretary's Commission on Achieving Necessary Skills (SCANS), 181–182
Sesame Street, 34–35, 37–38
Seven Oaks Elementary School (Lacey, Wash.), 164–165
Shanker, Albert, 5, 10
Shared-management model, 169–170
Sheingold, K., 17, 19, 21, 22, 218
Simulation, 29–30, 31–32, 103–105, 145
  in mathematics, 159
  in science, 104–105
  in social studies, 103–104

Site-based management, 203–206
Sivin, Jay, 17, 25n.
Sizer, Theodore, 64–65, 163, 180, 186–187
Skill building, computers and, 27–29, 100–101
Social studies
  critical thinking in, 140–142
  database software in middle school, 118–120
  multiple resources in high school, 120–121
  simulation in high school, 103–104
Software. *See* Computer software
Spelling checkers, 156
Spreadsheets
  for elementary schools, 107–108
  for high schools, 108–109
  problem solving and, 99, 107–109
Square One, 38
Standards, 179–190
  America 2000, 180–184, 186
  issues concerning, 187–189
  mathematics, 100, 161, 185
  New Standards Project, 184–187
  in restructured schools, 189–190
State-level restructuring, 63, 171–175, 204
Statistics, critical thinking skills and, 144–145
Storyboarding, 83, 88
Student attitudes
  change process and, 223
  computers and, 25–26
  television and, 34–36
Student performance, computers and, 24–25, 26–27
Success for All Schools program, 175

Teachers
  continuing education for, 202–203
  and impact of technology in classroom, 17–22
  innovative, 9–11, 21–22
  preparation of, 191–202
  role with computers, 30–31
  tips for restructuring classrooms, 221–222
Teaching
  collaborative, 52–56, 201
  constructivist approach to, 9–11, 112–113
  in conventional versus restructured schools, 7, 9
  of critical thinking, 129–130
  impact of technology on, 17–22
  new approaches to, 9–11, 21–22
  team teaching, 56–58
  in technology-rich classrooms, 216–223
Teaching style, 20
Team teaching, 56–58
Technology
  appropriateness of, 16–17
  basic skills and, 149–150
  in communication, 69–70
  in conventional versus restructured schools, 7
  critical thinking and, 36–37, 130–132
  environment for effective use of, 20–21
  impact of, 14–15, 17–20
  integration into instructional program, 21
  types of, 12, 15
  See also Computers; Television; Video technology
Telecommunications, 18, 30, 58–60
Telephones, 15
Television, 15, 33
  cable programming, 15, 34, 61, 62
  critical thinking and, 36–37, 131, 138–140
  network programming, 34
  specialized programming, 61–62
  See also Video technology
Tierney, Robert, 25*n.*
Top-down management model, 168–169
Tracking, 210–213

Traditional instructional strategy, 5, 9–12, 18, 112–113
Tucker, Marc, 184
Turkel, S., 18
Turner Broadcasting Company, 62
Two-way communication, 16

University of California at Berkeley, 206–207
University of Chicago, 4
University of Colorado, 211–212
University of Washington College of Education, 199–202
University Terrace Elementary School (Baton Rouge, La.), 165–166
Urban Mathematics Collaborative, 175

Vanderbilt University, Peabody College, 207
Vermont, school-level restructuring in, 165
Video assessment, 66
Video Encyclopedia of the 20th Century, 87, 114, 120
Video technology, 12, 15, 33–40
  in arts programs, 88–95
  availability of, 16, 38, 60, 131
  classroom use of, 60–61
  communication and, 33–34
  critical thinking and, 36–37, 130–132, 138–140
  as educational resource, 37–39
  elementary school video projects, 117–118
  high school video projects, 83–86, 140–142
  influences on attitudes and behaviors, 34–36
  interactive. *See* Interactive video
  middle school video projects, 82–83
  visual literacy and, 36–37
  See also Multimedia presentations; Television
Video yearbooks, 76–77
Visual arts
  communication through, 88–93
  critical thinking and, 143
Visual literacy, 36–37
Voucher plans, 208
Voyage of the Mimi, The, 38, 102–103

Washington state
  district-level restructuring in, 166–171
  school-level restructuring in, 164–165
  state-level restructuring in, 171–172, 204–205
  University of Washington College of Education, 199–202
White, C., 19
Whittle Communications, 61, 62
Whole-class instruction, 16–17
  with computers, 31–32, 100–101, 152–154
Wigfield, A., 17
Willison Central School (Vt.), 165
Writing, 45–49
  basic skills in, 151–156
  composition in, 135–138
  criticism of, 47–49, 138
  essay, 135–138, 154–155
  grammar checkers, 156
  integration of reading and, 151–152
  paragraphs in, 154–155
  persuasive, 135–138, 154–155
  plot structure in, 152–154
  prompts, 156
  revision process, 47–49
  spelling checkers, 156
  story, 152–154
  technology and, 69–70
  topic sentences in, 154–155
  See also English; Reading
Writing academies, 77–78

Yearbooks, video, 76–77